Classical
Mythology
in Literature,
Art, and
Music

XEROX

COLLEGE

PUBLISHING

Waltham, Massachusetts
Toronto

Classical Mythology in Literature, Art, and Music

Philip Mayerson

New York University

(**Cover**) The dragon of Colchis disgorging Jason as Athena
looks on. The golden fleece hangs on a tree nearby. *Vase
painting, c. 475 B. C. Vatican Museum. (Alinari)*

(**End papers, front**) Perseus chasing Medusa. *Vase
painting, early fifth century B. C. Museum Antiker Kleinkunst, Munich. (Hirmer)*

(**End papers, back**) Perseus, accompanied by Athena, carries of Medusa's head. *Vase painting, 470–460 B. C. British
Museum.*

Contents

CHAPTER **VIII**
The Trojan War   **375**

CHAPTER **IX**
The Homecomings   **423**

CHAPTER

Aeneas and the Quest for a New Troy   459

Preface

There is no natural phenomenon and no
phenomenon of human life that is not capable
of a mythical interpretation, and which does
not call for such an interpretation.

Ernest Cassirer—*An Essay on Man*

It is no longer necessary, fortunately, to introduce a book on Greek and Roman mythology with a lament over the decline of interest in reading the classics in their original languages and the consequent loss to humanistic studies. Even when countless thousands were compelled to wrestle with participial constructions and conditional clauses, there were not many who enjoyed or extracted the essence of the "greats." And even those who now elect to study Greek and Latin do not necessarily acquire an overview of the field of Classical Mythology. For that matter, neither did the native speakers, the Greeks and Romans, have that overview, for they used handbooks of mythology to guide them through the labyrinths of their own heritage. In short, no apologies need be made for a book of this sort; nor need we worry that the intellectual and imaginative sources of Greece and Rome will run dry. Bookstore shelves are filled with modern translations of the classics, inexpensive and highly readable; poets and painters, let alone sculptors, novelists, and playwrights, are still inspired by mythological themes; and hardly does a season go by without an ancient drama finding its way to the stage.

The aims of this text are simple: to give the reader a working frame of reference in Greek and Roman mythology and to make more meaningful and enjoyable the vast number of works that have come under the influence of these ancient tales. The text, therefore, as its title suggests, is designed for a rather broad range of interests: for students of literature, art, and music. It should also serve as an introduction to those scholarly works which presuppose a background in the classics—for example, Douglas Bush's *Mythology and the Renaissance Tradition in English Poetry* and his *Mythology and the Romantic Tradition in English Poetry.*

The stories of the gods and heroes are prefaced by a chapter on the major sources for Greek and Roman mythology, an important chapter in our view because it introduces the reader to the great literary figures of the past and shows that from the very outset we are dealing with a body of material that is highly sophisticated, hardly primitive, and always changing from one writer to another and from one age to the next. It is also an antidote against those widesweeping and erroneus generalizations one so often hears about the Greeks and Romans.

The mythological material itself is treated systematically: chronologically (if that word can be applied to mythology) and genealogically. It begins with the creation of the primal powers, their offspring, and the struggles for power which ultimately lead to the victory of Zeus and the Olympians. We then proceed one by one through the gods of heaven, the Twelve Olympians. From heaven we go beneath the earth and examine the topography of the Underworld and the lore of the gods of death, Hades and others. Dionysus and Orpheus are given a special place of their own since they bridge the gap between heaven and earth, between life and death. Having explored the various divine regions and given the biographies of the gods, we pick up the tales of the "older" and "younger" heroes, that is, those who preceded the great Trojan War and those who took part in it. Like the gods, the heroes are treated genealogically, house by house, or family by family. Whatever logic there may or may not be in such a treatment, practice has shown that it is an effective way of understanding a much tangled collection of tales. Then on to the Trojan War: the major families involved in that earth-shaking event—for so it appeared to the ancients—and the story of the struggle as Homer, the greatest of all poets, related it in the *Iliad*. Upon the downfall of Troy there follow the tales of the returns of the surviving heroes and an account of the consequences of being away from home for a decade or two. This concludes the story of the Greek heroes. From the material of the Trojan cycle, the Romans wrote an epilogue and fabricated a legend of their own origins, a story which culminated in Vergil's epic, *The Aeneid*.

We treat the myths and legends as a good deal more than amusing and fantastic tales of an inventive but simple-minded folk. What we have before us is a kind of language, the language of mythology if you will, which the ancients put to a number of uses: to explain the origin of the universe, of gods, of ethnic groups, and of man himself; to detail legendary history, the function of deities, and man's relationship to deity, to the state and to his fellow man. Though all these elements will be touched upon, the historical remoteness of their origins prevents us from seeing them operating in their pristine state. Easier to recognize are certain motifs, or recurring themes, some of which have analogues all over the world. These too have been presented without excessive speculation as to their originating mechanism. Our explanation for a particular myth or its underlying theme has been influenced to a great extent by the commonsense approach of the British scholar, H. J. Rose. These explanations, however, together with those of other schools of thought on the subject, should not be taken as dogma; the scholarly world is still heatedly debating—probably more so today than at any other time—the meaning and function of myth in ancient and other cultures.

Following the explication of a myth, we have illustrated its use in later literature and the other arts. Here the volume of material has been overwhelming. What has been attempted is a selection of poems and passages from the literary greats and near greats of the Western world. (We can easily be faulted for omitting a particular masterpiece or favorite.) The illustrations are drawn mostly from literature in the English language. European writers, especially those of the twentieth century, are also represented since the availability of fine translations has removed the language barriers between Continental and English literature. We have also given rather full summaries of the major epics and dramas of classical antiquity. In doing so our object has been twofold: to provide fuller mythological background in a seminal work, and to guide the reader through the unfamiliar byways of an ancient literary masterpiece. The summaries are also presented in the hope that they will stimulate an interest in reading the complete work in translation. For this purpose, the bibliography cites a number of translations and translators of individual epics and dramas from which a selection may be made.

In the fields of art and music, representative selection becomes a problem once more. Limitations of space compelled us to select works of art which not only come from the hand of a master, but which also best illustrate the mythological narrative. Hence, we have made extensive use of ancient vase paintings since they, better than any other visual medium, tell the story at a glance. For the rest, our selection was guided by the need to illustrate the use of mythological themes in varying media from the past to the present, from the seventh century B.C. to the twentieth century A.D. As for music, admittedly it was given even shorter shrift than art, and we have had to limit ourselves to a relatively small number of operas and other musical forms whose inspiration was found in the myths of Greece and Rome. Oddly enough, this field of research has been largely neglected by scholars, a fact evident in the paucity of bibliographical references.

To keep the eye of the reader from being diverted from the main objective of this text, we have omitted footnotes, appendices, and other scholarly apparatus. These may be readily obtained from the handbooks, dictionaries, and encyclopedias listed in the bibliography. Similarly, to keep the reader's mind from being boggled by myriads of names and to keep the text from resembling a telephone directory, names of people and places have been held to a minimum, to those judged most important. In the matter of spelling names, we have attempted to give the form most commonly found in English and in English literature. However, there is considerable variance in the way in which Greek names are anglicized; most have come into English by way of Latin, others directly from the Greek, It is, of course, possible to transliterate Greek names into English (some translators insist on it), but to the reader unfamiliar with the peculiarities of the Greek language such names as Oedipus and Actaeon look strange when given as Oidipous and Aktaion. Where appropriate we have given alternate spellings of important mythological figures; for example, Tiresias (Teiresias), or Deianira (Deianeira, Dejanira).

Finally and without ritualistic intent, I wish to express my deep-felt thanks to those many scholars in various disciplines whose works have sustained me over the years. Had it not been for their help, this book could have been neither conceived nor written. And to the readers, these final words which paraphrase Cicero's statement on the Latin language: "It is not so much a distinction to know the myths of Greece and Rome as a shame not to know them."

PHILIP MAYERSON
New York University

Acknowledgments

The author expresses his appreciation to the publishers for permission to quote from the following copyrighted material:

A. WATKINS, INC. *Artemis to Actaeon and Other Verse* by Edith Wharton, copyright 1909.

ALFRED A. KNOPF, INC. *The Myth of Sisyphus and Other Essays* by Albert Camus, trans. Justin O'Brien, copyright © 1955. *Two Legends: Oedipus and Theseus* by André Gide, trans. John Russell, copyright 1950.

THE BODLEY HEAD. *Medea of Euripides*, trans. Rex Warner, copyright 1944.

BRANDT & BRANDT, INC. and E. P. DUTTON & CO., INC. *The Prodigal* by Jack C. Richardson, copyright © 1960 by Jack C. Richardson.

CAMBRIDGE UNIVERSITY PRESS. *Theocritus*, edited with a translation and commentary by A. S. F. Gow, copyright 1950.

THE CLARENDON PRESS. *The Dialogues of Plato*, Fourth Edition 1953, trans. Benjamin Jowett, copyright 1920.

COLLINS-KNOWLTON-WING, INC. and A. P. WATT & SON. "Galatea and Pygmalion" and "Prometheus" by Robert Graves, copyright © 1955 by Robert Graves.

DODD, MEAD & COMPANY, INC. "Menelaus and Helen," from *The Collected Poems of Rupert Brooke*, copyright 1915 by Dodd, Mead, & Company, Inc., copyright 1943 by Edward Marsh.

DOUBLEDAY & COMPANY, INC. "Dialogues of the Gods," from *Selected Satires of Lucian*, trans. and ed. Lionel Casson, copyright © 1962.

FABER AND FABER, LTD. "The Oracle," "Perseus," and "Thyestes," from *The Collected Poems of Louis MacNeice*, ed. E. R. Dodds, copyright © 1966 by The Estate of Louis MacNeice.

GERALD DUCKWORTH & CO. "Children of Zeus," from *Legends and Pastorals* by Graham Hough, copyright 1961.

GROVE PRESS, INC. *The Poems of Catullus*, trans. Horace Gregory, copyright © 1956. "Demeter" and "Adonis," from *The Collected Poems of H.D.*, copyright 1925 and © 1953 by Norman Holmes Pearson and reprinted by his permission.

HARCOURT BRACE JOVANOVICH, INC. and FABER AND FABER, LTD. "The Waste Land," "Sweeney Among the Nightingales," "Sweeney Erect," "The Hollow Men," from *Collected Poems*, by T. S. Eliot, copyright 1936. "Little Gidding," from *Four*

Quartets, by T. S. Eliot, copyright 1943. *The Cocktail Party* by T. S. Eliot, copyright © 1950.

HARPER AND ROW. "Daphne," "Sonnet XXVII," and "Sonnet LII," from *Collected Poems* by Edna St. Vincent Millay, copyright 1922, 1931, 1950, 1958 by Edna St. Vincent Millay and Norma Millay Ellis. "Sonnet XXVII" and "Sonnet LII" are from *Fatal Interview*, which appears in *Collected Poems*. Reprinted by permission of Norma Millay Ellis.

HARVARD UNIVERSITY PRESS and THE LOEB CLASSICAL LIBRARY. *Apollonius Rhodius*, trans. R. C. Seaton, copyright 1912. *Callimachus and Lycophron*, trans. A. W. Mair, copyright 1921. *Hesiod, The Homeric Hymns and Homerica*, trans. H. G. Evelyn-White, copyright 1914.

HOGARTH PRESS. *Later Poems* by Rainer Maria Rilke, trans. J. B. Leishman, copyright 1938. Reprinted by permission of St. John's College, Oxford.

HOLT, RINEHART AND WINSTON, INC. "Tarry, delight; so seldom met," from *Collected Poems of A. E. Housman*, copyright 1936 by Barclays Bank, Ltd., copyright © 1964 by Robert E. Symons.

HOLT, RINEHART AND WINSTON, INC. and JONATHAN CAPE, LTD. "Pan With Us," from *The Poetry of Robert Frost* by Robert Frost, ed. Edward Connery Lathem, copyright 1934, © 1969 by Holt, Rinehart and Winston, Inc., © 1962 by Robert Frost. Reprinted by permission of the Estate of Robert Frost.

HOUGHTON MIFFLIN COMPANY. "Invocation to the Social Muse," and "Men of My Country Loved Mozart," from *Collected Poems 1917–1952* by Archibald MacLeish, copyright © 1952.

INDIANA UNIVERSITY PRESS and CALDER & BOYERS, LTD., LONDON. *Metamorphoses* by Ovid, trans. Rolfe Humphries, copyright © 1955 by Indiana University Press.

THE MACMILLAN COMPANY. *The Spoon River Anthology* by Edgar Lee Masters, copyright 1914, 1915, 1916, 1942 by Edgar Lee Masters. Reprinted by permission of Mrs. Ellen C. Masters. "Cassandra," from *Collected Poems* by Edwin Arlington Robinson, copyright 1916 by Edwin Arlington Robinson, renewed 1944 by Ruth Nivison.

THE MACMILLAN COMPANY and A. P. WATT AND SON. "Leda and the Swan" and "Two Songs from a Play" by William Butler Yeats, copyright 1928 by The Macmillan Company, renewed © 1956 by Georgie Yeats; "Lullaby" and "The Delphic Oracle upon Plotinus" by William Butler Yeats, copyright 1933 by The Macmillan Company, renewed © 1961 by Bertha Georgie Yeats. Reprinted from *Collected Poems* by William Butler Yeats by permission of Mr. M. B. Yeats and Macmillan & Co. (London).

NEW DIRECTIONS PUBLISHING CORP. and FABER AND FABER, LTD. *The Cantos* by Ezra Pound, copyright 1934 by Ezra Pound. "Speech for Psyche" and "Mr. Nixon," from *Personae* by Ezra Pound, copyright 1926 by Ezra Pound.

NEW DIRECTIONS PUBLISHING CORP. and INTERNATIONAL FAMOUS AGENCY. *Orpheus Descending* by Tennessee Williams, copyright © 1958 by Tennessee Williams.

OXFORD UNIVERSITY PRESS. "The Oracle," "Perseus," and "Thyestes," from *The Collected Poems of Louis MacNeice*, ed. E. R. Dodds, copyright © 1966 by The Estate of Louis MacNeice. *A Phoenix Too Frequent* by Christopher Fry, copyright 1949. *The Republic of Plato*, trans. F. M. Cornford, copyright 1941.

PENGUIN BOOKS. *Homer: The Iliad*, trans. E. V. Rieu, copyright 1950. *Lucretius: On the Nature of the Universe*, trans. Ronald Latham, copyright 1951. *Virgil: The Aeneid*, trans. W. F. Jackson Knight, copyright © 1956.

RANDOM HOUSE, INC. "Casino," from *The Collected Poems of W. H. Auden* by W. H. Auden, copyright 1945. "Cassandra," from *Double Axe and Other Poems* by Robinson Jeffers, copyright 1948. "The Cretan Woman," from *Hungerfield and Other Poems* by

Robinson Jeffers, copyright 1954. "Musée des Beaux Arts," from *The Collected Poems of W. H. Auden* by W. H. Auden, copyright 1945. "New Year Letter," from *The Double Man* by W. H. Auden, copyright 1941. "Science," from *Roan Stallion, Tamar, and Other Poems* by Robinson Jeffers, copyright 1954.

SECKER & WARBURG. *Two Legends: Oedipus and Theseus* by André Gide, trans. John Russell, copyright 1950.

UNIVERSITY OF CHICAGO PRESS. *Aeschylus: Agamemnon*, trans. Richmond Lattimore, copyright 1953. *Aeschylus: The Eumenides*, trans. Richmond Lattimore, copyright 1953. *Aeschylus: The Libation Bearers*, trans. Richmond Lattimore, copyright 1953. *Aeschylus: Prometheus Bound*, trans. David Grene, copyright 1942. *Euripides: Bacchae*, trans. William Arrowsmith, copyright 1959. *Euripides: Hippolytus*, trans. David Grene, copyright 1942. *Sophocles: Antigone*, trans. Elizabeth Wyckoff, copyright 1954. *Sophocles: Oedipus the King*, trans. David Grene, copyright 1942.

UNIVERSITY OF MICHIGAN PRESS. *Hesiod*, trans. Richmond Lattimore, copyright © 1959.

THE VIKING PRESS, INC. "Leander," from *Blue Juniata* by Malcolm Cowley, copyright 1929, renewed © 1957 by Malcolm Cowley. *Ovid: The Metamorphoses*, trans. Horace Gregory, copyright © 1958 by The Viking Press, Inc.

THE VIKING PRESS, INC. and LAURENCE POLLINGER, LTD. "For a Moment," "They Say the Sea is Loveless," and "Middle of the World," from *The Complete Poems of D. H. Lawrence*, Vol II, ed. Vivian de Sola Pinto and F. Warren Roberts, copyright 1933 by Frieda Lawrence. Reprinted by permission of the Estate of Mrs. Frieda Lawrence.

W. W. NORTON & COMPANY, INC. and INSEL VERLAG. *Sonnets to Orpheus* by Rainer Maria Rilke, trans. M. D. Herter Norton, copyright 1942 by W. W. Norton & Company, Inc., renewed 1969 by M. D. Herter Norton.

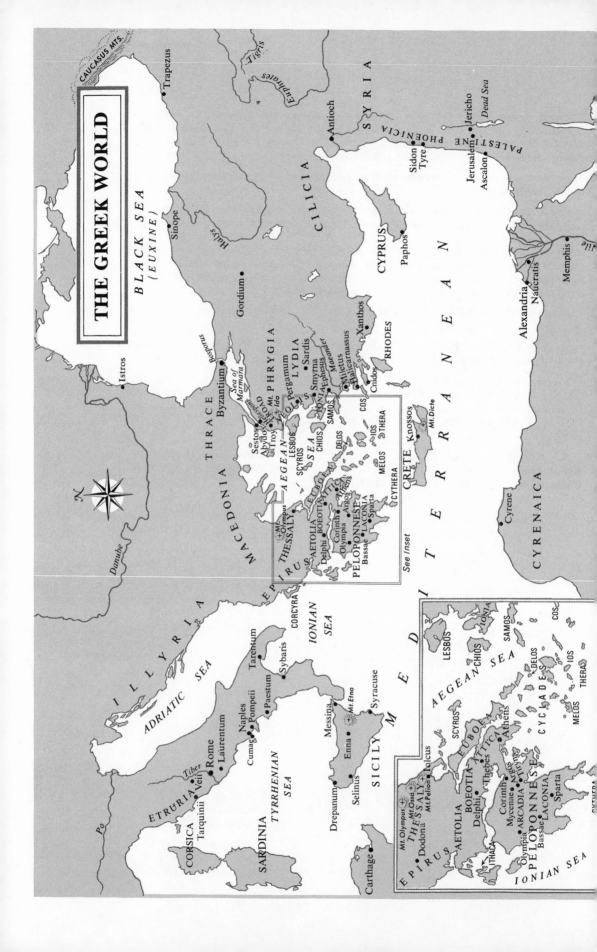

THE GREEK WORLD

CAUCASUS MTS.

Trapezus

BLACK SEA
(EUXINE)

Sinope

Istros

Byzantium

Sea of Marmara

THRACE

MACEDONIA

EPIRUS

Mt. Olympus
THESSALY

AETOLIA
Delphi BOEOTIA ATTICA
Olympia Corinth Athens
Bassae Argos
LACONIA
Sparta
PELOPONNESE

See Inset

IONIAN SEA

CORCYRA

ILLYRIA

ADRIATIC SEA

Danube

Tarentum

Sybaris

Naples
Cumae Pompeii
Paestum

Rome
Laurentum
Veii
Tiber
ETRURIA
Tarquinii

Po

CORSICA

SARDINIA

TYRRHENIAN SEA

Messina
Mt. Etna
Enna
Syracuse
Drepanum
Selinus
SICILY

Carthage

MEDITERRANEAN

Tigris

Euphrates

SYRIA

Antioch

PHOENICIA
Sidon
Tyre
PALESTINE
Jerusalem
Ascalon
Jericho
Dead Sea

CILICIA

CYPRUS
Paphos

Alexandria
Naucratis
Memphis
Nile

RHODES
Xanthos
Cnidos
Halicarnassus
Miletus
Maeander
Ephesus
IONIA
Smyrna
Sardis
LYDIA
Pergamum
Mt. Ida
Troy
Abydos
Sestos
TROAD
AEOLIS
PHRYGIA
Gordium
Halys
Bosporus

AEGEAN SEA
LESBOS
SCYROS
CHIOS
SAMOS
DELOS
EUBOEA
IOS
THERA
MELOS
COS
CYTHERA
CRETE
Knossos
Mt. Dicte

CYRENAICA
Cyrene

N

Inset

Mt. Olympus
Mt. Ossa
THESSALY
Dodona
Mt. Pelion
Iolcus
EPIRUS
ITHACA
AETOLIA
Delphi
BOEOTIA
Thebes
ATTICA
Corinth Athens
Mycenae Argos
ARCADIA Tiryns
Olympia
Bassae
PELOPONNESE
LACONIA
Sparta

IONIAN SEA

AEGEAN SEA
LESBOS
SCYROS
CHIOS
SAMOS
IONIA
EUBOEA
DELOS
CYCLADES
IOS
MELOS
THERA
COS

Myths and Mythographers of Greece and Rome

" . . . when telling a tale all men add something to it
because that increases pleasure."

Aristotle—*Poetics*

"Charm and beauty . . . often make the
unbelievable seem true."

Pindar—*First Olympian*

Here begins an odyssey through the world of classical mythology, starting with the creation of the world, proceeding to the divinities that once governed all aspects of human life and experience, and then on to the families of the heroes. This odyssey into the past is planned to provide an organized introduction to the main body of Greek and Roman mythology for a generation which may not have even Shakespeare's "little Latin and less Greek," but which nevertheless wishes to have a fuller appreciation of the literature, particularly English literature, and arts coming under its influence.

It is true that themes similar to the classical may be found in almost any corpus of mythology—American Indian, Chinese, Eskimo, Bantu—but it is classical mythology, the mythology of the ancient Greeks and its extension to Rome, that has the greatest fascination for the Western world. Its legacy has been rich in all fields of endeavor. Such names as Achilles, Hercules, Ulysses, Daedalus, Medea, and Helen of Troy have overtones of meaning and suggestion that range widely over the intellectual and emotional strings of our minds. The myth of Oedipus, for example, has so often been used as a touchstone for new psychoanalytical theories that his name, or the complex named after him, has become a household word. Even technology is not immune to the influence of Greece and Rome: rockets and space projects have been named after such mythological luminaries as Zeus, Jupiter, Apollo, Mercury, Atlas, Saturn, Pegasus, and the Gemini.

We need hardly mention the extent to which painters and sculptors such as Titian, Rubens and Rembrandt, Botticelli and Cellini, Poussin, Goya, Lipchitz and

1

Picasso have used and adapted classical mythology to illustrate the past, to reveal the human body, to express romantic or antiromantic ideals, or to symbolize any particular point of view. Novelists, poets, and playwrights—T. S. Eliot, Ezra Pound, Eugene O'Neill, Jean Anouilh, Albert Camus, James Joyce, to name a few of the twentieth century—have found similar uses for classical mythology, whether to express a view that life is absurd, to dramatize an antiwar theme, to portray moral dilemmas, or to expose pathological relationships. The themes of classical mythology cover virtually all human experience: love, hate, war, tyranny, treachery, courage, fate, man's relationship to man, to the state, or to divine powers. All these themes can be found in classical mythology and provide an endless source of inspiration for the creative imagination.

Homer

Whatever can be said of the influence of mythology upon writers or artists, Renaissance or modern, can also be said even of the earliest *littérateur* of the Western world, the Greek epic poet Homer (c. 750 B.C.). Homer's incomparable epics are not bare, historical, or even imaginative accounts of the Trojan War; rather, his *Iliad* and *Odyssey* take their themes from a large body of mythological material that by the eighth century B.C. had developed around the most celebrated war of antiquity. Surely the Trojan War, waged some four hundred years before Homer's time, was almost as ancient to him as it is to us. So confident is Homer of his audience's grasp of the details of the Trojan War, the abduction of Helen, and the multitude of other myths and legends merely touched upon in his narration, that the poet feels no obligation to elaborate upon them beyond the requirements of his art. Homer's interest lies not so much in the war but, as he tells us in the opening lines of the *Iliad*, in "the wrath of Achilles, Peleus' son, the ruinous wrath that brought on the Achaeans woes innumerable, and hurled down into Hades many strong souls of heroes." He then proceeds to relate, in human and psychological terms, the events in the final year of the long siege of Troy that led to tragedy. The *Odyssey*, similarly, is devoted to a theme which evolves from the Trojan War: the adventures of a man, renowned above all others for cleverness and sagacity, struggling to return home years after the fall of Troy. Behind this theme, Homer has struck yet another note, a moral one: that men and their wicked acts, not the gods, are the cause of most of the suffering humans endure. Many of the incidents in the *Odyssey* are designed to reflect this point of view which Homer has the great Olympian god Zeus state at the very outset of his poem.

In short, our earliest literary source for Greek mythology already shows a considerable amount of sophisticated manipulation of mythological material, not to speak of the consummate poetic craftsmanship of its creator, Homer—Byron's "blind old man of Scio's rocky isle." It is Homer and successive generations of Greek and Roman poets who, however much they have continued the process of reworking and enlarging upon a mythological core, have preserved for us those countless myths whose origins have been lost in the millennia of prehistory. But who were these Greeks and Romans? In planning an odyssey into the world of classical mythology, it would be well to prepare ourselves in advance by a brief introduction to these mythographers and myth-makers and to appreciate their own fascination with the imaginative past.

Hesiod

Second in importance to Homer is Hesiod (c. 700 B.C.), a contemporary, or near-contemporary, of the Western world's first poet. Before their time we possess only the names of mythical musicians and poets, such as Orpheus and Musaeus, whom the Greeks often associated with Homer and Hesiod as their earliest teachers and civilizers. Herodotus (c. 485–c. 425 B.C.), the Father of History, tells us that Homer and Hesiod were the first to compose theogonies and give the gods their epithets, to allot to them their several offices and powers, and to describe their forms. This well-known statement of Herodotus is not to be taken at face value, but as the opinion of an educated Greek of the fifth century who recognized the importance of Homer and Hesiod in giving system and order to the complex polytheism of the classical pantheon.

Hesiod, poet-theologian of Greece, prophet of justice and hard work, composed two poems, the *Theogony* and *Works and Days*, which may reasonably be considered his own creations. Many other poems have been attributed to him, principally because the weight of his name lent authority to any work on the subject of genealogy and mythology. The *Theogony*, an account of the origin and descent of the gods, is a conscious attempt on the part of Hesiod to organize the numerous traditions concerning the gods into an ordered and meaningful arrangement. It was not only a love to combine particulars into a whole, to give order and consistency of thought, which is so originally and characteristically Greek, that moved Hesiod to compose a "history" of the physical and divine universe. The real thrust of the *Theogony* is to exalt the god Zeus as the ultimate achievement in a historical process that began with the creation of the world and developed, through stages of anarchy and lawlessness, to an ordered universe in which Zeus is the source of power, wisdom, justice, peace, the joys of civilization, and the creative arts.

The design of Hesiod's *Works and Days* is quite different. Addressed to his brother Perses and the local rulers, it cries out for righteousness and hard work, for only through justice and work can men win a measure of happiness and security in a difficult world. In support of his thesis, Hesiod cites the myth of Prometheus and Pandora, the Five Ages of the World, and elaborates on the power of the great Olympian god Zeus.

The Rhapsodes and Lyric Poets

For about two centuries the fame and reputation of Homer were secured by rhapsodes, professional minstrels who recited his poems at festivals and public gatherings throughout Greek lands until at last they were committed to writing, according to tradition during the rule of the Athenian tyrant Pisistratus (546–527 B.C.). So great was the impact of the *Iliad* and the *Odyssey*—one good story always attracts another—that the heroic saga of Troy became the source of other epics designed to fill in the gaps of the story left open by Homer. Six epics, together with the *Iliad* and the *Odyssey*, made up the Trojan Cycle and were arranged chronologically, from the origin of the war to the death of Odysseus. The *Cyprian Lays* gave the first causes of the Trojan War and related events during the first nine years of the siege leading up to the *Iliad*; the *Aethiopis* contained the exploits of the Ethiopian Memnon and continued the story to the death of Achilles and the contest for his armor; the *Little Iliad* and the *Sack of Ilium*, from the contest for Achilles' arms to the capture of Troy including various incidents that took place during its fall; the *Home Comings*, the adventures of major and minor heroes returning home from Troy and leading up to those described in the *Odyssey;* the *Telegonia*, the death of Odysseus in Ithaca at the hands of Telegonus, his son by Circe, and the final settlement of the family after his death.

Of the six epics of the Trojan Cycle, which are believed to have been composed between the eighth and sixth centuries B.C., only fragments have survived to the present day, but they became a part, a living part, of Greek tradition and exercised an influence on later writers who have provided us with the preludes and sequels to the *Iliad* and the *Odyssey*. Equally influential was the Hesiodic tradition in genealogy and other epic compositions which, like the Trojan Cycle, were selected and arranged in "cycles" to make a complete story of famous legendary figures and their descendants (Oedipus, Danaus, Heracles, Theseus), of a momentous war (the struggle for Thebes), or of a grand adventure (the voyage of the Argonauts).

Homer also lent his name to a surviving collection of "hymns" which date close to the period of the Trojan Cycle. The *Homeric Hymns* owe their existence to the same rhapsodes—the so-called Homeridae (sons of Homer) who were responsible for preserving the *Iliad* and the *Odyssey* until they were put into writing. The rhapsodes often offered their own compositions as preludes to the recitation of Homer. These hymns, less devotional than literary, centered in epic style on the picturesque details in the mythological life of the deity being celebrated in song. One, the *Homeric Hymn to Hermes*, well-known through Shelley's translation, even has elements of burlesque and humor, which we would find strange in a hymn. Perhaps even more remarkable is the *Hymn to Aphrodite*, which relates with fine literary skill how Zeus humbled the goddess by having her fall passionately in love with the Trojan Anchises, "lest laughter-loving Aphrodite should one day softly smile and say mockingly among all the gods that she had joined the gods in love with mortal women who bear sons of death to the deathless gods, and had mated the goddesses with mortal men."

The popularity of mythology as a subject of literary compositions continued unabated even though the epic tradition began to recede and the mainstream of literary development turned toward the short poem generally called the lyric, the drama, and the prose narrative. Aeschylus (c. 525–456 B.C.), according to a later critic, admitted that his plays were "slices from the great banquets of Homer," while Aristotle (384–322 B.C.) in his *Poetics* says that in his days the finest tragedies were always on the story of some few legendary houses. However, the epic poets had created an age so remote in time, so removed from the reality and the concerns of later poets, that a new framework for mythological expression and new interpretations had to be fashioned.

Homer and his fellow-rhapsodes had glorified the past, a past whose continuity may well have been breached by migratory invasions of Dorian Greeks soon after the Trojan War (c. 1200 B.C.) bringing a Dark Age to Greece for about four hundred years. Out of the mythical and legendary flotsam and jetsam floating down the long stream of history, the epic poets created a society that could hardly have existed except in their own imaginations. From this debris of confused historical memories, folktales, rituals, and theologies of diverse ethnic groups, the so-called Heroic Age was fabricated, a society filled with tension and movement both on the mundane and divine levels. As we can see in the pages of the *Iliad* and the

Figure 1.   Zeus (or Poseidon). *Bronze
c. 460–450 B.C., recovered from the
sea off Cape Artemisium. National
Museum, Athens. (Hirmer)*

Odyssey, the poet has conjured up men and deeds considerably larger than life, gods and goddesses less so. Life for the gods on Mount Olympus mirrored, though not perfectly, the social and political organization of the Heroic Age. The Olympians, like kings, were sovereign by virtue of their strength and power, but Zeus won his right to rule the universe by defeating his own father. If men fight, bleed, cheat, feel jealousy or take sides, so do the gods but not as nobly, although Homer keeps their shortcomings from being observed by his heroes. Time and again the gods are said to live unlike mankind, without sorrows, yet Homer portrays them as having their own difficulties: they squabble, they complain, they are vindictive. Zeus himself is henpecked and has to threaten his wife Hera with corporal punishment if she continues to nag and disobey him. (Quite a contrast to the love that Hector and Andromache felt for each other!) Hera, in order to divert her husband's attention from the battlefield, seduces him by purely feminine wiles; and before he succumbs to his wife's charms, Zeus recalls his premarital relations with Hera and his extramarital affairs with mortal women and goddesses.

This scene of deception in Book XIV of the *Iliad* is considered by some historians of religion to represent a holy marriage (*hieros gamos*), a fertility ritual between an earth-goddess (Hera) and the weather-god (Zeus); to others it symbolizes, in the language of mythology, the historical union of peoples and religions of different ethnic backgrounds. But whatever the ritual background, Homer has transformed the episode, as he does with many others, into something quite different from what it was originally. In brief then, Homer presents us with a pantheon of gods who, by and large, were protectors of their favorites but who had no concern with morality as the later Greeks knew it.

Even as early as Hesiod the need was felt to explain away the differences between the two worlds, the heroic and the real. Hesiod resolved the problem by segregating the "godlike race of hero-men who are called demigods" into an age of its own.

For those heroes who did not die at Thebes fighting for the flocks of Oedipus or at Troy on behalf of Helen, Hesiod had Zeus transport them to the Islands of the Blessed where they lived in a kind of paradise without sorrow and without having to work for a living. Then, says Hesiod, Zeus made yet another generation—Hesiod's own—a race of iron, "and men never rest from labor and sorrow by day and from perishing by night; and the gods shall lay sore trouble on them."

As early as 500 B.C., Xenophanes of Colophon (c. 570–c. 480 B.C.) protested against the vivid anthropomorphism of the epic poets and their tales of the love affairs of the gods and about wars in heaven. Xenophanes also denounced the standards of athletic and military prowess, the *arete* (excellence) of the epic hero, as being less useful to society than intellectual achievement. From surviving fragments of his work we hear this unusual philosophic theologian and poet say:

> Homer and Hesiod have ascribed to the gods all the deeds that are shameful and disgraceful among men: theft and adultery and deceiving one another ... Men imagine the gods wearing clothes and talking like us ... The Ethiopians make their gods black and flat-nosed, the Thracians theirs grey-eyed and red-haired ... But if animals could paint and make things like men, horse and oxen too would make the gods in their own image ... It's no use to tell the tale of the battles of Titans and Giants or Centaurs—those fictions of our fathers' imaginations—nor wars of the gods; there's no good to be got from such subjects. One should always be thoughtful and right-minded about the gods ... Sound wisdom is better than brute strength. For if among the people there is one who is a good boxer or one who excels in wrestling or in the pentathlon, or in running, the city will not have better government on account of this man.

Xenophanes, however, was a prophet crying in the wilderness. Mythology was so much a part of the mental equipment of the Greeks, so much a part of their language and of their way of thinking, that it could not be purged in favor of Xenophanes' "supreme Deity who was one, greatest among gods and men, not like human beings either in body or mind, and who without stirring, sways all things by intellect." Yet there was a saving grace in that the tradition did not have the scriptual sacrosanctity that could reduce the tales of gods and heroes to dogma.

The lyric poet who succeeded the epic singer felt as free as his predecessor to manipulate familiar legendary material according to the demands of his theme. But unlike the minstrel or rhapsode, who usually related his story of the heroic past without intruding his own comments, the composer of the choral lyric connected the heroic past with the present. Between the seventh and fifth centuries B.C., the heyday of the lyric poets, choral poems infused with myth and legend were used to praise preeminent men (encomiums), to celebrate the victories of athletes at the sacred games (epinician odes), for dirges (elegies), for hymns to the gods (dithyrambs and paeans), and for a variety of other purposes. But since the poet was a teacher and the voice of the gods—Pindar could say: "Give me an oracle, Muse, and I will interpret the will of the gods"—the poem was also used to instruct and to draw moral maxims. Hence the poet might introduce new elements to well-known legends, embellish them with graphic details, or purge them of crudities, if they were inconsistent with his beliefs. The audience was accustomed to these changes and undoubtedly waited with anxious anticipation to see what new twists and turns the poet was going to give a story it knew so well.

A classic example of how freely a poet could treat familiar material is found in the lyric poet Stesichorus (early sixth century), a venerable authority on mythology.

When composing a poem in which he said that Helen of Troy had married and deserted her husbands two and three times, Stesichorus was struck blind, according to tradition, for his impiety and slander. Stesichorus then composed a palinode, a recantation, in which he boldly asserted that Helen never went to Troy at all, that Aphrodite, the goddess of love, had spirited her off to Egypt where she remained for seventeen virtuous years until her husband Menelaus found her on his way home from the Trojan War. What Paris had taken to Troy, so that its doom might be fulfilled, was only her phantom. Helen, it is said, was appeased by Stesichorus' palinode and restored his sight.

The greatest of the lyric poets was Pindar (518–438 B.C.) whose four books of victory odes (epinicians) have fortunately survived. His odes, celebrating the victory of an athlete at one of the sacred games (Olympian, Pythian, Nemean, Isthmian), were by and large religious hymns in which the victor would be presented to the gods. The opportunity was then taken, through the medium of myth, to glorify the heroic past, to stress the sanctity of religion, and to sound a strong moral note. For Pindar the athlete of his day, generally a young man of aristocratic background, had the same divine blood in his veins as the mighty men of old, and victory in one of the great national games was a fresh embodiment of that physical superiority (*arete*) displayed by epic heroes. But as respectful as Pindar was of the past, his gods were not the gay, irresponsible deities of Homer. If legend made the Olympians offensive to his standard of morality, then legend had to be reformed and improved. A notable example of this tendency is Pindar's rejection, in his *First Olympian Ode*, of the story that Pelops had been minced, cooked, and served as a feast for the gods. "I cannot understand how a god could gorge thus; I recoil!" he exclaims in horror, and refashions the story by claiming that Poseidon had carried off Pelops and that a spiteful neighbor had invented the story of his being eaten by the gods.

Aeschylus, Sophocles, and Euripides

Epic and lyric poetry had taken mythology far from its primitive origins, but another form of expression was to take it even further. Greek drama, one of the greatest achievements of the high-classical period (fifth century B.C.) had its roots in choral lyric and dance which were performed at religious festivals and, in particular, at the Great Dionysia at Athens. Said to have been invented by Thespis (fl. 534 B.C.), tragedy quickly developed from the simple interplay between one actor and the chorus into the highly sophisticated dramatic form now represented by the thirty-three extant tragedies of three prolific dramatists, Aeschylus (525–456 B.C.), Sophocles (c. 496–406 B.C.), and Euripides (485–406 B.C.). For the tragic poets, the myths and legends of the past provided the stockpile of plots for their dramas. Some used contemporary history for their plots, but Herodotus reports that when the fall of Miletus (494 B.C.) was dramatized, the Athenian audience burst into tears and the playwright was fined heavily for stirring up unhappy memories. Following Aeschylus' portrayal of happier events in Greek history (for instance, his *Persians*), heroic legend was used almost exclusively by tragic poets. Detailed episodes from the *Iliad* and the *Odyssey* were generally avoided; better dramatic material lay in legends which had less authority attached to them and which could be more freely adapted for either their moral or dramatic art. Of the more than 500 tragedies we know by title, about one-quarter were favorite themes, like the families of Oedipus and Atreus, and they were used over and over again.

Mythology, then, was the medium for the tragic poet, but the use he made of his medium was essentially for dramatic excitement, for stirring the emotions of his audience, and not merely for dramatizing a legend. However, as citizen and teacher, the poet also concerned himself with those persistent and universal problems affecting man and the world in which he lives. Mythology was called upon to serve both these ends. The heroic past, real and credible to the average Greek, permitted the tragedian to concentrate with great economy on the dramatic situation and to focus with great intensity on thought and meaning. Since his audience knew the outline of the plot, the poet was relieved of the burden of exposition; since the outcome was also known, the poet could achieve stunning ironic effects, as Sophocles did in his *Oedipus Tyrannus*. "The writer of tragedy is a lucky fellow," complains Antiphanes, a comic poet of the fourth century B.C. "The audience always knows the plot as soon as his play begins. All the poet has to do is to jog their memories. He just says 'Oedipus' and they know all the rest." The limitations imposed by the use of legendary material were overcome by embellishing old and familiar plots with new facets, new subtleties, and new meanings. Legendary material was no more a limiting factor for the Athenian playwright than old chronicles and romances were for Shakespeare.

Of the three great colossi of the Athenian stage, Sophocles was the most Homeric, telling a story largely for its inherent dramatic value. His tragic vision saw no need to challenge traditional values or the enigmatic ways of the gods and their oracles. He chose rather to dramatize individuals, noble and high-minded men and women, who were suffering as a result of some severe strain or terrible crisis. Whatever the reason for suffering—whether for guilt, excess, fulfillment of an oracle, or for something that happened in the past—Sophocles' legendary characters endure their agony, not with fatalistic resignation, but with heroic dignity. Out of their suffering a kind of balance is restored, for to Sophocles suffering serves some higher purpose, namely an educative and regenerative purpose. Antigone's self-sacrifice brings into more realistic balance the demands of the individual and the state; Philoctetes, afflicted by a loathsome disease, becomes the instrument of a great deliverance; Ajax' madness and suicide become a triumph of reason and humanity over hate; Oedipus, blinded by his own hand, gains insight, and at his death, absolution and divine grace.

While Sophocles dramatized the relationship of the individual to the higher powers ruling the universe, his predecessor, Aeschylus, had scaled Mount Olympus to fasion order out of the chaos created by the epic poets and their stories of battles and struggles between earlier dynasties of the gods. Two centuries earlier, Hesiod had attempted a similar theological reorganization in his generations of the gods, the *Theogony*. However, his vivid descriptions of the overthrow of Uranus by Cronus, and of Cronus and his Titan allies by Zeus and the Olympians had undoubtedly minimized his efforts.

In the public interest Aeschylus undertook to dramatize new and loftier ideas about the gods. The savagery of the age of the Titans had no place in his scheme of ordered government; for if order did not exist on Mount Olympus, how could it in humane, civilized, democratic Athens? Hence Aeschylus, as pious as Sophocles but not as conservative, undertook to purify the nature of godhead through dramatic representation. If religious truth demanded it, as it often did, he modified his legendary material to agree with that truth.

In the *Suppliants*, the myth of Danaus and his daughters provided Aeschylus with the plot to begin the process of purifying Zeus from the taints of anthropomorphism. His *Prometheus Bound*, though the only surviving play of a trilogy, concerns itself with the problem of evil and its relation to deity. Zeus is characterized as a tyrant, wielding brute power newly won by his victory over the Titans. He comes into head-on conflict with a beneficent but irreconcilable Prometheus, the giver of civilization to man. At the end of the trilogy it is conjectured that there was reconciliation and compromise between the two opposing forces and that Zeus evolved into a god who was both all-wise and all-powerful.

In his *Oresteia*—the only extant Greek trilogy, comprising the *Agamemnon*, *The Libation Bearers*, and the *Eumenides*—the issues are more complex. Out of the legendary sins of the house of Atreus, Aeschylus boldly creates a conception of civic and divine justice which exalted the civilized ideal as represented by the Athenian state. He dramatizes the chaos, both on earth and in heaven, that existed in the legendary past. Interwoven themes of violence, murder, and revenge gradually develop into a struggle between the old and the new order of gods. The Furies (Erinyes), whose office it is to protect the sacredness of the ties of blood, are members of old, anarchic forces. The justice they preach is harsh and vindictive—an eye for an eye and a tooth for a tooth—without regard for community good or social order. Opposing them is Apollo, spokesman for his father Zeus, the protector of the sovereign rights of king and city. Like Zeus in the *Prometheus Bound*, Apollo is yet unpolished and unschooled. He has commanded Orestes to avenge the death of his father Agamemnon by committing the horrendous act of matricide. The Furies, offended by the crime, demand their pound of flesh; Apollo insists upon revenge for the death of a king and father. The old and the new are brought into balance by Athena, daughter of Zeus and protectress of Athens. She conceives a higher ideal of justice in which the act of homicide is not to be avenged in the primitive way demanded by the Furies and young Apollo, but by a civilized instrument, a jury of Athenian citizens, which would preserve the fabric of society and would reconcile the claims of authority (Apollo) with the instincts of humanity (the Furies).

Sophocles had visualized the educative power of suffering for man, but Aeschylus' imagination had taken a bolder step: not only could man learn through suffering, but even Zeus himself could learn through experience and undergo a change of character in the course of time. This concept of a developing divine order, of religious evolution, was made possible for Aeschylus by the anthropomorphic nature of the Greek gods and the flexible, everchanging myths surrounding them.

The last and youngest of the great trio of tragic poets was Euripides, whose use of legendary material was far more startling than that of Aeschylus or Sophocles. An apostle of the new intellectualism that made man the center of its interest, Euripides maintained close relationships throughout his life with philosophers and a class of teachers known as Sophists. The latter were generally itinerant lecturers who were attracted to Athens by the wealth and political power the city had acquired by its victories over the Persians (490–479 B.C.). Although primarily practical teachers of how to be successful through the power of persuasive speech, they introduced into Athens a spirit of scepticism with regard to conventional religion and morality as revealed in the myths and legends of the gods. These professional purveyors of the new enlightenment are satirized by the comic poet Aristophanes (c. 447–c. 385 B.C.) in his play *The Clouds*.

A close friend of Euripides was the famous Sophist Protagoras (c. 485–c. 415 B.C.) whose dictum—Man is the measure of all things—centered on the doctrine of the relativity of all knowledge or opinion, thus making subjective experience the only valid ground for judgment. It was in the house of Euripides that Protagoras read his treatise on the nature of the gods which began with this sceptical statement: "As to the gods, I have no means of knowing either that they exist or that they do not exist. For many are the obstacles that impede knowledge, both the obscurity of the question and the shortness of human life."

Coming as he did under the influence of humanism and rationalism in a period which also saw the deterioration of Athenian ideals and character brought about by the Peloponnesian War (431–404 B.C.), Euripides was in sympathy with his educated contemporaries who questioned the morality of the gods of mythology and the existence of any divine government in the world. What mattered most to Euripides were the living individual and the elemental forces that were in conflict with the human psyche. Aristotle in his *Poetics* reports Sophocles as saying that he, Sophocles, portrayed men as they ought to be; Euripides, as they are. As a tragic poet, however, Euripides had inherited the tradition of expressing dramatic situations in mythological terms. Even though myths had little or no religious value to him, he exploited them as a medium for dramatizing ideas which the Athenian stage had never before witnessed. In the pursuit of his art, Euripides not only made use of lesser-known tales and legends, but also improvised freely on those which were popular and well-known. The death of Medea's children by her own hand, for example, is considered an invention of Euripides; according to local tradition, they were killed by the people of Corinth.

By treating the myths as if they had really happened to living individuals, suffering as living men and women suffer when subjected to shattering emotional experience, Euripides becomes the first realist of the stage and the forerunner of the psychological novelist. His interest in the minds and emotions of women have produced vivid portraits of deranged and brutalized victims of the cruelty of men and gods: Phaedra in the *Hippolytus*, Medea, Hecuba, Andromache, the Trojan Women, Electra, and Creusa in the *Ion*. Euripides' gods are often symbols of blind, irrational forces operative in human nature, quite indifferent to the demands of morality (Aphrodite and Artemis in the *Hippolytus*, Dionysus in the *Bacchae*). Whether in the foreground or background of his dramas, the gods are held up as being capricious, arbitrary, cruel.

Writing during the catastrophic Peloponnesian War, Euripides also used the dramatic vehicle of mythology to protest against the miseries of war and the agonies of defeat in the *Trojan Women*. Although a patriot of Athens, he violently opposed its demagogues in the *Suppliant Women*. He expresses his hatred for Athens' enemy Sparta in the *Andromache* and the *Children of Heracles*. Euripides is particularly bitter about Apollo, whose oracle at Delphi played politics by favoring the Spartan cause in the war. It was also Apollo who led Orestes to kill his mother, and in the *Ion*, Apollo is condemned as a liar and a ravisher of innocent girls. As a result of this critical treatment of the heroes and gods, Euripides strips them of their grandeur and glamor; for him true humanity lies with people of the lower classes, the honest working man and the slave.

The Hellenistic Age

When Euripides began to use mythology lightly and romantically, as he did in his *Iphigenia in Tauris* and *Helen*, he foreshadowed the spirit of the coming Hellenistic Age (323–146 B.C.). A century after Euripides, Alexander the Great (356–323 B.C.) brought about the end to the vigor and creative force of the Greek city-state (*polis*), the all-embracing community in which myth and thought had been bonded together in an intimate and meaningful relationship. Alexander carved out a huge empire in the Near and Middle East and founded numerous cities on the Greek model. Greek emigrations into the newly conquered territory spread a veneer of Hellenism over Asia as far east as India that was to last for more than a millennium. But lost in the historical movement were the pride and responsibilities of self-government. The *polis* became an administrative unit rather than a political organization; the citizen became an isolated individual and was no longer the political animal as Plato and Aristotle saw him. As the character of the community changed, so did the role of the poet and his art. The teacher and prophet who had a sense of civic responsibility was succeeded by the professional man of letters, the technical scholar, the researcher. Literature, which had been an integral part of the existence of the *polis*, became an agreeable diversion, a separate department for those educated in Greek language and culture.

Under the successors of Alexander the Great, new centers of culture arose in imitation of the famous institutions founded by Plato and Aristotle in Athens. The most celebrated of these was in Alexandria, Egypt, where the Museum and Library (founded c. 280 B.C.) housed and supported a large number of research scholars from all over the Greek East. The Royal Library in Alexandria became a center of literary production and criticism and gave the name "Alexandrian" to the literature of that age. Here scholars not only created new literary forms and imitated the old, but they also preserved the legacy of the past by copying, classifying, cataloging, and annotating older works of Greek literature. But as scholars, for whom mythology was a subject for advanced research and literature was for an audience of scholars and highly-educated laymen, they composed poetry abounding in myths and legends which became not instruments for thought, but ornaments for literary and pedantic ostentation.

The love story, little favored by earlier writers, was one of the favorite themes of the Alexandrians. To this was often added the scholarly interests of the age in antiquarianism, rationalizations of mythological lore, and library research. Apollonius Rhodius, head librarian at Alexandria (c. 260 B.C.), created a literary epic in which all these components were assembled to produce a narrative in imitation of Homer. His *Argonautica* is a scholar's tale of the heroic quest for the golden fleece and is made up of material gathered from many authorities and sources now lost to us. Apollonius transforms the myth of Jason and Medea into a highly elaborated romantic story of Medea's love for Jason and portrays her as a young girl experiencing the difficulties and doubts of a first love. (The romantic episode between Dido and Aeneas in Vergil's *Aeneid* owes much of its pathos and passion to Apollonius' account.) Apollonius fills out his narrative with local legends, explanations of ancient customs, stories of the founding of cities, descriptions of works of art, and a considerable amount of geographical data, which was one of the consuming interests of the Hellenistic Age.

Apollonius' adversary was his former teacher, Callimachus (c. 305–c. 240 B.C.), who was born in Cyrene, North Africa, librarian for the Royal Library, scholar-poet, and "poet-laureate" for the court of the ruling dynasty of Ptolemies in Egypt. To Callimachus, the long mythological narrative in the grand style was out of date. He rejected Apollonius' *Argonautica* with the caustic comment that "a big book is a bad book." He was the leading exponent of the school that advocated short poems, complete in themselves or loosely connected in a larger work, poems highly polished, refined in diction and learning, and, above all, removed from the commonplace and the trite. "I take no delight in ways where mobs hither and thither go," he declares in one of his epigrams, ". . . from public springs I never drink; I loathe all common things."

In imitation of the *Homeric Hymns*, Callimachus composed six hymns filled with recondite mythological lore, which not only "modernized" the gods and stripped them of classical seriousness, but which also served as political propaganda, comparing the glory, might, and accomplishments of the Ptolemies with those of Zeus and Apollo. His *Aetia* (Causes), a somewhat scientific or technical treatise in short epic form, continued the Hellenistic passion for rationalizing myths, history, and rituals. In other compositions, he used the barest outline of a myth (for example, Theseus and the Bull of Marathon in his *Hecale*) as an excuse for introducing elaborate effects in the forms of descriptions, digressions, or other ornamentation. Much the same technique is found in Shakespeare's *Lucrece* and Tennyson's *Oenone*.

On either side of these two schools of literature, Apollonian and Callimachean, the search for new forms of expression led Hellenistic poets to seek out local legends and folktales or to use mythological material in extraordinary ways. Theocritus (c. 310–c. 250 B.C.) created the literary pastoral (the idyll) and gave the form a long line of descendants from Vergil down to Spenser, Milton, Shelley, and Longfellow. Theocritus combined realism and romanticism in a setting of singing shepherds and simple country life. Mythology was turned into love stories: Daphnis, the idealized Sicilian hero of Greek pastoral, is punished by Aphrodite for boasting that love had no power over him; likewise the grotesque Cyclops Polyphemus—a monster in Homer's *Odyssey* and hardly a lover—is transformed into an amorous swain, desperately and hopelessly in love with the sea-nymph Galatea.

On the other side of the coin, Lycophron (born c. 320 B.C.) composed a long riddle-poem, the *Alexandra,* that outdid any other Greek poem in obscurity and in the use of recondite mythological material. Brought to Alexandria by Ptolemy Philadelphus to organize the collection of comedies in the Royal Library, Lycophron had the resources of the library at hand to collect the abstruse mythological allusions that were the vogue among the Alexandrian *literati.* The subject of the poem was a mysterious oracle of Alexandra (or Cassandra) reported to King Priam in a monolog by a messenger. The prophecy concerns the entire history of Troy and of the descendants of the Trojan and Greek heroes. Almost every theme of the Epic Cycle is touched upon, but in such a way that nothing and no one is called by any easily recognized name. Helen, for example, is referred to as "the madwoman of Pleuron's line, married five times." Pleuron was the great-grandfather of Helen's mother; the five men in Helen's life were Theseus, Menelaus, Paris, Deïphobus, and Achilles.

However much critics may deplore the literary production of the Hellenistic Age as lifeless, as a literature of exhaustion obsessed with elegance, erudition, and romantic love, the age was one in which the traditions of the past were collated and written down and thus preserved for succeeding generations. The passion of Hellenistic scholars for data of whatever kind led to the gathering of curious and exotic stories outside the mainstream of classical mythology. Mythological handbooks were also popular. The one which goes under the name of the *Bibliotheca* (The Library)—attributed incorrectly to Apollodorus of Athens, a learned scholar of the second century B.C.—undoubtedly had its source in a work of the Hellenistic period. The *Bibliotheca*, in its present form a work of the first or second century A.D., is an uncritical summary of traditional Greek mythology and contains unelaborated but reliable material on myths and legends collected from recorded literature. The interest of the age in astronomy also popularized star-myths, tales in which mythical characters were translated to the heavens and gave their names to constellations.

The rationalizing tendency of the time, foreshadowed by Euripides and exhibited in the works of Apollonius Rhodius, Callimachus, and other Hellenistic writers, produced an early anthropological theory on the origin of the gods. Euhemerus of Messene (fl. 300 B.C.) published a novel about a fictitious journey in which he claimed to have uncovered evidence that the major deities had originally been great kings and heroes of the past whose exploits, as revealed in myths and legends, were of such magnitude that mankind in a show of gratitude worshipped them as gods. To Euhemerus—from whom the word "euhemerism" is derived—Zeus became king of Crete by rebelling against and overthrowing his father Cronus who had previously held the throne. Euhemerism had a great vogue among the Romans who rationalized many of ther vague gods, such as Faunus and Saturnus, into early kings of the Italians. Among the Christian apologists, Lactantius in particular, Euhemerus' theory was exploited to show that even the pagans believed their gods to be nothing more than mere men.

The Roman Period

"Captured Greece captivated its crude conqueror," (*Graecia capta ferum victorem cepit*) is the verse by the Roman poet Horace with which historians inevitably introduce the Roman period. But the debt that Rome owed to Hellenic culture long antedated her military victory over Greece in 146 B.C. As early as the fifth century B.C. and before, Roman contacts with the Greek colonies in southern Italy and with the mysterious Etruscans to the north—who had in their own turn been influenced by the Greeks—transformed the vague and impersonal spirits of primitive Roman religion into full-fleshed Greek anthropomorphic gods. Some of their more personalized powers (Jupiter, Juno, Diana) were sufficiently similar to Olympian deities (Zeus, Hera, Artemis) to be identified with them. Gradually other Greek and Asiatic gods were introduced into the pantheon, either as new deities (Apollo, Aesculapius, Cybele) or under the names of nature gods with whom they were often identified superficially (Demeter = Ceres, Aphrodite = Venus, Persephone = Libera).

Virtually nothing remains of native Italian tradition that has not been influenced, invented, or overshadowed by the Greeks. This is particularly true of the myths concerning Roman gods; most were taken over from Greek writers or were fashioned on Greek models. Not only was Roman imagination no match for the Greek, but an early belief that all people worshipped the same gods, though under different names, accelerated the process of unrestrained borrowing. However, it was Rome's great victory over Carthage in the First Punic War (264–241 B.C.)

that stimulated her active pursuit of the arts; her second victory over the Carthaginians (201 B.C.) made the call of the Muses irresistible. In the words of the early Roman poet Porcius Licinus: "With the Second Punic War did the Muse in winged flight/Come to Romulus' crude people who in battle take delight."

The first models for early Roman writers were the Greek "classics": Homer, Euripides, and Sophocles. Livius Andronicus (c. 284–c. 204 B.C.), a Greek slave from southern Italy, translated the *Odyssey* into Latin and wrote tragedies on Greek models. But it was not long before the practical Roman mind put literature and legend to use in the glorification of the Roman state, a use that ultimately found its most perfect expression in Vergil. Naevius (c. 270–c. 201 B.C.) wrote a national epic on the First Punic War (*Bellum Punicum*) in which he drew on the Trojan Cycle and the Trojan War as an introduction to Rome's struggle with Carthage. Using Homer as a model, Ennius (239–169 B.C.), "the father of Roman poetry," composed a *Romaid*-like epic, the *Annals*, in which he glorified the great achievements of Rome from the time of Aeneas to his own day. Ennius also wrote some twenty tragedies based on Greek subjects and models, mainly on Euripides; his *Sacra Historia* followed Euhemerus in rationalizing old Greek mythology.

By the middle of the second century B.C., a new creative energy among Rome's educated sought its inspiration not so much in the classical works of Homer and Euripides, but in the technical perfection of the Alexandrians. It was not difficult to make the transition in a society that had become increasingly "Greek." Roman homes had Greek tutors and Greek libraries; to learn Greek was one of the major objectives of Roman education, and it was a Greek slave that walked beside the Roman child (hence the word "pedagogue") and talked with him in Greek. From the Alexandrians the new Roman poet took the cult of erudition, its interest in learning, mythological allusion, romance, emotion, and psychology. But the Roman poet, however much he strove to adapt Greek forms to the Latin, was not a slavish imitator. In the two main streams into which Roman literature flowed—romance and nationalism—Alexandrian learning was put to new and practical uses. The sentimental, light-handed romanticism of the Hellenistic Greek was converted into white-heat passion by such poets as Catullus (c. 84–c. 54 B.C.) and Propertius (c. 54–c. 16 B.C.). Yet Catullus earned the epithet of *doctus*, meaning that he was learned in Greek literature and mythology. Propertius, who encrusted his poems with Greek mythology, styled himself the Roman Callimachus, and found his inspiration in the *Aetia* of that renowned Alexandrian. To these and other poets who were too sensitive to bear the complexities and banalities of modern life, the imaginary and ennobling world of Greek mythology provided parallels either to cry out about lost virtues or to find support for their ecstasy in famous legendary loves.

Vergil and Ovid

The Alexandrian cult of "love and learning" was to find its two greatest Roman exponents in Vergil (70–19 B.C.) and Ovid (43 B.C.–17 A.D.). As a young man Vergil had tried his hand at the composition of various poetic genres, but these early attempts were overshadowed by his *Eclogues* (or *Bucolics*), pastoral poems modeled largely on the *Idylls* of the Alexandrian poet Theocritus. Roman temperament, however, made Vergil add elements which were hardly a part of the Theocritean landscape. In Vergil's hands the pastoral settings become more Italian; contemporary people and contemporary events, including the tragedy and suffering of Rome's civil war, were clearly alluded to. In the famous Messianic Eclogue, the fourth, which in the Middle Ages made him the herald of Christianity, Vergil prophesied the birth of a child who would bring peace to the world. The *Eclogues* were followed by the *Georgics*, a poetic treatise on farming, cited by Addison as "perfect" and by Dryden as "the best poem of the best poet." Greek in name and influenced by Alexandrian didacticism, the four short epics which made up the *Georgics* were designed to bring the spirit of Hesiod's *Works and Days* to Roman audiences. Again, Vergil's purpose was not merely to imitate the past, but to provide patriotic inspiration to his fellow-countrymen by recognizing in the farmer's hard work the basis for Rome's triumph and greatness. The climax of the fourth Georgic is a trio of mythical tales on death and rebirth; the most compelling and touching of them is the story of Orpheus' unsuccessful attempt to bring back from the land of the dead the wife he loved so much.

Turning from the pastoral and the didactic, Vergil undertook, with the encouragement of the new political establishment of Augustus, to compete with Homer in the epic. His aim was not to recreate another Achilles or Odysseus, but to sing the praises of the greatness of Rome, its past and its destiny. He worked for more than ten years on his *Aeneid* and then died before perfecting it to the point he wished. The material that went into the creation of this learned historic-patriotic epic were essentially Greek myths, Greek philosophy, Greek history, and even Greek romance. But in integrating and recombining hundreds of these elements, he turned out a work that was completely and uniquely Roman. Whatever he borrowed from the Greeks were altered in such a way that it actually became the opposite of what the Greeks, particularly the Alexandrians, stood for. *Timeo Danaos et dona ferentes*, "I fear the Greeks even when they bear gifts,"—this famous line is sufficient to show his anti-Greek sentiment. The romantic story of Dido and Aeneas, so appealing to St. Augustine and to modern readers, turns out on closer inspection to be anti-romantic. For the Roman audience, the romance undoubtedly suggested the catastrophe caused by the infatuation of a political leader for a foreign woman, Antony and Cleopatra. Roman loyalty and duty, symbolized by Vergil's hero Aeneas, demanded the subordination of personal inclinations to the responsibilities of mature leadership. By selecting the legend of Aeneas, Vergil firmly joined the nebulous early history of Rome with the attractive heroic past. But it was not the Homeric Greeks that Vergil made the ancestors of Rome's great leaders, but rather their enemies, the Trojans, whose defeat was avenged when Rome conquered Greece.

Alexandrian "love and learning" took quite a different turn with Ovid. Urbane, witty, and facile, a product of an age that had not suffered the searing effects of civil war, Ovid was temperamentally unsuited to take on the role of the solemn, patriotic seer, urging devotion to duty and faith in the mission of Rome. Lacking the puritanism and seriousness of Vergil, he also lacked the unrestrained passion of a Catullus or a Propertius. For his *Amores* he manufactured a beloved, Corinna, to whom he could direct his verses on the varying moods of love. Ovid was the detached sophisticate who coolly and without moral consciousness recorded the peccadilloes of Rome's high society. His mission was to amuse, to give pleasure;

his prime talent lay in the narration of mythology in a rapid and limpid style. His highly successful *Amores* (Loves) was followed by the *Heroides* (Heroines), letters mostly by famous women of mythology addressed to absent lovers or husbands. In this and other works Ovid shows himself to be a master of Alexandrian psychology, particularly of feminine psychology; but the psychological traits he describes, however vivid and Alexandrian, are not those of Greek but of sophisticated Roman women. Helen of Troy, for example, is portrayed as a society woman who protests Paris' outrage against her virtue but contrives at the same time to encourage him. In the *Ars Amatoria* (Art of Love), Ovid dubs himself the Professor of Love (*praeceptor amoris*) and with amused cynicism presents the Science of Love as if it were one of the didactic "how to" handbooks of his day.

Ovid's crowning achievement was his *Metamorphoses*, a mythological epic of baroque design in which he interwove two hundred and fifty stories, beginning with the creation of the world and ending with the elevation of Julius Caesar into a star. The mythical tales centered on the miraculous and magical transformation of people—usually motivated by a love episode—into animals, birds, trees, flowers, stones, water, or heavenly bodies. In addition, many of the stories were given in aetiological turn which would explain the existence of some natural or man-made phenomenon. The Alexandrian influence is obviously strong in Ovid. His manner of linking short stories into a continuous whole is fashioned on the technique Callimachus used in his *Aetia*; the compendium of mythical transformations was a favorite form among a number of Alexandrians. But Ovid's scholarship was not limited to the learned poets of Alexandria; it encompassed the vast corpus of mythological literature from Homer to Vergil; and to this he added no small amount of his own creative imagination. Although the *Metamorphoses* is somewhat of an anthology, it is no less an original work with the character of its creator strongly etched into it. Ovid's interest in feminine psychology, his sensuous vitality, capriciousness, and irreverence are all there. "He leads us," says a distinguished Ovidian scholar, "through romance, burlesque, splendor, horror, pathos, macabre, rhetoric, genre painting, debate, landscape-painting, antiquarian interest, patriotic pride—wherever his own fancy leads him." To these may be added, without exhausting the list: parody, sentimentality, legendary history, melodrama, humor.

The influence of the master poet of love and marvels reaches from his own day into the twentieth century. Ovid's works contributed to and gave authority to the ideal of romantic love in the Middle Ages, a concept which affects to a considerable extent the arts and even the morality of America and Europe. He inspired painters, from Poussin to Picasso, and writers such as Boccaccio, Chaucer, Shakespeare, Goethe, Rainer Maria Rilke, André Malraux, and T. S. Eliot. Of all the classics, Shakespeare, whether by his "small Latin" or through Golding's famous translation, knew Ovid's *Metamorphoses* best. Even Dante, whose *Divine Comedy* was moved by the solemn spirit of Vergil, ranked Ovid among the four great poets of antiquity.

With Vergil and Ovid, preparation for a journey into the world of mythology is approaching its end. It must be kept in mind, however, that only the high points have been touched upon; that almost every writer of antiquity, whether Greek or Roman, was so deeply versed in myth and legend that he became a resource for some otherwise unrecorded tale. Even early Christian writers, in their attempt to discredit their adversaries by pointing out the absurdities of stories about pagan gods, often transmit the learning of writers whose works have been lost to us. Sometimes a school text has come down to modern times—somewhat like the second century A.D. *Fabulae* or *Genealogiae* (Tales or Genealogies) mistakenly attributed to a certain Hyginus—which records, however imperfectly, the story of some lost work of a classical writer. Finally, there are the scholiasts, early commentators on Greek and Roman works, who often shed light on obscure mythological allusions in much the same way that modern scholars provide commentaries on the obscure symbols and abstruse quotations of a James Joyce, a T. S. Eliot, or an Ezra Pound.

The influence of classical mythology has waxed and waned throughout the ages, and though "faith of reason" may tell us that dryads no longer haunt our parks nor naiads rise from our oceans; still, as Coleridge insists, "the heart doth need a language, still/Doth the old instinct bring back the old names."

Myth, Legend, Folktale

Up to this point, the words "myth" and "legend" have been used rather loosely to describe those traditional narratives that have come down to us through Greek and Roman sources. This comes about because scholars, even within the same discipline, find it difficult to come to a common understanding on the definition of terms and the means of classifying the overwhelming variety of tales that are subsumed under the name of "mythology." There is however, increasing acceptance of a broad and convenient division of these stories into *myth* (sometimes called *myth proper*), *legend* or *saga*, and *folktale*. But it must be recognized from the start that, more often than not, no clear line of demarcation exists between these divisions; it is quite possible for one story to contain elements common to two or all three of these narrative forms.

Myths are stories of events, usually believed to have taken place in the distant past, that embody the traditions of a people concerning the universe and their religious beliefs. Myths deal with the actions of gods, their rituals, their relationships to one another, to heroes, and to the existence of natural phenomena. Gods or demigods are the main characters of these narratives. Myths should be understood not as amusing tales of an ill-informed people, but as a mode of perception by which man, at a certain stage in his development, made order out of chaos, made sense out of the manifold diversity existing in the world. "It is the object of myth, as of science," states Professor Pierre Grimal, "to explain the world, to make its phenomena intelligible."

Sir G. L. Gomme makes a similar observation when he says that myth explains matters in "the science of a prescientific age." Myth's most characteristic function, then, is explanatory of "aetiological" (*cf.* Callimachus' *Aetia*): how the universe was created, how man was brought into being, why a certain animal is the way it is (for instance, the myth of Arachne and the characteristics of the spider), how certain natural phenomena came into existence (such as the Pillars of Hercules), or how rituals began (for example, Prometheus' deception of Zeus to explain why certain parts of animals, and not others, are sacrificed to the gods of heaven).

Legends or Sagas—the Scandinavian word "saga" is often used, since "legend" has also acquired the very general meaning of story or narrative—are those tales which contain an element, no matter how minimal and tenuous, of historical fact. Unlike myths, the main characters of these narratives are human; the events described (a famous raid, a great migration, a dangerous hunt) have a basis in fact. But as the story passes from generation to generation, from singer to singer, and is ultimately put into writing, the original version has been so elaborated and so modified that it bears little resemblance to the actual event. A good illustration of the legendary narrative is Homer's *Iliad*. It has its setting in a very real war of the Late Bronze Age, the Trojan War, but the causes of the war, the intervention of the gods in its conduct, and the military strategy described by Homer, have no bearing on the historical facts of the war. Strabo (64 B.C. –c. 21 A.D.), a geographer and historian during the reign of Augustus, appositely remarks: "Homer took the Trojan War, a historical fact, and decked it out with his fanciful stories."

In contrast with myth and legend, whose function it was to record an ostensible truth and to be taken seriously, a great number of traditional tales were told principally and simply for the sake of amusement. Folktale is the term applied to this rather broad category of stories. The *Odyssey* is a collection of such stories that Homer has ingeniously woven into an epic of a man's return home after a long absence. Sir James Fraser, in the introduction to his editon of Apollodorus' *Bibliotheca*, defines the folktale and adds an appropriate word of caution:

> By folktales I understand narratives invented by persons unknown and handed down at first by word of mouth from generation to generation, narratives which, though they profess to describe actual occurrences, are in fact purely imaginary, have no other aim than the entertainment of the hearers and make no real claim on his credulity. . . . The zealous student of myth and ritual, more intent on explaining than on enjoying the more of the people, is too apt to invade the garden of romance and with a sweep of his scythe to lay the flowers of fancy in the dust. He needs to be reminded occasionally that we must not look for a myth or a rite behind every tale, like a bull behind every hedge or a canker in every rose.

All three forms of traditional narratives are rich in recurrent themes or motifs: unusual creatures and unusual physical phenomena, ogres, cruel stepmothers, life tokens, marvelous never-never lands, and the like. While these narratives and their motifs are of considerable interest to the psychologist, anthropologist and the comparative mythologist for insights into the human condition, no single theory has yet successfully explained the entire range of Greek and Roman mythology. The psychologist, for example, has made much over the motifs of violence and cruelty that persist in mythological forms, but as Stith Thompson has astutely perceived, ordinary life processes do not develop into folk motifs; there must be something within that process that people will remember and respect. In short, motifs develop from the dramatic, from the more than commonplace action. Getting dressed, eating breakfast, and going about one's day-to-day pursuits are not elements worth remembering and hence do not become folk motifs. But when a hero puts on a cap of invisibility, makes a magic journey to a marvelous land to kill a monster (as Perseus does when he slays the Gorgon Medusa), a number of motifs are involved, and each of them survives because it has been found satisfying to generations of storytellers. The recurrence of these motifs in different parts of the world may be due to similar thought processes. Sometimes they are historical and indicate a line of descent from one to the other or—as is the case in Homer's great popularity and the broad geographical distribution of his epics—from a common source.

Cosmogony and Theogony: Greek Myths of the Creation

Sing Heav'nly Muse . . .
In the beginning, how the heav'ns and earth
Rose out of Chaos.

Milton—*Paradise Lost*

From very early times the Greeks were interested in the beginnings of things, the genesis of the world and the origins of their gods. This interest, expressed first in myths and later by philosophy, arose not only from the well-known curiosity of the Greeks, but also from the caprices of history. The Greek-speaking people, coming comparatively late to the Mediterranean lands through a long series of migrations starting in the third millennium B.C., found on their arrival divinities and attendant mythologies of diverse ethnic populations from the manifold strata of the Bronze and Stone Ages. Even among the invading Greeks there was enough diversity in their religious beliefs to cause even further division when they intermingled and blended with the pre-Greek peoples. The result was a great but confusing pantheon of deities and cults. By Homer's time (c. 750 B.C.) the Olympians, with Zeus as their leader, had become—at least among the ruling classes—the dominant gods of the Greeks. But embedded in Homer's epics are a number of tales which tell of struggles and intrigues, within and without the Olympian household, to indicate that Zeus had considerable competition from other deities in his bid for power. Homer's objective, however, was not to sing of beginnings and hence his account merely touched upon the procreation of the gods. To Homer, benign old Oceanus, a river-god whose deep-flowing waters encircled the limits of the physical world, was the progenitor of the gods. Together with his wife Tethys, these two were the great-grandparents of all, as reflected in these lines of Spenser's *Faerie Queene*:

> Next came the aged Ocean and his Dame
> Old Tethys, th' oldest two of all the rest;
> For all the rest of those two parents came,
> Which afterward both see and land possest.

Rufinus, the fourth-century Christian apologist, tells us that there were many Greek writers on the subject of origins of the world, but two names stand out among

them: Orpheus and Hesiod. Of the two, Hesiod (c. 700 B.C.), the crusty bard of
Ascra in Boeotia, is by far the most important, since his mythical account of the
generation of the gods (*Theogony*) is the earliest, the most detailed, and the most
influential. In the invocation to his poem, the Muses of Mount Helicon assure
Hesiod that although they know how to speak many false things and give them the
semblance of truth (a caustic comment possibly directed against Homer), they also
know how to tell the truth (fig. 2). With this guarantee of inspirational integrity on
the part of the Muses, Hesiod proceeds to construct the universe and to give an or-

Figure 2.   Hesiod and his Muse. *Lithograph by Georges Braque, 1946,
illustrating Hesiod's* Theogony. *Spencer Collection, The New York Public
Library, Astor, Lenox and Tilden Foundation.*

derly development to the generations of gods culminating with the establishment of Zeus and the Olympians as the source of all that is good in life. His method is chiefly by genealogical classification, the traditional means, as within human families, of providing order and authority. To the anthropomorphic mind of the early Greeks, it was natural for the creation of the world to take place as a series of conceptions and procreations; that was the only way creation could be imagined in Hesiod's time. Stripped of its mythological disguise, genealogy easily becomes natural philosophy.

The Birth of the Universe

In the beginning, Hesiod tells us, Chaos came into being first, then broad-bosomed Gaea (Earth), dark Tartarus deep in the depths of the ground, and Eros (Love). From Chaos came forth Erebus (Darkness) and Nyx (Night); and from the union of Nyx and Erebus were born Aether (Light) and Hemera (Day). Gaea (Earth), "without sweet union of love," gave birth to Uranus (Heaven), Ourea (Mountains), and Pontus (Sea). In this simple way Hesiod fashions the physical outlines of the world, living quarters made ready for its divine inhabitants. He goes one step further by providing in the subcellar a kind of jail, Tartarus, for recalcitrant deities to be restrained and kept out of circulation. Tartarus as a Hell or a penal institution for human souls comes as a later development.

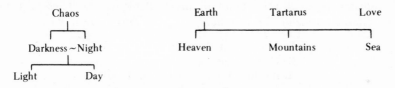

Chaos—related to the word "chasm" and sometimes best translated by that word —is yawning, gaping but substantial Space. Hesiod sidesteps the philosophical question of how or whether anything existed before Chaos; to him it is a starting point but not an absolute beginning. From Chaos and Earth all things are generated: the intangible and gloomy (Darkness and Night) from Chaos; the visible and solid (sky, sea, mountains, sun, stars) from primal Earth.

As successive generations of gods are brought into being, the universe gradually becomes more diverse and more complex. Eros (Love), on the other hand, has no offspring since he represents physical desire, a cosmic power that brings beings into physical union, the force of generation and reproduction. Aristotle, in his *Metaphysics*, suspected that Hesiod was the first to look for a prime mover in the universe and that he used Eros as the cause that from the first moved things and brought them together. Later philosophical speculation on Hesiod's cosmogony is reflected in Ovid's *Metamorphoses* where Chaos is considered a mixture of elements or potentialities of matter of all kinds.

The Birth of the Titans

When the primary elements of the physical world are brought into being, Earth mates with Heaven and produces a rather large family: the twelve Titans, the three Cyclopes, and the three Hecatoncheires (Hundred-Handed Ones).

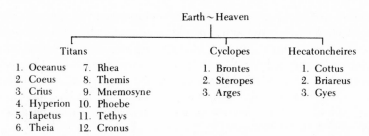

Of the Titans little is known with certainty except that they are mostly very ancient, primeval powers that were little worshiped in historical Greece. In the Hesiodic account, however, they form an early ruling dynasty and become the parents and grandparents of later gods. Oceanus and Tethys, as we have seen, are mentioned by Homer as the progenitors of the gods. Hyperion apparently was a sun-god.

Themis, on the authority of Aeschylus, is the same as Gaea and hence another form of Earth. Phoebe, whose name means "bright," possibly had some association with the moon as did her granddaughter Artemis, while Aeschylus tells us that she possessed the Delphic oracle before Apollo. Mnemosyne can hardly be more than an abstraction since her name means nothing more than Memory. Little can be said of the functions or the meanings of the names of Coeus and Crius. The names of Cronus, Iapetus, Oceanus, Tethys, and Rhea apparently are not derived from the Greek language and in all probability are pre-Hellenic deities. These obscure gods receive a humorous touch in Christopher Fry's *A Phoenix Too Frequent:*

> *Tegeus:* I swear, I swear . . .
> By Coeus, Crius, Iapetus, Cronus, and so on—
> By the three Hecatoncheires, by the insomnia
> of Tisiphone, by Jove, by jove . . .
>
> *Dynamene:* You needn't labor to prove your secondary education.

As for the Cyclopes and Hecatoncheires, these grotesque creatures are brought into existence in the remote beginnings of Hesiod's world and later serve as agents and allies of Zeus. The Cyclopes (Round-Eyes) each had one eye in the middle of their foreheads. The names Brontes (Thunder), Steropes (Lightning), and Arges (Flash) are descriptive of three aspects of the same phenomenon. Further in the narrative the Cyclopes as divine smiths fashion Zeus' attributes: thunderbolt and lightning. In later poets, the Cyclopes are associated with the artisan-god Hephaestus as his workmen (fig. 37). So in Marlowe's *Edward II* when the king says:

> My heart is an anvil unto sorrow,
> Which beats upon it like the Cyclops' hammers
> And with the noise turns up my giddy brain. . . .

In Homer, however, they are uncivilized, savage, cannibal shepherds, and later on we shall see how the civilized Odysseus matches his wits against an "un-Noble Savage," a Cyclops whom Homer calls Polyphemus.

Not much can be said about the Hecatoncheires, the hundred-handed giants, except that they become Zeus' secret weapon in his struggle against the Titans. In the *Iliad* we hear that one of these stalwarts, Briareus, is brought up from the sea to help Zeus put down a palace revolt plotted by Hera, Poseidon, and Athena. It has been conjectured that the octopus, a favorite theme in early Greek art, has suggested the monstrous shape of the Hecatoncheires, but it is likely that they were conceived purely in the imagination as creatures many times more powerful than ordinary beings, just as the eminent historian Arnold Toynbee calls the modern computer "a hundred-handed giant" and "an electronic Briareus."

The Overthrow of Uranus (Heaven)

Hesiod has now set the stage for a series of dramatic actions interspersed with further creations and elaborations of the divine universe. Heaven, very unpaternally, found begetting children was not to his liking, and as they were born he hid them in the great body of Earth and would not let them see the light of day. Earth, in great pain, devised a plan and a weapon that would help ease her straitened condition. She then called upon her Titan children for help. All were frightened and would not volunteer for the dangerous mission, all except the youngest Titan, Cronus. Now, in Hesiod's own words:

> . . . vast Earth rejoiced greatly in spirit, and set and hid Cronus in an ambush, and put in his hands a jagged sickle, and revealed to him the whole plot. And Heaven came, bringing on night and longing for love, and he lay about Earth spreading himself full upon her. Then the son from his ambush stretched forth his left hand and in his right took the great long sickle with jagged teeth, and swiftly lopped off his own father's members and cast them away to fall behind him. And not vainly did they fall from his hand; for all the bloody drops that gushed forth Earth received, and as the seasons moved round she bare the strong Erinyes (Furies) and the great Giants with gleaming armor. . . . And so soon as he had cut off the members with flint and cast them from the land into the surging sea, they were swept away over the main a long time; and a white foam spread around them from the immortal flesh, and in it there grew a maiden. First she drew near holy Cythera, and from there, afterwards, she came to sea-girt Cyprus, and came forth an awful and lovely goddess, and grass grew up about her beneath her shapely feet. Her gods and men call Aphrodite. . . . And with her went Eros, and comely Desire followed her at her birth at the first and as she went into the assembly of the gods.

We have no way of knowing whether Hesiod was ever aware of the original significance of this crude myth of emasculation. Variant forms of it are told all over the world to explain the separation of heaven and earth. A common motif is the physical link, a tree or a navel-string, and some scholars would interpret the story of Jack and the Beanstalk as one such tale of how the sky was separated from the earth. In the Hesiodic myth, anthropomorphized Heaven and Earth (Uranus and Gaea) are bound together in a sexual union, and it is Cronus' act of violence that irrevocably severs the bond between them. The analog to this tale comes from as far away as New Zealand: the Maori myth of Rangi and Papa (Heaven and Earth) who cling together and keep their children in darkness between their bodies until one of their sons forces them apart and allows the children to see the light of day. Similar motifs in Babylonian and Hittite texts of the second millennium B.C. have led to a current view among scholars that there exists a direct line of descent between tales from the Near East to those of Hesiod's day. Among psychoanalysts of the Freudian persuasion, Cronus' primeval crime dramatizes the Oedipal striving of the son for sexual freedom through the elimination of his father-rival.

Heaven's tragedy is not in vain, however, for a god never loses an intimate part of himself or bleeds without new life springing forth from his limbs or blood. The mutilation of Heaven leads to the birth of the Erinyes—better known by their Roman name: Furies—from the drops of blood that spatter the ground. This creation from the primal act of violence is most appropriate since the Erinyes are the spirits that avenge wrongs, especially the high crime of murder committed aginst a blood relative. Their origin is not very clear: some think they developed from the ghosts of those wrongfully put to death; others consider them embodied and personalized curses. Aeschylus calls them "blood hounds," and at Orestes' trial for matricide in the *Eumenides*, the poet has the chorus of Erinyes sing these words:

> We hold we are straight and just. If a man
> can spread his hands and show they are clean,
> no wrath of ours shall lurk for him.
> Unscathed he walks through his life time.
> But one like this man before us, with stained
> hidden hands, and the guilt upon him,
> shall find us beside him, as witnesses
> of the truth, and we show the clear in the end
> to avenge the blood of the murdered.

Aeschylus' description of the Furies has strongly influenced later artists and writers to portray them as terrifying creatures with serpents for hair and carrying torches and scourges in their hands. These are some of Aeschylus' words for them in the *Eumenides:*

> . . . they are black and utterly
> repulsive, and they snore with breath that drives one back.
> From their eyes drips the foul ooze, and their dress is such
> as is not right to wear in the presence of the gods'
> statues, nor even into any human house.
>
> . . . those gray
> and aged children, they with whom no mortal man,
> no god, nor even any beast, will have to do.
> It was because of evil they were born, because
> they hold the evil darkness of the Pit (Tartarus) below
> Earth, loathed alike by men and by the heavenly gods.

The result of these descriptions is that the Furies become part of the scenery of many a poet's Hell, the best known of which is Dante's Inferno in the *Divine Comedy:*

> . . . for my eye had drawn me wholly to the high
> tower with glowing summit,
> where, all at once had risen up three Hellish
> Furies, stained with blood; who had the
> limbs and attitude of women,
> and where girt with greenest hydras; for hair
> they had little serpents and vipers, where-
> with their horrid temples were bound.

And he (Vergil), knowing well the handmaids of the
    Queen of everlasting lamentation (Persephone),
    said to me: "Mark the fierce Erinyes!
This is Megaera on the left hand; she, that weeps
    upon the right is Alecto; Tisiphone is in the
    middle . . . ."

In the Alexandrian poets and their successors we find the following names assigned to this trio of creatures sprung from Heaven's spilled blood: Alecto (Un-
resting), Megaera (Grudger), and Tisiphone (Avenger).

The grim myth recorded by Hesiod has yet another surprising sequel, one which
transforms an ugly scene into one of beauty. When Heaven's members are cast
into the sea, foam gathered about them and a startling creation takes shape in the
form of the goddess of love, Aphrodite. Hesiod passes over any comment on her unnatural birth, but rather speaks of the feminine powers associated with this mighty
goddess: "the whisperings of maidens and smiles and deceits with sweet delight
and love and graciousness." After being formed in the sea—Hesiod connects
Aphrodite's name with *aphros*, the Greek word for foam—she is wafted first to the
island of Cythero off the coast of Sparta, and then to the island of Cyprus, both of
which claim her as their own. Hence, Aphrodite is also called Cyprian, Cypris,
or Cytherea. Shakespeare calls her Cytherea in the *Winter's Tale* to help describe
Perdita's garland:

               . . . violets dim,
    But sweeter than the lids of Juno's eyes
    or Cytherea's breath.

The primitive origins of Aphrodite, whom the Romans called Venus, is further
transformed into an event of rare beauty by the Renaissance painter Sandro Botticelli. His *Birth of Venus* (fig. 3), painted about 1480, shows a nude but ethereal
goddess being blown lightly ashore by two wind-gods, who look more like angels
than gods, and about to be received by the personification of Spring, the symbol of
rebirth. Coming under the influence of Renaissance Neoplatonism, Botticelli's
painting was capable of a wide range of allegorical interpretations which could
link the pagan past—even Hesiod's version of how the goddess of love came into
being—with the Christian symbols of the painter's own time.

The Reign of Cronus

With Heaven removed from the scene of action, Hesiod is ready for a new phase
in the development of the divine universe. Cronus and his fellow-Titans now represent the ruling powers and during their tenure a spate of new deities are brought
into being. A large number of these are personifications of evils. Many others represent specific natural phenomena such as rivers, winds, and heavenly bodies as
opposed to the primary elements brought into being during the first stage of creation. Hesiod also introduces during Cronus' reign the creation of a repertoire of
mythological monsters, creatures that will test the mettle of legendary heroes or that
will be found as residents in many a literary Underworld. Finally, at the end of this
phase of creation, the first generation of Olympians—the gods who will form the
ruling dynasty of the final period—is born. Hesiod's logic should not be overlooked. The malevolent deities of evil come to life immediately after Cronus acts

Figure 3. Botticelli. The birth of Venus. *Painting, c. 1480. Uffizi Gallery, Florence. (Alinari)*

violently against his father; the nature divinities are balanced between the beneficent aspects and the frightening and destructive elements of the physical world;
the Olympians and their allies, in contrast to the tyrannical and cruel Cronus, represent ethical and anthropocentric deities.

Night, the offspring of Chaos, brings forth a host of what we would mostly
call abstractions or personifications: Doom, Fate, Death, Sleep, Dreams, Blame,
Old Age—just to name a representative few of the catalog of fifteen. In Hesiod's
time, and even in Plato's, there was no understanding of what abstractions were.
Although they were invisible, they had a great influence in human affairs, and
hence they must be gods and must be given their due honor. The association of
these powers with Night is explained in this way: Night is the mother of Death
because they are so alike; she is the mother of the Fates (Moerae) and the goddesses
of Vengeance (Keres) because of their affinity with Death; she is the mother of
Sleep because sleep is the brother of Death and takes place at night; she is the
mother of Dreams since they too come at night; she is the mother of Deceit and Sex
which are generally practiced at night; she is the mother of Blame, Pain, Retribution (Nemesis), Old Age, and Strife (Eris) because they are dark and dreadful; she
is the mother of the Hesperides because both live in the far west "beyond the
glorious Ocean."

Another catalog of evil progeny is produced from one of the children of Night,
namely Strife (Eris). Most of her children are logical offspring because strife
or discord is their underlying cause. Like her mother Night, Strife does not need
the assistance of a male consort to produce a brood such as this: Fightings, Battles,
Murders, Quarrels, Lying Words, Disputes, Lawlessness, and Ruin. Some of
Strife's children also appear as unavoidable afflictions which beset mankind: Toil,
Forgetfulness, Hunger, and Suffering.

The scene of creation now shifts to Pontus (Sea) and his descendants. Pontus mates with Earth and produces three sons and two daughters: Nereus, the kindly Old Man of the Sea, Thaumas (Wondrous), Phorcys, Ceto (Sea-Monster Woman), and Eurybia (Mighty).

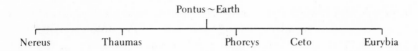

Pontus ~ Earth

Nereus   Thaumas   Phorcys   Ceto   Eurybia

Pontus' descendants have two sides to their character. One is beneficent, as represented by the sea-nymphs who are descended from Nereus. The other side is less pleasant. With but few exceptions we hear of terrifying mythological monsters who derive their descent either from Thaumas or from Phorcys and Ceto. To Hesiod, who openly discourages seafaring as an occupation, these monsters signify perhaps the destructive and death-dealing aspects of the sea.

Nereus and Doris, the daughter of Oceanus—we need not be disturbed by the fact that Hesiod has not yet introduced the Oceanids—become the parents of the Nereids, the nymphs of the sea. Hesiod says that there are fifty of these goddesses and gives a long list of their names that, by and large, are descriptive of the sea and the land surrounding it. Examples are Speo (Cave), Eulimene (Good Harbor), Halia (Salty), and Cymo (Wavy). Included in this catalog are the names of the traditional sea-nymphs who play important roles in various mythological dramas: Thetis, Galatea, and Amphitrite. Thaumas, like his brother Nereus, takes an Oceanid for a wife and begets three daughters who in one way or another are related to strong winds.

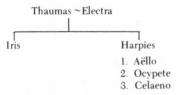

Thaumas ~Electra

Iris   Harpies
                        1. Aëllo
                        2. Ocypete
                        3. Celaeno

Swift, gold-winded Iris is the goddess or spirit of the rainbow. The Greeks and Romans thought of the rainbow as a sign of rain, and hence Iris is occasionally brought into a marital relationship with Zephyrus, the rain-producing west wind. The two concepts of rainbow and rain are brought together by Milton in his *Comus*:

> Iris there with humid blow
> Waters the odorous banks, that blow
> Flowers of more mingled hue
> Than her purpled scarf can shew
> And drenches with Elysian dew
> . . . .
> Beds of hyacinth and roses.

Iris, however, is best known in classical literature as a messenger both to gods and men. In the *Iliad* she is Zeus' personal messenger; in later poets her employer is Hera, Zeus having replaced her with Hermes. Iris' name survives in English as the name of a flower and of the colored portion of the eye, as well as in such words as "iridescent."

As their names clearly indicate, Iris' two sisters are personifications of the storm winds: Aëllo (Stormwind) and Ocypete (Swiftwind); later poets add a third with the appropriate name of Celaeno (Dark). Collectively these three sisters are known as the Harpies (Snatchers), and as such they are capable of carrying off various people and things. This is how the Harpies must have appeared to Hesiod. However, the words "wind," "spirit," and "soul" are closely related in Greek, Latin, and in Hebrew as well, and this relationship gives rise to the view that originally the Harpies were also considered souls of the dead. Their representation in art as birds with faces of women, a well-known form of the soul in popular belief, and the widespread notion that the souls of the dead can snatch away the souls of the living, further support this view.

The Monstrous Offspring of Phorcys and Ceto

Phorcys, styled an Old Man of the Sea in the Homeric poems, mates with his sea-monster sister Ceto and begets a host of monstrous creatures. On the principle of like begetting like, these in turn produce several generations of other monsters. Hesiod appears anxious to bring all this unnatural and unattractive offspring into existence early so as not to make them near-relations of the great Olympian god Zeus. In genealogical form, these are the generations of strange creatures whom we meet again in the adventures of such heroes as Heracles, Perseus, and Beller-ophon. Spenser identifies Phorcys in the *Faerie Queene* as ". . . the father of that fatall brood/By whome those old Heroes wonne such fame."

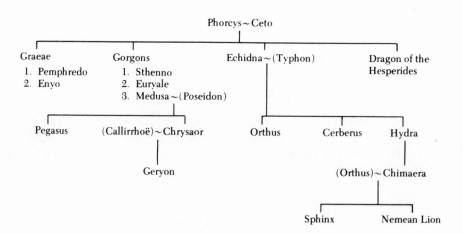

(Some interpreters of Hesiod's text make Echidna a sister of Geryon, and Echidna and Orthus the parents of the Sphinx and the Nemean Lion.)

The Graeae—the name is derived from the Greek word for "old" or "old wom-an"—apparently are the personifications of old age. Hesiod says that they were gray-haired from birth; later accounts make them blind and toothless or having only one eye and one tooth between them. William Morris (1834–1896), in his *Earthly Paradise*, imagines them like this:

There sat the crones that had the single eye,
Clad in blue sweeping cloak and snow-white gown;
While o'er their backs their straight white hair hung down
In long thin locks; dreadful their faces were,
Carved all about with wrinkles of despair;
And as they sat they crooned a dreary song,
Complaining that their lives should last so long,
In that sad place that no one came anear,
In that wan place desert of home and fear;
And singing, still they rocked their bodies bent,
And ever each to each the eye they sent.

More frightening than the Graeae are the Gorgons, creatures so nightmarish that a person who looks upon them is turned to stone. Medusa, the mortal one of the terrifying trio and best known in mythology, had the sea-god and horse-god Poseidon for her lover. Being pregnant with his child when the hero Perseus severed her head from her body, she produced the winged horse Pegasus and the little-known Chrysaor from her bloodied trunk (fig. 4). In early Greek art, the Gorgon Medusa is shown with hair done up in a coiffure of hissing snakes, flat-nosed, grinning horrendously, tongue protruding, and with fixed, wide-open eyes. Her head was often depicted on Greek buildings and shields, presumably to frighten enemies and to ward off the evil eye or evil spirits. A reasonable interpretation of the origin of Medusa and her sister-Gorgons is that they were personifications of nightmares, the kind that petrify the dreamer and scare him to death. Under the influence of later Greek artists, particularly the Alexandrians and their successors, Medusa's head is modeled along more attractive lines and given gentle features. The bronze statue of Benvenuto Cellini (1500–1571) in the Loggia dei Lanzi at Florence (fig. 5) shows how far removed Medusa has become from the frightening mask of earlier times.

In the context of the Gorgon's ability to transfix, petrify, and destroy, we can appreciate such literary allusions in Spenser's *Epithalamion* when the poet describes the effect his bride has on him:

> . . . stand astonisht lyke to those which red
> Medusaes mazeful hed.

Figure 4. The Gorgon Medusa holding Pegasus, the winged horse. *Terracotta relief, early sixth century B.C. National Museum, Syracuse. (Hirmer)*

Figure 5.   Benvenuto Cellini. Perseus holding the severed head of Medusa. *Bronze, 1554. Florence. (Alinari)*

And MacDuff in Shakespeare's *Macbeth* calling upon others to view Duncan's body: "Approach the chamber and destroy your sight/With a new Gorgon." Then in Ezra Pound's *Canto XV:*

> To the door,
> Keep your eyes on the mirror!
> Prayed we to the Medusa,
>   petrifying the soil by the shield,
> Holding it downward
>   he hardened the track
> Inch before us, by inch,
>   the matter resisting,
> The heads rose from the shield,
>   hissing, held downwards.
> Devouring maggots,
>   the face only half potent,
> The serpents' tongues
>   grazing the swill top,
> Hammering the souse into hardness,
>   the narrow rast,
> Half the width of a sword's edge.

The remaining descendants of Phorcys and Ceto bear little resemblance to human beings; rather they are a mixture of monstrous animals and hideous hybrids. Cerberus (fig. 6) and Orthus (sometimes Orthrus) are of the canine species. Cerberus is described by Hesiod as a flesh-eating creature, "the brazen-voiced hound of Hades, fifty-headed, relentless, and strong." He guards or is the doorkeeper at the home of the god of the lower world, and "on those who go in he fawns with his tail and both his ears, but suffers them not to go back out again, but keeps watch and devours whomsoever he catches going out." The number of heads on Cerberus varies from author to author and from artist to artist: some give him as many as one hundred, others a more conventional and practical three. To make him even more frightening, artists often embellish his tail and mane with snakes.

Cerberus is clearly one of the grim aspects of Death, a flesh-devouring hellhound, welcoming visitors but not permitting their return to the living. Orthus, although not as popular as Cerberus, appears to be one other such demonic dog of the lower world. His master is Geryon, a three-headed or three-bodied monster, whose home is far to the west at the edge of the world, a common death residence. Geryon is most probably another death figure and, like Hades, he has his own hellhound.

In the reptile family there is Echidna and her equally unattractive spouse Typhon. Echidna is half-human and half-snake, "great and awful, with speckled skin, eating raw flesh beneath the secret parts of the holy earth." Her husband Typhon—called Typhaon and Typhoeus by Hesiod—is a child of Earth and Tartarus and even more frightening than Echidna. Hesiod describes him thus:

> From his shoulders grew a hundred heads of a snake, a fearful dragon, with dark, flickering tongues, and from under the brows of his eyes in his marvelous heads flashed fire, and fire burned from his heads as he glared. And there were voices in all his dreadful heads which uttered every kind of sound unspeakable; for at one time, they made sounds such that the gods understood, but at another, the noise of a bull bellowing aloud in proud ungovernable fury; and at another, the sound of a lion, relentless of heart; and at another, sounds like whelps, wonderful to hear; and again, at another, he would hiss, so that the high mountains re-echoed.

Figure 6.   William Blake. Cerberus the Hellhound. *Watercolor, 1826, an illustration for Dante's* Inferno. *Tate Gallery, London.*

A fitting offspring of this couple is Hydra (Water Snake) who lived in the swamps near Lerna until Heracles killed her. Hesiod does not describe her appearance, but later writers and artists represented her as polycephalic, with heads ranging from five to one hundred, nine being a popular number (fig. 62).

The Lernean Hydra brought forth the Chimaera (She-Goat), a tripe-bodied monster who, says Hesiod, "breathed raging fire, a creature fearful, great, swift-footed and strong, who had three heads, one of a grim-eyed lion, another to a goat, and another of a snake, a fierce dragon; in her forepart she was a lion, in her hinder-part, a dragon; and in her middle, a goat, breathing forth a fearful blast of blazing fire." In art the Chimaera was represented with a lion's head and a serpent's head budding from the end of the tail, with the head and neck of a goat protruding from the middle of the creature's back (fig. 60). We shall later witness the end of this monstrosity at the hands of the hero Bellerophon.

The Chimaera mates with the hound Orthus to bring forth yet another mixed creature, the Sphinx. Hesiod merely tells us that she is deadly and that she destroyed the Cadmeans, as the people of Thebes were called. However, her figure is a well-known type that came to Greece from Egypt by way of the Levant. The Sphinx (Strangler or Choker) became "immortal" through the riddle that she put to Oedipus (fig. 74). She is usually represented as a winged creature with the head of a woman and the body of a lion. As the name implies, the Sphinx is a death figure, and as such Sphinxes were early thought to be present at battles and to carry off young men. Like the head of the Gorgon Medusa, the representation of a Sphinx on tombs and shields was designed to terrify people and frighten them away.

In Vergil's *Aeneid* the descendants of Phorcys and Ceto, as well as the evil sons and daughters of black Night and other monsters, become hideous phantasms in the poet's conception of the vestibule of the Underworld. This is Vergil's description, translated vividly by the seventeenth century poet John Dryden:

> Just in the gate and in the jaws of hell,
> Revengeful Cares and Sullen Sorrows dwell,
> And pale Diseases, and repining Age,
> Want, Fear, and Famine's unresisted rage:
> Here Toils, and Death, and Death's half-brother, Sleep,
> Forms terrible to view, their sentry keep;
> With anxious Pleasures of a guilty mind,
> Deep Frauds before, and open Force behind;
> The Furies' iron beds; and Strife, that shakes
> Her hissing tresses and unfolds her snakes.
> Full in the midst of this infernal road,
> An elm displays her dusky arms abroad:
> The God of Sleep there hides his heavy head,
> And empty dreams on ev'ry leaf are spread.
> Of various forms unnumber'd specters more,
> Centaurs, and double shapes, besiege the door.
> Before the passage, horrid Hydra stands,
> And Briareus with all his hundred hands;
> Gorgons, Geryon with his triple frame;
> And vain Chimaera vomits empty flame.

As for Cerberus, we find him in the Underworld proper, doing his job as a watchdog:

> No sooner landed in his den they found
> The triple porter of the Stygian sound
> Grim Cerberus, who began to rear
> His crested snakes, and arm'd his bristling hair.

And in order to get by him unscathed, Aeneas' guide tranquilizes the monster with a honey cake:

> . . . she cast before
> His greedy grinning jaws, just op'd to roar,
> With three enormous mouths he gapes, and straight,
> With hunger press'd, devours the pleasing bait.

Milton would like to make his Hell even more frightening than this, but he cannot compete with the ancient repertoire of mythological monsters and must be content with a comparison. From his *Paradise Lost:*

> A Universe of death, which God by curse
> Created evil, for evil only good,
> Where all life dies, death lives, and Nature breeds,
> Perverse, all monstrous, all prodigious things,
> Abominable, inutterable, and worse
> Than Fables yet have feign'd, or fear conceiv'd
> Gorgons and Hydras, and Chimeras dire.

The Birth of Nature Deities

With this bizarre and extravagant phase completed, creation proceeds along more natural lines with the mating of the Titans, mostly with their own kind, and with the begetting of a large number of nature divinities and the first generation of Olympian deities. First, a genealogy of the more apparent nature-gods, representing a further elaboration of the physical universe:

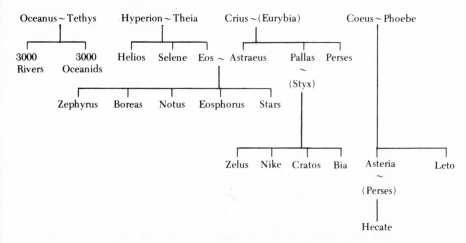

Oceanus and his wife, the Titaness Tethys, bring into existence an immense number of children: three thousand sons and three thousand daughters. The number three thousand should be taken to mean simply "countless" in the same sense that "million" and "billion" are often used today. These innumerable children of prolific parents are the divinities of rivers, streams, and springs in contrast with the Nereids who are nymphs of the sea. Oceanus himself is the fresh-water stream that encircles the earth, and out of his seed are generated sons who are river-gods; his daughters are nymphs of streams and springs. Hesiod names only twenty-five rivers and comments that the others are known only to those who live beside them. Of the twenty-five, the best-known in Greece are Achelous, Evenus, Alpheus, Ladon, and Peneus; other rivers located outside of Greece are the Nile in Egypt, and the Rhesus, Granicus, Aesopus, and Scamander in Asia Minor. Of the three thousand daughters—the Oceanids as they are called after their father Oceanus—Hesiod names forty-one. Most of their names are descriptive of streams and springs, just as many of the Nereids were named for qualities of the sea: for example, of flowing water, Callirrhoë (Beautifully Flowing); of color and light, Electra (Clear); of topography, Calypso (Hidden); of the beneficence of streams, Doris (Giver); and of wisdom and prophetic power, Metis (Wisdom). Then there are famous nymphs whose names have no descriptive meaning: Dione and Styx.

There are, of course, numerous other nymphs whose names are not listed in Hesiod's catalog. In mythology, nymphs are often willing or unwilling favorites of amorous gods, and they in turn press their affection on willing and unwilling mortals. For a song in his *Comus*, Milton coins the name of a nymph and places her in a beautiful pastoral setting:

> Sabrina fair,
>   Listen where thou art sitting
> Under the glassy, cool, translucent wave,
>   In twisted braids of lilies knitting
> The loose train of thy amber-dropping hair;
>   Listen for dear honour's sake,
>   Goddess of the silver lake,
>   Listen and save!
> Listen, and appear to us.
> In the name of Great Oceanus. . .

But to T. S. Eliot the symbolic beauty of the nymphs is lost in the crass materialism of modern life. Instead of beautiful nymphs and sylvan shores, he finds rats, slime, and industrial structures. In the "Fire Sermon" of *The Waste Land*, he jars us with these lines:

> The nymphs are departed.
> . . . .
> Sweet Thames, run softly, till I end my song.
>
> . . . .
> A rat crept softly through the vegetation
> Dragging its slimy belly on the bank
> While I was fishing in the dull canal
> On a winter evening round behind the gashouse. . .

So far, Hesiod has concerned himself with the lower floors of his cosmic structure: the basement where he has housed all the descendants of Night, the bogeymen of life, and the first floor where we find the familiar topographical features of land and sea. There remains for him to tend to the upper floors, to wit, the heavens. The poet remedies this by turning his attention to celestial phenomena. Hyperion and Theia (or Thea), both Titans, become the parents of three conspicuous aspects of the heavens: Helios (Sun), and Selene (Moon), and Eos (Dawn, Roman Aurora). The latter's epithets of "rosy-fingered" and "saffron-robed" reflect the color of the sky at dawn. Eos then mates with Astraeus (Starry), a child of Crius and Eurybia, and becomes the mother of the Winds, Eosphorus (Morning Star), and all the other nameless stars. Dawn quite naturally is closely related to the Morning Star—Shakespeare calls the Morning Star "Aurora's harbinger"—and a common belief in Greece that winds spring up at dawn also makes Eos an appropriate mother for Zephyrus (West Wind, Roman Favonius), Boreas (North Wind, Roman Aquilo), and Notus (South Wind, Roman Auster). Although in the *Iliad* Zephyrus is called blustery, from the *Odyssey* on he is gentle, the bringer of spring, as in Chaucer's Prologue to the *Canterbury Tales*:

> Whan that Aprille with his shoures soote
> The droghte of Marche hath perced to the roote
> And bathed every veyne in swich licour
> Of which vertu engendred is the flour,
> Whan Zephirus eek with his sweete breeth
> Inspired hath in every holt and heeth
> The tendre croppes. . .

And in Spenser's *Prothalamion*:

> Calme was the day, and through the trembling ayre,
> Sweete breathing Zephyrus did softly play
> A gentle spirit, that lightly did delay
> Hot Titans beames. . .

The offspring of Coeus and Phoebe (Bright) are in many respects similar to those of Hyperion and Theia. We have already mentioned Phoebe's possible association with the moon, and in later authors her name is often used for the Moon, as is her granddaughter's name Artemis (Roman Diana). Artemis' twin brother Apollo was from fairly early times identified with the Sun. Asteria (Starry), another daughter of Coeus aad Phoebe, gives birth to Hecate upon whom Hesiod heaps the highest praise as a power capable of helping man in all his endeavors. Hecate is generally associated with the mysterious and the afterlife, a not infrequent concern of a fertility spirit. Appearing at night she becomes identified with the moon as well as with witchcraft. However, these are later developments and we have no way of knowing whether to Hesiod she was a moon-goddess or another form of Artemis and Selene. But more about these figures later on.

The Birth of the Olympians

With the creation of the celestial phenomena and the winds, Hesiod's cosmic house is complete. But who is to be the ultimate master of the house? In anticipation of a struggle for dominance, Hesiod brings into being certain powers who will side with Zeus, the eventual *pater familias* of this household, in his battle against the Titans. These powers are to be provided through the descendants of Crius and Eurybia. Crius has to go outside the family of Titans for a wife, as does

Iapetus, largely because two Titanesses, Themis and Mnemosyne, are reserved for Zeus' bed and a higher calling. Crius mates with the nymph Eurybia and begets Astraeus, already mentioned in connection with Eos, and two sons. The Oceanid Styx is joined to one of these sons, and the resultant issue is four children, or more properly, four abstract powers; the competitive spirit Zelus (Eager Rivalry), Nike (Victory), Cratos (Strength), and Bia (Might). The introduction of Styx at this juncture is rationalized by aetiology, an explanation of why the gods swear their inviolable oaths by Styx. Hesiod replies by saying that this was her reward for siding with Zeus at a time when he was in desperate need of help in his struggle against the Titans. But since Styx herself could be of little help in an epic conflict of this kind, she sent her mighty children: Strength, Might, Victory, and Eager Rivalry. These powers, Hesiod tells us, remained with Zeus forever. In Aeschylus' *Prometheus Bound*, Cratos and Bia are two thug-like creatures of Zeus who drag Prometheus to a rocky gorge in the Scythian mountains.

The dramatic moment has arrived for the birth of the first generation of Olympians, the children of Rhea and Cronus, the grandchildren of Earth and Heaven. Cronus, the ruling power in the universe at this time, sires these three sons and three daughters:

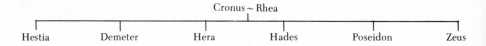

Cronus ~ Rhea

| Hestia | Demeter | Hera | Hades | Poseidon | Zeus |

Post-partum difficulties immediately arise for Rhea—as they had for her mother —when Cronus begins to swallow her children as each is born. Francisco Goya (1746–1828) paints a literal description of this traumatic and nightmarish episode (fig. 7). But let Hesiod tell the story in his own words:

> . . . Rhea was subject in love to Cronus and bare splendid children, Hestia, Demeter, and gold-shod Hera, and strong Hades, pitiless in heart, who dwells under the earth, and the loud-crashing Earth-Shaker (Poseidon), and wise Zeus, father of gods and men, by whose thunder the wide earth is shaken. These great Cronus swallowed as each came forth from the womb to his mother's knees with this intent, that no other of the proud sons of Heaven should hold the kingly office amongst the deathless gods. For he learned from Earth and starry Heaven that he was destined to be overcome by his own son, strong though he was. . . Therefore, he kept no blind outlook, but watched and swallowed down his children: and unceasing grief seized Rhea. But when she was about to bear Zeus, the father of gods and men, then she besought her own dear parents, Earth and starry Heaven, to devise some plan with her that the birth of her dear child might be concealed, and that retribution might overtake great, crafty Cronus for his own father and also for the children whom he had swallowed down.

Rhea was advised by her parents to go to Crete when she was about to bear Zeus. This she did and entrusted the newborn child to her mother to bring up. In place of the child, Rhea gave Cronus a huge stone wrapped in swaddling clothes which he mistook for Zeus and which he greedily swallowed. After a number of years when Zeus had grown to physical maturity, Earth, by some unstated trick, induced Cronus to regurgitate and disgorge the stone and the five

Figure 7. Goya. Cronus (Saturn) devouring one of his children. *Painting c. 1819–1823. Prado Museum, Madrid. (Anderson-Mansell)*

offspring he had so unpaternally swallowed. The stone was given an honored place at Delphi where it was seen in historical times by the noted geographer and traveler Pausanias (fl. 150 A.D.). Zeus then set free his uncles, the Cyclopes—apparently they had been put into shackles by Cronus—who in gratitude gave the young god his powerful weapons, lightning and thunder, which he put to good use in his later struggles.

An exegetical note is appropriate here lest, like Goya, we may be led to take Hesiod's tale too literally. The story just narrated is a composite of historical elements and folktale motifs. It is now generally agreed that Zeus, a migrant-god who came to Greece with the Indo-European Hellenes, was assimilated to an important native or near native Cretan (that is, a Minoan and pre-Hellenic) god of vegetation who was born and died annually. The ancient Cretans told of the birth and death of Zeus and actually had a locus for his grave. The Indo-European god, on the other hand, was a sky or weather-god whose name often signified "sky" or "bright sky" as in Greek Zeus, Latin Ju-piter, and German Ziu (*cf.* Tuesday). Certain features in Zeus' mythical biography which were not alien to the character of the Olympian god—for example, his birth (but not his death) on the island of Crete—were borrowed from the Cretan god of vegetation. Perhaps of more significance in the development of the myth is the influence of folktale motifs which apply to gods and heroes alike. A good example is the father who fears a prophecy that he will be unseated by one of his children and who attempts to bypass the oracle by getting rid of the child. Then there is the motif of a hero or, in this instance, a god, who is cast out but grows up and returns to avenge himself on his persecutor. Another is a man who is swallowed by a monster but, like the Biblical Jonah, manages to survive intact and alive.

Yet another common motif is that of the ogre who cannot be overcome by brute force but is easily taken in by a trick. All these will be repeated in one form or another in various Greek myths.

As for venerable Cronus, little is known of his cult or early history. It has been conjectured that Cronus was a pre-Hellenic divinity, largely because the gruesome tales of his violence against his father and his cannibalism are so unlike the usual run of Greek myths. The association of his name with an agricultural festival would indicate his function as a god of agriculture. In ancient art, the few representations we have of him show a morose but majestic old man holding in his hand what appears to be a sickle, the instrument he used to emasculate his father. The picture is further confused by another group of stories, as we shall soon see, that makes Cronus a king of the Golden Age or a ruler of a remote wonderland or paradise. Hence a certain amount of ambivalence arises in the minds of poets as to whether he is a villain or a fallen angel.

Among the Romans, Cronus was identified with Saturnus or Saturn whose origins are as obscure as those of the Greek Titan. However, Roman rationalists readily created a biography for him. As a refugee from Greece after his defeat by the Olympians, he was welcomed as an early king of Italy where he introduced agriculture, civilized life, and morality. As a result, the whole country was called Saturnia or the Land of Plenty. Under the influence of still later theorists, Saturnus was allegorized as Time, the devourer of all things. His Greek name Cronus was casually taken for the Greek word for time, *chronos*, and hence we find him represented in art, down to our own day, as Father Time, an old man with an hour glass holding a scythe in his hand.

What we know of the character of Cronus' sister-spouse Rhea depends mostly upon other deities with whom she is identified. Among the Greeks she was commonly equated with their goddess of the earth, Gaea or Ge, or with the great mother-goddess Cybele of Asia Minor. Aeschylus calls her: "Earth—she is one but her names are many." Among the Romans her mythological name was Ops, the goddess of plenty. In short, Rhea undoubtedly is one of the many manifestations common in the Mediterranean of the female principle of nature and of the power of fertility. As the embodiment of the fruitful earth, she is the giver of life and fertility to plants, animals, and men—the Alma Mater, the Mother of All. This is how she is addressed in the *Homeric Hymn*.

> I will sing of the well-founded Earth, mother of all, eldest of all beings. She feeds all creatures that are in the world, all that go upon the goodly land, and all that are in the paths of the seas, and all that fly: all these are fed of her store. Through you, O queen, men are blessed in their children and blessed in their harvests, and to you it belongs to give means of life to mortal men and to take it away. Happy is the man whom you delight to honor! He has all things abundantly: his fruitful land is laden with grain, his pastures are covered with cattle, and his house is filled with good things.

When Hesiod has reached this point in his account of the conflict between Cronus and his children, he does not go on, as we might expect, to describe the Titanomachy, the battle between the Titans and the Olympians. Instead, the poet looks ahead to a time when Zeus is king and has to contend with a recalcitrant subject, Prometheus. The arrangement should not be regarded as an attempt to develop suspense; the epic style, even in the form of a catalog, does not depend upon suspense to sustain interest. Since the audience is well aware of the events that will take place, the poet does not strive for hanging uncertainty as to what will happen, but for dramatic anticipation. Hesiod places the last phase of creation among the Titans at this juncture where it serves as the introduction to a crescendo of conflicts that will culminate in Zeus' final victory and lordship over the universe. These, then, are the children of the last Titan, Iapetus.

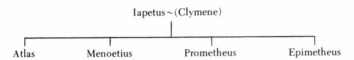

Iapetus takes the Oceanid Clymene for his wife—other writers provide him with an assortment of women for wives—who presents him with four sons. Hesiod mentions the fate of Menoetius and Atlas very briefly. Zeus has condemned Menoetius to Erebus (Darkness) because of his arrogance, while Atlas has been assigned the unpleasant task of carrying the heavens on his shoulders (fig. 8). The poet does not tell us why they were punished; presumably, like their brother Prometheus, they rebelled against Zeus and received stiff penalties. The difficulties of Zeus with Prometheus, like those with Cronus and Typhon are described at length. Here begins an important stage in the mature life of Zeus, one that is brightly reflected in literature and art from Hesiod's time to our own.

Battles of the Titans and the Rise of Zeus

With the birth of Iapetus' children, Hesiod halts temporarily the process of creation and relates three struggles of the first generation of Olympians to establish themselves as the dominant powers of the universe. The outcome of these struggles is no mystery. Zeus and the Olympians will triumph, first in a conflict with an individual, Prometheus; then with the existent powers, Cronus and his Titan allies; and finally with a mighty serpent, Typhon or Typhoeus, who may represent for Hesiod the powerful and nigh-uncontrollable forces of nature. (Later writers also tell of a struggle between the Olympians and the Giants.) Only after these battles were won, does Hesiod renew the process of creation, but creation now is of a different order from what it was in the past. We can anticipate the establishment of a just and stable government under Zeus, the creation of divinities embodying ethical forces characteristic of organized society, and, finally, the genesis of the familiar gods of the Olympian pantheon.

Part 1: Zeus versus Prometheus

Say why
That ancient story of Prometheus chained
To the bare rock, on frozen Caucasus;
The vulture, the inexhaustible repast
Drawn from his vitals? Say what meant the woes
. . . .
Tremendous truths! familiar to the men
Of long past times, nor obsolete in ours.

Wordsworth—*The Excursion*

As Hesiod tells the story in the *Theogony*, Prometheus' rebellion is presented as a challenge to the authority and wisdom of Zeus. On two occasions he out-smarts Zeus, apparently on behalf of mankind, and for his presumption and to teach him that the mighty Olympian cannot be trifled with, he is severely punished.

For the first time in the *Theogony* we hear that man, but not woman, is on earth. We shall also witness the creation of earth's first woman whom flinty Hesiod will call "a beautiful evil thing" (*kalon kakon*). Much the same material appears in Hesiod's *Works and Days*, but here the intent of the poet is not to stress the act of rebellion, but rather to explain why the world has become what it is, why men have to endure hardship in their lives. We need not be surprised to find a woman as the cause of the world's difficulties. In both poems Hesiod uses mythological material that undoubtedly was traditional in his own time. In the main, the mythical fabrics are aetiological, explanations of how man acquired the use of fire, why certain parts of the animal are sacrificed to the gods, and what were the origin and nature of woman. Prometheus is a combination of culture-bringer and trickster who brings the elements of civilization to man. In doing so, a culture-hero comes into conflict with the gods since what he gives to man was originally the jealously guarded property of the gods. Prometheus' name, although not deciphered to every scholar's satisfaction, apparently meant Forethought to Hesiod; his brother, Epimetheus, seems to have been invented as a foil for Prometheus, and his name is taken to mean Afterthought or Hindsight.

Once in the reign of Zeus, Hesiod starts his story, when gods and men were disputing with one another, Prometheus cut up an ox and divided it into two parts. He wrapped the best cuts of meat in the skin of the animal and placed the stomach, which is one of the worst parts, on top to make it look unappetizing. The second heap consisted of bones of the animal covered with rich, delectable fat. When Zeus pointed out to him that the division was inequitable, Prometheus invited Zeus to choose between the two portions. Zeus became angry, and though he saw through Prometheus' stratagem—Hesiod could never bring himself to admit that Zeus could be fooled—he chose the heap of bones covered with fat, and this is the reason why men sacrifice bones and fat to the immortal gods on their altars.

In revenge and anger, the Olympian god withheld fire from men, but wily Prometheus stole a spark of fire, hid it in the hollow stalk of a fennel plant, and gave it to man. When Zeus saw men using fire, he was even more furious and contrived what he must have considered the ultimate punishment for man, his final revenge upon the human race. He called upon his artisan-god Hephaestus to mix earth and water and to fashion from this plastic material a beautiful woman modeled after the immortal goddesses. Zeus then had his other divine minions deck her out in fine clothes, instruct her in woman's work, endow her with sex appeal, and teach her shamelessness, cunning words, lies, and deceitfulness. Then the Olympian gods each gave her a "gift": miseries for mankind, which were enclosed in a huge jar. The name of the lovely creature was Pandora, the All-Endowed or All-Giver. She was led to Prometheus' dull-witted brother, Epimetheus, who disregarded Prometheus' earlier warning to beware of any gift from Zeus and to refuse it if offered for fear that the gift might be harmful to man. But true to his name, Epimetheus accepted the gift without giving it a second thought. The result was calamitous for man, as Hesiod tells us in the *Works and Days*:

> For before this the tribes of men lived on earth remote and free from ills and hard toil and heavy sicknesses which bring the Fates upon men; for in misery men grow old quickly. But the woman [Pandora] took off the great lid of the jar with her hands and scattered all these, and her thought caused sorrow and mischief to men. Only Hope remained there in an unbreakable home within, under the rim of the great jar,

and did not fly out at the door; for ere that, the lid of the jar stopped her, by the will of Aegis-holding Zeus who gathers the clouds. But the rest, countless plagues, wander amongst men; for earth is full of evils and the sea is full. Of themselves diseases come upon men continually by day and by night, bringing mischief to mortals silently; for wise Zeus took away speech from them. So is there no way to escape the will of Zeus.

In the *Theogony* we have a similar bitter denunciation of womankind who was given to man as the price for fire and to place a would-be bachelor on the horns of a dilemma:

For from her is the race of women and female kind: of her is the deadly race and tribe of women who live amongst mortal men to their great trouble, no helpmates in hateful poverty, but only in wealth . . . And he [Zeus] gave them [men] a second evil to be a price for the good they had: whoever avoids marriage and the sorrows that women cause, and will not wed, reaches deadly old age without anyone to tend his years, and though he at least has no lack of livelihood while he lives, yet, when he is dead, his kinsfolk divide his possessions amongst them. And as for the man who chooses the lot of marriage and takes a good wife suited to his mind, evil continually contends with good; for whoever happens to have mischievous children, lives always with unceasing grief in his spirit and heart within him; and this evil cannot be healed. So it is not possible to deceive or go beyond the will of Zeus.

For Prometheus, Zeus decreed a most cruel punishment. His hands were bound and a shaft was driven through his midsection. In addition, an eagle was set over him to devour his liver by daytime, while by night his liver was restored to the extent that the eagle had eaten it during the day (fig. 8). This punishment continued until Heracles killed the eagle and freed the suffering Titan, an act not of pity on the part of Zeus nor a sign that he had relented, but rather for the greater glory of Heracles.

This is the story as Hesiod tells it. In Aeschylus' *Prometheus Bound*, the sole surviving play of a trilogy, a new confrontation takes place between Zeus and Prometheus. Aeschylus adds new features to the superhuman struggle between his protagonists: Zeus, fresh from his victory over the Titans, is raw power and a ruthless tyrant; Prometheus is not only the fire-giver and friend of man, but also the inventor of the useful arts and an omniscient seer. For man's good, Prometheus has taken away his knowledge of the future and substituted hope in its place. He has

Figure 8.   Atlas and Prometheus being punished by Zeus. *Vase painting.* *Vatican Museum.*

also acquainted man with astronomy, architecture, mathematics, the art of writing, animal husbandry, navigation, medicine, the art of prophecy, and all the other arts. In short, he is a true culture-hero. Although a Titan himself, Prometheus sided with Zeus in his struggle against the Titans and claims that he was instrumental in making the Olympian lord of the universe. But he comes into a head-on conflict with Zeus when he opposes Zeus' plan to wipe out the whole race of man and create a new one. Prometheus alone prevented the execution of the scheme and saved the human race from destruction, as he tells the chorus of Oceanids:

> As soon as he [Zeus] ascended to the throne
> that was his father's, straightway he assigned
> to the several Gods their several privileges
> and portioned out the power, but to the unhappy
> breed of mankind he gave no heed, intending
> to blot the race out and create a new.
> Against these plans none stood save I: I dared.
> I rescued men from shattering destruction. . . .

However, since Prometheus has thwarted Zeus' will, the Olympian orders Hephaestus to chain him to a rock in Scythia. This he does in the presence of Cratos (Strength) and Bia (Might), the two sons of Styx. Prometheus is visited by Io, a nymph who is suffering from Zeus' amorous advances, and is told by a prophesying Prometheus that there is more anguish for her to bear. Hermes then appears and demands that Prometheus reveal details of a prophecy concerning a marriage of Zeus that would result in his being driven from power. (We hear more about this prophecy in an Isthmian Ode of the poet Pindar: if Zeus or Poseidon has a son by the sea-goddess Thetis, this son will be stronger than his father. The prediction is bypassed by marrying Thetis off to a mortal, Peleus, who fathers the mightiest man of all, Achilles.)

Prometheus rejects Hermes' demands and lashes him and the Olympians with these words:

> Your speech is pompous sounding, full of pride,
> as fits the lackey of the Gods. You are young
> and young your rule and you think that the tower
> in which you live is free from sorrow: from it
> have I not seen two tyrants thrown? the third,
> who now is king, I shall yet live to see him
> fall, of all three most suddenly, most dishonored.
> Do you think I will crouch before your Gods,
> —so new—and tremble? I am far from that.
> Hasten away, back on the road you came.
> You shall learn nothing that you ask of me.

His refusal to bend to the authority and will of Zeus comes to a dramatic end. Wagnerian lightning, earthquakes, windstorms shatter the scene leaving Prometheus crying out to his goddess-mother to witness how unjustly he is suffering at the hands of Zeus.

Although Aeschylus' resolution to the drama, contained in his *Prometheus Unbound* and *Prometheus the Firebringer*, is lost to us, we are fairly certain that a reconciliation came about between the two adversaries in which Prometheus and the young, immature Olympian gained wisdom—as should man—through their suffering, a theme that the poet restates in the *Oresteia*. Aeschylus, for whom Zeus was the great and almighty god of justice, could not have continued to portray Zeus as a tyrant, but rather saw him outgrowing the heedless violence described by Homer and Hesiod. Prometheus, too, must have learned something about blind intransigence and disobedience to authority higher than himself.

In fragments of the lost plays we learn that Heracles shot the eagle gnawing at Prometheus' vitals and released the Titan from his bonds. Later accounts tell us that Prometheus returned from Tartarus, whence he had been plunged by a vengeful Zeus, to endure a fresh round of suffering, for he was now fastened to a crag on Mount Caucasus and tormented by an eagle or a vulture plucking at his liver. This state of suffering was to last until some other god would willingly take his place in Tartarus. This came about when the Centaur Chiron, who had been incurably wounded by one of Heracles' arrows, received permission from Zeus to replace Prometheus. According to yet other accounts, Zeus himself freed Prometheus when the Titan was finally prevailed upon to reveal to him the prophecy concerning the threat to his sovereignty if the Olympian were to beget a child through Thetis.

Following Aeschylus' treatment of the Prometheus myth, we find yet another version in one of Plato's dialogues, the *Protagoras*, in which the famous Sophist, who gives his name to the dialogue, presents the myth as if it were a socio-anthropological document. When the gods created all mortal creatures, man and beast, out of earth and fire, the task of assigning proper characteristics to these new creations was given to Prometheus and Epimetheus. Epimetheus, however, begged his brother for permission to handle the job all by himself. Prometheus found to his regret, that although Epimetheus had done a good job with the animals, he had left man naked, homeless, and defenseless. When man was about to be turned loose in the world, Prometheus, in order to give him the means to support life, stole fire and the mechanical arts from the workshops of Athena and Hephaestus, a felony for which he was later prosecuted. But men were lacking one quality which Prometheus could not provide; they lacked political wisdom which happened to be the sole property of Zeus. Threatened by destruction by wild beasts, men gathered in cities for self-defense; but having no sense of justice, they began to destroy one another. Zeus, in fear that the entire human race might be exterminated, sent his messenger Hermes to distribute the principle of reverence and justice to all men. Hence the development of man as a political animal.

Early accounts speak of Prometheus as the benefactor of man; later ones make him his creator as well. According to Ovid and Apollodorus, Prometheus created man out of earth and water at the very beginning of things; according to others, Zeus ordered Prometheus and Athena to make men out of mud and the winds and to breathe life into them after mankind had been snuffed out by the Deucalion flood (fig. 9). At one place in Greece, near Chaeronea in Boeotia, tourist guides pointed out two great stones to the gullible Greek traveler and geographer of Roman times, Pausanias. He duly reports that the stones were the remains of the clay used by Prometheus to mould man. And, says Pausanias, the stones even smelled like the flesh of a man. Apollodorus also reports that it was at Prometheus' suggestion that Deucalion, the classical Noah, built a chest or a ship and provisioned it so that he and his wife Pyrrha could support themselves during the

Figure 9.   Prometheus, in the presence of the Olympian gods, creates man.
Bas-relief from a Roman sarcophagus. National Museum, Naples. (Alinari)

flood. The Roman writer of the late fifth century, Fulgentius, says that Prometheus also created Pandora.

*   *   *   *

It can be readily seen that the figure of Prometheus is capable of a wide range of interpretations; he may be a creator, savior, prophet, thief, benefactor, fallen angel, rebel, and more. To the early defenders of the Christian faith—if they did not take issue with the pagan view of the creation of man as against the "true Prometheus" of the Old Testament—Prometheus' suffering became a mystical symbol for the Passion of Christ. Later writers took equal liberty with their interpretations of the character of Prometheus. Spenser has him create man "of many partes from beasts derived" and steal fire from the gods to animate his creation. For this he was punished by being deprived of his freedom and "hart-strings of an Aegle rived." In *Paradise Lost* the rugged individualism of Milton's Satan, who vows never to "repent or change," owes much to Aeschylus' Prometheus; the same is true of his tragedy *Samson Agonistes* which was modeled chiefly after the Greek dramatist's *Prometheus Bound*. On the other hand, the Irish-born satirist Jonathan Swift has no such bold conception; his Prometheus is nothing more than an old thief.

The number of "modern" versions of Prometheus beggars description. From the seventeenth century to the present, his name appears in titles to dramas, novels, epic poems, lyrics, statues, paintings, and music. On the Continent there are, among many others, *La Estatua de Prometeo* (The Statue of Prometheus) of the Spanish dramatist Pedro Calderón de la Barca (1600–1681), the *Prometheus* of the German poet Johann Wolfgang von Goethe (1749–1832), the *Prometeo* of the Italian Vincenzo Monti (1754–1828), the *Prometheus and Epimetheus* and *Prometheus the Sufferer* of the Swiss Nobel Prize winner Carl Spitteler (1845–1924), and the *Prométhée mal enchaîné* (Prometheus Drops His Chains) of the French novelist André Gide (1869–1951). Beethoven's Opus 43, the *Prometheus Overture*, was composed in 1800 as incidental music to a ballet of the same name. Gabriel Faure composed an opera *Prométhée* in 1900 and F. Wohlfahrt an oratorio, *Die Passion des Prometheus*, in 1955.

In English literature, the character of Prometheus was a strong and early attraction for both Byron and Shelley. Byron's *Prometheus*, a poem of only fifty-nine lines, was written in the revolutionary spirit of the early nineteenth century when Prometheus became a symbol of protest against traditional religion and morality, against any limitation to human endeavor, against prejudice and the abuses of political power. Goethe's Prometheus was an intellectual and a creative artist; Shelley's a humanitarian idealist and an earthly lover; Monti's a Napoleonic champion of political liberty. Byron's hero is a foe of the religious doctrine of his time which stifled the human spirit. His Prometheus becomes a symbol of struggling humanity, "humanity more sinned against than sinning," but the struggle, however hopeless, is worth the price, even the price of death.

> Titan! to whose immortal eyes
>   The sufferings of mortality,
>   Seen in their sad reality,
> Were not as things that gods despise;
> What was the pity's recompense?
> A silent suffering, and intense;
> The rock, the vulture, and the chain,
> All that the proud can feel of pain,
> The agony they do not show,
> The suffocating sense of woe,
>   Which speaks but in its loneliness,
> And then is jealous lest the sky
> Should have a listener, nor will sigh
>   Until its voice is echoless.

> Titan! to thee the strife was given
>   Between the suffering and the will,
>   Which torture where they cannot kill;
> And the inexorable Heaven,
> And the deaf tyranny of Fate,
> The ruling principle of Hate,
> Which for its pleasure doth create
> The things it may annihilate,
> Refused thee even the boon to die:
> The wretched gift eternity
> Was thine—and thou hast borne it well.
> All that the Thunderer wrung from thee
> Was but the menace which flung back
> On him the torments of thy rack;
> The fate thou didst so well foresee,
> But would not to appease him tell;
> And in thy Silence was his Sentence,
> And in his Soul a vain repentance,
> And evil dread so ill dissembled,
> That in his hand the lightnings trembled.

Thy Godlike crime was to be kind,
   To render with thy precepts less
   The sum of human wretchedness.
And strengthen Man with his own mind;
But baffled as thou wert from high,
Still in thy patient energy,
In the endurance, and repulse
   Of thine impenetrable Spirit,
Which Earth and Heaven could not convulse,
   A mighty lesson we inherit:
Thou art a symbol and a sign
   To Mortals of their fate and force;
Like thee, Man is in part divine,
   A troubled stream from a pure source;
His own funereal destiny;
His wretchedness, and his resistance,
And his sad unallied existence:
To which his Spirit may oppose
Itself—and equal to all woes,
   And a firm will, and a deep sense,
Which even in torture can descry
   Its own concenter'd recompense,
Triumphant where it dares defy,
And making Death a Victory.

In Shelley's lyric drama *Prometheus Unbound*, the Aeschylean struggle between Prometheus and Zeus is transformed into a conflict between the spirit of good and the spirit of evil. Shelley's champion of suffering mankind is, in his own words, "the type of the highest perfection of moral and intellectual nature, impelled by the purest and truest motives to the best and noblest ends." Jupiter—Shelley uses Roman names for his deities—is at the opposite end of the spectrum: cruel and tyrannical, he is responsible for all the evils in the world, evils that Hesiod would attribute to the descendants of Night or that he would say were loosed in the world by Pandora. Jupiter's reign has succeeded Saturn's in which man lived a beautiful but vegetable-like existence:

As the calm joy of flowers and living leaves
Before the wind or sun has withered them
And semivital worms; but he refused
The birthright of their being, knowledge, power,
The skill which wields the elements, the thought
Which pierces this dim universe like light,
Self-empire, and the majesty of love;
For thirst of which they fainted. Then Prometheus
Gave wisdom, which is strength, to Jupiter,
And with this law alone, "Let man be free,"
Clothed him with the dominion of wide Heaven.

But Jupiter gave man a wretched life:

> And in their desert hearts fierce wants he sent
> And mad disquietudes, and shadows idle
> Of unreal good, which levied mutual war,
> So ruining the lair wherein they raged.

To counterbalance the evils of Jupiter's reign, Prometheus rushes to the assistance of man by sending Hope, concealing Death, and . . .

>   . . . Love he sent to bind
> The disunited tendrils of that vine
> Which bears the wine of life, the human heart.

Then he gave man the use of fire, the mechanical arts, and ever so much more:

> He gave man speech, and speech created thought,
> Which is the measure of the universe;
> And Science struck the thrones of earth and heaven,
> Whick shook, but fell not; and the harmonious mind
> Poured itself forth in all-prophetic song;
> And music lifted up the listening spirit
> Until it walkt, exempt from mortal care,
> Godlike, o'er the clear billows of sweet sound;
> And human hands first mimickt and then mockt,
> With moulded limbs more lovely than its own,
> The human form, till marble grew divine;
> And mothers, gazing, drank the love men see
> Reflected in their race, behold, and perish.

Yet, in spite of these gifts, man is still pursued by "Evil, the immedicable plague," and its symbol or servant Jupiter still reigns. Prometheus withholds his secret from Jupiter and allows him to marry Thetis. The result is quite un-Aeschylean: Jupiter is unseated and sinks into a deep abyss. When Hercules appears to unbind Prometheus and restore him to Asia—a figure that Shelley introduces as the equivalent of Venus and Nature—man is freed from the restraints of civilized society, free to join spirit of creation and love, free—

> The loathsome mask has fallen, the man remains
> Sceptreless, free, uncircumscribed, but man
> Equal, unclast, tribeless, and nationless,
> Exempt from awe, worship, degree, the king
> Over himself; just, gentle, wise: but man
> Passionless; no, yet free from guilt or pain
> Which were, for his will made or suffered them,
> Nor yet exempt, tho' ruling them like slaves,
> From chance, and death, and mutability,
> The clogs of that which else might oversoar
> The loftiest star of unascended heaven,
> Pinnacled dim in the intense inane.

Shelley ends his drama with an ode beseeching man to love, to forgive, to hope, and to fight for his Utopia:

> To suffer woes which Hope thinks infinite;
> To forgive wrongs darker than death or night;
>   To defy Power, which seems omnipotent;
> To love, and bear; to hope till Hope creates
> From its own wreck the thing it contemplates;
>   Neither to change, nor falter, nor repent;
> This, like thy glory, Titan, is to be
> Good, great and joyous, beautiful and free;
> This is alone Life, Joy, Empire, and Victory.

Robert Bridges (1844–1930), poet laureate of England from 1913 until his death, was also attracted to the Aeschylean version of Prometheus, but like Shelley, he could see no reconciliation between Zeus and the Titan. In his *Prometheus the Firegiver* (1883), Zeus is the enemy and oppressor of man, and by withholding fire from him keeps man in a brutish condition. Prometheus, whose gift of stolen fire will be a spiritually liberating force, contrasts his love for man with Zeus's hatred in these lines:

> Could I but win this world from Zeus for mine,
> With not a god to vex my happy rule,
> I would inhabit here and leave high heaven:
> So much I love it and its race of men,
> Even as he hates them, hates both them, and me
> For loving what he hates, and would destroy me
> Outcast in the scorn of all his cringing crew,
> For daring but to save what he would slay:
> And me must first destroy.

The ultimate victory will not belong to Prometheus, even though he expunges Zeus' name from the altar and substitutes his own. A being greater than Zeus will rule the world in love and peace—unquestionably a veiled reference to the coming of Christianity—as the chorus sings its final ode:

> And he [Zeus], if he raise his arm in anger to smite them,
> And think for the good thou hast done with pain to requite them,
> Vengeance I heard thee tell,
> And the curse I take for my own,
> That his place is prepared in Hell
> And a greater than he shall hurl him down from his throne.
>   Down, down from his throne!
> For the god who shall rule mankind from the deathless skies
> By mercy and truth shall be known,
> In love and peace shall arise.
> O then, if I crouch or start,
> I will press thy loving kindness more to my heart,
> Remember the words of thy mouth rare and precious,
> Thy heart of hearts and gifts of divine love.

Shelley's lyric drama has since become one of the landmarks in English literature. A novel by his wife on the theme of Prometheus, published in 1818, two
years before her husband's drama, was to become through the medium of the cinema a landmark of a different kind, though few would attach the name of Mary
Shelley to it. When Byron and the Shelleys were spending a rainy summer in Switzerland, they amused themselves by reading and writing ghost stories. The short
story Mary Shelley wrote, and later expanded into a novel, turned out to be the
progenitor of a long line of horror stories and films. Her title for her novel was
Frankenstein, or the Modern Prometheus.

Among American poets to take up the Promethean theme for major works are
Henry Wadsworth Longfellow (1807–1882) and James Russell Lowell (1819–
1892). The latter's *Prometheus*, far removed from any classical rendering, uses the
Titan as a symbol of human suffering which is resolved through optimism:

> Therefore great heart, bear up! thou art but type
> Of what all lofty spirits endure, that fain
> Would win back to strength and peace through love;
> Each hath his lonely peak, and on each heart
> Envy, or scorn, or hatred, tears lifelong
> With vulture beak; yet the high soul is left;
> And faith, which is but hope grown wise, and love
> And patience which at last shall overcome.

Longfellow composed a *Prometheus, or The Poet's Forethought* and an *Epimetheus, or The Poet's Afterthought*, both of which are concerned with the human
condition of the poet.

> All is but a symbol painted
>   Of the Poet, Prophet, Seer;
> Only those are crowned and sainted
> Who with grief have been acquainted,
>   Making nations nobler, freer.
>
>   . . . .
>
> Ah, Prometheus, heaven-scaling!
>   In such hours of exultation
> Even the faintest heart, unquailing,
> Might behold the vulture sailing
>   Round the cloudy crags Caucasian.

This is Longfellow's statement in his *Prometheus*, the soaring spirit of
the creative poet struggling and suffering on behalf of humanity. *Epimetheus*,
on the other hand, is the weaker brother—the anticlimax, the depression that so
often follows the act of creation—who has only Hope as a remedy for his dis-
illusionment.

Contemporary with Longfellow and Lowell was one of the American literary titans, Herman Melville (1819–1891), whose *Moby Dick* is a cosmic
tragedy in which pagan gods play an important role. To one critic, the myth
of Prometheus, its similarities and differences as personified in the monoma-
niac Captain Ahab, is central to the entire novel. The likelihood, is, however,
that Melville, who was caught up in the new revelations of nineteenth-century
research in comparative religion and mythology, fused and even parodied

mythical figures from all over the world. So for example, Captain Ahab may be compared not only to one savior, Prometheus, but also to Perseus, and to Noah, and to the Persian Zoroaster as well as to Christ. Similarly, one can take the White Whale as a tyrannical Zeus against whom Ahab utters these Promethean words: "I now know that thy right worship is defiance"; he can also be a host of other incarnations of evil.

Melville knows another form of Prometheus, not the transfigured Creator Ahab, but the mechanical man, the ship's blacksmith who is explicitly addressed as the Titan when Ahab is being fitted for his artificial leg:

> I do deem it now a most meaning thing that that old Greek, Prometheus, who made men, they say, should have been a blacksmith and animated them with fire. . . . While Prometheus is about it, I'll order a complete man after a desirable pattern. Imprimis, fifty feet high in his socks; then, chest modelled after the Thames Tunnel; then, legs with roots to 'em, to stay in one place; then, arms three feet through at the wrist; no heart at all, brass forehead, and about a quarter of an acre of fine brains; and let me see—shall I order eyes to see outwards? No, but put a skylight on top of his head to illuminate inwards.

Earlier in the novel, Ahab awakes from a nightmare and compares himself to the suffering Prometheus:

> God help thee, old man, thy thoughts have created a creature in thee; and he whose intense thinking thus makes him a Prometheus; a vulture feeds upon that heart for ever; that vulture the very creature he creates.

The motif of the eagle—later transformed into a vulture—sent by Zeus to punish Prometheus for his deception and intransigence almost has a literary life of its own. In André Gide's sequel to the well-known story of Prometheus, *Prometheus Drops His Chains*, the eagle is not destroyed but is kept by the Titan as a pet that continues to live off his innards, a symbol perhaps of a friendly but gnawing conscience. The sculptor Jacques Lipchitz, in a relatively recent work (1943, fig. 10), presents us with yet another variation on the theme: Prometheus strangling

Figure 10. Jacques Lipchitz.
Prometheus strangling the vulture.
*Bronze, 1923. Walker Art Center,
Minneapolis.*

the eagle or vulture with his own hands—freedom from any limiting force self-attained. On the other hand, Robert Graves' vulture, in his short poem *Prometheus*, is love's torturer:

> Close bound in a familiar bed
> All night I tossed, rolling my head;
> Now dawn returns in vain, for still
> the vulture squats on her warm hill.
>
> I am in love as giants are
> That dote upon the evening star,
> And this lank bird is come to prove
> The intractability of love.
>
> Yet still, with greedy eye half shut,
> Rend the raw liver from its gut:
> Feed, jealousy, do not fly away—
> If she who fetched you also stay.

Pandora. Something must also be said for Pandora, the millstone around the neck of Hesiod's hardworking farmer. Like Prometheus, she could be allegorized by early Christian apologists into acceptable Christological doctrine without reference to Hesiod's cynicism. However, Pandora provided a ready-made parallel to the doctrine of original sin and hence is often compared to Eve. Origen (c. 184–254) compares Pandora's jar with the fruit in the Garden of Eden; Gregory of Nazianzus (c. 326–390) holds her up as an example of various deadly sins and outdoes Hesiod's "a beautiful evil thing" by calling Pandora "a deadly delight." Spenser could not forget these sinister implications when he invokes the image of Pandora in a private love poem, *Amoretti:*

> When I behold that beauties wonderment,
> And rare perfection of each goodly part:
> of natures skill the onely complement,
> I honor and admire the makers art.
> But when I feele the bitter balefull smart,
> which her fayre eyes unwares doe worke in mee:
> that death out of theyr shiny beames doe dart,
> I thinke that I a new Pandora see;
> Whom all the Gods in councell did agree,
> into this sinfull world from heaven to send:
> that she to wicked men a scourge should bee,
> for all their faults with which they did offend.
> But since ye are my scourge I will intreat,
> that for my faults ye will me gently beat.

In *Paradise Lost* Milton continues the tradition of a glamorous but fatal Eve-Pandora with this description of the world's first marriage:

> ... Here, in close recess,
> With flowers, garlands, and sweet-smelling herbs,
> Espousèd Eve decked her first nuptial bed,

And heavenly choirs the hymenaean sung,
What day the genial Angel to our sire
Brought her in naked beauty more adorned,
More lovely than Pandora, whom the gods
Endowed with all their gifts, and O too like
In sad event, when to the unwiser son
Of Japhet [= Iapetus] brought by Hermes, she ensnar'd
Mankind with her fair looks, to be aveng'd
On him who had stole Jove's authentic fire.

In Calderón's *La Estatua de Prometeo* and in Voltaire's libretto for the opera *Pandore* (1740), Pandora is a beautiful statue in the studio of the sculptor Prometheus and, like Pygmalion's creation, comes to life. For Calderón, she is the reincarnation of the goddess Minerva, brought to life by a stolen ray of Apollo's sun. Ultimately, Apollo forgives Prometheus' theft and permits his marriage to Pandora, thereby bringing about the blissful union of the creative mind (Prometheus) and the embodiment of art and spiritual enlightenment (Pandora-Minerva). Voltaire's Pandora comes to life and reciprocates Prometheus' love when she is touched by love's sacred flame. However, through her frailty and for the sake of love, but not out of curiosity or self-interest, she subjects mankind to all kinds of evil. Cupid and Hope come on the scene unexpectedly and save the situation, signifying to the audience that Love, with Hope's help, can conquer the power of Jupiter and Fate.

The poet-painter Dante Gabriel Rossetti (1828–1882) saw in Pandora the "beautiful evil thing" of Hesiod, and the "deadly delight" of Gregory of Nazianzus. As one critic put it, Rossetti seems to be obsessed with the evil of beauty and the beauty of evil. His paintings of this *femme fatale* conform to the pre-Raphaelite conception of beauty, a kind of sentimental but intense siren from the era of the silent films. In her hands she holds a box from which evils escape in dense, smoky vapor. The poet Swinburne eulogized one of Rossetti's paintings of Pandora with these words: "The whole design is among Rossetti's mightiest in godlike terror and imperial trouble of beauty, shadowed by the smoke and the fiery vapour of winged and fleshless passions crowding from the cascet in spires of flame-lit and curling cloud round her fatal face and mourning veil of hair." Rossetti composed this sonnet for his painting:

What of the end, Pandora? Was it thine,
The deed that set these fiery pinions free?
Ah! wherefore did the Olympian consistory
In its own likeness make thee half divine?
Was it that Juno's brow might stand a sign
Forever? and the mien of Pallas be
A deadly thing? and that all men might see
In Venus' eyes the gaze of Proserpine?
What of the end? these beat their wings at will,
The ill-born things, the good things turned to ill—
Powers of the impassioned hours prohibited.
Aye, hug the cascet now! Whither they go
Thou may'st not dare to think: nor canst thou know
If Hope still pent there be alive or dead.

The personality of Pandora undergoes yet another change in *The Fire-Bringer* by William Vaughn Moody (1869–1910), the three-act verse play which helped win for the poet a leading place among American poets of his day. Influenced by Euripides' *Bacchae* and the Nietzschean view of Greek drama, and conscious of the battle between the flesh and the spirit, Moody pleads for an enriched life for man: the union of Dionysus, Eros and Apollo—the trinity embracing the pleasure-giving and life-giving powers of Eros and Dionysus, and the spirituality and rationality of Apollo.

For the story line of *The Fire-Bringer*, Moody goes to Apollodorus and his version of the myth of Prometheus. According to this account, Deucalion and Pyrrha —the Mr. and Mrs. Noah of Greek mythology—managed, on information supplied by Prometheus, to survive the flood sent by Zeus to wipe out the human race. Deucalion, son of Prometheus, and Pyrrha, daughter of Epimetheus, repopulate the earth by magical means; they cast stones over their heads. Those cast by Deucalion become men; those by Pyrrha, women. Moody, unlike Aeschylus and Shelley, focuses on the events immediately following the flood and prior to the successful theft of fire and Prometheus' punishment. Mankind is now living in a spiritual and physical wasteland, having lost fire, the spark of love and life. Prometheus has already made one attempt at helping mankind and has not succeeded in stealing fire from Heaven. The Titan is wounded and dejected. It is Pandora who becomes the major figure in the play. She is no longer the woman who brought affliction to man leaving him only with the delusive gift of hope. In her song "of wounds and sore defeat I made my battle stay," she gives courage and aspiration to a dispirited mankind. She also raises up the dejected Prometheus and provides him with the hollow fennel stalk for a second assault on Heaven. When he returns after a successful mission and tells Pandora, "Thou gavest me the vessel; it is filled," her reply is, "I am the vessel, and with thee 't is filled." These significant lines emphasize Moody's view of Pandora as the prophetess of positive hope, the true All-Giver and All-Endowed, the synthesis of the flesh and the spirit. The play ends with a chorus of youths singing its praise of the trinity of Dionysus, Eros, and transcendent Apollo:

Although Moody and other poets make little or no mention of Pandora's Box, it has come into our language and into almost all European languages, to denote any source of multiple troubles. What was to Hesiod a large storage jar (*pithos*) becomes confused in medieval and renaissance times with a box or small urn (*pyxis*); and hence its transformation into Pandora's Box, a symbol of destruction caused or not caused by the female sex. From Ben Jonson's *The Execution of Vulcan:*

> Pox on thee, Vulcan, thy Pandora's pox
> And all the Evils that flew out of her box
> Light on thee. . .

In art Pandora's Box also has an independent life. Paul Klee's *Pandora's Box as a Still Life* (1920) is an urn-shaped vase with psychoanalytical overtones of the Pandora–Eve tradition. The *Pandora's Box* of Max Beckmann (1947) is a symbol of the horrors of the atomic age, the "black box" that lets loose an explosive destruction on the entire world.

Part 2: Zeus versus Cronus and the Titans

Divine ye [Titans] were created, and divine
In sad demeanour, solemn, undisturb'd
Unruffled, like high Gods, ye liv'd and ruled:
Now I behold in you fear, hope, and wrath;
Actions of rage and passion; even as
I see them, on the mortal world beneath,
In men who die.

Keats—*Hyperion*

Having made short shrift of Prometheus and his brothers, second-generation Titans, Zeus now has on his hands a deadly and prolonged conflict with Cronus and other first-generation Titans. Hesiod picks up the story not *in medias res* but at its dramatic conclusion, when Zeus frees his secret allies, the Hecatoncheires, the hundred-handed children of Earth and Heaven. The Titanomachy—the usual name for the battle between the Olympians and the Titans—has been foreshadowed for us earlier when Hesiod described how the Cyclopes gave Zeus his lightning and thunderbolts and how Styx and her children were rewarded for helping Zeus in his battle with the Titans. We now find that the war has been raging for ten years without a victory for either side. The Olympians fight from a vantage point, their citadel on Mount Olympus, the Titans from theirs on Mount Othrys. The Olympian gods are now humanized divinities and as such their manner of life resembles that of mankind; they live and fight like the heroes of epic poetry, a distinct change from the older generations of the gods and their primitive means of gaining power.

At a critical moment in the campaign, Zeus liberates the Hecatoncheires who apparently had been overlooked when Cronus freed the other children of Earth from Heaven's smothering oppression. But before entering the battle, the Hecatoncheires have to be fed. This Zeus tends to by providing them with the food of the gods, nectar and ambrosia. After reviving and refreshing them, Zeus exhorts the three hundred-handers (Cottus, Gyes, and Briareus) to fight on his side. They agree to do so out of gratitude for having been set free. Hesiod then spends all his poetic power in describing the final awesome battle between the old and new generations of gods, and just as any epic poet praises the courageous deeds of his hero, Hesiod sings of the might of Zeus:

> Now Zeus no longer held in his strength,
> > but here his heart filled
> deep with fury, and now he showed
> > his violence entire
> and indiscriminately. Out of the sky
> > and off Olympus
> he moved flashing his fires incessantly,
> > and the thunderbolts,
> the crashing of them and the blaze
> > together came flying, one after

> another, from his ponderous hand,
>> and spinning whirls of inhuman
> flame, and with it the earth,
>> the giver of life, cried out
> aloud as she burned, and the vast forests
>> in the fire screamed.
> All earth was boiling with it,
>> and the courses of Ocean
> and the barren sea, and the steam
>> and the heat of it was engulfing
> the Titans of the earth, while the flames
>> went up to the bright sky
> unquenchably, and the blaze
>> and the glare of thunder and lightning
> blinded the eyes of the Titan gods,
>> for all they were mighty.
> . . . .
> The winds brought on with their roaring
>> a quake of the earth and dust storm,
> with thunder and with lightning
>> and the blazing thunderbolt,
> the weapons thrown by great Zeus,
>> and they carried the clamor
> and outcry between the hosts opposed,
>> and a horrible tumult
> of grisly battle uprose,
>> and both sides showed power in the fighting.
> Then the battle turned. . . .

With the extraordinary firing power of the Hecatoncheires in his possession—the mythical equivalent of a battery of automatic weapons—Zeus soon routs the Titans and carries the field (fig. 11). The defeated gods are relegated to the dungeons of Tartarus where they are chained and guarded by the Hecaton-cheires. Hesiod takes the occasion to describe the Titans' prison. To reach Tartarus would take an anvil falling from heaven full nine days to reach earth, and then another full nine to reach Tartarus. It is a dark, dank place surrounded by a triple wall of bronze; its inhabitants, beside the Titans, are none other than the unpleasant children of Night. While on the subject, Hesiod feels impelled to touch upon other aspects beneath the earth: the house of Hades, Cerberus the hellhound, and the river Styx. With the mention of Styx and the terrible oath which gods swear by her—if they swear falsely they are cut off from the gods, their councils, and their banquets for nine years—Hesiod completes the cycle of the tale of the Titanomachy, which started with the mention of Styx and her children.

Hesiod, focusing as he does on Zeus and his rise to power in the divine hierarchy, does not name the Titans who oppose the Olympians although by implication Cronus appears as their leader. We know that Themis and Mnemosyne could not have been in the ranks of the adversaries since, as we have said and shall soon see, they have been reserved for Zeus' bed and a higher calling. Nor

Figure 11.   Peter Paul Rubens. The Fall of the Titans. *Drawing, c. 1635.*
Royal Museum, Brussels.

could it be Oceanus and his wife Tethys for their mythological biographies
indicate no hostility to Zeus; in fact, it is said that Hera was placed in their care
during the Titanomachy. As for Hyperion, he continues to shine as the sun, or is
an epithet for the sun in Homer and in later poets. Homer knows of the Titans
and cites two of them as inhabitants of Tartarus. Zeus, in one of his angry spats
with his goddess-wife Hera, bursts out that he does not care for her sulking,
not even if she went off to the depths of the world were Iapetus and Cronus sit in
the pit of Tartarus. Earlier in the *Iliad*, Homer has Hera swearing "by all the
gods who are down in Tartarus and are called Titans."

The Greeks, who took their myths seriously, viewed the battle between Zeus
and Cronus not as an Oedipal conflict but in terms of its moral implications. It
troubled and confused many of the brighter minds. Xenophanes, the early
critic of Hesiod and Homer, cried out against wars between the gods as giving
an improper view of the nature of divinity. Much of Aeschylus' theological
dramaturgy is directed toward purging Olympianism of stories of violence in the
household of the gods and toward showing the progressive change in the character of Zeus. The comic poet Aristophanes, satirizing the Sophists and their influence in the *Clouds*, gives an example of how the clever, cynical Sophists used
old myths to batter down their opposition—a case of the devil citing the
Bible. In the warmup to a full debate between Old and New Reasoning, between Traditional Education and the New "Progressive" Intellectualism, the
Sophist poses a question to the traditionalist: "Where is justice?" Without
thinking, the traditionalist gives the orthodox answer: "With the gods in heaven,
of course." Comes back the quick sophistic reply: "If justice is there, how is it that
Zeus could put his father in chains and yet live among the gods free and without punishment?" The traditionalist has no adequate reply.

Plato and Socrates were also very much concerned with the influence of this
old myth of the internecine struggle between Zeus and Cronus on morality
and on understanding the true nature of deity. In an early dialogue, the *Euthyphro*, Plato portrays Socrates in an earnest discussion with a young man Euthyphro who has brought up his father on a charge of murder even though the

father was not directly responsible for the man's death. The subject is piety, and Socrates is trying to get at its essence and arrive at a definition of piety. This is Plato's account of the conversation:

Socrates: And what is piety, and what is impiety?

Euthyphro: Piety is doing as I am doing; that is to say, prosecuting anyone who is guilty of murder, sacrilege, or of any similar crime—whether he be your father or mother, or whoever he may be—that makes no difference; and not to prosecute them is impiety. And please to consider, Socrates, what a noble proof I will give that this is law, a proof which I have already given to others:—of the principle, I mean, that the impious, whoever he may be, ought not to go unpunished. For do not men regard Zeus as the best and most righteous of the gods?—and yet they admit that he bound his father [Cronus] because he wickedly devoured his sons, and that he too had punished his own father [Uranus] for a similar reason, in a nameless manner. And yet when I proceed against my father, they are angry with me. So inconsistent are they in their way of talking when the gods are concerned, and when I am concerned.

Socrates: . . . Tell me, for the love of Zeus, whether you really believe that they [the stories about the gods] are true.

Euthyphro: Yes, Socrates; and things more wonderful still, of which the world is in ignorance.

Socrates: And do you really believe that the gods fought with one another, and had dire quarrels, battles, and the like, as the poets say, and as you may see represented in the works of great artists? . . . .

Euthyphro: Yes, Socrates; and, as I was saying, I can tell you, if you would like to hear them, many other things about the gods which would quite amaze you.

Socrates: I dare say; and you shall tell me them at some other time when I have leisure.

Euthyphro, of course, conveniently—perhaps conventionally—rationalizes Zeus' punishment of Cronus as just payment for having devoured his children, but Socrates is aware of the whole range of myths that deal with battles of the gods. In a later work, the *Republic*, Plato has Socrates take a firmer stance when he insists to his interlocutor Adeimantus that in the perfect state most of the old myths will have to be discarded. Ademantus is puzzled:

Adeimantus: What tales?

Socrates: Those which are narrated by Homer and Hesiod, and the rest of the poets, who have ever been the great story-tellers of mankind.

Adeimantus: What are the stories you mean?

Socrates: First of all . . . There was that greatest of all falsehoods on great subjects, which the misguided poet told about Uranus—I mean what Hesiod says that Uranus did, and how Cronus retaliated on him. The doings of Cronus, and the suffering which in turn his son (Zeus) inflicted upon him, even if they were true, ought certainly not to be lightly told to young and thoughtless persons; if possible, they had better been buried in silence. But if there is an absolute necessity for their mention, a chosen few might hear them in a mystery rite. . .

. . .For if our young men seriously listen to such unworthy representations of the gods, instead of laughing at them as they ought, hardly will any of them deem that he himself, being but a man, can be dishonored by similar actions; neither will he rebuke any inclination which may arise in his mind to say and do the like. And instead of having any shame or endurance, he will be always whining and lamenting on slight occasions.

The Five Ages. With the decline of Olympianism, interest in the theological implications of the Titanomachy also declined. But the character of Cronus was strongly conditioned by yet another story told by Hesiod. In the *Works and Days* the poet tells his wayward brother Perses a parable, much like the one he told him about Prometheus and Pandora, to illustrate the present state of man. It is the story of the Five Ages.

The gods first made a golden race of men who lived when Cronus reigned in heaven. These lived in a kind of Garden of Eden; whatever they needed was provided for them without their having to lift a hand. When that generation died out and became spirits who watched over the deeds of men, the Olympians created another race of men, this time men of silver. But this was a race of simpletons, childlike, given to wronging one another and not rendering the gods their due. Zeus in his anger put them away but, nevertheless, gave them the job of being spirits of the Underworld. Zeus then created another race of men, men of bronze, who were monstrous, warlike; that generation came to an end when they destroyed one another. The fourth generation of men was the race of heroes. Zeus created them, and for those who were not killed at Troy or before Oedipus' Thebes, the Olympian had a wonderland, a paradise—the Islands of the Blessed, a far-off land at the edge of the world-encircling river. There they lived "happy heroes for whom the grain-giving earth bears honey-sweet fruit flourishing thrice a year, far from the deathless gods, and Cronus rules over them; for the father of men and gods released him from his bonds." Then came the fifth age, Hesiod's own, Zeus-created. It is an age of iron in which men have to live by the sweat of their brow, suffering and sorrowing, in which good is mixed with evil. This age will come to an end when Decency and Respect forsake the earth and depart to Olympus. Hesiod, having made his point, does not say what is in store for us after the iron age comes to an end.

Cronus and the Golden Age. The picture of Cronus ruling during the Golden Age or as the sovereign power over the Islands of the Blessed, is picked up by other Greek and Roman poets and then transmitted to later *litterateurs*. Homer, however, has another tradition in which Cronus has no part. In the *Odyssey*, Homer's paradise is the Elysian Fields—compare the French *Champs Élysées*—and like the Islands of the Blessed, it is located at the world's end. Menelaus, Helen's husband, is told by the prophesying Old Man of the Sea Proteus (p. 104) that he will not die in Argos but that he will be sent, apparently alive, to this wonderland, a distinction he merits not for any act of virtue or piety on his part, but in recognition of his being Helen's husband and Zeus' son-in-law.

The fifth-century poet Pindar has another point of view on the kind of person who will merit a place in an aristocratic paradise. For him, the Islands of the Blessed are ruled over by Cronus and reserved for those mortals who have kept their souls free of sin through three incarnations. There they will join such celebrities as Achilles, his father Peleus, and Cadmus, the founder of Thebes.

Among the Romans, Saturnus or Saturn—their equivalent of the Greek god Cronus—is mainly associated with a golden age in Italy (p. 38). Vergil, who continues in the rationalizing spirit of the Alexandrians, views Saturn as coming to Italy after his defeat at the hands of the Olympians. There he becomes an early king, civilizes the then-primitive people, and gives them a long, peaceful rule—golden centuries in Latium, the name he gave to Italy. Vergil could see in Emperor Augustus another such savior for Italy "who shall establish for Latium a golden age in that very region where Saturn once reigned."

Ovid in his *Metamorphoses* places Saturn at the head of his four ages—he omits Hesiod's age of heroes—each of which he assigns to a metal of lesser value: gold, silver, bronze, and iron. His description of the Golden Age owes much to Hesiod but he adds a good deal more, including the death of Saturn with the end of the age:

> The first millennium was the age of gold:
> Then living creatures trusted one another;
> People did well without the thought of ill:
> Nothing forbidden in a book of laws,
> No fears, no prohibitions read in bronze,
> Or in the sculptured face of judge and master.
> Even the pine tree stood on its own hills,
> Nor did it fall to sail uncharted seas;
> All that men knew of earth were shores of home,
> No cities climbed behind high walls and bridges;
> No brass-lipped trumpets called, nor clanging swords,
> Nor helmets marched the streets, country and town
> Had never heard of war: and seasons travelled
> Through the years of peace. The innocent earth
> Learned neither spade nor plough; she gave her
> Riches as fruit hangs from the tree: grapes
> Dropping from the vine, cherry, strawberry
> Ripened in silver shadows of the mountain,
> And in the shade of Jove's miraculous tree,
> The falling acorn. Springtide the single
> Season of the year, and through that hour
> The soft breath of the south in flowering leaf,
> In white waves of the wheat across the meadows,
> Season of milk and wine in amber streams
> And honey pouring from the green-lipped oak.
>
> After old Saturn fell to Death's dark country
> Straitly Jove ruled the world with silver charm,
> Less radiant than gold, less false than brass.

*   *   *   *

In the Middle Ages and the Renaissance, Saturn was allegorized, moralized, associated with astrology, and euhemerized. Like many other "dead" gods of the classical pantheon, he assumed a variety of personalities such as Time, Heaven, God the Father, and Virtue. To be born under the star of Saturn made one "saturnine," gloomy and morose; Saturn's day became fixed in our calendar as Saturday; and the Roman festival established in his honor, the *Saturnalia*, the merriest of the year, was taken over in large part as Christmas. However, in yet later literary tradition, Saturn's associations were limited mostly to the Golden Age or to the defeat of an early race of gods. In the prologue to the fifth book of his *Faerie Queene*, Spenser describes a Golden Age over which a benign Saturn ruled:

> For during Saturnes ancient raigne it's sayd,
> That all the world with goodnesse did abound:
> All loved vertue, no man was affrayd
> Of force, ne fraud in wight was to be found:
> No warre was knowne, no dreadfull trompets sound,
> Peace universall rayn'd mongst men and beasts,
> And all things freely grew out of the ground:
> Justice sate high ador'd with solemne feasts,
> And to all people did divide her dred beheasts.

With a satirical touch and with considerable humor, Byron in *Beppo* has another view of the Golden Age.

> Oh, Mirth and Innocence! Oh, Milk and Water!
>   Ye happy mixtures of more happy days!
> In these sad centuries of sin and slaughter,
>   Abominable Man no more allays
> His thirst with such pure beverage. No matter,
>   I love you both, and both shall have my praise:
> Oh, for Old Saturn's reign of sugar-candy!—
> Meantime I drink to your return in brandy.

For John Keats (1795–1821), however, the idea of a decline from the Golden Age and man's fall from grace was incompatible with his faith in a universal law of change that imperiously legislates progress and enlightenment. To illustrate the working of this law, Keats took the battle of the Titans as the theme for his *Hyperion*, a poem that was never to be finished. His portrayal of the Titans, especially Saturn, is sympathetic and benign. They are not brutal and tyrannical gods; they are rather majestic, but unfortunate and humanly frail beings who represent one of the links in the upward evolution to a higher ideal. Even Hyperion, the one unconquered Titan, eventually has to give way to Apollo, a god superior in beauty, beneficence, and intellect. Keats picks up the story after the Titans—Keats has a roster of twenty-six mythical beings whom he classifies as representatives of the deposed rulers of the Universe—have been defeated by the Olympians and imprisoned in Tartarus:

> Deep in the shady sadness of a vale
> Far sunken from the healthy breath of morn,
> Far from the fiery noon, and eve's one star,
> Sat gray-hair'd Saturn, quiet as a stone,
> Still as the silence round about his lair;
> Forest on forest hung about his head
> Like cloud on cloud. No stir of air was there,
> Not so much life as on a summer's day
> Robs not one light seed from the feather'd grass,
> But where the dead leaf fell, there did it rest.

Several of the Titans are urging the use of force against the Olympians in order to regain their lost power. Saturn is in a quandary as to what course of action to take and appeals to Oceanus for advice:

O Titans, shall I say, "Arise!"—Ye groan:
Shall I say "Crouch!"—Ye groan. What can I then?
O Heaven wide! O unseen parent dear!
What can I? Tell me, all ye brethren Gods,
How we can war, how engine our great wrath!
O speak your counsel now, for Saturn's ear
Is all a-hunger'd. Thou, Oceanus,
Ponderest high and deep; and in thy face
I see, astonied, that severe content
Which comes of thought and musing: give us help!

It is through Oceanus that Keats expresses his belief in the progressive evolution of the world toward higher aesthetic ideal. Oceanus, "God of the Sea, sophist and sage from no Athenian grove" replies to Saturn:

We fall by course of Nature's law, not force
Of thunder or of Jove. Great Saturn, thou
Hast sifted well the atom-universe. . .
[And] first as thou wast not the first of powers
So art thou not the last; it cannot be. . .
As Heaven and Earth are fairer, fairer far
Than Chaos and blank Darkness, though once chiefs;
And as we show beyond that Heaven and Earth
In form and shape compact and beautiful. . .
So on our heels a fresh perfection treads,
A power more strong in beauty, born of us
And fated to excel us, as we pass
In glory that old Darkness. . .
. . . . for 'tis the eternal law
That first in beauty should be first in might.

The poem breaks off at the point where Apollo, in a virtually dissociated state often attributed to his priestesses, is inspired by Mnemosyne (Memory) and goes into an ecstasy that is both prophetic and creative:

"Knowledge enormous makes a God of me. . .
Creations and destroyings, all at once
Pour into the wide hollows of my brain,
And deify me, as if some blithe wine
Or bright elixir peerless I had drunk,
And so become immortal."—Thus the God,
While his enkindled eyes, with level glance
Beneath his white soft temples, steadfast kept
Trembling with light upon Mnemosyne.
Soon wild commotions shook him, and made flush
All the immortal fairness of his limbs;
Most like the struggle at the gate of death;
Or liker still to one who should take leave

Of pale immortal death, and with a pang
As hot as death's is chill, with fierce convulse
Die into life: so young Apollo anguish'd:
His very hair, his golden tresses famed
Kept undulation round his eager neck.
During the pain Mnemosyne upheld
Her arms as one who prophesied.—At length
Apollo shriek'd;—and lo! from all his limbs
Celestial. . . . .

Algernon Swinburne (1837–1909) was drawn to Keat's poetry, as Shelley
had been, and composed a *Hyperion* of his own. Although Swinburne followed
Keats' outline in having the setting in Tartarus and a call to arms against the
Olympians, he rejected the philosophy of progressive change and aesthetic
idealism. His own view was colored by the Greek philosophy of a relentless,
blind fatality and world destiny which man cannot alter, a world in which man
can attain happiness in the intellectual contemplation of truth—a kind of
retreat to the Garden of Epicurus. These are the words which Swinburne
puts into the mouth of Saturn:

Thro' all the circling universe of life
One inmost Power, unwearied, never sleeps
But circles ever thro' the lifeless deep
Life warm and radiant; hence, when bright-eyed Spring
Makes the green buds flush to their sunny core,
The green life gushes thro' Earth's parched veins,

. . . .

[And] thrills the huge void with immortality,
And whirls forever, changing life with life,
Round the vast orb of being. Herein we lived,
Throned in the unseen sky, or thundered out
In glorious darkness, o'er the trembling world.
Herein, and thrust by this vast hand of that
Which men call Time, or Fate, or Chance, or God.
Nameless and unresisted, tho' unknown,
We fell and newer glories took the place
Of our Supreme; Think ye no inward will,
Self-strong and self-created, wheels along
Existence on its void and fathomless way?
Fools are we, this not knowing, that the same
Is Life and Destiny, nor without one
Exists the other regent of itself:
More fools indeed, would we now wrestle it down,
But yielding in our inward power made strong,
And smiling down the restless rule of Change;
We shall be kings indeed and supreme gods,
Sitting upon calm thrones of Knowledge, strong
In perfect reason and matured peace,
Regal, unmoved, shall we forever reign,
And triumph in our being's perfectness.

Part 3: Zeus versus Typhon, the Hundred-Headed Dragon

. . . when the bold Typhoeus scal'd the sky
And forc'd great Jove from his own heaven to fly,
(What king, what crown from treason's reach is free,
If Jove and heaven can violated be?)

Dryden—*Astraea Redux*

Figure 12.   Zeus battling Typhon.
*Vase painting, third quarter of the sixth
century B.C. Museum Antiker
Kleinkunst, Munich. (Hirmer)*

Thanks to help he had received from the Hecatoncheires, Zeus was able to defeat the Titans. He now has to face, this time alone, one more challenger for power over men and gods, the draconian monster spawned by Earth and Tartarus. Hesiod gives him the name of Typhoeus, but he is also known as Typhon, Typhaeon, and Typho; and as Typhon he has mated with the equally monstrous Echidna, the half-snake and half-human mother of the two hellhounds Orthus and Cerberus, the Lernaean Hydra, and the Chimaera. Hesiod lavishes his descriptive power on nightmarish Typhoeus: arms and feet untiring and invincible, shoulders from which grew a hundred serpents' heads all flashing with fire and uttering human and bestial sounds (fig. 12). Apollodorus adds some further details by telling us that up to his thighs he was human in form and that he towered above the mountains up to the stars. Below his waist he had great coils of serpents which flashed fire from the hundred dragon heads projecting from his arms. All the gods, Zeus excepted, fled in terror before him and made for Egypt where they changed themselves into animals—an apparent rationalization by the Greeks to explain why the Egyptians worshiped animals and to account for the identification of certain Greek gods with Egyptian deities.

The battle between a supreme god or culture hero and a physical or moral monster is a mythological motif for which there are analogs the world over; Saint George and the dragon is the one which comes most readily to mind. Appropriately for his last battle with various challengers to his power,

Hesiod has Zeus take on Typhoeus alone and in a single combat. This is Hesiod's description of that final battle:

> But now, when Zeus had headed up
> > his own strength, seizing
> his weapons, thunder, lightning,
> > and the glowering thunderbolt,
> he made a leap from Olympus, and struck,
> > setting fire
> to all those wonderful heads set about
> > on the dreaded monster.
> Then, when Zeus had put him down
> > with his strokes, Typhoeus
> crashed, crippled, and the gigantic earth
> > groaned beneath him,
> and the flame from the great lord
> > so thunder-smitten ran out
> along the darkening and steep forests
> > of the mountains
> as he was struck, and a great part
> > of the gigantic earth burned
> in the wonderful wind of his heat,
> > and melted . . .
> So earth melted in the flash
> > of the blazing fire; but Zeus
> in tumult of anger cast Typhoeus
> > into broad Tartarus.
> And from Typhoeus comes the force of winds
> > blowing wetly . . .
> and burst upon the misty face
> > of the open sea bringing
> heavy distress to mortal men
> > and rage in malignant
> storm . . .
> And then again, across the limitless
> > and flowering
> earth, they ruin the beloved works
> > of ground-dwelling people
> by overwhelming them with dust
> > and hard tornadoes.

To Hesiod, the victory of Zeus over Typhoeus undoubtedly symbolized the Olympian's superiority over the wild, untamable forces of nature particularized in the storm winds. There are, of course, other versions of this struggle, most of which have to do with the final resting place of the monster. Homer has him lying prostrate in the mythical land of the Arimi; Aeschylus and Pindar bury him under Mount Etna in Sicily where he is held responsible for the eruptions of that famous volcano. The combination of winds and volcanic action were not unrelated to the Greeks; as early as Aristotle, and even earlier, it was thought that eruptions and earthquakes were caused by powerful subterranean winds. Apollodorus adds yet other elements to the story. In the titanic contest between the two powers, Typhon managed to grip Zeus in his coils and cut the sinews of his hands and feet with the sickle he had wrestled out of Zeus' hand. Typhon then carried off the crippled god to Cilicia in Asia Minor where he hid him in a cave and put a dragon to guard the sinews which he had wrapped in a bearskin. The sinews were stolen or retrieved through a ruse, and Zeus was made whole again. (Note the parallels between the Uranus-Cronus and Cronus-Zeus episodes.) The Olympian pursued Typhon to Mount Nysa where the monster was tricked into eating forbidden food. In Thrace he overturned a mountain out of which a stream of blood gushed, thereby giving an explanation for the name of the mountain, Haemus (blood, gore). When Typhon reached Sicily, Zeus buried him under Mount Etna which to this day continues to issue blasts of fire from the thunderbolts that were thrown in that mighty contest.

*   *   *   *

Matthew Arnold (1822–1888), poet and critic, knew the version of Apollodorus and used the episode of the Typhon in his dramatic poem *Empedocles on Etna*. Arnold, like many a poet, concealed a personal torment, a personal dilemma, in the impersonality of the characters and settings of the classical past. In Empedocles, the Greek philosopher and poet of the fifth century B.C., he found a symbol for that part of his life which had been rendered moribund by rationalism and materialism, his imagination shriveled by the loss of mystery and myth-belief, his soul and world no longer in harmony. He hears the poet Callicles as he sings mythological refrains of an idyllic world in which he can no longer believe. When Callicles tells the myth of Typhon, Empedocles sees the defeated rebel as himself, burned out, oppressed by cunning and by the invincibility of "littleness united." He reasons himself from depression into suicide and plunges into the crater. This is Callicles' song on the myth of Typhon:

> The lyre's voice is lovely everywhere;
> In the court of Gods, in the city of men,
> And in the lonely rock-strewn mountain-glen
> In the still mountain air.
>
> Only to Typho it sounds hatefully;
> To Typho only, the rebel o'erthrown,
> Through whose heart Etna drives her roots of stone
> To imbed them in the sea.
>
> Wherefore dost thou groan so loud?
> Wherefore do thy nostrils flash,
> Through the dark night, suddenly,
> Typho, such red jets of flame?
> Is thy tortured heart still proud?
> Is thy fire-scathed arm still rash?
> Still alert thy stone-crush'd frame?
> Doth thy fierce soul still deplore
> Thine ancient rout by the Cilician hills,

And that curst treachery on the Mount of Gore?
Do thy bloodshot eyes still weep
The fight which crown'd thine ills,
Thy last mischance on this Sicilian deep?
Has thou sworn, in thy sad lair,
Where erst the strong sea-currents suck'd thee down,
Never to cease to writhe, and try to rest,
Letting the sea-stream wander through thy hair?
That thy groans, like thunder prest,
Begin to roll, and almost drown
The sweet notes whose lulling spell
Gods and the race of mortals love so well,
When through thy caves thou hearest music swell?

Milton, in describing how Satan and his host were cast out of Heaven by the Son of God and his army of Angels, combines the two Hesiodic episodes of the Titanomachy and the undoing of Typhoeus. Like Zeus' powerful Hecatoncheires who rained stones on the Titans, the Angels match that and more. They

. . .plucked the seated hills, with all their load,
Rocks, waters, woods, and, by the shaggy tops
Uplifting, bore them in their hands.

But the Son of God alone, gives Satan and his followers a not so pleasant *coup de grâce*:

. . . Full soon
Among them he arrived, in his right hand
Grasping ten thousand thunders, which he sent
Before him, such as in their souls infixed
Plagues. They, astonished, all resistance lost,
All courage; down their idle weapons dropped . . .
Yet half his strength he put forth, but checked
His thunder in mid-volley; for he meant
Not to destroy, but root them out of Heav'n . . .
Nine days they fell; confounded Chaos roared,
And felt tenfold confusion in their fall
Through his wild anarchy; so huge a rout
Encumbered him with ruin. Hell at last,
Yawning, received them whole, and on them closed.

As early as the fifth century B.C., the Greeks—like most people fascinated by the unfathomable antiquity of Egypt and its religion—identified Typhon with the Egyptian god Seth. By the first century A.D., Plutarch, in an essay on the Egyptian deities Isis and Osiris, represents Typhon as the power of evil and destruction as opposed to the power of good in the person of Osiris, his brother. Typhon entraps his brother in a chest until Horus, the foster-son of Isis, the wife of Osiris, defeats Typhon in a singlehanded combat. Plutarch also tells of a city in Egypt that hunts down crocodiles in the belief that Typhon escaped from Horus in that form.

Both Milton and Melville knew this syncretistic version of the myth of Typhon. Much of Melville's symbolism in *Moby Dick* centers on the Osiris legend of death and resurrection. To this Melville adds another interesting element. The English word "typhoon" is derived from the Chinese word for *great wind* and influenced by the Greek *Typhon*. Melville was apparently aware of this connection between Typhon and typhoon; in *Moby Dick* the word is capitalized and Typhoon is addressed as a god by Captain Ahab. By extension, Typhoon becomes for Melville not only Hesiod's storm winds, but every manifestation of evil and destruction—the sea, Moby Dick.

In Milton's *On the Morning of Christ's Nativity*, the list of Egyptian gods is taken from Plutarch's essay but the Greek description of Typhon remains:

> Nor is Osiris seen
> In Memphian grove or green,
> Trampling the unshowered grass with lowings loud;
> Nor can he be at rest
> Within his sacred chest;
> Nought but profoundest Hell can be his shroud;
> In vain, with timbreled anthems dark,
> The sable-stolèd sorcerers bear his worshiped ark.
> He feels from Judah's land
>
> The dreaded Infant's hand;
> The rays of Bethlehem blind his dusky eye;
> Nor all the gods beside
> Longer dare abide,
> Not Typhon huge ending in snaky twine:
> Our Babe, to show his Godhead true,
> Can in his swaddling bands control the damnèd crew.

Part 4:   Zeus versus the Giants—the Gigantomachy

Like as Minerva, being late returned
From slaughter of the Giaunts conquered;
Where proud Encelade, whose wide nosethrils burnd
With breathed flames, like to a furnace red,
Transfixed with speare, downe tombled ded
From top of Hemus, by him heaped hye . . .

Spenser—*Faerie Queene*

With the downfall of Typhon, Hesiod brings to an end his version of the struggles Zeus had to face before being assured of his sovereignty on Mount Olympus and in the universe. Later sources, however, tell of other difficulties the Olympians had to endure before they could be secure in their power; in particular, it is a battle against certain giants. Hesiod produced a race of giants from the blood of Uranus which fell on the earth, and Homer knows of a breed of gigantic, savage men who were wiped out because of their insolence towards the gods, but neither poet speaks of a contest for power. The struggle between the Giants and the Olympians, generally called the Gigantomachy, becomes a popular theme from the early seventh century B.C. on through classical antiquity. The myth undoubtedly

Figure 13. The Gigantomachy. Athena striking down the giant Enceladus. *Detail from the frieze of the Great Altar of Zeus at Pergamum, c. 180 B.C. Pergamum Museum, Berlin.*

started as a variation of the popular motif of tribes or early gods attempting to dethrone established divinities; on a more advanced cultural level, the myth was interpreted as the struggle of civilization against barbarism. Because of the obvious parallel with the Titanomachy, later poets and mythographers frequently confuse Giants and Titans.

It appears that Earth became indignant at the fate of her former children, the Titans, at the hands of the Olympians. She mated with Uranus and brought forth a monstrous brood of giants with frightening faces and serpents for feet. Apollodorus names thirteen of them, of whom he singles out Porphyrion and Alcyoneus as surpassing the rest of their brothers. Alcyoneus was immortal as long as he fought in his native land; as for the others, the gods were informed that they would not be able to overcome a single giant unless they had the help of a mortal. When Earth heard of this new development, she discovered a herb which would serve as an antidote against the possibility of her children being killed by mortal hands. Zeus, however, kept the earth in darkness by forbidding Helios and Eos to shine. He took the herb for himself and then invited the most famous hero of all time, Heracles, to assist the Olympians in their struggle against the giants. Heracles killed Alcyoneus, but as the latter fell on the ground he came to life again. On Athena's advice Heracles dragged Alcyoneus from his native land and thus was able to kill him once and for all.

Folklore motifs that fill the story of Alcyoneus are not prominent in the denouement of the other giants. Porphyrion attacked Heracles and Hera, but was killed by Zeus and Heracles acting in unison, Zeus using his lightning bolt, Heracles his arrows. Another giant, Enceladus (fig. 13), attempted to run away but Athena picked up the island of Sicily and threw it upon him. One by one, the Olympians killed off the remaining giants; Zeus struck those unnamed with his thunderbolts, and Heracles finished them off with his arrows.

*   *   *   *

Keats employs the character of Enceladus in his *Hyperion* as a foil for Oceanus and Saturn. It is he who issues a call to arms to his imprisoned colleagues to resist the might and power of the Olympians. This is Keats' description of the brooding giant:

> . . .on a crag's uneasy shelve,
> Upon his elbow rais'd, all prostrate else,
> Shadow'd Enceladus; once tame and mild
> As grazing ox unworried in the meads;
> Now tiger-passion'd, lion-thoughted, wroth,
> He meditated, plotted, and even now
> Was hurling mountains in the second war,
> Not long delay'd, that scar'd the younger Gods
> To hide themselves in the forms of beast and bird.

The allusion to the "second war" is to Typhoeus' battle with Zeus; Keats' authority is apparently following Apollodorus' account which lists the Gigantomachy first, then Typhoeus who "scar'd the younger Gods to hide themselves in the forms of beast and bird" in Egypt, and lastly, as we shall see, the assault on heaven by the Aloadae. Here are some of the angry words of Enceladus as he attempts to stir up a fresh revolt:

> . . .shall we listen to the over-wise,
> Or to the over-foolish, Giant-Gods:
> Not thunderbolt on thunderbolt, till all
> That rebel Jove's whole armoury were spent,
> Not world on world upon these shoulders piled,
> Could agonize me more than baby-words
> In midst of this dethronement horrible.
> Speak! roar! shout! yell! ye sleepy Titans all.
> Do ye forget the blows, the buffets vile?

Longfellow had another view of Enceladus: he is called upon to be the savior of Italy in her struggle against the Austrians. Longfellow composed the poem in 1859 during Italy's difficulties with Austria and entitled it *Enceladus*:

> Under Mount Etna he lies,
>   It is slumber, it is not death;
> For he struggles at times to arise,
> And above him the lurid skies
>   Are hot with his fiery breath.
>
> The crags are piled on his breast,
> The earth is heaped on his head;
> But the groans of his wild unrest,
> Though smothered and half-suppressed,
> Are heard, and he is not dead.
>
> And the nations far away
> Are watching with eager eyes;
> They talk together and say,
>   "To-morrow, perhaps to-day,
>   Enceladus will arise!"

And the old gods, the austere
　　Oppressors in their strength,
Stand aghast and white with fear
At the ominous sounds they hear,
　　And tremble, and mutter, "At length!"

Ah me! for the land that is sown
　　With the harvest of despair!
Where the burning cinders, blown
From the lips of the overthrown
　　Enceladus, fill the air;

Where ashes are heaped in drifts
　　Over vineyard and field and town,
Whenever he starts and lifts
His head through the blackened rifts
　　Of the crags that keep him down.

See, see! the red light shines!
　　'Tis the glare of his awful eyes!
And the storm-wind shouts through the pines
Of Alps and of Apennines
　　"Enceladus, arise!"

A most vivid Enceladus is found in Melville's novel *Pierre* in which the hero, having fallen into a semi-conscious state, has a dream vision of the giant on the "Mount of Titans." To Melville, Enceladus is a God-hating and God-assulting figure; that and much more. Note, too, that his mutilation like that of Captain Ahab in *Moby Dick* is emphasized.

You saw Enceladus, the Titan, the most potent of all giants, writhing from out the imprisoning earth;—turbaned with upborne moss he writhed; still, though armless, resisting with his whole striving trunk, the Pelion and Ossa hurled back at him; turbaned with upborne moss he writhed; still turning his unconquerable front toward that majestic mount eternally in vain assailed by him, and which, when it had stormed him off, had heaved his undoffable incubus upon him, and deridingly left him there to bay out his ineffectual howl. . . .
Such was the wild scenery—the Mount of Titans, and the repulsed group of heaven-assaulters, with Enceladus in their midst shamefully recumbent at its base;—such was the wild scenery, which now to Pierre, in his strange vision, displaced the four blank walls, the desk, and camp-bed, and domineered upon his trance. But no longer petrified in all their ignominious attitudes, the herded Titans now sprung to their feet; flung themselves upon the slope; and anew battered at the precipice's unresounding wall. Foremost among them all, he saw a moss-turbaned, armless giant, how despairing of any other mode of wreaking his immitigable hate, turned his fast trunk into a battering-ram, and hurled his own arched-out ribs again and yet again against the invulnerable steep.
　　"Enceladus! it is Enceladus!"—Pierre cried out in his sleep. That moment the phantom faced him; and Pierre saw Enceladus no more; but on the Titan's armless trunk, his own duplicate face and features magnifiedly gleamed upon him with prophetic discomfiture and woe. With trembling frame he started up from his chair, and woke from that ideal horror to all his actual grief.

Otus and Ephialtes, the Aloadae.   Where Melville speaks of "Pelion and Ossa" he is alluding to an incident involving yet another group of giants who attempted to assault the Olympians. This time their number is but two, the Aloadae, so-called descendants of Aloeus. They were Otus and Ephialtes, the two sons of Aloeus' wife and the god of the sea Poseidon. From their youth on, both were known for their extraordinary strength and daring. They were prodigously huge, even as children. When only nine years old, Homer reports in the *Odyssey*, they were more than ten feet broad and over forty feet high. At this tender age Otus and Ephialtes attacked the Olympian gods and tried to assualt heaven by piling Mount Ossa on Olympus and Mount Pelion on Ossa. Had they waited until maturity, these two giants might have attained their objective but Apollo destroyed them in their youth "before the down had bloomed beneath their temples, and darkened their chins with the blossom of youth."

"Piling Pelion on Ossa" has become proverbial in English for adding difficulty to difficulty, and for exceedingly strenuous activity. Shakespeare has Hamlet use the allusion to Laertes to prove his love for Ophelia:

> Be buried quick with her, and so will I.
> And if thou prate of mountains, let them throw
> Millions of acres on us, till our ground,
> Singeing his pate against the burning zone,
> Make Ossa like a wart!

In the *Iliad*, Homer tells of another feat by Otus and Ephialtes. It seems that they put the god of war Ares in chains and kept him a prisoner in a bronze jar for thirteen months. Ares would have died, had it not been for Hermes, the messenger of the gods, who heard of Ares' difficulties and freed him at the point of total exhaustion. Apollodorus also tells of the assault of the Aloadae upon the Olympian gods. According to him, they actually piled the mountains on top of one another and threatened to change the land into sea and the sea into land. They met their end not for this attempt but rather for their presumption in daring to woo Hera and Artemis. We also hear that they grew over a foot in breadth and almost five feet in height every year. In later times their bones were said to have been seen in Thessaly, a common motif in attributing the bones of some prehistoric creature to the giants.

Part 5: The New Regime of Zeus

King of Kings, of those blessed
the most blessed, might most supreme—
O happy Zeus!

Aeschylus—The Suppliants

The enemies of the Olympians have been routed, the wars are over, Cronus has been forced to retire. Hesiod is now prepared to enter Zeus on a new phase of his divine career: the consolidation of his power, the characterization of his new regime, and the creation of the second generation of Olympian deities. At the conclusion of the wars, the gods, on the advice of Earth, urge Zeus to become their king and rule over them. To this he agrees and distributes portfolios of power among them. This is as far as Hesiod takes us in this aspect of the new regime.

Homer gives us another view and some further details of the division of power. In the *Iliad* we hear that Zeus is not the youngest but the oldest son of Cronus, and that when the time came to divide the universe among the sons of Cronus, lots were cast to determine the apportionment. Zeus won for himself the sky and the upper air, Poseidon the sea, and Hades the infernal regions; earth and Olympus were to be common territory—neutral ground so to speak—for all three gods. In Homer's patriarchal family, the three daughters of Cronus had no property rights and were exluded from the division. And although the three gods were supposed to be equal in power, Poseidon, piqued at having been told by Zeus' messenger not to take part in the Trojan War, was forcibly reminded that Zeus was physically stronger and had on his side the Furies who always support the older member of the family.

After assigning spheres of influence in the universe, Zeus undertakes a series of "marriages" which will, through his dispensation, provide the hallmarks of civilization, namely, peace, good government, enjoyment, and artistic creation. To Hesiod, a civilized state means the effective combination of law, the intellectual pursuits, and even the art of war. We need not concern ourselves over the nature of these marriages and the question of polygamy versus monogamy. In the language of mythology Hesiod merely means to indicate that all these benefits are derived from Zeus, they are the "seed" of Zeus. Homer and other poets portray the Olympian as monogamous, the marital relationship most acceptable to the Greeks. His relations with goddesses and mortals were viewed tolerantly as extramarital affairs. Perhaps Ovid's words best fit the situation: "the gods have their own laws." In tabular form these are the results of the seven marriages of Zeus as Hesiod gives them:

~ Metis	Athena
~ Themis	Horae (Hours or Seasons)
	1. Eunomia (Order)
	2. Dike (Justice)
	3. Eirene (Peace)
	Moerae (Fates)
	1. Clotho (Spinner)
	2. Lachesis (Assigner)
	3. Atropos (Irreversible)
~ Eurynome	Charites (Graces)
	1. Aglaia (Radiance)
	2. Euphrosyne (Joy)
	3. Thalia (Festivity)
~ Demeter	Persephone
~ Mnemosyne	Muses
	1. Clio (Celebrator)
	2. Euterpe (Charming)
	3. Thalia (Festivity)
	4. Melpomene (Songstress)
	5. Terpsichore (Delight in dance)
	6. Erato (Lovely)
	7. Polyhymnia (Many songs)
	8. Urania (Heavenly)
	9. Calliope (Beautiful voice)
~ Leto	Apollo, Artemis
~ Hera	Hebe, Ares, Eileithyia

The Birth of Athena. The first of the series of Zeus' brides was the Oceanid Metis (Wisdom). It was a marriage fraught with impending danger for the Olympian. He was told by his thoughtful grandparents Gaea and Uranus (Earth and Heaven) that the offspring of his marriage with Metis would be exceedingly clever and that a mighty son would be born to her who would overthrow the Olympian and become the new king of gods and men. On his grandparents' advice Zeus beguiled Metis with cunning talk, and when she was about to give birth to Athena he swallowed his wife "that the goddess might point out to him both good and evil." Zeus then gives birth to Athena from his head. Hesiod describes Athena as a war-goddess: a leader of the army, untiring, one who delights in wars and battles. Later accounts tell that the birth of Athena from the head of Zeus was accomplished by a kind of lobotomy or trepanning operation. Pindar says that the craftsman-god Hephaestus split open his head with an ax and that Athena sprang forth with a mighty warshout (fig. 14); others relate that the delivery was effected by Prometheus or Hermes and that the goddess sprang out fully armed uttering a war whoop.

Hesiod's tale of this first marriage on Olympus is a complex of themes involving both allegory and mythological history. First and foremost, Hesiod had to maintain the invincibility of Zeus; he could not be subject to the same cycle of succession that had afflicted his grandfather Uranus and his father Cronus. Therefore, any possibility of the Olympian's being deposed, any threat to his eternal rule, had to be removed at the very beginning of his reign. Pindar and Aeschylus record a similar motif in the secret that Prometheus stubbornly withheld from Zeus, namely that if Zeus married the sea-nymph Thetis, a child of that marriage would depose

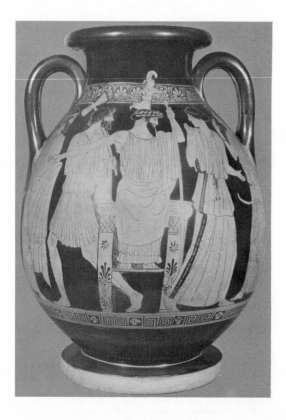

Figure 14.   The birth of Athena from the head of Zeus. *Vase painting, mid fifth century B.C. British Museum.*

him. This threat was bypassed by marrying off Thetis to a mortal. Hesiod took this motif and combined it with a kind of allegory. By swallowing Metis before Athena is born, Zeus not only forestalls the birth of a successor to his power but he also takes within himself the attribute of the Oceanid, wisdom or good counseling. The Olympian himself gives birth to a goddess who now combines the attributes of the father: a militant guardian of cities and a deity renowned for wisdom. Athena becomes a worthy addition to the earlier powers that allied themselves with Zeus: in particular the children of Styx—Zelus (Eager Rivalry), Nike (Victory), Cratos (Strength), and Bia (Might).

The swallowing motif is readily recognizable as a doublet of the one involving Cronus and his children; but there is a significant difference. Cronus' act is primitive and without lasting effect. Zeus, on the other hand, assimilates the virtue of Metis and, importantly, he retains it and always has wisdom within him. Since water-nymphs were also supposed to possess prophetic power, wisdom also implied prophecy. The *metis* of Zeus becomes one of his major characteristics, a distinct change from earlier divinities—including Zeus before his marriage to the Oceanid—who possessed only physical strength.

The myth which Hesiod used to enhance the power and invincibility of Zeus comes from an early historical stratum, from the time when the invading Greeks came upon an important and powerful pre-Greek deity. Athena was of a type, like Artemis, that was represented as unmarried and with no close ties to any kind of male consort. In coming to terms with this goddess, the myth-making imagination of the early Greeks subordinated her to their great god Zeus by making her his daughter, but they avoided subordinating her to another goddess by giving her a mother or, at least, a birth of the usual kind.

In *Paradise Lost* Milton makes good use of the myth of Athena's birth from the head of Zeus in paralleling the birth of Sin as springing from the head of Satan, who is described as suffering from a terrible headache:

> All on a sudden miserable pain
> Supris'd thee, dim thine eyes, and dizzie swumm
> In darkness, while thy head flames thick and fast
> Threw forth, till on the left side op'ning wide,
> Likest to thee in shape and count' nance bright,
> Then shining heav'nly fair, a Goddess arm'd
> Out of thy head I sprung.

Themis. Having ingested Metis and her wisdom, Zeus takes a second wife, Themis, one of the two Titanesses who had not been matched up with a Titan brother in the earlier period. She is reserved for Zeus mainly because of the high regard in which the Greeks held her. In the *Homeric Hymn to Apollo* she is present at Apollo's birth and feeds the newborn god nectar and ambrosia. To Aeschylus she is the daughter of Earth and succeeds her mother as the prophetess of the great oracle at Delphi, and from her the oracle ultimately descends to Apollo. In Aeschylus' *Prometheus Bound* Themis is said to be the mother of the suffering Titan, and it is she who first receives the prophetic word about a possible successor to Zeus' throne. Her name is related to the word "steadfast" or "firm," a characteristic of the earth as in *Terra Firma*. In short, Themis unquestionably has her origins in the form of an earth-goddess, an *Alma Mater*, who quite appropriately should mate with the fructifying sky-god Zeus.

The Horae (Hours). The offspring of this marriage are, fittingly, the Horae or Hours, personifications of the seasons of the year, and therefore connected with growth, fertility, and the fruits of the earth. In Homer they serve Zeus as his gate-keepers on Olympus where they roll aside the clouds, a mythological way of saying that they influence the weather and the seasons. Their names vary, and they number from two to four, but most often their number is given as three. Because of their beneficent powers, the Horae are always invited to be guests at marriages and births of gods and heroes, and they are often found as companions of many gods who in one way or another are associated with fertility.

By Hesiod's time—or it might even have been the poet's own invention—Themis was also regarded as the goddess of justice and righteousness; that is, of "established" custom or law. The connection between fertility and justice is not so far-fetched as it may sound: the rewards for being just are peace, good crops, fat flocks, healthy children, and all other good things in life, as Hesiod tells us in the *Works and Days*. A similar sentiment is expressed by Homer in the *Odyssey*. By coupling Themis and Zeus, the goddess of righteousness and the god of justice, Hesiod establishes the basis for prosperity and sound government. The issue of this marriage are two sets of triplets, the Horae (Hours or Seasons) and the Moerae (Fates). The names Hesiod gives to the Horae are not those which one would expect to be associated with the seasons of the year; rather, the names Eunomia (Order), Dike (Justice), and Eirene (Peace) are the civic virtues that produce stable government and just administration. They are the ethical qualities that characterize the new government of Zeus.

The Moerae (Fates). The second set of triplets are the Moerae or Fates whom, curiously enough, Hesiod has already called the daughters of Night and the sisters of the Keres, the goddesses of Vengeance. Hesiod is not nodding. In the language of mythology the poet tells us that under the new dispensation and government of Zeus, the Fates are now subordinated to the laws of justice as personified by the two gods. With Dike as a sister they are also the just administrators of human fortunes. Even as good fortune will fall upon the just, so evil will fall upon the unjust.

Derived from the Greek word *moira* meaning "lot" or "share," the Moerae are the "allotters," the powers that assign man his lot or share in life. In Latin the word *fatum*, "that which is spoken," signifies the decree of the gods, and from its plural we derive the Fates. Homer speaks of only one Moera who spins out the thread of man's future life when he is born. The association of the Fates with birth led the Romans to identify them with their own spirits of birth, the Parcae, derived from the Latin word *parere*, "to bring forth." The Greek Moerae were, in all likelihood, similar birth spirits who would visit a new-born child and determine what his lot in life would be.

Beginning with Hesiod, the number of the Fates is regularly three, and from the very beginning they were regarded as spinners, drawing out the thread of life. The names Hesiod assigns to them preserve the metaphor: Clotho, the spinning Fate; Lachesis, the one who assigns to man his fate; and Atropos, the fate that cannot be reversed or avoided, sometimes interpreted as the one who cuts the length of thread that has been spun and measured out. Later poets will vary the role of these three in the spinning process, but the Fates are consistently regarded as spinners. Sometimes, however, they are represented as writing the book of fate or reading from it. As the concept of fate changed from age to age, so did their parents and the deities whom the Fates served as children or companions, such as Eileithyia, the goddess of birth, Ananke (Necessity), Tyche (Latin Fortuna, Chance), and Thanatos (Death).

For the end of the *Republic* Plato manufactured an elaborate myth, the Vision of Er, in which the philosopher reaffirms his belief in the immortality of the soul and its implications for the human individual. In the afterlife, Plato's souls see a model of the universe in the form of a huge spindle resting on the knees of Necessity and moved by the Fates, the daughters of Necessity. Although the three sisters know the present, past, and future, man is not relieved of the responsibility of making his own choices, and his life is neither predetermined nor lacking in free will.

Round about, at equal distances, were seated, each on a throne, the three daughters of Necessity, the Fates, robed in white with garlands on their heads, Lachesis, Clotho, and Atropos, chanting to the Sirens' music, Lachesis of things past, Clotho of the present, and Atropos of things to come. . . .

The souls, as soon as they came, were required to go before Lachesis. An interpreter first marshalled them in order; and then, having taken from the lap of Lachesis a number of lots and samples of lives, he mounted on a high platform and said: "The word of Lachesis, maiden daughter of Necessity. Souls of a day, here shall begin a new round of earthly life, to end in death. No guardian spirit will cast lots for you, but you shall choose your own destiny. Let him to whom the first lot falls choose first a life to which he will be bound of necessity. But Virtue owns no master: as a man honors or dishonors her, so shall he have more of her or less. The blame is his who chooses; Heaven is blameless."

*   *   *   *

Although Milton makes some use of Plato's myth in the *Arcades*—the Fates being subdued by the music of the Spheres and the figure of the adamantine spindle —the theme most poets employed was the implacability of the Fates, or Destiny, and their chore of spinning out the thread of man's life. So does Spenser in the *Faerie Queene*, where he lodges the Fates in the abyss of Chaos and has them boasting of their superiority over gods and men:

There . . . all sitting round about
The direfull distaffe standing in the mid,
And with unwearied fingers drawing out
The lines of life, from living knowledge hid.
Sad Clotho helde the rocke, the whiles the thrid
By griesly Lachesis was spun with paine,
That cruell Atropos eftsoones undid,
With cursed knife cutting the twist in twaine:
Most wretched men, whose dayes depend on thrids so vaine.

To the mother who begged for a change in the fate of her children, Lachesis replies:

. . . Fond dame that deem'st of things divine
As of humane, that they may altred bee
And chaung'd at pleasure for those impes of thine.
Not so; for what the Fates do once decree,
Not all the gods can chaunge, nor Jove him self can free.

Shakespeare uses the Fates with and without their thread of life; and indeed some see the three witches in *Macbeth* modeled in part on the three sisters. In the play within a play in *A Midsummer Night's Dream*, Pyramus cries out these words, a parody or a burlesque on classical themes, when he sees Thisbe's body:

> O dainty duck! O dear!
> Thy mantle good,
> What, stain'd with blood!
> Approach, ye Furies fell!
> O Fates, come, come,
> Cut thread and thrum
> Quail, crush, conclude, and quell!

In a similar vein, the comic servant Launcelot Gobbo in *The Merchant of Venice* pretends to his blind father not to be his son:

> Talk not of Master Launcelot, father; for the young gentleman, according to the Fates
> and Destinies and such odd sayings, the Sisters Three and such branches of learning, is
> indeed deceased, or, as you would say in plain terms, gone to heaven.

Robert Browning (1812–1889) uses the Fates as the adversary of Apollo in his poetic dialogue *Apollo and the Fates*. When the Fates refuse Apollo's request to prolong the life of Admetus, claiming that death is a release from the illusions which the god gives man, Apollo plies the Fates with wine, gets them tipsy and ready to admit that man's struggle is no defeat but a triumph; that the elixir of life involves compounding fancy and fact. Browning keeps to the conventional portrayal of the Fates as spinners, but they are not very sympathetic to the human condition, at least when they are sober. As each describes her part in the spinning process, Atropos ends by saying:

> My shears cut asunder: each snap shrieks "One more
> Mortal makes sport for us Moirai who dangled
> The puppet grotesquely till earth's solid floor
> Proved firm he fell through, lost in Nought as before."

Edgar Lee Masters (1869–1950), who had a passion for the classics, sees his father in the character of Henry C. Calhoun asking him to punish Spoon River for the wrongs people did him. But the pursuit of wealth and power to attain this objective only leads him to a kind of hell. Masters, curiously enough, portrays the Fates as weavers and as instruments of revenge; the envenomed robe is also an instrument of revenge used unwittingly against Heracles by his wife. From the *Spoon River Anthology*:

> I reached the highest place in Spoon River,
> But through what bitterness of spirit!
> The face of my father, sitting speechless,
> Child-like, watching his canaries,
> And looking at the court-house window
> Of the county judge's room,
> And his admonitions to me to seek
> My own in life, and punish Spoon River
> To avenge the wrong the people did him,
> Filled me with furious energy

> To seek for wealth and seek for power.
> But what did he do but send me along
> The path that leads to the grove of the Furies?
> I followed the path and I tell you this:
> On the way to the grove you'll pass the Fates,
> Shadow-eyed, bent over their weaving.
> Stop for a moment, and if you see
> The thread of revenge leap out of the shuttle,
> Then quickly snatch from Atropos
> The shears and cut it, lest your sons,
> And the children of them and their children
> Wear the envenomed robe.

The Charites (Graces). Now that Zeus has bestowed wisdom, law, and order on the universe, the divine state can be considered civilized. But Hesiod is also aware that men, or even gods, need something more than an ordered society; that however well-regulated the state there is need for pleasure and joy to offset the dire and pestilential children of Night. Zeus is quick to remedy the situation. Mating with the Oceanid Eurynome, he brings into existence the Charites—better-known by their Roman name, the Graces—radiant goddesses of happiness and festivity: Aglaia, Euphrosyne, and Thalia.

Homer and other poets vary the number of Graces, their names and maternal parents, but there is sufficient evidence to see behind these figures ancient goddesses of vegetation who make the ground productive and cause joy and delight in the hearts of men. In Athens they were worshiped as Auxo (Increaser) and Hegemone (Leader, that is, she who brings forth plants). In the *Iliad*, Charis, the singular form of Charites, is the wife of Hephaestus. This is little more than an allegorical way of indicating the union of grace with craftsmanship. The Graces often accompany Aphrodite as personal attendants, and in the *Homeric Hymn* to the goddess of love we have a typical picture of this association:

> The ready Graces wait, her baths to prepare,
> And oint with fragrant oils her flowing hair.

The Graces are also associated with the Muses and are fond of poetry, singing, and dancing. It is quite natural, therefore, that, like the Hours, they would accompany various gods and goddesses and be welcome guests and entertainers at festivals and happy occasions, as for example, at the wedding of Peleus and Thetis where they joined in song with the Muses.

*   *   *   *

Following the Hellenistic period, the Three Graces were represented in art as nude or very lightly-draped figures. However much nudity was disparaged in late antiquity, the allegorical myth-interpreters of the time, such as Fulgentius and Servius, found an easy way out of the difficulty by interpreting the nudity of the Graces as a symbol of unspoiled beauty, simplicity, and sincerity. In a similar manner, the Platonizing humanists of the Renaissance could find a philosophical rationalization for the nakedness of the Three Graces and other gods and goddesses. The painting of the Graces by Francesco Vanni (1565–1609) shows them in

Figure 15.   Aristide Maillol. The Three Graces. *Bronze, Norton Simon Collection, Los Angeles County Museum of Art.*

their traditional pose with intertwined arms. Tintoretto (1518–1594), and particularly Rubens (1577–1640), found the Three Graces an appropriate subject for their canvases. More recent renderings, which preserve the simplicity and the serenity of the classical style, come from the hands of the sculptor Aristide Maillol (1861–1944) (fig. 15) and the painter Pablo Picasso (1881–   ).

The myth-interpreters of the late classical period cast their influence even as late as the eighteenth century. The fashionable women of the First Republic in France dressed "like the Graces," transparent and revealing. John Lemprière's *A Classical Dictionary* (1788), which influenced Keats and Leigh Hunt and many other poets by its subsequent editions, incorporates much of the late classical rationalizations in the article "Charites":

They were generally represented naked, because kindness ought to be done with sincerity and candour. The moderns explain the allegory of their holding their hands joined by observing that there ought to be a perpetual and never-ceasing intercourse of kindness and benevolence among friends. Their youth denotes the constant remembrance that we ought ever to have of kindnesses received; and their virgin purity and innocence teach us that acts of benevolence ought to be done without any expectation of restoration, and that we ought never to suffer others or ourselves to be guilty of base or impure favours.

To Spenser the Graces are "Venus Damzels" and he calls them by their Hesiodic names. However, late antiquity also infects his interpretation. From the *Faerie Queene*:

> These three on men all gracious gifts bestow,
> Which decke the body or adorne the mynde,
> To make them lovely or well favoured show,
> As comely carriage, entertainment kynde,
> Sweete semblaunt, friendly offices that bynde,
> And all the complements of curtesie:
> They teach us, how to each degree and kynde
> We should our selves demeane, to low, to hie;
> To friends, to foes, which skill men call Civility.
>
> Therefore they alwaies smoothly seeme to smile,
> That we likewise should be mylde and gentle be,
> And also naked are, that without guile
> Or false dissemblaunce all them plaine may see,
> Simple and true from covert malice free:
> And eeke them selves so in the daunce they bore,
> That two of them still froward seem'd to bee,
> But one still towards shew'd her selfe afore;
> That good should from us goe, then come in greater store.

For Matthew Arnold the blush is off the rose; myths of classical antiquity no longer have the power to stir the spirit and excite the heart. In *The New Sirens* he addresses the Graces:

> And you too, O worshipp'd Graces,
> Sylvan Gods of this fair shade!
> Is there doubt on divine faces?
> Are the blessed Gods dismay'd?

In a poem which Arnold first entitled "Indifference" but later named after one of the Graces, *Euphrosyne*, the poet hides the name of an unhappy love. Euphrosyne is Marguerite, beautiful, blithe, unconcerned, pagan:

> I must not say that thou wast true,
> Yet let me say that thou wast fair:
> And they, that lovely face who view,
> Why should they ask if truth be there?

The Muses. After Zeus has brought joy and festivity into the world, he takes Demeter for his fourth wife who gives birth to Persephone, the eventual bride of Hades, god of the Underworld. This marriage comes as a brief interlude in Hesiod's account of the blessings Zeus has bestowed on a now-civilized world. For his fifth wife the Olympian takes the Titaness Mnemosyne who, after Zeus visits her bed for nine successive nights, gives birth in due time to the Nine Muses. Here we have a clear piece of allegory: by the divine help of a beneficent Zeus, Memory produces the arts and intellectual pursuits. In the long proem to the *Theogony*, Hesiod invokes the Muses and gives them ample praise. He tells of their birth in Pieria near Mount Olympus, gives their names, and relates how they visited him on Mount Helicon in Boeotia and inspired him to sing of the present, past, and future. Any singer, he tells us, who chants the glorious deeds of heroes and the gods, cheers the heart of a man who is depressed by anxieties and cares.

Among early poets the belief was that the Muses could fill anyone with the power to sing, to prophesy, to dance. The likelihood is that in origin the Muses were water-spirits, more specifically spirits of mountain springs, who knew the present, past, and future; that is, they were wise and could tell the future. The belief is widespread that water, or the spirits that inhabit it, is an agency of prophecy. And let us recall that the Metis, whom Zeus swallowed, was an Oceanid, a fresh-water nymph. The two springs on Mount Helicon, Aganippe and Hippocrene, were sacred to the Muses who were said to have frolicked about the Pierian springs soon after their birth. The Castalian spring on Mount Parnassus was also sacred to them. On occasion the Romans identified the Muses with the Italian water-deities, the Camenae.

The names, number, and parents of the Muses vary throughout classical antiquity but Hesiod's influence remains the strongest. He established the canonical number of nine; the names he gave them persevered; Mount Helicon, the place of their epiphany to Hesiod, became the focus of their worship. Hesiod also anticipated the time when Apollo would be associated with the Muses as their leader—Apollo is called Musagetes, Leader of the Muses. Because of the Muses' relationship to Apollo, Mount Parnassus and the Castalian spring near Apollo's oracle at Delphi become favorite haunts of the Muses. Quite naturally the Muses are called upon to sing for the gods on Mount Olympus and on all happy occasions, but they can also be found singing a dirge, as they did at the funeral of Achilles' comrade-in-arms Patroclus.

On several occasions the prerogatives and talents of the Muses are challenged by presumptuous mortals. The Thracian bard Thamyris boasted that he could surpass

Figure 16.   The Nine Muses, each shown with her attribute. *Bas-relief on a Roman sarcophagus. Louvre. (Alinari)*

the Muses in song. For his presumption the jealous deities crippled him and deprived him of his ability to sing and to play the harp. The nine daughters of Pierus also presumed to rival the Muses; for their rashness, they were metamorphosed into birds. And when the Sirens tried to compete with the goddesses of song, they were stripped of their wing feathers.

While Hesiod does not assign to the Muses their specific spheres of influence in the arts and sciences, later poets and artists (fig. 16) departmentalize them and give them attributes as follows:

Clio	History	Wears a wreath and carries a scroll
Euterpe	Music	Flute
Thalia	Comedy and pastoral poetry	Comic mask, shepherd's staff, or wreath of ivy
Melpomene	Tragedy	Tragic mask, vine leaves, cothurnus (shoe worn by tragic actors)
Terpsichore	Dance	Lyre and plectrum
Erato	Lyric poetry	Lyre
Polyhymnia	Sacred songs and hymns	Veiled and thoughtful
Urania	Astronomy	Globe
Calliope	Epic poetry	Tablet and stylus

*   *   *   *

Homer, Hesiod, and other early poets invoked the Muses at the beginning of their poems in the sincere belief that the poet was merely the instrument or mouthpiece of the deities. After calling upon his Muse to tell him of Odysseus and his difficulties Homer could say: "Tell me about all these things, O daughter of Zeus, from whatever source you may know them." When poets, old and new, no longer took their Muses seriously, they continued to call on them in formal imitation of the ancient mode. Lord Byron could dismiss them humorously and offhandedly in the opening of a canto in *Don Juan* with "Hail, Muse! *et cetera.*" In the prologue to Shakespeare's *King Henry V*, the chorus calls for an unconventional and noncanonical Muse:

> O for a Muse of fire, that would ascend
> The brightest heaven of invention,
> A kingdom for a stage, princes to act
> And monarchs to behold the swelling scene!

Walt Whitman (1819–1892) in *Song of Myself* calls upon himself as his own Muse and source of inspiration:

> I celebrate myself, and sing myself,
> And what I assume you shall assume,
> For every atom belonging to me as good belongs to you.

In another poem, *Song of the Exposition*, Whitman asks the Muse, the "dame of dames," to take leave of Greece and migrate to the New World. He asks the same of all Old-World inspirations so that their inspiring presence may come to the Philadelphia Centennial Exposition of 1876 for which the poem was composed:

> Come Muse, migrate from Greece and Ionia,
> Cross out please those immensely overpaid accounts,
> That matter of Troy and Achilles' wrath, and Aeneas', Odysseus'
>   wanderings,
> Placard "Removed" and "To Let" on the rocks of your snowy Parnassus,
> Repeat at Jerusalem, place the notice high on Jaffa's gate
>   and on Mount Moriah,
> The same on the walls of your German, French, and Spanish castles,
>   and Italian collections,
> For know a better, fresher, busier sphere, a wide, untried
>   domain awaits, demands you.

Milton makes Urania, his "Heav'nly Muse," the inspirer of Moses on Mount Horeb and Mount Sinai; his *Paradise Lost* was not "to be obtained by the invocation of dame memory and her siren daughters, but by devout prayer to that eternal spirit who can enrich with all utterance and knowledge . . ." Pagan or Christian, the Muses would be called upon not only to inspire the poet to compose sublime verses, but also to lament over the state of current literary production. Spenser's *The Teares of the Muses* falls into the category of a lament, a "mone":

> Rehearse to me, ye sacred Sisters nine,
> The golden brood of Great Apolloes wit,
> Those piteous plaints and sorrowfull sad time,
> Which late ye powred forth as ye did sit
> Beside the silver Springs of Helicone,
> Making your musik of hart-braking mone.

The same theme is repeated humorously in Shakespeare's *A Midsummer Night's Dream* as Theseus reviews a choice of material to celebrate his marriage:

> "The thrice three Muses mourning for the death
> Of Learning, late deceased in beggary."
> That is some satire, keen and critical
> Not sorting with a nuptial ceremony.

In a more serious vein, William Blake (1757–1827) in *To the Muses* complains that the "Fair Nine" have forsaken poetry:

> How have you left the ancient love
>   That bards of old enjoyed in you!
> The languid strings do scarcely move,
>   The sound is forc'd, the notes are few!

Lord Byron was more ambivalent about his Muse. In 1807 he composed his *Farewell to the Muse*, ending with "eternal Adieu"; but in 1812 he invoked her with due modesty in the opening lines of *Childe Harold's Pilgrimage:*

> Oh thou! in Hellas deem'd of heavenly birth,
> Muse! form'd or fabled at the minstrel's will!
> Since shamed full oft by later lyres on earth,

> Mine dares not call thee from thy sacred hill:
> Yet there I've wander'd by thy vaunted rill;
> Yes! sigh'd o'er Delphi's long-deserted shrine,
> Where, save that feeble fountain, all is still;
> Nor mote my shell awake the weary Nine
> To grace so plain a tale—this lowly lay of mine.

Keats, on the other hand, can see a native English Muse patiently waiting for "home-bred glory." From the opening lines of Book IV of *Endymion*:

> Muse of my native land! loftiest Muse!
> O first-born on the mountains! by the hues
> Of heaven on the spiritual air begot:
> Long didst thou sit alone in northern grot,
> While yet our England was a wolfish den;
> Before our forests heard the talk of men;
> Before the first of Druids was a child;—
> Long didst thou sit amid our regions wild
> Rapt in a deep prophetic solitude.
> There came an eastern voice of solemn mood:—
> Yet wast thou patient. Then sang forth the Nine,
> Apollo's garland:—yet didst thou divine
> Such home-bred glory, that they cry'd in vain . . .

The haunts of the Muses, Parnassus and the Pierian springs, were also invoked by the poets as symbols of inspiration and learning. Alexander Pope (1688–1744) in his *Essay on Criticism* gives critics a piece of advice with these lines: "A little learning is a dang'rous thing:/Drink deep, or taste not the Pierian spring."

On the Continent, a group of idealistic poets who loved Greco-Roman culture took Parnassus as the symbol of their devotion to the arts apart from the material concerns of the world. Between 1866 and 1876 these poets published their work in a periodical called *Le Parnasse contemporain*, or *The Modern Parnassus*.

Archibald MacLeish (1892–   ) closes our sampler of the wide-ranging influence of the Muses. In his *Invocation to the Social Muse*, he issues a *caveat* to poets, cautioning them not to write social and political events into their poetry:

> SEÑORA, it is true the Greeks are dead:
>
> It is true also that we are Americans:
> That we use the machines: that a sight of the god is unusual:
> That more people have more thoughts: that there are
> Progress and science and tractors and revolutions and
> Marx and the wars more antiseptic and murderous
> And music in every home: . . .
> Does the lady suggest we should write it out in The Word?
> Does Madam recall our responsibilities?
>
> . . . .
>
> The things of the poet are done to a man alone
> As the things of love are done—or death when he hears the
> Step withdraw on the stair and the clock tick only.

The Conclusion of the Theogony.   Now that tranquility and the amenities of life have been introduced into the world, Hesiod rapidly brings his generation of the gods to a close. The succeeding marriages and relationships produce the traditional Olympians of the second generation whose mythological lives were apparently so well known that Hesiod felt no need to elaborate upon them. Mating with Leto as his sixth wife, Zeus becomes the father of Apollo and Artemis. The positioning of his marriage so close to that with Mnemosyne would suggest the intimate association of Apollo, the patron of the arts and learning, with the Muses. Zeus marries Hera as his seventh and final wife. The children of this supposedly auspicious union are not so illustrious or renowned as we might have been led to expect. Three children are born to Zeus and Hera: Hebe, the cupbearer of the gods; Ares, the god of war, and Eileithyia (also Ilithyia), the goddess of childbirth. The latter, although said to be of Cretan origin (that is, a pre-Greek Minoan goddess), is merely another aspect of Hera herself who presides over all phases of the life of women and who was worshiped under the name of Hera Eileithyia. As we shall see, Hera was able to delay the births of Apollo and Heracles and hasten that of Eurystheus. Similarly Hebe, whose name means "youth, adolescence," is a logical offspring of Hera who is also concerned with this important aspect of womanhood. Milton catches this youthful, adolescent aspect of Hebe in *L'Allegro* when he calls for the help of mythological forces to dispel melancholy, invoking the Grace Euphrosyne:

> Haste thee, Nymph and bring with thee
> Jest and youthful Jollity,
> Quips and Cranks, and wanton Wiles,
> Nods, and Becks, and Wreathed Smiles,
> Such as hang on Hebe's cheek,
> And love to live in dimple sleek.

As the young lady in the Olympian household, Hebe is the cupbearer of the gods and performs various domestic duties in her father's house. In *Endymion*, Keats gives this sensuous picture of the cupbearer of the gods:

> . . . arch Hebe brings
> A full-brimmed goblet, dances lightly, sings
> And tantalizes long; at last he drinks
> And lost in pleasure at her feet he sinks,
> Touching with dazzled lips her starlight hand.

When Heracles brings his mortal life to an end and is apotheosized, he is given Hebe as a wife. The deified hero, Spenser relates in *The Ruines of Time*, now enjoys "All happinesse in Hebes silver bowre,/Chosen to be her dearest Paramoure."

As the spirit of youth, Hebe has the power to rejuvenate. Heracles is said to have induced Hebe to make him young again; his nephew Iolaus, old and wrinkled, also had her help in rejuvenating himself. Among the Romans, Hebe was worshiped under the name of Juventas, "Youth."

As for Ares, it is somewhat of a mystery why the god of war—in particular Ares, who is not a popular figure in epic tales—should be a son of Zeus and Hera, unless he is a reflection of Hera in her aspect as a martial protectress of cities, especially of Argos. Perhaps, too, Ares is a reflection of the domestic quarreling and squabbling between Zeus and Hera. In the *Iliad*, when Ares comes to him whining and complaining, Zeus angrily accuses his son of lusting for quarrels and battles and of having inherited his mother's uncontrollable temper. There seems to be no love lost, at least in Homer, between Zeus and his son or, for that matter, between Zeus and Hera. This suggestion of antagonism between the divine couple is given some support in the episode which immediately follows the birth of the three children. Hesiod says that Hera was angry at Zeus for having brought Athena into existence in a most unusual manner, right out of his head. In retaliation Hera gave birth to Hephaestus "without union with Zeus." The most plausible explanation of this event is that Hesiod wished to avoid making Zeus the father of a cripple, as the god of craftsmen was popularly depicted in mythology. However, Hera's jealousy and antagonism become standard motifs in Greek mythology.

After citing the marriages of Zeus, Hesiod list those of two other Olympian gods. Poseidon takes the Nereid Amphitrite as his wife; their son is Triton. Aphrodite and Ares wed and have three children: Phobos (Fear), and Deimos (Panic)—suitable off-spring for a god of war—and a daughter Harmonia (Harmony) who later marries Cadmus, the king of Thebes. More will be said of these later. Hesiod briefly returns to Zeus, almost as an afterthought, to report the birth of several other prominent second-generation Olympians. Zeus takes as his consort Maia, the daughter of Atlas —Hesiod does not tell us who her mother is, but Maia's name seems to mean "mother" or "nurse"—and becomes the father of the god Hermes. Zeus then takes a mortal woman, Cadmus' daughter Semele, to his bed and sires the god Dionysus. And finally, with another mortal woman, Alcmene, the Olympian begets the great-est hero of all times, Heracles. Thus Hesiod ends the role of Zeus in the genera-tion of the gods.

CHAPTER IV

The Gods on Mount Olympus

Blessed is the man . . . the servant of the Muses,
singing the glorious deeds of the men of old
and the blessed gods who live on Mount Olympus . . .

Hesiod—*Theogony*

And Zeus went into his own home. All the gods
rose up from their seats to greet their father;
no one dared to remain seated as he approached,
but all stood up to meet him.

Homer—*Iliad*

On the east frieze of the Parthenon, the gods are portrayed as having come down from Mount Olympus to help celebrate the quadrennial Panathenaic festival. Waiting to receive the worship of city officials and citizens from their vantage point high on the Acropolis overlooking Athens are the Olympian gods, the Twelve: Zeus, Poseidon, Hephaestus, Hermes, Ares, Apollo, Dionysus, Hera, Athena, Artemis, Aphrodite, and Demeter. The spinster goddess of the hearth, Hestia, is missing from this list; she was left at home so that a place might be made for the god Dionysus who was admitted to the circle of the Olympians at a rather late date. Dionysus could hardly be refused a place on the Acropolis which overlooks his theater, the birthplace of drama and a source of great pride for the Athenians. However, in the canonical lists of the Twelve Olympians, which in Athens date back to the time of Pisistratus in the mid-sixth century B.C., Hestia has her due place along with her brothers and sisters, nephews and nieces. Two gods are conspicuous by their absence, Hades and his wife Persephone. These two, however, live in the dark Underworld and are concerned with the dead; they do not belong to life and light which so characterize the Olympians. The list of the Twelve was not so crystallized that other localities could not make substitutions. At Olympia, for example, Cronus and Rhea and the river-god Alpheus took the places of Hephaestus, Demeter, and Hestia.

The established number of Twelve Olympians—it should be noted that there were also twelve Titans—has stirred considerable speculation: to some it signified the number of months in the year, to others the twelve signs of the zodiac; both suggestions are found in Plato's *Laws* and *Phaedrus*. However that may be, the corporate nature of the Twelve undoubtedly had something to do with the varied aspects and ideals of the political, social, and economic life of a Greek city: political administration (Zeus), defense (Ares and Athena), crafts (Athena and Hephaestus), arts (Apollo), physical beauty (Aphrodite), commerce (Hermes), seafaring (Poseidon), agriculture (Demeter), animal husbandry (Artemis and Apollo), family life and the sacred hearth (Hera and Hestia). When Alexander the Great came to the end of his march into India, he set up an altar to the Twelve to show his dedication to Greek ideals. These, then, are the canonical Twelve Olympians and their Roman opposite numbers:

Zeus (Jupiter, Jove)	Ares (Mars)
Hera (Juno)	Aphrodite (Venus)
Poseidon (Neptune, Neptunus)	Hermes (Mercury, Mercurius)
Demeter (Ceres)	Athena (Minerva)
Apollo (Apollo)	Hephaestus (Vulcan, Vulcanus)
Artemis (Diana)	Hestia (Vesta)

The Olympians, of course, take their name from their traditional home on Mount Olympus. Although some fourteen other mountains in Greece, Cyprus, and Anatolia bore the same name—the number of mountains called Olympus is responsible for the suggestion that the name is a pre-Greek word meaning simply "mountain"—legend has established the divine community of Zeus and his colleagues on the tallest mountain in Greece. Situated on the border between Thessaly and Macedonia, Olympus rises almost ten thousand feet into the air with its cloud-capped peak often lost to sight, giving the impression that the mountain's summit was not part of the physical earth but rather of heaven itself. Hence, the divine inhabitants of Mount Olympus are sometimes called the "heavenly gods" (*ouranioi*), although strictly speaking the gods did not dwell in heaven (*ouranos* = *uranus*) but rather in the upper air (*aether*). It was this region that the giants Otus and Ephialtes tried to reach when they piled Mount Ossa on Olympus and Mount Pelion on Ossa. Shakespeare alludes to the great height of Olympus in a number of his plays. Leaping into Ophelia's grave, Hamlet cries out:

> Now pile your dust upon the quick and dead
> Till of this flat a mountain you have made
> T' o'ertop old Pelion or the skyish head
> Of blue Olympus.

Tullus Aufidius in *Coriolanus* says:

> ...My mother bows,
> As if Olympus to a molehill should
> In supplication nod;

And Othello declares the extent of his passion to Desdemona with these words:

> ... Oh my soul's joy!
> If after every tempest come such calms,
> May the winds blow till they have waken'd death!
> And let the labouring bark climb hills of seas
> Olympus-high and duck again as low
> As hell's from heaven!

Homer, Hesiod, and other poets modeled the divine community, the city of gods, on the legendary communities of the epic heroes. Zeus, therefore, has his palace and stronghold on top of Mount Olympus, as if it were an acropolis. There he holds his councils with the other gods who, like the Phaeacian nobles in the *Odyssey*, sit on their thrones in the court of the great king of the gods. The splendid homes of the other Olympians, built for them by the master-architect Hephaestus, are in the town below the acropolis. The gates to the city of gods were guarded by the Horae; the royal households had divine servants who waited on and entertained the gods. The Horae ministered to Zeus, Iris to Hera, Deimos and Phobos to Ares. Messenger service was provided by Iris and later by Hermes, entertainment by the Muses and the Graces. The gods even had a physician in attendance, Paiëon (or Paeon). Homer reports that he was called upon to heal Ares who was wounded by Diomedes during the Trojan War, and that Hades had to come up to Olympus to be ministered to by the gods' physician when Heracles had put an arrow through his shoulder.

The gods also have their homes away from home, generally in places where they were celebrated in worship. Zeus rules from Mount Ida as well as from Mount Olympus; Poseidon has a palace in the depths of the sea at Aegae; and Apollo could be found at home in Lycia, Chryse, Killa, or Tenedos. In these homes the gods slept and ate, and if married, lived with their wives. Although their life was much the same as that of human beings, the gods were set apart from men by special powers, possessions, and foods. They were neither omniscient nor omnipresent, but they could see from great distances, cover ground very rapidly, and hear the prayers of mortals in their far-off homes. Their food was not the kind that mortals ate; it was nectar and ambrosia. They bled when wounded; but it was not blood that flowed from their veins, but an ethereal substance called "ichor." The one overriding and dominating difference between the gods and the life-loving Greeks was the matter of mortality. The gods are "deathless," "ever-living," and "immortal," whereas men have to face the grim trauma of death.

One final point should be noted in the general life of the gods: their connection with one or more animals. Zeus is associated with the eagle, Hera with the peacock and the cow, Apollo with the raven and the swan, Aphrodite with the dove and the sparrow, Poseidon with the bull and the horse, Artemis with the deer and the bear, and so forth. The knotty problem of whether the gods were worshiped in animal form at an early stage of their development has never been satisfactorily resolved. As to the question of totemism, or the identification of a family or clan with a particular animal, no convincing evidence has yet been adduced to prove that any of the Greek gods was an animal totem.

1. Zeus (Jupiter, Jove)

In fleshing out the biography of the foremost of the Olympian Twelve, only those details need be mentioned that were not touched upon when his birth and rise to power were described. Of all the gods in the Greek pantheon, Zeus is the only one whose Indo-European identity can be established with a degree of certainty. At the root of his name is the element *DI*—as can be seen from the genitive or possessive case *Dios*, "of Zeus" —a linguistic stem meaning "bright," "sky," "heaven" in the family of Indo-European languages. The same element can be seen in Sanskrit *Dyaus*, Latin *dies* (day) and *Jupiter* (= *Diou*-piter), and Germanic *Ziu*. Zeus' attribute *pater* (father) is also found among the Romans (Ju-*piter* and

Figure 17.   Zeus about to hurl a bolt
of lightning. *Bronze from Dodona, c.
470 B.C. State Museum, Berlin.*

Dies-*piter*), Indians (Dyaus *pita*), and the Illyrians of the western Balkans
(Dei-*patyros*).

In origin, Zeus, like his Roman counterpart Jupiter, was a weather-god as we can
see from some of his titles: Rainer, Lightener, Thunderer, Cloud-Gatherer,
Sender of Fair Winds (fig. 17). He is concerned with the sky insofar as thunder,
lightning, rain, and other atmospheric phenomena were manifested in a particular
region. Since weather signs were observed about the peaks of mountains, it was
natural to think that the god made his home on the crests of the highest mountains.
The intimate association of weather, particularly of rain, with the life cycle led to the
Olympian's connection with all the phenomena of nature and to his lordship over
the family of gods and men. It is in the latter sense that his title of "Father" should
be taken, that is, lord and master, protector and ruler. In a fragment of a lost play
we have Aeschylus' reverent summation of the varied aspects of the great Olympian: "Zeus is the air, Zeus earth, and Zeus the sky,/ Zeus everything, and all that's
more than these."

On earth Zeus was the power who protected the family and the household, and
who maintained the customary laws (*diké*) of guest and suppliant. The Greek city
(*polis*), rooted as it was in the family, considered Zeus as the god who granted
kings their authority, guarded their power and rights, and in association with
Athena protected the city. Above all, Zeus was the guardian of law and morals,
as Hesiod never tires of asserting. In the *Works and Days* he inveighs against
the "bribe-devouring princes" in the manner of an Old Testament prophet:

> You princes, mark well this punishment you also . . . For upon the bounteous earth Zeus
> has thrice ten thousand spirits, watchers of mortal men, and these keep watch on judg-
> ments and deeds of wrong as they roam clothed in mist all over the earth. And there is
> virgin Justice [Dike], the daughter of Zeus, who is honored and reverenced among the
> gods who dwell on Olympus, and whenever anyone hurts her with lying slander, she sits
> beside her father, Zeus the son of Cronus, and tells him of men's wicked heart, until

the people pay for the mad folly of their princes who, evilly minded, pervert judgment and give sentence crookedly. Keep watch against this, you princes, and make
straight your judgments, you who devour bribes; put crooked judgments altogether
from your thoughts . . . The eye of Zeus, seeing all and understanding all, beholds
these things too, if so he will, and fails not to mark what sort of justice is this, that the
city keeps within it.

The most exalted conception of Zeus is found in Aeschylus who sees the Olympian
as the god of gods, righteous and omnipotent, yet mysterious and enigmatic. In the
Hellenistic period, when the Greeks took a more cosmopolitan view of the world,
Zeus' name was often combined with the main deity of a foreign tribe or region.
Thus, the Greek Zeus became Zeus-Amon-Re in Egypt, Zeus-Baal Shamayim in
Syria, and Zeus-Jupiter in Italy. The leading philosophers of this age of syncretism,
the Stoics, identified Zeus with the principles of Reason and Fire, both of which
permeate and animate the universe.

Zeus had a famous oracle at Dodona, in the mountainous region of Epirus in northern Greece. The story goes—it is a cult-myth to explain the origins of the oracle—
that a pigeon flew away from Thebes in Egypt and alighted on an oak tree at
Dodona where in a human voice it directed the people to found the oracle of Zeus.
The god made his will known through the rustling of the leaves of his sacred tree.
Other signs, such as the cooing of sacred pigeons, the nature of their flight, and the
murmuring of the sacred spring were probably used in a determination of the will
of Zeus. The god's consort at this site was the nymph Dione who Homer and other
poets—but no Hesiod—held to be the mother of Aphrodite.

There is another side to the life of Zeus, the lover and paramour of goddesses and
mortals, the progenitor of famed heroes and heroines. While Hesiod, Aeschylus
and other poet-prophets saw the moral and universal character of Zeus transcending
the human frailties of his mythical background, other poets with a more fanciful imagination, Homer in particular relished the less savory episodes in the
Olympian's career. The critic and poet Graham Hough (1908–   ) belongs to this
latter tradition and sees in the amours and marriages of Zeus nothing more than
pure lasciviousness. From his *Children of Zeus*:

> Ageless, lusty, he twists into bull, ram, serpent,
> Swan, gold rain; a hundred wily disguises
> To catch girl, nymph, or goddess; begets tall heroes
> . . . All that scribe or sculptor
> Chronicle is no more than fruit of his hot embraces
> With how many surprised recumbent breasts and haunches.

In all fairness to Zeus, however, we should attempt to understand how the Olympian acquired this reputation for reckless amours and multiple marriages. To do so
we must also try to penetrate the fog of pre-historic and pre-literary Greece and see
what likely interaction took place between the invading Hellenes and the native
population. Prior to the appearance of the Greeks in the Aegean, the predominant
religion centered on the female principle in nature, the mother-goddess as the
source and protector of all life (p. 38). The rituals associated with this religion
were often a form of magic designed to secure and guarantee the fertility of the earth
and its living creatures. By a simple equation of "like producing like"—sympathetic
magic—rituals and myths were fashioned, which would assure the continuum of life.
The all-productive Earth Mother or fertility goddess was given a male consort, gen-

erally a minor figure, and what took place in myth or in ritual act—impregnation and fecundity—made the worshiper and his community confident that the means of life would be assured.

The paradigm for the interaction of myth and ritual is found embedded in the poems of Homer and Hesiod, although we may doubt whether these two poets were aware of the implications of the story they narrated. In the *Odyssey* the nymph Calypso, ordered by the Olympian to let Odysseus return home, bitterly resents having to give up her mortal lover. She attributes the decree to the jealousy of the gods and takes the occasion to cite other cases in which goddesses were forced to give up their mortal lovers. Among these is Demeter who, Calypso says, lay with her lover Iasion in a thrice-plowed fallow field, but when Zeus heard of it, he struck the man dead with one of his thunderbolts. Hesiod adds two other details: that the incident took place in Crete and that Demeter gave birth to Plutus, a beneficent god who bestows wealth upon those who have the good fortune to meet him.

This story is undoubtedly the mythical form of a Cretan fertility ritual which was once acted out (with human participants?) on a "thrice-plowed fallow field"— that is, earth ready to receive the seed. The result of the union of the goddess of grain Demeter with the male Iasion produced Plutus, the Greek word meaning "wealth." The ritual has long since disappeared but the mythical form of it, its libretto so to speak, has survived; its meaning is made clear from analogs from other lands. Scholars call a "marriage" of this kind a *hieros gamos*, a "sacred marriage," and attribute myths like that of Demeter and Iasion to a pre-Greek stratum. When mythical mortals are the mates of deities, they are either completely enervated by the relationship or they perish by one means or another; rarely ever do they remain as consorts after the one all-consuming experience. This motif has very early origins in the Mediterranean region and continues to be found in all literary strata. Thus we find in Homer that Iasion is killed by Zeus. In the *Homeric Hymn to Aphrodite*, Anchises, the father of Aeneas by Aphrodite, says after learning that he had unknowingly shared Aphrodite's bed: "I beg you not to have me lead an enfeebled life among men. Take pity on me, for the man who lies with a deathless goddess loses all his strength afterwards."

When the invading Greeks came upon the Aegean scene with their patriarchal and very masculine chief-god Zeus, conflict and confusion must have taken place; unquestionably the Greeks could never have considered subordinating Zeus to any female deity. What seems to have taken place was a shift of emphasis: either Zeus became the dominant partner in the marriage, or the female deity was demoted to the status of a mortal and a minor figure, a case of reversal of the pre-Greek form of the fertility goddess with her minor male consort. A deity of this class is generally called a "faded goddess." However, neither the functional aspect of the "sacred marriage" nor the analogy between the human act of procreation and the fertility of the land were forgotten. Zeus was the fertilizing rain which made the seed germinate and which fructified the earth. An accommodation between the new and the old deities was gradually formulated, but the role and the initiative of the male was emphasized. Zeus' many love affairs are mythological expressions of this accommodation as the new cult of Zeus spread from locality to locality.

There are yet other aspects to Zeus' attraction to the fairer sex which are unrelated to ritual or to the conflict between differing cultures. A not uncommon desire of royal and not-so-royal families for a distinguished pedigree, made a love affair between Zeus and one of their real or mythical ancestors the beginning of an illustrious family line. Romantic inclinations were attributed to other Olympians so that a ruling dynasty could boast of divine ancestry. The propriety of the relationship was of course not put to question; the passage of time conveniently obscured the blot on the family escutcheon. Poets, however, glorified kings with epithet *diogenes*, "sprung from Zeus," a title that gave authority and prestige to their reigns since it also meant that Zeus had ordained and upheld them. Not only were kings called "scions of Zeus," but with the help of mythical family trees the Greeks could show that various races were sprung from the seed of their chief god. It was a case of mythology serving the cause of rationalism and ethnic chauvinism. The model which best illustrates these tendencies is found in the myth that tells of the consequences of the attention Zeus paid to a hapless girl from Argos, Io. As we shall soon see in more detail, it was from this indiscreet romance that a family of kings can be traced (Danaus, Perseus, Heracles) as well as the eponymous founders of the Egyptians, the Phoenicians, the Libyans, and the Cilicians. Small wonder then that, knowing of Zeus' wide experience in the affairs of the heart, the Roman poet Tibullus (48?– 19 B.C.) could say of the Olympian god of justice, *Perjuria ridet amantum Jupiter.* Juliet cites these same words when she begs Romeo for surer evidence of his love: ". . . at lovers' perjuries,/They say, Jove laughs." And again by Dryden in *Palamon and Arcite* and *Amphitryon*: "And Jove but laughs at lovers' perjury."

2. Hera (Juno)

The legendary and legitimate spouse of the great Olympian—keep in mind Ovid's injunction that the gods have their own rules—was his sister Hera. During the struggle with the Titans, young Hera was placed in the care of Oceanus and Tethys; but after Zeus had established himself as the supreme god, he courted her and, as Homer tells us, had a lover's tryst with the young goddess without their parents' knowledge. Various places in Greece competed with one another in pointing out the spot where the marriage was consummated. The scene of the marriage was said to be Euboea, or Cnossus in Crete, on Mount Thornax in Argolis. Pausanias and other late raconteurs of backyard mythology tell us that Mount Thornax was the place where Zeus transformed himself into a cuckoo so that he might sneak up on her unawares. Hera took pity on the shivering bird and warmed it by holding it against her breast. Quick as a wink, Zeus shed his disguise and tried to force his attentions on her. Hera resisted, but when Zeus promised to marry her, she discreetly surrendered. The wedding night for this auspicious couple is said to have lasted three hundred years.

Hera's character was mainly fixed by Homer. When she became the wife of Zeus she was treated with great reverence by the other Olympian gods. In terms of power, however, she was far inferior to Zeus who expected unconditional obedience, not only from his wife but from the other gods as well. She was not the queen of heaven, as later poets conceived her, but simply the wife of the great god of Mount Olympus. Homer's portrait of Hera is not that of a loving and devoted wife, but that of an obstinate, quarrelsome, and jealous shrew. It was this disposition of hers that often made Zeus shake with anger and frustration. On one occasion Hera conspired with Poseidon and Athena in a kind of palace revolt and plotted to put her husband in chains. On another, when she did not like the way Zeus interfered with the course of the Trojan War, she deliberately vamped and seduced him so as to divert his attention from actions on the battlefield. But when Zeus awoke and realized that he had been taken in by her wiles, he threatened her with a whipping and reminded her of the time when he had to punish her by shackling her hands to the clouds and suspending two anvils from her feet.

The classic example of the stormy relationship between Zeus and his wife took place on Mount Olympus after Achilles' mother Thetis had begged Zeus to allow the Trojans to get the upper hand so that the Greeks, realizing how egregiously they had affronted Achilles, would repay him with the rewards and respect due a great warrior. Zeus, knowing full well that this would run counter to Hera's wishes, reluctantly assented because of the debt he owed Thetis for her help in putting down the palace revolt mentioned earlier. Hera, always suspicious, rounds on her husband and charges him with treachery and plotting behind her back and with never taking the trouble of discussing things with her. Zeus loses all patience, reminds her that he is the master of the house and that if he wants her to know anything he will tell her. He then threatens her with the back of his hand. Dryden's paraphrase of Zeus' outburst has all the charm and rich vocabulary of the seventeenth century. In the tradition of the time Roman names are substituted for the Greek:

> My Houshold Curse, my lawful Plague, the Spy
> Of Jove's Designs, his other squinting Eye;
> Why this pain prying, and for what avail?
> Jove will be Master still and Juno fail.
> Shou'd thy suspicious Thoughts divine aright,
> Thou but becom'st more odious to my Sight,
> For this Attempt: uneasy Life to me
> Still Watch'd, and importun'd, but worse for thee.
> Curb that impetuous Tongue, before too late
> The Gods behold, and tremble at thy Fate.
> Pitying, but daring not in thy Defence,
> To lift a Hand against Omnipotence.

Compare the same passage in this unrhymed twentieth-century translation by Richmond Lattimore:

> Dear lady, I never escape you, you are always full of suspicion.
> Yet thus you can accomplish nothing surely, but be more
> distant from my heart than ever, and it will be the worse for you.
> If what you say is true, then that is the way I wish it.
> But go then, sit down in silence, and do as I tell you,
> for fear all the gods, as many as are on Olympus, can do nothing
> if I come close and lay my unconquerable hands upon you.

It is obvious that, at least for Homer, this marriage was never made in heaven. However, the Homeric characterization etched itself deep into the poetic imagination of the Greeks. Hera's jealousy became a popular motif in many mythological episodes involving Zeus' mistresses and their children. Her vindictiveness knew no limits and even extended to those who merely lent aid and comfort to Zeus in his unflagging pursuit of the opposite sex. Because of her husband's divided attention, the goddess remorselessly pursued such hapless mythical personages as Io, Callisto, Semele, Athamas, Echo, and particularly Heracles.

Mythology is one thing, cult another. In ritual, Hera was solemnly revered as

Figure 18.   The marriage of Zeus and
Hera. *Metope from Temple E at
Selinus, mid fifth century B.C. National
Museum, Palermo. (Alinari)*

the goddess of marriage and childbirth. Aristophanes speaks of her as "guarding
the keys of wedlock." As the guardian and patron of marriage she was naturally interested in the formality of the institution and the legitimacy of children. Here is one
likely explanation of why Zeus' philandering causes this particular goddess so much
anxiety. Her marriage with the great Olympian was annually celebrated in many
parts of Greece as a *hieros gamos*, a sacred marriage (fig. 18). The rite was unquestionably designed to be a pattern for human marriage. The Attic month Gamelion,
the "marriage month," which corresponds to our January, was sacred to Hera. Her
child by Zeus, Eileithyia, was the goddess of childbirth and another aspect of Hera's
concern for her own sex. This daughter—or daughters since Homer speaks of them
in the plural, the Eileithyiae—and the goddess herself attended women in childbirth. In Arcadia, Hera was called Maiden, Wife and Widow, three titles which
summarized her concern with all conditions of womanhood. The Roman goddess
Juno was similarly concerned with the primary aspects in the life of women, and
from very early times she was identified with the Greek Hera.

Hera's original function before the Greeks arrived is not known with any degree of
certainty although there is little doubt that she was a prominent and powerful
goddess of the native population in the Peloponnese. Homer calls her Argive Hera
and tells us that her favorite cities were Argos, Mycenae, and Sparta, all of them located in the Peloponnese. The consensus among scholars is that the early Greek invaders came to an accommodation with this powerful native goddess by marrying her off—and at the same time subordinating her—to their chief god Zeus.
Some interpret the perpetual squabbling of this divine couple as a historical memory of a not-too-happy accommodation between the Indo-European and Aegean
cultures.

As for her name, the most accepted interpretation is that Hera is the feminine
form of the Greek word "hero" and, hence, means "Great Lady" or "Our Lady."
Whether this was a translation of her original name is not known; it is possible that
the common reluctance to call a great divinity by his right name may have had
some part in the formulation of Hera as a title for this powerful goddess. The

peacock and the cow were her favorite animals. Her sobriquet was "ox-eyed" or "cow-faced," and sacred herds of cows were kept at the Heraeum (the temple of Hera) in Argos. In addition to her association with bovine creatures, she was fond of flowers, the lily in particular. A late tale connects Hera with her favorite flower and the creation of the Milky Way. The story is told that when the infant Heracles was placed to the breast of sleeping Hera, some of her milk fell upon the earth and changed the color of lilies from purple to a beautiful white. Some of her milk is said to have remained in the heavens and to have appeared among the constellations as the Milky Way.

Another side of Hera's character was brought out by the allegorizers of late antiquity who were convinced that myths contained hidden philosophical truths. Thus Hera's tempestuous outbursts against her husband were interpreted as disturbances in the atmosphere. In an elaborate exegetical note on the seduction scene in the fourteenth book of the *Iliad*, a scholiast of this school turns the *hieros gamos* into an allegory wherein Hera represents the lower air (surrounding the earth) and Zeus the upper air (aether). The mingling of Zeus and Hera produces the season of spring and its flowers, as in Milton's *Paradise Lost* when he compares the first physical meeting of Adam and Eve with the embrace of Zeus and Hera:

> He [Adam], in delight
> Both of her Beauty and submissive Charms
> Smil'd with superior Love, as Jupiter
> On Juno smiles, when he impregns the Clouds
> That shed May Flowers; and press'd her Matron lip
> With kisses pure.

In the same allegorizing spirit, the Italian painter Correggio (1494–1534) was permitted to portray a nude goddess in a nunnery, the Camera di San Paolo in Parma. His *Punishment of Juno* follows the account in Homer: she is suspended by her hands with a heavy anvil tied to her feet, a reminder of her punishment by Zeus for having persecuted Heracles. What edifying purpose could such a representation serve in a nunnery? To impress upon nuns the punishment that might await them if they were tempted to forsake their vows.

The philosopher/essayist Francis Bacon (1561–1612), a contemporary of Shakespeare, was one of the latter-day allegorizers of classical mythology. In his *De Sapientia Veterum* (*On the Wisdom of the Ancients*) Bacon finds ". . . concealed instruction and allegory was originally intended in many of the ancient tales." In his treatment of Juno and her suitor, he considers the goddess a symbol of the haughty and contemptuous nature of a man with limited gifts and endowments:

> The poets tell us that Jupiter, to carry on his love-intrigues, assumed many different shapes; as of a bull, an eagle, a swan, a golden shower, etc.; but when he attempted Juno, he turned himself into the most ignoble and ridiculous creature—even that of a wretched, wet, weather-beaten, affrighted, trembling, and half-starved cuckoo. Explanation. This is a wise fable, and drawn from the very entrails of morality. The moral is, that men should not be conceited of themselves, and imagine that a discovery of their excellences will always render them acceptable; for this can only succeed according to the nature and manners of the person they court, or solicit; who, if he be a man not of the same gifts and endowments, but altogether of a haughty and contemptuous behavior, here represented by Juno, they must entirely drop the character that carries the least show of worth, or gracefulness. . .

In Spenser, however, we return to a more sober side of the goddess and an appreciation of her early classical duties. In the *Epithalamion*, which he composed to celebrate his own marriage, he calls upon the ancient deity to bless and solemnize his marriage to Elizabeth Boyle:

> And thou great Juno, which with awful might
> The lawes of wedlock still dost patronize,
> And the religion of the faith first plight
> With sacred rites has taught to solemnize:
> And eeke for comfort often called art
> Of women in their smart,
> Eternally bind thou this lovely band,
> And all thy blessings unto us impart.

3. Poseidon (Neptune)

What classical deity is more familiar to us than the god of the sea! We know him well from Shakespeare's *Macbeth* in these guilt-ridden lines:

> Will all great Neptune's ocean wash this blood
> Clean from my hand? No, this my hand will rather
> The multitudinous seas incarnadine. . .

Or in this description of England from the not-so-well-known *Cymbeline*: "As Neptune's park, ribbed and paled in/With rocks unscalable and roaring waters"; And in the anonymous *Love Will Find Out the Way:*

> Over the mountains,
> And over the waves,
> Under the fountains
> And under the graves;
> Under floods that are deepest,
> Which Neptune obey,
> Over rocks that are steepest,
> Love will find out the way.

From Homer to the present, Poseidon and his Roman counterpart Neptune have had an undisputed control over the sea and his name is a symbol for the briny deep. But there is an enigma connected with both Poseidon and Neptune. Was the sea their original area of responsibility? The present scholarly consensus is that it was not. It is believed that originally both Poseidon and Neptune were deities not of salt water but of fresh water, and that they shared something of the personality of their celestial brothers Zeus and Jupiter. The question of which came first need not detain us long except to note that details in the life of this deity deal not only with the sea but with springs and rivers as well. And because of the ancient view that the elements under his control in some way caused earthquakes, Poseidon assumed responsibility for this geophysical phenomenon; he was god of earthquakes with the fearful epithet of "Earth-shaker." Adding to the enigma is the question of why Poseidon is associated with the horse. The Greek word for horse (*hippos*) appears frequently in his epithet *Hippios* and in the names of various springs—Hippe, Hippocrene, Aganippe—with which the god, as "ruler over springs" and "leader of the nymphs," has a close connection. No consensus has been reached on explaining Poseidon's relationship to horses.

Scholars have also fought long and hard over the meaning of the name Poseidon. One German scholar pointed out that, though the number of etymologies for his name has multiplied, certainty as to its meaning has not. The most popular etymologies are: "consort or husband of Earth" (*Posis Das*); the first two syllables of his name are related to the Greek word for river (*potamos*); his name means "Lord Zeus" indicating that at one time Zeus and Poseidon were identical. Beyond these *a priori* speculations, we know from recently deciphered tablets from the Bronze Age that Poseidon had a prominent position in cult and, in fact, seems to have been more important than Zeus. In view of this, the fourth-century B.C. historian Ephorus is being listened to more attentively when he says that in ancient times the Peloponnese seems to have been the home of Poseidon and that the land was considered sacred to him.

One theory attempting to explain all these inconsistencies holds that during the periodic migrations beginning about 2000 B.C., an early branch of Greeks, the Minyans, preceded the advance of the Zeus-worshiping Achaeans into the peninsula of Greece. These Minyans were a formidable foe since they had succeeded in taming the wild horse of the Eurasian steppes, and with horse and wheeled transport they advanced swiftly into Greece. Their chief god was Poseidon who was worshiped in equine form. Generations later, the Achaeans came with their chief god Zeus who in the course of time superseded Poseidon, much to the resentment of the Minyan deity. This clash between the two gods is said to be reflected in Homer's *Iliad* where we often find Poseidon at odds with Zeus, claiming equal power with the great Olympian. Although the migrating Greeks had little to do with the sea when they first entered the peninsula, the Minyans had gradually become experienced sailors. When they turned to seafaring as a major occupation, their god Poseidon also transferred his sphere of activity to the sea. Prior to this he had an earth-goddess as his mate who had difficulty in accommodating herself to this new medium, "the fruitless sea," or "the unharvested deep," as it is often called in Homer. A new spouse was arranged for Poseidon, Amphitrite, daughter of the former god of the sea Nereus. The mythological support for this view is found in the ancestry of the mortal who undertook the first voyage on the sea, Jason. His uncle Pelias was sired by Poseidon, and when Pelias was born his mother exposed him on a mountain where he was found and reared by horsewranglers or suckled by a mare.

As was mentioned earlier, Poseidon, like his Olympian brothers and sisters, was swallowed by his father and then disgorged when Zeus tricked Cronus into taking an emetic potion of some kind. According to an Arcadian tradition, however, his mother Rhea hid him in a flock of lambs and then pretended to have given birth to a young horse which Cronus proceeded to swallow in place of the newborn infant. The parallel with the ruse Rhea practiced to save Zeus from a similar fate should be noted. Other accounts have the newborn Poseidon cared for by certain semi-divine beings called Telchines of Rhodes—the island of Rhodes was a well-known maritime center—and have these Telchines forge the trident with which the god split rocks, caused springs to gush forth, and raked the seas into fierce storms. After the Titanomachy and the downfall of Cronus, Poseidon drew the sea for his realm, undoubtedly displacing Nereus, the Old Man of the Sea, in the process. The new god had a grand underwater palace near Aegae—compare the word "Aegean"—on the island of Euboea. In its stables he kept his white horses with bronze hooves and golden manes. He hitched these glorious creatures to a golden chariot whenever he wished transportation over the waves of the sea.

Poseidon and King Laomedon. Together with Apollo, Poseidon had a labor contract with Laomedon, the legendary father of Priam, king of Troy during the Trojan War. While Apollo tended the flocks, the sea-god built the walls of Troy, "the topless towers of Ilium." Some say that Zeus meted out this punishment to Poseidon because he had taken part in a palace revolt. In any event, Laomedon reneged on the contract and refused to pay the stipulated price upon completion of their labors; he even threatened to put the gods in chains, to cut off their ears, and to sell them off as slaves. It was for this reason that Poseidon hated the Trojans and took an active part in the war. He sided with the Greeks, sometimes viewing the progress of the war from the heights of Thrace, at other times interfering by disguising himself as one of the heroes and spurring on his favorites. When Zeus allowed the gods to choose sides, Poseidon joined the Greeks and caused the earth to tremble. At one point he challenged his nephew Apollo to fight and took him to task because he was not hostile to the Trojans after the insolent treatment he had received at the hands of Laomedon. Apollo judiciously and philosophically parried the challenge by claiming that it was beneath his dignity to fight with his uncle over mere mortals. So Homer reports. Later accounts tell us that Poseidon sent a sea-monster against Laomedon which would have devoured his daughter Hesione had Heracles not been johnny-on-the-spot and killed the creature. Laomedon gave Heracles the same treatment he had given Poseidon: he refused to pay the agreed price for his services. In revenge Heracles returned to Greece, raised an army, and to his renown was the first to take Troy.

Poseidon versus Athena and Hera. In Greece itself, Poseidon challenged a number of gods for control over certain territories, a possible historical memory of the time when the god was supreme on the peninsula. In a competition with Athena for control over Athens, he demonstrated his power by striking a rock on the Acropolis with his trident and by causing a spring of sea-water to gush forth. As her gift to the city, Athena planted an olive tree which much impressed the gods who sat in judgment. When the city was awarded to Athena, Poseidon became so angry that he sent a flood over one of the city's plains. He was later reconciled to Athena and shared a temple with her on the Acropolis. Poseidon also was Hera's rival for control over Argolis. The dispute was submitted to the local river-gods who decided in favor of Hera. This time, instead of sending a flood to demonstrate his anger at the decision, Poseidon dried up the rivers so that forever after their beds were dry in the summer. The latter is a bit of aetiology to explain a common topographical feature of semi-arid Greece. Another account has him inundating Argos with a flood until he was finally persuaded by Hera to check the waters. Because of this he was called The Flooder, and a sanctuary of Poseidon the Flooder was built at the point in Argos where the flood was said to have ebbed. Other competitions took place at Corinth and Troezen, at Aegina, Naxos, and Delphi; these were generally resolved by compensations and compromises of various sorts.

Poseidon's Offspring. Whether on sea or on land, the mythical nature of Poseidon is fairly consistent: he is violent, rough, savage, and ill-tempered. In his love affairs he was equally ungentlemanly, and the male offspring of these amours, where they were not justifications of royal dynasties, were like their father, rough and tough. He fathered the one-eyed monster, the Cyclops Polyphemus, whom Odysseus blinded much to his later regret, since Poseidon made life difficult for him and kept him from returning home. Antaeus, the invincible giant wrestler who was finally outwrestled by Heracles, was a son of his through Earth. Likewise, by Iphimedeia, wife of Aloeus, he sired the two giants Otus and Ephialtes who tried to assault the Olympians by piling Ossa on Olympus and Pelion on Ossa. Even the hundred-handed giant Briareus, who according to Homer men called Aegaeon, was said to be a son of Poseidon.

In Arcadia, the story was told that Poseidon came upon Demeter—some scholars claim that she was the original or early wife of Poseidon—as she was searching for her lost daughter Persephone. Very much taken with her, the god began making amorous advances which Demeter attempted to avoid by changing herself into a mare. Poseidon met the challenge by taking the shape of a stallion and forced his will on her. The offspring of this union was a horse whom the Arcadians called Arion, a name that appropriately seems to mean "very swift." Practically the same story was told at another place in Arcadia where Demeter was portrayed as black and horse-headed, but the child of this relationship was a girl called Despoina, the Mistress, one of the names of the Queen of the Underworld. In this respect the female offspring resembled her mother for we will find a daughter of Demeter as the wife of the dreaded lord of the afterlife.

Early poets had very little to say about how Poseidon courted his wife Amphitrite, but later writers eagerly filled in the details. The god's interest first centered on Amphitrite's sister Thetis, and Poseidon is said to have competed with Zeus for her love. However, when they learned of the oracle which predicted that Thetis would bear a son greater than the father, their ardor for the nymph cooled very quickly. Poseidon then courted Amphitrite, but she would have nothing to do with him and fled to escape his attentions. Through an intermediary Delphinus (Dolphin), the sea-god managed to convince her of his honorable intentions and she agreed to marry him (fig. 19). As a reward for his good work, Poseidon translated Delphinus to the stars as the constellation Dolphin. The child of this marriage was Triton, a merman, half-human and half-fish. In poetry and in art Triton's chief characteristic was a conch shell which he blew at the command of Poseidon to calm the waves of the sea. Like other minor mythological figures, he becomes more than one and Tritons are found serving other divinities of the sea. No certain etymology has been found for his or his mother's name; the element *tri* in both names is thought to be pre-Greek for "water."

After his marriage Poseidon tried to be as philoprogenitive as his brother Zeus. When Amphitrite heard of his interest in the sea-nymph Scylla, she put some magic herbs into her rival's bath which turned her into a hideous monster with six dogs' heads, each head having three rows of sharp teeth, and with twelve feet. (Ovid's *Metamorphoses* makes the merman Glaucus the errant lover and Circe the jealous woman.) Through this transformation Scylla became a threat of all seamen who had to sail by her cave, for she would seize six men at a time and devour them. In later times, Scylla was rationalized as a rock or other marine hazard. She is commonly paired with Charybdis, a whirlpool or maelstrom, the two of them being traditionally localized at the Straits of Messina between Italy and Sicily. "To be caught between Scylla and Charybdis" has become proverbial for being caught between equally dangerous alternatives.

Figure 19.   Poseidon and his wife Amphitrite riding in triumph over the
waves. *Roman mosaic from the Villa Stabiae, Pompeii. Louvre. (Marburg)*

Poseidon also wooed the Gorgon Medusa (p. 29), once a beautiful young girl, but because the god made love to her in one of Athena's temples, the goddess transformed her into a snaky-haired Gorgon. Medusa was with child when Perseus came on his mission to decapitate her, and from her spilled blood sprang Chrysaor, who sired the monster Geryon, and the winged horse Pegasus.

Love also gave divine sanction to aristocratic families. The origins of the family line of Jason the Argonaut, and of Nestor the renowned king of Pylos, can be traced back to an affair of the heart. Homer tells the story of Tyro, daughter of Salmoneus, who had fallen in love with the river-god Enipeus. She often wandered on the banks of his stream until one day Poseidon happened to take notice. He disguised himself as the river-god and made love to her at a place where the river rushes out to the sea. A mountain-high wave curled over them and hid them from sight. Afterwards Poseidon informed her of what had happened and told her that she would have beautiful children since a god's embrace is always fruitful. The children of the sacred marriage were Neleus and Pelias, the father of Nestor and the uncle of Jason.

Ezra Pound incorporates part of this Homeric tale in these lines from *Canto II*:

> . . . by the beach-run Tyro,
> Twisted arms of the sea-god,
> Lithe sinews of water, gripping her, cross-hold,
> And the blue-gray glass of the wave tents them,
> Glare azure of water, cold-welter, close cover.

More obvious is a myth that apparently came into being when the city of Athens became an important maritime center. A connection between the city's great hero Theseus and the god of the sea was needed. Accordingly a story was told about Aethra, wife of King Aegeus—note that the king's name is similar to Aegae, the Aegean Sea, Aegaeon, all names linked in one way or another to Poseidon. Aethra was told in a dream to wade across to the island of Sphaeria where Poseidon came upon the young woman and made love to her. In due time she gave birth to a son, the Athenian hero Theseus. Others claim that Theseus was the son of King Aegeus, but Aegeus, in all likelihood, is a humanized form of Poseidon of Aegae. In any event, Poseidon and his wife Amphitrite often stand by Theseus when he is in danger or in a tight spot.

In the *Faerie Queene*, Spenser takes particular care to give us a vivid picture of the god of the sea, his chariot, his triton, and some of his loves. This is Neptune's portrait on the tapestries in the house of Busirane:

> His face was rugged, and his hoarie hed
> Dropped with brackish deaw; his three-forkt Pyke
> He stearnly shooke, and therewith fierce did stryke
> The raging billowes, that on every syde
> They trembling stood, and made a long broad dyke,
> That his swift charet might have passage wyde,
> Which foure great Hippodames did draw in temewise tyde.
>
> . . . .
> And like a winged horse he tooke his flight,
> To snaky-locke Medusa to repayre,
> On whom he got faire Pegasus, that flitteth in the ayre.

And then for the wedding of the Thames and the Medway, Spenser has Neptune and his wife leading the procession. They are followed by the descendants of the sea-god—five stanzas worth, including Albion, of whom Spenser says with national pride: "the sonne of Neptune was." Here is the beginning of that procession:

> First came great Neptune with his threeforkt mace,
> That rules the Seas, and makes them rise or fall;
> His dewy lockes did drop with brine apace,
> Under his Diademe imperiall:
> And by his side his Queene with coronall,
> Faire Amphitrite, most divinely faire,
> Whose yvorie shoulders weren covered all,
> As with a robe, with her owne silver haire,
> And deckt with pearles, which the' Indian seas for her prepaire.

> These marched farre afore the other crew;
> And all the way before them as they went,
> Triton his trompet shrill before them blew,
> For goodly triumph and great jollyment,
> That made the rockes to roare, as they were rent.
> And after them the royall issue came,
> Which of them sprung by lineall descent:
> First the Sea-gods, which to themselves doe clame
> The powre to rule the billowes, and the waves to tame.

Proteus. Before leaving Poseidon, mention must be made of his associate Proteus. Although later writers make him a son of Poseidon, Homer, whose tale of Proteus is best known, makes him an Egyptian spirit, a *daimon*, living on the island of Pharos near the mouth of the Nile. In the *Odyssey*, he is the servant of Poseidon, the herdsman of the god's flocks of seals, a wise and prophetic old man of the sea. To get him to prophesy, one has to grab the slippery old fellow and hold onto him while he goes through a series of transformations. Menelaus, Helen's husband, found that the god's magical repertoire included transformations into a bearded lion, a snake, a panther, a boar, running water, and a leafy tree. Later tradition makes Proteus a king of Egypt who provided hospitality and a home for Helen after she was abducted by Paris.

Modern poets are attracted to Proteus' changes, his chaotic shapes, and the ultimate truth that comes to those who hold fast and persist. His name has given the English language an adjective, "protean": like Proteus, capable of assuming various shapes, variable and changeable. One of the fickle gentlemen in Shakespeare's *Two Gentlemen of Verona* is appropriately given the name of Proteus. Archibald MacLeish sees the power of music in making men shed their transformations, "all cheats and falsehoods of our vain escape." In his *Men of My Century Loved Mozart* he says:

> Changed by this last enchantment of our kind
> That still has power with our Protean souls—
> This keeping charm that could constrain the mind
> As nymphs in amber or in woody boles
> Of oak the live limbs by the spell confined—
> Changed to ourselves by this enforcing hand

> We lay like silver naked Proteus on the sand.
> The pelt fell from us and the sea-cow's shape
> The fish's scarlet the shark's wrinkled skin
> The seal's eyes and the brine encircled nape
> The foam's evasion the down-diving fin—
> All cheats and falsehoods of our vain escape:
> Changed to ourselves, sea-sleeked and dripping yet
> Our limbs lay caught and naked in the taking net.

For Wordsworth, Proteus and Triton are symbols of the untainted beauty and harmony of Hellenic life, in contrast with the crass commercialism and unfeeling materialism of his own day. From his *The World Is Too Much With Us*, this passionate outburst, a *cri de coeur:*

> Great God! I'd rather be
> A Pagan suckled in a creed outworn;
> So might I, standing on this pleasant lea,
> Have glimpses that would make me less forlorn;
> Have sight of Proteus rising from the sea;
> Or hear old Triton blow his wreathèd horn.

An episode in the *Ulysses* of James Joyce (1882–1941) has a marked analogy with the story of Proteus in Homer's *Odyssey*. Joyce transfers the shiftiness of Proteus to the shifting shapes of things and the difficulty of perceiving the truth in mere appearances. It is on this, the "ineluctable modality of the visible," that Stephen Dedalus speculates as he walks along "Sandymouth strand."

4. Demeter (Ceres)

The goddess Demeter, or Ceres as she was known among the Romans, was another child of Cronus and Rhea whose origins are still uncertain. Part of her name, *-meter*, incontestably seems to mean "mother"; but what of the *De-* or *Da-* element? Is it related to the Greek word for "earth"? Or is it another form of the word for "barley" or "spelt"? Does Demeter's name mean "Earth Mother" or "Grain Mother"? Is she a former wife of Poseidon? Is she a native goddess or a Hellenic deity who came to Greece during the early migrations of the Minyans? No sure answer has been provided to these questions, although in cult the goddess is clearly concerned with the cultivated soil, and in many parts of Greece she is specifically associated with grains such as wheat and barley (fig. 20). For this reason, she is often called a Corn Goddess, the British word for grain being corn.

Persephone (Proserpina). With the exception of the myths already mentioned—her pursuit by Poseidon in the guise of a stallion and her sacred marriage with the mortal Iasion—Demeter's mythological biography is inseparable from that of her daughter Persephone, also known as Kore or Cora (variously translated as Young Girl, Maiden, Virgin). In Roman mythology the young girl's name is Proserpina, a mispronunciation of the Greek Persephone compounded with a false etymology, as if derived from the Latin word *proserpere*, to spring forth. Persephone is the daughter of Demeter by Zeus. Greek mythology is unusually silent about how the god wooed and won the goddess. There is no recorded *hieros gamos*, no

Figure 20.   Demeter (Ceres), the goddess of grain, rising from the earth.
Terracotta. Term Museum, Rome. (Alinari)

hint of scandal in the Olympian household, no tale of a jealous Hera to make life difficult for an expectant mother. Either the story of Persephone's abduction eclipsed all other episodes in the life of Demeter, or the goddess was so revered that the lips of her worshipers were as sealed in silence as they were in connection with the final revelation of the Eleusinian mysteries in which the goddess played a major role. We can understand why Homer has so little to say about her, for she has little to do with warring epic heroes. In the *Odyssey*, Calypso mentions Demeter's love affair with Iasion and the thrice-plowed fallow field, the goddess' marriage bed; in the *Iliad*, brief mention is made of her sanctuary in flowering Pyrasus and of the fact that Zeus once loved her. When Homer speaks of "the yield of Demeter," it is a synonym for bread. The poet calls her fair-haired, and in a beautiful simile he describes how yellow Demeter blows the wind to sift the chaff from the grain on the holy threshing floor. To Hesiod, agricultural labors such as plowing, sowing, and harvesting are the "works of Demeter," and he tells farmers to pray to Demeter and Zeus-in-the-earth (Pluto) for flourishing grain fields.

Shelley, whose classical training brought him close to the sources of Greek mythology, views Demeter as Mother Earth and the source of all creation. In the *Song of Proserpine*, he calls on her to shed her divine influence on her daughter:

> Sacred Goddess, Mother Earth,
>   Thou from whose immortal bosom,
> Gods, and men, and beasts have birth,
>   Leaf and blade, and bud and blossom,
> Breathe thine influence most divine
> On thine own child, Proserpine.
>
> If with mists of evening dew
>   Thou dost nourish these young flowers
> Till they grow, in scent and hue,
>   Fairest children of the hours,
> Breathe thine influence most divine
> On thine own child, Proserpine.

The Rape of Persephone. The mother and daughter—the Mother and the Maid as they are sometimes called—are distinct personalities, but in the strange way in which mythological forms develop, they are in reality two aspects of a single nature. Demeter and Persephone (or Kore) are combined in the life cycle of grain: the seed and its sprouting are represented by Kore, the young girl; the mature, ripe grain by the mother, "yellow Demeter." The Roman goddess Ceres gives her name to the English word "cereal." The drama in the life of Demeter and Persephone is the birth, death, and rebirth of the vital foodstuff which becomes the staff of life; in mythical form it becomes the story of the abduction of Persephone, the Rape of Persephone, by the god of the Underworld. The myth is best preserved in the *Homeric Hymn to Demeter*, composed in the latter part of the seventh century B.C. to celebrate the famous cult of Demeter at Eleusis, a town about twelve miles west of Athens and later incorporated into the Athenian state. Hades or Pluto, god of the Underworld, appears to be the villain of the piece, but let us recall Plutus (Wealth) who, Hesiod tells us, was the child of Demeter and Iasion. Pluto has the identical meaning linked with his name, "the Rich One." Pluto's connection with wealth had to do not only with the seed planted in the earth—in this respect he was a fertility spirit—but also with the farmer's wealth, his crop, which was stored in large jars in underground chambers. The scene of the abduction in the Homeric hymn is Nysa in Asia Minor; later authorities place it near Eleusis or in the neighborhood of Enna in Sicily. The worship of Demeter had been introduced into Sicily at a very early date by Greek colonists. Here is how the hymn tells the story:

Zeus, without consulting Demeter, promised Persephone to Pluto for his wife. While the young girl was gathering flowers, among them an extraordinarily beautiful one which Zeus had ordered to grow in order to tempt the girl, the earth suddenly opened and out sprang the god of the Underworld. He caught the reluctant Persephone (fig. 21) and carried her off in his golden chariot. The young girl's

Figure 21. Hades carrying off Persephone. *Enlarged impression from a scaraboid gem, c. 460 B.C. The Metropolitan Museum of Art, The Cesnola Collection, purchased by subscription, 1874–76.*

cries were heard by no one except Hecate and Helios the sun; Demeter heard only their echo. The distraught mother immediately set out to search for her daughter. For nine days she wandered about without taking any nectar and ambrosia and without bathing. On the tenth day she met Hecate who told her that she had heard the cries of Persephone but that she did not know who had carried her off. The two goddesses then went to Helios who told them that Pluto, with Zeus' consent, had seized Persephone and forcibly taken her for his wife.

Resentful and angered, Demeter refused to take her place among the gods on Olympus; instead, she spent her time on earth disguised as an old woman. With her head veiled and wearing a dark cloak, she came to Eleusis where she was kindly received by the daughters of King Celeus. Pretending to be an old woman from Crete, who had escaped from pirates after having been abducted, she said she was looking for a job as a nurse or housekeeper. The girls took pity on her and introduced the disguised goddess to their mother, the queen. When hospitality was offered, Demeter refused to sit on a high couch, but instead seated herself close to the earth on a low stool. When offered wine, she likewise refused and asked for a mixture of flour and water flavored with mint. Demeter then became the nurse of the king's youngest son, and in her care the child grew like a god. Without his parents' knowledge, she would anoint the child with ambrosia during the day, while at night she would plunge him into the heart of a fire to burn away his mortal nature. The child's mother became suspicious, and when from a hiding place she saw Demeter thrust the child into the fire, she cried out in anxiety. The goddess snatched the child from the fire, turned on the mother and said that she had intended to make the child immortal and unaging, but that now he would have to face death. She then revealed her divinity to the queen and ordered the people of Eleusis to build a great temple in her honor.

Demeter now turned her anger against mankind and caused the fertile earth to be barren. Plants would not grow, oxen worked the fields to no effect, grain was sown in vain. Demeter would have destroyed the entire race of man through famine, and consequently would have deprived the Olympian gods of gifts and sacrifices, had Zeus not decided that it was time to intervene. He first sent Iris to plead with Demeter, but she vowed she would never set foot on Olympus again unless she could see her daughter Persephone once more. Zeus then sent Hermes to the Underworld with orders to the god to release the young girl. Pluto allowed Persephone to return to her mother but first secretly gave her a pomegranate to eat. When mother and daughter were reunited, Demeter asked Persphone if she had eaten anything while she was with Pluto; if she had, she would have to return to the god of the subterranean regions for a third part of the year and spend the two remaining parts with her and the other gods. As the Homeric hymn puts it: "But when the earth shall bloom with fragrant flowers, then from the realm of darkness and gloom shall you come up once more to be a wonder for the gods and mortal men." Persephone admitted that the god had secretly put a pomegranate seed into her mouth and that he had forced her to take it against her will (fig. 22).

Zeus and Demeter finally came to terms and agreed that Persephone would spend one-third of the year with the god of the Underworld and two-thirds with her mother and the other gods. Demeter then allowed the earth to become fertile once again. She returned to Eleusis where she taught her rites to the king's sons and revealed to them all her mysteries, mysteries which, the hymn says, are "full of awe, which no one may in any way transgress or pry into or utter for deep awe

Figure 22. Dante Gabriel Rossetti (1828–1882). Persephone holding the pomegranate given her by Hades. *Tate Gallery, London.*

of the gods checks the voice." The hymn closes with this reverent statement: "Happy is he among men upon earth who has seen these mysteries; but he who is uninitiate and who has no part in them, never has lot of like good things once he is dead, down in the darkness and the gloom."

The Thesmophoria. The myth of the rape of Persephone was taken very seriously in ancient times and was central to both the solemn festival of the Thesmophoria and the Eleusinian mysteries. The Thesmophoria was a fertility festival, or rather a form of fertility magic. It was primarily concerned with the autumn-sowing of the grain, a critical time in the life of the community, for if anything went wrong with the seed it spelled disaster. The participants in the Thesmophoria were exclusively married women who dramatized the myth of Persephone's abduction and acted out much of Demeter's suffering. A period of nine days of strict chastity was observed, pomegranates and garlands of flowers were forbidden, and on the most solemn day of the festival the women fasted and sat on the ground in deep sadness. The final day was given over to rejoicing and dancing and sacrifices to celebrate the return of Persephone and the assurance that the year would be a fruitful one. The solemnity of the Thesmophoria is reminiscent of the words of the psalmist in Psalm 126: "They that sow in tears shall reap in joy. He that goeth forth and weepeth, bearing precious seed, shall doubtless come again with rejoicing, bringing his sheaves with him."

The Thesmophoria celebrates the ascent of Persephone (or Kore) prior to the commitment of the seed to the soil. She is brought together with her mother, the union of the seed and the harvest, the two vital elements—the alpha and the omega —of the grain-growing cycle. As in most important agricultural festivals, the celebrants perform elaborate rituals and take all kinds of precautions so as to assure the success of the undertakings. The two-thirds of the year Persephone spends with her mother is the period between sowing the seed in September–October and reaping and threshing the crop in May–June. From June to the time of the autumn-sowing, the fields are barren and desolate; they are burned and parched by the sun. It is during these four months that Persephone the Grain Girl is absent; that is the one-third of the year she spends with Pluto when the seed is stored in underground silos. In Sicily, a festival called the Descent of Kore was celebrated at the time the grain was threshed which was also the time when the seed-corn was stored. That women played a prominent part in these functional rituals is ancient man's response to nature, the formula that guided him to the desired result. In spite of Plato's observation that the earth does not imitate woman but woman imitates the earth, early and not-so-early man saw the parallel between begetting and sowing, and he called upon woman to communicate the power of her fertility to the soil.

The Eleusinian Mysteries. The Eleusinian mysteries, the highest bloom of Greek religion, had its origins in an ancient ritual very much like the Thesmophoria. The old agricultural myth and its associated magic were applied to the human condition. The grief and sorrow of Demeter over the loss of her daughter and the despair of her search touch upon the deepest feelings of man. Demeter is rightfully called the *mater dolorosa* of Greek religion, and in works of art she is represented as grave, tender, and sympathetic. The ability of the worshiper to identify himself with a god guarantees him an experience similar to that of the god. The birth-death-rebirth cycle, implicit in the Demeter and Persephone myth, has a meaning for man that transcends its original agricultural function. Unlike the gods, about whom Homer never tires of telling us that they are deathless and ever-living, Demeter and Persephone have that close association with death which is ever-present for man. Persephone's absence is death; her return is rebirth and life. The renewal of life is the central idea of mystery worship, its connection with the agricultural or seasonal cycle a widespread phenomenon. We can be reminded of the words in the gospel of Saint John: "Except a corn of wheat fall into the ground and die, it abideth alone: but if it die, it bringeth forth much fruit." And of Saint Paul: "That which thou sowest is not quickened, except it die."

The complex rituals and formulae of the Eleusinian mysteries do not concern us here except to note that, unlike the Thesmophoria, the reenactment of the myth of Demeter and Persephone involved both sexes, and the mystery worship at Eleusis attracted people from all over the Mediterranean world. So well-kept was the final revelation that to this day we are not sure of what took place at the climax of the ceremony in the hall of mysteries at Eleusis. Clement of Alexandria (c. 150–c. 216 A.D.,), who had celebrated the Eleusinian mysteries prior to his conversion to Christianity, tells us that the votaries acted out the drama of Demeter and Persephone, fasted, touched holy objects, and drank the sacramental *kykeon*, a combination of flour, water and mint which Demeter drank in the house of King Celeus when she was mourning the loss of her daughter. If we can believe Clement, the final revelation, which the votaries glimpsed after an exhausting religious ordeal, was a cut stalk of grain. Whatever the final revelation, the mimetic performances and the symbolical representations seem to have given the participants that identification or contact with a divine power which provided them with comfort and an assurance of escape from the fear and gloom thought to await the soul after death. Let us recall the words at the very end of the Homeric hymn: "Happy is he among men upon earth who has seen these mysteries; but he who is uninitiate and who has no part in them, never has lot of like good things once he is dead, down in the darkness and the gloom."

Triptolemus. The old agricultural cult of Demeter and Persephone had given its believers effective fertility magic and a belief in the eternity or continuity of life. It also provided a theory on the civilizing effects of agriculture. The Homeric hymn had mentioned a prince of Eleusis, Triptolemus, whom Demeter had taught her mysteries. This hero joins the two goddesses in a kind of trinity (fig. 23). His name which means "thrice warring" was taken to mean "thrice plowing," and Triptolemus develops into the hero of the thrice-plowed field, the inventor of the plow and agriculture, and of civilization which is the result of it. The threshing floor of Triptolemus is mentioned as the cradle of agriculture where grain was sown for the first time. On vase paintings he is often shown seated on a winged car and flanked by Demeter and Persephone who offer him the cup of farewell as they send him out on his worldwide mission to propagate agriculture. Since Eleusis was a part of Athens, the Athenians considered their city to be the cradle of civilization by virtue of Demeter's gift to Triptolemus. The great orator Isocrates (436–338 B.C.) speaks of the two greatest gifts given to the Athenians by Demeter: grain, which is the reason why men do not live like wild beasts, and the mysteries, from which the people derive higher hopes for their life.

*   *   *   *

In modern literature, Milton, in a letter to Diodati (1637), compares his efforts to seek out the beautiful with those of the goddess who searched for her daughter: "Not with so much labour, as the fables have it, is Ceres said to have sought her daughter Proserpina as it is my habit day and night to seek for this idea of the beautiful. . ." In *Paradise Lost*, the garden from which Proserpina was abducted offers a point of comparison with the idyllic beauty of the Garden of Eden. As usual Milton uses Roman names, including Dis for Hades.

> Not that fair field
> Of Enna, where Proserpine gathering flow'rs,
> Herself a fairer flow'r, by gloomy Dis
> Was gathered, which cost Ceres all that pain
> To seek her through the world . . .

In *The Winter's Tale*, Shakespeare has Perdita wish merely for the flowers which the young goddess let fall when she was carried off:

> O Proserpina,
> For the flowers now that, frighted, thou let'st fall
> From Dis's wagon!

Figure 23.   The Eleusinian Trinity. Demeter, Kore (Persephone) and
Triptolemus. *Bas-relief, fifth century B.C. National Museum, Athens.*
(Alinari)

The poets of the nineteenth century, and in particular the Victorians, were very
much attracted to the myth of Demeter and Persephone. Shelley's poem has already been cited; his wife, Mary, wrote a drama called *Proserpine*. George Mere-

dith (1828–1909) composed two poems on the myth of the mother and daughter:
The Day of the Daughter of Hades and *The Appeasement of Demeter*. In the
former, which Meredith considered his best poem, considerable liberties are taken
with the ancient tale. The poet gives Hades and Persephone a daughter, Skiageneia,
who roams about the world with a handsome mortal, Callistes. Together they exult
in the loveliness of the living earth until Hades comes to fetch his errant daughter
and takes her back to the realm of death. Callistes is left only with a vision and with
a longing to be reunited with the daughter of death. Meredith's *The Appeasement
of Demeter* focuses on the curse of sterility that the goddess had called down on the
earth when Persephone was carried off. However, when Demeter sees two animals
attempting to stir up their mating spirit, she bursts into laughter and breaks the
spell. For Meredith it is laughter, not the *hieros gamos*, which revives the spirit of
fertility:

> Uprose the blade in green, the leaf in red,
> The tree of water and the tree of wood:
> And soon among the branches overhead
> Gave beauty juicy issue sweet for food.
> O Laughter! beauty plumped and love had birth.
> Laughter! O thou reviver of sick Earth!
> Good for the spirit, good
> For body, thou! to both are wine and bread!

Alfred Lord Tennyson published his *Demeter and Persephone* late in life, at
the age of eighty, when he was faced with the hard reality of man's condition.
With the Homeric hymn as his main source, he speaks through Demeter.

> So, in this pleasant vale we stand again,
> The field of Enna, now once more ablaze
> With flowers that brighten as thy footstep falls,
> All flowers—but for one black blur of earth
> Left by that closing chasm, thro' which the car
> Of dark Aïdoneus [Hades] rising rapt thee hence.

However, Tennyson is not happy with the present arrangement of man's fate; he
calls for a change in the divine establishment:

> Yet I, Earth-Goddess, am but ill-content
> With them who still are highest. Those gray heads,
> What meant they by their 'Fate beyond the Fates'
> But younger kindlier Gods to bear us down,
> As we bore down the Gods before us? Gods
> To quench, not hurl the thunderbolt, to stay,
> Not spread the plague, the famine; Gods indeed,
> To send the noon into the night and break
> The sunless halls of Hades into Heaven?

Algernon Swinburne takes the myth of Demeter and Persephone on yet another
tack, or perhaps on three others, since he composed three poems on the goddesses.
In the *Hymn to Proserpine*, Swinburne uses the classical myth to continue his impassioned battle on the side of Pan against Christ. Demeter and Persephone are
hardly more than symbols of his neo-pagan view of the world, sceptical yet sensuous.

> Will thou yet take all, Galilean? but these thou shalt not take,
> The laurel, the palms and the paean, the breast of the nymphs
>   in the brake;
> Breasts more soft than a dove's, that tremble with tenderer
>   breath;
> And all the wings of the Loves, and all the joy before death;
> . . . .
> Goddess and maiden and queen, be near me now and befriend.
> O daughter of earth, of my mother, her crown and blossom of birth,
> I am also, I also, thy brother; I go as I came unto earth.

In *The Garden of Proserpine*, the world is too much with Swinburne; he is "tired of tears and laughter." The Garden of Proserpine is Swinburne's Epicurean land of death where there is no heaven and no hell and where Proserpine is a death-goddess.

> Though one were strong as seven,
>   He too with death shall dwell,
> Nor wake with wings in heaven,
>   Nor weep for pains in hell;
> . . . .
> She [Proserpine] waits for each and other,
>   She waits for all men born;
> Forgets the earth her mother,
>   The life of fruits and corn;
> And spring and seed and swallow
> Take wing for her and follow
> Where summer song rings hollow
>   And flowers are put to scorn.

At Eleusis is Swinburne's version of the Homeric hymn, given a high burnish of lyricism. Following a tradition which made Triptolemus the child Demeter nursed in the house of King Celeus, Swinburne describes the episode of the goddess plunging the child into the heart of the fire. The goddess speaks:

> [I] lit around
> Fire, and made crawl the white worm-shapen flame,
> And leap in little angers spark by spark
> At head at once and feet; and the faint hair
> Hissed with rare sprinkles in closer curl,
> And like scaled oarage of a keen thin fish
> In sea-water, so in pure fire his feet
> Struck out, and the flame bit not in his flesh,
> But like a kiss it curled his lip, and heat
> Fluttered his eyelids; so each night I blew
> The hot ash red to purge him to full god.

Robert Bridges was also indebted to the Homeric hymn for his mythological drama *Demeter* (1905). Bridges' belief in the progressive march from evil to good, from selfishness to selflessness, leads him to transform Demeter's hostility toward Zeus and man into sympathy for the human race, and Persephone's heedless innocence into knowledge of the ultimate goodness in the world. The Imagists, whose movement for clarity of expression through precise images flourished from 1910 to 1918, represented a reaction to Victorian romanticism. Their leading mythological poet was H. D. (Hilda Doolittle, 1886–1961), the only one among a distinguished list of poets—Ezra Pound, James Joyce, Amy Lowell, and William Carlos Williams among others—to survive as an Imagist. H.D. composed a *Demeter* that captured the spirit of the goddess as a *mater dolorosa*:

> Though I begot no man child
> all my days
> the child of my heart and spirit,
> is the child the gods desert—
>
> . . . .
> Ah, strong were his arms to wrest
> slight limbs from the beautiful earth,
> young hands that plucked the first
> buds of the chill narcissus,
> soft fingers that broke
> and fastened the thorny stalk
> with the flower of wild acanthus.
>
> Ah, strong were the arms that took
> (ah, evil the heart and graceless),
> but the kiss was less passionate!

Notable among the musical versions of the abduction is Igor Stravinsky's *Persephone* which is called a melodrama for reciter, tenor, chorus, and orchestra. Produced in 1934, it had a libretto by André Gide, and as we would expect of Gide's treatment of mythological themes, the "rape" of Persephone is inverted into an act of voluntary self-sacrifice; unforced, she goes to the realm of the god of the underworld where she will bring a little light of day and love to the human spirits suffering there.

5. Hestia (Vesta)

The life story of Hestia is a short one. Unlike her brothers, sisters, and relatives, about whom the Greeks told innumerable tales of love and hate, of disputes and intrigues, little was said of the old maid of the Olympians. In Homer there is not a word; in Hesiod only that she was the firstborn of Cronus and Rhea. In Plato's myth of the flight of the divine soul in the *Phaedrus*, the philosopher tells us that Hestia stayed at home while Zeus led the remaining members of the twelve Olympians to the dome of heaven. Hestia, however, is not the Cinderella of Greek mythology; her celibacy was of her own choosing, for we hear that Poseidon and Apollo once asked for her hand. In the *Homeric Hymn to Aphrodite*, we have her full biography. The poet tells of Aphrodite's power to stir the passions of both gods and men, but of Hestia he says that she would have none of "Aphrodite's works":

She was the first-born child of wily Cronus . . . a queenly maid whom Poseidon and Apollo sought to wed. But she was wholly unwilling, nay, stubbornly refused; and touching the head of father Zeus who holds the aegis, she, that fair goddess, swore a great oath which has in truth been fulfilled, that she would be a maiden all her days. So Zeus, the Father, gave her a high honor instead of marriage, and she has her place in the midst of the house, and has the richest portion. In all the temples of the gods she has a share of honor, and among all mortal men she is the chief of the goddesses.

Hestia is the goddess of the hearth; more specifically, of the fire burning on the hearth. The Roman goddess Vesta was her etymological twin; both were of Indo-European origin and shared similar practices in cult. Greek Hestia and Roman Vesta never evolved into fully anthropomorphized deities—Ovid says that we should never think of Vesta as anything other than the living flame—and hence their mythological portraits are sketches with hardly any detail.

The character of the goddess and her cult developed from a number of almost universal ideas about fire: its identification with life, its purifying properties, and the importance of the hearth-fire as the center of family life. "She has her place in the midst of the house," is the way the Homeric hymn puts it. Important in family life, Hestia and Vesta became important goddesses in the cult of the state. Hestia presided at all sacrifices, and as the goddess of the sacred fire of the altar, she was invoked first and the first part of the sacrifice was offered to her. When the Greeks established a colony in a distant land, the colonists took the fire that was to burn on the hearths of their new homes from the mother-city, the "metropolis." If the sacred hearth-fire in the sanctuary of the goddess died out, it could not be relighted by ordinary means, but generally by the age-old process of the friction of wood.

Among the Romans, Vesta was inseparably connected with the Penates, the guardian spirits of the family larder. Taken together they represented the material vitality of the family or the state. And when the myth of the Roman state was fashioned, Aeneas was honored for having brought the sacred fire of Vesta from Troy to Italy along with the images of the Penates. In the ancient Roman household, the hearth was the center of family life and around it members of the family assembled for their common meal. A special offering for Vesta was laid on a holy dish and then thrown into her flames. The worship of Vesta united all the citizens of the state into one large family. The sacred fire of the Roman goddess burning on the public hearth or altar was her living symbol and was tended by a number of virgin-priestesses called Vestals.

In modern literature, the anonymity of the goddess of the hearth was respected. In Milton's *Il Penseroso*, Saturn and Vesta are called the parents of Melancholy, an invention which has been much disputed but which is undoubtedly tied to polyphonic associations of all three figures in the mind of the poet. The attendants of the Roman goddess, the Vestals, were given greater recognition in English literature, the word "vestal" having a range of connotative meanings which include nun, purity, virgin, and devoted to goodness. In *Venus and Adonis*, Shakespeare speaks of "Love-lacking vestals and self-loving nuns . . ." In *Romeo and Juliet*, the youthful lover complains about his being estranged from Juliet but that carrion flies

> may seize
> On the white wonder of dear Juliet's hand,
> And steal immortal blessing from her lips,
> Who, even in pure and vestal modesty,
> Still blush, as thinking their own kisses sin.

And in Alexander Pope's *Eloisa to Abelard* vestal is synonymous with nun: "How happy is the blameless vestal's lot!/The world forgetting, by the world forgot."

Figure 24. Apollo. *A detail from the center of the west pediment of the Temple of Zeus at Olympia, c. 460 B.C. Olympia Museum. (Hirmer)*

6. Apollo

With Apollo we come to the second generation of the gods who ruled from Mount Olympus. Together with Artemis, Athena, Ares, Aphrodite, Hermes, and Hephaestus, Apollo represents the younger set of the Olympians; they were gods who, according to most traditions, were sired by the great Olympian himself. Unlike most other Greek deities for whom the Romans could find an opposite number in their own pantheon, Apollo had no close Roman counterpart; consequently, he was adopted with his Greek name and his Greek epithet Phoebus (Bright, Shining). The latter is identical in meaning with the name of his grandmother, the Titaness Phoebe.

Apollo was the god of the flocks, of archery, of medicine, of music, of prophecy; he was the founder of cities, the promoter of colonization, the giver of laws, the punisher of wrongs, the god of the sun. The origin of this multifaceted god is as enigmatic and ambiguous as some of the responses that came from his celebrated oracle at Delphi. Did he come from Asia Minor, or did he come from the mysterious land to the north, the land of the Hyperboreans? The question is still being debated. The likelihood is that in the course of several millennia the personalities of several gods were blended into one until Apollo emerged in the form most characteristically Greek of all the gods (fig. 24). In the last verse of Shelley's *Hymn of Apollo*, the virtues of the god are summed up in these lines:

> I am the eye with which the Universe
>   Beholds itself and knows itself divine;
> All harmony of instrument or verse,
>   All prophecy, all medicine are mine,
> All light of art or nature;—to my song,
> Victory and praise in their own right belong.

The story of Apollo's birth and early years is found in a Homeric hymn, the *Hymn to Apollo*, which contains two traditions: the Delian (from the island of Delos) which tells primarily of the difficulties his mother had in bringing him into the world; the other, the Pythian, which celebrates the founding of Delphi as the seat of the oracle of Apollo. When the Titaness Leto (Roman Latona) was about to bear Apollo, she wandered over mountains and islands trying to find a place where she might give birth. No land, however, would receive her, for Hera in her jealousy had commanded that Leto could not bear her child in a place where the sun shone. Leto finally came to the island of Delos, but Delos hesitated to offer her a refuge for fear that her son-to-be would despise the desolate island and thrust it down into the depths of the sea with his foot. When the goddess swore that the island would have the god's great temple, she was allowed to give birth to him there. For nine days and nights Leto suffered labor pains, and although many goddesses came to offer sympathy and help, Leto could not deliver her son for Hera kept Eileithyia, goddess of childbirth, on Mount Olympus. The goddesses sent Iris on a special mission of mercy to Eileithyia, who finally came and served as Leto's midwife. Leto then knelt on the ground, grasped a palm tree, and painlessly gave birth to Apollo. The goddess bathed the child in water and clothed him in a white garment embroidered with gold. Fed by the goddess Themis with nectar and ambrosia, the infant-god burst his swaddling clothes and declared that the curved bow and the lyre would be his and that he would in the future announce the will of Zeus. The goddesses were amazed and Delos shone golden and its earth blossomed.

Apollo was born on the seventh day of the month, and ever after the number seven was sacred to him, and sacrifices were made to him on the seventh of each month. The palm tree under which he was born was one of the famous sights of antiquity from the time of Homer on. Other places in the Greek world, of course, claimed to be his birthplace—Ephesus in Asia Minor and towns in Boeotia and Attica—but Delos is generally honored as the scene of Apollo's nativity. The island, which before Apollo's time had been a floating piece of land, now became fixed and was fastened to the roots of the earth.

Apollo now ascended to Olympus where he joined the other gods and played to them on his lyre. His twin sister Artemis sang, and the Graces, Harmonia, Hebe, and Aphrodite danced. Having made himself known to the Olympians, Apollo set about to find a suitable place for his temple. He found Telphusa a favorable site, but the nymph of the place was unwilling to share honors with the god and persuaded him that the trampling of horses and the general noisy confusion of Telphusa were not suitable for the god's temple. At her suggestion Apollo went on to what later became known as Delphi and laid the foundation of his great temple at the foot of Mount Parnassus. At a nearby spring he fought and killed a monstrous she-dragon. As the body of the creature rotted away, the place acquired the name of Pytho, according to popular etymology meaning "corruption." Another tradition names the dragon Python, and from it Apollo was given the epithet of Pythian, a name which was also given to his priestesses.

As Apollo looked around for priests to serve him, he saw, in the distance, a ship from Crete on its way to trade with the people of Pylos. The god, in the shape of a dolphin, leaped into the ship and steered it toward the port of Delphi. (As a result of this incident, the god was called Delphian—again popular etymology.) With another great leap he sprang from the ship into his shrine and appeared before the Cretans as a young man. He enrolled the Cretans as priests of Apollo, but when they saw the rocky wilderness in which they were to live, they were afraid that the region could not sustain them. Apollo assured them that they would always have the rich gifts men would soon bring to honor his divinity. He told his priests to show others his will and not to commit wrongful acts or utter false words; if they did, he warned, they would be conquered by others and be subject to them forever.

Apollo had another struggle for supremacy over the famous oracle, possibly a reference to an actual historical conflict with invading Dorians (1100 B.C.) who dubbed themselves the descendants of Heracles. The story is told that Heracles and Apollo fought over the tripod of Delphi. Heracles, in one of the fits of madness Hera cast on him, flung a young man from the walls of Tiryns. The king purified him of the crime but Heracles was still plagued by disease. He went to the oracle at Delphi to learn how he might be cured. When the Pythian priestess refused to say anything to him, Heracles seized the tripod upon which the priestess sat and threatened to set up his own oracle. Apollo rushed onto the scene to defend his priestess. Heracles boldly attacked the god. Zeus separated them by hurling a thunderbolt between them, and the priestess hurried to tell Heracles how he could rid himself of the disease. The theme of the contest between Apollo and the hero was popular among vase painters of antiquity.

What can be said of Apollo's attributes and functions that would explain his development from a god of flocks—usually considered his earliest concern—to a deity of advanced morality? A reasonable hypothesis is that throughout the Dark Ages, from about 100 to 750 B.C., the Aegean people evolved their views about their gods from many sources. Apollo seems to have entered the Aegean from Asia Minor or from that fabled place beyond the north wind, the land of the Hyperboreans; he probably made a number of appearances during successive waves of migration. The myths that tell of his triumphs over other deities at Delphi and elsewhere may be historical reflection of his increasing popularity through the Dark Ages and in particular the increasing popularity of the oracle and his worship at Delphi.

As the god of flocks Apollo would well have deserved the epithet of Lyceus— if it does not mean "coming from Lycia" in Asia Minor. As Lyceus, the wolf-god, shepherds would have worshiped him for his power to keep wolves away from their flocks, or to bring wolves down on the flocks of their enemies. With the epithet Nomios, Apollo is the protector of the grazing animals; his attribute is the bow which keeps away wolves, wild animals, and rustlers. As a shepherd-god concerned with the well-being of the herd, he acquires the power of healing and becomes a physician-god. Apollo's interest in music also develops from his association with shepherds since music was their favorite pastime.

Apollo at Delphi.   All Apollo's early functions fade into the background once he takes possession of the oracle at Delphi. In the prologue to *Eumenides*, the concluding play of the *Oresteia*, Aeschylus has Apollo's priestess, the Pythia, recount how Apollo became the god of prophecy at Delphi.

> I give first place of honor in my prayer to her
> who of the gods first prophesied, the Earth; and next
> to Themis, who succeeded to her mother's place

of prophecy; so runs the legend; and in third
succession, given by free consent, not won by force,
another Titan daughter of Earth was seated here.
This was Phoebe. She gave it as a birthday gift
to Phoebus, who is called still after Phoebe's name.
And he, leaving the pond of Delos and the reef,
grounded his ship at the roadstead of Pallas, then
made his way to this land and a Parnassian home.

. . . .

He came so, and the people highly honored him,
with Delphus, lord and helmsman of the country. Zeus
made his mind full with godship and prophetic craft
and placed him, fourth in a line of seers, upon this throne.
So, Loxias is the spokesman of his father, Zeus.

According to this tradition, Apollo inherited the Delphic oracle from his grand-mother Phoebe who had succeeded her sister Themis, and she in turn her mother Earth (Gaea). Apollo, then, replaced a number of earlier female divinities who, as we have seen, appear to have been pre-Hellenic deities. When the Greek gods came to Delphi and when Apollo took over the oracle, the site undoubtedly had had a long history for prophetic utterance. Further witness to its antiquity was the *omphalos*, the navel stone, in the innermost sanctuary of the Temple of Apollo at Delphi (fig. 101). Stones of this kind are associated with the most primitive re-ligions of the Aegean; they appear to have been relics or cult objects connected with the worship of early earth-goddesses. Of course the Greeks were quick to tell a story of how the stone came there and why Delphi was considered the navel or center of the world. Zeus, in the spirit of academic inquiry, wished to find the center of the earth. He turned two eagles loose, one from the eastern edge of the world, the other from the western. Having been released at the same time and flying at the same speed, they met over Delphi and a stone was placed there to mark the spot. Delphi also housed another famous stone: the one which Cronus swallowed in place of Zeus. When he regurgitated it along with his children, the stone was sent to Delphi—so the story goes—where it was reverently anointed every day.

The legend of how Apollo killed the great she-dragon and of how its putrid re-mains gave rise to the name Pytho is an aetiological tale to explain an early name for Delphi and the reason why the god was called Pythian Apollo and his priest-ess Pythia. Although only the inspired priestess at Delphi was entitled to that name, other women who had the spirit of divination used the title, such as the young slave-girl who followed Saint Paul and who is described in *Acts* as having *pneuma Pythona*, a Python spirit. In historical times the Python had a prominent place in the tradition and ritual of Delphi. A great festival, known as the Step-teria, was held every eight years; it included a "drama" in which a lightly-built hut, called the palace of Python, was burned down. Apollo, represented by a handsome and well-born Delphian, pretended to go into exile. Accompanied by attendants, the young man was purified at Tempe to the north of Delphi, and then returned via the sacred route called the Pythian Way, crowned with Apollo's sacred plant, the laurel. At the Pythian games, second in importance only to the

Olympian games, one of the events was a musical contest on the subject of the fight between the god and the monster. These rituals with their accompanying mythological texts may well be historical reminiscences of the usurpation of the famous oracle by an invading Greek god. The Python, or the priestess bearing the name of Pythia, appears to be the reflection of a pre-Hellenic female cult—possibly that of a Minoan snake-goddess—that in early times possessed the oracle.

In the course of time Apollo's oracle at Delphi commanded considerable respect, not only in the Hellenic world but among non-Greeks as well. We know, for example, that the Lydians of Asia Minor, and particularly their last ruling king Croesus (c. 560–546 B.C.), were fond of applying to the oracle for political advice, for which they showed their gratitude by showering the god with rich gifts. According to tradition, the law codes of many Greek cities—such as the constitution of Lycurgus at Sparta—were attributed to Apollo and Delphi. The Delphic priesthood was especially proficient at these tasks since over the centuries the archives of the god's sanctuary had become filled with information of all kinds. The source of its intelligence were petitioners and envoys, as well as correspondence from several hundreds of Greek city-states and foreign principalities bordering the wide reaches of the Mediterranean. Delphi's "State Department" was kept well informed.

Politically Apollo came to the fore during the period of colonization (c. 750–550 B.C.) when Greek cities approached the god for advice on a choice of sites for their colonies. With the kind of information available at Delphi, the priests of Apollo generally made sound recommendations. The colonists were also advised to worship the gods of their mother-city and to honor Apollo the Founder by building him a temple on the soil of their new home. Naturally, a successful colony would demonstrate its gratitude by sending gifts to the god at Delphi. So grateful were cities and individuals that the precinct of the god soon became crowded with statues and other offerings; and added to these were other tokens of gratitude commemorating victories and outstanding events. Some twenty cities maintained "treasuries" at Delphi, small temple-like buildings which housed the treasured records and religious objects of a particular city or community. Some idea of the number of dedicatory works of art that crowded Apollo's holy precinct can be gauged from the high number of statues Emperor Nero (A.D. 54–68) removed to Rome: five hundred of them.

Apollo at Delphi gave pagan antiquity its high religious ethic. He emphasized purity of spirit rather than of ritual, of intention behind the deed rather than the bare act itself. Although he encouraged the worship of the Olympian deities, he did not neglect those outside that circle, advising petitioners to worship gods according to the customs of their ancestors or of their city. Inscribed on his great temple were the two famous precepts of the god: "Know thyself" and "Nothing in excess." Yet the god of moderation could also welcome Dionysus, the god of excess and ecstasy, into a partnership at Delphi. Undoubtedly the frenzied priestesses of the god had some influence in welcoming Dionysus into Apollo's home, if he had not actually lived there before the Olympian deity arrived. The grave of Dionysus was shown in the inner sanctuary of the temple, and for three winter months Apollo was said to hand over the shrine to Dionysus while he retired to the far north, to the fabled land of the Hyperboreans. The festival of Dionysus at Delphi was orgiastic, but characteristically of Apollo and his priesthood, the rituals were regulated and given a limited form of expression. Apollo recognized ecstasy but instead of suppressing it, he moderated it by limiting it to official women representatives from Greek cities and by making it a biennial celebration.

There was yet another side, a less advanced side perhaps, to the god at Delphi. Apollo was a god of catharsis, a god of purification, particularly from acts, such as homicide, which can infect and pollute an entire community. As early as Hesiod, we hear of how the sin of one man may cause suffering for a city:

> Often . . . a whole city suffers for a bad man who sins and devises presumptuous deeds, and the son of Cronus lays great trouble upon the people, famine and plague together, so that the men perish away, and their women do not bear children, and their houses become few, through the contriving of Olympian Zeus. And again, at another time, the son of Cronus either destroys their wide army, or their walls, or else makes an end of their ships on the sea.

This doctrine of pollution and communal responsibility is very prominent in the works of Aeschylus, Herodotus, and Sophocles. In the latter's *Oedipus Tyrannus*, the city of Thebes suffers because of Oedipus' crime, and it continues to suffer, until his physical presence is removed from the city. It is significant to note that Homer, who gives us a thumbnail description of the Oedipus myth in the *Odyssey*, says that Oedipus continued to rule in Thebes after the truth of his crime became known.

Apparently Delphi was also responsible for propagating a philosophy of life that is sometimes called "archaic pessimism." The nature of deity is enigmatic and no mortal can expect to know for sure how the god will act. "Know thyself" did not mean self-examination, but rather the recognition of how limited man was, how insignificant he was with respect to deity. Men felt their consciences oppressed by transgressions on divine prerogatives, and they attributed their suffering to punishment for some excess or overconfidence (*hybris*). In Aeschylus' *Agamemnon*, we can see how guilty Agamemnon feels when Clytemnestra lures him to step on the blood-red carpet:

> And as I crush these garments stained from the rich sea
> let no god's eyes of hatred strike me from afar.
> Great the extravagance, and great the shame I feel
> to spoil such treasure and such silver's worth of webs.

When first invited to step on the carpet, Agamemnon had expressed views which were more in keeping with the Apollonian doctrine. He tells his wife not to

> . . . cross my path with jealousy by strewing the ground
> with robes. Such state becomes the gods, and none beside.
> I am a mortal, a man; I cannot trample upon
> these tinted splendors without fear thrown in my path.
> I tell you, as a man, not god, to reverence me.

This was the true Greek way and was in keeping with Apollo's precept of "Know thyself." And since deity is mysterious and enigmatic, the vicissitudes of life are equally beyond man's comprehension. Life becomes chancy and unstable, as Herodotus has Solon (c. 640–c. 560 B.C.) say to King Croesus in a meeting which never could have taken place: "Look to the end, no matter what it is you are considering. Often enough deity gives a man a glimpse of happiness, and then utterly ruins him." Herodotus, for whom Croesus was an exemplar of *hybris*, reports this supposed conversation between Solon, the noted Athenian lawgiver, and the Lydian king, when Solon visited the latter's realm. After Croesus had displayed his vast wealth, he asked the Athenian whom he considered the happiest man in the world. Solon, a disciple of the Apollonian doctrine, cited an unknown Greek, Tellus of Athens, who lived a long and healthy life, had many children and grandchildren, and died gloriously in the defense of his city. Croesus had, of course, expected quite a different answer. He then asked Solon whom he considered happiest after Tellus. To demonstrate further to the king that no one can call himself happy until he knows how he dies, Solon mentioned two young men, Cleobis and Biton. These were two dutiful sons who, when their mother had no means of getting to the temple of Hera for her devotions, harnessed themselves to a cart and transported her to the temple some five miles away. In response to the mother's prayer that the goddess bestow on her sons the highest blessing as a reward for their piety, Cleobis and Biton fell asleep in the temple and never again awoke. Solon cites this tale as evidence of an enviable death and divine proof of how much better death is for mortal men than life.

The Delphic Oracle. How did the god make his will known and who helped formulate his doctrine? Unlike the oracle of Zeus at Dodona where the god spoke through the wind in the trees, Apollo's medium at Delphi was an elderly woman, the Pythia. At first there was only one Pythian priestess, but as the oracle became better known and the demand for responses from the god increased, there were usually two or three Pythias on hand to take their turn in the oracular vault of the temple of Apollo. A story is told to explain the age and dress of the priestess. It seems that originally the Pythia was a young girl, but when a rough mountaineer from Thessaly attacked her, it was decreed that thenceforth the Pythia had to be over fifty years of age, yet that she was to be dressed as a young girl.

When a question was to be put to the god, the priestess descended into the oracular vault of the temple, the innermost sanctuary, the holy of holies, where the priestess took her position on a tripod. The priestess was attended by an exegete, a priest-interpreter. When the chamber was filled with the fumes of burned barley, hemp, and laurel leaves—the priestess may have also chewed bay leaves or drunk the holy water of the Castalian spring—she fell into a trance and was then in communion with Apollo. When the priest put the question to her, she talked or babbled incoherently. The priest listened to her intently and memorized or took down her words. The response was turned over to another priest who issued the final form of the oracle, usually in metrical form or in prose. There was yet another priest who could explain to the postulant the obscurities of the god's response. The obscurities earned Apollo the epithet "Loxias," the Ambiguous One.

Responses to questions of a political nature were particularly ambiguous. For example, when Croesus asked if he should undertake an expedition against the Persians, the oracle replied that if he did he would destroy a great empire. This was no Pythia talking, but a priest-politician who was uncertain about the balance of power in the Near East. Croesus, who of course was not well-versed in Apollonian doctrine, did not inquire of the oracle whose empire would be destroyed, his or the Persian. To his regret he found out later that it was his own. On another occasion, he approached the oracle, as usual through a messenger, and asked whether his kingdom was to last long. The oracle replied that he had nothing to fear until a mule would be king of Persia. Confident that he was secure, Croesus undertook a war against the Persians and was defeated by Cyrus. Challenging the oracle for having misled him, he was informed that Cyrus was that "mule," the child of parents of different ethnic backgrounds. The folklore element in these oracles is very evident and is reminiscent of the prophecy given to Macbeth that he need not fear defeat until "great Burnam wood to high Dunsinane hill shall come against him."

These oracles as reported by Herodotus, a firm believer in their validity, illustrate the ruin to which overconfidence (*hybris*) produced by prosperity may lead man. To exalt oneself in anything, small or great, to overstep oneself, to take anything in life for granted—all are violations of the Olympian creed as revealed through the spokesman of Zeus, Apollo. These views were strongly felt in the Archaic Period (c. 750–500 B.C.)—hence the phrase "archaic pessimism"—and continued to be felt in varying degrees in subsequent ages.

It is said that the last of Apollo's oracular responses was given during the reign of Emperor Julian (A.D. 360–363), the philosopher-soldier and apostate who attempted to restore the worship of the pagan gods after the Roman Empire had officially become Christian. To Julian's messenger who had been sent to Delphi, the oracle—or perhaps a priest of Apollo who had become a Christian—replied:

> Say you to the Emperor: "Our beautifully-built house has fallen to the ground;
> Phoebus no longer has his dwelling place, his mantic laurel.
> His speaking spring—yes, even the water that spoke—has departed.

The spring referred to is the Castalian spring, named after the nymph Castalia who, like many others, was pursued by amorous Apollo. The nymph found refuge in a cave or spring on the slopes of Mount Parnassus and from that time on, the water of the spring had the power of inspiring those who drank it.

*　　*　　*　　*

In *The Last Oracle*, Swinburne has the Greek text of this last Delphic oracle as a preface to the poem in which he once more takes up the cudgel against "the pale Galilean" and Christian doctrine which "made the whole world moan with hymns of wrath and wrong." Milton, on the other hand, finds the power of Christ so overwhelming that pagan gods run before "the dreaded Infant's hand," and the "pale-eyed priest" of Apollo is made silent. From *On the Morning of Christ's Nativity*:

> The oracles are dumb;
> No voice or hideous hum
> Runs through the archèd roof in words deceiving.
> Apollo from his shrine
> Can no more divine,
> With hollow shriek the steep of Delphos leaving.
> No nightly trance, or breathèd spell,
> Inspires the pale-eyed priest from the prophetic cell.

Of more recent vintage is the treatment of Apollo's prophesying priestess by the French Symbolist poet, Paul Valéry (1871–1945). *La Pythie* (The Pythian Priestess) is concerned with the agonies of creation and the creative artist. The Pythia, or the poet, is possessed both physically and intellectually, painfully and ecstatically, by the power of creation, Apollo. The struggle, virtually a physical possession, is humiliating and hideous but ends in a harmony or union of the forces that are in conflict within the creative spirit.

Louis MacNeice (1907–1963) has no such resolution. His poem, *The Oracle*, speaks first of Delphi and then of other oracular means of divining the truth, but for the wry poet that he was, the question of truth in the oracle is not answered.

> The oracle
>   High between the cliffs,
> The tripod over
>   The mephitic cleft,
> Or the sybil's cave
>   Where the winds blow
> The dead leaf answers
>   To and fro:
> Where shall we find truth in an oracle?
> The oracle
>   Among the talking oaks,
> The flight of birds,
>   The examination of guts,
> Luck of the cards,
>   Lines of the hand,
> Call of the raven
>   In a sallow land:
> Where shall we find the truth in an oracle?

Cassandra. The many faces of Apollo—shepherd, prophet, healer, singer, and lover—are seen in the numerous myths with which the ancient world illustrated the life of the young god. As a lover he was not very successful, and to the women who rejected him he gave rather tragic lives. Perhaps best known of these is Cassandra, daughter of Priam and Hecuba, king and queen of Troy. One tradition has it that when she was but a child, her parents left her in the sanctuary of the Thymbraean Apollo along with her young brother Helenus. The next morning, the two of them were found entwined with serpents that were purifying the children's ears so that they might be able to understand the sounds of nature and the voices of the birds. They were in effect being given the power to interpret the will of the god.

When Cassandra grew up, so the more traditional version goes, Apollo taught her the art of prophecy on the condition that she yield to his amorous embraces. Cassandra promised, but did not keep her word. The god then ordained that for having gone back on her promise she would have the gift of prophecy but that no one would believe her. With the approach of the Trojan War, Cassandra continually announced the calamities that would befall Troy, but her prophecies were disregarded. Her father Priam even looked on her as a madwoman and had her shut away and guarded. After the fall of the city, Cassandra was given to Agamemnon as his share of the booty. She arrived with Agamemnon at Mycenae only to be brutally murdered by Clytemnestra (fig. 99). In a series of stirring passages in Aeschylus' *Agamemnon*, Cassandra is vividly dramatized as a priestess of Apollo, possessed by the god and in a mantic state. With emotionally packed words she tells the chorus of the sinful past of Agamemnon's family and of what is taking place in the palace and prophesies her own death. Of course, she is not believed or her words are misinterpreted. Before entering the palace to meet her end, Cassandra is again possessed by the god, painfully so, and then tears off the symbols that mark her as a divining priestess.

> Oh, flame and pain that sweeps me once again! My lord,
> Apollo, King of Light, the pain, aye me, the pain!
> This is the woman-lioness [Clytemnestra], who goes to bed
> with the wolf [Aegisthus], when her proud lion [Agamemnon] ranges far away,
> and she will cut me down; as a wife mixing drugs
> she wills to shred the virtue of my punishment
> into her bowl of wrath as she makes sharp the blade
> against her man, death that he brought a mistress home.
> Why do I wear these mockeries upon my body,
> this staff of prophecy, these flowers at my throat?
> At least I will spoil you before I die. Out, down,
> break, damn you! This for all that you have done to me.

*   *   *   *

The tragic life of Cassandra has been attractive to modern poets such as Meredith, Rossetti, Masefield, and H. D. Four operas were written bearing her name, and Johann Christian Bach (1735-1782) composed a cantata entitled *Kassandra*. Robinson Jeffers (1887–1962), for whom ancient myth was a medium of expression for his unconventional views on humanity, shortened Aeschylus' *Oresteia*, at least its first two plays, into a dramatic poem, *The Tower Beyond Tragedy*. In it the spirit of the murdered Agamemnon possesses the body of Cassandra and through her voice calls for the death of the she-wolf, Clytemnestra. Jeffers' poem *Cassandra*, while not characterized by the physical violence and lust of his other works, expresses his condemnation of poets and politicians, and humanity in general; his identification is with Cassandra, the prophet whom no one believes.

> The mad girl with the staring eyes and long white fingers
> Hooked in the stones of the wall,
> The storm-wrack hair and the screeching mouth: does it matter, Cassandra,
> Whether people believe
> Your bitter fountain? Truly men hate the truth; they'd liefer
> Meet a tiger on the road.
> Therefore the poets honey their truth with lying; but religion-
> Venders and political men
> Pour from the barrel, new lies on the old, and are praised for kindly
> Wisdom. Poor bitch, be wise.
> No: you'll still mumble in a corner a crust of truth, to men
> And gods disgusting.—You and I, Cassandra.

Edwin Arlington Robinson (1869–1935), in the manner of Old Testament prophets, denounces America for her complacent materialism, her egotism, and her blindness to the past and the future. Of course, his words will be ignored like the prophecies of Cassandra. From his *Cassandra*, written during the early years of World War I:

> I heard one who said: "Verily,
>   What word have I for children here?
> Your Dollar is your only Word,
>   The wrath of it your only fear.
>
> . . . .
>
> "Your Dollar, Dove and Eagle make
>   A trinity that even you
> Rate higher than you rate yourselves;
>   It pays, it flatters, and it's new.
>
> "And though your very flesh and blood
> be what your Eagle eats and drinks,
> You'll praise him for the best of birds,
>   Not knowing what the Eagle thinks.
>
> "The power is yours, but not the sight;
>   You see not upon what you tread;
> You have the ages for your guide,
>   But not the wisdom to be led.
>
> "Think you to tread forever down
>   The merciless old verities?
> And are you never to have eyes
>   To see the world for what it is?
>
> "Are you to pay for what you have
> With all you are?"—No other word
> We caught, but with a laughing crowd
> Moved on. None heeded, and few heard.

The Sibyl.   Another unfortunate young girl who crossed paths with Apollo was a certain Sibylla or Sibyl. Like Cassandra's, her story and others of the same stamp generally explain a characteristic of the mantic priestesses of the god of prophecy: their age, their virginity, their dissociated mental state when they serve as Apollo's medium. T. S. Eliot, in the epigraph to *The Waste Land*, borrows a quotation from the Latin novelist Petronius Arbiter (first century A.D.) which tells of the fate of the best-known of the Sibyls—there were a number of these, ranging from four to ten—the Cumaean Sibyl, who allegedly had come to Italy from the East. The quotation translates as follows:

> Yes, with my very own eyes I have seen the Cumaean Sibyl suspended in a bottle, and when the children asked, "Sibyl, what do you want?" she replied, "I want to die!"

Eliot is referring to an old folktale that explains why a priestess of Apollo is an old crone. In the romantic story told by the Roman poet Ovid, Apollo was very much taken by the Sibyl, then a young girl, and offered to make her immortal if she would give in to his charms. To make the offer even more attractive, the god promised her anything she wished. The Sibyl scooped up a handful of sand and asked to live for as many years as there were grains of sand in her clutched fist. However as is common in folktales, she forgot to ask that she remain young through the years, and to make matters worse she rejected Apollo's amorous overtures. As the years passed by the hundreds, the Sibyl gradually shriveled up so that she became small enough to be hung up in a bottle. Hence, when children asked her what she wanted, her response—the one that so attracted T. S. Eliot—was "I want to die!"

It was the Cumaean Sybil whom Aeneas sought as a guide through the land of the dead. He found her in a vast cave, about to prophesy. Vergil gives this description of the mantic priestess of Apollo as she becomes possessed by the god:

". . . the god, the god is here!" As she spoke her face, her color changed suddenly—her hair started from its braid—her bosom heaves and pants, her wild soul swells with frenzy—she grows larger to the view, and her tones were unearthly as the breath of the divine presence comes on her nearer and nearer. . . .

But the prophetess, not yet Phoebus' willing slave, is storming with giant frenzy in her cavern, as though she hoped to unseat from her bosom the mighty god. All the more sharply he plies her mouth with his bit till its fury flags, tames her savage soul, and moulds her to his will by strong constraint. . . .

Such are the words with which the Cumae's Sibyl from her cell shrills forth awful mysteries and booms again from the cavern, robing her truth in darkness—such the violence with which Apollo shakes the bridle in her frenzied mouth and plies her bosom with his goad. Soon her frenzy abated and the madness of her lips grew calm.

The prophecies of the Cumaean Sibyl reportedly were written down on palm leaves which were collected into books. A well-known tale of antiquity tells of how nine books of Sybilline oracles were offered to an early king of Rome, Tarquinius Priscus. He tried to bargain with the Sibyl, but ended up paying the same price for three books as he would have for all nine. These three books are said to have survived until 83 B.C. when they were destroyed by fire. They were replaced by a new collection which, though extant, are mostly a mixture of Jewish-Hellenistic and Christian material from the second century B.C. to the third century A.D. The last time the Sibylline books were officially consulted was in A.D. 363 at the end of the reign of Emperor Julian. However, the influence of Vergil—the Sibylline prophecy appears in the fourth of his *Eclogues*, the celebrated "Messianic Eclogue"—and of the late Sibylline books in medieval and later times assured the Sibyls an honored place along with the prophets of the Old Testament.

Daphne.   Apollo was attracted to another young girl who rebuffed his advances and like Cassandra and the Sibyl, ended up in an adjunct relationship to the god of prophecy. The girl in this instance was Daphne (Laurel) whose parentage is variously given. According to one tradition, she was a tree nymph and an ancient priestess of Delphi; according to another, she was the daughter of Tiresias, the noted seer of antiquity, and was called by the name of Manto (Prophetess); according to yet another, Daphne was the daughter of the river-god Peneus and Earth. On either side of her family, she was endowed with the potential for prophecy. Being very beautiful, Daphne was pursued by a smitten Apollo. As Spenser put it: "Fayre Daphne Phoebus hart with love did gore." Just as she was about to be overtaken by the god, she prayed to her mother, Earth, who opened the ground and received her. So that Apollo would not leave empty-handed and disgruntled, Earth created the laurel (=Daphne) which the god adopted as his sacred plant and made a wreath of its leaves. Since then, wreaths of laurel crowned victors of the Pythian games. We have already observed how the laurel was used in various religious and prophetic rituals of the god.

Ovid, in true Alexandrian style, embellishes the tale with purple patches and baroque romantic details. According to the poet of the *Metamorphoses*, Daphne was Apollo's first love and Cupid the prime cause of the god's difficulties. It seems that Apollo foolishly jeered at Cupid's power with bow and arrow. The wily god of love, determined to show Apollo his might, shot a golden, love-exciting arrow into the god's heart, and a leaden, love-repelling arrow into Daphne's. Apollo, burning with passion, pursued an unwilling Daphne, and just as he was about to catch her, she prayed to her father Peneus for help. The river-god obliged by transforming his daughter into an evergreen laurel. This is Ovid's description of the metamorphosis of Daphne and its effect on Apollo:

> . . . her limbs grew numb and heavy, her soft breasts
> Were closed with delicate bark, her hair was leaves,
> Her arms were branches, and her speedy feet
> Rooted and held, and her head became a tree top,
> Everything gone except her grace, her shining.
> Apollo loved her still. He placed his hand
> Where he had hoped and felt the heart still beating
> Under the bark; and he embraced the branches
> As if they still were limbs, and kissed the wood,
> And the wood shrank from his kisses, and the god
> Exclaimed: "Since you can never be my bride,
> My tree at least you shall be! Let the laurel
> Adorn, henceforth, my hair, my lyre, my quiver. . . ."

*   *   *   *

Ovid's *Metamophoses* passed into the Middle Ages along with many other works of antiquity, and by the twelfth century it became acceptable through the agency of allegory for Christian moralizing. By this time, all mythology, even Ovid's frivolous and light-hearted legends, became a form of moral philosophy. At the beginning of the fourteenth century, the *Ovide moralisé* (Ovid Moralized) appeared in France, and within it the story of Daphne and Apollo with a moral commentary. Daphne, as the daughter of a river, was cold by temperament and represents virginity. She was changed into a laurel because, like virginity, it is ever green and produces no fruit. As the Virgin Mary, Daphne is loved by Apollo, the true sun. When he places the laurel wreath on his head, it is God assuming the flesh of the woman whom he made his mother.

This treatment of ancient mythology did not go unopposed. In the prologue of *Gargantua*, Rabelais (c. 1494–1553) objected to allegorizing Homer, saying that Homer could no more have had this in mind than Ovid could have been thinking of the Gospel Sacraments in his *Metamorphoses*. Martin Luther (1483–1546), the German religious reformer, attacked the moralizers of Ovid who "turned Apollo into Christ and Daphne into the Virgin Mary." These admonitions went unheeded and allegory continued strong throughout the Renaissance. Further, allegory was the means by which a poet or an artist could avoid censure for telling a licentious story or for depicting pagan forms. Thus we find on the base of the statue of

Figure 25.   Giovanni Lorenzo Bernini.
Apollo pursuing Daphne. *Marble,
1622–1623. Borghese Gallery, Rome.
(Alinari)*

Daphne (fig. 25) carved by Giovanni Lorenzo Bernini (1598–1680) this moral inscription as an antidote to the sensual appeal of the nymph: "Any lover who follows the pleasures of ephemeral appearance, fills his hands with leaves or plucks bitter berries."

The theme of Apollo and Daphne has been popular in every century. Operas were composed on it, the latest being Richard Strauss' *Daphne* produced in 1938. The god and nymph were also portrayed on canvas; Nicolas Poussin's *Apollo and Daphne* (c. 1664) is one of the best. And of course, poets used the theme in numerous ways. Ezra Pound begins one part of his poem *Mr. Nixon* in this way:

> "Daphne with her thighs in bark
> Stretches toward me her leafy hand,"—
> Subjectively. In the stuffed-satin drawing-room
> I await The Lady Valentine's commands.
>
> Knowing my coat has never been
> Of precisely the fashion
> To stimulate, in her,
> A durable passion.

Edna St. Vincent Millay (1892–1950) gives us a purely feminine approach, as if Apollo is some kind of masher who must be rebuked and told off. This is her *Daphne:*

Why do you follow me?—
Any moment I can be
Nothing but a laurel-tree.

Any moment of the chase
I can leave you in my place
A pink bough for your embrace.

Yet if over hill and hollow
Still it is your will to follow,
I am off;—to heel, Apollo!

Asclepius (Aesculapius). So much for those women in Apollo's life who reflect aspects of the god's power to divine the future and to act as the spokesman of Zeus. There were yet others whose favors the god sought and with whom he was sometimes successful or nearly so. Apollo was a little more fortunate with Coronis, a beautiful young girl who came from Thessaly in the rough northernmost reaches of Greece. Her father was Phlegyas, a son of the war-god Ares; her brother was Ixion who had the effrontery to attempt to ravish Hera. We shall find him attached to a fiery wheel and punished by revolving eternally in the deepest pit of Tartarus.

Coronis was bearing Apollo's child and the god took pleasure in the girl as long as she was faithful, or as Ovid cynically remarks, "thought to be." The news was brought back to Apollo by a white raven to which the god had assigned the job of keeping an eye on the girl. The raven reported that Coronis had taken up with a mortal. According to other accounts, Apollo discovered her transgression through his own powers of prophecy. Since the raven had not avenged him on the spot by plucking out Coronis' eyes, Apollo punished the raven by changing his feathers from white to black. And there lies the mythical explanation for the raven's coloring. As for Coronis, she was killed by Apollo, or his sister Artemis. The god regretted his hasty action, but it was too late; he could do nothing to bring her back to life. When her body was on the funeral pyre, Apollo snatched his unborn child from the flames. (To be snatched unborn from the flames is a sure sign of near immortality and the bringing into being of an extraordinary person.) This was the unusual origin of Asclepius, the legendary healer of antiquity. When Rome suffered from a plague in 293 B.C., he was brought to the city on the advice of the Sibylline Books, reinforced perhaps by an oracle from Delphi. The Greek name on Roman lips became Aesculapius.

Apollo, not having the facilities to rear the child, turned him over to the good centaur Chiron. Centaurs were generally wild, lustful, and hard-drinking hybrid creatures—human to the waist, a horse in the lower part of the body—who inhabited the rough country of Thessaly and Arcadia. Chiron, however, was an exception to the general rule. The son of Cronus and the Oceanid Philyra, Chiron was a kindly old man, wise in the ways of medicine and other arts, to whom the education of such great heroes as Achilles and Jason was entrusted (fig. 82). Asclepius had, of course, inherited his father's skill in medicine which was furthered by the training he received from his foster-father Chiron. Asclepius' fame as a physician soon became widespread; he not only cured the sick but also gained the reputation of being able to bring the dead back to life. Apollodorus names six mythical personages who were brought back to life by Asclepius' skill. Asclepius managed this feat by virtue of a life-giving drug given to him by Athena: the blood which had flowed from the right side of the body of the Gorgon Medusa.

According to a much later tradition, Asclepius was ordered to bring back to life Glaucus, son of the king of Crete Minos, and for this reason was put into a secret prison. While pondering what to do, he observed a snake creeping up his staff. Without thinking, Asclepius killed it. Later, another snake came out of the ground carrying an herb in its mouth, placed it on the head of the dead snake, and *mirabile dictu* the serpent stirred into life. Asclepius, using the same herb, raised Glaucus from the dead. And so the snake—that uncanny creature that is in communication with the land of the dead and the land of the living—coiled around a staff became a common attribute for the great healer (fig. 26). When the son of Apollo came to Rome, legend has it that he came in the form of a snake and took up residence on the island in the Tiber River where a temple was dedicated to him on January 1, 292 B.C. A snake coiled around a staff persists to this very day as the symbol for physicians, although in the United States it inappropriately became confused with the attributes of Hermes (Mercury).

The cult of Asclepius rapidly spread throughout the Greek-speaking world. Temples were dedicated to him at places known to promote health, or near wells and springs believed to have healing powers. These temples, the most famous of which was at Epidaurus, were not so much places of worship as the ancient equivalent of hospitals or spas. Dedicatory plaques discovered at these sanctuaries attest to the cures effected by Asclepius and his priests: some were miracles, others were accomplished by auto-suggestion and by such accepted therapeutic methods as the regulation of diet and exercise. The most prominent cure was by incubation, that is, through sleeping in the sanctuary and having the dreams of the sick person interpreted by the priest of Asclepius who suggested the proper remedy for the illness.

Figure 26.   Asclepius and his daughter Hygieia. *Roman sculpture. Vatican Museum. (Alinari-Mansell)*

The question of whether Asclepius was originally a god or a man has not been settled. The present consensus is that he was a historical figure who became so renowned in the art of healing that he was worshiped as a god. Greek imagination soon manufactured the mythical material to prove his divinity. This form of legend was not uncommon in ancient Greece: the great man, the hero, who was so powerful that he could conquer death, or rake hell and bring back the dead. The most conspicuous among these, as we shall see, was Heracles, some of whose "labors" attest to his ability to conquer the unconquerable, death. Homer, however, speaks of Asclepius as "excellent" or "noble," a term never used for a god. His two sons, Podaleirius and Machaon, were physicians with the Greek army at Troy; the Trojan heroes had Apollo himself as their physician. Asclepius also had a number of daughters who are nothing more than abstractions of his profession: Hygieia (Health), Iaso (Healing), and Panacea (Cure-all). Note how the oath, attributed mistakenly to Hippocrates (c. 460–c. 377 B.C.) and sworn to by physicians entering their profession, brings together Apollo, his son and his grandchildren in its invocation:

> I swear by Apollo the Physician, by Asclepius, by Hygieia, by Panacea, and by all the gods and goddesses, making them my witnesses, that I will carry out, according to my ability and judgment, this oath and this indenture. . . .

Admetus and Alcestis. Asclepius' talent for reviving the dead and departed triggers a series of events that ultimately leads to the bittersweet story of Admetus and Alcestis. When Hippolytus died (p. 370), so goes the most common version, the goddess Artemis appealed to Asclepius to bring her favorite back to life. He did so, but since the great healer had violated the first law of nature, Zeus killed him with a flash of lightning. Other accounts have Hades registering the complaint that if Asclepius did not stop his nefarious practice of reviving the dead, his kingdom would be seriously depopulated. Pindar, in his third Pythian Ode (c. 474 B.C.), tells the story for the benefit of the ailing tyrant of Syracuse. As a staunch believer in the Olympian creed as revealed by Apollo, Pindar uses the myth in support of a moral thesis that the gods always mix sorrow with happiness, and that often more sorrow than happiness is rationed out to mortal man; also, mortals must be satisfied with what they have and not anger the gods by looking for more. Even Coronis, Asclepius' mother, by seeking another marriage while she was bearing Apollo's child, illustrates the principle that punishment and suffering follow when mortal limits are exceeded. As for Asclepius, he went beyond mortal limits when he perverted his art and allowed himself to be seduced by a handsome fee to restore a dead person to life.

Apollo, in anger over the severe punishment meted out to his son, killed the Cyclopes who had forged Zeus' thunderbolts. Zeus would have sent Apollo to Tartarus, had Leto not intervened and begged Zeus to have mercy on her son. The Olympian relented and sentenced Apollo, as if he were being punished under Greek law for having taken the life of someone of his own clan, to serve a mortal man in the lowly status of a serf for the period of one year. Fortunately, the god was assigned to the kindly king of Pherae, Admetus, for whom he worked in his old profession as a herdsman. Admetus' flocks and herds benefited by having their patron god watch over them: the animals flourished and increased in number since they bore twins or would give birth twice a year. Because of the respectful treatment he received at the hands of Admetus, Apollo helped him to overcome serious obstacles in gaining Alcestis for his bride. However, as folk motifs would have it, Admetus forgot to honor Artemis at his wedding. In anger the goddess declared through various portents that the king had to die. Apollo went to plead Admetus' case with the Fates, plied the stern old women with drink, and got them to agree to spare the king's life on condition that he find someone to take his place.

Euripides ALCESTIS. At about this point Euripides picks up the thread of the story for his tragicomedy *Alcestis*, produced in 438 B.C. When the fatal day arrives, Admetus has found no one who would agree to take his place; even his aged mother and father refuse him. Alcestis, however, volunteers to serve as her husband's substitute. Apollo, who has to leave the palace because of her approaching death, comes face to face with Thanatos (Death). Thanatos berates the god for cheating him out of his legitimate prey. Apollo, in bantering tones, attempts to dissuade Thanatos from taking Alcestis but without success. He takes his leave but first he foreshadows the coming of Heracles who will take Alcestis from Thanatos by force. Alcestis and Admetus tearfully make their farewells. Alcestis asks that her husband never marry again so that their children will be spared the cruelty and jealousy of a stepmother. Admetus vows never to remarry, that she will always be in his heart, and that when his time comes to die, he will be buried in the same tomb with her. Alcestis then dies and passes on to the Underworld. While the palace is in mourning, Heracles appears on his way to perform one of his difficult labors. He is courteously and hospitably received by a grieving Admetus who refuses to tell Heracles the cause for all the lamentation in the palace. Heracles is finally persuaded to stay.

During the funeral procession, Admetus has an angry interchange with his father who, like a Sophist, defends himself against the charge of not being a true father. He places the blame for Alcestis' death squarely on the shoulders of Admetus. Heracles appears on the scene deep in his cups, reeling with drink and chiding everyone for being so depressed and sad. When he hears from a servant that they are mourning the death of Alcestis, he recoils with shock and remorse. He leaves vowing to repay Admetus for his hospitality and kindness. He soon returns leading a veiled woman whom, he says, he has won in a wrestling match. He asks Admetus to take her into his house and care for her. Unaware that Heracles has brought back Alcestis from the land of the dead, Admetus is at a loss as to what to do, although there is something about the veiled woman that reminds him of Alcestis. Heracles insists that he take his prize and finally gets Admetus to see that he has brought Alcestis back from the grave. Dramatically, Alcestis does not say a single word during this interchange. The excuse is that she will not be able to speak for three days until she has paid off her obligations to the gods of the Underworld.

The semi-tragic story of Admetus and Alcestis combines several folk motifs. The central theme of the willingness of the wife to sacrifice herself for her husband holds a practical lesson for a male-oriented culture, namely, that a man's best friend is a good wife. Superimposed on this were the popular motifs of the raking of hell by an extraordinary hero, and the recovery or near-recovery of one of a pair of lovers. Euripides, in his sophisticated rendering of the myth, shifted the emphasis to a character study of the heroes and heroines of ancient legends from the standpoint of the moral standards of his own day. Without forgetting that Euripides had an audience to deal with—there is a good deal of melodramatic sentimentality in the speeches of Admetus and Alcestis—his penchant for discrediting and disparaging the popular heroes of mythology makes him portray Heracles and Admetus as less than sympathetic, less than attractive human beings.

* * * *

Over the centuries the myth of Admetus and Alcestis has been variously interpreted. More than twenty operas were written on the theme, the best-known being
Christoph Gluck's *Alceste* (1767), the latest an operatic version of Thornton Wilder's
Alcestiade (1962). In the prologue to Chaucer's *Legend of Good Women*, Alcestis is
portrayed as the wife of the god of love. She urges the poet not to tell of the infideli-
ties of women but rather to praise their virtues. As a paragon of virtuous womanhood
she is appropriately chosen by Chaucer to plead for her sex. Milton used the myth
to communicate the experience of a personal tragedy, the loss of his wife in the
second year of their marriage. Although he had been blind before they met, Milton
sees her in a dream, coming back to him from the grave just as Alcestis had. From
his twenty-third sonnet:

> Methought I saw my late espousèd saint
>   Brought to me like Alcestis from the grave,
>   Whom Jove's great son to her glad husband gave,
>   Rescued from Death by force, though pale and faint.
> Mine, as whom washed from spot of child-bed taint
>   Purification in the Old Law did save,
>   And such as yet once more I trust to have
>   Full sight of her in Heaven without restraint,
> Came vested all in white, pure as her mind.
>   Her face was veiled; yet to my fancied sight
>   Love, sweetness, goodness, in her person shined
> So clear, as in no face with more delight.
>   But, oh! as to embrace me she inclined,
>   I waked, she fled, and day brought back my night.

Robert Browning also seems to have found something in the classical story of Alcestis that touched upon his personal life. *Balaustion's Adventure* is, in Browning's
words, a "transcript" of Euripides' play as told by a young girl Balaustion, a fictitious
poetess from the island of Rhodes. Concerned for the safety of her kinfolk during
the Peloponnesian War, Balaustion persuades them to leave the island, but their ship
is forced to take refuge at Syracuse, the bitter enemy of the Athenians. Balaustion, a
great admirer of Euripides, wins over the hostile Syracusans by reciting Euripides'
Alcestis. Browning glosses over Euripides' cynicism and his interest in feminine psychology in favor of a reformed Admetus whose character gains strength and nobility
from his earlier weakness. When Heracles unveils Alcestis

> It was the crowning grace of that great heart,
> To keep back joy; procrastinate the truth
> Until the wife, who had made proof and found
> The husband wanting, might essay once more,
> Hear, see, and feel him renovated now—
> Able to do, now, all herself had done,
> Risen to the height of her: so, hand in hand,
> The two might go together, live and die.

Browning changes the carefree and carousing Heracles of Euripides into a muscular knight-errant who rescues Alcestis, as he had Elizabeth Barrett, from the grave. This is Browning's description of Heracles as he comes on the scene:

> Happy, as always; something grave, perhaps
> The great vein-cordage on the fret-worked front,
> Black-swollen, beaded yet with battle-dew
> The yellow hair o' the hero!—his big frame
> A-quiver with each muscle sinking back
> Into the sleeping smooth it leaped from late.

At the end of the poem Browning has his poetess recast the myth: Alcestis is rejected by Persephone, the goddess of the lower world, because her soul is so much a part of her husband's that she cannot die while he still lives:

> "Two souls in one were formidable odds:
> Admetos must not be himself and thou!"
>
> And so, before the embrace relaxed a whit,
> The lost eyes opened, still beneath the look;
> And lo, Alcestis was alive again,
> And of Admetos' rapture who shall speak?

In the twentieth century, the American novelist and dramatist Thornton Wilder (1897–   ) became deeply interested in the myth of Alcestis. For him Alcestis is a Christ-like figure whose act of self-sacrifice helps mankind feel and understand love (Apollo). In *The Woman of Andros* (1930), the courtesan Chrysis, questioning the nature of suffering, says that the answer will come after her death, when "I shall be among the shades underground, and some wonderful hand, some Alcestis, will touch me and will show me the meaning of all these things. . . .   In another novel, *The Ides of March* (1948), Wilder has the Roman poet Catullus recite a "lost" *Alcestiad* after the first attempt was made on the life of Julius Caesar. The latter prefigures *The Alcestiad*, a drama which had its first performance at Edinburgh in 1955 as *A Life in the Sun*. Wilder constructed the play along the lines of a Greek tetralogy but alters the myth and the characters to suit his own purposes. *The Alcestiad* is called an existentialist allegory in which Wilder, in contrast with such Existentialists as Sartre and Cocteau, offers a religious affirmation of human and divine relationships. The mystical union of divine love, Apollo and Alcestis, cannot be obtained without a commitment, no matter how meaningless it may seem, to human love and human self-sacrifice, without finding and realizing oneself in others.

T. S. Eliot's approach to the myth of Alcestis was considerably more oblique than Wilder's. When his play *The Cocktail Party* was produced in 1949, no one was aware that Euripides' *Alcestis* had provided him with the framework for his drama until he revealed it two years later. Only then did critics notice how Eliot exploited and reinterpreted the dramatic material inherent in Euripides' play. Even the names bear phonetic relationships to the mythical characters: Edward = Admetus, Lavinia = Alcestis, and Harcourt-Reilly = Heracles. Alcestis' death is paralleled by Lavinia's desertion of her husband; Admetus is grief-stricken, Edward is mortified and deeply disturbed; Admetus receives Heracles hospitably, Edward carries on with the cocktail party; just as Heracles drinks and sings, so does the Unidentified Guest. For Eliot death of the body is of less importance than death of the spirit. The departure of

Lavinia, the break in the marriage, the estrangement, separation, and isolation are all psychological and metaphysical representations of death. Eliot has Edward say: "I am not afraid of the death of the body/But this death is terrifying. The death of the spirit." When the Uninvited Guest, who turns out to be the psychiatrist Sir Henry Harcourt-Reilly, places on Edward responsibility for what happened, there is an allusion to Alcestis' return from the dead. Eliot enlarges on this phenomenon and turns it into a metaphysical statement:

> Guest: You set in motion
> Forces in your life and in the lives of others
> Which cannot be reversed. That is one consideration.
> And another is this! it is a serious matter
> To bring someone back from the dead.
>
> Edward: From the dead?
> That figure of speech is somewhat . . . dramatic,
> As it was only yesterday that my wife left me.
>
> Guest: Ah, but we die to each other daily.
> What we know of other people
> Is only our memory of the moments
> During which we knew them.

Marpessa and Idas.   The many women Apollo pursued without much success may be concluded with Marpessa, the daughter of Ares' son Evenus. However, unlike other members of her sex whose stories are in one way or another connected with the cult of Apollo, Marpessa's tale illustrates the wisdom of avoiding physical contact with a divine being, the wisdom of realizing mortal limitations. Our earliest reference to Marpessa appears in Homer who tells us that Idas, "the strongest of men" fought with Apollo with bow and arrow for her hand. What else Homer knew of this story is not told, but if it had been told by anyone else, we should have expected to find the mortal punished for his presumption in competing against a god. Later embellishments are given to us in an abridged version of the story by Apollodorus. Marpessa had attracted the eye of Apollo and he set out to woo her. Idas apparently had the same idea and carried her off in a winged chariot provided by Poseidon. Marpessa's father chased them in his own chariot but he could not catch up with the fleeing lovers. Seeing himself defeated, Evenus slaughtered his horses and threw himself into the river Lycormas which ever after was called by his name, the Evenus. Idas and Apollo came face to face in Messene where the god would have robbed him of Marpessa. Idas stood his ground and the two, mortal and god, fought for the girl's hand. Zeus interfered at this moment and gallantly allowed Marpessa to make her own choice, god or mortal. Marpessa, fearing that the god would desert her when she became old and gray, made a wise choice by taking Idas for her husband. The daughter of this marriage was Cleopatra who became the wife of Meleager, the valiant leader of the Calydonian boar hunt.

The Victorian poet Stephen Phillips (1864–1915), who was prematurely hailed as the savior of poetic drama and the grand style, found in the story of Marpessa and Idas the full range of human experience with all its sorrow. His *Marpessa* (1897) is romantic and sentimental, more in harmony with the Hellenistic spirit than with the Homeric or the Classical. Apollo makes Marpessa an offer of immortality since she is too beautiful ever to taste sorrow and death; she would help him bring bliss to struggling men and sorrowing women. Idas cannot match Apollo's bid for her favor; he can only offer his love, love not so much for her beauty alone but "Because Infinity on thee broods;/ And thou art full of whispers and of shadows;" and because her voice is music, her face mystery beyond his power to comprehend:

> O beauty lone and like a candle clear
> In this dark country of the world! Thou art
> My woe, my early light, my music dying.

Marpessa responds to the humble approach of the transcendent Idas. Turning to Apollo she thanks him for his kind offer and indicates her choice of Idas. As for that "existence without tears for evermore" which the god promised, she philosophizes that sorrow is the natural state for man, and that it is out of sadness that men have created beauty in the world.

> Yet I being human, human sorrow miss.
> The half of music, I have heard men say,
> Is to have grieved.

Hyacinth. Greek imagination left nothing undone. If Apollo was unfortunate in his relationships with women, the same motif was carried over to men. A highly romantic story is told of Apollo's affection for young Hyacinthus, or Hyacinth. So taken was the god with the young man, son of the king of Sparta, that he abandoned Delphi and his interest in the lyre and bow. Instead he spent his time with the youth, hunting and fishing and roaming over the rough mountain trails. One day, Apollo and Hyacinth competed in discus-throwing, but as luck or fate would have it, Apollo's discus ricocheted off a stone, struck Hyacinth's head and killed him. Apollo, in anguish over losing the man he loved, promised that his death would not go unremembered, that Hyacinth would be reborn as a flower whose petals would be marked with the god's own words of grief: *Ai Ai*, Greek for *Alas!* No sooner said than done. From Hyacinth's blood sprang the flower which bears his name—probably our iris or larkspur. Other versions place the onus for Hyacinth's death on Zephyrus, the West Wind, who was also in love with the young man. In a fit of jealousy he let loose a puff of wind which caused Apollo's discus to veer off course and strike Hyacinth full in the face.

This is the story that has come down to us from rather late sources, from the Hellenistic period on, and for that reason heavy emphasis is placed on the romantic involvements. The earliest reference to Hyacinthus appears in Euripides' *Helen*, where no mention at all is made of love or romantic attachment but where it is merely said that the god ordained a festival in honor of Hyacinth's death, a bit of aetiology to explain the Dorian festival called the Hyacinthia. Curiously enough, Apollo had no significant role in the ritual of the Hyacinthia. From the non-Greek combination of sounds in Hyacinth's name—the *nth* which also appears in "Corinth"—and from other evidence, we are quite sure that the festival dates back to pre-Dorian times, that is, prior to the first millennium B.C., and that it had its origins among the non-Greek population of the region surrounding ancient Sparta. The Hyacinthia, so far as it can be reconstructed, was a three-day celebration. The first day was a very solemn one, not very different from holy days of special significance in many religions. Sacrifices were offered to the dead—a sure sign of solemnity, anxiety, and crisis—the death of Hyacinth was lamented, the wearing of garlands was forbidden, sexual continence was observed, and the singing of hymns of praise was forbidden. On the second day, offerings of cakes, that is, of unleavened bread, were made at the tomb of Hyacinth. On the third day, there were contests of various sorts, horse races, sacrifices, and "joyful solemnity" existed throughout the land. The combination of rites of mortification, purification, and reinvigoration assures us of the importance of the festival in honor of Hyacinth. Just how important it was to the Lacedaemonians, the people of Sparta and its neighboring regions, can be seen from the fact that they always returned home at the approach of the Hyacinthia, even when they had taken the field against the enemy. Once, an armistice of forty days was declared so that the Lacedaemonians could return home to celebrate their national festival.

The Hyacinthia was celebrated at about the time of the summer solstice, late June or early July, and it was therefore interpreted by some scholars to express the ancients' concern over the drying up of vegetation by the heat of summer and the loss of fertility to the land. Whatever the particular concern—the summer drought, the shortening of the days beginning with the summer solstice—the fear of the loss of divine providence, as seen in terms of the seasonal cycle of death and resurrection, moved the ancients to perform these rituals in order to reassure the continuing rhythm of life in all its manifestations. It is for this reason that the Hyacinthia was celebrated by the Lacedaemonians and their predecessors as a solemn and serious festival. In historical times, the cult of Hyacinth was subordinated to that of Apollo and the death of the youthful Hyacinth was given a romantic aetiology which was made increasingly more fanciful as the significance of the festival disappeared from view. The poetic associations of Hyacinth, however, have endured. For his description of the Gardens of Adonis in the *Faerie Queene*, Spenser speaks of how

> . . . all about grew every sort of flowre,
> To which sad lovers were transformd of yore:
> Fresh Hyacinthus, Phoebus paramoure,
> And dearest love . . .

In *Lycidas*, Milton picks up the allusion to the hyacinth as a flower of mourning: "that sanguine flower inscrib'd with woe." In his poem *On the Death of a Fair Infant*, the myth is given greater elaboration:

> For so Apollo, with unweeting hand,
> Whilom did slay his dearly-lovèd mate,
> Young Hyacinth, born on Eurotas' strand,
> Young Hyacinth, the pride of Spartan land;
> But then transformed him to a purple flower.

Keats, in a pastoral scene from his *Endymion*, pictures shepherds at a game of quoits which brings to mind the tragedy of the youthful prince:

> . . . pitying the sad death
> Of Hyacinthus, when the cruel breath of
> Zephyr slew him,—Zephyr penitent,
> Who now, ere Phoebus mounts the firmament,
> Fondles the flower amid the sobbing rain.

D. H. Lawrence (1885–1930), on the other hand, uses the name of Hyacinthus as a symbol of idealized beauty inherent in the commonplace and mundane. This is from his *For a Moment*:

> For a moment, at evening, tired, as he stepped off the tram-car,
> —the young tram-conductor in blue uniform, to himself forgotten,—
> and lifted his face up, with blue eyes looking at the electric
>   rod which he was going to turn round,
> for a moment, pure in the yellow evening light, he was Hyacinthus.

Again elevating the comonplace by mythological allusion, Lawrence finds esthetic pleasure in the sight of a girl hurriedly removing her wash from a line:

> In the green garden darkened by the shadow of the coming rain
> and a girl ran swiftly, laughing breathless, taking in her white washing
> in rapid armfuls from the line, tossing in the basket,
> and so rapidly, and so flashing, fleeing before the rain
> for a moment she was Io, Io, who fled Zeus, or the Danae.

Apollo Musagetes. As the patron-deity of song and music, Apollo provided the musical entertainment for the Olympians at their banquets and at the weddings of distinguished heroes. In this role he was often joined by other divinities connected with the pleasurable arts of music and dance: the Muses, the Graces, and the Hours. His epithet *Musagetes* (Leader of the Muses) indicated his dominant position in the field of the arts; and since Greek poetry and music were intimately related, Homeric bards and other poets claimed their art from Apollo or the Muses. The god's musical instrument was the lyre, also called phorminx or cithara; from the latter are derived the names of the present-day cithern, zither, and guitar. Apollo came by the lyre, as we shall presently see, through a barter arrangement with the god Hermes who is usually given credit for inventing the instrument. The Alexandrian poet Callimachus has a novel story which cleverly ties in Apollo's favorite number with the number of strings on the lyre. In his hymn *To Delos*, Callimachus tells how the Muses sent their sacred birds to celebrate the birth of the god:

> . . . and with music the swans, the gods' own minstrels . . . circled seven times around Delos, and sang over the bed where the child would be born, the Muses' birds, the most musical of all birds that fly. Hence the child later strung the lyre with just so many strings—seven strings—since seven times the swans sang over the pangs of birth.

Shakespeare has an equally fanciful description of Apollo's "lute" in *Love's Labour's Lost*. Love, he says, is

>   . . . as sweet and musical
> As bright Apollo's lute, strung with his hair;
> And when Love speaks, the voice of all the gods
> Make Heaven drowsy with the harmony.

The ancient poets put Apollo in competition with other deities to see who was the better musician. The mythical motif in these tales evidently reflects a competitition between two modes of music, two kinds of instruments, two kinds of gods: one that moderates and calms the spirit (Apollo and his lyre), the other that stimulates the senses and is highly emotional (Marsyas-Pan and the flute). When Apollo wins these contests, it is a victory for the god of *sophro-syné* (moderation), and indicates his superiority over those gods, usually portrayed as foreign, whose worship was accompanied by emotional excesses.

Apollo versus Marsyas. Marsyas, a satyr or silenus (p. 250) from Phrygia in Asia Minor, challenged Apollo to a musical contest, the terms of which were that the winner could do whatever he wished to the loser. Marsyas' instrument was the flute, in reality a reed instrument related to the clarinet or oboe. How he came by the flute is told in another story. Athena had invented the instrument, but when she saw how it distorted her features when she played it, she threw it away in disgust. Marsyas picked up the flute and was so delighted by its sounds and his success in playing it that he challenged Apollo. The Muses were chosen as judges in the contest and they decided in favor of Apollo when he added his voice to the music of the lyre. As a just punishment for the presumption of Marsyas in challenging a god, Apollo tied him to a tree and flayed him alive. It is said that his blood, or the tears of his mourners, became the river Marsyas in Asia Minor.

The story of Marsyas' presumption in challenging Apollo soon became an instructive symbol of the punishment that is handed out to the ignorant and the proud. For his ideal state Plato would have preserved only two modes of music: one would inspire courage and deeds of valor in times of war and difficulty, the other would suggest to citizens restraint, temperance, and peaceful actions. He rejects the use of the flute and concludes by saying that there is nothing new in preferring Apollo and his instrument to that of Marsyas.

*　　*　　*　　*

During the Renaissance the contest symbolized the victory of the mind (Apollo) over the dark world of matter (Marsyas). However, in Matthew Arnold's *Empedocles on Etna*, the story is sung by Callicles as an illustration of the cruelty of the god of intellect and thought. Marsyas, like the poet-philosopher himself, is a victim of Apollo's cruelty. Borrowing from late sources which make Marsyas the music teacher of a young man named Olympus, the song ends with these words:

> Therefore now Olympus stands,
> At his master's piteous cries
> Pressing fast with both his hands
> His white garment to his eyes,
> Not to see Apollo's scorn;—
> Ah, poor Faun, poor Faun! ah, poor Faun!

It is at this point that Empedocles, the poet-philosopher, rejects the god of intellect:

> And lie thou there,
> My laurel bough!
> Scornful Apollo's ensign, lie thou there!
> Though thou has been my shade in the world's heat—
> Though I have loved thee, lived in honouring thee—
> Yet lie thou there,
> My laurel bough!

> I am weary of thee.
> I am weary of the solitude
> Where he who bears thee must abide—
> Of the rocks of Parnassus,
> Of the gorge of Delphi,
> Of the moonlit peaks, and the caves.

Oscar Wilde (1854–1900), in the *Burden of Itys*, looking longingly for the pagan past to mitigate his unhappiness with the Christian present, views Marsyas as an unwelcomed intruder into his dream of beauty: "No more thou wingèd Marsyas complain,/Apollo loveth not to hear such troubled songs of pain!" And in Wilde's dramatic essay on esthetics, *The Decay of Lying*, Apollo is the symbol of pure art, Marsyas the world about us and "the singer of life."

> Art never expresses anything but itself. This is the principle of my new aesthetics. . . .
> Of course, nations and individuals, with that healthy natural vanity which is the secret
> of existence, are always under the impression that it is of them that the Muses are talk-
> ing, always trying to find in the calm dignity of imaginative art some mirror of their
> own turbid passions, always forgetting that the singer of life is not Apollo, but Marsyas.

Apollo versus Pan and the Story of Midas.   Apollo has another musical contest, this time with the woodland deity Pan. Again the scene takes place in Phrygia in Asia Minor, which to the Greeks was the region of the highly emotional and orgiastic cults of Cybele, Dionysus, and other oriental deities. Although Pan's native home was Arcadia in Greece—his life's story will presently be considered—he became associated with the entourage or revel-rout of Dionysus. A god of the flocks and shepherds, Pan was pictured as having horns, beard, a pug nose, goat's feet, and as being covered with hair. The favorite instrument of this half-goat/half-man deity was the panpipe or syrinx, an instrument still popular with shepherds. It seems that Apollo and Pan were having a music contest, Apollo playing his lyre and Pan his pipes. This time two judges were selected to decide the winner: Tmolus the god of the mountain bearing his name and Midas the mythical king of Phrygia. Some versions have King Midas as an unrestrained member of the audience. Tmolus cast his vote in favor of Apollo but Midas stubbornly judged in favor of Pan. Apollo, according to the popular account, caused the ears of a donkey to grow from Midas' head as appropriate for one who was such an ass as to prefer the music of Pan to that of Apollo (fig. 27). In the *Metamorphoses* Ovid tells the story of the consequences of Midas' insistence on favoring Pan. Ovid finds Pan's song "barbaric" and Midas "stupid." Apollo, on the other hand, is described in growing terms:

> Apollo's hair,
> Golden, was wreathed with laurel of Parnassus,
> His mantle, dipped in Tyrian crimson, swept
> Along the ground. His lyre, inlaid with jewels,
> With Indian ivory, his left hand held;
> His right hand held the plectrum. You could tell
> The artist from his bearing. With his thumb
> He plucked the strings, and charmed by that sweet music,
> Tmolus ordered Pan to lower his reeds,
> Submissive to the lyre, and all approved
> The judgment of the holy god of the mountain,

Figure 27.   Apollo, Midas, and Pan.
*A rendering by Cima da Conegliano
(c. 1460–1508) of the mythical music
contest. R. Pinacoteca, Parma. (Alinari)*

All except Midas, who began to argue,
Calling it most unfair. Such stupid ears
Apollo thought, were surely less than human,
And so he made them longer, stuffed them full
Of gray and shaggy hair, and made their base
Unstable, giving them the power of motion.
The rest of him was human; this one feature
Alone was punished, and he wore the ears
Of the slow-going jackass. So, disfigured,
Ashamed, he tried to hid them with a turban,
But when he had his hair cut, then his barber
Saw, dared not tell, and wanted to, and could not
Keep matters to himself, no more than barbers
Today can do, and so he dug a hole
Deep in the ground, and went and whispered in it
What kind of ears King Midas had. He buried
The evidence of his voice, filled up the hole,
Sneaked silently away. But a thick growth
Of whispering reeds began to grow there; these,
At the year's end full-grown, betrayed the sower,
For when a light breeze stirred them, they would whisper
Midas has asses' ears! You can still hear them.

Ovid has given a humorous turn to the story of Midas, and of his barber as well.
The story has all the markings of a folktale. Midas in fact becomes a kind of stock
character as the foolish and intemperate king whom the Greeks quite naturally place
in a foreign locale. Another well-known story of Midas, which links his proverbial
greed with a bit of aetiology, is also told by Ovid. Midas had been very kind to a
member of Dionysus' revel-rout, a silenus who had gotten drunk and had strayed
into the hands of some unfriendly people. He was bound in wreaths of flowers and

brought to Midas who received him most hospitably and entertained him for a period of ten days. When Midas returned the silenus to Dionysus, the god asked the king if there was any favor he wished granted. Midas foolishly asked that everything he touched be turned to gold. It was granted. Ecstatically the king went about touching all kinds of things: twigs, stones, clods of earth, grain, apples, stone columns, water—all turned to gold. But when he sat down to eat and his servant brought him his food, that too turned to gold. Midas begged the god to take back the favor. Dionysus then ordered him to bathe in the upper reaches of the Pactolus river near Mount Tmolus. The bath saved Midas, but from that time on the golden touch of Midas was to be found in the gold-bearing sands of the Pactolus.

*   *   *   *

Chaucer knew the Ovidian version of Midas and his unfortunate ears. In the *Canterbury Tales*, the voluble and lusty Wife of Bath, to prove her statement that women cannot keep a secret, gives an abbreviated version of the story but substitutes the king's wife for the babbling barber. Midas' wife whispers his secret to the water of a marsh: "Myn housbonde hath long asses erys two"; for the rest of the story the Wife of Bath advises the reader to consult "Ovide." Jonathan Swift was fond of both tales concerning Midas and combines them to satirize the venality of the Duke of Marlborough in *The Fable of Midas* (1712):

> Midas, we are in Story told,
> Turn'd ev'ry thing he touch't to Gold:
> He chip't his Bread, the Pieces round
> Glitter'd like Spangles on the Ground.
>
> . . . .
>
> Two Gods their Skill in Musick try'd,
> And both chose Midas to decide;
> He against Phoebus Harp decreed,
> And gave it for Pan's oaten Reed:
> The God of Wit to shew his Grudge,
> Clap't Asses Ears upon the Judge,
> A goodly pair, erect and wide,
> Which he could neither Gild nor hide.
>
> . . . .
>
> Our Midas too has Asses Ears;
> Where every Fool his Mouth applies,
> And whispers in a thousand Lies;
> Such gross Delusions could not pass,
> Thro' any Ears but of an Ass.
> But Gold defiles with frequent Touch,
> There's nothing fouls the Hands so much:
> And Scholars give it for the Cause,
> Of British Midas dirty Paws.

Percy Shelley's wife, Mary, was also attracted to the story of Midas and wrote a dramatic vignette on the theme. Following Ovid for the general outline of the story, she embellished his play with new incidents and a moral. In place of the barber and Chaucer's wife, Mary Shelley entrusts Midas' secret to his Prime Minister who tattles it to some green reeds. The gift Dionysus gives the king turns into a curse, and after he is freed from his golden touch, Midas has learned his lesson. The play *Midas* ends with this moral:

> None but the meanest peasants shall have gold.
> It is a sordid, base and dirty thing:—
> Look at the grass, the sky, the trees, the flowers,
> These are Jove's treasures and they are not gold—
>
> . . . .
>   . . . we have lost
> Man's curse, heart-bartering, soul-enchaining gold.

Linus.   An unusual association of the god of music is that with a young man named Linus. The story of that relationship is an excellent example of the ability of the Greeks to personify and to mythologize on almost any aspect of the human experience. In this instance Linus is a song, usually a dirge, sung during the harvesting of a crop. On good evidence the name Linus is a Hellenized form of a Semitic ritual cry: *ai lanu*, "woe to us"; and as a dirge it expressed not general sorrow, but the wailing of reapers or vintagers as they cut the grain or plucked the grapes from the vines. Reaping was equated with death—compare out expression "the grim reaper"—and among early peoples there was a fear of offending the spirit inherent in the vine or grain. The expression of sorrow, the dirge of the harvester, was an attempt to avoid the consequences of offending the vegetation spirit who might not return the following year. The historian Herodotus, who always had an eye for parallels with Greek religion, comments that Linus is celebrated in song under different names in Phoenicia, Cyprus, and other places, and that in Egypt his name was Maneros, very probably meaning "Come back!" The Greeks took this ritual cry of harvesters, personified it, and described the death of the young man to account for the dirges sung in his honor.

At Argos in the Peloponnese, Linus was called the son of Apollo and Psamathe, daughter of king Crotopus. Finding herself with the child of the god and terrified of her father, Psamathe exposed the infant on a mountainside. Linus was discovered by shepherds who reared him, but unhappily he was later torn to pieces by dogs. Psamathe, grief-stricken at the fate of her child, told her father what had happened, but instead of receiving sympathy, she was condemned to death. Apollo was indignant at Crotopus' cruelty and caused a plague to fall upon Argos. As was usual in such circumstances, the oracle was consulted on how to end the plague. Apollo answered that the Argives had to propitiate Psamathe and Linus. Sacrifices were offered, women sang dirges which were called Linus songs, and a festival was established in honor of the young man. The plague, however, did not cease until the cause of the pollution, Psamathe's father, left Argos.

Another version was told in Central Greece, in Boeotia, where Linus was held to be a son of the Muse Urania and Amphimarus, a son of Poseidon. According to this tradition, Linus dared to challenge Apollo in a musical contest and for his high presumption Apollo killed him. On Mount Helicon, the home of the Muses, a funeral sacrifice was offered for him and dirges, Linus songs, were sung in his honor before sacrifices were offered to the Muses. The city of Thebes in Boeotia claimed to be the site of his tomb, Argos claimed the same honor, as did Chalcis in Euboea.

There is yet another story of Linus' death. Linus, a skilled musician, was brought in to teach Heracles the intricacies of lyre-playing. Heracles was neither a good pupil nor a patient one. He snatched the lyre from Linus' hand and hit him on the head with it. That was the end of Linus. Under the influence of euhemerism, the Alexandrians viewed Linus as a historical figure and attributed to him a number of poetical works.

Phaethon. Not only were the Greeks capable of transforming a ritual cry into a human personality, they could also take the epithet or surname of a deity and change it into a living person, complete with life history. In Homer, the sun-god Helios bears the epithet *phaethon*, "shining"; we soon hear of it as Phaethon, son of Helios by the Oceanid Clymene or the nymph Rhode. But how does Apollo become connected with the sun, one of his most popular representations in modern literature? As early as the fifth century B.C., Apollo was conjectured to be the sun, an association that undoubtedly came about through the belief that the god, like Helios, knew everything. Greek poets, however, hardly ever had Apollo ride in the sun-chariot through the heavens, an idea that is generally found in Roman literature after the time of Vergil. Helios was the god who drove the chariot of the sun across the sky from east to west; and since the earth was considered to be flat and surrounded by Oceanus' stream, he made the return trip to the east by floating around the earth's disk in a huge cup. Helios, in fact, had no regular cult within Greece although he was given due reverence along with other heavenly bodies. It was only on the island of Rhodes, which had close affinities with the Near East and their sun-gods, that Helios had a vigorous cult. Representations of Apollo with rays around his head characterizing him as the sun belong to the time of the Roman Empire, particularly under Elegabalus (A.D. 218–222), who tried to make the Eastern sun-god the chief deity of the Romans.

The story of Phaethon (or Phaeton) and his tragic end is best known through Ovid's *Metamorphoses*. The tale as told by Ovid is an Alexandrian tour de force full of geographic and astronomical lore, transformations, and pathos. The story opens with the youthful Phaethon boasting to a friend that his father was the sun-god. He had been told this by his mother Clymene who at that time was married to Merops, king of Ethiopia. The friend replied in effect, "You're a fool if you believe everything your mother tells you; all that boasting about your father being the sun!" Phaethon was abashed at having been disbelieved and went to his mother with a plea for proof that his father was really the sun-god. Clymene swore that she had told him the truth and suggested that he visit his divine father to get his word for it.

After a long trip to the east, Phaethon arrived at the royal palace of Apollo, god of the sun. He was well received by his father who owned up to his parenthood and acknowledged Phaethon as his true son. To give the young man even further reassurance, Apollo said that he would grant him any favor he wished and he swore an inviolable oath by the river Styx that it would be granted. In true folklore style, young Phaethon asked for the impossible: to be allowed to drive the sun-chariot for one day. Too late for Apollo to retract his offer, and too little time for the god to give his son the proper instruction. As the time for daybreak grew near, Phaethon put on his father's solar crown and climbed into the chariot. It was not long before the horses of the sun felt an unfamiliar hand on the reins; they took off as if there was no one to check them and left the usual track of the sun's course. The northern constellations were the first to feel the effects of the wild and unrestrained chariot: Ursa Minor and Ursa Major for the first time felt the heat of the sun; the Serpent, usually torpid and harmless, began to warm up and become threatening; and Boötes the plowman ran away even though he was hindered by his plow and not used to moving quickly.

Phaethon was thoroughly frightened by the strange and monstrous creatures of the constellations—the Scorpion, reeking with black sweat, seemed ready to sting him with his bent tail—and in panic and stark terror he dropped the reins of the chariot. The horses were now completely out of control and the chariot careened wildly over the sky. The moon looked on in amazement, clouds began to smoke, the earth burst into flames, and great fissures appeared in its crust. Cities ignited and forest fires raged on the mountains. The heat became unbearable for Phaethon; it was equally intolerable for nymphs of the springs and rivers. The water of the deep could hardly shelter the fish, while its surface was littered with the carcasses of seals. Deserts were created and the men of Ethiopia had their skins turn black.

Earth, overcome with heat and thirst, appealed to the great Olympian for help. Zeus quickly tossed a bolt of lightning at Phaethon who fell from his chariot, his hair aflame, and like a shooting star plunged into the Eridanus river (the Po). His half-sisters grieved for him and were transformed into poplars on the banks of the river; their tears became the amber that exudes from these trees. Phaethon's best friend Cycnus also mourned for him until he was changed into a swan. The Naiads of Italy raised a tomb for the young Phaethon and carved an epitaph which commemorated not only his failure but also his great daring in attempting to drive his father's sun-chariot. Apollo was distraught over the loss of his son and allowed the earth to go without light for one whole day. It was only when the great Olympian apologized for having let loose his bolt of lightning against Phaethon, and after he added a few threats, that Apollo yoked the team of horses once more and put the sun-chariot on its regular daily course.

*   *   *   *

The allegorizers of the Renaissance were not so sympathetic to Phaeton as Ovid had been. At an earlier time the story had undoubtedly been an Apollonian symbol of man's limitless desires and his finite power. This in turn seems to have been framed on a number of explanatory tales and primitive anxieties over eclipses and speculations of what would happen if the sun should ever break from its regular path across the sky. When the *Metamorphoses* was moralized, the daring of Phaethon was seen in quite a different light. Ovid's impetuous adolescent became the fallen angel Lucifer who dared to revolt against God. He was also interpreted as an arrogant philosopher, or as the anti-Christ in opposition to the sun which stood for Christ. According to some scholars, the three drawings by Michaelangelo of the fall of Phaethon (fig. 28), which were tendered to the young nobleman Tomasso Cavalieri, symbolize the "presumption" and "rashness," of a Platonic lover approaching the object of his affection. In 1655, Thomas Hall translated Ovid's story to serve as a school text for the edification of the young. Its long title left no room for doubt as to Hall's intention: "Phaetons folly, or, the downfal of pride: being a translation of the second book of Ovids Metamorphoses . . . where is lively set forth the danger of pride and rashness, with the safety of moderation. . . ."

Moral considerations aside, Phaethon's fiery ride through the heavens gave poets a handy metaphor or simile to fit a number of different occasions. Shakespeare's contemporary, George Chapman (c. 1559–1634), described the hair of Ovid's literary mistress Corinna in *Ovid's Banquet of Sense* in this way:

> The downward-burning flame
> Of her rich hair did threaten new access
> Of venturous Phaeton to scorch the fields. . .

In Shakespeare's *Two Gentlemen of Verona*, the Duke, upon uncovering plans of Valentine to elope with his daughter Silvia, pointedly reminds the young man of his presumption and mortality when he emphasizes "for thou art Merops' son":

> Why, Phaeton,—for thou art Merops' son—
> Wilt thou aspire to guide the heavenly car
> And with thy daring folly burn the world?
> Wilt thou reach stars, because they shine on thee?

In *Romeo and Juliet*, an impatient and eager Juliet cannot wait until Romeo appears, and she pleads for time to pass swiftly with these decorative words:

> Gallop apace, you fiery-footed steeds,
> Towards Phoebus' lodging; such a waggoner
> As Phaeton would whip you to the west
> And bring in cloudy night immediately.

Richard the Second, who met his downfall at the hands of the rebel Bolingbroke, makes this appropriate comparison: "Down, down I come, like glist'ring Phaeton,/ wanting the manage of unruly jades."

As the sun-god, Apollo's epithet Phoebus has virtually become a synonym for the sun. We find such poetic ornaments as "ruddy Phoebus gins to welke in the west"; "redd'ning Phoebus lifts his golden fire"; "Phoebus fiery carre"; and "Phoebus' fire scarce thaws the icicles." Spenser borrows from the nineteenth Psalm the image of the sun "which cometh forth as a bridegroom out of his chamber, and rejoiceth as a giant to run his course" and fuses it with the classical allusion to produce his effect:

> At last the golden Orientall gate
> Of greatest heaven gan to open faire,
> And Phoebus fresh, as bridegrome to his mate,
> Came dauncing forth, shaking his deawie haire:
> And hurld his glistring beames through gloomy aire.

Thus throughout the ages, from his very beginnings to the present, Apollo had different meanings for different people. Aeschylus saw him as a new moralist for the Olympians; Euripides considered him a liar and a ravisher of innocent girls. He could be allegorized as Christ or viewed, as did the seventeenth century poet Abraham Cowley, as a fiend. For the Romantics he symbolized the intellect. Keats made him a god of progress, of self-control, of knowledge; Swinburne calls him "the word, the light, the life, the breath, the glory." Matthew Arnold, on the other hand, found the Apollonian ideal too much to bear. For the twentieth century Imagist H. D., Apollo is cool, beautiful, and perfect, the bringer of mystical illumination, the idealized hero.

MICH·ANG·FLOR·INV·

Figure 28.   Michelangelo. The fall of Phaethon. *Chalk drawing, 1533.*
(Radio Times Hulton)

7. Artemis (Diana)

Artemis, according to most mythologists, was the daughter of Leto (Latona) and twin-sister of Apollo. Having been born on Mount Cynthus on the island of Delos, she was also called Cynthia or Delia. Whether the close sibling relationship of Artemis with Apollo came about because she shared similar attributes with the god— both were armed with bow, quiver and arrows, and both sent plagues and death among men and animals—cannot be stated with any degree of certainty. However, the nonmythological evidence strongly suggests that Artemis had been a resident of Greece long before Apollo and the Indo-European Greeks arrived on the scene. Her association with wild animals connects her with the Minoan goddess called *potnia theron*, Mistress of Wild Animals. She, or a goddess like her, appears on Minoan-Mycenaean gems armed with a bow or spear and leading savage and strange-looking beasts. Sometimes she is represented as receiving the homage of a male worshiper as she stands pedestaled on a mountain or hilltop. Homer appears to have had no great affection for Artemis. His attitude toward the goddess has led some scholars to view her as an unassimilated or unnaturalized goddess in the early Greek pantheon: a goddess of a conquered race who, unlike Hera and others, had not been accepted by the conquerors and hence a bit of *odium theologicum* was attached to her. The best evidence for those who hold this position is found in the twenty-first book of the *Iliad*. The gods and goddesses have been battling with one another, some participating on the side of the Greeks, others fighting in favor of the Trojans. Poseidon, the god of the sea, has just challenged Apollo to a fight. The later disdainfully refuses to pick up the gauntlet; he will not fight for men, those wretched creatures "who flourish like leaves, but for a short time and then droop and fade." His sister Artemis angrily turns on him, accuses him of cowardice and of refusing to fight like a man. But before Apollo can reply, Hera charges in abruptly and gives Artemis a substantial piece of her mind.

"Impudent hussy! Are you proposing to stand up to me? I know your bows and ar-rows, and what a lioness you are to women, whom Zeus allows you to destroy at your discretion; but if you match yourself with me you will regret it. You would find it better sport to slaughter wild deer in the mountains than to fight with your superiors. But since you dare me and would like to try conclusions, let this teach you how much stronger I am."

Hera broke off, and with her left hand seized Artemis by both wrists, while with her right she swept the bow and arrows from her shoulders. Then she boxed her on the ears with her own weapons, smiling as her victim writhed and the arrows came tum-bling out of the quiver. Artemis burst into tears and fled from her...

It is, however, difficult to accept the poet Homer as an authority on early Greek history and religion; hardly any of the gods in the *Iliad* are models of good deport-ment, not even Zeus, the one god whom we can confidently call a native Greek. The likelihood is rather that Homer had a general dislike for any deity that is wild and irrational: the god of war Ares is called a "butcher," Aphrodite a "hussy," and Artemis is described as a lioness and an indiscriminate killer of women and animals. But whatever her nature and in spite of Homer's unfavorable characterization, the classical Artemis was a goddess of wildlife and especially of the young of all living things. She was also revered as a goddess of birth and as such was invoked by women in labor. In this respect she shares some of the functions of Eileithyia, the daughter of Hera and the goddess of childbirth. At times she is even called Artemis

Eileithyia. According to one tradition, she was born earlier than Apollo so that she might assist her mother in giving birth to her brother.

Artemis' connection with the life of women led to her identification with the moon; the moon was commonly thought to exercise a powerful influence over the physical life of women. In this latter aspect Artemis is taken for her mother's cousin, Selene the moon-goddess. Hesiod, as we have seen, has put these two goddesses in a very close family relationship: Selene's father is the Titan sun-god Hyperion; Artemis' grandmother is the Titaness Phoebe (Bright) whose name is often used for the moon and, in later writers, for Artemis or her Roman counterpart Diana. A further development takes place: having acquired lunar functions, Artemis then becomes linked with the goddess Hecate who is a niece of Leto and Artemis' cousin. Hers is the realm of the mysterious and uncanny that take place at night, of sorcery and black magic, and of the crossroads that are universally haunted. Hecate is usually represented as triformed, either three-headed or triple-bodied. Vergil speaks of "Hecate with her triple form who is the maiden Diana with three faces." These three faces were interpreted to represent the three personalities united in one goddess: Selene in heaven, Artemis on earth, and Hecate in the infernal regions. It is not surprising, therefore, to find Diana allegorized in the Renaissance as the Trinity. Hecate, of course, retains her own personality, and after Euripides has Medea admit that Hecate was her patroness in the black arts, she becomes prominent in literature as a leading witch and an inhabitant of the sulfurous infernal regions. Shakespeare uses her in two chilling scenes in *Macbeth*; in *Hamlet*, her arts are described in the play which Hamlet has the traveling actors put on to "catch the conscience of the king." As the player Lucianus is about to pour the poison into the ears of King Gonzago, he says:

> Thoughts black, hands apt, drugs fit, and time agreeing;
> Confederate season, else no creature seeing;
> Thou mixture rank, of midnight weeds collected,
> With Hecate's ban thrice blasted, thrice infected,
> Thy natural magic and dire property
> On wholesome life usurp immediately.

Apart from the lunar and the infernal, Artemis was above all the goddess of wild and undomesticated nature (fig. 29). Her animals were the bear and the wolf, the boar and the lion, the hare and the stag; her sacred haunts were the lakes, marshes, streams, groves, and forests. Roman Diana was also particularly fond of wooded places and was commonly worshiped in groves. Rough and uncultivated Arcadia was Artemis' special country. She was called Parthenos (Virgin, Unmarried), a distinctive title which, of all the major Greek deities, only she and her stepsister Athena bore. At one time in the early stages of her development, Artemis, like Athena, may have had a male partner, but if she did he was not very prominent and faded quickly out of the mythological picture. It is also possible that she had different male partners at different places, and since they were not well known, their names never became closely linked with that of the goddess. However that may be, the sexual inviolability of Artemis became so fixed in the Greek mind that we hear very little of her experiences with male deities or mortals. As a consequence, the storytellers of old had to resort to a form of mythological subterfuge to bypass the difficulty of producing an illustrious ancestor or a name-giving hero from a virgin goddess. In Arcadia where Artemis reigned supreme, the problem was resolved by taking an

Figure 29.   Artemis the Huntress, the
so-called "Diana of Versailles." *A
Roman work, perhaps a copy of a
Greek original. Louvre. (Alinari)*

Figure 30.   François Boucher. Zeus,
in the guise of Artemis, wooing Callisto.
*Painting, 1769. Wallace Collection,
London.*

attribute of the goddess and transforming it into a full-fleshed human being. The myth-making mechanism is similar to that by which Apollo's sacred plant was transformed into the unwilling Daphne, and by which the Semitic ritual cry *ai lanu* was personified as Linus.

Callisto. The Arcadian Artemis was known as Artemis Calliste, Artemis the Fairest. We soon hear in mythology of a Callisto, daughter of King Lycaon who established the worship of Zeus Lycaeus in Arcadia. At the root of the names Lycaon and Lycaeus is the Greek word *lykos*, "wolf." Callisto was a huntress and a companion of Artemis. Zeus, upon seeing Callisto, was very much taken by her and disguised himself as Artemis so that he might take advantage of her innocence (fig. 30). But in order to keep the affair secret from his madly jealous wife, he changed Callisto into a she-bear. According to another version, Artemis discovered Callisto's pregnant condition in the bath and metamorphosed her into a bear. Hera, however, was not deceived by the disguise and saw to it that Callisto was killed by Artemis during a chase; or she caused Callisto to trespass on a sacred precinct of Zeus and had to be killed by Artemis. The child of this relationship, Arcas, survived and was given by Zeus to the mother of Hermes, Maia, to rear. The Olympian then translated Callisto to the stars as the constellation Ursa Major, the Great Bear. Ovid tells yet another version. Juno (Hera) had transformed Callisto into a bear, and when Arcas came upon his mother during a hunt and was about to kill her, Jupiter (Zeus) placed both among the stars as constellations. Hera's jealousy was yet unmitigated; she could not bear the thought of the honor given to Callisto and her son Arcas, and she persuaded the god of the sea Poseidon never to allow their stars to bathe in his waters. For this reason the Great Bear and the Little Bear—some say that Arcas became Arctophylax or Arcturus—do not sink below the horizon. Star mythology of this kind is usually the product of the Hellenistic age when interest in astronomy ran high.

Such was the tragic romance of Zeus and Callisto. In antiquity, the Arcadians showed the tomb of Callisto on a hill, and on top of the hill was a sanctuary of Artemis Calliste (Fairest). Since the tomb of Callisto was connected with the temple of the goddess, it is clear that Callisto is only another form, a by-form, of Artemis Calliste. The symbol of Arcadian Artemis was the she-bear, the animal into which Callisto had been transformed. Artemis was also honored at Athens by young girls performing a bear-dance at the festival called the Brauronia. Arcas, who descended from Zeus, gave his name to the Arcadian people and became their eponymous hero. It is also of interest to note that a descendant of Arcas is the Arcadian Atalanta who, as we shall see in the episode concerning the Calydonian boar hunt, had all the characteristics of Arcadian Artemis.

The fate of Callisto's father was far more tragic than that of his daughters. Lycaon was a curious mixture of piety and impiety. Although he established the worship of Zeus Lycaeus in Arcadia, he was said to have been turned into a wolf for sacrificing a child on the altar of the god. Ovid adds other elements. When Zeus visited on earth and made his divinity known to mankind, Lycaon was so impious as to mock the prayers which the people offered the god. He went even further: not only did he try to murder Zeus, but he also tried to trick him into eating the flesh of a human hostage that he had boiled and roasted. The Olympian punished the king by turning him into a ravening and rapacious wolf. Lycaon's actions so disillusioned Zeus that he decided to destroy the entire race by a deluge. According to Ovid, this was the great flood which engulfed the earth and which only Deucalion and Pyrrha, the children of Prometheus and Epimetheus, survived.

The savagery of the remote regions of Arcadia became traditional in early antiquity. For example, when Plato wished to characterize the most degenerate form of government in the *Republic*, he cited the legend of the ritual of Zeus Lycaeus and how anyone who tasted a piece of human flesh mixed with the entrails of a sacrificial victim, would be changed into a wolf. This, he says, is the fate of the man whom the people put forward as their deliverer and protector, the tyrant who, once he has tasted blood becomes a human wolf. Yet it was not long before Arcadia became a symbol of nostalgic pastoralism, of the simple and quiet life, of rusticity and guileless shepherds. The pastoral as a literary form had its start in the third century B.C. with the *Idylls* of Theocritus, but it was Vergil who discovered Arcadia as the land of love, song, and rustic simplicity, as can be seen in the seventh and tenth of his *Eclogues* (39 B.C.). Jacopo Sannazaro (c. 1458–1530) was the Neapolitan rediscoverer of idealized country life; his *Arcadia* influenced the work of the Portuguese poet Jorge de Montemayor (c. 1521–1561) whose *Diana* introduced the pastoral to Spain, and by way of translation, to other European countries. Montemayor inspired, among many others, the *Arcadia* of Sir Philip Sidney (1554–1586), elements within the *Don Quixote* of Miguel de Cervantes (1547–1616) and Shakespeare's *The Two Gentlemen of Verona*.

Iphigeneia. Another mythological figure who had close connections with Artemis was Iphigeneia (or Iphigenia) who, like Callisto, may have been a by-form of the goddess. In mythology, however, she was the daughter of Agamemnon, commander of the Greek forces in the Trojan War, and his infamous wife Clytemnestra. Agamemnon had offended Artemis before the Greek ships had set sail for Troy. The offense is variously given: he had once killed a stag in the grove of Artemis; he had boasted that the goddess could not have done better with her bow; the year Iphigeneia was born, he had vowed that he would sacrifice to her the most beautiful thing the year might produce, but that he had afterwards refused to fulfill his vow. For one of these reasons, Artemis sent an adverse wind or becalmed the Greek fleet at Aulis and so prevented it from sailing to Troy. The expedition's seer Calchas declared that Artemis had been affronted and that she could be appeased only by the sacrifice of Iphigeneia. At first Agamemnon resisted the command, but he finally consented to having Diomedes and Odysseus fetch her to Aulis under the pretext that she was to be married to Achilles. At this point tradition divides: according to some, particularly in Aeschylus' *Agamemnon*, the sacrifice of Iphigeneia was duly carried out; according to others, Artemis interceded just at the point when Ipigeneia was being sacrificed. The goddess substituted a stag or a bear for her and carried her off to Tauris in the Crimea where she was made to serve the goddess as her priestess (fig. 31).

The subsequent adventures of Iphigeneia are told by Euripides in his drama *Iphigeneia in Tauris*. Among the barbaric Taurians, strangers and shipwrecked sailors were sacrificed to Artemis in a most savage manner. When Orestes, Iphigeneia's brother, and his comrade Pylades arrived in Tauris, they were captured and brought before Iphigeneia to be sacrificed. Orestes had come to Tauris on instructions to fetch the local cult-image of Artemis and bring it back to Greece so that he could rid himself of the Erinyes (Furies) plaguing him for the death of his mother. Iphigeneia, however, recognized her brother and fled with him and

Figure 31. The sacrifice of Iphigeneia at Aulis. *Roman wall painting, 63–79 A.D., in the House of the Tragic Poet, Pompeii. National Museum, Naples. (Alinari)*

the statue of Artemis. When they arrived in Greece, Iphigeneia carried the statue to the Attic town of Halae where she instituted the rites of the Taurian Artemis. However, instead of human sacrifice, a pretense of it was made by making a slight cut in a man's throat and drawing a drop of blood. Iphigeneia continued in the service of the goddess until her death.

Victorian poets were sympathetic toward Iphigeneia and played upon the pathos of her hapless plight at Aulis. Walter Savage Landor (1775–1864), in *Iphigeneia and Agamemnon*, presents us with a very noble Iphigeneia who says when she is about to be sacrificed: "O father! grieve no more: the ships can sail." Tennyson has Iphigeneia blaming Helen for her difficulties, her youth being blasted by a curse. From *A Dream of Fair Women:*

> I was cut off from hope in that sad place
>   Which men call'd Aulis in those iron years:
> My father held his hand upon his face;
>   I, blinded with my tears,
>
> Still strove to speak: my voice was thick with sighs
>   As in a dream. Dimly I could descry
> The stern black-bearded kings with wolfish eyes,
>   Waiting to see me die.
>
> The high masts flicker'd as they lay afloat;
>   The crowds, the temples, waver'd, and the shore;
> The bright death quiver'd at the victim's throat—
>   Touch'd—and I knew no more.

Iphigeneia was probably celebrated more in opera than in any other art form. More than twelve operas were written between 1699 and 1915 on either Iphigeneia in Aulis or Iphigeneia in Tauris, the most notable being the two by Christoph Willibald Gluck in 1774 and 1779.

Actaeon. The next story about Artemis takes us to Boeotia and the city of Thebes where we hear of the misfortunes of a young hunter, Actaeon, in an encounter with the goddess. Actaeon was the son of Aristaeus and Autonoë, and the grandson of Cadmus, the celebrated founder of Thebes. It was his fate to be torn to pieces, a fate that is usually reserved in mythology for an unwilling worshiper of the god Dionysus. Because of this we hear of him as a competitor of Zeus for the hand of Semele, the mother of Dionysus. To prevent him from marrying his aunt—she happened to be the sister of Actaeon's mother—Artemis had him torn apart by his hunting dogs. Other versions attribute Actaeon's punishment to other forms of presumption, such as wishing to marry Artemis or boasting that he was a better hunter than the goddess. However, the most famous account of the tragic end of Actaeon is found in Ovid's *Metamorphoses* where the story is told in lavish detail, including the names of almost all fifty dogs in Actaeon's hunting pack.

One day, Ovid's story goes, Diana and her attendant nymphs went to her sacred haunt, a secret sylvan nook surrounded by thick cypresses and pines. Within it there was a spring of crystal-clear water which flowed into a silvery pool. It was here that the goddess was accustomed to refresh herself and bathe after a long day's wearying hunt. Diana and her nymphs were frolicking in the bath when all of a sudden Actaeon, who had been idly wandering through the forest after a successful hunt, came upon the goddess and her attendants (fig. 32). When the nymphs saw

Figure 32. Titian. Artemis (Diana) and her nymphs surprised in their bath by Actaeon. *Painting, 1559. National Gallery, Edinburgh (Anderson-Mansell)*

him, they let out a scream and rushed toward the goddess to hide her with their bodies. But Diana was a head taller than the rest of them, and being taken by surprise, she blushed from head to toe. Instinctively, she reached for her bow and arrows, but they had been laid aside before she went into her bath. Instead, the goddess splashed water into the face of the intruding Actaeon, saying, "Now go and tell, if you can, that you have seen Diana in the nude." Immediately a pair of stag's horns sprouted from Actaeon's head, his neck grew longer, his ears became sharp-pointed, his hands turned to feet, his legs and his body were covered with a hairy spotted hide. Thus transformed, Actaeon was in a state of panic; he did not know where to go or where to hide. His hunting dogs, however, had no such hesitation; they pursued him over rocks and cliffs, through seemingly impassible mountain gorges. Finally they overtook him and began to tear him to pieces. Actaeon's hunting companions, not knowing what had taken place, cheered on the dogs and called for Actaeon to see the sport. He heard his friends, of course, but could do nothing to make them aware of what had happened. Diana was pitiless, and her anger was only appeased after the dogs had torn the life out of the young man who had intruded upon her bath.

Actaeon's offense lay in seeing the goddess unrobed and without her permission. In fact, to come upon any deity uninvited courts disaster. Hunters in Greece were therefore well advised to be careful when they approached woodland swimming holes or mountain grottos. If they came upon a mortal girl or a nymph, there was no great risk, but if they happened upon a goddess, it invited certain disaster. Witness also what happened to Tiresias, the great Theban prophet, when he chanced to come upon Athena as she was bathing. He was young at the time and on a hunting trip when it happened. Athena blinded him by sprinkling water into his eyes. Tiresias' mother begged the goddess to restore his sight, but the goddess could not rescind her action. She did, however, give Tiresias the power to understand the voices of the birds, that is, to have the power of prophecy, and she gave him a staff with which he could walk as safely as if he had his eyesight.

In general, groves and woodland pools have something eerie and awesome about them, a feeling that John Steinbeck was able to capture in his novel *To a God Unknown* (1933). A human being must be careful, very careful, how he approaches such places for fear that he may be treading upon sacred and tabooed ground. This feeling is best expressed in Vergil's *Aeneid*. As Evander points out to Aeneas the future site of Rome, he comes to the Capitol, one of the hills of Rome, which was then covered with forest undergrowth, "Even in those old days," says Vergil, "that spot held a sinister awe of its own, which used to inspire fear and alarm into the countryfolk who then as now trembled at the trees there and the rocks. Evander continues: 'This wooded hill with its leaf-clad crest is the habitation of some god, but it is not known which god he is.' "

*   *   *   *

Actaeon's transformation and punishment for violating a taboo did not go for nought. His story has had a long and durable history in literature and art. A popular theme among vase painters of antiquity, Actaeon's "passion" was also represented on a metope of Temple E at Selinus (460–450 B.C.). Diana and Actaeon were equally popular among Renaissance masters such as Titian (fig. 32) and Rembrandt. And when Ovid's story was moralized, Actaeon was seen as Jesus Christ. The rationalizers among Elizabethan writers could interpret Actaeon's hunting dogs as the young man's emotions, a figure of speech that Shakespeare appropriates for a speech by the love-torn Orsino in *Twelfth Night*:

> O, when my eyes did see Olivia first,
> Methought she purg'd the air of pestilence!
> That instant was I turn'd into a hart,
> And my desires, like fell and cruel hounds,
> E'er since pursued me.

In *Adonais*, Shelley's elegy for Keats, the Elizabethan metaphor is transferred from the heart to the intellect. Shelley sees in Keats—and especially in himself—the poet who, Actaeon-like, is able to gaze on Nature (Artemis) most intimate, only to be pursued and preyed upon by his thoughts (Actaeon's hounds).

> ... he, as I guess,
> Had gazed on Nature's naked loveliness,
> Actaeon-like, and now he fled astray
> With feeble steps o'er the world's wilderness,
> And his own thoughts, along that rugged way,
> Pursued, like raging hounds, their father and their prey.

For Oscar Wilde, Actaeon symbolized the scientist, the man of clay, who destroys by his discoveries the beauty inherent in nature. Wilde, the last Endymion, will look on the moon without a telescope! From *The Garden of Eros*:

> Methinks these new Actaeons boast too soon
>   That they have spied on beauty; what if we
> Have analysed the rainbow, robbed the moon
>   Of her most ancient, chastest mystery,
> Shall I, the last Endymion, lose all hope
> Because rude eyes peer at my mistress through a telescope!

Robinson Jeffers follows the same theme for his poem *Science*. Actaeon is a scientific man who has created giants, but because of his inward conflicts he cannot manage them; he can only use them for self-destruction:

> His mind forbodes his own destruction;
> Actaeon who saw the goddess naked among leaves and his
>   hounds tore him.
> A little knowledge, a pebble from the shingle,
> A drop from the oceans: who would have dreamed this
>   infinitely little too much?

Edith Wharton (1862–1937), in an epistolary poem, *Artemis to Actaeon*, takes another stance. She finds in Actaeon's fatal adventure—"fashioned for one hour's high use"—his one soaring and glorious experience, far transcending immortality or achievements to be looked back upon:

> For immortality is not to range
> Unlimited through vast Olympian days,
> Or sit in dull dominion over time;
> But this—to drink fate's utmost at a draught,
> Nor feel the wine grow stale upon the lip,
> To scale the summit of some soaring moment,

> Nor know the dulness of the long descent,
> To snatch the crown of life and seal it up
> Secure forever in the vaults of death!

And then T. S. Eliot's parody of these lines from *The Parliament of Bees* by John Day (fl. 1606):

> When of a sudden, listening, you shall hear,
> A noise of horns and hunting, which shall bring
> Actaeon to Diana in the spring,
> Where all shall see her naked skin . . .

In *The Waste Land*, that intricate tangle of the learned and the popular and the vulgar, Eliot transforms the idyllic lines of John Day into symbols of the ugliness of industrialized society. Hunting horns become automobile horns, Actaeon the repulsive Sweeney, and chaste Diana and her nymphs appear in Mrs. Porter and her daughter who bathe their feet in a solution of bicarbonate of soda:

> But at my back from time to time I hear
> The sound of horns and motors, which shall bring
> Sweeney to Mrs. Porter in the spring,
> O the moon shone bright on Mrs. Porter
> And on her daughter
> They wash their feet in soda water . . .

Niobe.   Artemis and Apollo were quick to act in concert in two instances in which their mother Leto was gravely offended. One offense involved the presumption of a mortal; the other, violence on the part of a giant offspring of Earth. Best known of the two stories is that of Niobe, wife of Amphion, king of Thebes, and the mother of many sons and daughters. She was the daughter of another mythical personage who had offended a god, Tantalus, and the sister of Pelops, the grandfather of two leading figures in the Trojan War, Agamemnon and Menelaus.

Niobe, in her pride and arrogance, boasted that she had given birth to many children whereas Leto had only Apollo and Artemis. Leto called upon her children to avenge this insult. They did so with obedience and dispatch (fig. 33); their arrows

Figure 33.   Artemis and Apollo slaying the children of Niobe. *Vase painting, mid fifth century B.C. Louvre. (Hirmer)*

killed every one of Niobe's children, leaving only a tearful Niobe who was changed into a pillar of stone still dripping with her tears. The story is as early as Homer. In the *Iliad*, Achilles invites the mourning Priam, who had come to ransom the body of his son Hector, to eat something. Achilles reminds Priam that Niobe had taken nourishment following her tragedy. From the prose translation of Samuel Butler (1835–1902):

> Even lovely Niobe had to think about eating, though her twelve children—six daughters and six lusty sons—had been all slain in her house. Apollo killed the sons with arrows from his silver bow, to punish Niobe, and Artemis slew the daughters, because Niobe had vaunted herself against Leto. She said Leto had borne two children only, whereas she had herself borne many—whereon the two killed the many. Nine days did they lie weltering and there was none to bury them, for the son of Cronus turned the people into stone; but on the tenth day the gods in heaven themselves buried them, and Niobe then took food, being worn out with weeping. They say that somewhere among the rocks on the mountain pastures of Sipylus, where the nymphs live that haunt the river Achelöus, there, they say, she lives in stone and still nurses the sorrows set upon her by the hand of heaven.

Later writers have modified and enlarged the simple story told by Homer. The number and the names of Niobe's children vary in different accounts. Homer gives the number of children as twelve; other writers speak of her as the mother of four, six, fourteen, eighteen, or even twenty children. According to Ovid, the sons were killed when they were engaged in gymnastic exercises, whereas the daughters met their fate during their brothers' funeral. For genealogical reasons—in order to keep the line of the king of Thebes alive—some writers allow one daughter and one son to survive. Yet another tradition has Niobe ask Zeus to change her into a stone which will always shed tears; and in later times people still believed that they could see the petrified figure of Niobe on Mount Sipylus in Lydia, just as Lot's wife can be seen as a pillar of salt on the shores of the Dead Sea.

Niobe soon became a stock figure of sorrow and bereavement. The theme was popular among vase painters of antiquity. In various museums in Europe there are Roman copies of a group of sculptured figures, originally from the fifth to fourth century B.C., of Niobe and her children (fig. 34). "Like Niobe, all tears" is Hamlet's description of his mother as she followed the body of her husband. Lord Byron transfers the figure of Niobe to the Church of Rome. In *The Age of Bronze* he says bitingly: "Lo! Mother Church, while all religion writhes,/Like Niobe, weeps o'er her offspring, Tithes." But in *Childe Harold*, he passionately cries:

> Oh Rome, my country! city of the soul!
> . . . .
> The Niobe of nations! there she stands,
> Childless and crownless, in her voiceless woe.

Tityus. The presumption and arrogance of Niobe was insignificant in comparison with the offense of the giant Tityus. He was the son of Earth (Gaea) and, as Homer tells us in the *Odyssey*, he tried to assault Leto as she was traveling to Delphi to visit her famous son. When Odysseus toured the Underworld, he found Tityus stretched out and pinned to the ground, his length covering nine acres, and a pair of vultures sat on either side of him plucking continuously at his liver. To

Figure 34. Niobe trying to shield her youngest daughter from the wrath of Apollo and Artemis. *Roman copy of a work of the fourth century B.C. Uffizi Gallery, Florence. (Alinari)*

Homer, Tityus—together with Tantalus and Sisyphus—is one of the trio of arch-sinners in the House of Hades. All three are eternally punished for having attempted in one way or another to poach upon the prerogatives of the gods. This is the first reference in Western literature to punishment in the afterlife, but it should be noted that it is punishment for offenses committed against the gods, not against man. In later traditions, we hear that Hera—jealous, of course, that Zeus had given Leto his affection—urged Tityus to commit his infamous deed. Tityus was quickly dispatched by the arrows of either Artemis or Apollo, or of both, and sent on his way to Tartarus. His tomb was shown near the spot where he supposedly attempted to assault Leto. However, such "tombs" likely were those of Bronze Age kings, like the great circle graves and beehive tombs at Mycenae. A later age, having forgotten the original inhabitants of these tombs, made them out to be the burial places of "giants."

The story of Tityus' punishment was taken by early rationalizers to symbolize not the eternal torment of the sinner in the afterlife, but rather the agonies of the living overwhelmed by sensual passions. Lucretius (94–55 B.C.), the Roman apologist and apostle of Epicurean philosophy, fervently denied the existence of Hell or Tartarus; in the punishment of Tityus and others, he saw a paradigm for those who create a hell for themselves on earth by the pursuit of their sensual pleasures. "Tityus is here among us," he says, "laid low by love, lacerated by birds of prey, eaten up by uneasy anxiety or torn by some other passion." The same theme was picked up in the Renaissance by Michelangelo. A drawing of Tityus' torment was presented by the artist to Tomasso Cavalieri in 1532 which bore upon Michelangelo's own doubts and anxieties concerning profane love. Then, because Prometheus and Tityus were subjected to similar penalties, the two often are confused. Rubens used Michelangelo's drawing of Tityus when he painted his Prometheus in 1613. A painting by Titian (c. 1549) in the Prado Museum is often cited and reproduced as his Prometheus, even though it is known that he painted a series of canvases on the trio of Homeric sinners plus one other, Ixion. The representation of a snake in a lower part of the painting makes it even more certain that the scene takes place in the lower regions and that it is Tityus who is being punished, not Prometheus.

Orion. Another giant whose fate was determined by Artemis was Orion. His mythical occupation as a hunter undoubtedly had much to do with his connection with the goddess of the hunt; but this was rather incidental since most of his life's story has to do with his prominence as a constellation. The asterism Orion is the most brilliant of all constellations with its two first-magnitude stars, Betelgeuse and Rigel, and the other bright stars that make up his belt and his sword. The Pleiades, another important star cluster among all people of ancient times, precede Orion, as if running from him. The mighty hunter is accompanied by the brilliant Dog Star, Sirius, and Procyon (the Foredog). As a constellation, Orion is known as early as Homer and Hesiod. In the *Iliad*, he is called "mighty Orion" and his constellation decorates the shield of Achilles. In the *Works and Days*, Hesiod summarizes the work of the farmer by the rising and the setting of Orion: at its appearance in June, the harvesting of grain; when in mid-heaven in September, the vintaging of the grapes; and when it begins to set at the end of October, the time for plowing the soil. In the *Odyssey*, Homer gives us fragments of Orion's mythological biography: he is finer than Otus and Ephialtes, the two giants who tried to mount heaven by piling Ossa on Olympus and Pelion on Ossa; Calypso, bitter at having to release her lover Odysseus, cites the death of Orion at Artemis' hands as one of the instances in which gods were unfair toward those deities who had love affairs with mortals. Later accounts piece together two traditions: one from the wine-producing island of Chios in the Aegean, the other from Boeotia.

Orion was the son of Poseidon and Euryale, and as the child of the sea-god, he was given the power of walking across the deepest waters. His first wife was Side (Pomegranate) whom Hera sent to Hades for her presumption to compare her beauty with that of the goddess—a possible mythical explanation for the ripening and picking of the pomegranate in the season when Orion is visible in the evening sky. Orion then went to Chios where he fell in love with Merope, the daughter of Oenopion (Wineface), king of the island. The great hunter cleared the island of wild animals and brought the spoils of the chase to Merope. But when he asked for her hand in marriage, Oenopion kept putting him off until one day Orion got drunk and tried to force his attentions on the king's daughter. Oenopion, incensed by his behavior, called upon the god of the vine Dionysus to help him avenge the insult. Satyrs caused Orion to fall into a deep sleep, thereby giving Oenopion the opportunity to blind him and cast him out on the seashore. Orion, instructed by an oracle, made his way to Hephaestus' workshop on the island of Lemnos where the god of craftsmen took pity on him and gave him a young helper to act as his guide in seeking out the home of the sun-god. With the young man on his shoulder, Orion traveled eastward until he reached the source of the sun's rays. His vision was restored by staring into the sun. It was in the east that the goddess of dawn Eos (Roman Aurora) fell in love with him and carried him off to an island where she lived with him until, as Homer tells us, the gods decreed that Artemis kill him with one of her arrows. Orion's relationship with Eos produced Keats' line in the *Endymion*: "blind Orion longing for the morn."

As to Orion's death, there are a number of different versions. Some say that he presumed to challenge Artemis in the sport of throwing the discus; or that he made love to one of Artemis' nymphs and that she killed him or sent a monster scorpion to sting him to death. The latter story is an explanation of why Orion's constellation sets as Scorpio rises into the sky. Yet another version tells us that Artemis fell so madly in love with Orion that she forgot her duties and displeased her brother. One day, Apollo saw Orion as he waded through the sea with his head just above the water. Apollo pointed out the black object to his sister and said that she could not hit it. Artemis let fly one of her unerring arrows which killed him. The archer-goddess placed Orion among the stars where he appears as a giant with a belt, sword, lion's skin, and club. She gave him Sirius the Dog Star as his hunting dog, "fierce Orions hound" is what Spenser calls him in the *Faerie Queene*. And T. S. Eliot in *Sweeney among the Nightingales*: "Gloomy Orion and the Dog/Are veiled; and hushed the shrunken seas."

The Boeotian version, mostly from the time of Ovid and Hyginus, tells us how Orion was named and how he pursued the Pleiades. Apart from a rather flippant story of how he acquired his name from a far-fetched etymology or pun, the tale contains serious mythological elements involving the visit of stranger-gods, a hero born from the liquid of the gods, and birth from the earth. His father Hyrieus, a Boeotian hero, was childless but a man of upstanding character. One day he was visited by three gods, Zeus, Poseidon, and Hermes, who posed as strangers in the land. Hyrieus received them so hospitably that they granted him any wish he might have. He asked for a son. The gods fulfilled his desire in a most unique way: they took an oxhide, urinated on it, and then instructed Hyrieus to bury the hide for ten months. He did so, and the earth gave birth to his son who was first named Urion to commemorate the act of the gods (*ourein* in Greek); the child's name was later changed to Orion.

When Orion grew to manhood, Pleione and her daughters became an object of his passion. She was the wife of Atlas and the mother of seven daughters who were called collectively the Pleiades. Pursued by Orion as they traveled through Boeotia, Pleione and her daughters fled before the mighty hunter. Their prayers reached the ears of Zeus who metamorphosed them into doves and then placed them in the heavens as the star-cluster, the Pleiades, where they can still be seen being pursued by the constellation Orion. Six of the stars are visible to the naked eye; the seventh is dim or invisible because, as the story goes, one of the Pleiades, Electra, is weeping for the downfall of Troy, the city founded by her son Dardanus. Others say that the star is Merope who is blushing because of all the sisters, she alone had a mortal for a husband. This phenomenon in the Pleiades accounts for Lord Byron's line: "Like the lost Pleiad seen no more below."

The rising of the Pleiades in spring was the signal for the reopening of navigation, and early Greek sailors guided their ships by sighting this cluster of stars. Hence there is some plausibility in deriving the names of Pleione and the Pleiades from the Greek word *plein*, to sail. In the third century B.C. a group of seven Alexandrian poets took the name of the constellation and called themselves the Pleiad or the Tragic Pleiad. In the latter part of the sixteenth century, seven French poets—Pierre de Ronsard (1524–1585) was their leading light—formed their own *Pléiade* in the interest of improving French poetry through experimentation, originality, and inspiration by the writers of antiquity.

Figure 35. Artemis Polymastos (Diana of Ephesus). *Roman copy of the third century A.D. National Museum, Naples. (Alinari)*

Artemis at Ephesus. When Artemis was taken overseas by colonizing Greeks, it was possible for her Hellenic character to undergo a startling change. At Ephesus, an Ionian city on the coast of Asia Minor, her cult was more Near Eastern than Greek. Here she was revered and represented as Artemis Polymastos, Many-breasted Artemis, a mother-goddess of the Oriental type (fig. 35). A legend was told that the city had been founded by an Athenian prince about 900 B.C. when the Dorian invasions forced the earlier Hellenic populations to migrate to the western coast of what today is Turkey. Intermarriage with the local population produced not only a hybrid ethnic group, but also a hybrid cult of Artemis. The goddess was worshiped in a great temple at Ephesus which later became known as one of the Seven Wonders of the World. Not only was Artemis held in great veneration here, but a small sacred stone as well. This stone was believed to have fallen from Zeus in heaven and was known as the *diopetes*, "Zeus-fallen." We have already seen two such sacred stones: one which Cronus was supposed to have swallowed in place of Zeus; the other , the *omphalos* or navel-stone within the temple of Apollo at Delphi. Likewise reputed to have fallen from heaven was the Palladium, a statue of Pallas on which the safety of Troy was said to depend.

The missionary activities of Paul of Tarsus at Ephesus brought him into conflict with the artisans whose livelihood depended on selling representations of the goddess. In *Acts* we hear of Artemis, her temple and the *diopetes*—the King James version uses Roman names for the Greek—when Demetrius the silversmith harangues his fellow-craftsmen:

> So that not only this our craft is in danger to be set at nought; but also that the temple of the great goddess Diana should be despised and her magnificence should be destroyed, whom all Asia and the world worshippeth.

And when they heard these sayings, they were full of wrath, and cried out saying, Great is Diana of the Ephesians.

After a considerable uproar, a certain Alexander addressed the people of the city, saying:

> Ye men of Ephesus, what man is there that knoweth not how that the city of the Ephesians is a worshipper of the great goddess Diana, and of the image which fell down from Jupiter?

The cult of this strange goddess then traveled to Southern France when Greek colonists from Asia Minor founded (c. 600 B.C.) the city of Massilia, or Marseilles as it is known today. From Massilia the cult made its way to the Aventine hill of Rome where the Greek geographer Strabo (63 B.C.–A.D. 21) tells us that the temple of Diana had a statue of the Ephesian type.

Arethusa. Artemis was also exported to Syracuse in Sicily when that city was founded by Greek colonists at a very early date (c. 734 B.C.). There she was known as Artemis Arethusa, Arethusa being the name of several springs in Greece—one is named in the *Odyssey* on the island of Ithaca—whose waters well to the surface from underground sources. Such springs often arise from the pressure created by rivers, such as the Alpheus in Elis, which plunge into subterranean passages and do not reappear for considerable distances. From very early times, as early as the poets Pindar and Ibycus, the story was told that the waters of the river Alpheus passed unmixed under the sea and rose as the spring of Arethusa in Syracuse. The fabled course of the Alpheus River undoubtedly influenced the description of the river Alph in the *Kubla Khan* of Samuel Taylor Coleridege (1772–1834):

> In Xanadu did Kubla Khan
> A stately pleasure-dome decree:
> Where Alph, the sacred river, ran
> Through caverns measureless to man,
> Down to a sunless sea.

To account for the spring that surfaced on an island in the harbor of Syracuse and to link the Greek colony with its Hellenic homeland—Elis in the northwest of the Peloponnese had a spring called Arethusa—a highly romanticized episode was created under the name of Arethusa. She was a woodland nymph, a huntress in the retinue of Artemis. One day, after a tiring and heated hunt, Arethusa undressed and refreshed herself with a swim in the waters of the Alpheus river. The god of the river soon felt the presence of the nymph and by a murmuring of his waters made known his amatory interest in the swimmer. Arethusa became terrified and fled naked before the pursuing god who attempted to embrace her. When she felt herself tiring and could sense the hot breath of the god on her back, she called upon Artemis for help. The goddess clothed the nymph in a cloud of mist and carried her off to Ortygia, an island in the harbor of Syracuse. There the goddess split the earth and transformed Arethusa into a spring which gushed forth from the earth. Alpheus did not give up the chase. He changed from his human form into watery shape and plunged underneath the earth, made his way under the sea, and then arose on Ortygia where he mingled his waters with those of Arethusa. It was believed, as the Greek geographer Strabo tells us, that a cup thrown into the Alpheus would make its reappearance in the spring of Arethusa in Ortygia.

Shelley and Keats were attracted to the myth of Arethusa. Shelley's *Arethusa* is a fanciful retelling of the story with many liberties taken with the details of the ancient myth. Lyricism, pastoral ambience, and escapism are what Shelley presents us with in this poem, as can be seen even in the first stanza:

> Arethusa arose
> From her couch of snows
> In the Acroceraunian mountains,—
> From cloud and from crag,
> With many a jag,
> Shepherding her bright fountains.
> She leapt down the rocks,
> With her rainbow locks
> Streaming among the streams;—
> Her steps paved with green
> The downward ravine
> Which slopes to the western gleams:
> And gliding and springing
> She went, ever singing,
> In murmurs as soft as sleep;
> The earth seemed to love her,
> And Heaven smiled above her,
> As she lingered towards the deep.

Keats, on the other hand, questing for definitions of ideal beauty and ideal love in the mythical landscapes of his *Endymion*, comes upon a tormented Alpheus, passionately pleading with Arethusa for her love. The scene is one of sensuous earthly passion. Arethusa is fearful of Diana and holds off the river-god at arm's length. Alpheus pleads painfully:

> O that I
> Were rippling round her dainty fairness now,
> Circling about her waist, and striving how
> To entice her to a dive! then stealing in
> Between her luscious lips and eyelids thin.
> O that her shining hair was in the sun,
> And I distilling from it thence to run
> In amorous rillets down her shrinking form!
> To linger on her lilly shoulders, warm
> Between her kissing breasts, and every charm
> Touch raptur'd!—See how painfully I flow.

Endymion. As lunar characteristics became firmly attached to Artemis in late antiquity, her name or her epithets became interchangeable with those of the goddess of the moon, Selene. Hence in the myth of Endymion and Selene it is not at all unusual to find Artemis, Diana, Phoebe, Cynthia, or Luna (Moon) substituted for the name of moon-goddess. Endymion was a handsome young man who gained a renowned reputation by the perpetual sleep in which he spent his life. One tradition about Endymion takes us to Elis; another to Caria in Asia Minor. At Elis he is said to have been a king and the father of three children who gave their names to people of various districts in Greece: Aetolus to the Aetolians, Paeon to the Paeonians, and Epeius to the *Epeioi* or Epeans. Endymion, however, was especially beloved by Selene by whom he had fifty daughters. Some scholars see in these fifty daughters the fifty lunar months that comprised the four-year period of an Olympiad, the interval between games at Olympia in Elis. As for Endymion's three sons, the question of who would succeed him as king was solved by a race at Olympia. The three sons competed and the race was won by Epeius who succeeded to the kingdom and gave his name to the people of Elis, the Epeans.

The Carian tradition holds that Endymion came from Elis to Mount Latmus in Caria where his occupation is variously given as a king, shepherd, or hunter. According to the popular account, Selene came upon the handsome youth as he slept in a cave on Mount Latmos and fell in love with him. She kissed him and watched over him as he slept. Selene's attraction to Endymion caused her to forget her lunar obligations; more and more frequently she was absent from her station in the heavens, and toward morning she was even paler and more tired out from her vigil. When Zeus discovered the cause of Selene's strange behavior, he gave Endymion the choice between death in any way he preferred or perpetual sleep together with eternal youth. Endymion opted for immortality through eternal sleep and everlasting youth. He fell asleep in his cave on Mount Latmus but he still received nocturnal visits from the goddess of the moon. Other versions have it that Endymion was punished by Zeus for having dared to fall in love with Hera when he was received among the gods of Olympus; or that Selene, so overwhelmed by his good looks, sent him into a deep sleep so that she might be able to kiss him without being observed. In later times, Endymion's tomb was shown in a cave on Mount Latmus; at Elis, however, he was said to have been buried at Olympia.

*   *   *   *

The myth of Endymion has had a long and varied history since its inception. During the Renaissance, representations of Diana and Endymion were painted by Tintoretto (c. 1575–1580), Van Dyck (c. 1626), and Rubens (c. 1636). Michael Drayton wrote his *Endimion and Phoebe* in 1595, a Platonized version of the myth in which Diana was vested with all the attributes of divine love who bestows upon her lover gifts not of the flesh but of the spirit. In 1606 he rewrote the story as *The Man in the Moone*. Both versions influenced Keats in varying degrees when he undertook his epic *Endymion*, the poet's own confession of his internal struggles and conflicting desires. Diana was his dream-goddess, his symbol of beauty in all its manifestations, of the real and ideal. Sir Francis Bacon saw in the myth of Endymion a concealed meaning, an explanation for the varied behavior of rulers. Other poets and writers similarly allegorized, Platonized, or simply romanticized the story of Endymion's relationship with the goddess of the moon. William Basse, chiefly known for his epitaph on Shakespeare, attributes the notion of the man in the moon to the story of Endymion. From his *Urania* (c. 1606):

> For when Endymion once in Latmos slept
> The Moone (some say) came downe and kis'd him there,
> Erronious Fame reports that she hath kept
> Him ever since within her spotlesse Sphere.
> And of this falshood, so profusely blowne,
> The generall tale of Man i' the' Moone is growne.

In Shakespeare's *The Merchant of Venice*, Portia describes the moonless night: "The moon sleeps with Endymion,/And would not be awak'd."

Matthew Arnold, disillusioned with love, rushes to solitude and loneliness; he identifies not with Endymion but with Luna the moon. He writes in *To Marguerite*:

> Back! with the conscious thrill of shame
> Which Luna felt, that summer-night,
> Flash through her pure immortal frame,
> When she forsook the starry height
> To hang over Endymion's sleep
> Upon the pine-grown Latmian steep.
>
> Yet she, chaste queen, had never proved
> How vain a thing is mortal love,
> Wandering in Heaven, far removed.
> But thou hast long had place to prove
> This truth—to prove, and make thine own:
> 'Thou has been, shalt be, art, alone.'

Without symbolic value, but with eloquence and lyrical richness, Edna St. Vincent Millay retells the myth of Endymion for a twentieth-century audience. From Sonnet XXVII of *Fatal Interview*:

> Moon, that against the lintel of the west
> Your forehead lean until the gate be swung,
> Longing to leave the world and be at rest,
> Being worn with faring and no longer young,
> Do you recall at all the Carian hill
> Where worn with loving, loving late you lay,
> Halting the sun because you lingered still,
> While wondering candles lit the Carian day?
> Ah, if indeed this memory to your mind
> Recall some sweet employment, pity me,
> That with the dawn must leave my love behind,
> That even now the dawn's dim herald see!
> I charge you, goddess, in the name of one
> You loved as well: endure, hold off the sun.

And from the final sonnet of *Fatal Interview*:

> Oh, sleep forever in the Latmian cave,
> Mortal Endymion, darling of the Moon!
> Her silver garments by the senseless wave
> Shouldered and dropped and on the shingle strewn,
> Her fluttering hand against her forehead pressed,
> Her scattered looks that trouble all the sky,
> Her rapid footsteps running down the west—
> Of all her altered state, oblivious lie!
> Whom earthen you, by deathless lips adored,
> Wild-eyed and stammering to the grasses thrust,
> And deep into her crystal body poured
> The hot and sorrowful sweetness of the dust:
> Whereof she wanders mad, being all unfit
> For mortal love, that might not die of it.

As an epilogue, it is not inappropriate to cite Ben Jonson's (1573–1637) hymn to Diana from *Cynthia's Revels*:

> Queen and Huntress, chaste and fair,
>   Now the sun is laid to sleep,
> Seated in thy silver chair,
>   State in wonted manner keep:
>   Hesperus entreats thy light,
>   Goddess excellently bright.
>
> Earth, let not thy envious shade
>   Dare itself to interpose;
> Cynthia's shining orb was made
>   Heaven to clear when day did close:
>   Bless us then with wishèd sight,
>   Goddess excellently bright.
>
> Lay thy bow of pearl apart,
>   And thy crystal-shining quiver;
> Give unto the flying hart
>   Space to breathe, how short soever:
>   Thou that mak'st a day of night,
>   Goddess excellently bright.

8. Athena (Minerva)

Athena, the goddess who sprang fully-armed from the head of Zeus with a mighty war shout, was the daughter of Zeus and Metis (fig. 14). The unusual way in which she came into the world and the significance of Zeus swallowing Metis when she was pregnant with the goddess, have been treated in connection with Hesiod's *Theogony*. Homer, who has no less respect for the goddess than Hesiod, but who generally has a distaste for the bizarre and the irrational, has nothing to say about her mother or the way in which she was born. On the island of Crete the story was told that Athena came forth from a cloud which Zeus burst with a bolt of lightning. In other versions she is said to have been the daughter of the river Triton, an apparent attempt to account for her title Tritogeneia (Water?-born). The first two syllables of this epithet have some connection with water as can be deduced from the names of the nymph Amphitrite, the spouse of the sea-god Poseidon, and her son Triton. Wherever there was a river or lake by the name of Triton, as in Libya and Boeotia, the inhabitants claimed that Athena was born there. Among the Romans she was identified with Minerva, their goddess of handicrafts, an important deity in their triad of divinities in which she appears with Jupiter and Juno.

As in the case of many second-generation Olympians, Athena's origins are veiled by the uncertainties of the Bronze Age civilizations of the Minoans and the early Greeks. However, like her stepsister Artemis, Athena can be traced to pre-Hellenic forms. And like Artemis she was dedicated to celibacy and chastity; if she ever had been associated with a male partner, he has been long since faded out of the mythological picture. Athena did, however, preserve and maintain the duties prominent among Minoan-Myceaean deities: protection and fertility, but protection seems to have been her main sphere of activity. In the manner of Minoan deities she occasionally takes the form of a bird, as in the *Odyssey* where she changes herself into a sea-eagle. Her favorite theriomorphic form is the owl, the denizen of the rocky crevices of hill-top citadels. The Mycenaeans, the successors to the Minoans, seem to have represented their protective or tutelary divinity as a shield-goddess, and it was from this form that Athena's later appearance as a fully-armed goddess most likely descended. As the tutelary goddess of a ruling prince of early times, she dwelt in his house on a citadel or acropolis where she exercised her influence not only in warfare but in all the activities of the royal household. An echo of this relationship can be heard in the *Odyssey* where Homer has Athena return to the wide streets of Athens and enter the house of Erechtheus, the ruler of the city. Later, when the temple of the goddess replaced the royal palace on the citadel, as archaeological investigation has shown, she receives rulers and other worshipers in the house that she formerly shared with the ruling prince.

When Athena protected the interests of early princes, her shrine was deep within the royal palace and her cult-statue had special significance for the city which she protected. The image of the goddess was called the Palladium, the name taken from an epithet of Athena, Pallas. The meaning of Pallas is probably related to the Greek word for "young girl" or "maiden," but in mythology Athena is said to have acquired the name from Pallas, one of the giants whom she killed during the battle between the Olympians and the Giants. Another account has it that Pallas was the daughter of Triton and a friend of Athena. The goddess accidentally killed her and made the Palladium in commemoration of her friend. It is said that Zeus threw down the Palladium from heaven when Dardanus was founding the city of Troy—note the comparison with the *omphalos* at Delphi and the *diopetes* in the Temple of Artemis at Ephesus. From that time the Palladium became a pledge or talisman for the safety of the city. During the Trojan War, the image had to be removed from the city before it could fall. The assignment to remove this life-token of the city was given to Odysseus and Diomedes who made their way to the citadel and stole the image from the temple of Athena (fig. 93). Later, when it became necessary to link the legendary past of Troy with Rome, myth-makers invented a second Palladium which was taken to Italy by Aeneas and deposited in the temple of Vesta at Rome. Many cities in Greece and Italy laid claim to possessing the original and genuine Trojan Palladium.

Matthew Arnold transfers the symbol of the Palladium to the soul where it serves as the life token of the individual. His poem is appropriately entitled *Palladium*:

> Set where the upper streams of Simois flow
> Was the Palladium, high 'mid rock and wood;
> And Hector was in Ilium, far below,
> And fought, and saw it not—but there it stood!
>
> It stood, and sun and moonshine rain'd their light
> On the pure columns of its glen-built hall.
> Backward and forward roll'd the waves of fight
> Round Troy—but while this stood, Troy could not fall.
> . . . .
> Still doth the soul, from its lone fastness high,
> Upon our life a ruling effluence send.
> And when it fails, fight as we will, we die;
> And while it lasts, we cannot wholly end.

Two other aspects of Bronze Age Greece seem to have survived in the worship and mythology of Athena: the snake-goddess and the tree-goddess. From very early times the snake was viewed as the protector of the household, and in Minoan domestic shrines images of snake-goddesses or snake-priestesses were uncovered by archaeologists. The snake in association with Athena continued to be revered well into historical times. The historian Herodotus reports that the "house-protect-ing snake" left Athena's temple on the Acropolis when the Persians approached the city (480 B.C.). This snake was said to have lived in the temple of the goddess and to have been fed a honey-cake once a month. And when the renowned Athenian sculptor Phidias (or Pheidias) portrayed the goddess as Athena Parthenos, he carved a snake wreathed around her shield. This colossal cult-image, made of ivory overlaid with gold, was housed in Athena's great temple, the Parthenon, after its completion in 432 B.C. As for Athena's connection with tree-goddesses of early times, she is said to have created the olive tree when she contested with Poseidon for possession of Attica. She struck the rocky and bare soil of the Acropolis with her spear, and there suddenly sprang into being the tree for which Athens became famous. Herodotus also reports that when the Persians burned the temples on the Acropolis, the sacred olive tree which grew by Athena's temple put forth a shoot a yard long in one night.

In Homer, Athena appears in the two roles for which she is best known: a protec-tress of heroes and a goddess of good counsel. Odysseus is her special favorite since he is the embodiment of that special kind of wisdom that Homer idealizes in the *Odyssey*. He is inventive, tricky, deceptive, and cunning, qualities which Athena herself admits to possess. In mythology at large, Athena will be found at the side of such heroes as Heracles, Perseus, and Jason, giving them her advice, protection, and guidance. Neither did Homer pass over Athena's skill in domestic arts and in-dustries. In the *Iliad*, when Hera decides to vamp her own husband so as to distract his attention from the field of battle, she decks herself out in a fine, new dress which Athena, *couturiére* of the Olympians, had made with her own hands. And when Hesiod recounts the creation of the first woman on earth, Pandora, it is Athena whom Zeus calls upon to dress her and to teach her the art of needlework and weaving.

Arachne. In this area of her special competence, a story is told of a mortal challenger, a Lydian girl by the name of Arachne. She was the daughter of Idmon, a famous dyer of cloth, and she had become so skilled in the art of weaving and embroidery that even the nymphs would leave their usual haunts to view her work. When a high compliment was paid to Arachne, that Athena herself must have taught her, she denied it and dared the goddess to compete with her. Athena heard the challenge and immediately appeared before Arachne in the disguise of an old woman. She advised the younger girl to take on a mortal challenger and to ask for-giveness of the goddess. Arachne rudely rejected the advice and repeated her challenge. Athena dropped her disguise and the contest began. Spenser, borrowing liberally from Ovid's version of the myth, describes the confrontation between goddess and mortal in the *Muiopotmos*:

> For the Tritonian Goddesses having hard
> Her blazed fame, which all the world had fil'd,
> Came downe to prove the truth, and due reward

> For her prais-worthie workmanship to yeild
> But the presumptuous Damzel rashly dar'd
> The Goddesse selfe to chalenge to the field,
> And to compare with her in curious skill
> Of workes with loome, with needle, and with quill.
> Minerva did the chalenge not refuse,
> But deign'd with her the paragon to make:
> So to their worke they sit, and each doth chuse
> What storie she will for her tapet take.

For her main theme Athena took her contest with Poseidon for possession of Attica; she represented the twelve Olympians in their majesty and might as part of her design, and in the four corners of the web she portrayed punishments meted out by the gods to presumptive mortals. Arachne, unafraid, produced a piece of cloth on which she had woven the illicit and deceitful amours of the gods. Athena could find no flaw in Arachne's weaving, but incensed at her theme she tore the work to pieces and drove Arachne to hang herself. The goddess loosened the rope and saved the young girl's life, but she transformed her into a spider, condemned forever to hang on a thread and to spin her web. And thus, as told by Ovid in the *Metamorphoses*, we have an explanation of the origin of the spider—which belongs to the order of arachnids—and of its ability to spin webs. This aetiological motif is combined with that of the presumptive mortal who is punished for daring to compete with a divinity and for being so foolhardy as to illustrate the illicit loves of the gods.

Athena at Athens. Athena was especially venerated in the city which was her namesake, and as Athens developed into a kind of industrial center of the Aegean world, so did Athena's prominence as a patroness of arts and crafts. She was not only concerned with spinning and weaving, as might be expected of a goddess of women's work, but her influence extended to all kinds of trades and she was worshiped or regarded as a teacher of such artisans as potters and goldsmiths. In connection with these crafts she earned the title of *Ergane*, "the workwoman." Clearly, her influence among craftsmen overlapped that of Hephaestus who was equally held in high regard by the artisans in Athens. Therefore, when the Athenians sought to produce an indigenous child from whom they could trace their ancestry, the two divinities of arts and crafts were brought into an amatory relationship. But how could the problem of Athena's commitment to celibacy be overcome? The story was told that Hephaestus announced his wish to marry the goddess. Zeus consented to the arrangement but allowed Athena to reject Hephaestus' advances. When Hephaestus tried to embrace the goddess, she resisted. Hephaestus' seed fell on the earth which thus became impregnated and in due time produced a boy. Athena took charge of the child, half-man and half-serpent, when Earth refused to have anything to do with her extraordinary son. Athena placed him in a chest and gave it to the daughters of Cecrops—Cecrops being the mythical founder of Athens after having come from Egypt—with instructions not to open it. They disobeyed, and at the sight of the serpentine child, they became terrified and leaped off the Acropolis and died. The child was called Erichthonius, "child of the earth" or the equivalent of "native son." Erichthonius—some confuse him with Erectheus or they may possibly be the same—took up his residence in the Erectheum, the oldest temple on the Acropolis, and from this time on it was said that serpents were kept in the temple in his honor. From this child of native Athenian soil sprang the line of legendary kings of Athens. Erichthonius is also said to have instituted in honor of his foster-mother, the Panathenaea, the festival in which the Athenians took such great pride. Later its sacred procession was represented on the frieze of the Parthenon.

Athena as the Goddess of War. As Athena extended her influence into every phase of urban life she became known as the protectress of the city, the inventor of instruments necessary and useful for the maintenance of civilized life, the symbol of wisdom and of the intellect. She was characterized by epithets and titles which expressed all these qualities, as for example: Polias (Guardian of the City), Paeonia (Healer), Hygieia (Health), Pronoia (Forethought), Boulaea (Councilor), Soteira (Savior), Promachos (Front-line, Champion), Nike (Victory), Xenia (Hospitable), Agoraea (Of the Market Place), and Mechanitis (Inventive). But it was in connection with her character as a goddess of war that she was best known and most often represented. Unlike the god of war Ares, who was the personification of the frenzy of battle or the warlike spirit, Athena represented the ordered battle which saves the city, the goddess of courage combined with prudent and intelligent tactics. In art, therefore, she is often portrayed as fully-armed, wearing a helmet or carrying it in her hand, protected by her aegis, a kind of breastplate which commonly is decorated with the head of the Gorgon Medusa. Perseus is said to have given it to his patroness after his encounter with the frightful and deadly maiden (fig. 36). The

Figure 36. Athena Promachos. Her right hand held a spear; left hand holds her aegis with its Medusa head and border of snakes. *National Museum, Naples, (Alinari)*

most ideal representation of Athena as the goddess of war, and one which was to influence generations of artists, was the Athena Parthenos of Phidias. This celebrated colossal statue of the goddess in ivory and gold was housed in the Parthenon. She was represented in a standing position, holding a Nike (Victory) in her left hand, a spear in her right, her shield at her feet, and the snake appearing from its inner side.

When Byron attacked Lord Elgin for having removed the sculptured decorations from the Parthenon to the British Museum between 1801 and 1803, he pictured Phidias' Athena appearing before him to complain bitterly of the plundering of her temple. From Byron's *The Curse of Minerva:*

> Long had I mused, and treasured every trace
> The wreck of Greece recorded of her race,
> When lo! a giant form before me strode,
> And Pallas hail'd me in her own abode!
>
> Yes, 't was Minerva's self; but, ah! how changed
> Since o'er the Dardan field in arms she ranged!
> Not such as first, by her divine command,
> Her form appear'd from Phidias' plastic hand:
> Gone were the terrors of her awful brow,
> Her idle aegis bore no Gorgon now;
> Her helm was dinted, and the broken lance
> Seem'd weak and shaftless e'en to mortal glance;
> The olive branch, which still she deign'd to clasp,
> Shrunk from her touch and wither'd in her grasp;
> And, ah! though still the brightest of the sky,
> Celestial tears bedimm'd her large blue eye;
> Round the rent casque her owlet circled slow,
> And mourn'd his mistress with a shriek of woe!

Byron attacks Lord Elgin again the second canto of *Childe Harold*, and prefaces it, with an elegy for the passed greatness of Athens:

> Come, blue-eyed maid of heaven! —but thou, alas!
> Didst never yet one mortal song inspire—
> Goddess of Wisdom! here thy temple was
> And is, despite of war and wasting fire,
> And years that bade thy worship to expire:
> But worse than steel, and flame, and ages slow,
> Is the dread sceptre and dominion dire
> Of men who never felt the sacred glow
> That thoughts of thee and thine on polish'd breasts bestow.
>
> Ancient of days! august Athena! where
> Where are thy men of might? thy grand in soul?
> Gone—glimmering through the dream of things that were:
> First in the race that led to Glory's goal,
> They won, and pass'd away—is this the whole?

A schoolboy's tale, the wonder of an hour!
The warrior's weapon and the sophist's stole
Are sought in vain, and o'er each mouldering tower,
Dim with the mist of years, gray flits the shade of power.

9. Hephaestus (Vulcan)

Of all the blessed and happy gods that were said to live on Mount Olympus, Hephaestus was probably the least blessed and the least happy. His mythological biography can easily confirm this: deformed from birth, unsure of his parentage, buffeted about by both his mother and father, unlucky in love, and fated never to be exalted in religion nor in literature with ethical and cultural virtues. By way of compensation, if such it can be called, Hephaestus could never have suffered from an identity-crisis or from ambivalent feelings as to his place in the divine universe: in historical times he was clearly the god of craftsmen and the god of the fire of the forge. The brief Homeric hymn honoring the god—possibly offered when his temple, the Hephaesteum, was built at Athens between 450 and 440 B.C.—places him in a tandem relationship with Athena, but with his specialty clearly defined:

> Sing, clear-voiced Muse, of Hephaestus famed for his skill. With bright-eyed Athena he taught men glorious crafts throughout the world,—men who before used to dwell in caves in the mountains like wild beasts. But now that they have learned crafts through Hephaestus the famed worker, easily they live a peaceful life in their own houses the whole year round. Be gracious, Hephaestus, and grant me success and prosperity!

Crafts, however, were not Hephaestus' original concern. A study of the distribution of his cult indicates that the god began his career as an Asian deity of volcanic fire, possibly in Anatolian Lycia, and then traveled to the volcanic island of Lemnos in the Aegean where he was particularly loved and revered. From there his cult spread to Greece and to various regions colonized by Greek settlers. Some scholars believe that at Athens, he replaced Prometheus as a god of fire. The original volcanic nature of Hephaestus can best be recognized in his Roman counterpart, Vulcan or Volcanus, who gave his name not only to a physical phenomenon, the volcano, but also to the process for treating rubber and its compounds, vulcanization. Among the Romans, Vulcan was also called Mulciber (Soother) and Quietus (Quiet One), and they married him off to Mater Stata (Steady Mother). The hopeful intention of his worshipers in appealing to him by these names was, of course, to seek his cooperation in keeping the powerful and destructive forces of the volcano under control. His marriage to Mater Stata was likewise expected to have a stabilizing influence upon their unpredictable god.

Although Roman religion kept the early character of Vulcan as a god of destructive volcanic fire in view, the Greeks virtually had no reminiscence of their deity serving in this capacity. They did, however, locate Hephaestus' workshop underneath various volcanos; but this idea might easily have arisen in popular imagination from seeing smoke rising from the volcanic peaks and explaining it as the smoke coming from the chimney of Hephaestus' forge. From very early times, then, the Greeks saw in Hephaestus their divine craftsman, the patron-deity of metal-workers and artisans of all kinds. To Hesiod he is skilled in crafts beyond all other Olympians, and when Zeus wished to create a bane to mankind, he assigned Hephaestus the task of moulding a woman out of earth and water. In the *Odyssey*, the hero of the epic, coming face to face with Penelope after his long ordeal, has his appearance altered and enhanced by Athena; the work of the goddess is compared to that of an artisan who is instructed in the secrets of his art by Athena and Hephaestus and painstakingly puts a beautiful finish to his work by overlaying silver with gold. Hephaestus continued to be held in high regard in the ancient world as long as the social class of the artisans maintained an esteemed position in the eyes of the public; but when the status of the craftsman began to sink during the Hellenistic period, and when Hephaestus began to be identified with the Roman volcano-god, the god's divinity likewise suffered a loss of prestige.

In myth Hephaestus was pictured as club-footed and lame, characteristics which were incorporated into his epithets. As one might expect in early societies, the lame and the halt were little suited for occupations such as agriculture or warfare; their place was in the workshop just as the blind found an occupation as minstrels. To account for Hephaestus' deformity, the story was told that when he once came to his mother's assistance during one of her domestic squabbles with Zeus, the Olympian in anger seized him by the foot and flung him from heaven. After falling for a full day he landed on the island of Lemnos where he was picked up half-dead by the local inhabitants and cared for. Milton makes good use of this theme in his *Paradise Lost*; he parallels the fall of Satan and the palace he built in Hell with Hephaestus' ejection by Zeus and his well-known talent as an architect of the homes of the Olympian gods:

> Nor was his name unheard or unador'd
> In ancient Greece; and in the Ausonian land
> Men call'd him Mulciber; and how he fell
> From Heav'n, they fabl'd, thrown by angry Jove
> Sheer o'er the crystal battlements: from morn
> To noon he fell, from noon to dewy eve,
> A summer's day; and with the setting sun
> Dropt from the zenith like a falling star,
> On Lemnos th' Aegean isle.

Hesiod tells an odd story of Hephaestus' birth. Hera, jealous and resentful of Zeus because of the unorthodox manner in which he brought Athena into the world, gave birth to the divine craftsman parthenogenetically, without her husband's assistance or cooperation. Although Hesiod makes no comment on Hephaestus' deformity, the likelihood, as we have already stated, is that the poet could not conceive of the great Olympian siring anything but a perfectly formed child.

There are yet further difficulties in store for Hephaestus. His mother Hera tried to to do away with him because he was a cripple and threw him out of heaven—both stories of his ejection are related in Homer's *Iliad*. Fortunately, however, he landed in the sea where he was cared for by two nymphs, Thetis and Eurynome, who sheltered him for nine years. Hephaestus repaid his benefactors by making bronze ornaments, bracelets, pins, and necklaces for them.

According to a late tradition, Hephaestus sprang from the thigh of Hera and for a long time was kept in ignorance of who his parents were. Unhappy at this state of affairs, he decided on a plan by which he could surely extract the information from his mother. One day Hera received a gift from her son, an exquisitely wrought golden throne. She sat on it with delight, but when she tried to rise again, she was suddenly gripped by invisible bonds. Hera cried out for help and the gods tried to extricate her from the throne; but to no avail since Hephaestus was the only one who could release her, and he refused to leave the depths of the sea where he was living with Thetis and Eurynome. The god of war Ares tried to drag him up by force, but Hephaestus drove him off by throwing burning brands at him. The god of the vine Dionysus was more successful; he plied the craftsman-god with wine, made him tipsy, and brought him back to Olympus perched on a mule—a favorite scene of vase painters in antiquity. Hephaestus still refused to budge; he would not release his mother until she revealed to him the secret of his birth. Other accounts make him demand the goddess Aphrodite or Athena for a bride as a condition for Hera's release.

The story of Hephaestus' amatory adventure with Athena has already been told. In Hesiod's *Theogony*, the god made the youngest of the Graces, Aglaea, his wife; in the *Iliad*, it is Charis (Grace), the singular form of Charites (Graces), whereas in the *Odyssey*, Aphrodite (Venus) is said to be his wife. These "marriages" should be considered little more than allegory: Beauty or Grace joined or wedded to Craftsmanship. But Homer is not content to let it go at that; to him, Hephaestus outside of his workshop is an object of ridicule. In the *Iliad* the gods on Mount Olympus burst out laughing when they see him bustling up and down the hall as he serves them nectar from a huge bowl. In the *Odyssey* the blind bard Demodocus entertains the court of King Alcinous by singing of how Aphrodite made a cuckold out of her husband Hephaestus. The sun-god Helios told Hephaestus that his wife was having a love affair with the god of war Ares, the tryst taking place whenever Hephaestus left his palace. The god resolved to trap the lovers *in flagrante delicto*, in the very act of committing adultery. He went into his workshop and forged an invisible but unbreakable net which he draped over the bedposts and hung from the rafters. Pretending to leave for Lemnos, he returned unannounced to find Aphrodite and Ares caught, embarrassingly so, in his clever device. Hephaestus then summoned the gods—the goddesses out of modesty stayed at home—to witness how Aphrodite and Ares were caught in each other's arms. The gods roared with laughter at the sight. Hephaestus, insisting that Zeus pay back the bride-price he had given him for Aphrodite, was pacified when Poseidon assured him that he would stand surety for the adulterer's fine that Ares would have to pay him as the injured husband. Homer's spicy tale of adultery on Mount Olympus, taken together with the tragedy that befell Agamemnon because of his adulterous wife Clytemnestra, makes a compelling contrast with the ideal marriage of Odysseus and his devoted Penelope.

In the workshop, however, Hephaestus had no peer, and his prodigious activity was equaled only by his skill. He was continuously at work on some masterpiece. He built the palaces of the Olympian gods, Zeus' golden throne, his sceptre, and even his thunderbolts were the creation of the craftsman-god. He made the winged chariot of Helios the sun, the arrows of Apollo and Artemis, Demeter's sickle, the armor of the great heroes, weapons for Athena, a necklace for Harmonia which she wore at her wedding to Cadmus, and Agamemnon's scepter. When Thetis approached him to fabricate new armor for her son Achilles, Hephaestus gladly acceded to her request because she had been so kind to him when Hera had thrown him out of heaven. Homer spends the good part of the eighteenth book of the *Iliad*

Figure 37. Hephaestus and the Cyclopes forging armor for Achilles.
Athena stands behind Hephaestus; Thetis, Achilles' mother, is on the right.
Roman bas-relief. Conservatori Museum, Rome. (Alinari)

in describing Hephaestus' workshop and the magnificent armor he made for Achilles. Although later accounts place his workshop under volcanic mountains, such as Mount Etna and assign the three Cyclopes to him as his workmen (fig. 37), Homer places his home and shop on Mount Olympus where Thetis finds him at work in his highly-automated shop. This is the way Homer describes the scene:

> . . . Thetis of the Silver Feet made her way to the palace of Hephaestus, which the god of the Crooked Foot had built with his own hands of imperishable bronze. It shines like a star and stands out among the houses of the gods. She found Hephaestus hard at work and sweating as he bustled about at the bellows in his forge. He was making a set of twenty three-legged tables to stand round the walls of his well-built hall. He had fitted golden wheels to all their legs so that they could run by themselves to a meeting of the gods and amaze the company by running home again. They were not quite finished. He had still to put on the ornamental handles, and was fitting these and cutting the rivets.

When Thetis came and was greeted by Charis, Hephaestus asked his wife to entertain the goddess while he put away his tools. Hephaestus then

> raised his monstrous bulk from the anvil. He limped, but he was nimble enough on his slender legs. He removed the bellows from the fire, collected all the tools he used, and put them in a silver chest. Then he sponged his face and hands, his sturdy neck and hairy breast, put on his tunic, picked up a thick staff and came limping from the forge. Golden maidservants hastened to help their Master. They looked like real girls and could not only speak and use their limbs but were endowed with intelligence and trained in handwork by the immortal gods. Supported by his toiling escort, the Lord Hephaestus made his clumsy approach to the spot where Thetis was seated, and himself sat down on a polished chair, took her hand in his and greeted her.

Thetis explained the purpose of her visit and asked him to make a set of armor for her son Achilles. Hephaestus readily agreed and said that he would turn out a set of armor that would astonish everyone:

> With that, Hephaestus left her and went back to his forge, where he turned the bellows on the fire and bade them get to work. The bellows—there were twenty of them

—blew on the crucibles and gave a satisfactory blast of varying force, which increased at critical moments and subsided at others, according to Hephaestus' requirements and the stage that the work had reached. He cast imperishable bronze on the fire, and some tin and precious gold and silver. Then he put a great anvil on the stand and gripped a strong hammer in one hand and a pair of tongs in the others.

During the Renaissance, Hephaestus in his Roman guise was a popular subject for the great masters. Tintoretto painted Vulcan surprising Mars and Venus, the theme which Homer had elaborated in the *Odyssey* and which Ovid had transmitted to later generations. Another of his canvases shows Vulcan and his workmen, probably the Cyclopes, toiling at the forge. Rubens portrayed Vulcan hard at work fashioning the lightning bolts of Jupiter; Velásquez and Van Dyck have him busily at work in the smithy. In literature the god was usually associated with aspects of his workshop. Spenser uses his name as a synonym for fire: "Vulcanes flaming light" or "fiers Vulcans rage to tame." Shakespeare's allusions to the god are connected with his workshop: "As black as Vulcan in the smoke of war;" and Hamlet speaks of his tortured imagination as "foul as Vulcan's stithy." But Marlowe has not forgotten Ovid's version of Homer's tale of adultery among the gods; in *Hero and Leander,* one of the scenes represented in the temple of Venus is that of "Blood-quaffing Mars heaving the iron net,/Which limping Vulcan and his Cyclops set."

10. Ares (Mars)

Ares, the Greek god of war, like his brother or stepbrother Hephaestus, never developed moral or theological virtues; above all, he never learned any of the social graces. In contrast with Athena who was also a deity of war, but whose cool and considered strategy was designed to protect the community, Ares represented the passionate response to battle, the uncontrolled and irrational frenzy of the fight, the tumult, the confusion, and the horrors of war. Hesiod, as we have already seen, has made him the son of Zeus and Hera, and the husband of the goddess Aphrodite. The poet has no comment on these family ties, and we can only speculate that his mating of Ares and Aphrodite signified the union of the two most uncontrollable of passions within the human breast, possibly the tempestuousness of the sexual union. The daughter of this marriage is Harmonia, a Greek word meaning love and harmony as well as the absence of strife or discord. Mythologically she may represent little more than the result of the purging of these human emotions. The sons of Ares and Aphrodite are Deimos (Panic or Terror) and Phobos (Fear), who obviously take after their father, and often attend him in battle.

The Romans had no such view of their god of war Mars or Mavors whom they considered second in importance to Jupiter and whom they made the father of Romulus, the mythical founder of Rome. Unlike his Greek counterpart, Mars seems to have been from very early times a protector of the community and its fields, and his festivals indicate that he had agricultural functions as well. In the calendar of the early Romans, the agricultural year began with the month to which his name was attached, Martius, which has found its way into English as March. Whatever indigenous mythology that may have attached itself to Mars was lost when the Greeks captivated the Romans with their stories of the gods.

It is Homer who has painted the definitive picture of Ares as a god who loves war for its own sake, as one who takes an absolute delight in the din and roar of battles, in the slaughter of men and in the destruction of towns. In the *Iliad*, Ares spurs on the Trojan forces accompanied by his two sons and by Eris (Strife) who, Homer says, is his sister who helps him in his bloody work by sowing discord among men. And when Ares hears that a son of his, Ascalaphus, has been killed in battle, he impetuously orders Panic and Fear to harness his horses and arms himself to avenge his son's death even though Zeus had forbidden the gods to take part in the war. Athena, far more reasonable than Ares, snatches the helmet from his head, the shield from his shoulder, and the bronze spear from his hand. She berates him with such words as "Blockhead!" and "Maniac!" and shouts at him that he has lost all reason and restraint. Earlier in the *Iliad*, when gods and men fight among themselves, Diomedes—guided and inspired by Athena—wounded the god with his spear. Ares let out a bellow as loud as nine or ten thousand battling men, and then rushed to his father to complain of what Athena had done to him. Zeus gave him a black look and said:

> You turncoat, don't come to me and whine. There is nothing you enjoy so much as quarrelling and fighting; which is why I hate you more than any god on Olympus. Your mother Hera too has a headstrong and ungovernable temper—I have always found it hard to control her by word of mouth alone. I suspect it was she that started this business and got you into trouble. However, I do not intend to let you suffer any longer, since you are my own flesh and blood and your mother is my wife. But if any other god had fathered such a pernicious brat, you would long since have found yourself in a deeper hole than the sons of Uranus.

Zeus then sees to it that his son's wound is ministered to by the physician of the Olympian gods. But so unpopular was Ares that the Greeks seem to have taken pleasure in inventing stories in which the war-god gets the worst of the encounter. At another stage of the Trojan War, Athena opposed Ares and laid him low with a stone. Homer tells us that his body stretched out on the ground covered seven acres. We have already witnessed his unsuccessful attempt to rescue Hera when Hephaestus had her trapped in his magical chair: Ares was sent flying by Hephaestus' burning brands. On another occasion Otus and Ephialtes, the two giants who attempted to scale heaven by piling mountains upon one another, imprisoned Ares in a bronze jar for thirteen months. That would have been the end of him had his mother not gotten Hermes to rescue him in the nick of time.

Ares is the father of numerous children by various women. They are mostly sons who are like their father, violent and warlike: Diomedes of Thrace, whose horses ate flesh until Heracles finished them off by feeding them their master; Cycnus, a highwayman who waylaid travelers bringing gifts to Delphi and who used the skulls of his victims to build a temple to his father or to Apollo. Heracles killed him in battle and in the process wounded Ares in the thigh. The war-god was also the father of Phlegyas, the name-giver to a whole tribe of impious and ferocious raiders, the Phlegyae. Phlegyas himself was killed by Apollo and condemned to a tortured existence in Tartarus for having defiled the god's temple.

Two lesser-known deities who accompany Ares in his sanguinary pursuits are Enyo and Enyalius. The latter's name was used frequently by Homer as an epithet of the god meaning "warlike." He was identified by the Romans with Quirinus, an Italic deity with functions similar to those of Mars; and when Romulus died, he appeared to a friend to announce that he was thenceforth to be known by the name of the god Quirinus. Enyo was identified with the Roman war-goddess

Figure 38. Ares and Aphrodite.
Roman wall painting, 80–11 B.C.
Pompeii. National Museum, Naples.
(Alinari)

Bellona, the companion of Mars and sometimes said to be his sister or wife. In *Macbeth*, Shakespeare calls Mars "Bellona's bridegroom." The Romans invoked Bellona to inspire them with warlike spirit and enthusiasm which no enemy could resist. Vergil describes her as armed with a bloody scourge, while others represent her as driving the chariot of the god of war. In *Paradise Lost*, Milton describes the din that Satan hears coming up from Hell:

> Nor was his ear less pealed
> With noises loud and ruinous (to compare
> Great things with small) than when Bellona storms
> With all her battering engines, bent to rase
> Some capital city.

In literature and art Ares is known to us in the two roles which Homer assigned to him, warrior and lover (fig. 38). Under his Roman name of Mars, he is virtually a synonym for war and for anyone taking pleasure in its bloody aspects. The great painters of the Renaissance delighted in representing him either alone (Rubens, Velásquez, and Rembrandt) or together with his inamorata, the goddess of love (among others, Botticelli, Tintoretto, Veronese, and Rubens). Spenser sums up the dual personality of the god of war with these words in the *Faerie Queene:*

> . . . Mars is Cupidoes frend,
> And is for Venus loves renowed more
> Then all his wars and spoiles, the which he did of yore.

The romantic side to the god's nature is again stressed by Spenser in his introduction to the same work:

> . . . and with you bring triumphant Mars,
> in loves and gentle jollities arrayd,
> After his murdrous spoiles and bloudie rage allayd.

11. Aphrodite (Venus)

The unique and uncommon birth of Aphrodite resulting from Cronus' act of violence against his father Uranus, holds a dramatic place in Hesiod's cosmogonic and theological speculations. Following her trip from Cythera to Cyprus and her birth from the sea, the goddess was given an entourage of Eros (Love)—the aboriginal creative impulse in Hesiod's universe—and Himeros (Desire) to escort her to the assembly of the gods where she was received as one of them. Other writers fill out Aphrodite's company of attendants with the Charites (Graces) and the Horae (Hours or Seasons). Hesiod's crude tale of the creation of the goddess of love was refined and sublimated by later poets who pass over Uranus' mutilation and tell only of her association with the sea, as does one composer of a Homeric hymn honoring the goddess: "There the moist breath of the western wind wafted her over the waves of the loud-roaring sea in soft foam, and there the gold-filleted Horae welcomed her joyously. . ." Another poet starts his hymn to the goddess with these simple words: "I will sing of Cytherea, born in Cyprus."

But as can be anticipated, Homer rejected Hesiod's version of how Aphrodite came into being—he undoubtedly would have deplored the bad taste of the Boeotian farmer-poet—for to him the goddess was the daughter of Zeus and the Oceanid Dione. Since the name of the nymph appears to be etymologically related to that of her Homeric husband, some scholars see in Dione the original consort of Zeus–Dios, a wife whose place in Zeus' bed was usurped by the pre-Greek goddess Hera. On mythological grounds at least, there is good reason to suspect that Homer, in preferring to introduce Aphrodite to the world by the more accepted method of procreation, did not preserve an early historical tradition but simply

Figure 39. Aphrodite rising from the sea. *Bas-relief, c. 460 B.C. on the so-called "Ludovisi Throne." Terme Museum, Rome. (Alinari)*

reported another version or invented one which offended him less than the Hesiodic tale. Had there been a strong tradition concerning Zeus and Dione, Homer and
other poets would hardly have missed the opportunity to elaborate upon a relationship that resulted in the birth of the goddess who was the personification of
the sex drive and the power of passion. Mythology offers nothing in the way of
pursuit, competition, resistance, or jealousy. In any event, the story of Aphrodite's
ascent from the sea was far more appealing to the sculptors and painters of antiquity
than the rather prosaic and undramatic account of her lineage in the epics of
Homer. It was from the former tradition that Aphrodite was given the epithet
Anadyomene, "coming up (from the sea)." On the base of his famous statue of
Zeus at Olympia, Phidias represented the goddess as being received from the sea by
Eros and one of the Graces, while the spectacle was being witnessed by an assem-
blage of the great gods. The celebrated artist of the fourth century B.C., Apelles,
painted an *Aphrodite Anadyomene* in which the goddess is shown wringing out her
hair as she arises from the sea, the falling drops of water forming a transparent veil
of silver around her body. The painting had been commissioned for the temple of
Asclepius on the island of Cos, but it was later taken to Rome by Augustus who set
it up in the temple he dedicated to Julius Caesar. Although these works have been
lost to us, we can still see the poetic charm of Aphrodite Anadyomene on the Ludovisi throne (fig. 39), perhaps one of the finest renderings of the theme in the fifth
century B.C.

Hesiod seems to have made a point of emphasizing the geographical direction
in which Aphrodite traveled as she was being formed in the foam of the sea: from
the island of Cythera off the coast of the Peloponnese, eastward to Cyprus where
she "came forth a revered and beautiful goddess and grass grew beneath her delicate feet." No matter how much the Hesiodic tradition tried to place Aphrodite's
"conception" near Hellenic soil, the origin of the goddess points decisively in
another geographical direction. She had her beginnings as an Oriental goddess
who then made her way not eastward but westward from the Near East to the
islands of the Aegean and then to Greece. Aphrodite is akin to the Semitic fertility
goddess known to us under such names as Ishtar, Astarte, or Ashtoreth; her
husband or lover was called Bel or Baal (Lord), Tammuz, Adonis. On the island of
Cyprus, however, the goddess shed some, but not all, of her Semitic character
and gradually became more and more Hellenized, until the Greeks adopted her as
their very own. Homer calls her "Cypris" or "the Cyprian"; other poets will similarly recall her birth on the island of Cyprus in the epithet "Cyprus-born." The
historian Herodotus, however, is quick to recognize her eastern antecedents,
when he speaks of the temple of Aphrodite Urania at Ascalon as being reputed to
be the oldest temple of the goddess. On further inquiry, he is told that the
temple of the goddess on Cyprus was derived from the one at Ascalon, and that
the one in Cythera was built by Phoenicians who had come from the region of
Ascalon in what was called Syria. The name Aphrodite Urania or Heavenly
Aphrodite also owes much to the Oriental goddess of fertility who was worshiped
in connection with one of the heavenly bodies, most often the moon or the planet
Venus. She is the "queen of heaven" about whom the Old Testament prophet
Jeremiah complained that the women in the cities of Judah and in the streets of
Jerusalem made offerings to her in the form of cakes.

The Greek-acculturated Aphrodite owed much to the great goddess of fertility
of the Syro-Phoenicians, Babylonians, and other Asiatics, but as was often the case

Figure 40.   The Aphrodite of Cnidos by Praxiteles. *A Roman copy of the original of c. 340 B.C. Vatican Museum. (Alinari)*

with the Greeks, the character of the goddess was reinterpreted, sublimated, and idealized by their philsophers, poets and artist. In cult, to be sure, Aphrodite was called upon, as she was in the Near East, to help in the essential process of generation and fertility for all living things. The poets, however, began to see her more as the personification of the sex drive, the power of love, the rapture of the love embrace, the pleasures and the joys of lovemaking. In the Homeric hymn honoring the goddess, the poet invokes his Muse in these words: "Muse, tell me the deeds of golden Aphrodite the Cyprian, who stirs up sweet passion in the gods and subdues the tribes of mortal men and birds that fly in the air and all the many creatures that the dry land rears, and all that the sea: all these love the deeds of rich-crowned Cytherea." Yes, even the gods were subject to her power, all except Hestia, Artemis, and Athena. The same hymn tells us that Zeus was very much aware of Aphrodite's power and did not want her to mock the gods by saying that she had caused them to have love affairs with mortal women. To remedy this situation, the Olympian caused her to fall in love with a mortal, the Trojan Anchises, and later she gave birth to a great son, Aeneas (p. 4).

Greek artists continued the naturalization of Aphrodite as a Hellenic deity by idealizing her beauty and charm, in contrast with Semitic representations which emphasized and exaggerated the sexuality of the goddess of fertility. The climax to this mode of Hellenization was reached in the work of the fourth-century B.C. sculptor Praxiteles whose *Aphrodite of Cnidos* (c. 340) became a model for numerous Aphrodites of Hellenistic and Roman times: the popular *Venus de Milo*, the *Aphrodite of Cyrene*, the *Crouching Venus*, and various others which go under the name of *Venus Genetrix*.

The Roman encyclopedist and polymath Pliny the Elder (A.D. 23–79) has recorded the story—virtually a legend—of how the people of Cnidos acquired Praxiteles' masterpiece. The sculptor had made two statues of Aphrodite, one draped, the other showing the goddess as she was laying aside her dress on a water jar before taking a bath (fig. 40)—the first convincing representation of the beautiful female nude. In Praxiteles' opinion, they were both of equal value and consequently offered them for sale at the same price. The people of the island of Cos, who were known for their conservatism, bought the draped figure of the goddess; the Cnidians, apparently unabashed by nudity, purchased the other. To the good fortune of the Cnidians, their Aphrodite was not only hailed as the finest statue to come from the hand of Praxiteles and of the whole world, but it also became a tourist attraction and people traveled to Cnidos from remote parts of the world to view the great work of art. So highly did the Cnidians value their treasure, Pliny says, that when King Nicomedes of Bithynia offered to buy it from them at a price that would pay off their whole public debt, which was considerable, the Cnidians preferred to endure any hardship rather than part with the work which gave their city its great renown. The *Aphrodite of Cnidos*, now known to us only through Roman copies, was later carried off to Constantinople where it was destroyed by fire, along with many other art treasures, during the reign of the emperor Justinian (A.D. 525–565).

In the hands of philosophers and poet-philosophers, the character of the eastern deity was to take yet other turns. In the *Symposium* (Banquet), a philosophical dialog on the nature of Eros (Love), Plato makes use of the two contradictory versions of Aphrodite's birth in his effort to arrive at an understanding of what love is and what it should be. Through the mouth of one of the guests at the banquet we hear of a new interpretation of love as represented by two titles of Aphrodite: Urania and Pandemos (of all the people). The former owes something to the Semitic "queen of heaven" and to the myth of her birth from the mutilated Uranus; the latter was originally an extension of the idea of Aphrodite as the goddess of the family and of the political community. Plato, however, uses the two forms of Aphrodite to illustrate two different kinds of love, and the interpretation by a certain Pausanias at the banquet anticipates Plato's concept of the highest form of love: that is, an Eros or desirous longing to ascend the ladder of love to the supreme reality of Beauty, Beauty eternal and perfect. This is how the subject of the two kinds of love is introduced by Pausanias:

> For we all know that Love (Eros) is inseparable from Aphrodite, and if there were only one Aphrodite there would be only one Love; but as there are two goddesses there must be two Loves. And am I not right in asserting that there are two goddesses? The elder one, having no mother, who is called Heavenly Aphrodite—she is the daughter of Uranus; the younger, who is the daughter of Zeus and Dione—her we call Common (Pandemos); and the Love who is her fellow-worker is rightly called Common, as the other Love is called Heavenly (Urania).

Pausanias goes on to rationalize his view that homosexual love of a higher order—in which a strong bond of intellectual comradeship joins the lover and the beloved—finds its justification in Aphrodite Urania since she is derived solely from the male, and being the older of the two has nothing of gross wantonness in her. On the other hand, the Eros who is the offspring of Aphrodite Pandemos represents common love: love of the body rather than of the soul. The goddess who is his mother is much younger than Aphrodite Urania, and having been born of the male and female (Zeus and Dione), partakes of both.

Poets with a philosophical bent of mind saw in Aphrodite something approaching a universal law, an impersonal nonmoral force, a state of mind. Euripides, in his tragedy *Hippolytus* (428 B.C.), says that Aphrodite is no goddess but something more, something stronger; that she crushes those who repress or reject the power of love; that she is a generative force from which all things take their birth.

These are the words he puts into the mouth of the nurse who attempts to convince her mistress Phaedra, a tragic victim of the goddess, to enter into an illicit relationship with her stepson Hippolytus:

> The tide of love,
> at its full surge, is not withstandable.
> Upon the yielding spirit she comes gently,
> but to the proud and the fanatic heart
> she is a torturer with the brand of shame.
> She wings her way through the air; she is in the sea,
> in its foaming billows; from her everything,
> that is, is born. For she engenders us
> and sows the seed of desire wherof we're born,
> all we her children living on the earth.

The Romans had no love-goddess, a situation that was remedied by identifying a latecomer to their pantheon, Venus, with the Greek Aphrodite. Venus, originally, seems to have been a spirit who saw to it that gardens were neat and tidy; her name, if from the Latin *venustus*, would be the equivalent of the Greek Charis (Grace or Charm). Aphrodite came to Rome from Mount Eryx in western Sicily where there was a famous temple of Astarte-Aphrodite—the Semitic influence having been introduced by the Carthaginians and other Phoenician settlers. Adopted by the Romans together with all her alien mythological trappings, Venus became as Greek as Aphrodite. Also influential in introducing her worship into Rome was the Julian family, the most illustrious of patrician families, which claimed descent from Venus. By etymological manipulation it was contended that the Julii were descended from Iulus, a son of Aeneas and grandson of Aphrodite (Venus). (Iulus was also known by the name of Ascanius.) To Iulus had been attributed the founding of Alba Longa, the home not only of the Julian family but also of Romulus and Remus, the legendary founders of Rome. Julius Caesar, the most celebrated member of the Julii, took pride in the divine origin of his family and often placed a head of Venus on Roman coins. He also dedicated a temple to the goddess on the Palatine, and at times used "Venus Genetrix" (= mother of the Julian family) as a password with his soldiers. Venus Genetrix later became prominent in Imperial cult as the mother of all the Romans. It is not surprising, therefore, to find Greek and Roman elements blended and harmonized by the Roman didactic poet Lucretius. In the invocation to this poem on Epicurean philosophy he calls on Venus as the progenitor of the Romans, as the spirit of creation, and as the wife of the god of war, the power capable of neutralizing the frenzy of strife:

Mother of Aeneas and his race, delight of men and gods, life-giving Venus, it is your doing that under the wheeling constellations of the sky all nature teems with life, both the sea that buoys up our ships and the earth that yields our food. Through you all living creatures are conceived and come forth to look upon the sunlight. . . . Since you alone are the guiding power of the universe and without you nothing emerges into the shining sunlit world to grow in joy and loveliness, yours is the partnership I seek in striving to compose these lines *On the Nature of the Universe*. . . . Meanwhile grant that this brutal business of war by sea and land may everywhere be lulled to rest. For you alone have power to bestow on mortals the blessings of quiet peace. In your bosom Mars himself, supreme commander in this brutal business, flings himself down at times, laid low by the irremedial wound of love.

Thomas Gray (1716–1771), in these few lines from the *Hymn to Adversity*, combines the Euripidean and Lucretian aspects of the goddess of love as a torturer and a tamer:

> Daughter of Jove, relentless power,
> Thou tamer of the human breast,
> Whose iron scourge and tort'ring hour
> The bad affright, afflict the best.

Anchises. In spite of the efforts of the Greeks and Romans to adopt Aphrodite as their own, the mythology of the goddess remained firmly based in eastern tradition and eastern locales. The four men of some prominence with whom mythology has her romantically involved in one way or another—Anchises, Paris, Adonis, and Pgymalion—are either from the Near East or from the island of Cyprus. Anchises' main claim to fame was his "marriage" to Aphrodite on Mount Ida near ancient Troy. According to the Homeric hymn in honor of the goddess, Zeus had arranged for Aphrodite to fall in love with this member of the royal house of Troy as he was pasturing sheep on Mount Ida. The goddess had approached Anchises in the disguise of a daughter of a Phrygian king, but upon consummating their marriage, the goddess revealed her true identity and announced that he would be the father of a son, Aeneas. He was commanded, however, to announce that the child was a son of a nymph. To this the goddess added the threat that if he ever betrayed the real mother, Zeus would destroy him with a flash of lightning. According to later traditions, Anchises, having had too much to drink, boasted of his love affair with the goddess and was struck by lightning, some say fatally. Others insist that it only blinded or maimed him. In the *Aeneid*, Vergil has Anchises survive the capture of Troy, and Aeneas dutifully carries his father on his shoulders from the burning city. On his way to Italy, Vergil tells us, Anchises died soon after the first arrival of Aeneas in Sicily and was buried on Mount Eryx which was sacred to Aphrodite.

Paris. Another Trojan shepherd to whom Aphrodite showed her favor and goodwill was Paris (also known as Alexander), the son of Priam and Hecuba, king and queen of Troy. The young man, destined to be the cause of the Trojan War and to be celebrated in literature for his seduction of Helen, was implicated in a beauty contest of which more will be told in the treatment of the Judgment of Paris and the myths concerning the Trojan War. Briefly, when Zeus singled out Paris to judge which of three goddesses—Athena, Hera, or Aphrodite—deserved to be given the golden apple inscribed with the words "For the Fairest," the youthful shepherd awarded the prize to Aphrodite since she had promised to procure for him Helen, the most beautiful woman in the world. Later, when Paris and Helen's husband Menelaus fought a duel to settle the issue of the Trojan War, the goddess' favorite was on the verge of being killed by Menelaus when Aphrodite, as Homer tells it, "snatched up Paris, very easily as a goddess may, and hid him in thick darkness, and set him down in his own perfumed bedroom." And when the goddess approached Helen to inform her that her lover awaited her in his bedroom, Helen turned on Aphrodite and bitterly accused the goddess of being used to satisfy her romantic interest in mortal men. If she loves Paris so, Homer has Helen say in this unusual speech, "Go yourself and sit by his side, and depart from the way of the gods; neither let your feet take you back to Olympus, but suffer for him and look after him until he makes you his wife or perhaps his slave."

Pygmalion. The myths of Aphrodite which have as their locale the island of Cyprus combine, as can be expected by the proximity of the island to Asia Minor, Semitic and Hellenic forms of her worship. An eastern feature of the goddess was the cult of sacred prostitution, a religious practice that traveled along the commercial routes, probably by way of Cyprus, to Corinth in Greece and to Mount Eryx in Sicily. Another oriental aspect of the goddess was her association with a youthful lover Adonis whose name is derived from the Semitic word *adon*, "lord." Adonis was the title of the Babylonian Tammuz who is the prototype of all fertility-gods who die and rise again in the annual cycle of vegetation. As his cult moved westward to the Mediterranean, the name of Adonis, either by misinterpretation or for fear of mentioning the divine name, was used for the god. Adonis was worshiped at Amathus in Cyprus, and it appears that his cult was carried from Cyprus to Athens by the fifth or sixth century B.C. The cycle of myths in which Aphrodite is localized on Cyprus, although recorded in rather late sources and hence highly romanticized, bears on the more Semitic side of the goddess. It is to the writers of the Roman period, especially Ovid in the *Metamorphoses*, that we owe a connected account of these presumably Cyprian or Syro-Phoenician myths.

The story is told of Pygmalion, the legendary king of Cyprus, who was so filled with disgust at the shocking vices of the women on his island that he decided to remain a bachelor. However, having considerable skill as an artist, he carved a statue of his ideal of womanhood out of ivory, and the more he looked upon his exquisite creation, the more he fell in love with it. At a festival in honor of Aphrodite, he prayed to the goddess for a wife like this ivory statue. When Pygmalion returned home and kissed the image he had created, much to his amazement, it was alive and became the woman of his dreams and prayers. She was given the name of Galatea (Milk-white?). To this idyllic couple a son was born, Paphos, who gave his name not only to the famous city on the island of Cyprus but also to Aphrodite who is said to have risen out of the sea at Paphos and hence is often called "Paphian."

*   *   *   *

Pygmalion's unusual experience has appealed to many writers and composers. Between the years 1608 and 1865, more than a dozen operas, operettas and cantatas were composed on the theme of Pygmalion and Galatea. Among the Elizabethan poets, John Marston (1575–1634) wrote a rather heavy-handed erotic burlesque on the Ovidian version of the tale which he called *The Metamorphosis of Pigmalion's Image*. Whereas Marston overplayed the sensual, the Victorian poet William Morris, in his treatment of the theme for *The Earthly Paradise*, has Pygmalion observe all the proprieties of his day. Instead of passionately bringing the statue to life by kisses and caresses, as do Ovid and Marston, Morris' Pygmalion finds the statue alive on his return from the temple of Venus, and Galatea is decorously clad in the clothes which Pygmalion offered the goddess in her temple. An earlier nineteenth-century poet, Thomas Lovell Beddoes (1803–1849), takes Pygmalion as the symbol of the frustrations of a creative artist. In his *Pygmalion*, prayers go unanswered during the artist's lifetime; it is only when the artist dies that the statue comes to life. Similarly, the poetess H. D. takes considerable liberties in her handling of the myth of the ancient sculptor. In her *Pygmalion*, we see a sculptor-hero who is not obsessed with the love of a woman but in conflict with the results of his art. His goddess is

Athena, patroness of the arts, not Aphrodite, and he carves statues of gods who, when they come to life, abandon him leaving him in a quandary as to whether he creates his art or is manipulated by it. Robert Graves (1895–   ) wrote two poems with the Cyprian artist in mind. In *Pygmalion and Galatea*, the sculptor asks for a woman to be lovely, merciful, constant, various, and a woman. In *Galatea and Pygmalion*, Graves takes a more cynical view:

> Galatea, whom his furious chisel
> From Parian stone had by greed enchanted,
> Fulfilled, they say, all Pygmalion's longings:
>   Stepped from that pedestal on which she stood,
> Bare in his bed laid her down, lubricious,
> With low responses to his drunken raptures,
>   Enroyalled his body with her demon blood.
>
> Yet young Pygmalion had so well plotted
> The art-perfection of his woman monster
> That schools of eager connoisseurs beset
>   Her famous person with perennial suit;
> Whom she (a judgement on the jealous artist)
> Admitted rankly to a comprehension
>   Of themes that crowned her own, not his repute.

In a lighter mood, W. S. Gilbert (1836–1911)—better known as the librettist of the popular Gilbert and Sullivan comic operas—wrote a comedy called *Pygmalion* in which the sculptor, who is married, uses his wife as the model for his statue. The statue comes to life, falls in love with her creator, and then realizing the impossibility of the relationship, turns back into marble of her own accord. And finally, we have the *Pygmalion* of George Bernard Shaw (1856–1950), who has given us in the form of a comedy the most popular version of the ancient myth. Instead of a sculptor, Shaw's Pygmalion is Henry Higgins, a professor of phonetics who creates not a statue out of stone but an elegant lady out of Eliza Doolittle, a Cockney girl of the lowest social class. Through the professor's skill and training, she passes as an equal of the snobbish aristocrats of the day. Shaw's play has also had great success when transformed into the musical comedy *My Fair Lady*.

Adonis.   The story of the Cyprian Aphrodite continues with the mythical king Cinyras, a son of Paphos. According to most accounts, he founded the cult of Aphrodite-Astarte on Cyprus and built her celebrated temple at Paphos. He was also the ancestor of the priests of Aphrodite at Paphos who were called the Cinyrades, the descendants of Cinyras. His daughter was Myrrha, also called Smyrna, who fell madly and passionately in love with her own father. The cause of this forbidden passion is variously given: some say that Myrrha's mother boasted that her daughter was more beautiful than Aphrodite herself; others say that Myrrha neglected the worship of the goddess. In the usual course of events in mythology, Aphrodite punished the mother for her presumption, or the daughter for her neglect, and caused Myrrha to fall in love with her own father. With the help of her nurse, Myrrha was brought to her father at night and in darkness; other accounts have Myrrha approach her father in disguise or when he had too much to drink. After several meetings, Cinyras discovered that his lover was his own daughter and was so filled with horror that he tried to kill her. Myrrha fled from her tortured father, and just at the moment that he was about to overtake her, she prayed to the gods to save her. Instantly she was metamorphosed into a tree, a myrrh tree. It is the shade of this tragic girl that Vergil points out to Dante in the Inferno of the *Divine Comedy:*

> That is the ancient spirit of flagitious Myrrha
>   who loved her father with more than rightful love;
> She came to sin with him disguised in alien forms.

Myrrha had been with child when she was transformed into the incense-producing tree, and in the course of time the trunk of the tree burst open—or was ripped open by a wild boar—and the child Adonis was born. Aphrodite was so charmed by the beauty of the child that she concealed him in a chest and entrusted him to Persephone, the goddess of the Underworld. But when Persephone opened the chest and discovered the beautiful child, she refused to surrender him. The case was brought before Zeus, or the Muse Calliope, who decided the dispute by declaring that during four months of the year Adonis should be left to himself, for four months he should belong to Persephone, and for the four remaining months to Aphrodite.

When Adonis grew to youthful manhood and became a handsome hunter, Aphrodite fell in love with him. The goddess, fearing for his life, cautioned him to avoid ferocious beasts, but the thrill of the hunt was overpowering for the youthful Adonis. His dogs flushed out a wild boar which he was able only to wound with his spear. The boar turned on the young hunter and savagely tore him to pieces. From Adonis' blood that spilled on the ground grew the blood-red flower, the anemone. In the Near East, the anemone is one of the first flowers that bloom in early spring, and like Adonis, having bloomed early it quickly fades and dies. A number of variations to the story of Adonis are related by different poets: that Cinyras split open the bark of the myrrh tree with his sword; that the child was reared by nymphs who anointed him with the tears of his mother; that Ares was jealous of the attention that Aphrodite was giving to the young man and turned himself into an avenging boar; that following his death, Adonis was permitted to return to Aphrodite for six months of the year, but the other six had to be spent in the Underworld.

In the whole cycle of stories from the island of Cyprus, from Pygmalion to Adonis, the goddess Aphrodite is in one way or another connected with the four major mythological figures. Behind the veil of mythological embroidery stand Pygmalion and Cinyras who, tradition holds, were king-priests of the cult of Aphrodite-Astarte in Cyprus. Myrrha (or Smyrna), apart from her obvious transformation into the tree that provides the incense and perfume associated with the worship of Aphrodite, might also represent the priestess of Aphrodite and the cult of sacred prostitution that Cinyras is said to have introduced at Paphos.

Adonis, on the other hand, is the typical young male figure, associated with Aegean and Near Eastern fertility goddesses whose death marks the withering of vegetation, the harvesting of crops, or more generally, the temporary withdrawal of divine providence. The death of Adonis causes the earth to become barren; his return, symbolized by the blooming of the anemone in spring, announces the renewal of life and the return of divine providence. Women annually commemorated the passing of Adonis with rites of mourning, weeping of the kind that the Old Testament prophet Ezekiel observed on behalf of Tammuz in front of the temple at Jerusalem. By the fifth century B.C., the cult of Adonis was firmly established at Athens. Aristophanes, in his antiwar play *Lysistrata*, satirized the women who were attracted to this foreign cult; an Athenian official complains bitterly about wanton women who whirl about and shriek "Ai, Ai Adonis!" and "Beat your breasts for Adonis!" And when the Athenian fleet was about to sail on the ill-fated expedition to Syracuse in 415 B.C., Plutarch tells us: "... not a few were troubled because the days on which the fleet set sail happened to be the time when the women celebrated the death of Adonis; there being everywhere exposed to view images of dead men, carried about with mourning and lamentation, and women beating their breasts." The historian Ammianus Marcellinus, who wrote in the fourth century of this era, relates the mourning and weeping of the women to the rites of Adonis when speaking of the burial of King Grumbates' son near Persia: "For seven days ... the women woefully beating their breasts and weeping in the accustomed manner, loudly bewailed the hope of their nation cut off in the bloom of youth, just as the priestesses of Aphrodite are often seen to weep at the annual festival of Adonis, which as the mystic lore of religion tells us, is a kind of symbol of the ripened grain."

The annual mourning for Adonis was part of a festival, the Adonia, which took its name from the youthful lover of Aphrodite. Evidence for the worship of Adonis comes from Athens, Byblos, and Alexandria. Byblos in Phoenicia was especially sacred to Adonis, and the Adonia was celebrated in the spring, the time when Adonis returned to spend his six months with Aphrodite, the mythical expression for the return of fertility and divine providence. His death, it was said, made the river of Byblos run red every year. At Alexandria in Egypt, the ritual of the festival is preserved in the form of a pastoral poem composed by Theocritus early in the third century B.C. In spite of artificialities of the poem which characterize the sophisticated literary forms of the Hellenistic period, the idyll preserves the main features of the ritual: the sacred marriage (*hieros gamos*), the symbols of fertility, the death and disappearance of the youthful lover, and the plea for his return. Here is an abbreviated version of Theocritus' idyll.

Lady Aphrodite of the golden toys ... see how after a year the Seasons have brought you back Adonis from Acheron s ever-flowing stream [a river in the Underworld] ... the dear Seasons, tardiest of the Blessed Ones, yet ever longed for is their coming, and ever for all men do they bring some gifts. Lady of Cypris, Aphrodite, you changed Berenice [queen of Egypt] from mortal to immortal by dropping ambrosia into her woman's breast. And for your sake, Lady of the many names and many shrines, Berenice's daughter, lovely as Helen of Troy, pampers Adonis with all things good. By him in their season are all that fruit-trees bear, and delicate gardens in silver baskets guarded [the so-called Gardens of Adonis in which quickly-growing and quickly-decaying plants were placed as a symbol of the brief duration of Adonis' life], and golden flasks of Syrian perfume. And all the cakes that women fashion on the kneading tray, mingling every hue with fine white wheat-flour, are there, and those they make of sweet honey and smooth oil. All the creatures of the earth and air are there. And green bowers have been built, laden with tender dill and boyish Loves flit overhead like young nightingales that flit upon the tree from spray to spray. . . .

In Adonis' rosy arms Aphrodite, the Cyprian, lies, and he in hers ... the golden down is still upon his lip; his kisses are not rough. And now farewell to Aphrodite as she clasps her lover. But all together, at daybreak, with the dew, will we bear him out to the waves that splash upon the shore; and there with ungirt hair, breasts bared and clothing falling to the ankle will we begin our clear song. "Dear Adonis, you alone of the demigods, visit both earth and Acheron ... Look on us with favor next year too, dear Adonis. Happy has your coming found us now, Adonis, and when you come again, dear will be your return.... Farewell beloved Adonis, and I hope you'll find us happy when you come again."

Another idyll which continued the tradition of romanticizing elements of the ritual of the Adonia comes from the hand of Bion, a bucolic poet who was active about 100 B.C. This poet of shepherds and lovers focuses on the death of the youthful Adonis and the lament of Aphrodite for her lost love. Here is a sampling from Bion's *Lament for Adonis* which depicts the scene following the death of the handsome hunter:

... When she saw, when she marked the bleeding wound of Adonis, when she saw the bright red blood about his thigh, she lifted up her hands and moaned, "Stay with me, Adonis, poor Adonis. stay with me! . . . Awake, Adonis, for a little while and kiss me yet again, the latest kiss! . . . This kiss will I treasure, even as you, poor ill-fated Adonis, are fleeing and going to Acheron to that hateful and cruel king . . . Persephone, take my husband, for you are stronger than I, and all beautiful things drift down to you. But I am ill-fated, my anguish is inconsolable; and I lament my Adonis, dead to me, and I have no rest for sorrow. . . ."

.... A tear the Paphian sheds for each blood-drop of Adonis, and tears and blood on the earth are turned to flowers. The blood brings forth the rose; the tears the anemone.

Woe, woe for Adonis, he has died, the handsome Adonis!

... Cytherea, cease your lamentations; today refrain from your dirges. You must again bewail him, again must weep for him another year.

*   *   *   *   *

From literary sources such as these, later poets borrowed components of the mythologized ritual of Tammuz-Adonis. The Adonis-garden, which symbolized the cycle of the seasons, of death and resurrection, is taken by Spenser in the *Faerie Queene* as a kind of Platonic paradise where after a period of a thousand years souls transmigrate into bodies.

> There wont faire Venus often to enjoy
> Her deare Adonis joyous company,
> And reape sweet pleasure of the wanton boy;
> . . . .
> And sooth it seems they say: for he may not
> For ever die, and ever buried bee
> In balefull night, where all things are forgot;
> All be he subject to mortalitie,
> Yet is eterne in mutabilitie,
> And by succession made perpetuall,
> Transformed oft, and chaunged diverslie:
> For him the Father of all formes they call;
> Therefore needs mote he live, that living gives to all.

Spenser's Adonia-garden, a symbol of love which uses but ultimately transcends the senses, is taken over by Milton for his masque *Comus*. In the Attendant Spirit's epilogue, we are presented with a vision of Adonis attended by the Heavenly Aphrodite—Milton's "Assyrian Queen"—which, in Spenserian symbolism, is to anticipate that higher form of Platonic love as represented by the union of Cupid (Love) and Psyche (Soul) and their children Youth and Joy. All live in "Gardens fair":

> Where young Adonis oft reposes,
> Waxing well of his deep wound
> In slumber soft, and on the ground
> Sadly sits th' Assyrian Queen;
> But far above in spangled sheen
> Celestial Cupid, her fam'd son, advanc't,
> Holds his dear Psyche sweet intranc't
> After her wand' ring labours long,
> Till free consent the gods among
> Makes her his eternal Bride,
> And from her fair unspotted side
> Two blissful twins are to be born,
> Youth and Joy; so Jove hath sworn.

In *Paradise Lost*, however, Milton alludes to the Adonis-garden, but without allegorical meaning. When Satan sees Eve among her flowers, she is in a

> Spot more delicious than those gardens feigned
> Or of revived Adonis. . . .

In the same poem Milton elaborates on the Semitic form of Adonis, including the explanation why the river Adonis near Byblos ran red:

> Thammuz came next behind,
> Whose annual wound in Lebanon allured
> The Syrian damsels to lament his fate
> In amorous ditties all a summer's day,
> While smooth Adonis from his native rock
> Ran purple to the sea, supposed with blood
> Of Thammuz yearly wounded: the love-tale
> Infected Sion's daughters with like heat,
> Whose wanton passions in the sacred porch
> Ezekiel saw, when by the vision led
> His eye surveyed the dark idolatries
> Of alienated Judah.

The Venus-Adonis motif in its most popular form was the romantic one which the Hellenistic tradition had inspired. In the *Faerie Queene* of Spenser, the love of the two mythological figures is woven on a tapestry which hung in Castle Joyeous:

> In which with cunning hand was pourtrayed
> The love of Venus and her Paramoure
> The faire Adonis, turned to a flowre,
> A worke of rare device, and wondrous wit.
> First did it shew the bitter balefull stowre,
> Which her assayd with many a fervent fit,
> When first her tender hart was with his beautie smit.
> Then with what sleights and sweet allurements she

> Entyst the Boy, as well that art she knew,
> And wooed him her Paramoure to be;
>
> . . . .
>
> Lo, where beyond he lyeth languishing,
> Deadly engored of a great wild Bore,
> And by his side the Goddesse groveling
> Makes for him endlesse mone, and evermore
> With her soft garment wipes away the gore,
> Which staines his snowy skin with hatefull hew:
> But when she saw no helpe might him restore,
> Him to a dainty flowre she did transmew,
> Which in that cloth was wrought, as if it lively grew.

Shakespeare's *Venus and Adonis*, probably his first published work (1593), is an expansion and elaboration of the story as told by Ovid in the tenth book of the *Metamorphoses*. For his Elizabethan audience, however, Shakespeare added a variant note to the common tradition: Adonis became a chaste and reluctant young man pursued by a passionately amorous Venus (fig. 41). Borrowing motifs freely from several other Ovidian tales and from stock situations in Italian pastoral poetry, Shakespeare turned out—apart from whatever symbolic and metaphysical elements scholars seem to detect in the poem—a spicy and intellectually erotic narrative which soon became a handbook for lovers. A brief example of the nonclassical antithesis between a cold Adonis and a warm Venus:

> Look how a bird lies tangled in a net
> So fast'ned in her arms Adonis lies.
> Pure shame and aw'd resistance made him fret,
> Which bred more beauty in his angry eyes.
> > Rain added to a river that is rank
> > Perforce will force it overflow the bank.
>
> Still she entreats, and prettily entreats,
> For to a pretty ear she tunes her tale.
> Still is he sullen, still he low'rs and frets
> 'Twixt crimson shame and anger ashy-pale.
> > Being red, she loves him best; and being white,
> > Her best is better'd with a more delight.

Keats, in his treatment of the theme in *Endymion*, combines the reluctant youth of Shakespeare and the Hellenistic literary treatment of the Adonia. Before his death Keats' Adonis had rejected Venus' overtures, but when resurrected he becomes a willing lover. The story is sung by a Cupid to the accompaniment of a lyre:

> . . . my poor mistress went distract and mad,
> When the boar tusk'd him: so away she flew
> To Jove's high throne, and by her plainings drew
> Immortal tear-drops down the thunderer's beard;
> Whereon, it was decreed he should be rear'd
> Each summer time to life. Lo! this is he,
> That same Adonis, safe in the privacy
> Of this still region all his winter-sleep.

Figure 41.   Titian. Adonis taking leave from Aphrodite (Venus). The artist
possibly anticipates the reluctant lover of Shakespeare's *Venus and Adonis*.
Painting, 1553. Widener Collection, National Gallery of Art, Washington, D.C.

> Aye, sleep; for when our love-sick queen did weep
> Over his waned corse, the tremulous shower
> Heal'd up the wound, and, with a balmy power,
> Medicined death to a lengthened drowsiness:
> . . . .
> And soon, returning from love's banishment,
> Queen Venus leaning downward open arm'd:
> Her shadow fell upon his breast, and charm'd
> A tumult to his heart, and a new life
> Into his eyes. Ah, miserable strife,
> But for her comforting! unhappy sight,
> But meeting her blue orbs! Who, who can write
> Of these first minutes? The unchariest muse
> To embracements warm as theirs makes coy excuse.

The death of Keats in the springtime of his life occasioned Shelley's lament for the
young poet, *Adonais*. Imitating Bion's threnody on the death of Adonis and a similar elegy written on Bion's death, Shelley used the ancient pastoral form of the
Adonis-dirge to honor the passing of Keats. For melodic effect, Shelley added a syllable to Adonis' name and produced the more rhythmic Adonais.

> I weep for Adonais—he is dead!
> Oh weep for Adonais! tho' our tears
> Thaw not the frost which binds so dear a head!
> And thou, sad Hour, selected from all years
> To mourn our loss, rouse thy obscure compeers,
> And teach them thine own sorrow!

Adonis was to influence literature from yet another quarter. Sir James George Frazer (1854–1941), classical scholar and anthropologist, ransacked mythological treatises in his search for the survival of primitive ritual patterns. Behind the myths of such figures as Adonis, Hyacinth, Linus, Persephone, the Egyptian Osiris, and the Anatolian Attis, Frazer perceived spirits or genii of fertility, personifications of grains and fruits, whose death and resurrection allegorized the seasonal cycle of growth and decay. His research was published between 1890 and 1915 in a *magnum opus* of twelve volumes, *The Golden Bough*. Although Frazer's theory of the Dying and Reviving God has undergone much modification, it has deeply influenced a whole body of historians of literature, scholars who have attempted to detect behind certain literary genres Frazer's theme of death and resurrection. Gilbert Murray and F. M. Cornford subjected ancient tragedy and comedy to an anthropological analysis and revealed what they considered to be the primitive ritual drama underlying the later sophisticated forms. The same treatment was extended to such genres as European Mummers' plays by R. J. Tiddy, the Scandinavian Elder Edda by Bertha Philpotts, and the legend of the Holy Grail by Jessie L. Weston. The analysis went so far as to see primitive ritual drama in the Punch-and-Judy show and in the pre-Shakespearean legend of Hamlet!

These anthropological analyses, which like Frazer's theory have also undergone modification, were to influence not only historians of literature but poets as well. One critic, commenting on T. S. Eliot's *The Waste Land*, states: "Here we have classic myth, in addition to medieval and occult lore, used not only for reference but for frame and background. There is Adonis, the slain vegetation god, who is merged with Christ; but Adonis has more to do with Frazer than with Venus. . . ." T. S. Eliot himself is quick to acknowledge his debt to Frazer, and indirectly to Adonis, in this opening note to *The Waste Land*:

> Not only the title, but the plan and a good deal of the incidental symbolism of the poem were suggested by Miss Jessie L. Weston's book on the Grail legend. . . . To another work of anthropology I am indebted in general, one which has influenced our generation profoundly; I mean *The Golden Bough;* I have used especially the two volumes *Adonis, Attis, Osiris.* Anyone who is acquainted with these works will immediately recognise in the poem certain references to vegetation ceremonies.

The anthropological influence is also strong in H. D.'s *Adonis*, a poem concerned not with love and Aphrodite, but with the cycle of death and resurrection. However, the poetess transfers the symbol of Adonis from the seasonal rhythm of vegetation and fertility to the cycle of anguish and happiness in the human heart:

> Each of us like you
> has died once.
> each of us like you
> has passed through drift of wood-leaves,
> cracked and bent

> and tortured and unbent
> in the winter frost,
> then burnt into gold points,
> lighted afresh,
> crisp amber, scales of gold-leaf,
> in the sun-heat. . . .

Cupid and Psyche.   Three other tales associated with Aphrodite are unusual in that they influenced literature and art more in later times than in antiquity. The story of Cupid and Psyche is known to us only in the version of the first-century A.D. writer Apuleius; the story of Hero and Leander is cited by Vergil and Ovid but is elaborated in epic form by a Greek poet of the fifth century A.D., a certain Musaeus Grammaticus; and for Pyramus and Thisbe we have to rely solely on Ovid who tells us in the fourth book of his *Metamorphoses* that the story is not too well known.

Eros—Cupid is the Latinized form (from *cupere*, to desire) of the Greek god of Love—and Psyche (Soul) are brought together rather late in the classical period. We have already seen how Hesiod employed Eros as a cosmic principle in the early stages of his cosmogony, and that after the birth of Aphrodite he attended her along with the Hours and the Graces as she went to the company of the gods. Later poets make him a son of the love-goddess and even speak of several Erotes or Cupids. To Homer, Eros is little more than physical desire, the passionate kind that drives Paris to Helen. Later poets make him a cunning and cruel power that can affect the body or unhinge the mind; yet he can be sweet and endearing and bittersweet. Early Greek artists represented Eros in the flower of boyhood—the statue of the late classical sculptor Praxiteles being the best known. But as time went on artists made him ever younger until by the Hellenistic period he becomes the chubby winged child armed with arrows made familiar to us by rococo art. Shakespeare's "pretty dimpled boys, like smiling Cupids" is taken from North's translation (1579) of the *Parallel Lives* of Plutarch (c. 46–c. A.D. 120) "pretty fair boys apparelled as painters do set forth god Cupid. . . ."

When the nature of love became a topic for philosophical discussion at the beginning of the fourth century B.C., as in Plato's *Phaedrus* and *Symposium*, a depersonalized Eros was brought into relationship with the soul (psyche). At about the same time, Eros and Psyche were being portrayed in art in an atmosphere of harmony and quietude. Hellenistic poets and artists were of two minds on this relationship: by some, Eros and Psyche were united in harmony, a motif that seems to have been carried over into Roman and early Christian art as a symbol of heavenly happiness; others considered the soul as the seat of passion and portrayed Eros as a torturer of Psyche, passion dominating the soul. In the hands of Apuleius the motif of the torment of Psyche was combined with a variety of widespread folktale themes—Beauty and the Beast, fairy bridegroom, violation of taboo, search for the lost husband, accomplishing impossible tasks, the perilous journey, and so on— into an allegorical fairy tale of the quest of the human soul for love, of attaining true and pure happiness through the purification of the soul by suffering and misfortune. The story of Cupid and Psyche is but one part of Apuleius' novel the *Metamorphoses*, better known as *The Golden Ass.* The hero of this sole Latin novel that has come down to us complete is a certain Lucius who is accidentally metamorphosed into an ass, and in this disguise he is able to observe and hear many strange things. He hears the story of Cupid and Psyche recited by an old crone in a den of thieves.

Once upon a time, the story goes, a certain king and queen had three beautiful daughters of whom the youngest, Psyche, was the most beautiful. Psyche's beauty caused many people to think she was an incarnation of Venus herself, and she received so much adoration that the worship of the goddess was neglected and all but disappeared. Venus angrily ordered her son Cupid to punish Psyche by causing her to fall in love with some contemptible and loathsome man. Cupid, however, was so stricken by the girl's beauty that he himself fell in love with her. In the meantime Psyche's two sisters had married royalty, but no one courted or showed any interest in Psyche. Her father, in fear that the gods might have been offended, consulted the oracle of Apollo at Miletus and was told that his daughter was not going to be the bride of a mortal husband but of a monster who neither gods nor men could resist; that her husband awaited her corpse on the top of a mountain. Dressed in mourning clothes and conducted to the mountain with funeral music and lamentations, Psyche awaited her fate. A gentle breeze lifted her off the ground and carried her to a pleasant valley where she fell asleep on a bed of flowers.

In that secluded valley she discovered a fabled palace so beautiful that she knew it must be a god's residence. An invisible being announced that all she was looking at was to be her own and that she would be served by a host of unseen servants. Magically, a table appeared covered with delicacies of all kinds; instrumental and choral music drifted throughout the palace but no performers could be seen. With much trepidation Psyche undressed and went to bed, but a gentle whisper in the dark of the night announced the presence of her invisible and unknown husband. At night Cupid would come to her and lie with her in the dark, but he would be gone before dawn, leaving Psyche perplexed as to the identity of her lover. She did, however, manage to get his consent to a visit by her two sisters, but he imposed a condition: she must not attempt to find out what he looked like no matter how much they pressed her. She agreed. The West Wind brought the sisters to Psyche's new home, and filled with envy they asked her about her husband. The ingenuous Psyche, drawing from her imagination, described him as being a handsome youth who spent his time hunting. Her husband again emphasized the dangers in receiving visits from her sisters, and that this child which she was now bearing would be a god only if she kept his secret. After giving her sisters contradictory versions about her husband, she had to confess that she really did not know his identity. Stirred by jealousy, the two sisters aroused fears in Psyche that her husband was the monster prophesied by Apollo. And what of the child she was bearing? They advised her to provide herself with a lamp and a sharp knife, and if she discovered her invisible lover to be a monster, to kill him.

One night, disregarding the taboo that Cupid had imposed, she lit a lamp, armed herself with a knife, and approached her sleeping husband. The light revealed the youthful god Cupid in all his glory. But as Psyche bent over him, a drop of burning oil fell from the lamp onto the shoulder of the sleeping god. He awoke and instantly flew away to the top of a cypress tree. Pausing momentarily to reproach her with "Love cannot live with suspicion," he flew off and was gone. Gone too were the palace and the gardens. Now in a highly emotional state, the unhappy young girl attempted to drown herself, only to have the river reject her. Filled with remorse, Psyche wandered off until she came to the city in which one of her sisters lived. Psyche told her what had happened and added that Cupid would accept the sister in place of herself. The sister eagerly ran to the top of the mountain and called on the West Wind to carry her at once to Cupid's palace. With that she leaped headlong from the mountain, only to be dashed to pieces. The same fate met Psyche's other sister.

While Psyche searched for her lost lover, Cupid lay heartsick and groaning in his mother's home. Venus had the news of her son's unhappiness brought to her by a sea gull as she bathed in the sea. Furious at what had happened, she rushed home and berated Cupid for having disobeyed her orders and for having formed an amorous relationship with her enemy. She asked Juno and Ceres, who happened to be on the scene, for their help in finding and punishing Psyche. The goddesses, however, fearing Cupid's love-tipped arrows, rationalized his behavior as being that of a young man coming of age; and fearing Venus' anger they avoided offering Psyche any help when she came to them with her prayers. At last Psyche arrived at the temple of Venus where she was seized and brutally maltreated by Venus' servants Custom, Anxiety, and Sadness. Even Venus herself reviled the girl and physically abused her though she was pregnant with Cupid's child.

Not content with this kind of punishment, the goddess then imposed on Psyche a number of nigh-impossible tasks. First she was led to the storeroom of the temple and was ordered to separate an enormous heap of mixed grain before nightfall. Venus then left for a banquet. Psyche was completely at a loss as to how to accomplish this formidable task, but Cupid stirred up an army of ants to sort out the different kinds of grain. When Venus returned from her party at midnight and saw that the grain had been sorted, she knew that her son had had a hand in helping Psyche. She threw the girl a piece of black bread for her supper and left. The following morning the goddess ordered Psyche to bring her a piece of wool from a dangerous flock of golden sheep that fed on the bank of a neighboring stream. For this second perilous task Psyche again had divine help: a green reed in the river dissuaded her from approaching the animals when the rising sun made them most vicious. Instead, the reed instructed her to wait until they had been lulled by the murmuring of the stream and the heat of the day, and then she was to pluck the golden fleece from the bushes through which the flocks had passed. Psyche did as she was told and returned to Venus with her arms full of golden wool.

The goddess was resolved to put the girl to the ultimate test. She pointed to a distant mountain peak and ordered Psyche to bring back a jar full of water from the stream which burst forth from the rock and plunges down to the Stygian marshes and feeds the Cocytus, a river to the Underworld. When the hapless girl reached the summit of the mountain, she saw to her horror that the stream was guarded by monstrous serpents. In this moment of her greatest peril Psyche was served by divine providence: Jupiter, owing a debt to Cupid for having helped him win Ganymede as his cup-bearer, sent his eagle who took the jar and filled it with water from the forbidden stream. When Psyche returned to Venus with her task completed, she learned that there was yet another. The goddess put a small box into her hand and told her to go to the Underworld and to get Proserpina to put a bit of her beauty into it so as to compensate for what she had lost in taking care of her sick son. Psyche was sure that all was now lost. She went up into a high tower and resolved to go to the Underworld by jumping to her death. Just then, the tower miraculously broke into speech and advised her how to make the perilous journey without committing suicide. The tower directed her to a hellmouth at Taenarum and gave her specific instructions on how to cross the river of the dead—she was to carry two coins in her mouth to pay for her round-trip passage on Charon's ferry—and how to get by Cerberus the hellhound—she was to throw him a piece of barley-bread soaked in water and honey on entering and leaving the domain of the dead. The talking tower also gave Psyche a long list of caveats so as to avoid being made a permanent resident of the Underworld. Of prime importance was the warning that once Proserpina had given her what she had come for, she was under no circumstances to open or even look at the box. Psyche did as she was told, and when she was about to leave the Underworld the desire came over her to possess some of the beauty she thought the box contained. She opened the box and instantly fell into a deep death-like sleep. Cupid, now recovered, came to her rescue and revived her with the touch of an arrow.

As Psyche was on her way to finish this final task set for her by Venus, Cupid appealed his case before Jupiter. The god summoned the other gods and goddesses to a council where it was decreed that it was time for Cupid to settle down even though he had chosen a mortal woman for his wife. Psyche was brought up to heaven (fig. 42) where she was given a cup of nectar—the drink of the gods—which made her immortal. Venus relented, and at the great wedding feast Jupiter had ordered, the goddess danced on the occasion of her son's formal betrothal. So, with due rites, Psyche passed into the power of Cupid; and their child was a daughter whom men called Voluptas (Pleasure).

*   *   *   *

Cupid and Psyche, but one episode in Apuleius' *Metamorphoses*, soon attracted allegorizers of late antiquity and the Renaissance. The story of the two lovers became an iconographic motif for pagan and Christian alike, a symbol of the immortality of the soul and its hope for a future life of happiness after death. Yet, it was also possible to place another construction on the tale of the romantic pair, as did the fifth-century mythographer Fulgentius who identified Psyche with Lust and Cupid with both Earthly and Divine Love. During the Renaissance, Apuleius became very popular, partly because of interest in him as a Platonist and partly because of Boccaccio (1313–1375) who, in his encyclopedic work on the genealogy of the gods, not only related the story but also added an allegorical interpretation of it. The Italian painter Raphael (1483–1520) took twelve scenes from the story of Cupid and Psyche for the frescoes he designed for the Villa Farnesina, the palace of Pope Leo X (fig. 42).

It was not long before Apuleius' *Metamorphoses* was translated into Italian, French, and German, and then finally into English by Thomas Aldington in 1566. Shackerley Marmion (1603–1639) composed *The Legend of Cupid and Psyche*, an embroidered version in heroic couplets of the story as told by Apuleius and Fulgentius. In Spenser's Adonis-garden, we find Cupid and Psyche.

> . . . now in stedfast love and happy state
> She with him lives, and hath borne a chyld,
> Pleasure, that doth both gods and men aggrate,
> Pleasure, the daughter of Cupid and Psyche.

Milton, influenced by Spenser's symbols of ideal love, has Psyche give birth not to Pleasure but to twins, Youth and Joy, apparently shying away from the earthy connotations of the Latin word Voluptas as inappropriate for the end of the *Comus*.

Figure 42.   Hermes (Mercury) conducts Psyche to Olympus. *Fresco by
Raphael, 1518, one of the panels illustrating the story of Cupid and Psyche.
Farnese Palace, Rome. (Alinari)*

The theme of Cupid and Psyche also had a great vogue on the Continent among writers and composers of the seventeenth century. Among others, the celebrated French fabulist La Fontaine wrote a poem on the theme, *Les Amours de Psyché et de Cupidon* (1669), and the two greats of the Grand Siecle, Molière and Corneille, collaborated on the dialogue for Lulli's opera *Psyche* (1671). But the nineteenth century saw a spate of revivals in England. In 1819 Keats wrote his *Ode to Psyche* which omitted the traditional allegory; the poet instead plays upon the pastoral scene and the joy of "warm Love."

> 'Mid hush'd, cool-rooted flowers, fragrant-eyed,
>   Blue, silver-white, and budded Tyrian,
> They lay calm-breathing on the bedded grass;
>   Their arms embraced and their pinions too;
>   Their lips touch'd not, but had not bade adieu,
> As if disjoined by soft-handed slumber,
> And ready still past kisses to outnumber
>   At tender eye-dawn of aurorean love:
>   The winged boy I knew;
>   But who wast thou, O happy, happy dove?
>   His Psyche true!
>
> . . . .
> Yes, I will be thy priest, and build a fane
>   In some untrodden region of my mind,
> Where branched thoughts, new grown with pleasant pain,
>   Instead of pines shall murmur in the wind:
> Far, far around shall those dark-cluster'd trees
>   Fledge the wild-ridged mountains steep by steep;
> And there by zephyrs, streams, and birds, and bees,
>   The moss-lain Dryads shall be lull'd to sleep;
> And in the midst of this wide quietness
> A rosy sanctuary will I dress
> With the wreath'd trellis of a working brain,
>   With buds, and bells, and stars without a name,
> With all the gardener Fancy e'er could feign,
>   Who breeding flowers, will never breed the same:
> And there shall be for thee all soft delight
>   That shadowy thought can win,
> A bright torch, and a casement ope at night,
>   To let the warm Love in !

Elizabeth Barrett Browning (1806–1861), for whom the old gods of antiquity were dead and Christianity was a worthy myth and poetically acceptable, found Apuleius' *Metamorphoses* attractive enough to paraphrase portions of the Cupid and Psyche episode. William Morris (1868-1870) gives an extravagant rendering of the story for his *Earthly Paradise*; the robustly romantic story of Apuleius is decorated and adorned with Victorian bric-a-brac, as for example the almost complete zoo which Psyche produces to entertain her sisters: it holds elephants, rhinoceroses, lions, leopards, tigers, eagles, peacocks, swans, and apes. Robert Bridges also turned his hand to the theme of the two lovers for his *Eros and Psyche*, a poetic narrative composed in 1885 and revised in 1894. Not only does Bridges turn the

Latin names of Apuleius into their Greek equivalents, but he also adds a considerable number of mythological details from ancient and modern literature. Although the poet claimed his work to be "in all essentials a faithful translation of
Apuleius' story," his success may be judged from a letter that Gerard Manley
Hopkins wrote to Bridges: "The story you have not elevated but confined yourself
to make it please. Eros is little more than a winged Masher, but Psyche is a success,
a sweet little 'body,' rather than 'soul.' "

   At the opening of the twentieth century, T. Surge Moore wrote two dramas on incidents taken from Apuleius, *Pan's Prophecy* (1904) and *Psyche in Hades* (1930),
which are poetic discourses on the nature of true love and the complexities of life
and soul. Between these two dramas, the Imagist-poet Richard Aldington in *Images*
(1915) took the two lovers in the form of a statue of Eros and Psyche to contrast the
beauty of the past with the ugliness of the contemporary urban scene.

   Ezra Pound, in a simple expression of Psyche's feeling when united with her
lover, composed these words for her in his *Speech for Psyche in the Golden Book
of Apuleius*:

> All night, and as the wind lieth among
> The cypress trees, he lay,
> Nor held me save as air that brusheth by one
> Close, and as the petals of flowers in falling
> Waver and seem not drawn to earth, so he
> Seemed over me to hover light as leaves
> And closer me than air,
> And music flowing through me seemed to open
> Mine eyes upon new colours.
> O winds, what wind can match the weight of him!

   Finally, a late revival of interest in Apuleius has come about through modern
translations; among the latest is one by the well-known poet and mythographer
Robert Graves under the popular title *The Golden Ass* (1951).

Hero and Leander.   In contrast with the story of Cupid and Psyche, the romance
of Hero and Leander is little more than a straight tale of tragic love, a literary genre
that had its origins in the Hellenistic period. Vergil makes brief mention of the
tragedy in his *Georgics*; Ovid develops the theme in two poetic epistles in the
Heroides, a collection of imaginary letters of mythical heroines. This is all that we
know about the story until the fifth century A.D. when the Greek poet Musaeus,
surnamed the Grammarian, wrote a miniature epic on the romance of Hero and
Leander. Then by a quirk of scholarship during the Revival of Learning, this Musaeus was identified with the legendary poet and teacher of hoary antiquity, Musaeus, a forerunner of Homer and Hesiod. Scaliger (1540–1609), the ranking
scholar of the Renaissance, said that if the poet of *Hero and Leander* had written
the *Iliad* and *Odyssey*, he would have done far better than Homer. Aldus Manutius
(1449–1515), scholar and printer-publisher, when attempting to publish the
whole corpus of Greek literature, began with *Hero and Leander*, being "desirous
that Musaeus, the most ancient poet, should form a prelude to Aristotle and other
sages. . . ." Musaeus' work was soon translated into French, Spanish, and English;
and by 1592 Abraham Fraunce was able to say that "Leander and Heroes love is in

every mans mouth." It was this case of mistaken identity, an instance where a late work was given the authority of a mythical poet who was said to be a son of the Muses, that resulted in the great popularity of Hero and Leander in literature.

Once, so the story goes, Eros struck a young man and a girl with one of his love-tipped arrows. The girl, Hero, was a priestess of Aphrodite and lived in a tower at Sestos on the European shore of the Hellespont (Dardanelles); the boy, Leander, lived on the Asian side at Abydus. It chanced that the two met at a festival of Adonis and fell madly in love with each other. When Hero told the youthful Leander that she lived on the other side of the Hellespont, he insisted upon keeping his tryst with her. He would swim across the dangerous passage if Hero would keep a lighted lamp in her tower window to guide him across the dark waters. Throughout the summer nights Leander would cross the Hellespont for a passionate meeting— blessed only by the dark night— with his beloved Hero. But at the approach of winter, the sea turned stormy, and though reason should have kept Hero from lighting the lamp, her desire to see Leander drove her to light it. One fatal night, Leander plunged into the stormy Hellespont and fought against tide and waves, and not only did his strength fail him but Hero's lamp was blown out by fierce gusts of wind. Dawn came and Leander had not reached the tower. Hero scanned the sea for some sign of her lover. No sign of him, but there at the base of her tower was his body, torn by the rocks and lifeless. Beside herself with grief, the young girl plunged from a cliff into the sea so that she might join her lover in death.

*   *   *   *

Musaeus told his simple straightforward tale of tragic love in some three hundred and forty lines of poetry. Marlowe, who was to give the story its finest rendering in the English language, took over eight hundred lines and yet left his *Hero and Leander* unfinished—George Chapman was to complete it in 1594. Instead of playing, as does Musaeus, upon the pathos of star-crossed lovers joined together without the benefit of marriage rites, Marlowe focuses upon the physical and sensual aspects of young love as well as upon the Machiavellian tactics by which an eager Leander convinces a chaste Hero to surrender herself to her emotions. To this Marlowe adds epigram, moralizing, mythological ornamentation, and lavish word-painting—literary trappings derived in large part from the influence of Ovid upon Elizabethan poets. Marlowe sets the mood in the very opening of the narrative:

> On Hellespont guiltie of True-loves blood,
> In view and oposit two citties stood,
> Seaborderers, disjoin'd by Neptunes might:
> The one Abydos, the other Sestos hight.
> At Sestos, Hero dwelt; Hero the faire,
> Whom young Apollo courted for her haire,
> And offred as a dower his burning throne,
> Where she should sit for men to gaze upon.
> The outside of her garments were of lawne,
> The lining purple silke, with guilt starres drawne,
> Her wide sleeves greene, and bordered with a grove,
> Where Venus in her naked glory strove,
> To please the carelesse and disdainfull eies

Of proud Adonis that before her lies.

. . . .

Some say, for her the fairest Cupid pyn'd
And looking in her face, was strooken blind.
But this is true, so like was one the other,
As he imagyn'd Hero was his mother.
And oftentimes into her bosome flew,
About her naked necke his bare armes threw,
And laid his childish head upon her brest,
And with still panting rockt, there tooke his rest.

After the two meet and fall in love, Leander, "like to a bold sharpe Sophister," attempts with arguments such as these to convince Hero "Venus Nun," to give up her vow of chastity:

Ah simple Hero, learne they selfe to cherish,
Lone women like to emptie houses perish.

. . . .

Wilt thou live single still? one shalt thou bee,
Though never-singling Hymen couple thee.
Wild savages, that drinke of running springs,
Thinke water farre excels all earthly things:
But they that dayly tast neat wine, despise it.
Virginitie, albeit some highly prise it,
Compar'd with marriage, had you tried them both,
Differs as much as wine and water doth.

. . . .

This idoll which you terme Virginitie
Is neither essence subject to the eie,
No, nor to any one exterior sence,
Nor hath it any place of residence,
Nor is't of earth or mold celestiall,
Or capable of any forme at all.
Of that which hath no being doe not boast,
Things that are not at all are never lost.
Men foolishly doe call it vertuous,
What vertue is it that is borne with us?

And Leander goes on in this vein, supporting his sophistic arguments with mythological citations, until Hero "swallow'd Cupids golden hooke." In short, Marlowe's rendition of the idyll is a sixteenth-century picture of the amorous pursuit of a lady of the court who swoons, is revived by a kiss, and drops "her painted fanne of curled plumes, thinking to traine Leander therewithall."

Shakespeare, in As You Like It, has a rather cynical Rosalind tell Orlando that no one dies because of love; citing the story of Hero and Leander, Rosalind gives it a humorous twist:

Leander, he would have liv'd many a fair year though Hero had turn'd nun, if it had not been for a hot midsummer night; for (good youth) he went but forth to wash him in the Hellespont, and being taken with the cramp, was drown'd; and the foolish chroniclers of that age found it was 'Hero of Sestos.' But these are all lies. Men have died from time to time, and worms have eaten them, but not for love.

Far less reverent is Thomas Nashe's prose burlesque of the story of the ill-fated lovers, *Prayse of the Red Herring* (1599). Nashe is quick to pick up the inconsistencies in the ancient tale—for example, why didn't Leander take a boat instead of swimming?—and makes short shrift of Hero's hesitation to fall into her lover's arms. And when Hero discovers the body of Leander, Nashe describes it as "sodden to haddocks meate"; and the young girl's emotional state "a franticke Bacchanal outright, and made no more bones but sprang after him, and so resignd her Priesthood, and left worke for Musaeus and Kit Marlowe."

The poets of the nineteenth century found the story of Hero and Leander especially appealing to their sense of the romantic. Byron, who had proudly duplicated Leander's feat by swimming the Hellespont in May of 1810, treats the theme both seriously and humorously. In the *Bride of Abydos*, the locale of his Turkish romance leads the poet to introduce the second canto with these lines:

> The winds are high on Helle's wave,
>   As on that night of stormy water
> When Love, who sent, forget to save
> The young, the beautiful, the brave
>   The lonely hope of Sestos' daughter
>
> . . . .
>
> That tale is old, but love anew
> May nerve young hearts to prove as true.

In a lighter spirit, Byron compares his experience in the Hellespont with that of Leander. From *Written after Swimming from Sestos to Abydos*:

> If, in the month of dark December,
>   Leander, who was nightly wont
> (What maid will not the tale remember?)
>   To cross thy stream, broad Hellespont!
> If, when the wintry tempest roar'd,
>   He sped to Hero, nothing loth,
> And thus of old thy current pour'd
>   Fair Venus! how I pity both!
>
> For *me*, degenerate modern wretch
>   Though in the genial month of May,
> My dripping limbs I faintly stretch,
>   And think I've done a feat today.
>
> . . . .
>
> 'T were hard to say who fared the best:
>   Sad mortals! thus the Gods still plague you!
> He lost his labour, I my jest;
>   For he was drown'd, and I've the ague.

Keats, whose poetry was often inspired by works of art as well as literature, describes the death of Leander in his sonnet *On an Engraved Gem of Leander*:

> Sinking bewilder'd' mid the dreary sea:
> 'Tis young Leander toiling to his death;
>   Nigh swooning, he doth purse his weary lips
>   For Hero's cheek, and smiles against her smile.

> O horrid dream! see how his body dips
> > Dead-heavy; arms and shoulders gleam awhile:
> He's gone: up bubbles all his amorous breath!

There follow narrative poems on the tale of the two lovers by Thomas Hodd (1827) and Leigh Hunt (1819); and in German there is Schiller's *Hero und Leander* (1801) which Hunt seems to have known. Tennyson's *Hero to Leander* (1830) is a brief but passionate plea by Hero to her lover not to leave her since she knows that he will be doomed "and the billow will embrace thee with a kiss as soft as mine." Later in the century, Dante Gabriel Rossetti places Hero's lamp in a shrine of Anteros (Love returned) where it will remain unlit until "some one man the happy issue see of a life's love." From Rossetti's sonnet *Hero's Lamp:*

> That lamp thou fill'st in Eros' name to-night,
> > O Hero, shall the Sestian augurs take
> > To-morrow, and for drowned Leander's sake
> To Anteros its fireless lip shall plight.
>
> . . . .
>
> That lamp within Anteros' shadowy shrine
> > Shall stand unlit (for so the gods decree)
> > Till some one may the happy issue see
> Of life's love, and bid its flame to shine:

In the twentieth century, A. E. Housman (1859–1936), classical scholar and poet, uses the tale of Hero and Leander as a symbol of the transient nature of happiness. In "Tarry, delight, so seldom met" from *More Poems:*

> By Sestos town, in Hero's tower,
> > On Hero's heart Leander lies;
> The signal torch has burned its hour
> > And sputters as it dies.
>
> Beneath him, in the nighted firth,
> > Between two continents complain
> The seas he swam from earth to earth
> > And he must swim again.

To the American poet Malcolm Cowley, Hero's lover is enticed by the sea to surrender to its rhythms and mysteries; Hero is to be comforted by knowing that Leander will become part of the living and ever-moving sea. From Cowley's *Leander* (1929):

> Between the waves, out of the sight of land,
> at nightfall toward an unseen beacon swimming;
> the sea flung her arms about his arms
> in foam, mingled her hair with his
> and clung against his breast;
> against his lips the salt pulse of the sea.
>
> . . . .
>
> He lingered to the rhythm of the waves,
> a last time felt the rain against his cheek,
> then slowly filled his lungs with water, sank
> through immense halls of darkness, infinite

chambers of dream, a white thing that drifts
southward with the current, a cold body
whittled by the sea.

And Hero
waiting in her desolate chamber, Hero
be comforted;

for they have taken the dead whose flesh you loved
and dressed him in the plunder of the sea;
his hair is wreathed with algae; his eyes gleam
luminous with jellyfishes; coral
blooms on his thighs; his arms are braceleted
with pearl, and scars of kisses on his breast.

Pyramus and Thisbe.   The last story in this triad of tales is that of Pyramus and
Thisbe. They have no immediate connection with Aphrodite except that their story
is one of love, tragic love. Our earliest and sole source for the story is Ovid's *Metamorphoses* where we find the daughters of Minyas staying at home, occupying
themselves with domestic work and telling stories after they had refused to take
part in the holy but orgiastic rituals of Dionysus. The tragic fate of Pyramus and
Thisbe, a story of true love, precedes Ovid's treatment of Aphrodite's extramarital affair with Ares, a story of inconstant and meretricious love. The locale of
the tale is Babylon, and the likelihood is that Ovid derived it from the work of a
Hellenistic poet at either Alexandria or Syrian Antioch.

Pyramus and Thisbe, the handsomest youth and the most beautiful girl in the
East, lived in adjoining houses in Babylon. Their nearness to one another brought
them together and they fell in love. They would have married if their parents had
not been opposed to it; but though their parents prevented their seeing each
other, they kept their love alive by conversing through a chink in the garden wall
that separated the two houses. Finally they decided to defy their parents and to
meet in secret outside the city walls near a mulberry tree that grew beside the tomb
of the Babylonian king Ninus. Thisbe stole out of her house in the dark of night and
was the first to arrive at the trysting place. As she waited for her lover she was
frightened away by a lioness whose jaws were dripping with the blood of a recent
kill. Thisbe ran to the shelter of a cave, dropping her veil as she ran off. The lioness,
after drinking her fill at a nearby spring, turned toward the woods, and seeing the
veil on the ground, tossed and ripped it with her bloody mouth. When Pyramus
arrived on the scene and saw the blood-stained veil, he was sure that some ravening
beast had killed his beloved Thisbe. In grief, and blaming himself because he had
asked Thisbe to meet him in secret, he drew his sword and plunged it into his heart.
As he lay dying under the mulberry tree, his blood stained the white berries of the
tree, and sinking to the roots of the tree his blood also tinged the hanging berries
with its dark red color. When Thisbe found it safe to return, she discovered
Pyramus in the last throes of death. She embraced him and resolved to die with
her lover. Seizing the sword with which Pyramus had killed himself, she prayed
to the gods and then fell on the sword's point (fig. 43). The gods answered her
prayer: the color of mulberries which until then had been white were from this
time on to be dark red when ripe. The two lovers were finally reunited when their
parents placed their ashes in a common urn.

Figure 43. The tragic end of Pyramus and Thisbe. *Roman wall painting, first century A.D. Pompeii. (Alinari)*

The tragedy of Pyramus and Thisbe has been immortalized by Shakespeare in his burlesqued version for the play-within-a-play in *A Midsummer Night's Dream*, a play which Bottom and his company of amateurs call "The Comedy of Pyramus and Thisbe." And lest the ladies be frightened by the sight of Pyramus drawing his sword to kill himself at "Ninny's tomb," Bottom calls for a special prologue:

> . . . and let the prologue say, we will do no harm with our swords, and that Pyramus is not kill'd indeed; and for the more better assurance tell them that I Pyramus am not Pyramus, but Bottom the weaver. This will put them out of their fear.

But long before Shakespeare had read Ovid's story in his school books, Pyramus' and Thisbe's love was in every man's mouth. In the twelfth and thirteenth centuries, Provençal troubadours sang *"l'autre diz de Piramus,"* and French and Italian poets were attracted to the theme. Boccaccio refashioned the story for his novel *Fiammetta*; John Gower (c. 1330–1408), one of the fathers of English literature, was so moved by the fate of the two lovers that he included them in his *Confessio Amantis* (Confession of a Lover). Chaucer made good use of Ovid's lovers in *The Legend of Good Women* in which he had Pyramus serve as an exemplar of "A man that can in love been trewe and kynde," and Thisbe of a woman who "dar and can as wel as he." An allegorized version of Ovid's *Metamorphoses*, written by a certain Petrus Berchorius in the fourteenth century, transforms Pyramus into the son of God, Thisbe into the soul, sin was the garden wall that stood between them, the mulberry tree turns into the cross, the spring into a baptismal font, and the lion into the devil. When Pyramus commits suicide, the allegorizer turns this into Christ enduring death for the human soul and Thisbe's demise becomes the soul's imitation of his death accompanied by the same mental anguish. In terms of motif—lovers separated by parents, their meeting in secret, each dying thinking that the other is dead—the story of Pyramus and Thisbe is essentially the same as that of Romeo and Juliet and many other tragic romances. It could also serve for a poetic allusion, as in Shakespeare's *Merchant of Venice* when Shylock's daughter, Jessica, says in an antiphonal response to Lorenzo:

> In such a night
> Did Thisbe fearfully o'ertrip the dew,
> And saw the lion's shadow ere himself
> And ran dismay'd away.

Following the Elizabethan period, interest in Pyramus and Thisbe waned except in the field of operatic composition; from the late seventeenth to the twentieth century, ten operas were produced on the theme, the best known being perhaps Gluck's *Piramo e Tisbe* (1746).

12. Hermes (Mercury)

The youngest of the Olympian clan was Hermes, the messenger of the gods, the leader of the souls to the Underworld, the guide of travelers, the god of speech, of thieves, of businessmen, the reputed inventor of the lyre, the syrinx, numbers and the alphabet, the giver of fertility, and the protector of athletes. Young though he was from a mythological point of view, the likelihood is that Hermes was one of the oldest and most nearly primitive of all Greek gods; and though his name is one of the few in Greek mythology that has a plausible etymology—"he of the stone-heap"—his nature and functions were, in the main, fashioned by a very early pre-Greek population.

In naming their equivalent to Hermes, the Romans focused on his commercial aspect and called him Mercurius or Mercury. This name is probably derived from the Latin word *merces*, "merchandise, wares." As Roman armies and merchants made their way into Gaul and parts of Germany, the god Mercury, either by identification or acculturation, became one of the chief deities of the Celts and Teutons. Julius Caesar was to comment on the Celtic gods of Gaul that Mercury was their first and foremost god, that he was regarded as the inventor of all the useful arts, the protector of roads and travelers, all-powerful in business and money matters. The cult of Celtic Mercury was very widespread; his name appears in such place-names as Mercurey, Mercueil, Mercœur, and Montmartre (Mount Mercury). Among the Germans, Mercury was identified with the great Teutonic god Wodanaz, known also as Odin in Norse and Woden in Old English. "Woden's day" or "Wednesday" was also related to Mercury since it was the fourth day of the week, the number four being sacred to the god, the day of his birth.

In yet another part of the ancient world, Hermes was equated with the Egyptian god of knowledge and letters, Thoth. During the third and fourth centuries of this era, certain writers of a religio-philosophic sect known as the Gnostics, falling under the spell of the supposed wisdom of very ancient Egypt, attributed to the god a collection of treatises called the *Hermetica*, and other works on magic, astrology, and alchemy which are a medley of Greek, Egyptian, Platonic, and Christian elements. This exotic form of the god was called Hermes Trismegistus, "Hermes Thrice Great."

The line of reasoning that joins together all the varied characteristics and functions of Hermes appears to have had its start in his earliest representation as the spirit, the *daimon*, which resided in the heap of stones that marked the grave-mound and the pillar of stone that sometimes was placed on top of the mound. Such mounds and gravestones tend to become landmarks, particularly in a country without roads, and help guide the traveler to his destination. Hence, the spirit within these stones became the protector and guide of travelers; and in recognition of the resident *daimon* it was the custom for anyone who passed such markers to add his stone to it. And since the mound was also a grave, Hermes served as a guide not only for the living but for the dead as well, showing their souls the way to the land of the dead. Then, his association with the Underworld makes him a fertility spirit—if he was not one to begin with—since anyone who can go to the realm of the dead and return usually becomes associated with the cycle of life and death. And since tradition and cult make Hermes a native of Arcadia, the land of shepherds, he was called upon to help promote the increase of flocks, a function that he shared with his half-brother Apollo. The early representation of Hermes was a simple monumental stone called a "herm"; later, the herm was squared and given a human head, and marking his connection with fertility, a phallus. This was his most popular representation and herms were often found at cross-roads, byways, before houses and temples, and in marketplaces.

Other functions associated with Hermes are an extension of the old *daimon* who helped travelers, living and dead. Knowing his way from one place to another, Hermes became the messenger and herald of the gods, and any human emissary came under his protection. In his capacity as a messenger, it was necessary for him to be an eloquent and persuasive speaker, and on occasion to plead the case of those who sent him. From very early times, therefore, Hermes was skilled in the art of speaking, and anyone who wished to acquire proficiency in that art would offer the god the tongue of a sacrificial animal. In the course of time, Hermes' talent in the field of oratory was combined with the lyre, which he invented, to make him a general patron of literature; later, the Roman poet Horace would designate men of his profession as "Mercury's men." As for businessmen and thieves, their connection with Hermes comes from the use of the roads which also fell under the god's divine jurisdiction. Merchants, of course, especially appreciated Hermes' influence in making them effective salesmen. However, in associating with thieves and merchants, Hermes had some of their less socially desirable characteristics rub off on him, thereby making it difficult for the god ever to acquire strong moral qualities. His mythological biography also reflects the kind of company he kept; he is often portrayed as sly and cunning both in word and deed, a trickster given to cheating and lying, although he performed these actions with a considerable amount of skill, dexterity, and grace.

Hermes' connection with young men, their gymnastic exercises and games, is less evident than some of his other functions. This concern of the god is generally linked to his being a god of good luck; good luck is needed by athletes who compete against one another. The relationship is explained either as an offshoot of Hermes as a god of fertility or his being a god of commerce, since both have something to do with people who come into sudden and unexpected wealth. And as a giver of wealth and good luck, Hermes also presided over games of chance, particularly the game of dice. In his capacity as a patron of young men and their exercises, Hermes was represented in statuary fully anthropomorphized as a youth.

This youthful Hermes can best be seen in Praxiteles' celebrated *Hermes Carrying the Infant Dionysus* (fig. 44) in which the sculptor seems to have put into marble Homer's description of the god "looking like a young prince at that most charming age when the beard first starts to grow."

Generally, when on a mythological mission Hermes can be recognized by his several attributes: the *petasus*, a traveling hat with a broad brim which in later times was given two little wings, his winged sandals or shoes, and the herald's staff or caduceus (fig. 45). In Homer's epics the caduceus is frequently mentioned as a kind of magic wand with which the god opened and closed the eyes of mortals. Usually the caduceus was represented as a simple staff wound about with two white ribbons, a symbol of the authority and inviolability of the herald who came under the divine protection of the god. Later artists transformed the ribbons into snakes; still later artists added wings to the caduceus.

The early life and adventures of Hermes are related in a Homeric hymn which was composed about 600 B.C., possibly for a festival honoring the god or to celebrate his birthday on the fourth day of the month. The hymn, as this literary genre is conventionally called, is one of the longest of those that have survived. It has often been called enchanting and humorous, light and playful, typical of the Greek attitude in not groveling before any power, human or divine. The central motif which the unknown poet selected for the hymn was Hermes the Trickster who by his cunning outwits the great god Apollo. His mother is regularly given as Maia, a daughter of Atlas. She was a shy goddess who avoided the company of the other gods. Zeus would visit her at night in her cave on Mount Cyllene in Arcadia while his wife Hera slept unaware of her husband's philandering. Maia then conceived and gave birth, as the poet tells us, to a son

> . . . of many shifts, blandly cunning, a robber, a cattle driver, a bringer of dreams, a watcher by night, a thief at the gates, one who was soon to show forth wonderful deeds among the deathless gods. Born with the dawning, at mid-day he played on the lyre, and in the evening he stole the cattle of far-shooting Apollo on the fourth day of the month; for on that day queenly Maia bare him. So soon as he had leaped from his mother's heavenly womb, he lay not long waiting in his holy cradle, but he sprang up and sought the oxen of Apollo.

As this unusual infant stepped from the cave of his birth at noon, he discovered a tortoise, killed it, and using the shell as a sounding board fashioned a new instrument, the lyre. Without any need for instruction he broke into song, singing of his own mother's love affair with Zeus. Shelley, whose translation of this Homeric hymn is one of his best efforts, gives us this rendering of the episode:

> He sung how Jove and May [Maia] of the bright sandal
>   Dallied in love not quite legitimate;
> And his own birth, still scoffing at the scandal,
>   And naming his own name, did celebrate;
> His mother's cave and servant maides he planned all
>   In plastic verse, her household stuff and state,
> Perennial pot, trippet, and brazen pan,—
> But singing, he conceived another plan.

Having finished his song, Hermes, yet in the first day of his life, had a craving for meat. That same evening—for it is in the dark of night that thieves and knaves

Figure 44. Hermes holding the infant Dionysus. *An original work by Praxiteles, c. 340 B.C. Olympia Museum. (Alinari)*

Figure 45. Hermes winging his way over the waves. He holds his magic rod in his right hand; his left holds the lyre, an instrument he invented. *Vase painting, British Museum.*

practice their art—he sneaked out of his cave on Mount Cyllene and traveled far north to Mount Pieria in Thessaly where this young cattle-rustler stole fifty of Apollo's cows. In order not to be tracked, he made the cattle walk backwards, and to confuse the tracks even more, he made a special pair of shoes for himself out of twigs. Hiding the cattle in a cave, he sacrificed two of them to the Olympian gods and stretched out their hides on the walls of the cave. Hermes then hurried back to his cave on Mount Cyllene where he tucked himself in his cradle just as dawn was beginning to break.

> There he lay, innocent as a new-born child,
>   As gossips say; but tho' he was a god,
> The goddess, his fair mother, unbeguiled
>   Knew all that he had done being abroad:
> "Whence come you, and from what adventure wild,
>   You cunning rogue, and where have you abode
> All the long night, clothed in your impudence?
> What have you done since you departed hence?"

Hermes answered his mother that he planned for them to take their rightful place among the gods and to share in the wealth that was legitimately theirs. He will not live out the rest of his life in a gloomy cave, and if Zeus will not honor him by making him a prince of thieves, he will become one by his own efforts. In the meantime Apollo had discovered who was behind the theft of his cattle and charged angrily into Maia's cave. There he found Hermes in his crib, wrapped in his swaddling clothes, pretending to be asleep. When Apollo charged him with the theft of his cattle, the young god cleverly argued that even if he knew what the word "cattle" meant, he was much too young to steal anything; all he wanted was sleep and his mother's breast. Some traditions hold that it was on this occasion that Hermes stole Apollo's bow and arrows. Finally, Zeus ordered the child to return the cattle, but when Apollo heard Hermes play on the lyre which he had invented, he was so charmed by the instrument that he allowed the young god to keep the animals and the remainder of his herd in exchange for the instrument. Apollo also gave Hermes his golden staff and made him a divine protector and keeper of herds. The two then became steadfast friends. Other traditions relate that Apollo also taught Hermes the art of throwing dice and the power of divination, but only to the extent that chance could help in foretelling the future.

Such was the uncommon infancy of a god. Zeus appointed Hermes as the messenger both for himself and his brother Hades, the god of the Underworld. In the *Iliad*, however, Hermes is a divine guide to the living while Iris carries messages for Zeus. Zeus, for example, sends Iris to King Priam to prepare the ransom which will reclaim the body of his dead son Hector, and it is Hermes who is given the job of guiding Priam unseen to the tent of Achilles. In the closing book of the *Odyssey* we find Hermes again serving as a guide, but this time as a guide for the dead. Using his golden wand he stirred up the souls of the suitors whom Odysseus had killed upon his return to Ithaca, and like a shepherd he guided the disembodied souls down to the Underworld. When later traditions introduced Charon as the aged and unkempt ferryman who transported the shades of the dead across the rivers of the Underworld, Hermes usually deposited his charges on the banks of the river Styx (fig. 47), and if they could pay their fare and had been given a proper burial, Charon would take over from that point. In his role as a guide of the dead,

Hermes was often called *psychopompos* "leader of souls." W. H. Auden, in the *New Year Letter*, refers to Hermes by this epithet. The reference to Janus is to the Roman deity associated with doorways, openings, and beginnings.

> And often when the searcher stood
> Before the Oracle, it would
> Ignore his grownup earnestness
> But not the child of his distress,
> For through the Janus of a joke
> The candid psychopompos spoke.

As a guide and messenger and as the youngest in the Olympian household, Hermes was often called upon, mostly by Zeus, to perform various useful services for the gods. When Ixion violated the laws of hospitality on Mount Olympus and attempted to attack Hera, Hermes was called upon to affix him to a fiery wheel to revolve eternally in the deepest reaches of Tartarus (fig. 49). And when the giants Otus and Ephialtes imprisoned Ares in a bronze jar for thirteen months, it was Hermes who was sent on a mission of mercy to free the god of war (p. 180). Hermes also acted as Zeus' intermediary when the great Olympian came into a head-on conflict with Prometheus (p. 43). On still another occasion the young god had to act as a kind of midwife for his father, for when mortal Semele was incinerated by the blazing majesty of Zeus, some say that Hermes snatched the unborn Dionysus from the flames and later helped Zeus give birth to the child from his thigh (fig. 52). On yet another occasion, he was called upon by Zeus to kill the hundred-eyed monster Argos which Hera had placed over Io, whom Zeus loved and had transformed into a heifer to avoid her being detected by his prying wife. For this service Hermes was given the title of *Argeiphontes*, "Slayer of Argos."

Hermes also accompanied Zeus when the gods walked among men in the guise of mortals. The tradition carried over into historical times, for when the Apostle Paul healed a cripple in a Greek city of Asia Minor, the people cried out, as recorded in the King James version of *Acts*: "The gods are come down to us in the likeness of men. And they called Barnabas, Jupiter; and Paul, Mercurius, because he was the chief speaker." However, of all the services that Hermes performed for the gods, none is more celebrated than his role in the Judgment of Paris. In one of the most famous scenes in literature and art, Hermes, at the bidding of Zeus, conducted Hera, Athena, and Aphrodite to the presence of a young Trojan shepherd, Paris, who was asked to judge which of these three goddesses deserved to be awarded the golden apple inscribed with the words "For the Fairest" (fig. 85). This episode, a *casus belli*, will be dealt with in more detail in the legends concerning the Trojan War.

Hermes appears to have had a soft spot in his heart for that crafty and cunning man of Homer's epic, Odysseus. When the latter's adventures led him to the island of the enchantress and goddess Circe, he might have been turned into a swine, as had a number of his men, if not for Hermes. The god not only provided him with a magical plant, *moly*, which prevented the sorceress from working her magic on him, but also advised Odysseus on how to avoid being unmanned and stripped of courage when sharing the goddess' bed. Hermes' tender regard for the welfare of Odysseus was that of a great-grandfather for one of his descendants, and Odysseus had inherited much of his cunning and craft from his divine ancestor and from his grandfather on his mother's side, Autolycus. Autolycus was a son of Hermes—he was the most accomplished liar and thief of his day according to Homer—to whom the god had given the power of making himself and the things he stole invisible or giving them new forms. Odysseus' grandfather was invincible in his profession until he met another master thief and trickster, Sisyphus, to whom Homer also gave the accolade "the craftiest of mortals." Autolycus' reputation did not pass Shakespeare unnoticed; he becomes a humorous character in *The Winter's Tale*, a singing rogue and peddler, a "snapper-up of unconsidered trifles":

> My father nam'd me Autolycus, who being, as I am, litter'd under Mercury, was likewise a snapper-up of unconsidered trifles. With die and drab I purchas'd this caparison, and my revenue is the silly cheat.

Pan.   Autolycus is typical of one branch of Hermes' descendants, that given to larceny and trickery. As for the god's connection with pastures and fertility, it is best represented by another of his reputed sons, Pan, the great god of flocks and shepherds. Hermes is most often cited as his father, but his mother is variously given. She may be Dryope, Callisto, Oeneis, or Thybris. Some fanciful accounts make Pan the child of Penelope by Hermes in the form of a ram, by Odysseus, or even more fantastically by Penelope and all her suitors. It is quite possible that Penelope was the name of a nymph who became confused with the heroine of the Homeric epic. In any event, Pan was a rustic deity of Arcadia, the land of sheep and goats and shepherds, and accordingly he inherited the characteristics of the animal with which he was most often associated. From birth Pan was fully developed, a goat from the waist down, a turned up nose, goat horns, and a beard. His mother, so the story goes, was so frightened by his appearance that she ran away from him, leaving him to be brought up by nymphs. Pan's appearance was not only goatish but so was his temperament: he was frisky, short-tempered, and lustful. His name also bore some relationship to his function, being related to Greek and Latin roots meaning "to feed"; hence Pan was "the Feeder" or the pasturer of the flocks. In the hands of ancient theologians, Pan's name was derived from the Greek word *pas, pan*, meaning "all," and this minor deity of the pastures became a symbol of the universe, a universal god.

In his native haunts of Arcadia, however, Pan was the god of the forests, pastures, flocks, and shepherds; he lived in caves, wandered on the summits of mountains and rocks, and amused himself by leading the dances of the nymphs or taking part in the hunt. Pan was accustomed to taking his siesta at noontime, and anyone who disturbed his rest would be terrified by his shout. Shepherds, therefore, were very careful not to play upon their pipes at midday when the rustic god was taking his nap. Pan also had the power to induce "pan-ic," a state of unreasoning terror, especially felt by travelers in lonely and desolate places, which makes people act like a stampeding herd of animals. E. M. Forster (1879–1970) has taken this side of Pan's character as a theme for his short story, *The Story of a Panic*, in which he gives a vivid description of Pan-inspired fear.

Among the Romans, Pan was identified with their god of forests and herdsmen, Faunus. But under the influence of Hellenistic rationalism, Faunus was treated as one of the legendary kings of Latium, the son of Picus and the father of Latinus, and one of the great founders of the religion of Latium. During his reign Faunus promoted agriculture and the breeding of cattle; and it was during his supposed lifetime that Arcadian Evander and Heracles were said to have migrated to Italy. In addition to being worshiped as Pan's Roman counterpart, Faunus was revered as an oracular and prophetic divinity. To those who covered themselves in the skins of sacrificial animals and slept in his sacred precincts, he communicated his prophecies through the eerie sounds of the forest and through dreams. Another Roman divinity who was often confused with Faunus was the rustic Silvanus (or Sylvanus). He originally watched over the boundaries of fields and uncultivated lands but gradually acquired pastoral functions similar to Faunus. Like many of the other spirits of the wild who lived in the woods and upon the hills, these Greek and Roman deities were often pluralized into Pans, Fauni (or fauns) and Silvani. These nature-spirits became an indelible part of the pastoral tradition in literature and art. Milton thinks of them when describing the nuptial place of Adam and Eve in *Paradise Lost:*

> . . . In a shadier bower
> More sacred and sequester'd, though but feign'd,
> Pan or Sylvanus never slept, nor nymph
> Nor Faunus haunted.

The French poet and leader of the Symbolist movement, Stéphane Mallarmé (1842–1898), made the faun a symbol of all that is paradoxical in the human male. His *L'Après-midi d'un faune* (The Afternoon of a Faun) is the monologue of a faun who chases nymphs, sleeps during the noonday heat and has erotic dreams of women, reverences beauty, and is a musician and poet and dreamer. Mallarme's poem inspired Claude Debussy's *Prelude to the Afternoon of a Faun* (1894) which Nijinsky made into a ballet (1912). In art of the twentieth century, the work of the Spanish artist Pablo Picasso (1881–   ) includes a number of small sculptures of fauns; his *Joy of Life* (1947), a painting of a faun and a centaur dancing with a nymph transforms an ancient sylvan scene into a contemporary expression of animal *joie de vivre*. Of course the distinction between Pan and Faunus among artists and poets has been blurred, but the lines from Ben Jonson's *Pan's Anniversary* will take us back to Hermes' offspring:

> Of Pan we sing, the best of leaders, Pan,
>   That leads the Naiads and the Dryads forth;
> And to their dances more than Hermes can.

Pan and Syrinx.   The favorite instrument of this gamesome god, as befitted a patron of shepherds and pastures, was the syrinx, also called appropriately the panpipe. Pan's musical competition with the god Apollo, the pipe versus the lyre, has already been described. The story of how Pan invented this popular instrument of shepherds, an invention that was also attributed to Hermes, is told by Ovid in his *Metamorphoses*, a story that combines amorous pursuit, transformation, and aetiology. The Roman poet introduces the tale as a story-within-a-story. When Jupiter called upon Mercury to dispatch the hundred-eyed monster Argos that Juno had placed over Io, the Olympian's love transformed into a heifer, the god first tried to close Argos' hundred eyes in sleep by playing on his pipe of reeds and by telling him various stories. Among these was the tale of how the instrument on which he played was invented. There was a certain woodland nymph who lived on the mountain slopes of Arcadia. Her name was Syrinx, and she was actively pursued by the gods of the woodlands and fields. She would have none of them because she was devoted to the chaste goddess Diana. Pan, meeting her one day, was very much taken with her, but Syrinx rejected his amorous advances and fled before him until she reached the river Ladon. There, with Pan in hot pursuit, she begged her sister-nymphs to transform her. At that moment Pan caught up with her and embraced what he thought to be the nymph, only to find that he held a tuft of reeds in his arms. As he breathed a sad sigh of frustration, the air sounded through the reeds and produced a plaintive tone. Charmed with the novelty and with the sweetness of the sound, Pan said, "At least this much I have!" and took reeds of unequal lengths, bound them together, and named the instrument Syrinx in honor of the coy nymph he desired but could not have. Keats, in an early poem, *I Stood Tip-toe upon a Little Hill*, looks with longing admiration on the poet

> . . . who pull'd the boughs aside,
> That we might look into a forest wide,
> To catch a glimpse of Fauns and Dryades
> Coming with softest rustle through the trees;
> . . . .
> Telling us how fair, trembling Syrinx fled
> Arcadian Pan, with such a fearful dread.
> Poor nymph,—poor Pan,—how did he weep to find,
> Nought but a lovely sighing of the wind
> Along the reedy stream; a half-heard strain,
> Full of sweet desolation—balmy pain.

Elizabeth Barrett Browning gives us her poetic version of how Pan created the syrinx, omitting all reference to the nymph whom the god desired, and ends with a critical comment on paganism. From *A Musical Instrument* (1860):

> What was he doing, the great god Pan,
>   Down in the reeds by the river?
> Spreading ruin and scattering ban,
> Splashing and paddling with hoofs of a goat,
> And breaking the golden lilies afloat
>   With the dragon-fly on the river.
> . . . .
> Sweet, sweet, sweet, O Pan!
>   Piercing sweet by the river!
> Blinding sweet, O great god Pan!
> The sun on the hill forgot to die,
> And the lilies revived, and the dragon-fly
>   Came back to dream on the river.
>
> Yet half a beast is the great god Pan,
>   To laugh as he sits by the river,
> Making a poet out of a man:
> The true gods sigh for the cost and pain,—
> For the reed which grows nevermore again
>   As a reed with the reeds in the river.

Pan and Marathon.   Two stories about Pan which had more far-reaching consequences than his unrequited passion took place within historical times. Herodotus tells of how the Athenians came to dedicate a shrine to Pan under the Acropolis and to honor the god with annual torch races and sacrifices. On the eve of the Battle of Marathon (490 B.C.), the Athenian general sent a runner, Pheidippides by name, to Sparta with a message asking for help against the invading Persians. On the way, the messenger was approached by the god Pan on Mount Parthenium and was asked why the Athenians gave him so little honor in spite of all the friendliness and help he had shown them. Upon his return Pheidippides told the Athenians of his encounter with the god, and they were so impressed with the story that as soon as they could they dedicated a shrine to the god. The distance (about 150 miles) that Pheidippides covered in two days is commemorated in modern times by the "Marathon Race" in the Olympic games. Robert Browning, in one of his Dramatic Idyls entitled *Pheidippides*, resurrects the famous messenger for the Battle of Marathon and has him run again, this time twenty-six miles from the battlefield to Athens after the Persians have been defeated. The Athenians cried:

> ... To the Akropolis!
> Run, Pheidippides, one race more! the meed is thy due!
> "Athens is saved, thank Pan," go shout!

The "Death" of Pan. The indefatigable Plutarch, biographer and philosopher of the first century A.D., tells a story about the death of Pan. In the reign of Tiberius (A.D. 14–37), a ship from Greece on its way to Italy was driven near the coast of the island of Paxi. Suddenly the passengers heard a voice from the shore cry out, "Thamus!" This happened to be the name of the pilot of the ship. After the voice cried out the name of Thamus for the third time, the pilot answered. Then the voice said: "When you come to Palodes, say that the great Pan is dead." When the ship drifted near Palodes, the mariner shouted: "Pan the great is dead!" Immediately the air was filled with groans and lamentations. On arriving in Italy, the pilot was called before Tiberius who was very fond of the bizarre and supernatural. The emperor ordered an inquiry, but his astrologers and scholars were unable to explain the meaning of the announcement; they came to the conclusion that it did not refer to the god Pan but to another spirit of the same name.

The most plausible explanation of the strange story reported by Plutarch, if true in any part, is that the cry heard by the pilot had to do with the lamentation over the Semitic hero-god Tammuz (p. 188) whose annual death was being celebrated. The Greek word *pammegas*, "all-great," and referring to Tammuz was taken as *Pan megas*, "great Pan." What was intended to be heard was the ritual-cry: "Tammuz, Tammuz, the great Tammuz is dead."

*   *   *   *

However true or untrue Plutarch's account may be, early Christians seized upon it as signifying the victory of Christianity over paganism since both the crucifixion of Christ and the announcement of Pan's death occurred during the reign of Tiberius. There was yet another way in which these two episodes might be interpreted. As indicated, pagan theologizing based on a false etymology of Pan's name made the god into a symbol of the universe, of "all." Hence when Christ suffered his passion, the lord of the universe (Pan) also suffered. The identification of Christ with Pan was furthered by the religious associations of their real or figurative occupations as shepherds. Thus Spenser has no difficulty in making Pan into Christ in his *Shepheardes Calendar:*

And wonned not the great God Pan,
   upon mount Olivet:
Feeding the blessed flocke of Dan,
   which dyd himselfe beget?

An early commentator on Spenser, the virtually unknown E. K., glosses a similar passage as follows: " 'Great Pan' is Christ, the very god most rightly (methinks) applyed to him; for Pan signifieth all, or omnipotent, which is onely the Lord Jesus."

To Milton in *Paradise Lost* Pan carries the epithet "universal"; in *On the Morning of Christ's Nativity*, he follows Spenser in identifying the god of shepherds with Christ:

The shepherds on the lawn,
   Or ere the point of dawn,
Sat simply chatting in a rustic row;
   Full little thought they then
   That the mighty Pan
Was kindly come to live with them below.

On the other side of the coin, Pan was taken as a symbol of all that was pagan and evil. The conventional view of Satan's physical appearance—his cloven hoof in place of a foot, the horns on his forehead—owes much to the Arcadian god of shepherds. To Elizabeth Barrett Browning, the announcement of Pan's death signified the dethronement and death of the false gods of Greece, and that whatever Pan meant to Art and Poetry could now be found and realized in Christ. Her poem *The Dead Pan* revived Plutarch's old story which was taken as coincident with the crucifixion of Christ.

Gods of Hellas, gods of Hellas,
Can ye listen in your silence?
Can your mystic voices tell us
Where ye hide? In floating islands,
With a wind that evermore
Keeps you out of sight of shore:
              Pan, Pan is dead
. . . .
And that dismal cry rose slowly
And sank slowly through the air,
Full of spirit's melancholy
And eternity's despair!
And they heard the words it said—
"Pan is dead—Great Pan is dead—
              Pan, Pan is dead."

'Twas the hour when One in Sion
Hung for love's sake on a cross;
When His brow was chill with dying,
And His soul was faint with loss;
When His priestly blood dropped downward,
And His kingly eyes looked throneward—
              Then, Pan was dead.

By the love He stood alone
His sole Godhead rose complete,
And the false gods fell down moaning,
Each from off his golden seat;
All the false gods with a cry
Rendered up their deity—
           Pan, Pan was dead.

Ezra Pound also commemorated the death of the rude and shaggy son of
Hermes; his *Pan is Dead,* an apparent tongue-in-cheek poem, connects the death
of the god with the death of fertility and, perhaps, of creative inspiration. For
Robert Frost (1874–1963), Pan was not dead but a symbol of the contemporary poet
who had no place in the urbanized world. *Pan with Us,* written during the years of
Frost's literary apprenticeship, questions the validity of the pastoral tradition and
the myth of rural Arcadia in America.

Pan came out of the woods one day—
His skin and his hair and his eyes were gray,
The gray of the moss of walls were they—
    And stood in the sun and looked his fill
    At wooded valley and wooded hill.

He stood in the zephyr, pipes in hand,
On a height of naked pasture land;
In all the country he did command
    He saw no smoke and he saw no roof.
    That was well! and he stamped a hoof.

His heart knew peace, for none came here
To this lean feeding save once a year
Someone to salt the half-wild steer,
    Or homespun children with clicking pails
    Who see so little they tell no tales.

He tossed his pipes, too hard to teach
A new-world song, far out of reach,
For a sylvan sign that the blue jay's screech
    And the whimper of hawks beside the sun
    Were music enough for him, for one.

Times were changed from what they were:
Such pipes kept less power to stir
The fruited bough of the juniper
    And the fragile bluets clustered there
    Than the merest aimless breath of air.

They were pipes of pagan mirth,
And the world had found new terms of worth.
He laid down on the sun-burned earth
    And ravelled a flower and looked away.
    Play? Play?—What should he play?

Pitys and Echo. From time to time Pan was attracted to a number of nymphs who did not respond to his desires in the way the cloven-footed divinity wished. These episodes, clearly aetiological, did not become as popular as some of his other adventures. Pan, as a divinity of the high hills, was naturally associated with the pine-tree (*pitys*), and when the god approached the tree-nymph Pitys with amorous intent, she fled. She was spared his unwanted attentions by being transformed into the tree that bears her name, the branches of which the god Pan took for a garland. On another occasion Pan fell in love with an Oread, the mountain-nymph Echo, whom the god could neither convince nor catch. In frustration and revenge, Pan turned the shepherds on the mountain mad, and in their madness they tore the poor nymph to pieces, leaving only her disembodied voice to "echo" among the hills.

Echo and Narcissus. In a more familiar version of Echo's tragic life, Pan is not cited as the villain of the piece; it seems rather that the nymph brought on her own unhappiness, first by attempting to trick Hera and then by falling in love with the handsome but unfeeling youth Narcissus. As Ovid tells the story, Echo chattered away incessantly at Hera while Zeus was dallying with various nymphs. She hoped, of course, to keep the goddess at a distance so that she could not notice her husband's philandering. But Hera was not deceived; she punished Echo by depriving her of all power of speech, except that she could repeat the last sounds of what she heard. When the nymph came upon Narcissus in the forest, she fell passionately and uncontrollably in love. Narcissus was the son of the nymph Liriope of Thespiae whom the Boeotian river-god Cephisus had ravished when she was bathing in his waters. When the mother asked Tiresias, the celebrated prophet of Thebes, whether her child would live to old age, the seer replied: "If he never comes to know himself."

Narcissus grew up to be a handsome young man, but he was incapable of having any feelings of love. When Echo came upon Narcissus and was irresistibly drawn to him, she tried desperately to hold a conversation, but the speech defect which Hera had visited upon her caused the nymph considerable embarrassment. When, for example, Narcissus said to the love-pressed girl, "Take your hands off me! I would rather die than have you take advantage of me," all Echo could reply was, "Take advantage of me!" Spurned and shamed, Echo retreated to a cave in the woods and died of grief. She was seen no more; only her voice, which can still be heard in the mountains, lives on. As for Narcissus, he continued to reject lovers of both sexes until one young man prayed: "May he love and not possess the object of his love." Nemesis, the goddess of justice who punishes the proud and arrogant, heard his prayer. One day after a tiring hunt, Narcissus paused to refresh himself at a pool of water, and as he bent over to take a drink he caught sight of his reflection in the water. This is Ovid's description of how the young man reacted to what he saw:

> He loved the image that he thought was shadow,
> And looked amazed at what he saw—his face.
> Fixed, bending over it, he could not speak,
> Himself as though cut from Parian marble.
> Flat on the grass he lay to look deep, deeper
> Into two stars that were his eyes, at hair
> Divine as Bacchus' hair, as bright Apollo's,

At boyish beauty of ivory neck and shoulder,
At face, flushed as red flowers among white,
Enchanted by the charms which were his own.
Himself the worshipped and the worshipper,
He sought himself and was pursued, wooed, fired
By his own heat of love. Again, again
He tried to kiss the image in the well;
Again, again his arms embraced the silver
Elusive waters where his image shone;
And he burned for it while the gliding error
Betrayed his eyes. O foolish innocent!
Why try to grasp at shadows in their flight?
What he had tried to hold resided nowhere,
For had he turned away, it fell to nothing:
His love was cursed. Only the glancing mirror
Of reflections filled his eyes, a body
That had no being of its own, a shade
That came, stayed, left with him—if he could leave it.

This was the end for Narcissus. He pined away for himself until at last he died. The nymphs mourned for him. So did Echo who had echoed his last anguished cries. Death shut his eyes, but it is said that even in the Underworld, Narcissus' shade continued to gaze in self-love at his reflection in the Stygian waters. And when the nymphs came to give his body the last rites, it was nowhere to be found; instead, they found a flower with a yellow center surrounded by white petals, the narcissus.

*　　*　　*　　*

When Ovid came into his own during the late Middle Ages, his story of Echo and Narcissus was matched in popularity only by that of Pyramus and Thisbe. It continued to be held in esteem right into the twentieth century. During the Middle Ages and Renaissance, the fate of the two mythological figures was appropriately moralized to serve the ends of Christian teaching. The fourteenth-century *Ovide moralisé* took Echo as a symbol of virtue. The allegorized *Metamorphoses* by Petrus Berchorius (Thomas Waleys) saw in the mountain-nymph Echo those flatterers who frequent prelates and others in high places; she could also represent quarrelsome women and servants who have to have the last word. As for Narcissus, he symbolized pride; the pool of water, worldly prosperity which is impermanent and passes away, destructive to the life of the soul. In the fifteenth century, Marsilio Ficino saw in Narcissus a Platonic symbol of the futility of trying to find permanence in a transient and mundane world. In the sixteenth and seventeenth centuries Echo and Narcissus were portrayed on canvas by such master artists as Tintoretto, Caravaggio, and Poussin, the latter having painted four versions of the myth.

In England, a sixteenth-century translation of Ovid's tale of Narcissus added almost nine hundred lines of moralizing which stressed "richis and bewty be vayne"; "the transitory thinges of this world are not to be trustyd"; "all dysdayne ful folkes are compared unto Narcyssus." Earlier, Chaucer had retold the story when he translated the thirteenth-century French allegorical romance for his *Romaunt of the Rose*. There was a clear lesson to be learned from Narcissus' experience.

> This is the miror perilous,
> In which the proude Narcisus
> Saw al his face fair and bright,
> That made him sith to lye upright.
> For who-so like in that mirour,
> There may no-thing ben his socour
> That he ne shal ther seen som thing
> That shal him lede into loving.

Elizabethan poets freely adapted Ovid's story for poetic allusions. In *Hero and Leander*, Marlowe describes Leander's features as

> ... exceeding his
> That leapt into the water for a kis
> Of his owne shadow, and despising many,
> Died ere he could enjoy the love of any.

The non-Ovidian element of Narcissus' death by drowning goes as far back as the Middle Ages. Shakespeare retains the same allusion in his *Rape of Lucrece:* "That, had Narcissus seen her as she stood,/Self-love had never drown'd him in the flood." And in *Venus and Adonis:* "Narcissus so himself himself forsook,/And died to kiss his shadow in the brook."

The myth of Echo and Narcissus saw yet another revival, largely on the continent of Europe, during the late nineteenth and twentieth centuries. The story, however, no longer served to reveal the mysteries of the true Faith; rather it provided a new symbol for art, aesthetics, and psychoanalysis. In 1891 André Gide published his *Traité de Narcisse*, a defense in Platonic terms of the basic tenets of Symbolism, in which the poet is called upon to make manifest the eternal truths that lie behind the changing external symbols of the visible world. In looking into the pool of water, Gide's Narcissus discovers something more than his own reflection; he finds the moving panorama of life which he had not seen before. Paul Valéry, the French writer whose *La Pythie* has been mentioned above, composed three poems in which the figure of Narcissus symbolized varying aspects—mostly introspective and contemplative—of the human psyche: *Narcisse parle*, *Fragments du Narcisse*, and *Cantate du Narcisse*. The German poet Rainer Maria Rilke (1875–1926) also wrote a number of poems on the theme of Narcissus, and in the last year of his life translated Valéry's *Fragments du Narcisse*. To Rilke, Narcissus was the symbol of the poet who sacrificed his own life and identity in his service to mankind. These are the last two stanzas of his *Narcissus:*

> Narcissus perished as he gazed. His being
> evaporated from his mirrored beauty
> like perfume from an opened flask. But, seeing
> that just to see himself was all his duty,
>
> he loved back all that had begun to flee,
> left nothing for the open wind's reception;
> ecstatically short-circuited perception,
> cancelled himself, and could no longer be.

The myth of Narcissus and Echo was to serve masters other than poets and essayists. Just before the turn of the century, Havelock Ellis (1859–1939), *littérateur* and scientist, used the term "narcissism" to describe the pathological state of self-love and self-adulation, a term which psychoanalysts have since qualified to cover a number of neurotic manifestations in the human personality. Sigmund Freud also touched upon the nature of narcissism in his analysis of the childhood of Leonardo da Vinci (1910), and then four years later in more detail in his essay on the subject, *Zur Einführung des Narzissmus* (On Narcissism: an Introduction). Among composers the story of Echo and Narcissus has long served as a libretto for operatic and choral compositions, the latest being the musical idyl of Jules Massenet (1878). As for contemporary artists, the nymph Echo attracted representations by Vasili Kandinsky (1866–1944) and Max Ernst (1891–   ), while Salvador Dali (1904–   ), the leader of the surrealist school of painting, has given us one of the best-known interpretations of Ovid's story in his *Metamorphosis of Narcissus* (fig. 46).

Hermaphroditus.   The god Hermes had yet another son whose physical characteristics were as uncommon as those of Pan. Hermes mated with the goddess Aphrodite and sired a son, Hermaphroditus, who was to bear not only the name of both his parents but their sexual characteristics as well. Mythology has little to report of this relationship except that in Homer's *Odyssey* we hear Hermes say that he would

Figure 46.   Salvador Dali. Metamorphosis of Narcissus. Narcissus stares at his reflection in the pool while a narcissus blossoms from an egg. *Painting, 1937. Tate Gallery, London.*

have gladly changed places with Ares who was caught in bed with Aphrodite by Hephaestus' clever strategem. The concept of a bisexual divinity has been explained as due either to a Greek adaptation of Oriental deities that combine both sexes, or to a myth that was fashioned to explain certain marriage rites in which clothing was exchanged by the sexes. From the fourth century B.C. on, Greek sculptors took a fancy to representing Hermaphroditus as a handsome youth with female breasts or as an Aphrodite with male genitals.

Ovid, quite naturally, produced a story to explain this bizarre offspring of Hermes and Aphrodite. The motif he employed was similar to the one used for Echo and Narcissus: a passionate nymph and an unresponsive youth. When Hermaphroditus was fifteen years old he left the place of his birth and went to live among the Carians of Asia Minor. It chanced that the nymph Salmacis caught sight of the godling who had inherited the beauty of his father and mother. Overcome with passion and love for the youth, she begged to be his bride. He blushed. The nymph then begged for a kiss. His reply was: "Stop! or else I must run away from this spot and from you." Salmacis pretended to leave but followed him unseen. When Hermaphroditus came to a stream, the cool waters of a pool invited him to undress and to refresh himself in swimming. Salmacis, observing all from her hiding place nearby, saw her opportunity. Casting aside her clothing, she plunged into the waters and embraced the unwilling Hermaphroditus. As he tried to free himself from the clinging naiad, Salmacis prayed to the gods that the two of them never be separated. The gods granted her prayer. Their two bodies were joined, one face and one body for Salmacis and Hermaphroditus; they seemed neither man nor woman, yet resembled both. When Hermaphroditus realized his transformation, he called upon his mother and father to cause any man who came into these waters to lose his virility and to come forth a half-man. Hermes and Aphrodite heard and granted the prayer of their biformed son.

The story of Hermaphroditus' fate was not likely to influence many writers, although in the age in which there was a mania for allegory, the tale could be given an edifying interpretation. An Elizabethan translator, T. Peend (1565), added to his text a moralized analysis in which Hermaphroditus was taken as youthful purity, his newly-adopted home Caria as the mundane world, and Salmacis as all the enticements of vice. The myth could also be juggled, as it was in France during the early seventeenth century, to represent the Roman Church (Salmacis) inviting the Protestants (Hermaphroditus) to return to her bosom. However, it was the motif of the reluctant youth and the highly passionate maid—a motif similar to that of Echo and Narcissus—that was to influence the characterization of Shakespeare's *Venus and Adonis*. For Algernon Swinburne, the nineteenth-century pagan, the godling became a symbol of ambivalent love. An excerpt from his *Hermaphroditus* (1863):

> To what strange end hath some strange god made fair
>   The double blossom of two fruitless flowers?
> . . . .
> Yea, sweet, I know; I saw in what swift wise
>   Beneath the woman's and water's kiss
>   Thy moist limbs melted into Salmacis,
> And the large light turned tender in thine eyes,
> And all thy boy's breath softened into sighs;
>   But Love being blind, how should he know of this?

CHAPTER

The House of Hades:
Gods of the Underworld

The undiscover'd country, from whose bourn
No traveller returns . . . .

Shakespeare—*Hamlet*

The canonical Olympian Twelve just described have their place in the world of sun and light and the living. Life's sibling, Death, was alien and abhorrent to them. Apollo, as we have already observed, had to take his leave when Alcestis, wife of his favorite King Admetus, was approaching death. Similarly, the goddess Artemis had to leave her beloved Hippolytus when he was on the point of dying. Euripides has her say to him: "Farewell! It is not lawful for me to look upon death and to have my eyes polluted with the last gasps of the dying." This is the attitude of the Classical and post-Classical eras. It is true that Demeter had some connection with death, but only insofar as she was a power of fertility and concerned with the earth to which both the dead and the seed were entrusted. As for Hermes, even though he may have originated as the spirit who inhabited the burial mound, he was in historical times *psychopompos*, the guide of the dead spirits to the Underworld. As such he provided an essential service for the living, since such spirits could be a source of danger if permitted to wander about at large. Souls of the dead, to be sure, could legitimately return to the world of the living during certain festivals, particularly those involving critical operations of the seasonal cycle. On these All-Souls' days, the spirits of the dead were remembered, entertained, and propitiated. After appropriate rituals, assuring the worshipers of their assistance and cooperation, the spirits returned to their proper abode. A custom among Romans, borrowed from the Etruscans, facilitated the contact between the quick and the dead. When the foundations of a city were laid, a pit was dug in the center of the city which supposedly connected both realms. On three days of the year, sacred and holy days, the stone which covered the aperture, the *lapis Manalis*, was removed, thus giving the spirits of the dead free access to the upper world.

The Greeks, perhaps more than any other people, gave unrestrained expression to their love of life and they stocked their mythological accounts with stories of life's caprices and tragedies. Death was not accorded the same treatment. Here too the long shadow of Homer, which fell on so many aspects of Greek life, touched the mythological view of what lay before man when he finished his term of life. The Homeric epics describe the kingdom of the dead as empty nothingness. In death, man has no further contact with this world; his descendants can no longer reach him with gifts nor need they fear his ghost. And in that grim and gloomy region which Homer has reserved for the departed, the shade of the dead man, a pale and bodiless image (*eidolon*) of a living man, wanders about like a shadow or a ghost in a world of silence. The *locus classicus* for Homer's description of life beyond the grave is the eleventh book of the *Odyssey*. Of course Homer may incorporate in his epics earlier attitudes regarding the dead, although his explanation for a partic- ular ritual may differ from that of modern scholars. The passages most often cited is the burial of Patroclus in the twenty-third book of the *Iliad*. For the funeral pyre of his beloved comrade-in-arms, Achilles slays twelve Trojan prisoners, four horses, two of Patroclus' nine dogs, and a large number of oxen and sheep. To this are added numerous jars of honey and oil. Homer attributes the sacrifice of the twelve Trojans to Achilles' venting his anger on the enemy for the death of his friend. Scholars, however, see in the entire ritual the relic of an extravagant pre-Homeric funeral cult in which the things sacrificed—possessions, food, and slaves—were meant to serve the dead man in his after-life. But Homer did not interpret it in this way; and at the very end of the previous book, the touching lament of Andromache for the death of her husband Hector makes it clear that the poet did not understand the meaning of funeral gifts, at least as we understand them today:

> But now by the beaked ships, far from your parents, shall the wriggling worms devour you when the dogs have had their fill, as you lie there naked; yet in these halls lie your garments, delicate and fair, wrought by the hands of women. Yes, all these will I con- sume with burning fire—they are of no use to you since you will never lie in them—as a token of honor to you from the men and women of Troy.

As for the Homeric view on whether death is to be preferred to life, we need only cite the words of Achilles when Odysseus comes upon his shade in the kingdom of the dead. To Odysseus, who praises him as a mighty prince among the dead for whom death should have lost its sting, Achilles bluntly replies:

> Great Odysseus, spare me this talk about the comforts of death. I would rather live on earth as the serf of another, with a landless man who has no great livelihood of his own, than rule among all these dead men who have done with life.

This, then, was Homer's picture of life after death. The poet had, to be sure, men- tioned the Elysian Fields (or Elysium) as a kind of paradise, but this had been reserved for Menelaus simply because he was a son-in-law of Zeus; and it was a place to which he would be translated without experiencing the trauma of death. Hesiod had also mentioned a similar paradise, the Islands of the Blessed, to which the sur- viving heroes of a bygone age, the fourth in the poet's succession, would also be translated without death. However, the idea of the empty nothingness of the king- dom of the dead did not satisfy the emotional needs or eschatological outlook of later generations. Theologians, poets, and philosophers revived earlier ideas of the cult of the dead—they had never disappeared entirely from view—and added to

Homer's scanty description of the topography and community life in the region over which Hades ruled.

Hades, the third brother in the Olympian clan, was the son of Cronus and Rhea. In the division of the universe following the Titanomachy, he was awarded the nether world. Statius, a Latin poet of the first century A.D. who was much admired by Dante and Chaucer, has this wry comment on Hades' fortune in the lottery which gained him the guardianship of the spirits of the dead: "As he turned his chariot downward . . . he paled to look on Hell after having lost Heaven." Hades was rarely seen by his colleagues on Mount Olympus; on one occasion he came up from his dark realm to seek medical care after Heracles had wounded him.

Although a ruler of the dead, Hades is not to be confused with the Devil or Satan, a Judaeo-Christian tradition derived from the Near East. As a death-god, Hades is grim, inexorable, sternly just, irrevocable in his decrees; he is not evil in himself, not an enemy of mankind, nor a tempter of evil. However, in common with many cultures, the death-god—or for that matter any power which is feared and is to be avoided—was not to be called by his proper name; instead, a euphemism was often employed. The name-taboo is summed up in the popular saying: "Speak of the Devil and he appears." The name Hades, with poetical variation of Aïdes and Aïdoneus, means etymologically "the Unseen One," and is linguistically related to the Latin word *videre*, to see. He was also called Pluto (or Pluton), "the Rich One," a name that is either a euphemism or is connected with his being a spirit of fertility and wealth in the earth. Plato, in his dialog *Cratylus*, remarks with his usual insight: "Pluto is concerned with *ploutos* and means giver of wealth, because wealth comes out of the earth beneath. People in general use the term as a euphemism for Hades." By the fifth century B.C., the earliest occurrence of the name Pluto, Hades' name had apparently lost its euphemistic significance to the man in the street and Pluto was used as a substitute for the feared name. The lord of the dead was also called "the Host of Many," "Wise in Counsel," "Zeus Beneath the Earth," "the Unconquerable," and the all-embracing "He who has many names."

As for the Romans, their native death-god, if they ever had one, has been lost to us. Their concept of the Underworld and its gods was initially derived from the Greek-influenced Etruscans, and later more directly from the Greeks. In addition to adopting the name Pluto, they also translated it into Latin as Dis, a contraction of their adjective *dives* (wealthy). Their death-god was also called Orcus, a deity who forcibly carried off the living to the infernal regions. Orcus is probably related to the Greek Horcus (Oath), the avenging spirit who, according to Hesiod, was born of Eris (Strife) as a plague to men committing perjury. In the customary confusion of names, however, Pluto and Dis by popular use displaced Hades and Orcus as the Greek and Roman names for the lord of the dead, the latter two being used as the name of the realm over which they formerly ruled.

In classical mythology Hades had only bit parts to play. Even in the principal episode of his life, his atavistic marriage to Persephone, he is mentioned only in connection with her rape and her release; the myth really concerns Demeter and her alter-ego daughter more than the lord of the dead. Late tradition makes Aphrodite, not Zeus, the catalyst in this primitive marriage so that she could show her power even in the world of the dead. It is a tradition that Shakespeare follows in the *Tempest* where Ceres complains of Venus and Cupid that ". . . they did plot/ the means that dusky Dis my daughter got."

Late tradition also attributes to Hades a small number of extramarital adventures.

He fell in love with a nymph called Mintha (or Mentha), but his jealous wife turned her into a mint plant. Some say that it was Demeter who metamorphosed the unfortunate nymph, and another account says that she was turned into dust from which Hades caused the mint plant to spring forth. Another unfortunate nymph was Leuce (White), a daughter of Oceanus, whom Hades carried off. After her death she was changed into a white poplar and transferred to Elysium. The poplar tree, often found bordering cemeteries in Greece and Italy, has associations with death. In parts of Greece today, people avoid the shade of poplar trees for fear of malicious spirits that are supposed to be found lurking there. Let us recollect too that when the sisters of Phaethon were mourning his death, they were transformed into a grove of poplars. In Latin legend an aetiological story is told of Hercules who, having overpowered the giant Cacus, wore a victory wreath of poplar leaves. When he wore this crown on his journey to the Underworld, the heat of the infernal regions darkened the upper parts of the leaves, while the undersides turned silver due to the hero's own perspiration or radiance. And because Hercules went to the Underworld and returned, the white poplar became a symbol of the promise of life after death. Hence, the white poplar is used, in Ireland for example, for coffins and for rods that measure out graves.

Hades wore a magical hat or helmet that made him invisible, an appropriate mythological device for "the Unseen One." This helmet was given to him as a present by the Cyclopes, when the Olympians secured their release from Tartarus. It was at the same time that Zeus received his thunderbolts and Poseidon his trident. Hades parted with his helmet of invisibility on several occasions. Hermes borrowed it when he fought alongside the other Olympians in their battle against the Giants. Athena put on the helmet to be unobserved when she helped Diomedes wound Ares during the battle in which the gods took sides in the Trojan War. And one mortal, the hero Perseus, was permitted to wear the magical helmet when he went to oppose the petrifying Gorgon, Medusa. As a symbol of his power, Hades had a staff with which, like Hermes Psychopompos, he drove the shades of the dead into the infernal regions. His chariot, the same in which he had snatched up Persephone and taken her beneath the earth, was made of gold and was drawn by four black immortal horses. Black, naturally, was Hades' color. So were the sacrificial animals that were offered to him and his consort. Besides these horses, Hades was also said to have had herds of oxen in the lower world and on the island of Erytheia where they were attended by a herdsman called Menoëtes.

Erytheia and Geryon. An exegetical note is needed here on Erytheia (or Erythia) and the several cattle owners and their herdsmen in the Underworld. Erytheia (Red Island) is in origin a mythological never-never land, far to the west in the stream of the world-encircling Ocean. Taking its color from the setting sun, Erytheia is undoubtedly a land of the dead over which the triple-bodied or triple-headed Geryon ruled. He is the monster whom Hesiod has cataloged along with other descendants of Phorcys and Ceto who seem to have to do with death. Later, Erytheia is given a physical location in Spain, and this explains why Milton calls Spanish explorers "Geryon's sons." Geryon, like Hades, owned cattle which were cared for by a herdsman Eurytion. Significantly, Heracles, in one of his labors which mark him as the hero powerful enough to conquer death, kills Geryon, his herdsman Eurytion, and his hellhound Orthus. As for Hades' herdsman Menoëtes who pastured his cattle on Erytheia, he boldly challenged Heracles to a wrestling match. In the competition Heracles broke the herdsman's ribs and would have killed him if Persephone had not begged that his life be spared. Geryon, then, and the herdsmen Eurytion and Menoëtes are death-figures, possibly non-Greek or even Hellenic death-gods who lost their identity as such when Hades became supreme ruler over the land of the dead.

Thanatos. Another death-figure deserves to be mentioned here. Thanatos, the personification of Death, has little in the way of mythological dress. Hesiod calls him the son of Night and the brother of Sleep and Dreams. He is described as iron-hearted, of a pitiless disposition, and hated by all the gods. Once he seizes a man, he never lets him go. In effect, Thanatos is an agent or angel of death. In Euripides' *Alcestis*, he is the black-robed lord of the dead who comes with his sword to lop off a lock of hair of a dying person. It is he whom Heracles ambushes at the fresh grave of Alcestis, grapples with him and refuses to break his hold until he surrenders Alcestis—once again, as in the case of Heracles' match with Menoëtes, the motif of the death-conqueror. Had Heracles been unsuccessful in meeting Thanatos, Euripides tells us, he would have had to go into the Underworld and petition Hades and Persephone for Alcestis' release.

The Kingdom of Hades

Where was this kingdom over which Hades ruled, and what was it like? The land of the dead was generally conceived of as being far to the west, at the world's end, where the sun sinks into the world-encircling river Ocean, a subterranean land that was separated from the world of the living by a body of water. The usual approach to it was through a cave or hellmouth, such as the one at Taenarum near Sparta or where the river Styx in Arcadia plunges over a steep cliff. In Italy, access to the world of souls was through the cave of the Cumaean Sibyl near Lake Avernus. These were the entrances made famous by poets; other localities possessed their own hellmouth. For Homer, Hades' dank house was in the fogbound land of the fabled Cimmerians where "the shining sun never looks down with his rays." To reach it, Odysseus had to sail to the end of the world. These are the directions given to him by the enchantress Circe when Homer's hero is told that he had to consult the seer Tiresias in the land of the dead:

> Set up your mast, spread your white sails, and sit down in your ship. The North Wind will bear your vessel on her way, and when you have sailed your ship across the stream of Ocean, you will come to a waste shore and the groves of Persephone where the tall poplars grow and the willows shed their fruit prematurely. Beach your ship by the deep-eddying Ocean and go to the dank house of Hades. There the Pyriphlegethon and the Cocytus, a branch of the river Styx, flow into the Acheron; and there by a rock the roaring waters of the two streams meet.

In modern literature, Persephone's grove of poplars and willows turns into a garden abounding in all kinds of deadly flora. Spenser's "Gardin of Proserpina" in the *Faerie Queene* includes not only those plants that were "direfull deadly blacke both leafe and bloom," but also the fruit that tempted Eve, the golden apples of the Hesperides, and the apple which led to the Judgment of Paris and ultimately to the Trojan War. Keats' phrase "nightshade, ruby grape of Proserpine" in his *Ode on Melancholy* owes something to this development of Persephone's grove. And in Swinburne's melancholic *Garden of Proserpine* there is

> No growth of moor or coppice,
>   No heather-flower or vine,
> But bloomless buds of poppies,
>   Green grapes of Proserpine,
> Pale beds of blowing rushes
> Where no leaf blooms or blushes
> Save this whereout she crushes
>   For dead men deadly wine.

The Rivers of the Underworld. The infernal regions were not only subterranean but also set apart by a body of water. It was a view that was largely conditioned by transposing the geographical features of the visible world with those of the "unseen"; as if one were to take a picture of the world of the living and then use the photographic negative of it to represent the world of the dead. Of the five bodies of water traditionally held to separate the two worlds, four are known to Homer—Styx, Cocytus, Pyriphlegethon, and Acheron. A fifth, Lethe, becomes prominent by the fifth century B.C. and assumes an important place in the doctrine of the transmigration of souls. The meanings assigned to these bodies of water tell the sad tale of death: Styx was the Abhorrent or the Hated, Cocytus the Wailing, Pyriphlegethon (or Phlegethon) the Burning, Acheron the Sorrowful, and Lethe Forgetfulness. In *Paradise Lost* Milton neatly cites all five with the attributes assigned to them by classical tradition:

> Abhorrèd Styx, the flood of deadly hate,
> Sad Acheron of sorrow, black and deep;
> Cocytus, nam'd of lamentation loud
> Heard on the rueful stream; fierce Phlegethon
> Whose waves of torrent fire inflame with rage.
> Far off from these a slow and silent stream,
> Lethe, the River of Oblivion, rolls
> Her wat'ry labyrinth . . .

Of the five, the river Styx holds first place. By its waters the gods swore their inviolable oaths, oaths so sacred that to break them was punishable by banishment from the council of the gods for nine years. Styx, the Oceanid nymph of the stream, was also held in high regard by the Olympians for the help she gave Zeus in his struggle with the Titans (pp. 36; 43). The mythical river Styx had some connection with one by that name in Arcadia whose cold, mountain waters drop dramatically over a steep cliff into a deep gorge. Folk-belief attached remarkable properties to this water. To taste it was supposed to cause instant death, although some say that it was only harmful during daylight hours. The belief in the deadly nature of the water is a probable expanation of why the Arcadians and the gods swore their most solemn oaths by the river Styx. Its water was also said to be so corrosive that the only substance that could withstand its action was the hoof of a horse or mule.

Acheron and Lethe were also names of small rivers or springs in various parts of Greece: the former being described in literature as a river, marsh, or lake; the latter as a spring, river, or even a field. As for Cocytus and Pyriphlegethon, they appear to be completely mythical. Pyriphlegethon, the river of fire, in origin probably had reference to the flames of the funeral pyre which burned away the mortal flesh and gave release to the soul. Later, this igneous river was transformed into the infernal fire of sulphur and pitch which served to punish the wicked in their posthumous life —the flames of hellfire.

To those philosophers and theologians who looked for moral allegories in the myths invented by poets, the four rivers cited by Homer—Cocytus, Acheron, Pyriphlegethon, and Styx—represented different levels of expiatory punishment that awaited the human soul after death. This was the eschatological view of Plato as well as of Dante. To those philosophers and theologians whose doctrines led them to conclude that life on earth was the true hell, the four rivers symbolized those vices—sadness, remorse, anger, and hate—which tortured the life of man and destroyed the happiness of the soul. During the Renaissance, Neoplatonists took the rivers of hell as symbolizing the evils which spring from living in the material world. Marsilio Ficino (1433–1499), the influential Neoplatonist of the Renaissance, could speak of "the deep gorge of the senses always being shaken by the floods of Acheron, Styx, Cocytus, and Phlegethon." Another thinker of the time interpreted the rivers as the four elements: Air (Acheron), Fire (Phlegethon), Earth (Styx), and Water (Cocytus). This reversal of the mythical picture has led one scholar to give a new interpretation to the so-called river-gods that Michelangelo carved at the base of the tombs of Giuliano and Lorenzo de' Medici: in the complex Neoplatonic design of these two monuments, the river-gods are the four rivers of Hades that symbolize "the fourfold aspect of matters as a source of potential evil."

Lethe has a geographical disposition quite different from that of the other four infernal rivers. The introduction of a river of forgetfulness or oblivion into the hydrographical scheme of Hades' kingdom is a necessary concomitant for those eschatological doctrines which held that the soul after death passed into another body. Those souls which were prepared for a new incarnation were made to drink a certain amount of water from Lethe's stream so that they would have no remembrance, or at least only the dimmest and vaguest one, of their former existence. These views were in the main derived from religious movements, generally known under the name of Orphism and Pythagoreanism, that came into prominence during the fifth century B.C. and that were to have a deep impact on Plato and those who came under his influence. In the climax to the *Republic*, Plato's grand eschatological myth, the Vision of Er, souls selected a new corporeal existence after having been punished for a thousand years for their sins or rewarded for their virtues. They were then led to the plain of Lethe, a barren desert, where they encamped and finally drank of the river of Forgetfulness. In the sixth book of the *Aeneid*, Vergil has Anchises reveal a similar apocalyptic vision to his son Aeneas. In reply to Aeneas' query regarding the great number of shades he sees in a valley through which the river Lethe flowed, his father answers:

> They are the souls destined for new bodies, and there at Lethe's stream they drink of its waters which give release from anxiety and memory of the past . . . When all these (purified) souls have completed a cycle of a thousand years, God summons them to the stream of Lethe in a mighty procession so that, forgetful of the past, they may begin to wish to be reincarnated.

Dante has an important place for Lethe in his *Purgatorio*, the poet himself drinks of its waters to purge his memory of intellectual transgressions. Milton, in his catalog of infernal rivers in *Paradise Lost*, separates Lethe—as do his classical sources—from the four rivers of horror, but he takes no notice of the stream's function in metempsychosis:

> Far off from these, a slow and silent stream,
> Lethe, the River of Oblivion, rolls
> Her wat'ry labyrinth, whereof who drinks
> Forthwith his former state and being forgets,
> Forgets both joy and grief, pleasure and pain.

Other poets use Lethe as a symbol of forgetfulness or oblivion. Shakespeare, in *2 Henry IV*, has the new King Henry say of the indignities he has suffered: "May this be washed in Lethe and forgotten?" And when the Queen in *Richard III* asks the scheming Richard what he would bequeath her children, he replies:

> Even all I have—ay, and myself and all—
> Will I withal endow a child of thine,
> So in the Lethe of the angry soul
> Thou drown the sad remembrance of those wrongs
> Which thou supposest I have done to thee.

To Keats the deadening of the senses was closely connected with oblivion and death. In this mood he opens his *Ode to a Nightingale:*

> My heart aches, and a drowsy numbness pains
>   My sense, as though of hemlock I had drunk,
> Or emptied some dull opiate to the drains
>   One minute past, and Lethe-wards had sunk:

And similarly in his *Ode on Melancholy*:

> No, no, go not to Lethe, neither twist
>   Wolf's-bane, tight-rooted, for its poisonous wine;
> Nor suffer thy pale forehead to be kiss'd
>   By nightshade, ruby grape of Proserpine;

In *Don Juan* Byron comments on the ironies of the human condition which make the ability to forget an important part of life. The reference to the son of Thetis concerns the nymph's unsuccessful attempt to make Achilles immortal by immersing him in the river Styx.

> And if I laugh at any mortal thing,
>   'Tis that I may not weep,; and if I weep,
> 'Tis that our nature cannot always bring
>   Itself to apathy, for we must steep
> Our hearts first in the depths of Lethe's spring,
>   Ere what we least wish to behold will sleep:
> Thetis baptized her mortal son in Styx;
> A mortal mother would on Lethe fix.

No two maps of the Underworld are the same, nor are the accounts that list the permanent residents who served the god of the dead. There were landmarks the traveler sighted when approaching Hades' substanceless empire: the White Rock and the Gates (of the setting sun). At the Gates lay all those grim sons and daughters of Nyx (Night) and the monstrous brood of Phorcys and Ceto whom Hesiod cataloged in his generations of the gods. The path to the kingdom of the dead led to the shore of one of the infernal rivers, as T. S. Eliot expressed it in *The Hollow Men:*

In this last of meeting places
We grope together
And avoid speech
Gathered on this beach of the tumid river.

Charon. There on the beach the shades had to await transportation across the infernal streams, usually Acheron or the Styx, by the mythological figure in charge of the ferry, Charon. Charon is yet another death-spirit who, like Hades' hellhound Cerberus, guarded the entrance to his master's kingdom. The Etruscans, coming under the influence of the Greeks, called their demon of death Charun and depicted him as a half-human and half-animal monster who dispatched his victims with a heavy hammer. In modern Greek folklore he is called Charos and gallops about on horseback carrying off the young and the old. On ancient funerary urns Charon is often represented receiving the shade of a dead person from the hand of Hermes Psychopompos (fig. 47). Vergil describes Charon as "a grisly ferryman, frightful and foul; his chin an uncleared forest of hoary hair; his eyes a mass of flame; while his dirty garment hangs from his shoulders, gathered into a knot."

Charon accepted only those who had received a proper burial; others who had not received the ritual honors of the dead were doomed to wander on the banks of the stream for a hundred years or longer. There were, of course, notable exceptions

Figure 47.   Charon in his boat receives the shade of a woman from Hermes
Psychopompos. Vase painting, fourth century B.C. Staatliche
Antikensammlungen, Munich.

such as Heracles, Orpheus, and Aeneas who were able to convince Charon to transport them alive across the rivers of Hell. The fee charged by the grim ferryman was an *obolos* or some other coin of very small value, and for this reason a coin was placed in the mouth of the deceased before he was interred. T. S. Eliot's epigraph to *The Hollow Men*—A penny for the Old Guy—has as one of its several implicit meanings this ancient and widespread practice. "Charon's coin" is still a current tradition in the United States Navy; a penny is put in a dead seaman's mouth before he is committed to the water in a sea-burial. The penny is called "a coin for Charon." Related to this was the custom of placing a coin under the step of the mast of a new ship. Thus, if the ship were to meet with disaster, the fare of all on board would be paid. Similarly, the custom of placing "a penny piece on each eye," as Dickens describes it in *Martin Chuzzlewit*, probably has the same belief behind it, although it is rationalized as a means of keeping the eyelids closed as rigor mortis sets in.

Elysium and the Islands of the Blessed

Upon reaching the opposite shore, Charon deposited his passengers in Hades proper. Now the topography of the infernal regions becomes even more confused in our sources. At first, "Heaven and Hell" were separated, then they were brought together in one place, and in later antiquity they were separated once more. In the Homeric epics, there is no Charon, and all the dead, great and small, good and evil, dwell on the Plain of Asphodel. The asphodel, probably *Asphodelus ramosus*, is a fitting plant for the Underworld since it is a weed that thrives on arid wastelands. As noted in the introduction to this chapter (p. 228), Homer speaks of an Elysian Field, a special place at the world's end where a favored few are translated body and soul. The ruler of this land is the Cretan king Rhadamanthys, son of Zeus and Europa and famed as a judge of his people. There in Elysium is a sailor's paradise, as the sea-god Proteus prophesies for Menelaus; there

> . . . life is easiest for mankind. There no snow falls, no strong winds blow, nor is there ever any rain; instead Ocean sends the West Wind's whistling breeze to refresh its inhabitants.

Hesiod, the farmer from Boeotia, also has a paradise for those mortals of his fourth age, the age of heroes, who survived legendary wars. These heroes, also a favored few, were sent without death to the ends of the earth, to the Islands of the Blessed where, under the rule of Cronus, there is no sorrow and where the earth bears crops of honey-sweet fruit three times a year (pp. 6; 59)—a true farmer's paradise. However, by the time of Pindar in the early fifth century B.C., ethical and mystical concepts of the age become part of the picture of what befalls man in the world beyond. Pindar, poet and propagandist of aristocratic ideals, reserves a place on the Islands of the Blessed for those who have for three incarnations kept their souls free from sin. Under the guidance of both Rhadamanthys and Cronus, souls enjoy cool breezes, flowers are blazing with gold out of which they make garlands for their hands and wreaths for their heads. It is here, not in Homer's grim and gloomy Plain of Asphodel, that Pindar would assign Achilles, his father Peleus, and Cadmus. Presumably, like those who have merely led a good life while on earth, Pindar's paragons on the Islands of the Blessed would have all their material needs taken care of without their having to lift a finger. In a fragment of one of his dirges, Pindar paints a picture of a Greek paradise, possibly Elysium, where the soul, purged of all taint of evil, enjoys all the pleasures a Greek gentleman could wish for:

For them the sun shines bright and strong . . . and before their city, the meadows are deep red with roses and are shaded by incense trees heavy with golden fruit . . . Some take pleasure in horses and in wrestling, some with games of chance and lyre-playing, while among them blooms all manner of goodly happiness and bliss.

The end of this fragment is translated by Alfred Lord Tennyson for the close of his poem *Tiresias*:

> . . . and every way the vales
> Wind, clouded with the grateful incense fume
> Of those who mix all odor to the Gods
> On one far height in one far-shining fire.

As theological views changed so did the physical location of the Greek paradise, whether Elysium or the Islands of the Blessed. Homer and Hesiod had placed them at the world's end but quite apart from Hades; later accounts found a place for them either in the infernal regions or in the heavens. To those schools of religious thought, especially the Pythagorean, that emphasized moral purity, souls earned for themselves a home in a land of felicity and bliss if they had lived virtuously during their stay on earth. Man had a choice of two roads of unequal difficulty to travel, the path of virtue and the path of vice. The Pythagoreans symbolized this choice by the letter Y, Greek upsilon. The unbranched base of the letter was the common road which all men traveled before attaining the age of reason and responsibility; but when they reached the "crossroads," the point where the arms of the Y diverged, a choice had to be made between the right (virtue) and the left (vice). After death, the soul traveled a similar road on its journey to the beyond. At first it made its way along a common road, neutral ground, until it reached the crossroads where the judges of the souls sat. If the soul had led a pure life on earth, it was directed to the path on the right to Elysium. If the soul had chosen the easy path of vice during its mundane existence, it was driven to the left and the pit of Tartarus. The Pythagorean Y is reflected in Vergil's *Aeneid* where we hear the Sibyl saying to Aeneas as he came to a fork in the road of the Underworld: "This is the place where the road goes in two different directions. The path to the right skirts the dwelling place of mighty Dis [Pluto] and points the way to Elysium. The other to the left inflicts punishment on the wicked and sends them to godless Tartarus."

Other influences, mainly from the East, altered the traditional geography of the pagan's paradise. Astral religion and speculations of the physics of the soul tended to remove Elysium and the Islands of the Blessed from "the world's end" or the infernal regions and to locate them in the heavens. It was maintained that a relationship existed between souls and the stars, and that souls were particles of heavenly fire or burning breath. Upon death and release from the body, the soul attempted to ascend from its temporal sublunary abode to its celestial home among the heavenly bodies which were thought of as moving islands, other earths, enveloped in a luminous ether. The sun and the moon were readily identified with the Islands of the Blessed. The moon in particular was considered "ethereal," and in the moon or in the pure air surrounding it, were to be found the Elysian Fields. However, only pure souls could make the ascent to their prenatal home. Those stained by vice and sin had become heavy and gross, literally weighed down by their pollution. Such souls, like the heavy end of a balance, went down to the infernal regions and Tartarus where lay the instruments of punishment and purification. But when relieved of the weight of sin, the soul became light again and could ascend to the heavens and find peace in the luminous ether. There were, of course, many variations on the relationship of the soul to the planets and the stars, and such speculations in antiquity bequeathed a tradition to the Middle Ages, and later to the supreme poetical expression of these ideas in Dante's *Paradiso*. Finally, the Elysian Fields came to earth in Paris in the seventeenth century when its fashionable pleasure promenade was given the name *Champs Élysées*. In the eighteenth century, the German poet and dramatist, Friedrich von Schiller, made humanistic Joy "a daughter from Elysium." His poem, *An die Freude* (Ode to Joy), in which the poet envisaged the attainment of an Elysian community and a brotherhood of man, was taken by Beethoven for the final movement of his Ninth Symphony. The chorus opens the powerful movement signing:

> Freude, schöner Götterfunken,
> Tochter aus Elysium. . . .
> [Joy, lovely spark of the divine,
> Daughter from Elysium. . . .]

Tartarus

Tartarus, unlike Elysium or the Islands of the Blessed, had a far more fixed place in the mythological universe: it was a chasm or gulf deep within the bowels of the earth. We already witnessed the birth of Tartarus as one of the three primeval beings in Hesiod's *Theogony*, a being and yet a place into which the vanquished Titans and monstrous Typhoeus were cast. Hesiod describes it as surrounded with a wall of bronze and a triple thickness of night about its neck or throat. Above it were the foundations of the earth and sea. And so deep was Tartarus that a bronze anvil falling from heaven would take full nine days to reach the earth and yet another full nine days to the bottom of this almost bottomless pit. There, Hesiod tells us, is the residence of Night and Day, of Sleep and Death, of Hades and of Styx, and it is the place where Atlas stands as he supports the vault of heaven. Although the poet's description is no true map of the Underworld, it is clear that Tartarus served mainly as a dungeon, a kind of Olympian jail, for insubordinate and rebellious divinities. Homer has a similar view. In the *Iliad* we hear Zeus addressing the assembly of the gods and threatening anyone who disobeyed him with these words: "I will take and cast him far, far away into dank and murky Tartarus where is the deepest gulf beneath the earth; there are the gate of iron and the threshold of bronze, as far beneath Hades as heaven is high above earth."

It was not long before Tartarus became a place of post-mortem punishment and retribution, and housed not unruly deities but the souls of the wicked. Plato, in two eschatological myths which appear in the dialogs *Gorgias* and *Phaedo*, illustrates this new development and gives us a vivid picture of the Hellenic hell:

> Now in the days of Cronus, there existed a law respecting the destiny of man, which has always been, and still continues to be in Heaven,—that he who has lived all his life in justice and holiness shall go, when he is dead, to the Islands of the Blessed, and dwell there in perfect happiness out of reach of evil; but that he who has lived unjustly and impiously shall go to the prison-house of vengeance and punishment, which is called Tartarus.

This is Plato's introduction to the myth in the *Gorgias*. The same theme is picked up in the *Phaedo*:

Figure 48. A trio of sufferers in the Underworld: Sisyphus bearing the rock; Ixion fixed to a wheel; Tantalus attempting to satisfy his thirst. *Engraving, 1790. (Radio Times Hulton)*

. . . those who appear to be incurable by reason of the greatness of their crimes—who have committed many and terrible deeds of sacrilege, murders foul and violent, or the like—such are hurled into Tartarus, which is their fitting destiny, and they never come out. Those again who have committed crimes which, although great, are not irremediable—who in a moment of anger, for example, have done some violence to a father or a mother, and have repented for the remainder of their lives, or who have taken the life of another under the like extenuating circumstances—these are plunged into Tartarus, the pains of which they are compelled to undergo for a year, but at the end of the year the wave casts them forth—mere homicides by way of Cocytus, patricides and matricides by Pyriphlegethon—and they are borne to the Acherusian lake, and there they lift up their voices and call upon the victims whom they have slain or wronged to have pity on them, and to be kind to them, and let them come out into the lake. And if they prevail, then they come forth and cease from their troubles; but if not, they are carried back again into Tartarus and from thence into the rivers unceasingly, until they obtain mercy from those whom they have wronged: for that is the sentence inflicted upon them by their judges.

Tityus, Tantalus, and Sisyphus. This picture of Tartarus, which was to be so influential among all succeeding theologians and philosophers, was not created in the imagination of Plato; it developed when the Greeks turned their thoughts to moral principles and the responsibilities of individuals for their behavior. As usual, they looked to Homer to provide authority and examples of what happens to the unjust man. When the hero of the *Odyssey* traveled to the land of the dead, he was privileged to observe the punishment of three of its residents: Tityus, Tantalus, and Sisyphus. Of the three, Homer records only the indictment against Tityus, a giant and son of Earth: he dared to assault Leto, the mother of Apollo and Artemis. For his presumption and violence, he was stretched out—he covered nine acres—and two vultures continually plucked at his liver (pp. 160–162). As for Tantalus and Sisyphus, Homer is silent on the cause for their punishment although later antiquity eagerly furnished the evidence for their misdeeds and crimes. Tantalus, so Odysseus observed, suffered great agonies as he stood up to his chin in a pool of water. His thirst was unbearable, but whenever he stooped down in his eagerness to drink, the water disappeared (fig. 48). And whenever he tried to reach overhead for boughs heavy with delicious fruits, the wind would toss them far out of his reach. When Odysseus came upon Sisyphus, he found him grappling with a huge boulder which he strained to roll up toward the crest of a hill. Just as he was about to succeed in the backbreaking task, the weight of the stone became too much for him and down it came, making it necessary for Sisyphus to start all over again (fig. 48).

These were the original trio of sinners in the Underworld although Homer implied —as Plato observed in the *Gorgias*—that such punishment was reserved for kings and potentates, not for the common man. But what were the nefarious crimes of which Tantalus and Sisyphus were guilty? Both seem to have enjoyed the favor of the gods and then, being overly clever, offended them and were accordingly punished. In short, they fall into the category of "tricksters" who, like Prometheus, may have been culture-heroes in origin. Tantalus was said to have been a son of Zeus and the father of two well-known mythological figures, Pelops and Niobe. All traditions agree that he was a very weathy king in Asia Minor (Lydia, Phrygia, or Paphlagonia). On intimate terms with the gods, Tantalus was often invited to dine with the Olympians. It was at their table that he heard the divine counsels which were given to him in confidence. But he abused that confidence and was duly punished. It is to this abuse of confidence that Milton indirectly refers in *Samson Agonistes* when his protagonist cries out:

> . . . But I
> God's counsel have not kept, his holy secret
> Presumptuously have published, impiously,
> Weakly at least and shamefully—a sin
> That Gentiles in the parables condemn
> To their abyss and horrid pains confined.

Another version has it that while a guest at the table of the gods, Tantalus stole and gave to his mortal friends the celestial food of the gods, nectar and ambrosia, which conferred immortality on whoever tasted of it. Yet another popular tradition tells us how Tantalus tried to trick the gods—some say he wanted to test their omniscience—by getting them to eat food other than nectar and ambrosia. Accordingly, he cut his son Pelops in pieces, boiled them, and set them before the gods. The gods, with one exception, were not fooled. Demeter, however, who happened to be distracted by the disappearance of her daughter, absentmindedly ate part or all of the left shoulder. Pelops was later restored, and the part of him that Demeter had consumed was replaced with a piece of ivory. It is to this incident that Robert Herrick (1591–1674) alludes when, in his poem *To Electra*, he says that the skin of his mistress is whiter than "Pelops arme of yvorie." Spenser mentions Tantalus' high position in being invited to dine with the gods in these lines from the *Faerie Queene*:

> Most cursed of all creatures under skye,
> Lo Tantalus, I here tormented lye:
> Of whom high Jove wont whylome feasted bee,
> Lo here I now for want of food doe dye.

Pindar, who was revolted at the thought of the gods acting like cannibals, offers yet another explanation for Tantalus' difficulties. His great wealth led him into complacency and arrogance, and Zeus punished him by hanging over him the weight of a huge stone which forever is a constant threat to his peace of mind. Other accounts claim that a certain Pandareus had stolen a golden dog which Hephaestus had created to protect Zeus in his infancy. Pandareus turned the dog over to Tantalus for safekeeping, but when he asked for its return, Tantalus swore by Zeus that he knew nothing about the dog. For having sworn falsely by Zeus' name, Tantalus is said to have either been thrown down from Mount Sipylus or buried under it. Still yet another account attributes his difficulties to his cosmological theories. With a view similar to that of the philosopher Anaxagoras, Tantalus maintained that the sun was not a god but a fiery mass of matter. Tantalus' punishment was proverbial in ancient times, and the English language also has taken his name in the form of a verb "to tantalize," that is, to torment or tease by holding out something desirable which cannot be realized or attained.

The third member of Homer's trio of malefactors and sinners was Sisyphus, son of Aeolus and great-grandson of Deucalion, the Hellenic Noah. Sisyphus was connected with the city of Corinth and was said to have built the town of Ephyra, later known as Corinth; or that Medea handed over to him the reins of government after she had wreaked her vengeance on the ruling family of the city. As king of the city he is said to have promoted navigation and commerce and to have founded the Isthmian games. In the *Iliad*, Homer calls him "the craftiest of all men." But since Homer did not spell out the reason for his being condemned eternally to roll a rock up a steep hill, later writers give various reasons for his damnation. Some say that he betrayed the secrets of the gods to mortals; or that when Zeus carried off Aegina, the daughter of the river-god Asopus, Sisyphus reported the abduction to the girl's father in exchange for a supply of water on the citadel of Corinth. Others would have us believe that he was a highwayman who attacked travelers with huge blocks of stone until Theseus, the Athenian hero and civilizer, killed him. Yet another tradition reports that out of hatred for his brother Salmoneus, he lay with his sister-in-law Tyro and begot two sons. Tyro, however, killed them immediately after birth, and when Sisyphus took cruel vengeance on her, he was punished for it in the lower world.

Other episodes of Sisyphus' life in both worlds are related to his reputation for being the craftiest of all men. He is in fact the prototype of the trickster of popular tales. Zeus, to avenge the treachery done to him, sent Thanatos (Death) to Sisyphus, but the latter succeeded in putting Thanatos into chains so that no man died until Ares rescued him and put Sisyphus into his hands. But before dying, Sisyphus cleverly instructed his wife not to administer the obligatory funeral rites, but to cast out his body into the public streets. When Sisyphus arrived in the lower world, he complained bitterly to Hades or Persephone that he had not received the last rites due him and that he be permitted to return to earth to punish his wife. When permission was granted for his return, he naturally refused to leave the world of the living for the world of the dead. He is said to have died of old age and that his punishment was a device to keep him from escaping Hades' realm.

Brought into association with others of his own kind, Sisyphus has an encounter with Autolycus, Hermes' son (pp. 215–216). This master thief had been stealing Sisyphus' cattle, but because of his cleverness no evidence could be produced to prove it. Sisyphus outwitted him by attaching to the hooves of his cattle lead plates inscribed with the words "stolen by Autolycus," or with some other sign which enabled him to track the herds purloined by this archthief. When Sisyphus recovered his cattle, he avenged himself by seducing Autolycus' daughter, Anticleia (or Anticlea), who brought into the world another exceptionally crafty fellow, Odysseus. To Homer, Odysseus is the legitimate son of Anticleia and Laertes, but as early as Sophocles—by that time Odysseus' reputation had become somewhat tarnished— we hear of this new paternity for Homer's paragon of cleverness and sagacity.

The character of Sisyphus was very appealing to the French writer Albert Camus (1913–1960), Nobel Prize winner for literature in 1957. To Camus, life is absurd and life on earth is similar to that which Sisyphus endures in the lower world: endless punishment. But to men who are not aware of their hopeless state, life is neither heroic nor tragic. It becomes so only when one is aware and conscious of one's wretchedness. Sisyphus, on the other hand, is the absurd hero. He is always conscious of what he has to bear; his rock and his task are always before him as reminders of life's hopelessness. Happiness is to be found in the recognition of that condition, in the struggle to rise about it, and in the ability to meet any fate by scorn. Camus concludes *Le Mythe de Sisyphe: essai sur l' absurde* with this statement:

> I leave Sisyphus at the foot of the mountain! One always finds one's burden again. But Sisyphus teaches the higher fidelity that negates the gods and raises rocks. He too concludes that all is well. This universe, henceforth without a master, seems to him neither sterile nor futile. Each atom of that stone, each mineral flake of that night-filled mountain, in itself forms a world. The struggle itself toward the heights is enough to fill a man's heart. One must imagine Sisyphus happy.

Ixion. To Homer's three sinners a fourth was soon added, and the four become standard representatives of those suffering in Tartarus. As early as Pindar we hear of Ixion, the first man to shed the blood of a kinsman. Aeschylus also calls him the first murderer; he is the Greek equivalent of the Biblical Cain. Ixion's family background is variously given, but most often he is called a son of Phlegyas and consequently a brother of Coronis. Ixion was a Thessalian king who ruled over the Lapiths. When he asked for the hand of a young girl in marriage, he made her father lavish promises in the way of bride-gifts. But when asked to live up to his promises, Ixion treacherously invited his father-in-law to a banquet and then contrived to throw him into a pit filled with burning coals. By doing so Ixion was guilty not only of not honoring a contract, but also of murdering a member of his family, a deed that no one before had committed. The horror aroused by this crime was such that no one dared to purify Ixion. Of all the gods, only Zeus had pity on him. The Olympian purified and delivered him from the madness which had seized him following his crime. But Ixion proved ungrateful to the extreme. Upon being invited to the Olympian's table, he dared to make amorous overtures to Hera and attempted to force his attentions on her. Zeus, or Hera, negated his passion by fashioning a cloud-like phantom called Nephele (Cloud) which resembled Hera, and by Nephele Ixion became the father of Centaur, the progenitor of all other centaurs. As a punishment for his audacity and violence, Ixion was chained hands and feet to a fiery or winged wheel (p. 131) said to roll perpetually through the air—hence some considered Ixion to be a form of sun-god or meteorological phenomenon—or in Tartarus where he took his place by the side of the other great offenders (figs. 48, 49).

In the same poem, *To Electra*, in which Robert Herrick alludes to the fairness of his mistress' skin as being whiter than "Pelops arme of yvorie," the poet continues with an allusion to the cloud which Zeus served up to delude Ixion:

> True, I confesse; such whites as these
> May me delight, not fully please:
> Till, like Ixion's cloud you be
> White, warme, and soft to lye with me.

Milton also makes a reference to this cloud in *Paradise Regained*, but it is veiled and free of Herrick's sensuousness. Milton has Christ say in rejecting the values of Greek culture:

> Who therefore seeks in these
> True wisdom, find her not, or by delusion
> Far worse, her false resemblance only meets,
> An empty cloud.

Benjamin Disraeli, Prime Minister of England under Queen Victoria, composed a burlesque called *Ixion in Heaven* (1833), an amusing short tale of Ixion's visit to Olympus at the invitation of Zeus. Fifty years later, Robert Browning took a more serious and philosophical approach to the myth. His Ixion resembles Prometheus in conflict with Zeus. He is a heroic figure who, through his suffering, comes to a more exalted view of divine justice, a conviction that sin and evil do not merit perpetual punishment but are conditions that allow for the growth of the soul. Browning's *Ixion* concludes with these words:

Figure 49.   Ixion about to be fixed to a wheel for having affronted Hera. *Vase painting. British Museum.*

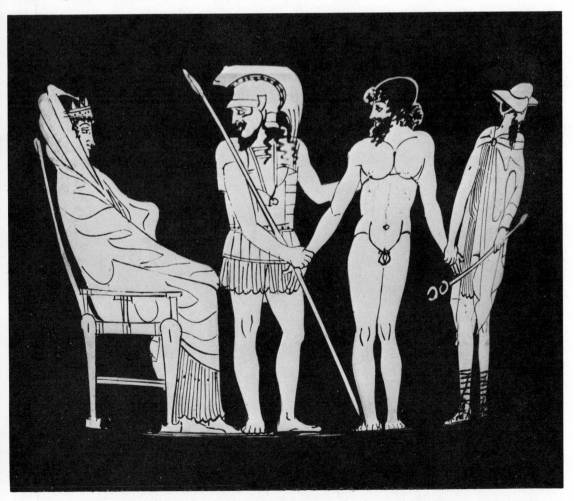

Out of the wreck I rise—past Zeus to the Potency o'er him!
  I—to have hailed him my friend! I—to have clasped her—my love!
Pallid birth of my pain,—where light, where light is, aspiring
  Thither I rise, whilst thou—Zeus, keep the godship and sink!

The forms of punishment in Tartarus become so well known among poets that the mere mention of the stone or wheel is sufficient to identify the sufferer, as in Tennyson's *Demeter and Persephone*. Tennyson, like Browning, sought a new form of godship to replace worship through fear. (The last line and a half is a translation from the *Odyssey* and describes Achilles taking his leave of Odysseus.) Instead of fear, punishment, and darkness, says Tennyson, a time will come when deity will accept

The worship which is Love, and see no more
The Stone, the Wheel, the dimly glimmering lawns
Of that Elysium, all the hateful fires
Of torment, and the shadowy warrior glide
Along the silent field of Asphodel.

In addition to Tityus, Tantalus, Sisyphus, and Ixion, there were others who became part of the catalog of sufferers in Tartarus. Salmoneus, a brother of Sisyphus and king of Elis, was presumptuous enough to consider himself an equal of Zeus: not only did he preempt sacrifices of the god and order them for himself, but he also imitated the thunder and lightning of the great Olympian by making a thundering noise with his chariot and by hurling lighted torches into the sky. Some scholars see in Salmoneus a wizard or priest-king who by means of imitative magic attempted to make rain; later generations misinterpreted his actions as blasphemy. Be that as it may, Zeus quickly dispatched him with a bolt of lightning and hurled him into Tartarus for his impiety and presumption. Also to be found in Tartarus were Theseus and his comrade Pirithous, king of the Lapiths. The latter, with Theseus' help, dared to invade the world of the dead and attempt the abduction of Persephone. For their overweening audacity, both men were either bound or held fast in magic chairs. Heracles later rescued Theseus when he descended to the lower world on another mission. And lastly, the Danaids, the many daughters of king Danaus, have a prominent place in Tartarus for having killed their husbands at their father's bidding. Theirs is the task of trying to fill a leaky jar or sieve with water.

Vergil reviews all these miscreants and sinners in the *Aeneid* when his hero makes a descent into the Underworld. Later, under the influence of the Roman poet, Spenser has Sansfoy (Faithless), the dead pagan in the *Faerie Queene*, see almost the same corps of sufferers:

There was Ixion turned on a wheele,
For daring tempt the Queene of heaven to sin;
And Sisyphus an huge round stone did reele
Against an hill, ne might from labour lin;
There thirstie Tantalus hong by the chin;
And Tityus fed a vulture on his maw;
Typhoeus joynts were stretched on a gin,
Theseus condemned to endlesse slouth by law,
And fifty sisters water in leake vessels draw.

The Judges in the Underworld

These then were the cardinal sinners on whom the gods avenged an insult to their person or prerogatives. But when the Greeks began to be concerned with moral values within a society that tended more and more toward individualism, the legendary offenders and their punishment became prototypes for men who committed crimes and sins against their fellowmen. And where punishment had to be meted out, there had to be judges. Homer had mentioned Minos as a judge in Hades' realm, a judge in the sense of one who exercises authority over those whom he rules and is called upon to settle the disputes of his subjects. Early poets had in like manner placed Rhadamanthys and Cronus in charge of those who were privileged to inhabit the Islands of the Blessed and the Elysian Fields. By Plato's time, however, the concern was not so much with the epic heroes of Homer and Hesiod or with Pindar's aristocrats, but with the man in the street and the kind of life he lived while a member of society. In the *Gorgias*, Plato uses mythological material to support his contention that the man who has lived unjustly and impiously has something to fear in the afterlife. Under the influence of Orphic and Pythagorean doctrines, he describes a tribunal of infernal judges who meet the souls of the dead as they approach that point in the road where one way leads to Paradise, the other to Hell:

> In the time of Cronus, and quite lately in the reign of Zeus, judgment was given on the very day on which men were to die; the judges were alive, and the men were alive; and the consequence was that cases were erroneously decided. Then Pluto and the authorities from the Islands of the Blessed came to Zeus, and said that the souls found their way to the wrong places. Zeus said: "I shall put a stop to this. . . . I will deprive men of the foreknowledge of death, which they possess at present. . . . therefore I have appointed sons of my own to be judges; two from Asia, Minos and Rhadamanthys, and one from Europe, Aeacus. And these, when they are dead, shall give judgment in the meadow at the parting of the ways, whence the two roads lead, one to the Islands of the Blessed, and the other to Tartarus. Rhadamanthys shall judge those who come from Asia, and Aeacus those who come from Europe. And to Minos I shall give the primacy, and he shall hold a court of appeal, in case either of the two are in any doubt:— then the judgment respecting the last journey will be as just as possible.

All three of Plato's judges, legendary sons of Zeus, won so great a reputation for their administration of justice during their stay on earth that they continued to exercise their juridical expertise in the afterlife. Minos and Rhadamanthys (Rhadamanthus) were sons of Zeus and Europa, and their activities centered on the island of Crete. Aeacus, the grandfather of Achilles, is generally called the son of Zeus and Aegina, the offspring of the affair that caused talebearing Sisyphus so much anguish in Tartarus. Aeacus earned such a reputation for justice and piety while he was king of Aegina—an island named after his mother—that he frequently was called upon to settle disputes not only among men, but even among the gods themselves. While it is characteristic of Plato to recommend specialization of duties—Rhadamanthys to handle souls from Asia, Aeacus to judge those from Europe, and Minos to act as an appeals-court judge—the assignment of judicial posts in the afterlife was based usually upon simpler considerations. Vergil, for example, speaks of Rhadamanthys as a judge in Tartarus who pitilessly compels each sinner to confess the crimes committed during his lifetime, crimes to be atoned for in Tartarus. Minos, on the other hand, presides over those who have been unjustly put to death and takes into account their earthly lives and earthly sins. Other poets and authorities simplify the process even further and make Minos the sole judge of sinners. By the time of Dante, medieval imagination had transformed Minos from a dignified judge into a devil grinning frighteningly: in the *Inferno*, Minos is the demonic judge who twists his tail around his body; the number of times he girds himself is an index of the circle in hell to which the sinner was to descend.

Punishment in Tartarus. The most common form of punishment in Tartarus was the application of fire and the lash to the sinner. In origin, both burning and whipping were magical means of purification and exorcism; later tradition was to view them primarily as penalties. The executors of infernal judgments were usually the Erinyes (Furies) who either scourged the guilty souls with whips and snakes or used their burning torches to punish the damned. Pyriphlegethon, the river of fire surrounding Tartarus, also served as an instrument of punishment. The Greeks and Romans, however, took no pleasure in descriptions of the tortures which a soul had to endure in Tartarus, nor did they draw up a penal code listing individual sins along with the appropriate penalty to be administered in Tartarus. Rather, it was the infernal eschatology of the East and its mystical sects which mingled and coalesced with Greco-Roman concepts that later produced the detailed assortment of atrocities conventionally associated with hell: demons succeeded the Erinyes, and Tartarus became a pit or gulf filled with volcanic fire, burning mud, and brimstone.

By the end of the first century B.C. the terrors of Tartarus began to lose their hold on many minds. Cicero and Seneca claimed that no one was childish enough to fear the gloomy regions of the dead or the monsters and spirits that were supposed to dwell there. Plutarch, a devout believer in the pagan gods, saw in the myths of infernal punishment of the wicked a means of frightening children, only tales told by nurses. Lucretius, the Roman apologist of Epicurean rationalism, argued vehemently that men by their anxieties created a Tartarus for themselves on earth. He interpreted the Homeric trio of sinners as prototypes of earthly terrors and anxieties rather than literal punishment of the damned: the boulder hanging over Tantalus' head as the irrational fear of the gods and the suffering that chance might bring; the suffering of Tityus as self-inflicted pain caused by excess of passion or jealousy; and the eternal torture of Sisyphus as the symbol of the ambitious politician who, repeatedly defeated in elections, comes back again and again for more punishment at the polls. But in spite of the inroads made by these and other sceptics, the belief in Tartarus and its tortures was kept alive in the lower strata of the population until the later interpreters of Plato, the Neoplatonists, revived and gave new vigor to the older doctrines and the myths connected with them. Neoplatonism, a synthesis of several philosophical schools dominated by the authority and "divinity" of Plato, became the leading philosophy of the pagan world from the middle of the third century A.D. and was to exercise a major influence on the thought of the Middle Ages and Renaissance. So it is that Tartarus, which started out as a place of confinement for rebel gods, was turned into a torture chamber and inferno for the souls of the damned. In *Paradise Lost* Milton combines the early and late characteristics of Tartarus, a jail and a fiery pit. He relates how the archangels Gabriel and Michael were urged to battle Satan and his corps of insurgent angels, and to

> . . . drive them out from God and bliss
> Into their place of punishment, the gulf
> Of Tartarus, which ready opens wide
> His fiery chaos to receive their fall.

William Butler Yeats (1865–1939), who saw in mythology the symbols and confirmation of his mystical and supernatural beliefs, combines Neoplatonic and Christian views of the afterlife in *The Delphic Oracle upon Plotinus*. His point of departure in the poem is an account of the response of the Delphic oracle on the journey of Plotinus, famed Neoplatonist of the third century A.D., to the Hellenic paradise. For Yeats, the continuity and renewal of spiritual forces are reflected in the mythology of one generation to the next, from one age to another. Plotinus, the symbol of the "Golden Race" of Greeks, has difficulty in reaching the Islands of the Blessed and the Neoplatonic choir of Eternal Love because of the crucifixion of Christ ("salt blood blocks his eyes"). Plotinus bears some relationship to Christ since both have come from the East; and it is the souls of the East, as we observed in Plato's *Gorgias*, who are judged by Rhadamanthys.

> Behold that great Plotinus swim,
> Buffeted by such seas;
> Bland Rhadamanthus beckons him,
> But the Golden Race looks dim,
> Salt blood blocks his eyes.
>
> Scattered on the level grass
> Or winding through the grove
> Plato there and Minos pass,
> There stately Pythagoras
> And all the choir of Love.

Dionysus and Orpheus: God and Man, Myth and Mystery

I saw a staring virgin stand
Where holy Dionysus died,
And tear the heart out of his side,
And lay the heart upon her hand
And bear that beating heart away;
And then did all the Muses sing
Of Magnus Annus at the spring
As though God's death were but a play.

Yeats—Two Songs from a Play

The above poetic statement of Yeats, compounded as it is with pagan and Christian symbols and with the ritual of the seasonal cycle, brings together in one myth the enigmatic character not only of Dionysus but also of Orpheus. Robert Browning admitted the difficulty when he claimed—with some license in spelling the names of the gods—that faith had no need "to puzzle out who Orpheus was,/ or Dionysius Zagreas." Orpheus, legendary poet and teacher, gave his name to Orphism, a religious movement, which developed in Greece in the sixth century B.C. or earlier. Much of Orphic doctrine—the transmigration of souls, good and evil in man, original sin, retribution in another life—was supported by a mythological apparatus that centered largely on the infancy of Dionysus: his birth, passion, and rebirth. As for Dionysus, although the Olympians treated him as a second generation god and a latecomer to their hierarchy, his worship goes back to a very early stratum, earlier than Zeus himself.

Dionysus

For a fuller appreciation of the character of Dionysus it is necessary to put aside the conception of the god made popular by Renaissance artists and poets, and to forget Keats' "god of breathless cups and chirping mirth." It was the poets and artists of the Hellenistic period and those of succeeding generations who crystallized the character of Dionysus as "jolly Bacchus"—Bacchus was his Lydian name—the tipsy god of wine and his reveling entourage of satyrs, sileni, and nymphs. This was the representation taken over by Renaissance painters such as Titian and Rubens. To the Greeks, Dionysus was a god of wine and much more than that, as his epithets and cult-titles confirm. He is *Dendrites* (of the Tree), *Liknites* (of the Winnowing Fan, an instrument used to separate the chaff from the grain), *Anthios* (the Blossom Bringer), *Karpios* (the Fruit Bringer), and *Phleus* (the Abundance of Life). In Attica he was known as the Ivy Dionysus; among the Lacedaemonians, there was the Fig Dionysus; and on the island of Naxos, his statue had a face made of fig wood. His epithets relate him not only to flora but to fauna as well, in particular to the bull. He is called bull-horned, bull-shaped, bull-faced, cow-born, horned, and two-horned. In other animal symbols he appears as a goat, panther, fawn, lion, tiger, ass, dolphin, or snake. In short, the domain of Dionysus is not limited to the vine, but extends to all nature and especially to its life-giving and seminal moisture: the sap rising in a tree, the blood pounding in the veins of a young animal, the liquid fire of the grape, all the mysterious and uncontrollable tides that flow and ebb in nature (fig. 50). By further extension, Dionysus becomes identified with the emotional and irrational, unrestrained frenzy and ecstasy, the removal of gulf between god and man, between the finite and the infinite.

The questions who Dionysus was and what his origins were, are obscured in the mists of antiquity. Was he indigenous to Greece or was he a latecomer from Thrace and Phrygia, the European and Asian regions flanking the Dardanelles? Scholars are not in agreement. Does his name mean "Zeus of (Mount) Nysa" or "Son of Zeus"? Scholars agree only that his name is a sacred and unfathomable symbol. Homer knows of Dionysus, but he is hardly noticed except in metaphor; this god has no place among the Olympians worshiped by Homer's warrior-gods. By the Classical Age, the figure of Dionysus was clothed in trappings borrowed from several gods, notably the Cretan Zeus and Zagreus, the Phrygian Sabazius, and other Eastern deities. That the god was a spirit of fertility there can be no doubt. He bears a

Figure 50. Dionysus, god of fertility, giver of wine to man, patron of drama and religious ecstasy. *Vase painting. Museum Antiker Kleinkunst, Munich. (Hirmer)*

resemblance to Hyacinthus, Linus, and the Semitic Adonis. Among the Phrygians of Asia Minor, the belief was held that Dionysus was bound or slept in the winter and that he was free or awake in the summer. The same idea is found at Delphi where the celebrants of Dionysiac worship, the Thyiades, performed a ceremony of awakening the child with a winnowing fan, the *liknites*. At the Anthesteria, the festival of flowers celebrated at the beginning of springtime in the Mediterranean, the rituals reflected both rejoicing and gloom. On the chief day, the new wine was brought in and ceremonially blessed before the god of wine. Everyone drank of his own jug. On the same day, a ship bearing the statue of Dionysus on wheels was brought into town. The wife of the leading citizen in town was then married to the statue of the god. In the evening, pots of cooked fruits were offered to the dead. All the rites associated with the Anthesteria attest to the importance of the festival: the drinking of the new wine which inspired the worshipers with its magic potency, the coming of the god at the critical time of the agricultural year, the holy marriage (p. 93), and the propitiation of the dead in order to gain their cooperation with the powers of fertility beneath the ground.

Attracted to Dionysus were certain fertility spirits of wildlife who help make up this "revel-rout": Satyrs, Sileni, Centaurs, Pans, and Fauns. The semi-equine centaurs and the hircine pans and fauns have already been described. As for satyrs and sileni, they also bore the bestial and lustful characteristics of the horse and goat. Classical writers constantly confused the two, but by the fourth century B.C., sileni are generally portrayed as old, inebriated, and with the ears of a horse. One of their number, like the centaur Chiron, is singled out for his intellectual talents. So it is that we find Silenus entrusted with the education of young Dionysus, or represented as a kindly old man who looks after the satyrs as if they were his children. When the ancients compared Socrates to Silenus, it was not only to the similarity in looks they were referring, but also to the wisdom and secrets which Silenus was thought to possess. However, the tipsy side of his character was better known. At the Anthesteria, Silenus appeared with Dionysus on the ritual ship and helped in the drinking of wine; and it was a drunken Silenus whom Midas saved from being captured by unfriendly people (p. 143). In the revel-rout he usually reclines on a wineskin or is so drunk that he has to be transported on an ass. Satyrs, on the other hand, are usually represented as young, highly amorous, goatlike creatures with small horns protruding from their forehead and a tail like that of a goat or horse.

Dionysiac Worship. The desire to move the spirit of fertility by sympathetic means—that is, by a form of magic that is imitative—produces yet another experience: communion with the god, the goal of all mysticism. A passive form of this religious phenomenon has already been observed in the myths of Demeter and Persephone, as applied in the Eleusinian mysteries. The worshipers of Dionysus engaged in certain rituals which we call "orgies" and "revels." The orgy (*orgia*) was a solemn act of homage to the god in which the celebrants were said "to revel" (*bakchuein*), that is, to be in communion with the god and to be transformed into Bacchus himself. Once divinity had entered into the celebrant, deity and devotee became one, god and man became one. Thus the barrier interposed by Apollo and Delphi between the human and the divine was shattered by Dionysus. Olympianism, as we know from the lips of Homer, Aeschylus, and Sophocles, had insisted that man realize the limitations imposed upon him by his mortality and the impossibility of ever closing the great interval between himself and the eternal majesty of the gods. Dionysus now made it possible to close that gap and to guarantee man a life similar to that of the god. So it is that Plutarch, biographer and philosopher of the first century A.D., could console his wife on the death of their infant daughter by reminding her of the immortality of the soul, as revealed in the mysteries of Dionysus.

The means by which the worshipers of Dionysus attained the state of communion with the god were wine or other sacramental intoxicants, dancing, and the excitation of music. Wine was the most commonly used sacrament, although the same effect could be attained through milk or even water. Drunkenness, as William James observed in the *Varieties of Religious Experience* (1902), "expands, unites, and says Yes: it brings the votary from the chill periphery of things to the radiant core: it makes him for the moment one with truth." Wine, thus, has a religious value: the worshiper of Dionysus who drinks it—or any other sacramental drink associated with the god—has taken the god within himself. The state in which god is in man, god-possessed, was described by the Greeks with the word *entheos* or *enthusiasmos*; from the latter is derived the English word "enthusiasm."

Dancing, like drinking the essence of the god, was ritualistic in origin and magic in character. Many people the world over dance to make their crops grow by sympathetic magic: the higher you leap, the taller your plants grow. But dancing also produces a concomitant religious experience: a sense of being possessed by an alien spirit. In many societies, there are people for whom, as Aldous Huxley says in *Ends and Means*, "ritual dances provide a religious experience that seems more convincing than any other. . . . It is with their muscles that they most easily obtain knowledge of the divine." Dionysiac dancing has been compared to that of the dervishes of the thirteenth century A.D., to that of the American Shakers, to the Jewish Hasidim, and to the Siberian Shaman. The founder of the sect of Dervishes, Jelaluddin Rumi, said that "he who knows the power of the dance dwells in God." To the dance must be added the compelling power of the highly emotional music produced by the Phrygian reedpipe, the drum, and the cymbals, all instruments associated with the god of frenzy. The myths of musical competitions between the followers of Dionysus and Apollo manifest the conflict between the two opposing forms of religious expression, Apollonian calm and control versus Dionysiac passion and abandon.

The combination of rhythmic dance and wild Dionysiac music is highly infectious and obsessive, capable of producing mass hysteria (fig. 51). It was particularly so among the women of ancient Greece whose lives were normally restricted in freedom and expression; to them the call of Dionysus made its strongest appeal. Women would abandon their looms and household duties to follow the priest of Dionysus to the wildest parts of the mountains to celebrate the *orgia* of the god. They draped themselves with the skins of animals, usually fawnskins; wreathed their heads with ivy or branches of oak and fir; brandished the *thyrsus*, a staff tipped with a pine cone and often wrapped with vine or ivy leaves. Some women grasped snakes in their hands; others had them wreathed around their bodies or entwined in their hair. In their frenzied state they became Bacchae and were so called. And because they were mad, frenzied, and possessed, they earned the name of Maenads or Thyiads, the former being related to Greek and English *mania*. The god Dionysus spurs them on to perform superhuman acts and to have visions: they uproot trees, kill wild animals, put armed men to flight, see the ground flowing with milk, wine, and honey. Regarding the latter, Plato in the *Ion* has Socrates imply that the

Figure 51.   A Dionysiac procession: Dionysus, Pan and Bacchant. *Roman
bas-relief. National Museum, Naples (Alinari)*

Bacchae draw honey and milk from the rivers only when they are possessed by the
god but not when they are in their right minds.

The Greek vase painters were best at capturing the rapt expression of the Bac-
chantes as they were seized by the savagery of the Dionysiac ecstasy: their heads
are turned up and thrown back, their mouths are wide open as they call the god with
"euoi!" "euoi!"; they brandish their thyrsi, beat upon the drum, or are engaged
with the satyrs and sileni in the devotional orgy to the god.

The climax to the Dionysiac orgy is the tearing to pieces (*sparagmos*) and the eating of the raw flesh (*omophagia*) of an animal. We have already observed a similar motif in connection with Cronus devouring his children and Zeus swallowing
Metis. The motif of the *sparagmos* is also present in the death of Actaeon, a cousin
of Dionysus according to mythological genealogies. But in the Dionysiac rites, a
deeper and more primitive stratum is plumbed. The animal that is rent and devoured is believed to be the incarnation of the god; and the sacramental eating of
the warm and bleeding flesh transfers to the worshiper the vital powers of the god
himself, in particular his divinity and his own life drama. The most usual victim is a
bull, the bull being one of the common forms of the epiphany of Dionysus. Other
animals which embodied the god—the goat, fawn, snake, and even the lion—served
as holy victims and a sacramental meal for the supreme mystery. If we are to believe
the testimony of the fourth-century Christian writer, Firmicus Maternus, the Cretans celebrated the funeral festival in honor of Dionysus in which they enacted the
life and death of the god in a passion play and "rent a living bull with their teeth."

Still more revealing is the fragment of a play of Euripides, the *Cretans*, preserved
by the Neoplatonist Porphyry, in which Dionysiac rites are fused with a mystic cult

of Cretan deities. The votary proclaims that he has become an initiate of the Zeus of Mount Ida, of night-wandering Zagreus—Zagreus is the Orphic name of the Underworld Dionysus—and of the Mountain Goddess (Rhea-Cybele). After he has fulfilled the "solemn rite of the banquet of raw flesh," the sanctified initiate robes himself in pure white clothing, avoids the taint of childbirth and funerals, abstains from meat, and most significantly, calls himself by the very name of the god, "Bacchus."

The extant play of Euripides, the *Bacchae*, produced in 406 B.C., reveals the extent to which the votary of the god rejoices at being one with his god and at calling himself by his name, the mystic union that is brought about by taking part in the Dionysiac *orgia*. But in addition to the glory and the transfiguration experienced by the celebrant, Euripides also portrays the horror and revulsion that overcomes the votary once the frenzy and ecstasy has departed and rationality returns. As in several of his other plays, Euripides views the ancient gods of the Greeks not as fiends or fictions but as blind natural forces operating within the individual. The Dionysiac is one such force, a force that runs contrary to the human faculty of reason. However, the failure to give expression to the irresistible surge of Dionysiac power, to repress or inhibit it, results in being overwhelmed by that power. André Gide has caught this side of the playwright when he reports in his *Journal* for August 21, 1940: "Euripides takes sides no more than does Ibsen, it seems to me. He is content to illuminate and develop the conflict between natural forces and the soul that claims to escape their domination."

All Greece recognized and worshiped Dionysus, but all Greece did not engage in orgiastic celebrations in honor of the god. For the most part, it was Apollo and his priests who regulated and institutionalized the worship of the god. The Dionysiac power was not suppressed; rather, it was recognized and moderated. At Delphi, for example, where the mantic priestesses of Apollo exhibited many of the symptoms of maenadism, Dionysus was supreme for the three winter months when the god of prophecy absented himself. And it was at Delphi, sacred to Apollo, that Dionysus was said to have a tomb (p. 121). The Dionysiac orgy was celebrated at Delphi, but it was restricted to alternate years when Thyiades were permitted to roam about on Mount Parnassus brandishing their thyrsi and torches in orgiastic frenzy. But even these Thyiades represented an official cult-association; it was not an open group to which any one seized by the spirit could join.

Dionysus at Athens.   At Athens and its surrounding region, there was no biennial winter awakening of the god; there was no mountain-dancing and no *omophagia*. The Athenians met this obligation by sending a delegation of women to represent them at the official cult-festival at Delphi. Dionysus at Athens was honored with celebrations that resembled country fairs mixed with a little old-fashioned magic. In addition to the Anthesteria mentioned above, there was the merry rustic festival of the Rural Dionysia with its dramatic performances, processions, songs, and country sports—for example, players trying to keep their balance while jumping on a slippery wineskin. Best known of these festivals is the City or Great Dionysia in honor of Dionysus Eleuthereus, a celebration which Pisistratus introduced into Athens late in the sixth century B.C. from the village of Eleutherae, close to the borders of Boeotia, which local legend claims was the birthplace of the god. Dionysus was worshiped there as *melanaigis* (of the black goatskin) and a "goatsong" (*tragōdia* = tragedy) was said to have been sung to lament the slain god.

As the City Dionysia developed at Athens, it became a religious festival sponsored by the state. It opened with a sacred procession in which the statue of Dionysus and representations of the phallus, the symbol of the god, were conducted to his temple where sacrifices were offered. In the theater of Dionysus, choral odes (dithyrambs) were sung in honor of the god and a set number of tragic dramas were performed. Shortly before 480 B.C. comedies were added. These too had their origin in the Dionysiac festival; the word comedy probably derives from the Greek "revel-song." The Athenian festival at which comedies were performed was called the Lenea; the Greek word from which it is derived, *lēnē*, is the equivalent of "maenad." The "revel-song" associated with the rites of Dionysus left its mark on early comedy by its uninhibited language and ribald merrymaking. All these Athenian festivals, when they were intimate community affairs, must have provided an emotional release for their participants without the need to take part in the Dionysiac *orgia*. But when they became more associated with the cultural and political greatness of Athens, when they became more social than religious, the Dionysiac temper sought satisfaction in other forms of worship. From the fifth century B.C. on, Attic literature begins to contain many references to foreign gods with orgiastic rituals—Attis and Cybele, Adonis, Sabazius—who offered the identification with deity that Dionysus had once promised.

Dionysus at Rome. Dionysus traveled to Rome, as had many of his fellow-deities, by way of the Greek colonists who had settled in Italy at an early date. Among the Italians the god was called by his Lydian name of Bacchus, or was identified with a native fertility-god, Liber Pater. The rural Bacchic rituals of Greece were transformed into religious societies in urban Rome. The mystical rites of the god, the Bacchanalia as the Romans called them, were celebrated in secret, a practice the conservative Roman establishment viewed with suspicion as a form of political subversion. Reports soon came to the Senate, which was always averse to foreign cults with orgiastic rites, that celebrants of the Bacchanalia were creating a public scandal, that they were engaging not only in gross improprieties and immoral practices, but in crimes of violence as well. In 186 B.C., the Senate issued a decree—the so-called *Senatus consultum de Bacchanalibus*—which suppressed all Bacchic societies in Rome and throughout Italy as being a conspiracy against the state. However, the worship of Dionysus by individuals under official supervision was not forbidden, as for example at the innocent festival of Bacchus, the Liberalia, which was celebrated on March 17th with feasts and merriment. It was at this festival that young men who had reached the age of sixteen were initiated into manhood and received the *toga virilis*. The Bacchanalia, however, acquired the reputation of being orgies in the modern sense of the word, and the word "bacchanal" has since become a synonym for drunken revelry and debauchery.

Orphism. There was yet another modification in the worship of Dionysus, one that is revealed in mythology and which was to have far-reaching effects in metaphysics and eschatology. Orphism, a religious movement that began to make itself known in the sixth century B.C., took its name from Orpheus, a legendary or mythical poet. Orpheus is either legendary or mythical, primarily because there has been no consensus among scholars as to whether he was a historical personage or another aspect of Dionysus. But the ancients had no such doubts: to them Orpheus was a real man, a great singer, a prophet and teacher, a reformer of the older and more primitive worship of Dionysus. It is clear, however, that both Dionysus and

Orpheus have ritualistic and mythological connections, and that Orphism attempted to synthesize elements of the two prevalent forms of religious beliefs, Apollo and Dionysus. From Apollo came the emphasis upon purification—the keynote of Orphic faith was consecration and purity—and from Apollo Orpheus took the lyre, the symbol of controlled emotion. From Dionysus came the belief of "god in man" and the divinity of the soul. The Orphic, however, altered the concept of how godhead was to be obtained. He sought to become Bacchus, but the grace he sought was spiritual ecstasy, not physical intoxication; the means he adopted were abstinence and purification through a system of rules that had to be observed every day of the votary's life, not the periodic sacramental drink, shrill music, and wild dancing. As for the eating of the raw flesh, the *omophagia*, there are differences of opinion as to whether the Orphic ever took part in this primitive ritual. The likelihood is that the practice varied from place to place. On the island of Crete, if the fragment of Euripides' *Cretans* describes an Orphic ritual, he may have taken part in the omophagy when he was initiated into the sect but forever after abstained from eating meat. In other places there may have been periodic sacrifices to the god when the prohibition was suspended and when the Orphics ate of the sacramental flesh. And in yet other places, the Orphics undoubtedly rejected entirely that part of the Dionysiac ritual. Orphism is also unique in the sense that, unlike Greek religion in general, it had a founder and that its tenets were laid down in books said to have been written by Orpheus himself. Again it is Euripides who reveals the essence of this new faith. In his play *Hippolytus*, which dramatizes the conflict between ascetic purity and ungovernable passion, Theseus, believing that his illegitimate son Hippolytus has violated his wife, rips into the young man and charges him with being an Orphic, but a hypocritical one.

> You are the veritable holy man!
> You walked with Gods in chastity immaculate!
> I'll not believe your boast of God's companionship:
> the Gods are not so simple nor so ignorant.
> Go, boast that you eat no meat, that you have Orpheus
> for your king. Read until you are demented
> your great thick books whose substance is as smoke.
> For I have found you out. I tell you all,
> avoid such men as he. They hunt their prey
> with holy-seeming words, but their designs
> are black and ugly.

Orphic theology added an element that was supported by neither Apollo nor Dionysus. Apollo had insisted upon placing the divine off-limits for mortals; Dionysus claimed the possibility of communion with the divine through his rituals. Orpheus took another tack: all mortals have a dual nature in which the divine is lodged within the soul and evil in the body. To support this contention, the Orphics developed their own mythological anthropogony, the creation of man. At the same time, they transformed the omophagy, the culminating rite of the Dionysiac orgy, into the primeval crime of the Titans. Briefly, the myth placed the responsibility of the death of the child Dionysus upon the Titans who killed the child and ate his body. In anger, Zeus incinerated the Titans with his lightning, and from the ashes of the Titans, containing as they did part of the divine Dionysus, the god ordered man to be created. Man, therefore, has within him both the divine (Dionysus) and evil

(Titans). The objective of the Orphics was to purify themselves of their "Titanic nature" so as to be made fit for communion with gods. To them the body was the tomb or prison-house of the soul, a doctrine which they summarized pithily in two words: *sōma* body), *sēma* (tomb). Plato, in the *Cratylus*, outlines this Orphic view of man's dual nature:

> For some say that the body is the tomb [*sema*] of the soul which may be thought to be buried in our present life . . . . it seems to me most probable that the Orphic poets were the inventors of the name, and they were under the impression that the soul is suffering the punishment for certain sins, and that the body is an enclosure or prison in which the soul is incarcerated, kept safe as the name *sōma* implies, until the penalty is paid . . . .

For the Orphic, then, the body was evil and a source of trial and punishment for the soul, and the ultimate hope of the Orphic was to free himself altogether from the prison of the body through ritual purification. However, the soul could not be fully purified in the course of one generation and had to be born again in another body. This cycle of incarnation could be terminated only after several generations of purification; until then the soul suffered in the body and in the Underworld. This was the contribution of the Orphics to making the Underworld a place of punishment for mortals. Pindar reflects the Orphic view of the cycle of generations when he says that man will go to the Islands of the Blessed if he has kept his soul free from sin for three incarnations in either world, in the world of the living or that of the dead. Plato also responded to Orphic ideals: the stress he placed upon the dualism between body and soul, and the virtually complete separation of the two; the aim of the philosophic soul to free itself from the limitations imposed upon it by the body. His dialog on the immortality of the soul, the *Phaedo*, is strongly charged with Orphic elements although Plato substitutes philosophy as the purifying agent rather than ritual. This is his apocalyptic vision, as stated by Socrates, after describing the punishment of souls in the afterlife:

> . . . those who have been pre-eminent for holiness of life are released from this earthly prison, and go to their pure home which is above, and dwell on the true earth: and of these, such as have duly purified themselves with philosophy, live henceforth altogether without the body, in mansions fairer still, which are not easily to be described, and of which the time now fails me to tell.

The Orphics also introduced into their theology a speculative cosmogony, an expansion and development of Hesiod's *Theogony*, in which the gods were given new functions. Our sources are late and not all agree on details, but the Orphic cosmogony has this outline. In the beginning stood Chronos (Time), which is ageless and never grows old. From Chronos—not to be confused with Cronus—were born Aether, Chaos, and Erebus (Darkness). From an egg, which Chronos fashioned in Aether (Upper Air), sprang forth Phanes, the Orphic equivalentof Eros, who became the creator of all things and the first ruler of the gods. From Phanes, Night was born; and from Night and Phanes, Uranus (Heaven) and Gaea (Earth) were brought into being. Then came the Titans. The Orphic story follows Hesiod for most subsequent details with the important exception that Zeus swallowed Phanes—once more the familiar motif of swallowing—and created all things anew. Zeus therefore becomes, in the words of the Orphic, "the beginning, the middle and the end of all," a phrase comparable to Milton's description of God in *Paradise Lost*: "Him first, Him last, Him midst and without end."

The Orphic story continues with the birth of Dionysus, his death at the hands of the Titans, his resurrection, and the creation of man. Demeter had a daughter by Zeus, Kore-Persephone. To the god of the Underworld Persephone bore the Furies; to Zeus she bore Dionysus who was also called Zagreus. The Olympian set his child upon his throne, placed his scepter in his hand, and declared to the new generation of gods that Dionysus was now to be their king. The Titans, however, were jealous of the child and plotted to unseat the son of Zeus. According to some, it was Hera who incited the Titans because her husband had given his affection to another woman. The Titans distracted the child-god with toys of various sorts, and while the child was absorbed with his playthings, they killed him, tore him to pieces (*sparagmos*), and ate his flesh (*omophagia*). The goddess Athena, however, saved the heart of the slain child, brought it to Zeus who swallowed it and gave birth to a new Dionysus, some say as the son of Semele. For their part in this unspeakable crime, the Titans were reduced to ashes by the lightning bolts of Zeus, and from the ashes of these wicked beings, man was formed.

This brings us back full circle to the poem of Yeats which serves as an epigraph to this chapter. *Two Songs from a Play* is taken from Yeats' play *The Resurrection*, in which the death and resurrection of Christ is taken as a reenactment of the mythical story of Dionysus. Yeats, however, used the Orphic version for his poem, and his "staring virgin" is, of course, Athena.

> I saw a staring virgin stand
> Where holy Dionysus died
> And tear the heart out of his side,
> And lay the heart upon her hand
> And bear that beating heart away;
> And then did all the Muses sing
> Of Magnus Annus at the spring
> As though God's death were but a play.

The Myths of Dionysus.   In turning to the mythological biography of Dionysus, it must be recognized that many of the motifs contained in it are projections of the Dionysiac ritual. The tearing apart or death of the young god (*sparagmos*) is reflected in his passion and in the penalties inflicted upon those who resist the worship of Dionysus. Rejection or resistance to the god's rites produces hallucinations or "madness" (*mania, enthusiasmos, ecstasis*), all manifestations of the religious experience of the worshipers of Dionysus. Some scholars see in the resistance-motif political opposition to the cult of Dionysus as it swept over Greece. The likelihood is, rather, that it expresses a psychological phenomenon in mythical form: that to resist the irresistible surge of Dionysiac power in one's nature is to invite punishment in the form of being overwhelmed by that same elemental force. This is the point of view Euripides expresses in the *Hippolytus* concerning Aphrodite, his symbol of passion as a nonmoral cosmic power:

> Upon the yielding spirit she comes gently,
> but to the proud and the fanatic heart
> she is a torturer with the brand of shame.

Other motifs deserve notice in the story of Dionysus' life and travels, taken as it is from a variety of sources and made into a continuous narrative: Hera's jealousy, the test of divinity, the exposure of a hero or infant god on a mountain or his being set adrift on the sea, the raking of hell, and, finally, the Hellenistic fondness for geographical aetiology—for example, how the Tigris river got its name.

The Birth of Dionysus. The story most commonly told of the birth and child-hood of Dionysus takes place at Thebes during the reign of Cadmus, founder of the city. Cadmus had four daughters—Semele, Ino, Autonoe, and Agave—all of whom in one way or another were involved in the life of the god. Semele had attracted the eye of Zeus and was now bearing his child. Hera, knowing of her husband's philandering ways, determined to avenge herself on Semele and her unborn child. She appeared to the ingenuous girl in the form of her aged nurse Beroe, and advised her to make sure of her lover's divinity by insisting that he visit her in the same splendor and majesty in which he appeared before his own wife. That night Semele begged Zeus for a favor, one that he had to grant. Zeus swore by the river Styx that the favor would be hers. When she asked him to appear before her as the great god of the Olympians, Zeus knew, only too late, that it would result in her death. He came to Semele in his true guise as the god of lightning. It was too much for a poor mortal to bear. The fire of Zeus' thunderbolts killed her but made her son with whom she was pregnant immortal. At the very moment that Semele's life was about to be snuffed out, Zeus snatched the unborn child from his mother's womb, sewed him into his thigh, and when the gestation period was ful-filled, the god Dionysus was born (fig. 52). Some say that Hermes acted as a kind of midwife in this unusual birth. Hermes, or according to others Persephone or Rhea, took the child to Semele's sister and brother-in-law, Ino and Athamas, to be brought up as a girl. Hera, her jealousy unabated, turned on Ino and Athamas and threw them into a state of madness: Ino flung herself into the sea with one of her two sons, while Athamas killed the other. In order to save the child Dionysus, Zeus changed him into a ram and carried him to the nymphs of Mount Nysa who brought him up in a cave. For Ino's kindness in acting as a nurse for the divine child, she was transformed into the sea-goddess Leucothea—the White Goddess.

Another version places the responsibility for Semele's difficulties upon her father. When Cadmus heard that Semele was the mother of a son by Zeus, he put her and the child in a chest and cast it into the sea. The chest was carried to the coast of Laconia, the southeastern region of the Peloponnese, near the town of Brasiae. Semele was found dead and was solemnly buried, but Dionysus was still alive and was brought up by Ino who happened to be at Brasiae at the time. For this reason, the plain of Brasiae was called the garden of Dionysus. Later in his life, Dionysus descended into Hades' realm and brought his mother back to life. To-gether they ascended Mount Olympus where they took their place among the gods. Semele was also known by the name of Thyone, and to many scholars she is the Thraco-Phrygian earth-goddess Zemelo whom the Greeks reduced in status to a mortal woman.

The Travels of Dionysus. Having been brought into the world in a most miracu-lous way, Dionysus was given Silenus as his tutor who helped him discover the secrets of nature and how to make wine. The youthful god then began his travels accompanied by Silenus and others of his revel-rout: satyrs, nymphs, woodland deities, and bands of frenzied women, the Maenads. This tour was said to have been occasioned by Hera who recognized him and drove him mad. In Egypt Dionysus was hospitably received by king Proteus, and in gratitude the god taught the inhabitants the cultivation of the vine. In Syria, on the other hand, he flayed

Damascus alive for opposing the introduction of the vine. Dionysus then traveled to India by crossing the Euphrates River by means of a bridge made of ivy and vines. When he came to another impassable stream, Zeus arranged for a tiger to carry him across, and for this reason the river was called the Tigris. In India, where he is said to have stayed many years, he instructed the inhabitants in viticulture and in the art of fruit-growing. Worshipers flocked to the god; even panthers and lions fell under his influence and willingly drew his triumphal chariot. Upon his return from India, Dionysus visited Phrygia where the goddess Cybele or Rhea purified him of murders he committed in his madness and taught him her mysteries and rites of initiation. It was also in Phrygia that the god was said to have adopted the dress connected with his worship: the animal skin draped around the body, the wreath of ivy or vine leaves for the head, and the thyrsus. Phrygia also gave the god the musical instruments used in his worship: the reedpipe, the drums, and the cymbals.

Dionysus versus Lycurgus.   Continuing his march to the west, Dionysus crossed the Hellespont and entered Thrace where Lycurgus, king of the Edonians, rejected the god and his worship. So hostile was Lycurgus that Dionysus was forced to leap into the sea where the nymph Thetis gave him refuge. In gratitude, he later gave the nymph a golden urn. In the meantime Lycurgus imprisoned the members of the god's revel-rout, his satyrs and frenzied women, but the women were suddenly set free. As a result of the maltreatment of Dionysus by his host, the country ceased to bear fruit and Lycurgus became mad. In his madness Lycurgus struck and killed his own son Dryas with an ax, imagining that he was cutting down a vine. According to another source, he cut off his own legs in the delusion that he was lopping a vine. As soon as Lycurgus had committed this act, he recovered his senses. The country, however, still remained barren. The god through an oracle declared that it would remain so until Lycurgus had been put to death. In despair, the Edonians took their king to a nearby mountain, Mount Pangaeum, where they bound him, and by the will of Dionysus, Lycurgus was torn to pieces by horses.

The mountain on which Lycurgus met his Dionysiac fate was also the scene of a

Figure 52.   The birth of Dionysus from the thigh of Zeus. Hermes prepares to receive the newborn infant. *Roman bas-relief. Vatican Museum. (Alinari)*

confrontation between Dionysus and Orpheus. From a fragment of a lost play of Aeschylus, the *Bassarids*—a Bassarid is a Thraco-Phrygian version of a Maenad— we learn how Orpheus met an end similar to that of Lycurgus. It seems that Orpheus, who was a native of Thrace, refused to honor Dionysus and preached a doctrine different from his. Orpheus believed that the sun, whom he called Apollo, was the greatest of the gods. It was Orpheus' custom to ascend Mount Pangaeum before dawn so that he might see and worship the sun as it rose in the sky. Dionysus was so enraged at the neglect of his divinity by Orpheus that he sent his Bassarids against him. They tore the dissenting young man to pieces and scattered his limbs far and wide. This is but one version of Orpheus' fate; others will be given in the fuller account of his life's story.

Dionysus at Thebes; Euripides BACCHAE. From Thrace, Dionysus turned his steps toward the place of his birth, Thebes, where Pentheus, son of Agave and grandson of Cadmus, was now reigning. But as in so many places, the divinity and rites of Dionysus were rejected. This particular episode is dramatized by Euripides in one of his finest plays, the *Bacchae*. In the prologue of the play, the god appears and announces that he has come to avenge the slanderous words of his mother's sister: that Semele had slept not with a god but with a mortal, and that she has passed off her shame on Zeus. In retribution, Dionysus has driven all the women of Thebes, including Cadmus' daughters, into a frenzied state of mind; possessed by the god, they wander on Mount Cithaeron wearing the symbols of the god's orgiastic rites. After Dionysus expresses his determination to prove to one and all that he is a god, the chorus makes its entrance. It is composed of Asiatic Maenads dressed in fawnskins, crowned with ivy and vine leaves, and carrying thyrsi and the musical instruments used in Dionysiac worship. They sing a hymn, a cult-hymn full of ritual phraseology which incorporates Greek and Near Eastern elements, a hymn that reflects the ecstasy of those who worship the god Dionysus willingly and rightly:

> Blessèd, blessèd are those who know the mysteries of god
> Blessèd is he who hallows his life in the worship of god,
>> he whom the spirit of god possesseth, who is one
>> with those who belong to the holy body of the god.
> Blessèd are the dancers and those who are purified,
>> who dance on the hill in the holy dance of god.
> Blesséd are they who keep the rite of Cybele the Mother.
> Blessed are the thyrsus-bearers, those who wield in their hands
>> the holy wand of god.
> Blessèd are those who wear the crown of the ivy of god.
> Blessèd, blessèd are they: Dionysus is their god!
> . . . .
> He is sweet upon the mountains. He drops to the earth
>> from the running packs.
> He wears the holy fawn-skin. He hunts the wild goat
>> and kills it.
> He delights in the raw flesh.
> He runs to the mountains of Phyrygia, to the mountains
>> of Lydia he runs!
> He is Bromius [the Noisy One] who leads us! *Euhoe!*

Although ecstasy is reserved for those who accept Dionysus, agony awaits those who reject him. Agave has already been driven out mad on to the heights of Mount Cithaeron along with her sisters and the other women of Thebes. Her son Pentheus, puritanical, disbelieving, the apostle of rationality, has denied the divinity of the god and declared his rites immoral and barbaric. Some of the Bacchae who are caught by Pentheus' men are imprisoned. A search is ordered for the stranger who has made the women of Thebes run amok, but the god voluntarily appears before Pentheus and allows himself to be maltreated and put under lock and key. News is then brought to the ruler of Thebes that the chains on the legs of the imprisoned women have miraculously fallen off and that the doors to their prison have opened by themselves. From within the palace Dionysus calls for an earthquake and the blazing thunderbolts of god. The palace totters and collapses; bolts of lightning flash and tongues of flame shoot up from the tomb of Semele. All tremble. The god appears amidst the rubble and calms his worshipers. Pentheus, in spite of himself and his stiff-necked attitude, is gradually and imperceptibly brought under the influence of Dionysus. He allows himself to be dressed as a woman so that he might spy on the women as they celebrate the orgy of the god on Mount Cithaeron. Dazed and completely under the spell of Dionysus, he addresses these words to the god:

> I seem to see two suns blazing in the heavens.
> And now two Thebes, two cities, and each
> with seven gates. And you—you are a bull
> who walks before me there. Horns have sprouted
> from your head. Have you always been a beast?
> But now I see a bull.

On Mount Cithaeron, Dionysus encourages Pentheus to climb a fir tree in order to get a better view of the women as they celebrate the rites of the god. When he is perched in the tree, Dionysus cries out to the women that their enemy and the one who mocks Dionysus and his worship is among them. "Punish him," he cries. The women, led by Pentheus' mother Agave, uproot the tree. They are in a frenzy, god-possessed, superhuman in their strength. Pentheus comes tumbling down from his perch and is torn apart by the women (fig. 53). This is how Euripides describes the *sparagmos* in his play; the report of the King's death is brought back to Thebes by a messenger:

> . . . and down, down
> from his high perch fell Pentheus, tumbling
> to the ground, sobbing and screaming as he fell,
> for he knew his end was near. His own mother,
> like a priestess with her victim, fell upon him
> first. But snatching off his wig and snood
> so she would recognize his face, he touched her cheeks,
> screaming, "*No, no, Mother! I am Pentheus,*
> *your own son, the child you bore to Echion!*
> *Pity me, spare me, Mother! I have done a wrong,*
> *but do not kill your own son for my offense.*"
> But she was foaming at the mouth, and her crazed eyes
> rolling with frenzy. She was mad, stark mad,

Figure 53. The death of Pentheus; probably a scene from Euripides' *Bacchae. Roman wall painting, 54–79 A.D. Pompeii. (Alinari)*

possessed by Bacchus. Ignoring his cries of pity,
she seized his left arm at the wrist; then, planting
her foot upon his chest, she pulled, wrenching away
the arm at the shoulder—not by her own strength,
for the god had put inhuman power in her hands.

After Euripides gives a grisly description of how Pentheus was torn to pieces by his aunts and other women of Thebes, he continues with the messenger's description of the frenzied mother's subsequent behavior.

> . . . His mother, picking up his head,
> impaled it on her wand. She seems to think it is
> some mountain lion's head which she carries in triumph
> through the thick of Cithaeron. Leaving her sisters
> at the Maenad dances, she is coming here, gloating
> over her grisly prize. She calls upon Bacchus:
> he is her "fellow-huntsman," "comrade of the chase,
> crowned with victory."

Agave returns to Thebes with the head of Pentheus impaled on her thyrsus. She is still in a dissociated state and believes that she carries the head of a lion as a trophy from the hunt. As she comes to her senses, as the Dionysiac frenzy leaves, Agave recognizes, to her horror, that her victim is not a lion but her own son. Agave, her father Cadmus, and the people of Thebes now recognize the power and divinity of Dionysus.

Dionysus and the Daughters of King Proetus. Having cleared his mother's name and established his worship at Thebes, Dionysus continued his travels in Greece. The god was well received at Argos where all the women joined in his worship except the daughters of King Proetus. Dionysus exacted his usual punishment: he drove them mad and they fled wildly over the mountains believing themselves to be cows. Other accounts say that Hera was responsible for their madness because the king's daughters had offended her; but it should be noted that in Argos many stories involving Hera and her priestesses involve transformations into cows or heifers. In any event, Melampus, the prophet and missionary of Dionysus in Argos, agreed to cure the king's daughters for a price, one-third of Proetus' kingdom. When the king refused, his daughters and other women went even madder and killed their own children. Proetus finally agreed to Melampus' terms, but by this time Melampus had raised the terms to include another third of the realm for his brother. The prophet, noted for his drugs and purifications, effected a homeopathic cure by driving the women down from the mountains with shouts and frenzied dance.

Dionysus and the Daughters of King Minyas. A tale similar to that of Proetus' daughters is told about the rejection of the god by the daughters of Minyas, king of Orchomenus in Boeotia. When the inhabitants of the city turned out to worship Dionysus, the king's daughters insisted upon staying at home and working at their looms. Dionysus appeared to them in the form a young girl and recommended that they give the god his due. When the king's daughters rejected the advice, Dionysus showed his power: he filled the room with the hallucinatory phantoms of a bull, a lion and a panther; wine and milk flowed from their spindles; vines sprouted from their looms; wild Dionysiac music filled the room. Succumbing to the god, the daughters of Minyas went mad, so mad that they had an insatiable desire to honor the god with his orgy. They cast lots to see whose son would be made into an offering. It fell to Hippasus, the son of Leucippe, who was torn to pieces. His death, it is said, was celebrated annually at Orchomenus with various rituals associated with the god. As for the daughters of Minyas, they were transformed into bats or some other form of nocturnal winged creature.

Dionysus and the Pirates. The last adventure of Dionysus takes place at sea. The earliest account is recorded in a Homeric hymn in honor of the god. In Ovid's *Metamorphoses*, the story is woven into the Roman poet's version of Euripides' *Bacchae*. Ovid introduces a young man Acoetes, son of a poor fisherman, who is a helmsman of the ship and who recognizes the god. Acoetes eventually becomes a priest of the god after having been initiated into the Bacchic mysteries. The story, however, is not designed to center on the son of a poor fisherman, but to show the power of the god. It seems that pirates from the coast of Thrace laid their hands on the young god thinking that they had captured the son of a king. Some accounts say that he hired a ship to transport him from Icaria to the island of Naxos; but instead of landing at Naxos the men steered for Asia where they intended to sell him into slavery. When Dionysus perceived his predicament, he quickly demonstrated his miraculous powers. Wine began to stream through the ship and its sweet fragrant bouquet spread all around. A vine heavy with grapes ran up the mast and spread out along the top of the sail. Ivy twined around the oars and the mast, and garlands hung from the oarlocks. The god turned himself into a lion and roared frighteningly while phantoms of other wild beasts appeared before the sailors. When the lion sprang at the master of the ship, the sailors in desperation jumped overboard and were turned into dolphins. The only man spared was the helmsman, called Acoetes by Ovid, who had at the very outset recognized that the unusual passenger was a god of some sort and had advised his fellow-sailors to release him. Debarking on the island of Naxos, Dionysus met and married Ariadne, the Cretan princess who had been abandoned by the Athenian hero Theseus. The biography of multifaceted Dionysus comes to an end with his divinity now universally acknowledged. Together with his mother whom he had raised from the dead, the god ascended Mount Olympus where he took his place among the twelve Olympians. Hestia, the spinster goddess of the hearth, graciously withdrew so as to make room for the new Olympian.

*   *   *   *

The theme of Dionysus floating in a vine-swathed boat surrounded by swimming dolphins has been given its finest visual representation by Exekias (or Execias), an Attic potter and painter in the black-figure style who flourished in the second half of the sixth century B.C. (fig. 54). On this libation cup Dionysus is portrayed as bearded and long-robed, a mature and solemn divinity, unlike later representations which show the god as weak and effeminate. Ovid, coming under this later influence, describes the god as "a young boy with the appearance of a pretty girl who seemed to stagger as if he were heavy with wine and sleep." On the other hand, D. H. Lawrence, who seems to have been familiar with the Homeric hymn of Exekias' painting, uses the theme as a symbol of the imperishable beauty of the past in contrast with the coal-burning and smelly ocean liners of his day. This is the first stanza of his *Middle of the World:*

> This sea will never die, neither will it ever grow old
> nor cease to be blue, nor in the dawn
> cease to lift up its hills
> and let the slim black ship of Dionysos come sailing in
> with grape-vines up the mast, as dolphins leaping.

In yet another poem, *They Say the Sea Is Loveless,* Lawrence is drawn back to the theme, perhaps by the sight of dolphins sporting in the sea:

> They say the sea is loveless, that in the sea
> love cannot live, but only bare, salt splinters
> of loveless life.
> But from the sea
> the dolphins leap round Dionysos' ship
> whose masts have purple vines,
> and up they come with purple dark rainbows
> and flip! they go! with the nose-dive of sheer delight;
> and the sea is making love to Dionysos
> in the bouncing of these small happy whales.

Figure 54.   The Voyage of Dionysus.
Interior of a red-figured cup by Exekias.
Mid sixth century B.C. Museum Antiker
Kleinkunst, Munich. (Hirmer)

For Ezra Pound, Ovid's version of Dionysus' adventure at sea in the third book
of the *Metamorphoses* forms a major portion of *Canto II:*

> The ship landed in Scios,
>   men wanting spring-water,
> And by the rock-pool a young boy loggy with vine-must,
>   "To Naxos? Yes, we'll take you to Naxos,
> Cum' along lad." "Not that way!"
> "Aye, that way is Naxos."
>   And I said: "It's a straight ship."
> And an ex-convict out of Italy
>   knocked me into the fore-stays,
> (He was wanted for manslaughter in Tuscany)
>   And the whole twenty against me,
> Mad for a little slave money.
>   And they took her out of Scios
> And off her course . . .
>   And the boy came to, again, with the racket,
> And looked out over the bows,
>   and to eastward, and to the Naxos passage.
> God-sleight then, god-sleight:
>   Ship stock fast in a sea-whirl,
> Ivy upon the oars, King Pentheus,
>   grapes with no seed but sea-foam,
> Ivy in the scupper-hole.
> Aye, I, Acoetes, stood there,
>   and the god stood by me,
> Water cutting under the keel,
> Sea-break from stern forrards,
>   wake running off from the bow,
> And where was gunwale, there now was vine-trunk,
> And tenthril where cordage had been
>   grape-leaves on the rowlocks,
> Heavy vine on the oarshafts,
> And, out of nothing, a breathing,
>   hot breath on my ankles,
> Beasts like shadows in glass,
>   a furred tail upon nothingness.
> Lynx-purr, a heathery smell of beasts,
>   where tar smell had been,
> Sniff and pad-foot of beasts,
>   eye-glitter out of black air.
> The sky overshot, dry, with no tempest,
> Sniff and pad-foot of beasts,
>   fur brushing my knee-skin,
> Rustle of airy sheaths,
>   dry forms in the *aether.*
> And the ship like a keel in ship-yard,
>   slung like an ox in smith's sling,

Ribs stuck fast in the ways,
                    grape-cluster over pin-rack,
                    void air taking pelt.
Lifeless air become sinewed,
                    feline leisure of panthers,
Leopards sniffing the grape shoots by scupper-hole,
Crouched panthers by fore-hatch,
And the sea blue-deep about us,
                    green-ruddy in shadows,
And Lyaeus: "From now, Acoetes, my altars,
Fearing no bondage,
                    fearing no cat of the wood,
Safe with my lynxes,
                    feeding grapes to my leopards,
Olibanum is my incense,
                    The vines grow in my homage."

Although Ezra Pound's Dionysus forms a part of the labyrinthine symbolism of the multiple hero of his *Cantos*, the most common association of the god was with revelry and wine. Robert Herrick and others celebrated the god in various drinking songs in which Bacchus becomes synonymous with the liquid grape and its intoxicating influence upon men. The following verse from Dryden's *Alexander's Feast* illustrates that particular genre:

The Praise of Bacchus then, the sweet Musician sung;
Of Bacchus ever Fair, and ever young:
The jolly God in Triumph comes;
Sound the Trumpets; beat the Drums:
Flush'd with a purple Grace
He shews his honest Face,
Now give the Hautboys breath; He comes, He comes.
Bacchus ever Fair and Young,
Drinking Joys did first ordain:
Bacchus Blessings are a Treasure;
Drinking is the Soldiers' Pleasure;
Rich the Treasure,
Sweet the Pleasure;
Sweet is Pleasure after Pain.

The American poet and philosopher, Ralph Waldo Emerson (1803–1882), celebrated the god in terms of his Pantheistic philosophy. In his poem *Bacchus*, Emerson calls upon a "Wine of wine,/Blood of the world," which would unite him with Nature and the essence of life. In the final verse, the poet asks the god to unite him with the memories of the past:

Pour, Bacchus! the remembering wine;
Retrieve the loss of me and mine!
Vine for vine be antidote,
And the grape requite the lote!
Haste to cure the old despair,—
Reason in Nature's lotus drenched,

> The memory of ages quenched;
> Give them again to shine;
> Let wine repair what this undid;
> And where the infection slid,
> A dazzling memory revive;
> Refresh the faded tints,
> Recut the aged prints,
> And write my old adventures with the pen
> Which on the first day drew,
> Upon the tablets blue,
> The dancing Pleiads and eternal men.

Not all poets subscribed or succumbed to this specialized form of the god. Milton, in *Paradise Lost*, calls upon his Muse Urania to "drive far off the barbarous dissonance/of Bacchus and his Revellers." Keats also prefers an inspiration other than Bacchus; he would rather have the intoxication of poetic imagination, as he tells us in the *Ode to a Nigntingale:*

> Away! away! for I will fly to thee,
>   Not charioted by Bacchus and his pards,
> But on the viewless wings of Poesy.

For Matthew Arnold, the Bacchanalia is a symbol of energetic youth teeming with energy and confident of surpassing past achievements. His *Bacchanalia; or, the new Age* (1867) recognizes the cycle of youth and age, present and past, new and old; but the poet, Arnold in this instance, is mindful of the past and how few of its achievements have survived. The bacchanalian scenes in Keats' *Endymion* and Leigh Hunt's *Bacchus and Ariadne* (1819) are notable for their poetic virtuosity. In the roundelay "O sorrow" of Book Four, Keats presents us with a Bacchic procession of his "Great God of breathless cups and chirping mirth":

> And as I sat, over the light blue hills
> There came a noise of revellers: the rills
> Into the wide stream came of purple hue—
>   'Twas Bacchus and his crew!
> The earnest trumpet spake, and silver thrills
> From kissing cymbals made a merry din—
>   'Twas Bacchus and his kin!
> Like to a moving vintage down they came,
> Crown'd with green leaves, and faces all on flame;
> All madly dancing through the pleasant valley,
>   To scare thee, Melancholy!
> O then, O then, thou was a simple name!
> And I forgot thee, as the berried holly
> By shepherds is forgotten, when, in June
> Tall chestnuts keep away the sun and moon:—
>   I rush'd into the folly!
>
> . . . .
>
> Within his car, aloft, young Bacchus stood,
> Trifling his ivy-dart, in dancing mood,
>   With sidelong laughing;

And little rills of crimson wine imbrued
His plump white arms, and shoulders, enough white
　　　For Venus' pearly bite:
And near him rode Silenus on his ass,
Pelted with flowers as he on did pass
　　　Tipsily quaffing.

Hunt's *Bacchus and Ariadne*, influenced by Ovid's "letters" of famous heroines (*Heroides*) as well as by the paintings of Titian and Poussin, is a sentimentalized rendering of Ariadne's abandonment by Theseus and her subsequent marriage to Bacchus. Ariadne hears the revel-rout of the god approaching, then

Suddenly from a wood his dancers rush,
Leaping like wines that from the bottle gush;
Bounding they come, and twirl, and thrust on high
Their thyruses, as they would rouse the sky;
And hurry here and there, in loosened bands,
And trill above their heads their cymballed hands:

. . . .

A troop of goat-foot shapes came trampling after,
That seemed, with tickling, stung to frisks and laughter;
Butting and mumming, they jumped here and there
With backward knees, and a strange tottering air;
And some eat grapes; some drank, and others chased
The women, or with leering heat embraced;
And some with reeds their smoothened lips beneath,
Jerked up and down them with a flickering breath.
In middle of the rout Silenus rode
Upon a stumbling ass,—a drunken load;
And as they held him, lolled and slipped about,
And giggled with close chin, and half peered out
From his fat eyes, and tried a feeble shout.

. . . .

Last, with the exception of some more of these
Who danced behind him, came in his fine ease
The god himself. Two shiny leopards drew him,
And others coursed about, or leaped up to him,
Trying to win a look from him: but he,
Reclining in his car of ivory,
Like a ripe world's divinest human flower,
Sat looking forward to the lady's bower.
Curls trembled in his neck; a crimson vest
Slung by two clasps, reached half way up his breast.
His fruity cheek was rounded off, and bent
Just near the dimpled chin; his eye intent,
And liquid dark, and from his ivy crown,
Mixed with his locks, some glancing grapes hung down.
Upon one arm he leaned, and from his hair
Short sunny beams broke sharply here and there;
His dark head glowing o'er his shoulders fair.

The women in the Bacchic procession easily lent their frenzied personalities to poetic and not-so-poetic allusion. Swinburne, in a fine alliterative rage against Harriet Beecher Stowe for her attacks on the personal life of Lord Byron, called her "a blatant Bassarid of Boston, a rampant Maenad of Massachusetts" in *Under the Microscope* (1872). Shelley compares the wild disordered hair of a Maenad to gathering storm clouds in his *Ode to the West Wind:* "Loose clouds ... Like the bright hair uplifted from the head/Of some fierce Maenad ..." In Spenser's *Faerie Queene*, the raging wife of the dead Souldan is compared to "that madding mother, mongst the route/Of Bacchus Priests her owne deare flesh did teare." And Vergil, describing Dido's emotional state when she got wind of Aeneas' unannounced departure: "All aflame and quite out of her mind, she raged throughout the city like some Thyiad ... when the Bacchic cry drives her to celebrate the orgies of the god and the nocturnal din on Mount Cithaeron beckons her."

The nineteenth century was to witness a revolutionary change in attitude toward Dionysus and yet another confrontation between Apollo and the god of wild forces in nature. For almost a century, Europe had been under the spell of Johann Winckelmann (1717–1768), the art historian who had laid down the canons of Greek art and who had discovered ancient beauty for northern Europe. His ideal of Greek art was Apollonian serenity and was summarized in his famous phrase "noble simplicity and quiet grandeur" (*edle Einfalt und stille Grösse*). In 1872 Friedrich Nietzsche (1844–1900) published his challenge to the tradition that Winckelmann had imposed on classical scholarship and poets. His book, *The Birth of Tragedy out of the Spirit of Music*, rejected Winckelmann,and his school, and claimed that the basis of Greek religion and art was not Apollonian and serene, but Dionysiac and tragic. To Nietzsche, Greek tragedy had its origins in the Dionysiac, and it was Dionysus who inspired the chorus which developed from the procession of the satyr-dressed votaries of the god. The Apollonian in tragedy, its intellectual component, was an afterthought, a later appendage to the Dionysiac chorus, and was represented by the dialogue. Both tragedy and art grew out of the tensions between the emotional and restless Dionysus and the calm, reflective Apollo; and the greatness of Greek art lay in the way in which the artist united the ideals of both gods, in the way in which the artist overcame his innate pessimism by imposing Apollonian order on the tragic and savage Dionysus. Nietzsche saw in Richard Wagner(1813–1883) and his early operas a new but Teutonic Aeschylus who would once again unite music and drama, myth and symbol, Dionysus and Apollo.

By the twentieth century, the work of Freud and his disciples in psychoanalysis was to add yet another dimension to the god of wild forces, specifically the wild forces in human nature. Turning back to Euripides' *Bacchae*, poets, playwrights and composers saw in it a vehicle for bringing psychosexual forces to the forefront. In 1968, an operatic version of Euripides' play, *The Bassarids*, was produced. It was composed by Hans Werner Henze with a libretto by W. H. Auden and Chester Kallman. The opera presents Pentheus as a religious fanatic, fearful of sex, a Puritan; his mother Agave, a sexually-repressed woman. A critic said of the opera that it "can be read as a study of the triumph of sexual instinct, represented by Dionysus and his followers (the Bassarids) over sexual sublimation and orthodox religion. By extension, the opera can be interpreted as the revolt of youth against the conservatism of their elders." It is well, however, to keep in mind the words that Euripides puts in the mouth of Tiresias when Pentheus charged that the worshipers of god were encouraged by his rites toward immorality:

Dionysus does not, I admit, *compel* a woman
to be chaste. Always and in every case
it is her character and nature that keeps
a woman chaste. But even in the rites of Dionysus,
the chaste woman will not be corrupted.

Orpheus

The name of Dionysus is known to us through the earliest literary sources
(Homer and Hesiod) and archaeological records (the Linear B tablets). The name
of Orpheus, on the other hand, first comes to our attention in a fragment of a poem
by a sixth-century B.C. poet, Ibycus, where we hear only of "the renowned Orpheus." Pindar makes a passing reference to him as a member of the expedition of
the Argonauts, a celebrated lyre player, the father of song. In the late fifth and early
fourth centuries B.C., the name of Orpheus heads a list of the four oldest poets,
the other three being the legendary Musaeus, Homer and Hesiod. With the development of Orphic doctrines, however, Orpheus comes into clearer focus as a
mythological personality. The story of his life, amplified by Hellenistic mythographers and later poets, has three main themes: the extraordinary power of his
musicianship, the descent to Hades to recover his wife, his tragic death.

Orpheus the Musician. Orpheus was born in Thrace, the son of Oeagrus and one
of the Muses, a most appropriate mother for a great musician and poet. Calliope,
the most dignified of the Muses, is most commonly given as his mother; occasionally
Polyhymnia or Clio is named as his mother. But since Orpheus was an outstanding lyre (or cithara) player, some mythographers make Apollo his father. Orpheus' fame with the lyre made some consider him to be its inventor, or to have aug-
mented the number of its strings from seven to nine in honor of his mother and
aunts, the nine Muses. As early as Aeschylus we hear that Orpheus captivated all
those who heard him: wild beasts would follow him, plants and trees would bend in
the direction of his voice, and he gentled the fierce hearts of wild men. The power
of his music on all aspects of nature— "music hath charms" in a very real sense—
became a common theme (fig. 55), and it passed from generation to generation and
from age to age into modern literature. Among others, it was a favorite of Shakespeare who used the theme as part of a song for *Henry VIII:*

And Orpheus with his lute made trees
And the mountain tops that freeze
   Bow themselves when he did sing.
To his music plants and flowers
Ever sprung, as sun and showers
   There had made a lasting spring.

Everything that heard him play,
Even the billows of the sea,
   Hung their heads, and then lay by.

In *The Merchant of Venice,* Lorenzo philosophizes on the "sweet power of music":

. . . Therefore the poet
Did feign that Orpheus drew trees, stones, and floods,

Figure 55. Orpheus charming the beasts by his singing. *Roman mosaic. National Museum, Palermo. (Alinari)*

> Since naught so stockish, hard, and full of rage
> But music for the time doth change his nature.

And Proteus, one of the two gentlemen in *The Two Gentlemen of Verona*, also knows the power of music and poetry, as he tells the Duke:

> For Orpheus' lute was strung with poets' sinews,
> Whose golden touch could soften steel and stones,
> Make tigers tame, and huge leviathans
> Forsake unsounded deeps to dance on sands.

Until his marriage, Orpheus' life was fairly uneventful. His one adventure beyond the borders of the Hellenic world took place when he was invited to become a member of the Argonauts on their voyage to Colchis to gain the golden fleece. Hardly the caliber of a "hero," Orpheus' most outstanding feat was to outsing the Sirens and thereby prevent the Argonauts from being lured to their destruction. This episode is enlarged upon by William Morris in *The Life and Death of Jason* (1867), the longest mythological tale in modern English poetry, in which Orpheus and the Sirens compete with one another in a prolonged series of antiphonal, but not bewitching, lyrics. In general, Orpheus' duty on board the Argo was not to "move stocks and stones," but to help the morale of the crew and to keep to men from quarreling, as Spenser reminds us in this passage from the *Amoretti:*

> When those renoumed noble Peres of Greece,
> through stubborn pride amongst themselves did jar
> forgetfull of the famous golden fleece,
> Then Orpheus with his harp theyr strife did bar.

Orpheus and Eurydice.　All these earlier episodes in the life of Orpheus pale before two others: the attempt to bring his wife Eurydice back from the realm of the dead, and the circumstances surrounding his own tragic end. (The quest for a lost spouse is a motif that is not limited to European culture; it is found as far east as Japan as well as among many North American Indian tribes.) Our main classical authorities for the concluding events in Orpheus' life are the Roman poets Vergil and Ovid, both of whom undoubtedly derived much of their material, including the accents of pathos and romance, from Alexandrian poets. In the fourth of Vergil's *Georgics*, a treatise on beekeeping in highly polished poetic form, the poet introduces the death of Eurydice by way of a literary digression as he tells the story of Aristaeus, a rustic deity or hero who had some connection with apiculture. Ovid also found the story much to his liking for he used Orpheus' quest for the beginning of his tenth book of the *Metamorphoses*, and developed the incidents involving the singer's death for the introduction of his eleventh book. Several centuries earlier, Plato had cited a unique version of the quest in the *Symposium* as part of a discussion on love. Alcestis' sacrifice for her husband was given as an illustration of a lover willing to die for her beloved. But not so Orpheus; unlike Alcestis he did not dare to die for love. Instead, according to Plato's interlocutor Phaedrus, he contrived to enter Hades alive, a mere lyre player, and the god punished Orpheus by presenting him with a phantom in place of his wife and later causing his death at the hands of women. Behind this account may lie the doctrine of punishment for the mortal who presumes to transgress the limits of his human condition.

The story made popular by Vergil and Ovid begins with the death of Eurydice, a Dryad or tree-nymph. Hotly pursued by Aristaeus, she ran before him, and in her haste to escape she stepped on a poisonous snake and received a fatal bite on her ankle. Her Dryad companions made Mount Rhodope and Pangaeum echo with their cries. Orpheus was grief-stricken at the loss of his wife and determined to bring her back from the Underworld. He descended to the land of the bodiless dead through the hellmouth of Taenarum and made his plea in song before Hades and Persephone. In the name of love, he asked that his wife be allowed to return to the world of the living, on loan so to speak, for she would have to return when old age made its claims on her. What was the effect of Orpheus upon those who heard him? This is how Ovid describes it:

> And with his words, the music
> Made pale phantoms weep: Ixion's wheel
> Was still, Tityus' vultures left the liver,
> Tantalus tried no more to reach for the water,
> And Belus' daughters [the Danaids] rested from their urns,
> And Sisyphus climbed on his rock to listen.
> That was the first time ever in all the world
> The Furies wept.

The triple jaws of Cerberus remained agape as Orpheus sang. Hades and Persephone did not have the heart to refuse such a touching plea. They brought Eurydice before them—she still limped a bit from the snakebite on her ankle—and gave her to Orpheus only if he would not look back at her until they had both passed out of the world of darkness into the light of day. Orpheus readily agreed and the two climbed upward to the land of the living. But at the moment when they were nearing the place that separated the two realms, Orpheus, out of eagerness and anticipation to be restored to his love, looked back. In an instant, Eurydice vanished, lost forever, leaving Orpheus stunned and inconsolable at the double death of his wife. Traumatized by this soul-shaking experience, Orpheus resolved to remain celibate

Figure 56.   Hermes, Eurydice and Orpheus. *A Roman copy of a Greek bas-relief of the fifth century B.C. National Museum, Naples (Alinari)*

and to have nothing more to do with women, even though many offered themselves to him. According to Ovid, he rejected the advances of the opposite sex and gave his love only to young men in the first bloom of youth. One day as he was singing, and as usual drawing the trees, beasts and stones after him, a group of Thracian women came upon him. They recognized the singer as the man who spurned the love of their sex. Acting more like Maenads than women, they tore Orpheus limb from limb and flung his head and lyre into the Hebrus river. Both head and lyre, still singing and playing, were carried by the stream into the sea until they reached the island of Lesbos, the home of Sappho and other famed lyric poets. When a serpent approached the head to bite it, Apollo interceded and turned the creature into stone. Dionysus then demanded vengeance upon the women who dared to kill his singer. The women were rooted to the ground and were transformed into oak trees.

The scene of that moment when Orpheus turned around to look at Eurydice is represented on a much admired Attic bas-relief of the second half of the fifth century B.C. and preserved in a Roman copy (fig. 56). The ancient sculptor portrayed three figures caught at that tragic moment when Orpheus has just turned around to catch an anxious glance of his beloved. Eurydice's left hand is placed on Orpheus' shoulder in a gesture of a loving farewell, while Hermes Psychopompos, the Guide of Souls, has taken hold of her right hand and is about to lead her back to the Underworld. This was the law of the powers of the nether world, the law of Persephone, for most mortals: only the voice could penetrate the realm of the departed, nothing else, as witnessed by sacrifices to the dead which were performed with faces averted.

Other variants in the narrative tell of how Orpheus took up an "Orphic way of life" after the second death of Eurydice, how he refused to eat flesh, and how he sang Orphic songs of the beginning of things and of the gods. During his visit to the Underworld, Persephone is said to have instructed him in mystery worship; but when he began to indoctrinate others into the mysteries, Zeus killed him with a thunderbolt. Already mentioned is Aeschylus' version of the poet's death at the hands of Thracian Bacchants, known as Bassarids, for having worshiped Apollo in the rising sun. After Orpheus was torn apart by women, the Muses gathered his remains and buried them at the foot of Mount Olympus. Nightingales nested on his tomb and sang there more sweetly than they did elsewhere in the world. Some also say that his singing head did not float to the island of Lesbos but to Smyrna, one of the birthplaces assigned to the great epic singer Homer. As for Orpheus' lyre, which could find no musician equal to its original owner, Zeus placed it in the heavens as the constellation Lyra.

*   *   *   *

The personality of the legendary Orpheus impressed itself deeply and profoundly upon Western culture. In the Judaeo-Christian tradition, the iconographical affinities between the Thracian singer and Biblical figures did not go unnoticed. Orpheus could represent the person of David, "a cunning player on a harp," as he charmed the sheep and wild beasts of the wilderness by the magic of his playing, a scene also suggested by the prophetic vision of Isaiah of the lamb lying down with the lion. Thus Orpheus became identified with the Prince of Peace, and in the Christian catacombs of Rome he is a familiar figure in paintings which show him as the Good Shepherd caring for his flock. In literature and in ballads as well, the popularity of Orpheus' story continued unabated through the Middle Ages, mainly because of the influence of Vergil and Ovid. But as can be anticipated, the classical legend was transformed by local beliefs and cultural patterns. For example, in the medieval *Lay of Sir Orfeo*, the Greek realm of Hades is turned into a Celtic land of enchanting and beautiful fairies; Hades himself becomes a fairy king of the Otherworld and is surrounded by knights and ladies dressed in white mounted on white horses. Heurodis, the medieval counterpart of Eurydice, is won over by the king of the Otherworld, not through death but because she falls asleep under a fairy tree.

Orpheus and Eurydice also enjoyed the distinction of participating in a number of literary and musical firsts. Their tale was the theme of the first secular drama in a vernacular language, *Orfeo* (1471), composed by the Italian humanist and friend of Lorenzo the Magnificent, Angelo Poliziano (Politian). In the field of music, Caccini and Peri composed the first true Italian opera, *Euridice* (1600), to celebrate the marriage of Henri IV. It was followed shortly by Monteverdi's *Orfeo* (1607). And when the need arose in the eighteenth century to revitalize opera because it had degenerated into a mere vehicle for displaying the vocal accomplishments of individual singers, Christoph Willibald Gluck chose the story of Orpheus and Eurydice in his attempt to return to the principles of Greek tragedy. *Orfeo ed Euridice*, first performed in 1762 and now considered the oldest opera in modern repertoire, revolutionized opera by making music and drama mutually dependent on each other, by making it a medium for conveying lyric and tragic feeling. Gluck's audience, however, demanded a happy ending which the librettist Ranieri Calzabigi provided. Just as Orpheus was about to put an end to his life after having lost Eurydice for a second time, Amor (Love) appears and thrusts aside Orpheus' sword. The god of love announces that for his constancy and courage, the gods have decreed that Eurydice be returned to him. Amor then brings Eurydice to Orpheus and bids them both to continue their journey back to earth.

Literary allusions to the tragic love and tragic death of Orpheus and Eurydice are legion. In the hands of Milton, the myth was capable of conveying varying shades of feeling and meaning. In *L'Allegro*, the poet invokes the goddess Mirth to allow him to live with her and to surpass Orpheus in song:

> Untwisting all the chains that tie
> The hidden soul of harmony;
> That Orpheus' self may heave his head
> From golden slumber on a bed
> Of heaped Elysian flow'rs, and hear
> Such strains as would have won the ear
> Of Pluto, to have quite set free
> His half-regained Eurydice.

In more somber tones Milton calls upon the goddess Melancholy in *Il Penseroso* for Peace and Quiet, Leisure and Contemplation. As he describes the pleasures of the scholarly life, he calls upon the sad goddess so that she might

> ... bid the soul of Orpheus sing
> Such notes as, warbled to the string,
> Drew iron tears down Pluto's cheek,
> And made Hell grant what Love did seek.

In *Lycidas*, an elegy in pastoral form on the death of Edward King, Milton reproaches the nymphs for not helping his friend when he was drowning; but then he recollects that the Muse could not save her own son Orpheus from his death.

> Ay me! I fondly dream
> 'Had ye been there,' ... for what could that have done?
> What could the Muse herself that Orpheus bore,
> The Muse herself, for her enchanting son
> Whom universal nature did lament,
> When, by the rout that made the hideous roar,
> His gory visage down the stream was sent,
> Down the swift Hebrus to the Lesbian shore?

Finally, in *Paradise Lost*, in yet deeper and more plaintive tones, Milton perceives the tragic parallel between himself and Orpheus, the tragedy of human greatness, and calls upon inspiration from heaven to protect him against all the evils and temptations of the temporal world.

Still govern thou my song,
Urania, and fit audience find, though few.
But drive far off the barbarous dissonance
Of Bacchus and his revelers, the race
Of that wild rout that tore the Thracian bard
In Rhodope, where woods and rocks had ears
To rapture, till the savage clamor drowned
Both harp and voice; nor could the Muse defend
Her son. So fail not thou who thee implores;
For thou art heav'nly, she an empty dream.

No English writer of the first rank, with the possible exception of T. Surge Moore, seems to have been attracted to the myth of Orpheus and Eurydice as a theme for a major work. Moore's *Orpheus and Eurydice*, published in 1909 as a play, exploits the story of the unfortunate couple as symbols of the Platonic conflict between the beauty of two worlds, between the transient and temporal (Orpheus) and the spiritual and eternal (Eurydice). On the Continent, however, French and German writers boldly reinvigorated the ancient myth with new meanings. Jean Cocteau (1889–1963), a leading spirit of the surrealist movement in literature and art, made of it a dramatic extravaganza both for the stage and the cinema. *Orphée*, first produced in 1926 and then made into a film in 1950, is a one-act play with thirteen scenes in which the theme of poetry and death is seen within the frame of the miraculous, the invisible, and the unreal. Orpheus defends an absurd oracular phrase which is tapped out by the foot of a horse—the initial letters of the phrase "*Madame Eurydice Reviendra Des Enfers*" form an anagram for a common French obscenity —a defense which results in his death at the hands of Bacchants. When Eurydice is about to die of poison administered by a competitor of her husband, Death appears on the stage. Instead of a skeleton in a winding sheet or the figure of the grim reaper, Cocteau represents Death as a beautiful young woman dressed in the latest fashion. She is assisted by two men dressed in surgeon's uniforms, masks and rubber gloves. As Death goes about her business of concluding the life of Eurydice, her two assistants manipulate mysterious machines that vibrate and hum. After Orpheus' death, Eurydice returns to reclaim what is left of her husband and leads him to heaven through a mirror—the mirror being Cocteau's device through which death comes and goes. In heaven Orpheus offers up a prayer of thanks which ends with these words:

We thank thee for having saved Eurydice, because, through love, she killed the devil in the shape of a horse, and in so doing she died. We thank thee for having saved me because I adored poetry, and thou art poetry. Amen.

The "German" poet Rainer Maria Rilke (1875–1926), born in Prague, died in Switzerland, and influenced by the French—in particular by the sculptor Rodin and the poet-philosopher Paul Valéry (p. 124)—made the myth of Orpheus central to his belief in Art and the Beautiful, in Poetry and Death. Instead of accepting the myth as the ancient symbol of the impassable gulf between the living and the dead, Rilke saw in it his own conception of death which rejects the notion of separation. An early poem, *Orpheus Eurydike Hermes* (1904), inspired by a Greek bronze group of figures at Naples, does not sound the Vergilian note of pathos on the unhappy separation of the two lovers; rather, Eurydice in death has already become part of a new life. And when Orpheus fatefully turns around, she no longer recognizes him; she utters just one word, "Who?"

Rilke's major work on the theme is *Die Sonette an Orpheus* (Sonnets to Orpheus), fifty-five poems in two parts, published in 1923 as a memorial for a young dancer who died at an early age. Rilke found in Orpheus the symbol of the poet as the heightened image of man's being, the singer through whom Nature herself speaks, through whom the world of changing appearances becomes transformed into the Real and the Absolute. Orpheus' song is creation, it exists on its own, it has roots both in life and death. And when Orpheus is torn limb from limb, his music enters and gives order to all things. From the concluding poem of the first part of the Sonnets:

But you, divine one, you, till the end still sounding,
when beset by the swarm of disdainèd maenads,
you outsounded their cries with order, beautiful one,
from among the destroyers arose your upbuilding music.

None of them there could destroy your head or your lyre,
however they wrestled and raged; and all the sharp
stones they flung at your heart
turned soft on touching you and gifted with hearing.

In the end they battered and broke you, harried by vengeance,
the while your resonance lingered in lions and rocks
and in the trees and birds. There you are singing still.

Oh you lost god! You unending trace!
Only because at last enmity rent and scattered you
are we now the hearers and a mouth of Nature.

Jean Anouilh (1910–   ), a French neo-Hellenic dramatist like Cocteau, turned to the myth of Orpheus not to sing of poetry and death but of the sordidness and grotesqueries of pelples' lives and loves. First produced in 1941 during the German occupation of France, Anouilh's *Eurydice* (English title: *Legend of Lovers*) is the ancient myth in a modern setting. Orpheus is a café musician, the son of a harp player without talent or money, an old roué; Eurydice is a touring actress in a fourth-rate company who travels with her mother and her mother's lover. As the two wait for their train in a railway station, they meet and fall deeply in love with each other, a love that is consummated in a cheap hotel room. Orpheus, however, persists in questioning Eurydice about her former lovers. In shame and confusion Eurydice runs away, only to be killed in a bus accident. A certain young man, a Monsieur Henri, who is present throughout the drama and who obviously represents Hermes Psychopompos, returns Eurydice to Orpheus on the condition that he not look at her before dawn. But Orpheus is still plagued by doubts and cannot restrain himself from questioning Eurydice about her past. Finally, even though aware of the consequences, he turns to her and looks her squarely in the face just before dawn's light. Eurydice is lost to him again. Monsieur Henri appears and tells Orpheus that death alone is a proper setting for love, that only there can Eurydice be given back to him, the eternally pure and young Eurydice of their first meeting. Orpheus sees the logic in what Monsieur Henri has said and goes to join Eurydice in death.

The American dramatist, Tennessee Williams (1911–   ), approached the ancient myth from yet another tack. *Orpheus Descending* (1957), a thoroughly revised

version of an early and unsuccessful play, *Battle of Angels* (1940), is a complex of
pagan and Christian archetypes in a modern American setting. Williams' Orpheus-
Christ is a guitar player-poet, Val Xavier (= Savior), a kind of wandering minstrel
whose presence rather than his music affects all those with whom he comes into
contact. The Eurydice to be raised from the Underworld is not one woman but
three local Magdalenes; it is an act that is motivated more by compassion than by
sexual love. And the hell from which these women are to be liberated is not the
world of the dead but the world of the lonely, a hell on earth, as these passionate
words of Lady Torrance tell us—Lady Torrance is unhappily married to a dying
man, Jabe, a symbol of Evil and Death:

> Ask me how it felt to be coupled with death up there, and I can tell you. My skin
> crawled when he touched me. But I endured it. I guess my heart knew that somebody
> must be coming to take me out of this hell! You did. You came. Now look at me! I'm
> alive once more!

But Val Xavier comes to a tragic end because of his compassion. Orpheus' looking back is transformed by Williams into Val's delaying too long in his attempts to
convince Lady Torrance to run away. Jabe shoots and kills his wife; the sheriff, who
misinterprets Val's sympathy for his deranged wife, stirs up a mob of men who lynch
and burn the guitar player.

A further sampling, without resorting to a catalog, of the wide application of the
myth of Orpheus shows that it covers virtually every field of artistic endeavor. In the
field of cinematography, Cocteau followed his *Orphée* by a sequel, *Le Testament d'-
Orphée* (1960); Tennessee William's *Orpheus Descending* was made into a film with
the title *The Fugitive Kind* (1960). An unusual film version of the ancient tale was
made from the work of the Brazilian poet and playwright Vinicius de Moraes.
Entitled *Black Orpheus* (1957), the scene is set in the city of Rio de Janeiro where a
guitar-playing streetcar conductor falls in love with a village girl who has come to the
city to escape a sinister stranger, Death. Death finds Eurydice at a street carnival
and carries her away, leaving Orpheus heartbroken. He tries unsuccessfully to find
her at the Bureau of Missing Persons, and then at the suggestion of a porter, he goes
to a house guarded by a dog named Cerberus where a seance is taking place. When
he hears a voice, Eurydice's voice, he insists, as did the original Orpheus, on turning
around to see his love once more. As he does, the voice which had been coming from
the mouth of an old crone, stops. After reclaiming Eurydice's body at the morgue,
Orpheus falls to his death from a cliff when a jealous girl friend throws a stone at
him which strikes him in the head. Children, whom Orpheus had told that he made
the sun rise by his playing, run to his home for his guitar so that they might make the
sun rise again.

Composers of various musical forms were also attracted to the myth of Orpheus as
themes for their compositions. Franz Liszt made it into a symphonic poem (1856)
and Igor Stravinsky into a ballet (1947). Hector Berlioz and Leo Delibes composed
cantatas (1827, 1878) on the death of Orpheus. Among the many operas, severa of
which have been named above as firsts, Jacques Offenbach's *Orphée aux Enfers*
(Orpheus in Hades), first performed in 1858, is a burlesque or travesty on the ancient
tale. Orpheus is portrayed as a music teacher in Thebes, unhappily married to
Eurydice who is in love with Aristaeus, really Pluto in disguise. Orpheus himself
loves a shepherdess Chloe. Contrary to all expectation, it is Jupiter who becomes
romantically attracted to Eurydice when he visits her in the Underworld disguised

as a fly. When Orpheus leads Eurydice back to life, the Olympian causes him to look back by flashing lightning before him. Jupiter wins Eurydice as a devoted Bacchante and Orpheus returns home a happy man. In a more serious key, Ernest Krenek composed an opera, *Orpheus und Eurydike* (1923), with a libretto by the German artist and writer Oscar Kokoschka. Kokoschka had earlier written a play with the same title (1919) in which the two lovers symbolized the conflict between the sexes, between the creative female and the dominant but tragic male. In Darius Milhaud's *Les Malheurs d' Orphée* (The Misfortunes of Orpheus), 1926, the myth is manipulated into a kind of Romeo and Juliet tragedy.

Three twentieth-century poets, all of whom happen to be women, interpret the character of Orpheus in quite different ways. The *Eurydice* of H. D. is the expression of a bitter and resentful woman who charges Orpheus with arrogance and ruthlessness for having denied her another chance at life. Why, she asks, did he hesitate, turn, and look back and so condemn her once more to a life among the gray lichens of death? Yet, in spite of it all, she would not change places with Orpheus; her hell is no worse than his. At least she has her thoughts and her uncompromising spirit, and no god can deprive her of that. Muriel Rukeyser, on the other hand, emphasizes the death of the poet in her *Orpheus* (1949), a death that is transformed into the birth of a god. Orpheus is the ritually slain god who is resurrected into the body of song and prophecy. In the *Orphic Voice* (1960), Elizabeth Sewell has written a wide-ranging book which explores the power of Poetry, particularized by the myth of Orpheus, power "not merely over words and hence over thoughts, but also in some way over natural objects and their behavior be they animate or inanimate . . ." Myth is living thought and the story of Orpheus is a reflection of myth in its own mirror, poetry thinking about itself.

Representations of Orpheus and the various episodes in his life were painted on vases and on canvas, carved in stone, and put into other media. One of the latest is a "stabile" of Orpheus made of small plates of a metal alloy by Richard Lippold (1962) and hangs, along with one of Apollo, from the ceiling of the grand promenade of the Philharmonic Hall of the Lincoln Center for the Performing Arts in New York City. Some of the better-known artists drawn to the mythical figure of Orpheus were Rubens, Poussin, and Breughel in the seventeenth century, Corot in the nineteenth, and Rodin in the late nineteenth and early twentieth century. And a painting by Lord Leighton of the couple looking longingly and intensely at each other, inspired Robert Browning, always moved by the theme of separation and reunion, to write this short lyrical poem, *Eurydice to Orpheus* (1864):

> But give them me, the mouth, the eyes, the brow!
> Let them once more absorb me! One look now
>   Will lap me round forever, not to pass
> Out of its light, though darkness lie beyond:
> Hold me but safe again with the bond
>   Of one immortal look! All woe that was,
> Forgotten, and all the terror that may be,
> Defied,—no past is mine, no future: look at me!

CHAPTER VII

The Age of Heroes

But their multitude I could not number nor
name—not if I had ten tongues and ten mouths,
not if I had a voice unbreakable and a heart of
bronze within me—if the Muses of Olympus,
daughters aegis-bearing Zeus, had not put
them into my mind. . .

Homer—*Iliad*

When Homer heralded the end of the Dark Ages for Greece, a host of heroes emerged from the shadows of history, a multitude so great that Homer had to seek inspiration from the Muses in order to number and name only those that came to fight before the walls of Troy. And so well known were many of these heroes by Homer's time that the poet felt no need to provide biographical and "historical" detail. In the *Iliad*, for example, Homer presupposes that his audience is fully acquainted with the causes of the Trojan War and all the events prior to the tenth year of the war; nor does he feel obligated to relate many of the earlier episodes in the lives of Achilles, Paris, Helen and others. In the invocation to his Muse in the *Odyssey*, Homer does not even mention the name of Odysseus; merely saying that he is telling the tale of that "resourceful" hero who after sacking Troy traveled widely and suffered much before reaching his home was enough to bring the name "Odysseus" to the mind of his audience.

But who were these heroes of mythology, and how much historicity is there in stories which, among many others, tell of the Trojan War, the voyage of the Argonauts, and the war against seven-gated Thebes? Scholars have reached no agreement on these questions. Some believe that behind these heroic legends are specks or motes of historical fact, the residue from a long period of oral transmission. In the course of being handed down from father to son and from bard to bard, the dry data of history, such as political, social and economic factors, were first eroded and then encrusted with highly imaginative detail until they were turned into the fascinating stories which have survived to this day. Scholars of this persuasion give the name of "saga" to a legend that supposedly evolved from an historical event (pp. 17–18). The Trojan war is most often cited as a prime example of a saga. It is commonly believed that the war had its origins in trade rivalries between the Greeks and Trojans, but Homer and poets before him attributed the cause of the war to the abduction of Helen by Paris, and thus, in the words of Christopher Marlowe, she "launched a thousand ships and burnt the topless towers of Ilium." However, since the decipherment in 1952 of the Linear B tablets—documents in the Greek language which come from the mainland of Greece and the island of Crete, and which are virtually contemporary with the supposed date of the most renowned legendary war of all time—difficulties have arisen in attaching some aspect of historicity to Homer's epics. Of the names listed on these tablets, almost a quarter of them are "Trojan"; that is, names cited by Homer and other epic poets as Trojan. Scholarly rationalizations, of course, can be provided to account for the phenomenon: the Greeks had a trading post at Troy VII A, the archaeological stratum at Hissarlik which has been identified with the Troy of Homer, and they borrowed Trojan local history; or Troy was occupied by a Greek-speaking people at the time of the Trojan War; or an old story of a siege of a city from the sea was given a new setting when historical Troy was attacked.

At the other end of the scholarly spectrum are those who see no trace of historical fact, speck or mote, in any of the adventures attributed to various heroes. To these scholars, heroes were gods at one time—a kind of reverse euhemerism—or their surrogates as divine kings. The legends which grew up about the god-kings are literary versions of ritual narratives, accounts of the rites which the divine king had to perform. So for example, the *Iliad* is derived from a ritual which embodies a sacred combat (Achilles versus Hector) and a holy marriage (Paris and Helen). The *Odyssey* also contains a sacred combat (Odysseus' single-handed attack on his wife's suitors); and the episode in which Odysseus contrives to blind Polyphemus the Cyclops with a burning brand is said to derive from a fire-making rite.

Heroic Motifs. The problem of what lies behind heroic mythology cannot be resolved into an easy formulation. The long-honored custom of trying to bridge the gaps of history with the tenuous threads of legends is treacherous; and those who see only ritual in the heroics of an Achilles or a Jason have equally slender support in their analogs and parallels. There is, however, agreement that many heroic legends contain motifs or patterns that are common in folklore, the repository of popular tradition. Some of these have already been seen in myths concerning the gods (pp. 23; 37–38). Myths, legends, ballads, and tales of common acceptance often show striking similarities in that their narratives tell of monsters, ogres, cruel stepmothers, witches, fairies, marvelous never-never lands, magical objects, and unusual physical phenomena. The widespread occurrence of these patterns of expression has led into the investigation of folk psychology, particularly by the psychoanalytical schools inspired by Sigmund Freud (1856–1939) and C. G. Jung (1875–1961). Both Freudians and Jungians see striking similarities between mythological motifs and those desires, dreams and memories that, in disguised form, exert a dominating influence on the personality of an individual. Both schools claim that at birth the individual has an inheritance from the dim and distant past, traces of the experiences of former generations, now glossed over and forgotten, and that the individual repeats important events of a process which occurred ages and eons ago. Hence the interpretation of dreams, which are but symbolic representations of inherited patterns, is the key to understanding what takes place in the unconscious mind. Freud considered myth, like the dream, the "royal road" to the understanding of the creations of man's unconscious. Freudians emphasize the repression of sexual desires and egoistical motives as being the dominant force in the creation of myths, dreams, fantasies, and substitutive gratifications.

To Freud, the story of Oedipus reveals the most powerful of these conflicts: the libidinal desire of the son for his mother and the jealousy of the father. Freud coined the term "Oedipus complex" in 1912 to describe this primal conflict within the human psyche, a conflict which if not resolved at an early age, results in a personality disorder in later years. Jung elaborated on Freud by positing a theory of "archetypes of the collective unconscious." These archetypes are the primordial images or mythical themes inherited by the individual from his human and animal antecedents—engrams (imprints), as Jung calls them—which lie dormant within the brain. These phylogenetic relics of psychic energy rise to the surface in dreams, delusions, fears, and in figures of speech. They are, according to the Jungian view, also responsible for the recurrence of mythological motifs, emotional disorders, literature and art and science, patterns of ritual, similarities in superstitions and religious beliefs. The theory of the archetypes is, as Jung himself points out, not his own creation. Of the many who foreshadowed Jungian concepts, one may be cited, the essayist Charles Lamb (1775–1834), who out of his own disturbed mental state anticipated Jung's archetypes. Using as his examples the monsters of classical mythology, the horrendous descendants of Pontus, Lamb wrote in *Witches and Other Night Fears:*

> Gorgons, and Hydras, and Chimaeras—dire stories of Celaeno and the Harpies—may reproduce themselves in the brain of superstition—but they were there before. They are transcripts, types—the archetypes are in us, and eternal.—These terrors—date beyond the body—or, without the body, they would have been the same.

As attractive as have been the speculations of Freudians and Jungians on the universality of mythological motifs, they have not stood the test of empirical investigation and consequently have received only a limited degree of acceptability. Possibly the strongest advocates of the two schools have been literary critics of recent years; and although the first flush of enthusiasm for psychoanalytic revelation has faded, the vocabulary of the critic is still rich with such terms as "tragic guilt," "father image," "primal father," "archetypal hero," and the omnipresent "Oedipus complex" or "Oedipal conflict." The theories of Freud and Jung, taken together with the investigations of Sir James Frazer and other cultural anthropologists into ritual patterns— the dying and resurrected man-god, the year-god, ritual combats and dramas —represent the major influences not only on critics but on poets, novelists, and playwrights as well. One historian of literary criticism comments: "Surely the hugest cloudy symbol, the most threatening of our last ten of fifteen years in criticism, is the principle of criticism by myth and ritual origins." As for the influence of the anthropologist, we have already seen it at work in connection with the myth of Adonis and T. S. Eliot's *The Waste Land.* In his play *The Family Reunion* (1939), based in part on Aeschylus' *Oresteia,* Eliot attempts to synthesize Greco-Christian ritual and modern psychology. Around Harry (= Orestes), the "hero" of the play, revolve the emotional dislocations caused by an unfortunate childhood and the rituals of salvation and purification. The Freudian element is far more pronounced in Eugene O'Neill's *Mourning Becomes Electra* (1931) which is also based on Aeschylus' trilogy.

The hero Orin—Orestes in New England—is a neurotic who suffers from an Oedipus complex and the further complication of an incestuous love for his sister Lavinia (Electra).

The unsuccessful attempts to find a common source or wellspring for the widespread distribution of mythological motifs should not blind us to the individual insights contributed by various academies into the character of ancient ritual, history, and the human personality. As for the motifs or patterns contained in the stories of the legendary heroes of Greece and Rome, we can observe striking similarities without necessarily being able to rationalize all their details. Prominent above all others is the unusual birth of the hero, usually through a divine agency, and the attempt to put an end to his life when yet an infant. The infant hero is exposed on a mountain or set adrift on water. He is then miraculously saved and brought up by human or animal foster parents. The exposure of a hero, along with supernatural conception, is one of the identifying marks of the true hero of legend. The cause for exposure is variously given: to avoid the fulfillment of a prophecy (Perseus and Oedipus), because of incestuous parentage (Aegisthus), because of a fateful dream (Paris), or because the father wanted a son instead of a daughter (Atalanta). Sometimes the mythographer gives no reason, as in the case of the twins Pelias and Neleus who were sired by Poseidon on Tyro. Oedipus was reared by foster parents at Corinth after having been saved by a herdsman; Aegisthus was suckled by a goat, Paris and Atalanta by a she-bear, Romulus and Remus by a she-wolf; Neleus and Pelias by a mare and bitch (or saved by horse wranglers). These fateful children of legend generally have an uneventful childhood, but when they reach maturity, they return to the scene of their origin or to the home of a parent and take their rightful position (Theseus), fulfill a prophecy (Oedipus), or rescue or avenge someone (Neleus and Pelias save their mother from her cruel stepmother Sidero; Aegisthus carries on the feud of his father Thyestes).

This popular theme was not exclusively reserved for legendary heroes for it crept into the biographies of the gods—it is very prominent in the myth of Zeus—and historical figures. The fifth-century B.C. historian Herodotus, for example, as he details the background of the Persian Wars, tells this story about the famous Persian king, Cyrus the Great, Before Cyrus was born, his grandfather Astyages had a dream that his pregnant daughter passed water in such quantities that it swamped all Asia. Another dream of his was that of a vine that grew from the intimate parts of his daughter's body and spread over all Asia. The king's magi were called in to interpret his dreams. They informed the king that his dream foretold the loss of his throne to his daughter's son. In order to interdict the event, Astyages gave orders to have the newborn child exposed on a mountain inhabited by wild beasts. The herdsman to whom the child was given took it to his home instead of exposing it as he had been ordered. Responding to his wife's pleas, he gave her the infant to replace the one she had just lost in childbirth. Later a story circulated that the infant Cyrus had been exposed on a mountain and was suckled by a bitch. At an early age Cyrus chanced to come before his grandfather and revealed his noble birth by the manner in which he conducted himself. Astyages was led into a sense of false security by his magi until his grandson fulfilled the prophetic dreams by deposing him and winning control over Asia (the Near and Middle East).

There are other motifs surrounding the legendary heroes of Greece which are found in the popular tradition: the life token in which the life span of a hero, or even of a city, coexists with an external object (the burning brand with Meleager, the purple lock of hair with King Nisus, the single thread of gold hair on the head of King Pterelaos, the Palladium with the city of Troy); immortality or rejuvenation through fire (Heracles' immolation on Mount Oeta) or through boiling (Jason's father Aeson through Medea's magic); magical impregnation, the wondrous and unnatural means by which a hero is conceived (Zeus visiting Danaë in a shower of gold). These and many other motifs are held in common by the ancient Greeks and people the world over. But there is a singularity in the character of heroes in Greek legends: their suffering and tragic mortality. The happy ending, the "wish-fulfillment," is conspicuously absent even though the patronage of the gods is bestowed upon the hero and even though the hero may exert his influence from beyond the grave. The tragic lives of Achilles, Agamemnon, Oedipus, Jason, and a host of others will attest to this condition among the heroes of Greek legend. There are, of course, rare exceptions: Perseus seems to have lived happily ever after, and Heracles after his tortured death ascended Mount Olympus to take his place among the gods. To all others, however, tragedy is the common lot. It arises most often from the concerns of the community, the family, blood relationships: a father's curse, a family quarrel, blood-revenge, incest or adultery, the abduction of a woman or theft of property, the violation of laws established by custom, antagonism between relatives or members of the same family, or disregard for the prerogatives of the gods.

Heroic Genealogy. In addition to "leitmotifs," Greek heroic mythology is also heavily weighted with pedigrees. Genealogical classification has been touched upon in connection with the generation of the gods and we have seen the use to which Hesiod put it in giving an orderly and systematic development to his ideas of the universe and the gods. Genealogy also has a prominent place in the legends of the heroes since the family tree is history in skeleton form. Greek poets and chronologers, apart from their reputed passion for order and reason, used pedigrees to explain ethnic origins, the names of cities or regions, to provide a ruler with a distinguished ancestor in the form of a god or hero, to rationalize a political situation, or to prove the concept of inherited sin. The Romans were quick to recognize the usefulness of genealogy, an example of which is Caesar's family tree (p. 186).

In the matter of authority for power and the historical right to rule, nothing was as effective as descent from a famous hero in remote antiquity. For example, the descendants of the Dorians legitimized their conquest of the Peloponnese (c. 1100 B.C.) by deriving their race from Heracles. But when legendary chronology was arranged, Heracles could not be brought into the immediate picture because traditionally he belonged to the period prior to the Trojan War— the Trojan War is a kind of meridian from which most legendary events were reckoned. Since the Dorian invasion took place after the Trojan War, it was accordingly ascribed to the descendants of Heracles, the Heracleidae, in the third generation. A story was told that after sundry adventures in which they were persecuted by Eurystheus, the ruler of the Peloponnese at that time, the sons of Heracles inquired of the oracle at Delphi when they might return. They were told to do so "at the third harvest." At first this was taken to mean "in the third year," but military reverses indicated that this was not the meaning of the oracle. A hundred years later, another descendant of Heracles asked the same question of the oracle and received the same response. This time, however, the "third harvest" was interpreted to mean the "third generation," an interpretation which harmonized more or less with the traditional chronology.

The Descendants of Deucalion and Pyrrha.   Greek mythographers derived the origin of their heroes from two main genealogical streams: from the descendants of Deucalion and Pyrrha, and from those of the river-god Inachus. Deucalion and Pyrrha, the pious son and daughter of Prometheus and Epimetheus, survived the flood with which Zeus, with Poseidon's assistance, wiped out an early race of sinful men (pp. 44; 153–154). When the ark carrying them came to rest on Mount Parnassus and the flood receded, they were approached by Themis or Hermes who told them to throw the bones of their mother behind them. Interpreting "bones" as stones and "mother" as earth, Deucalion cast stones which eventually turned into men while Pyrrha's stones became women. This is how the earth was repopulated. The direct male descendants of Deucalion and Pyrrha gave their names to the traditional divisions of the Greek people. Hellen gave his name to the "Hellenes" as the Greek people called themselves generically—"Greeks" (*Graeci*) was the word used by the Romans from their contact with the Greek inhabitants of southern Italy (*Magna Graecia*). Dorus gave his name to the Dorians, Aeolus to the Aeolians, Ion to the Ionians, and Achaeus to the Acheans and the region of Achaea. In this genealogy the mythographer has given us in effect an ethnological theory:

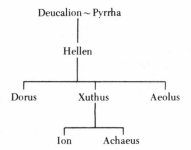

Aeolus—not to be confused with the Aeolus, king of the winds—was marvelously prolific, far more so than his brothers, having sired a dozen sons and daughters who gave him numerous grandchildren. Two of Aeolus' sons, Sisyphus and Salmoneus, occupy prominent places in the Underworld; others, such as Cretheus, Perieres, and Athamas, have mythologically important offspring. The descendants of Salmoneus and Cretheus culminate in that devoted couple, Alcestis and Admetus, in Jason, the leader of the Argonautic expedition, and in Nestor, the grand old man in the *Iliad,* "from whose tongue flowed speech sweeter than honey." Perieres is unimportant in himself, but his granddaughter Penelope will marry Odysseus, and his grandson Tyndareus will marry Leda, the mother of Helen and Clytemnestra, Castor and Polydeuces (Roman Pollux). Athamas will meet a tragic fate in Thebes, but his children Phrixus and Helle will be responsible for the name of the Hellespont and for planting the golden fleece in Colchis where Jason will have his greatest adventure. Sisyphus the trickster will be the grandfather of Bellerophon, the slayer of the Chimaera. Some say that Sisyphus was the father of Odysseus which would bring the Homeric hero into a closer genealogical relationship with Penelope; others more generally make Laertes Odysseus' father, some four generations removed from Aeolus. The following is the family tree of Aeolus, considerably pruned so as to show the mythologically important descendants of five of his sons:

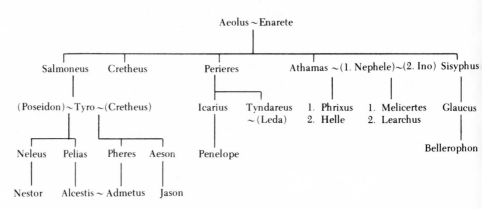

The distaff side of Aeolus' offspring was not ignored by genealogists. From his daughter Calyce came these notable descendants: her son Endymion who was beloved by Selene; Aetolus, the son of Endymion and reputed founder of the Aetolian people and the region of Aetolia; Calydon, the son of Aetolus, founder of the city in Aetolia which bears his name and which is remembered for a famous legendary hunt, the Calydonian Hunt; Oeneus and Althaea, the parents of Meleager, who made a name for himself in the Calydonian Hunt, and of Deianira, the second wife of Heracles and the unwitting instigator of his death; Diomedes, the son of Tydeus and grandson of Oeneus, a famous warrior in the Trojan War who, among his other accomplishments, attacked and wounded Ares in the battle between men and gods; and finally, Leda who married Aeolus' grandson Tyndareus, a man many generations her senior according to genealogists.

The Descendants of Inachus. The second main genealogical stream derives from the river-god Inachus, son of Oceanus and Tethys and eponym for the river Inachus in the Argolid. When Hera and Poseidon contended for possession of the land, Inachus cast his vote in favor of the goddess (p. 100). He is also said to have introduced the cult of the goddess into the land and to have raised the first temple in honor of Hera. Later rationalizers made Inachus a mortal and the ancestor of Argive kings. His son, Phoroneus, was viewed in local tradition as the first to bring men together to live in communities. His descendants were founders of such famous cities as Argos, Tiryns, and Epidaurus. Pelasgus, a grandson of Phoroneus, was the eponym for the Pelasgians whom the Greeks traditionally considered the native and aboriginal people of Greece. Pelasgus begot Lycaon whose impious ways were given as one of the causes of the great deluge. Lycaon's daughter was Callisto upon whom Zeus fathered Arcas, the eponym of Arcadia and the ancestor of the Arcadian people (p. 153). But notwithstanding the distinguished descendants of Phoroneus, it was Io, daughter of the river-god Inachus, who was to be the important ancestor of a long line of legendary houses and heroes. Her story, which was made popular by Ovid's account in the *Metamorphoses* and details of which are contained in Aeschylus' *Prometheus Bound*, deserves telling before tracing the line of heroes that descended from this daughter of Inachus.

Figure 57. Correggio. Zeus (Jupiter) and Io. The artist's interpretation of Ovid's "... the god hid the land in a thick, dark cloud, caught the fleeing girl and took her by force." *Painting, c. 1530. Kunsthistorisches Museum, Vienna.*

The Story of Io. Io, priestess of Hera at Argos and a young girl of outstanding beauty, became the object of Zeus' passion when the god noticed her returning from her father's stream. She fled from his unwanted embraces but it was to no avail. The Olympian surrounded the earth with a dark cloud so that he could ravish the young girl without being observed, particularly by his wife (fig. 57). Hera, however, noticed the cloud over Argos and the absence of her husband. She descended from heaven and dissipated the cloud. But Zeus had anticipated his wife's move and transformed Io into a young cow, a beautiful white heifer, which he claimed had sprung from the earth. Hera, still suspicious, asked for the heifer as a gift. Zeus could do little but give in to his wife's request. Hera set Argos Panoptes, the hundred-eyed monster, to guard the heifer. When Inachus searched for his daughter, all Io could do to let her father know of her situation was to inscribe the two letters of her name in the dust with her hoof. Inachus was powerless to save his daughter. Finally, Zeus took pity on the poor girl and sent Hermes to kill the ever-watchful monster. This was accomplished by first closing the eyes of Argos in sleep and then cutting off his head. Hera took the eyes and placed them on the tail of her favorite bird, the peacock. Hermes earned the title of *Argeiphontes* (Slayer of Argos) for having dispatched the monster (p. 215). However, Hera remained unappeased and sent a gadfly to torment Io. She fled across the sea which, tradition says, was named Ionian after the unfortunate young girl. In her travels, Io came upon a fellow-sufferer, Prometheus, who prophesied that she had still much suffering and wandering to endure, that he would be freed by a descendant of hers in the thirteenth generation (Heracles), that the place where she would cross from Europe into Asia would become known as the Bosporus (Cow's Ford, Ox-ford) and that the end of her tribulations would come in Egypt, where Zeus would restore her by a touch of his hand. All came about as Prometheus had foretold. In Egypt, Io gave birth to a son Epaphus, a name which the Greeks interpreted to mean "he of the touch."

In spite of all that we know about Io, there is no sure determination of her original function. It has been suggested that she was another form of "cow-faced" Hera, or that she had aspects of a moon-goddess as witnessed by her horns and her wanderings. Those tales which associate Io with several locales in the Mediterranean are interpreted by some as indicating the spread of the worship of Hera by Argive colonists. Because of Io's bovine characteristics, she became identified with the Egyptian goddess Isis who in turn had acquired her bovinity from the cow-goddess Hathor. And as early as Herodotus, Io's mythical difficulties were rationalized as one of the causes of the conflict between East and West. The Persians, according to Herodotus, claimed that Io was abducted and carried off to Egypt by Phoenicians who had come to Argos to trade. The Phoenicians, on the other hand, denied that they had used any violence; rather, Io had had an intimate relationship with the captain of the vessel, and when she discovered herself with child, she ran away so as to escape the shame and the reproach of her parents. Io's encounter with Zeus was tragic but not fruitless; her descendants would bring together in one family line various races bordering the Mediterranean as well as founders of important cities and royal houses.

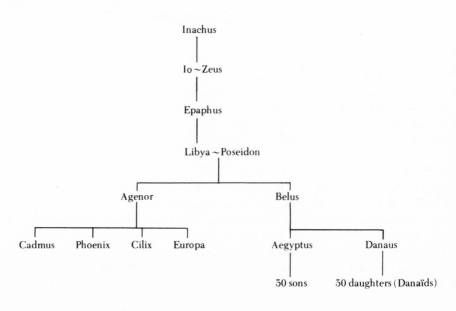

Libya (or Libye), the daughter of Epaphus, gives her name to the Libyans, as the Greeks called the people of North Africa. The twin brothers Agenor and Belus have Semitic connections: Agenor is a king of Tyre or Sidon; Belus is an oriental monarch but his name is merely a Hellenization of "Baal," a divine title of Semitic gods. Agenor's son Cadmus was to found the city of Thebes; his other two sons, Phoenix and Cilix, are little more than eponyms of the Phoenicians and Cilicians. Europa, Agenor's daughter, will not only give her name to the continent of Europe, but because of Zeus' amorous insistence, will establish the royal house of Minos on the island of Crete. Aegyptus and Danaus were twin sons of Belus: the former gave his name to that famous land of antiquity, Egypt; the latter to a race of Greeks known as the Danaans—Homer uses the Danaans, Achaeans, and Argives interchangeably for the Greeks involved in the Trojan War—and became the ancestor of a royal house.

The genealogical stream now divides into three major tributaries, the mythological dynasties founded by Cadmus, Europa, and Danaus. At Thebes the descendants of Cadmus take an active part in the myths concerning the god Dionysus and in the tragedy which engulfed Oedipus and his family.

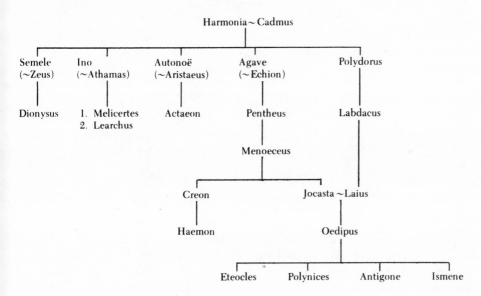

Europa, a sister of Cadmus, will provide the heroic ancestry for the island of Crete —her sons Minos and Rhadamanthys have already been observed serving special assignments in the Underworld. There will also exist a close connection between Minos and his offspring and the Athenian hero Theseus.

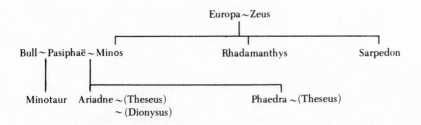

So much for the branches of the genealogical stream which had Agenor as their source. The latter's twin brother Belus had twin sons, Aegyptus and Danaus, whose fifty sons and fifty daughters were to come into an internecine conflict, as will soon be told, of whom only Lynceus and Hypermnestra survived to preserve the line. But from these two will come not only the most prestigious heroes of the Peloponnese and all Greece, Perseus and Heracles, but also a host of legendary tales bearing upon the life and times of the descendants of the royal house of Danaus. It should be noted how prominently Zeus is involved in continuing the line of Inachus through romantic associations with women descended from the river-god: Io, Callisto, Semele, Europa, Danaë, and Alcmene.

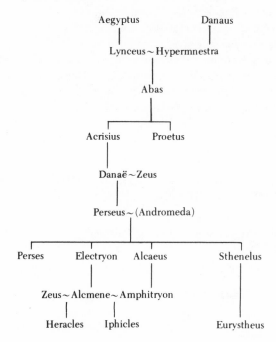

There are, of course, other pedigrees which will have to be considered in due course, in particular the family background of Theseus and the heroes who took leading roles in the Trojan War. Generally, those who were renowned either for individual heroics or for the part they played in the Voyage of the Argonauts or the Hunt of the Calydonian Boar—for example, Perseus, Heracles, Oedipus, Jason, Meleager, Theseus, Minos, and the parents of participants in the Trojan War—are known as the Older Heroes. The Younger Heroes were of a later generation and took part in such enterprises as the War of the Seven against Thebes, the Trojan War, the Wanderings of Odysseus, and the Adventures of Aeneas. The narratives dealing with the exploits of these legendary heroes form cycles of which the principal ones concern Heracles, Theseus, Jason, and leading figures in the Trojan War. Most of the action, it will be noted, takes place in centers that were prominent during the Bronze Age—Mycenae, Tiryns, Sparta, Thebes, Athens, Argos, Troy—a fact that has led some scholars to see an origin for most of these tales in the so-called Mycenaean period (19450–1100 B.C.) of that age. Finally, it should be observed that although the legendary tales had their origin in some half-remembered time, as they became enlarged and elaborated, the material became inextricably intermingled with half-forgotten rituals, folk-motifs, and very obvious aetiologies.

1. The House of Danaus

Pride of place must be given to the House of Danaus and to the two great descendants of that line, Perseus and Heracles. The story opens in Egypt at the time of the death of Belus, the reputed king of Egypt. Danaus and his twin brother Aegyptus had a falling-out over the terms of their inheritance. When Aegyptus suggested that the two families unite through the marriage of his fifty sons with Danaus' fifty daughters, Danaus, warned by an oracle that he would die at the hands of a son-in-law, fled with his children to his ancestral land Argos where he managed to become its ruler. He is said to have built the acropolis of the city and instructed the inhabitants in the art of digging wells, since Poseidon had dried up all the springs when Inachus awarded the land to Hera. The fifty sons of Aegyptus now arrived on the scene with orders from their father not to return home without their brides. When Danaus refused to agree to the mass marriage, the sons of Aegyptus laid siege to Argos until Danaus was forced to agree to their terms. However, he ordered his daughters to behead their bridegrooms on the wedding night and provided them with the instruments for the task. All obeyed except one, Hypermnestra, who was married to Lynceus. At the command of Zeus, Athena and Hermes purified the daughters of the murder of their husbands. The taint of their gory crime, even though they were purified, made it difficult for the girls to find other husbands. Danaus overcame the problem by offering his daughters as prizes to victors in public races. Their descendants became known as the Danaans or Danai. But there was still the matter of the prophecy that Danaus would die by the hand of one of his sons-in-law. The one son of Aegyptus, Lynceus, who had been spared by his wife, killed Danaus and took the throne.

Even though the Danaids, the daughters of Danaus, were said to have been purified, we hear later of their punishment in the Underworld for their crime. They were ordered by the judges in Tartarus to forever fill up jars of water that leaked like sieves (p. 244). Plato mentions that the carrying of water in broken jars was an Orphic conception of the punishment of the unrighteous in the afterlife. The plight of Danaus and his daughters when they arrived in Argos became the subject of the earliest surviving tragedy in European literature, Aeschylus' *Suppliants*, a play of uncertain date and the first of a trilogy whose other two plays on the same theme are lost to us. The eighteenth century was to see a flood of operas concerning Hypermnestra, the one Danaid who refused to kill her husband. This was due largely to the libretto of Metastasio (1698–1782), the phenomenally versatile Italian court poet whose *Ipermestra* was to provide the setting for eighteen operas by eminent and not-so-eminent composers. Chaucer incorporated the story of Hypermnestra into his *Legend of Good Women*, but he omits any reference to the other sons and daughters of Aegyptus and Danaus and inverts the parentage of Hypermnestra and Lynceus. To Chaucer, Ypermistre, who is married to Lino, is ordered by her father Egiste to "cut his throte a-two," a nefarious deed which she cannot bring herself to commit.

Perseus. Acrisius, a grandson of Lynceus and Hypermnestra, eventually became king of Argos. His twin brother Proetus was king of Tiryns, and the two had never gotten along well together; there was sibling rivalry even when they shared the same womb. Proetus' daughters, as has already been observed, had a tragic encounter with Dionysus when they refused to worship the god of ecstasy. In any event, Proetus is said to have seduced Danaë, the daughter of Acrisius, and after a furious

Figure 58. Acrisius orders a carpenter to prepare a chest for Danaë and the infant Perseus. *Vase painting, c. 450 B.C. Museum of Fine Arts, Boston.*

battle with his brother, he was forced to run for his life. Acrisius, quite concerned over the fact that he had no male heir, consulted the oracle. He was told that he would have no sons and that the son of his daughter would kill him. In order to prevent the oracle from being fulfilled, the king imprisoned Danaë in a subterranean bronze chamber—some say it was a bronze tower. To no avail, for Zeus took a fancy to the young girl and transformed himself into a golden shower which poured through the roof and fell into her lap.

In due course Danaë gave birth to a son, Perseus. Acrisius refused to admit that his daughter had conceived a son of Zeus, and having in mind the oracle, he made plans to get rid of the child without offending the gods. He had the mother and the child shut up in a chest (fig. 58) which was then cast into the sea. The chest, a floating ark, was washed ashore on the island of Seriphus where Dictys, a fisherman and brother of the king of the island, received Danaë and Perseus kindly and offered them the hospitality of his home. There they remained until Perseus grew to manhood. However, Polydectes, the brother of Dictys and king of Seriphus, fell in love with Danaë, but Perseus stood in the way. Polydectes cleverly contrived to send the young man on a dangerous mission: to fetch the head of one of the snake-haired Gorgons (pp. 28–30).

Perseus and Medusa. After a misleading start, Perseus received the help of Athena and Hermes who advised him to go after the head of Medusa, the mortal sister of the three grisly Gorgons. Hermes then led Perseus to the Graeae, the sisters of the Gorgons, who could provide him with further assistance and direction. At first the Graeae refused to inform on their sisters, but when the young hero took the one eye and tooth which they shared, they were forced to direct him to the nymphs who gave him the cap of invisibility (the cap of Hades), winged sandals, and a pouch in which to carry the head of the Gorgon. Hermes also provided an adamantine sickle. Outfitted in this way and given further directions by the Graeae, Perseus found the Gorgons asleep. With Athena guiding his hand, and using his shield as a mirror so as to avoid the petrifying glance of the grinning Gorgons, Perseus swiftly and safely lopped off the head of Medusa and put it into his pouch (inside covers). From the severed trunk of Medusa sprang the winged horse Pegasus and Chrysaor.

Perseus and Andromeda.   Now began another adventurous phase in the life of the hero of Argos. Although pursued by Medusa's sisters, Perseus easily evaded them by means of his winged sandals and his cap of invisibility. As he flew off carrying the snaky-locked head of Medusa, drops of her blood fell on the sandy deserts of Libya, and when they reached the ground, the blood became deadly snakes. This is the reason why Libya abounds in poisonous serpents. Perseus then flew three times around the world. On its western edge, the giant Atlas refused him hospitality in a most ungracious manner. Perseus thereupon un-covered the ghastly Medusa head and transformed Atlas into a huge moun-tain upon which the heaven and all its stars rest. At last, the hero flew to the Ethiopian realm of King Cepheus. He looked down and saw the king's daughter Andromeda chained to a rock. Smitten by her exquisite beauty and by love, Perseus learned that her unfortunate situation was due to her mother's sinful words; Queen Cassiopeia had boasted of her beauty and had offended the sea-goddesses. An oracle ordered King Cepheus to sacrifice his daughter to a sea-mon-ster that would be sent by Poseidon. When a monstrous dragon appeared on the scene, Perseus offered to kill the creature if Andromeda would become his wife. Cepheus and Cassiopeia readily agreed and promised in addition a kingdom and a dowry. At that Perseus swooped down on the monster and cut off his head with the marvelous sickle that Hermes had given him. The head of Medusa in the mean-time had been placed on the sand and covered with seaweed. In an instant, the sea-weed hardened and turned into coral.

Perseus and Andromeda returned in triumph to Ethiopia and made prepara-tions for the wedding. But as popular lore will have it, all did not go well: the wedding festivities were interrupted by Phineus, a brother of King Cepheus. It seems that Andromeda had been promised to Phineus, and when he heard of her betrothal to Perseus, he burst in on the festivities with several hundred men. Perseus refused to surrender his bride without a fight, but when he found him-self outnumbered, he took out the Medusa head from the pouch and turned Phi-neus and his men into stone. After the marriage Perseus returned to Seriphus with his wife only to find that Dictys and Danaë had been forced to take refuge in a temple because of Polydectes' cruelty. Perseus took his revenge by turning the king and his followers into stone, an event which is said to account for a circle of huge stones on the island of Seriphus.

After setting his kindly foster-father Dictys on the throne, Perseus set out for Argos with his mother and wife. Acrisius, hearing of the glorious exploits of his grandson and remembering the oracle that prophesied his end at the hands of his daughter's son, fled to Larissa where Perseus followed him. At the public games, either in honor of a funeral or in honor of Acrisius, Perseus took part in a discus-throwing event. His discus was deflected by the wind and struck Acrisius, killing him and fulfilling the oracle. Reluctant to return to Argos after this unfortunate accident, Perseus exchanged the kingdom of Argos, which he now had inherited, for that of Tiryns which was ruled over by a son of Proetus. As for the winged sandals and the cap of invisibility, Perseus handed them over to Hermes who returned them to the nymphs. The hero gave the nightmarish head of Medusa to his tutelary-goddess Athena who placed it on her aegis or shield. Perseus and Andromeda, unlike most legendary heroes and heroines, had many children and lived happily ever after.

By the fourth century B.C., many of the figures in this cycle of legendary adven-tures were elevated to the status of constellations: Perseus and his wife Andromeda, her parents Cepheus and Cassiopeia, Pegasus, and even the dragon which was given the name of Cetus (sea-monster). A century earlier, the Persian king Xerxes attempted to use the myth in a political gambit. According to Herodotus, he sent messengers to the city of Argos to plead for their neutrality in his war against the other Greek cities, claiming that the Argives and Persians came from the same bloodline, namely, Perseus and Andromeda and their son Perses who gave his name to the Persians.

*   *   *   *

By the time of the Middle Ages, the story of the arch-hero of Argos had been allegorized and moralized so as to make it acceptable as part of Christian doctrine. Boccaccio, one of the main links between the Middle Ages and the Renaissance, saw in Perseus' adventure not only the possibility of an actual event, but also moral and allegorical truths: a wise man's ascent to virtue (Perseus flying off on his winged sandals) after conquering sin (the decapitation of Medusa); allegorically, a symbol of Christ rising upward to his Father. Similarly, in the auto sacramental (dramatic religious pieces) of the Golden Age in Spain, the theme of Perseus was turned into an elaborate allegory. Calderón's *Andrómeda y Perseo* (1680) uses Andromeda to personify human nature, Perseus Christ, Phineus the Devil, Medusa Guilt and Death. Calderón also wrote a play, *Las fortunas de Andrómeda y Perseo*, in which the court dramatist freely expanded the legend to suit the romantic and theological inclinations of his audience. Earlier, Lope de Vega (1562–1635), creator of the Spanish secular play, had also elaborated the legend in his *El Perseo* to play upon his theme of love and honor. But it is to the artists of the Renaissance that the palm must be given for the use made of the legends surrounding Perseus. The famous bronze by Benvenuto Cellini showing Perseus holding the head of the Medusa (fig. 5) has been mentioned earlier. Titian (1554) and Rembrandt (1636) put on canvas highly sensual representations of Danaë as she awaited Zeus' visitation in a shower of gold. Others, such as Piero di Cosmo, Tintoretto, Titian, and Rubens (fig. 59) were attracted to scenes of Andromeda chained to a rock or of Perseus rescuing her from the threatening jaws of the dragon.

In later literature, the story of Perseus' adventures was given lengthy treatment by William Morris in *The Doom of King Acrisius* which forms a part of Morris' *Earthly Paradise*. Charles Kingley, who wrote *The Heroes* (1856), stories of Perseus, Theseus, and the Argonauts for young readers, also composed a vigorous and expanded *Andromeda* (1858). Robert Browning incorporated the story of Andromeda in a youthful poem of his, *Pauline* (1833), and Elizabeth Barrett Browning in *Aurora Leigh* (1857) shocked her Victorian public with this word-picture of Acrisius' daughter:

> A tiptoe Danae, overbold and hot,
> Both arms a-flame to meet her wishing Jove
> Half-way, and burn him faster down; the face
> And breasts upturned and straining, the loose locks
> All glowing with the anticipated gold.

Gerard Manley Hopkins (1844–1889), in an enigmatic sonnet *Andromeda*, seems to have used the rescue motif as a religious symbol, perhaps as the second coming of Christ (Perseus) to rescue the Church (Andromeda). Less enigmatic is Louis MacNeice's *Perseus* (1937) in which the head of Medusa symbolizes the poet's awareness

Figure 59.   Ruben's version of Perseus rescuing Andromeda. *Painting,*
1620–1621. Hermitage Museum, Leningrad. (Mansell)

of death and the petrifaction caused by time. The opening and closing stanzas of the
poem allude to the hero of Argos:

> Borrowed wings on his ankles,
> Carrying a stone death,
> The hero entered the hall,
> All in the hall looked up,
> Their breath frozen on them
> And there was no more shuffle or clatter in the hall at all.
> . . . .
> Ever to meet me comes, in sun or dull,
> The gay hero swinging the Gorgon's head
> And I am left, with the dull drumming of the sun, suspended and dead,
> Or the dumb grey-brown of the day is a leper's cloth,
> And one feels the earth going round and round the globe
>   of the blackening mantle, a mad moth.

   Herman Melville finds an early account of whaling in the legend of Perseus and
his slaying of the dragon Cetus. Keeping in mind that the Latin word *cetus*, derived
from Greek *kētos*, was used for any extraordinary sea-creature or leviathan, we
can appreciate the unusual interpretation Melville gives to the legend in
Moby Dick.

The gallant Perseus, a son of Jupiter, was the first whaleman; and to the eternal honor
of our calling be it said, that the first whale attacked by our brotherhood was not killed
for any sordid intent. Those were the knightly days of our profession, when we only
bore arms to succor the distressed, and not to fill men's lamp-feeders. Every one
knows the fine story of Perseus and Andromeda; how the lovely Andromeda was tied to
a rock on the sea-coast, and as Leviathan was in the very act of carrying her off, Perseus,
the prince of whalemen, intrepidly advancing, harpooned the monster, and delivered
and married the maid.

Pegasus. The winged horse Pegasus and the hero associated with him deserve a word. Pegasus, the remarkable creature that sprang from the truncated Gorgon (fig. 4), was said to have caused many a spring to gush forth from the earth at the point where he stamped his hoof. It must be kept in mind that Medusa had been with child by Poseidon when Perseus sealed her fate, and that Poseidon was connected both with fresh water and horses. The famous spring of the Muses on Mount Helicon, the Hippocrene (Horse-spring), was said to have been created by Pegasus, and at Corinth the spring Pirene was also said to have come from the ground when the winged horse struck it with his hoof. And it was with a hero from Corinth, Bellerophon, that Pegasus was to be intimately connected in legend, except in Homer who does not credit the winged horse with helping the Corinthian hero perform his mighty deeds. The story of Bellerophon starts at Corinth, travels to the court of King Proetus, Perseus' uncle, and ends with a series of bold adventures in Anatolian Lycia. In Bellerophon's experience with Proetus' wife can be seen the Biblical parallel of Joseph and Potiphar's wife, a motif that has analogs in many parts of the world.

Bellerophon. Bellerophon, or Bellerophontes as Homer calls him, was a descendant of Hellen and Aeolus. His grandfather was the famous trickster Sisyphus; his father Glaucus, a king of Corinth, was reputed to have been a fancier of racing horses which he fed on human flesh so as to make them more spirited and warlike. Glaucus met his fate by being torn to pieces by his beloved horses when they overturned his chariot. His son Bellerophon had the misfortune to kill a young man in Corinth and was forced to seek sanctuary with king Proetus. It was at the court of the Argive king that Proetus' wife Anteia—some give her name as Stheneboea—met and fell in love with Bellerophon. But when the young man rejected Anteia's passionate advances, she accused him to her husband of attempting to seduce her. Proetus would have killed Bellerophon on the spot had he not been afraid of violating the laws of hospitality. He chose instead to send Bellerophon to his father-in-law Iobates, king of Lycia, with written instructions to kill the bearer of the note. But Iobates also hestitated to take upon himself the burden of a homicide. He thought of another means of disposing of the young man: he sent him on a mission to kill the fire-breathing Chimaera, the monster that had the head of a lion, the tail of a slashing serpent, and the body of a goat (p. 32).

Bellerophon sought guidance from a seer who told him to secure, if possible, the horse Pegasus. By this time Pegasus had been caught and tamed by Athena and had been presented by her to the Muses. Bellerophon was also advised to spend a night in Athena's temple. While he slept the goddess brought him a golden bridle, and when he awoke Athena showed him Pegasus drinking at the spring Pirene. The winged horse allowed Bellerophon to put on the golden bridle; and seated on his back the hero sped off, found the Chimaera and dispatched it with arrows from his unassailable perch high in the air (fig. 60). Iobates was amazed at Bellerophon's success and sent him off to fight the Solymi, a famed mythical tribe of warriors, and the equally mythical Amazons, a race of female warriors. The hero was successful in both undertakings. Iobates then decided on more direct action: he sent his soldiers to ambush the young man, but Poseidon—some say that Poseidon was Bellerophon's father—sent a flood and drowned all the soldiers. Iobates was now convinced that he was not dealing with an ordinary mortal and gave up any further attempt to have Bellerophon killed. He made him heir to his kingdom

Figure 60. Bellerophon, mounted on Pegasus, about to kill the Chimaera.
Terracotta, fifth century B.C. British Museum.

and gave him one of his daughters in marriage. However, success was too much for Bellerophon; in his arrogance he decided to challenge the gods. Mounted on Pegasus he tried to fly up to Olympus, but Zeus met the challenge by sending a gadfly which stung Pegasus and caused him to throw his rider. Bellerophon fell to earth and was crippled and blinded by the fall. Pegasus continued his flight to Olympus where he served Zeus as the bearer of his thunder and lightning. Bellerophon, on the other hand, wandered wretched and lonely until he died.

Literary allusions to Pegasus are more plentiful than those to Bellerophon. The British had no qualms about naming one of their ships after the unfortunate hero from Corinth; it was on board the *H.M.S. Bellerophon* that Napoleon surrendered in 1815. From the story of Bellerophon, who was unconsciously the bearer of his own death-warrant, came the phrase "letters of Bellerophon" (*Bellerophontis litterae*) to describe a communication which is prejudicial to the one carrying it. Pegasus afforded more ready comparisons either with other equally remarkable horses or with poetic inspiration, the latter arising from his connection with the Muses. In Chaucer's *Squire's Tale*, a wondrous horse is "lyk the Pegasee,/the hors that hadde wynges for to flee." Shakespeare, in *1 Henry IV*, describes madcap Prince Hal vaulting into his saddle:

> As if an angel dropp'd down from the clouds
> To turn and wind a fiery Pegasus
> And witch the world with noble horsemanship.

For poetic inspiration, the spring Pegasus created is invoked by Keats in his *Ode to a Nightingale* when he asks for "a breaker full of the warm South,/Full of the true, the blushful Hippocrene." And Milton in *Paradise Lost* calls upon his heavenly

Muse who had helped him to soar "Above the flight of Pegasean wing," to bring him down to earth in safety. (The allusion to the Aleian Field is taken from Homer's version of what befell Bellerophon when he became hated by all the gods and wandered alone through the Aleian Plain—that is, the Plain of Wandering—eating out his heart and avoiding contact with mankind.)

> Return me to my native element
> Lest, from this flying steed unreined (as once
> Bellerophon, though from a lower clime)
> Dismounted, on th' Aleian Field I fall,
> Erroneous there to wander and forlorn.

Heracles (Hercules).   Several generations after the death of Perseus, the greatest and most popular of all Greek heroes was born: Heracles, hero of heroes, a man of Herculean strength, an honorary member of the Olympians after his death and apotheosis, widely admired and worshiped as a hero-god among the Greeks and in those most distant lands of antiquity influenced by the Greeks. The Romans called him Hercules, and in post-classical literary usage this was the most common form of his name. Around this descendant of Perseus there grew so many legends which, like the Gordian knot, have defied unraveling by scholars. Was he a ruler of Tiryns at the end of the Bronze Age, a vassal of the king of Argos, a prince so great that he attracted to himself a myriad of tales concerning his prowess among the quick and the dead? Was he merely a folktale figure, like Jack the Giant Killer, about whom clustered many stories of killing or seizing monsters and monstrous animals, exploits which corresponded to the life and times revealed in heroic literature? Or was he, since his name means "Glory of Hera," a pre-Hellenic godling or divine lover of the native fertility-goddess Hera who, with the coming of the Greeks and her marriage to the great god Zeus, changed her relationship with her lover to one of hostility and antagonism? As in the case of so many other Greek mythological figures, the answer is not a simple nor an assured one. The likelihood is that the stories surrounding the figure of Heracles incorporate all three possibilities and represent an unstratified synthesis of folklore, history, and ritual dramas. However that may be, the literature concerning the life of this sturdy and lusty adventurer is so rich that space can be given only to the legends of his birth and early years, the famous Twelve Labors, and to some of his "incidental labors," the *parerga* as they are known in Greek.

Although Heracles' closest associations were with the Peloponnese, his birth and early years have the city of Thebes as their setting, a creation undoubtedly of Theban myth-makers and genealogists who wished to link their city with the greatest of all Greek heroes. For this purpose stories were invented which would bring Heracles' mother Alcmene and her husband Amphitryon to Thebes. Then again by mythological invention the scene was shifted back to the Peloponnese and the cities of Argos, Mycenae, and Tiryns where Heracles would serve King Eurystheus and perform for him his remarkable labors (*athloi*)—*athloi* in Greek are contests or struggles or ordeals, conventionally translated as "labors." These from very early times were canonized as twelve in number, a number which the Greeks used for Titans, Olympians, signs of the Zodiac, and for the months of the year. Of the twelve canonical labors, six take place within the Peloponnese (Nemea, Lerna, Erymanthus, Ceryneia, Stymphalus, and Elis); the remaining six are outside the Peloponnese and Greek lands, either in foreign or in mythical lands. For some scholars, the fabled beasts in the labors of Heracles are death figures. Certainly those labors that involve the cattle of Geryon, Cerberus, and the Apples of the Hesperides have as a common theme the ability of the hero to conquer death. The strength and endurance of this hero *par excellence* were to lead in yet other directions: for the poets, Heracles' gargantuan appetite for food and women lent toward his becoming a comic figure; philosophers, on the other hand, took him as a paragon of virtue whose struggles were transformed into allegories in which the hero was able to overcome the seductive call of vice by philosophical fortitude. The man in the street, however, would call upon Heracles as the Averter of Evil (*Alexikakos*) and would write on his doors or walls this charm: "The son of Zeus, Heracles the Conqueror, lives here; let no evil thing enter."

The Events Preceding Heracles' Birth: Amphitryon and Alcmene.   The opening of the story has for its setting the ancient city of Mycenae and its king Electryon, one of the sons of Perseus and Andromeda. His daughter Alcmene, the mother-to-be of the great Heracles, was promised to her cousin Amphitryon, the son of Alcaeus (Valiant) who was the folk hero of Thebes and brother of Electryon. When Electryon became embroiled in a war with the cattle-rustling Taphians, he left his kingdom in charge of Amphitryon and promised him that if all went well he could have Alcmene as his bride. Upon his return he fell into a quarrel with Amphitryon over some cattle which the latter had recovered, and in the argument Electryon was "accidentally" killed. As a consequence Amphitryon was forced to leave Mycenae and went to Thebes with Alcmene where he was purified by King Creon. Alcmene, however, refused to consummate her marriage until Amphitryon avenged the death of her eight brothers who had been killed by the Taphians. Creon allowed Amphitryon to raise an army on condition that he first catch a ravaging fox which supposedly could not be caught. Amphitryon borrowed a remarkable dog for the purpose, a dog which supposedly could catch any animal it might pursue. To resolve the dilemma, the gods turned both fox and dog into stone. Amphitryon then attacked the Taphians, but he could not overcome them since their king Pterelaus had a familiar life token, a golden thread of hair which made him immortal and invincible. However, the king's daughter Comaetho fell in love with Amphitryon, and to earn his affection and gratitude, she cut or pulled out the fatal hair and Pterelaus died. For her treachery to her father Amphitryon killed the poor love-struck girl.

It was while Amphitryon was completing his campaign that Zeus appeared to Alcmene in the guise of her husband. Not aware that anything was amiss, she invited the false bridegroom into her bedroom where he told her of how he had avenged the death of her brothers and then consummated the long-delayed marriage in a night that he stretched into three. When Amphitryon arrived the following day and wanted to tell Alcmene of his accomplishments, he was astonished at her cool reception and that she already knew of what had happened. The famous seer Tiresias came to their help and solved the mystery. Some say that Amphitryon himself came to the realization that some divinity had slept with his wife and that thereafter he never shared her bed.

The theme of the false bridegroom is turned into a comedy of errors by the Roman comic poet Plautus (c. 250–184 B.C.). In his *Amphitryo*, Mercury also assumes a disguise, that of Amphitryon's slave Sosia, and sees to it that Jupiter is able to enjoy his night with Alcmene without intrusion. When the real Amphitryon and Sosia appear on the scene, confusion is compounded and Amphitryon is beside himself with jealousy and bewilderment. It is only after Alcmene has given birth that Jupiter appears and clarifies what had taken place. When Molière treated the theme in 1668—as did Dryden who used both Plautus and Molière for his adaptation in 1690—the comedy of errors was further complicated by the confrontation of two indistinguishable Amphitryons and Sosias and the sorting out of the true Amphitryon and Sosia. Jean Giraudoux's *Amphitryon 38* (1929)—38 allegedly representing the thirty-eighth version of the legend—is infused with Gallic wit, fantasy, and insight into the power of the weaker sex.

The Birth of Heracles.   Thus Heracles was conceived. But Hera as usual demonstrated her hostility toward her husband's philandering ways. This hostility was directed against Heracles even before he was born. On the day that Alcmene was to give birth, Zeus boasted : "This day shall bring to light a man sprung from my seed who shall rule over all the surrounding peoples." Hera, working her wiles, persuaded her husband to swear an inviolable oath that he would stand by his word. Zeus complied without being aware of his wife's subtle ways. Hera hurried to Argos where she induced the wife of Sthenelus, who was then with child, to give birth prematurely to Eurystheus. At the same time, she—or Eileithyia, the goddess of childbirth (p. 86)—delayed the birth of Heracles by crossing her legs and clasping her hands over her knees, a neat peice of sympathetic magic. By an equally neat folk device, the goddess was tricked. A friend of Alcmene dashed out and cried: "Alcmene has given birth to a boy!" In astonishment, the goddess stood up and uncrossed her legs, and at that instant Heracles was born. It is to this stratagem of Hera that Milton alludes in his *Areopagitica* where he inveighs against the licensing of books. Before this, he says:

> . . . books were ever as freely admitted into the world as any other birth; the issue of the brain was no more stifled than the issue of the womb: no envious Juno sat cross-legged over the nativity of any man's intellectual offspring.

Alcmene brought into the world not only Heracles, but one night later a twin brother Iphicles; the former was conceived by Zeus, the latter by Amphitryon. It is said that Alcmene, fearing Hera's anger, exposed her newborn son in a field near Thebes where he was found by Hera and Athena. Hera was prevailed upon to nurse the child for a while before returning him to his mother. Other accounts say that the child was brought to Olympus and put to the breast of Hera while she was asleep, but when the goddess awoke she pushed the child away, and the milk thus spilled produced the Milky Way (p. 97). When yet an infant Heracles demonstrated his prodigious strength by strangling two snakes that Hera had maliciously placed in his cradle. Others would make Amphitryon responsible for introducing the snakes so that he could determine which child was his and which was the god's.

Heracles' Early Years.   As a young man Heracles was provided with the finest tutors in chariot-driving, wrestling, archery, and military tactics. Training in the arts was not neglected; Heracles was placed in the care of Linus for instruction in the art of music. As already reported, Heracles was neither a talented pupil nor a patient one. When his lyre playing was criticized, he took the instrument and killed Linus with it. Heracles claimed self-defense, but his foster-father, determined to keep him out of further trouble, sent him to watch over his cattle, a job that occupied the youthful Heracles until he was eighteen years of age. While engaged in this occupation, Heracles had his first great adventure. It so happened that a ravaging lion roamed about Mount Cithaeron preying upon the flocks of Amphitryon and Thespius, the latter being king and eponym of the Thespians. Heracles took it upon himself to rid the country of the lion. Thespius, who had fifty daughters, offered him the hospitality of his palace as long as the chase lasted. The king, wishing to have the hero's progeny as his grandchildren, also invited Heracles to enjoy the favors of his fifty daughters. This was accomplished in fifty nights; or according to other versions, in seven nights, or in one night! The offspring of Thespius' daughters were said to have been the first colonizers of the island of Sardinia. As for the ravaging lion, the so-called Thespian lion, Heracles killed it and thereafter wore its hide as a garment and its mouth and head as a helmet (fig. 66). Some claim that it was not the Thespian lion but the Nemean lion that provided the hero's traditional costume.

Upon his return to Thebes, Heracles helped his father and the aged King Creon in settling family feuds and in disposing of armies sent against the city. The glorious manner in which Heracles had delivered the country won for him immortal fame among the Thebans, and Creon rewarded him with the hand of his eldest daughter Megara by whom he became the father of several children. It was at about this time that Hera visited him with a fit of insanity during which he imagined his wife and children to be his enemies. In his madness Heracles killed not only Megara and his children but also two children of his twin brother Iphicles. In his grief Heracles sentenced himself to voluntary exile and went to King Thespius who purified him by formal rites of the crime of homicide. Still not satisfied, Heracles sought the advice of the oracle at Delphi. It was there that the Pythian priestess called him by the name of Heracles; until then he had been called by the name of his renowned grandfather Alcides (or Alceides), "the descendant of Alcaeus." The prophetess then advised him to live at Tiryns and to serve Eurystheus for twelve years as a vassal, after which time he would win immortality. By this mythological device, Heracles' career at Thebes is brought to an end and a new phase opens up for him in the Argolid of the Peloponnese where his family had its origins.

The Labors of Heracles. The twelve labors which would earn for Heracles a place among the immortals were performed for Eurystheus, king of Argos or Mycenae, whom Hera had cleverly brought into the world by premature birth so as to forestall her husband's prophecy regarding his son by Alcmene. In historical terms, the relationship between Heracles and Eurystheus can best be explained as that between a vassal prince and an overlord. In many epic tales the opposing interests of the two are highlighted: the vassal who directs his animus against the authority and the supposed incompetence of a powerful king. This employee-employer relationship can best be seen in Homer's *Iliad* where the poet portrays Achilles as nurturing a gnawing hostility against Agamemnon for taking the best of the war booty while he has to do all the hard work. As for the tasks that Eurystheus sets for Heracles, they have the flavor of the Bronze Age with its representations of hunting scenes and men wrestling with bulls or lions. The art of the period corresponds so well with the exploits of Heracles that many scholars see in the labors a Mycenaean origin. The first six of these labors take place in the Peloponnese: the Nemean Lion, the Hydra of Lerna, the Erymanthian Boar, the Hind of Ceryneia, the Stymphalian Birds, and the Stables of Augeas; the remaining six have foreign or mythical locales: the Cretan Bull, the Horses of Thracian Diomedes, the Girdle of the Amazons, Geryon, Cerberus, and the Golden Apples of the Hesperides. As to the monsters involved in these *athloi*, we have already observed how Hesiod introduced five of them into the world as descendants of Phorcys and Ceto: the Nemean Lion, the Hydra, Geryon, Cerberus, and the Dragon of the Hesperides. In the art of the Classical Age, the finest representations of the twelve labors are found on the metopes of the Temple of Zeus at Olympia.

The Nemean Lion. The first task Eurystheus set for Heracles was to bring him the hide of the Nemean lion. In the valley of Nemea, not far from Argos, a certain Molorchus advised Heracles that the lion could not be overcome by ordinary weapons, that he had to be taken in a wrestling-match. Heracles tracked the lion to his lair, and after having used his club and arrows against the best without effect, he blocked up one of the two entrances to the den, and entering the other, he put his brawny arms around the neck of the creature and choked it to death (fig. 61). Heracles returned to Eurystheus carrying the dead lion on his shoulders—some say that he skinned the lion with its own claws and used the hide to cover his own body. Eurystheus was so terrified at the sight of the beast and at the extraordinary strength of Heracles that he fled and ordered the hero in the future to deliver the account of his exploits outside the gates of the city. He is also said to have had a bronze jar built under the earth where he hid and from where he conveyed his commands to Heracles by a messenger. Zeus honored his son by translating the monstrous beast to the heavens as one of the signs of the zodiac. Shakespeare alludes to the strength of this prodigious animal when Hamlet, after seeing the ghost of his father, cries out to Horatio who attempts to restrain him:

> My fate cries out
> And makes each petty artire [muscle] in this body
> As hardy as the Nemean lion's nerve [sinews].

The Hydra of Lerna. The second assignment handed out to Heracles by Eurystheus was to kill the many-headed Hydra (fig. 62). This gigantic watersnake lived in the swamps near Lerna and ravaged both flocks and countryside with its deadly breath. The difficulty in disposing of this monster lay in the fact that as soon as one head was cut off, two fire-breathing heads grew in its place. As Heracles struggled to overpower the Hydra, Hera sent a huge crab to annoy the hero by biting his feet. He crushed the crab with his foot, but Hera transferred the creature

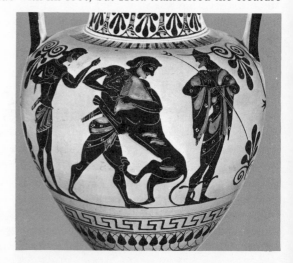

Figure 61. Heracles strangling the Nemean Lion while Iolas and Hermes look on. *Vase painting, late sixth century B.C. Museum of Fine Arts, Boston.*

Figure 62.   Pollaiuolo (1429–1498).
Heracles dispatching the Hydra of
Lerna. *Uffizi Gallery, Florence.*
(Alinari)

to the heavens where it became part of the zodiac as Cancer the Crab next to the Lion. Heracles shot fire arrows into the lair to force the Hydra out into the open. Having difficulties in decapitating the snake, Heracles called upon his nephew Iolaus to help him. As fast as the hero struck off one of the Hydra's heads, Iolaus cauterized the stump with a firebrand, thereby preventing any additional heads from sprouting. It is said that Iolaus used up almost an entire forest in the process. The immortal head was also cut off and buried under a huge boulder. After the monster had been disposed of, Heracles dipped his arrows in its blood or gall which was so lethal that it spelled certain death for anyone who was wounded by one of these arrows. Eurystheus, it is said by those who hold the canonical number of the labors to be ten, refused to recognize this exploit as legitimate because Heracles had had the assistance of Iolaus. Shakespeare found in the mythical watersnake an apt allusion for his historical play *1 Henry IV*. The Earl of Douglas challenges King Henry with these words:

> Another king? They grow like Hydra's heads.
> I am the Douglas, fatal to all those
> That wear those colours on them.

The Hind of Ceryneia.   The third and fourth commissions assigned by Eurystheus took Heracles back to hunting less spectacular beasts. The hero was asked to catch the hind of Ceryneia, an unusual animal in that females of the deer do not have antlers, much less golden antlers and bronze hooves. This extraordinary creature, which roamed the high ranges of the Parthenion (Virgin) and Artemision (Artemis' Mountain), was said to have been dedicated to Artemis by the nymph because the goddess had saved her from the pursuit of an overly amorous Zeus.

Heracles was ordered to bring the animal back to Mycenae alive. He tracked the animal for an entire year, from Mount Artemision to the river Ladon in Arcadia, the land sacred to Artemis. Having at last caught the animal, he was met by Apollo and Artemis as he was passing through Arcadia. The twin deities were terribly angry at him thinking that the hero was attempting to kill the hind sacred to the goddess. Heracles pleaded that he had been forced by Eurystheus to capture the animal and that he was taking it back alive. Apollo and Artemis were convinced that he told the truth and permitted the hero to complete his mission. Some say that the hind was turned loose at Mycenae; others say that Heracles killed it.

The Erymanthian Boar. The scene for the fourth labor and the next hunt turns to Mount Erymanthus in Arcadia and the Erymanthian boar, which Heracles was to bring back to Mycenae alive. Coupled with the hunt is an episode, one of the *parerga*, with the semi-human centaurs who inhabited the region. In his pursuit of the boar, the hero came to the cave of the centaur Pholus who received him hospitably. Dionysus had given this centaur a huge jar of excellent wine. Heracles insisted upon opening the jar contrary to the wishes of his host. The delicious bouquet of the wine attracted other centaurs and a drunken brawl ensued. Heracles drove them away, and with the hero in hot pursuit, they fled to the cave of Chiron, the grand old centaur (p. 131). One of Heracles' arrows tipped with the Hydra's poison, aimed at a fleeing centaur, missed its mark and hit Chiron. Heracles tried to heal him with his own medicines but without success. Even though Chiron was immortal and could not die, neither could he recover. In agony he prayed to Zeus to take away his immortality and give it to the tormented Prometheus. In this way Chiron was delivered of his burning pain and died. Pholus was also killed by one of the poisoned arrows when it accidently dropped on his foot. As for the Erymanthian boar, Heracles picked up the chase, drove the creature into deep snow, and snared the exhausted animal by means of a net. Vase painters of antiquity were fond of this scene, showing the hero with the wild boar on his back, offering the creature to a cowering Eurystheus as he peeped out of his bronze jar.

The Augean Stables. Eurystheus, now wishing to impose a servile and undignified task on Heracles for his fifth labor, ordered him to clean out the stables of Augeas (or Augeias) in a single day. Augeas was the king of Elis on the western coast of the Peloponnese who had inherited huge herds of cattle from his father and whose stables had not been cleared out for a good number of years. Without mentioning Eurystheus' order, Heracles made an offer to Augeas to remove all the dung from his stables in one day for a tenth of his cattle. The king of Elis could hardly believe his ears and readily agreed. Heracles sealed the bargain by bringing Phyleus, a son of Augeas, to witness the agreement. This done, the hero then cleverly diverted the course of two rivers, the Alpheus and Peneus, so that they ran through the stables and thereby flushed out the accumulated filth. When Augeas learned that Heracles had undertaken the task at the command of Eurystheus, he refused to abide by his agreement. Brought before a panel of arbitrators, the son of Augeas testified against his father and a judgment was given in favor of Heracles. In a rage the king ordered both the hero and Phyleus to leave Elis. Heracles vowed revenge and at a later date led an army against Elis, killing the king and his other sons. It was after this victory that Heracles is said to have marked out the sacred ground on which the Olympian games were to be celebrated—Olympia is situated in the region of Elis on the river Alpheus—and instituted the festival and games in honor of the Olympian Zeus. The sculptor of the metopes on the famous Temple of Zeus at Olympia honored this tradition with representations of the hero's Twelve Labors. For the one illustrating the Augean stables, the sculptor apparently had iconographic difficulties and portrayed Heracles using a more conventional instrument, a shovel, to accomplish his task. Eurystheus, according to some narrators, refused to accept this as a legitimate labor since Heracles had accepted a fee. William Wordsworth uses Heracles' hydraulic device as a poetic figure in *The Prelude*, describing those who followed Robespierre in the French Revolution as a clique:

> . . . who with clumsy desperation brought
> A river of Blood and preached that nothing else
> Could cleanse the Augean stable.

The Stymphalian Birds. As a finale for Heracles' labors in the Peloponnese, Eurystheus called upon the hero to rid a region in Arcadia of a flock of pestilential creatures, the Stymphalian birds. These took their name from the lake of Stymphalus, which was surrounded by a thick wood. The claws of the birds were of bronze and their feathers, which they could use as arrows, were made of iron. These fabled birds were so numerous that their filth covered the fields and meadows while their feathers took a toll of both men and beasts. Athena provided Heracles with a marvelous bronze rattle whose noise startled the birds from their roosting places in the wood, and as they attempted to fly away, Heracles picked them off with his arrows. According to other accounts, the hero did not kill the birds but only drove them away to the island of Aretias where they were found later by Jason and his fellow-Argonauts.

The Cretan Bull. The remaining labors set for Heracles by Eurystheus were to take the hero outside the Peloponnese. For his seventh task, according to one tradition, he was to go to the island of Crete to catch the bull which had carried Europa across the sea; according to another, it was the bull which Poseidon had sent from the sea and which Minos, to his and his daughter's regret, had refused to sacrifice in honor of the god. (The story of both bulls will be told in the account of the House of Minos.) With the permission of Minos, Heracles easily captured the Cretan Bull, hefted it to his shoulders—or rode on its back over the sea—and brought it to Eurystheus. The bull was set free and roamed about Greece until it came to the plain of Marathon where it earned the name of the Marathonian Bull. Later, the Athenian hero Theseus duplicated the labor of Heracles and disposed of the bull.

The Man-eating Mares of Diomedes. The locale for the next assignment for Heracles turns to Thrace, the land to the north and east of Greece, traditionally known for its barbarism. It was there that Eurystheus sent the hero for his eighth labor: to fetch and bring back alive to Mycenae the carnivorous horses of Diomedes. Diomedes, the son of Ares and king of the Bistones, had the barbaric custom of feeding the flesh of unfortunate strangers to his mares. On his way to Thrace, Heracles accepted the hospitality of King Admetus in Thessaly and helped the kindly monarch to recover his wife (p. 134). As for the man-eating mares of Diomedes, the hero cured them of their uncivilized diet by feeding them the flesh of their master. Thus tamed, the horses were brought back to Mycenae where they were dedicated to Hera, their breed reportedly lasting to the time of Alexander the Great. Others say that the horses were killed by wild beasts on Mount Olympus.

Hylas.   In the midst of his labors, Heracles paused to take part in the first maritime expedition, the voyage of the Argonauts. One account places this after his experience with Diomedes; another places it after his adventure with the Erymanthian boar. In any event, Heracles joined Jason and the other heroes in Thessaly and was accompanied by his favorite, Hylas, a young lad who father he had killed. When the Argonauts landed at Cios on the coast of Asia Minor, the young man was sent out to fetch water for Heracles. But, as the romanticizing poets would have it, his beauty attracted the nymphs of the spring, and they drew him down into the water. Heracles left the *Argo* to search for Hylas, roving over the land and calling out his name. It was in vain, but Heracles persisted and the *Argo* had to continue its voyage without the celebrated hero. In historical times, it is said, the people of Cios celebrated an annual festival in honor of the youth and roamed about the land calling out for Hylas. The likelihood is that Hylas—his name is probably a ritual cry of woe like that of Linus—was a deity of vegetation whose return was annually sought by various rituals. The Hellenistic poet Theocritus composed a romantic idyll, his thirteenth, on the loss of Hylas. In the *Faerie Queene*, Spenser compares Fancy in his mask of Cupid to

> . . . that same daintie lad, which was so deare
> To great Alcides, that when as he dyde,
> He wailed womanlike with many a teare,
> And every wood, and every valley wyde
> He fild with Hylas name; the Nymphes eke Hylas cryde.

The Girdle of the Amazon.   Heracles' ninth labor came about as a result of a wish of Admete, the daughter of Eurystheus: she wished to have the girdle which Ares had given to Hippolyte (or Hippolyta), queen of the Amazons, as a token of her superiority over all women. The king considered this request a suitable mission for Heracles. The hero called for volunteers and outfitted a ship for the expedition which attracted such heroes as Theseus, Telamon, and many of the original Argonauts. It also attracted mythographers and poets to the opportunity of introducing embellishments and minor adventures. After an incident on the island of Paros with the sons of Minos, and a military expedition on the coast of Asia Minor, Heracles crossed a body of water which he called Euxine, now known as the Black Sea. Having landed at the port of Themiscyra at the mouth of the Thermodon river, the hero was kindly received by Hippolyte who agreed to give him her celebrated girdle. But Hera was not content to let it go at that. She disguised herself as an Amazon and spread the report that the queen of the Amazons was being robbed by a stranger. The Amazons immediately rushed to help out their queen, and Heracles, thinking that Hippolyte had plotted against him, killed her and took the girdle from her dead body. According to another tradition, she survived and led an army of Amazons to invade Attica against Theseus.

Heracles, on his way back to Greece, had a number of adventures, the most significant one at Troy. When Laomedon, then king of Troy, had refused to pay Poseidon and Apollo their fee for building the walls of the city (p. 100), the two gods sent a sea-monster and a plague against Troy for breach of contract. An oracle commanded Laomedon to rid himself of these calamities by offering his daughter Hesione to the monster. Heracles arrived on the scene and offered to save Hesione for a price: the horse which Zeus had given him as a reward for allowing the god to carry off his son Canymede. Laomedon agreed. Heracles killed the monster and saved Hesione. Laomedon, however, refused as usual to live up to his part of the bargain. In revenge, Heracles later sailed against Troy with a fleet of ships—this was to be the first organized expedition of the Greeks against Troy—and killed Laomedon and all his sons except Priam who was fated to rule Troy during the great ten-year-war celebrated by poets in song.

Geryon. When Heracles returned to Mycenae with Hippolyte's girdle—in classical times, this relic was said to have been seen in the temple of Hera at Argos —Eurystheus planned an excursion for him to an even more mythical land than that of the Amazons. The last three labors, as already indicated, are clear examples of the hero's ability to harrow hell and to overpower death.

For his tenth assignment, Eurystheus sent Heracles across the world-encircling Ocean to Erytheia, the Red Island, which lay under the rays of the setting sun in the west. There lived Geryon (Geryones or Geryoneus) the triple-bodied grandson of the Gorgon Medusa, whose cattle were pastured along with those of Hades. It was Heracles' mission to fetch these oxen of Geryon. After the usual number of minor adventures, the hero traveled to the straits of Gibraltar where he set up two pillars on the sides of the strait which were hence called the Pillars of Heracles, or more familiarly the Pillars of Hercules. (These are still with us in the dollar sign [$]; it originated under Charles V of Germany to represent the Pillars of Hercules entwined with a scroll that bore his motto *Plus Ultra*, "Still Farther.") Finally, Helios the sun permitted Heracles to use his golden cup or boat to sail around the disc of the earth and reach his destination. On the island of Erytheia he came upon Geryon's herdsman Eurytion and his dog Orthus whom he dispatched with his club. As Heracles was driving off the cattle, another herdsman reported the theft to Geryon. Triple-bodied Geryon attacked the hero with three spears and protected himself with three shields, but to no avail: Heracles killed Geryon and continued on his way. He sailed with his booty to Tartessus where he returned the golden cup to Helios.

The return to the Peloponnese with Geryon's oxen was filled with many adventures which connected the hero with his widespread cult in Italy and Sicily. He crossed the Pyrenees and the Alps, and in the process founded cities in Gaul and became the father of the Celts. Among the Ligurians in southern France, an attempt was made to steal his cattle. After he had spent all of his arrows on his attackers, he prayed to Zeus for help. The Olympian assisted him with a shower of stones which drove off the Ligurians. The spot on which this happened became the stony Plaine de la Crau. Heracles continued his march through Italy by traversing Tyrrhenia, the country of the Etruscans. In southern Italy, one of his oxen jumped into the sea and swam to Sicily where Eryx, the son of Poseidon, put the creature into his own herd. Heracles went to Sicily and claimed the animal, only to have to engage Eryx in a wrestling match. By defeating Eryx three times in wrestling, he not only won the ox that he had lost, but also possession of the land. Colonists from Sparta later claimed possession of Sicily on the basis of this legend. When Heracles reached Thrace, Hera stampeded his cattle as a further obstacle to his safe arrival in Argos. After much difficulty, Heracles recovered his herd and took them to Eurystheus who sacrificed them to Hera. Thus ended the tenth labor. It is said that the ten labors occupied Heracles for eight years and one month. But since Eurystheus considered two of them as not legitimate, he required two additional tasks from the hero.

Figure 63.   Heracles, with the help of
Athena, supports the heavens for Atlas
who is bringing him the apples of the
Hesperides. *Metope from the Temple
of Zeus at Olympia, c. 456 B.C.
Olympia Museum. (Hirmer)*

The Golden Apples of the Hesperides.   For his penultimate task, Heracles was
asked to fetch the golden apples of the Hesperides, the apples which Hera had
received from Mother Earth at her wedding and which were entrusted to the Hesperides and guarded by the dragon of the Hesperides, called Ladon by some. This
was to be no small labor since the location of the garden where they were kept was
not known. The locus of the Hesperides is generally placed far to the west, "beyond
the glorious Ocean" as Hesiod tells us. Heracles made his way out of Greece to the
banks of the mythical river Eridanus. On the way he had his usual violent alterca-
tions with enemies of various sorts until he arrived at the stream where the nymphs
advised him to seek out the prophetic sea-god Nereus. Heracles came upon the
sleeping Nereus and, much in the same way that Menelaus engaged Proteus, wrestled with the reluctant sea-god who tried unsuccessfuliy to escape by a variety of
transformations. On advice from Nereus, Heracles traveled through Libya, Egypt,
Ethiopia, Asia, and Arabia until at last he arrived at that mountain in the Caucasus
where Prometheus was being tortured by an eagle plucking continuously at his liver.
Heracles shot the eagle, freed Prometheus, and offered in his place Chiron who had
agreed to die for the rebellious Titan. Prometheus then gave his savior some practical advice: not to fetch the apples himself but to send Atlas, the Titan who held the
heavens on his head (or shoulders). Heracles traveled far to the west where
he found Atlas suffering under his burden. He put his proposition to the Titan who
happened to be a neighbor of the Hesperides.

Atlas agreed to fetch the precious fruit on condition that the hero would take over his burden of holding up the heavens. As for the dragon who guarded the apples, Heracles had already disposed of him with one of his arrows. When Atlas returned with the golden apples (fig. 63), he refused to resume his former job and said that he himself would take the apples to Eurystheus. Heracles, a match for the Titan in cleverness, did not object. He asked Atlas to hold the heavens for a moment while he put a cushion on his head (or shoulders) so as to make the task of supporting the heavens more bearable. When Atlas fell for the ruse, Heracles picked up the apples and went off to deliver them to Eurystheus. The king made a present of them to the hero, but Heracles dedicated them to the goddess Athena who in turn sent them back to the garden of the Hesperides. The tradition that rationalized Atlas as a mountain, is mainly due to Ovid who relates that Perseus transformed him into the geographical feature of the same name by means of the petrifying head of Medusa.

During the Renaissance when classical mythology and the Bible were differentiated only to the extent that the former was considered a distortion of the revealed word, the story of the apples of the Hesperides was seen in terms of the temptation of Eve and the harrowing of hell by Christ. This is how it is stated in Sir Walter Raleigh's *History of the World* (1614):

> . . . so also was the fiction of those golden apples kept by a dragon taken from the serpent which tempted Evah: so was paradise itself transported out of Asia into Africa, and made the garden of the Hesperides: the prophecies, that Christ should break the serpent's head, and conquer the power of hell, occasioned the fables of Hercules killing the serpent of Hesperides, and descending into hell, and captivating Cerberus . . .

In *Paradise Regained*, Milton implicates "the ladies of the Hesperides" in the temptation of Christ. In *Comus*, however, Milton has a more romantic view "Of Hesperus, and his daughters three / That sing about the golden tree"; there, beauty is compared to the tree within the garden guarded by the dragon:

> But Beauty, like the fair Hesperian tree
> Laden with blooming gold, had need the guard
> Of dragon-watch with unenchanted eye,
> To save her blossoms, and defend her fruit
> From the rash hand of bold Incontinence.

Shakespeare, in *Love's Labour's Lost*, cites through one of his characters an apocryphal version of Heracles' eleventh labor. Berowne's long peroration on love includes: "For valour, is not Love a Hercules,/Still climbing trees in the Hesperides?"

Cerberus. The final and crowning achievement of Heracles—the only one of the twelve labors expressly cited by Homer—was to fetch Cerberus, the hound of Hades, from his lair in the lower world. After having been intiated into the Eleusinian mysteries and purified for having killed the centaurs, he was thus prepared to violate the inviolable: to enter the land of the dead as a living man. Accompanied by Athena and Hermes, Heracles descended into the realm of Hades through the hellmouth at Taenarum. Some traditions connect the descent of the hero to the lower world with his contest with Hades "in the Gate and among the dead" where he is said to have wounded the god. Other accounts tell of how Charon ferried him across the waters of Hades and was punished for it by having to spend a year in chains. Various ghosts of the dead fled before the hero. He then slaughtered one of Hades'

Figure 64.   Heracles bringing Cerberus the Hellhound to a terrified Eurystheus. *Vase painting, late sixth century B.C. Louvre. (Hirmer)*

oxen in order to give the shades blood to drink. His generosity was opposed by
Menoëtes, the herdsman of Hades' cattle. He challenged Heracles to a wrestling
match to his regret, for the herdsman found himself in a rib-crushing bearhug, and
escaped death only when the queen of the dead Persephone asked the hero to relax
his grip.

Making his way to Hades and Persephone, Heracles asked permission to take
Cerberus back with him to the upper world. The god of the dead agreed on condition that he do so without using any of his weapons. Heracles went to the gates
where the hellhound stood guard, put his brawny arms around the creature's throat,
and applied pressure until Cerberus went limp. Even then the beast tried to bite
him with his serpent's tail. Finally, he allowed Heracles to put him on a leash and
lead him out of the Underworld. As they passed the gate, he met Theseus and
Pirithous—their attempt to abduct Persephone will be related later—who begged
him to release them. Heracles managed to free Theseus, but when he attempted to
do the same for Pirithous, the earth began to tremble. Back in the land of the living,
Heracles showed the monster to Eurystheus as proof of his having fulfilled this last
labor (fig. 64). Having done so, the hero took Cerberus back to his post at the gate to
the lower world where the flesh-tearing beast continued to serve Hades as the
guardian of his realm.

Dante found a place for Cerberus in the third circle of his *Inferno* (fig. 6)
where gluttons and epicures were being punished; there

> Cerberus, a monster fierce and strange, with three throats,
>   barks dog-like over those that are emersed in it.
> His eyes are red, his beard greasy and black, his belly
>   wide, and clawed his hands; he clutches the spirits,
> flays, and piecemeal rends them.

Shakespeare's comic characters, as usual, play havoc with traditional mythology. In *Love's Labour's Lost*, Holofernes presents Moth as Hercules with the following pedantic lines:

> Great Hercules is presented by this imp,
> Whose club kill'd Cerberus, that three-headed canus;
> and when he was a babe, a child, a shrimp,
> Thus did he strangle serpents in his manus.
> Quoniam he seemeth in minority,
> Ergo I come with this apology.

Antaeus. Having thus completed the labors assigned him by Eurystheus, Heracles won this chance at immortality. But before telling how the imaginative Greeks set the stage for his dramatic apotheosis, mention must be made of several incidental labors which have not yet been woven into the narrative of the canonical twelve. On his way to procure the golden apples of the Hesperides, Heracles passed through Libya where he was met by Antaeus (the Hostile or Hateful One). He was the son of Gaea (Earth) and Poseidon, a giant of a man who not only challenged all those he met to a wrestling match, but who also used the skulls of his victims to build a temple in honor of his father. Antaeus' strength lay in his contact with his mother, and he was invincible as long as he touched the earth. Heracles discovered the source of his strength and overcame his antagonist by lifting him up from the earth and crushing him in the air. Later writers relate that the tomb of Antaeus was a man-shaped hill near the town of Tingis in Morocco, and that when the Roman Quintus Sertorius opened the supposed grave of Antaeus, he found a skeleton of sixty cubits (c. 90 feet). He was so struck with horror that he had it immediately covered again. The story of the mythical wrestling match attracted the artist-sculptor Antonio Pollaiuolo (1432–1498) who turned it into a piece of sculpture and a painting. Tintoretto also portrayed the struggle on canvas. In *Paradise Regained*, Milton uses the tale for a heroic simile to describe Satan's amazement when Christ's divinity is revealed:

> As when Earth's son Antaeus (to compare
> Small things with greatest) in Irassa strove
> With Jove's Alcides, and oft foiled still rose,
> Receiving from his mother Earth new strength,
> Fresh from his fall, and fiercer grapple joined,
> Throttled at length in the air, expired and fell . . .

Lityerses. During the same expedition, but this time in Phrygia, Heracles met another deadly antagonist, Lityerses, who was said to be the illegitimate son of King Midas. Like many of his ilk, he received all strangers kindly but then forced them to a deadly duel. His macabre device was to compel all those who passed his fields to help him reap the harvest, and when he outstripped them in the task, he mowed off their heads in the evening and hid their bodies in the sheaves of grain. This was done to the accompaniment of a song, a Lityerses-song, a literary version of which the Hellenistic poet Theocritus gives us in his tenth idyll. The story is told in other accounts of how the ideal Sicilian shepherd Daphnis loved a young girl named Piplea who was carried off by robbers. He followed them to Phrygia where he found her in the clutches of Lityerses. In order to win back his love, Daphnis took up the ogre's challenge to reap until one defeated the other, but he was no match for

Lityerses. Just as he was about to be put to death, Heracles appeared and saved the day by beating Lityerses at his own game. He cut off the head of his "grim reaper" and threw it into the Maeander river. Matthew Arnold recalls this episode between Lityerses and Daphnis in his poem *Thyrsis* a monody mourning the death of the poet Arthur Hugh Clough:

> Thou hearest the immortal chants of old!
> Putting his sickle to the perilous grain
> In the hot cornfield of the Phrygian king,
> For thee the Lityerses-song again
> Young Daphnis with his silver voice doth sing.

Cacus.   As the cult of Heracles gained acceptance among the Romans, adventures of the Greek hero were linked to their local traditions. Pallas, who gave his name to the best-known of the seven hills of Rome, the Palatine, is made a son of his by Evander's daughter. Hercules—it is now appropriate to use his Roman name—was on his way back to Greece with the cattle of Geryon. He was passing through the site destined to be the great city of Rome when the cave-dwelling monster Cacus stole some of his bulls and cows. He dragged them to his cave on the Aventine hill by their tails, thereby reversing their tracks and leaving no clue. This Cacus was a son of Vulcan, the god of volcanic fire, and was himself a fire-breathing demon. Hercules was on the point of continuing his journey without being aware of the theft, when he heard the stolen cattle bellowing from within the cave. Cacus blocked the entrance with a huge stone, but Hercules, undaunted, tore a gaping hole in the roof of the cave. Cacus met the hero with a volley of stones and belched forth flame and smoke from his jaws. Hercules flung himself through the fire, seized the troglodyte, applied his famous wrestling hold, "the knot of Hercules," and squeezed him to death. He freed his cattle and dragged Cacus into the daylight. Evander, who then ruled over the country, showed his gratitude by dedicating an altar, the Ara Maxima, to Hercules and thereby established his cult at Rome.

Heracles' Later Life and Apotheosis.   With Heracles' labors in hand, we pick up the story of the dramatic conclusion to the hero's life. He went to Oechalia where king Eurytus, who had taught Heracles the art of archery, had promised him his daughter Iole in marriage if he could best him and his sons in shooting with bow and arrow. Heracles engaged in the contest and, naturally, succeeded in demonstrating his superiority. Eurytus, however, refused to give his daughter to a man who had killed his children. Complications arose between the two which resulted in Heracles' having another fit of madness, and this time he killed the king's son Iphitus. In spite of being purified of the homicide, a severe illness sent him to Delphi to seek a cure with the help of the oracle. When the Pythian priestess refused to answer the question put to her, Heracles fought with Apollo (p. 119), and the two of them were not separated until Zeus let loose a bolt of lightning which settled the matter. Finally, the oracle advised Heracles to serve King Eurytus for a number of years: otherwise he would be sold as a slave and the money used to compensate Eurytus for the loss of his son. The hero was then sold to Omphale, a queen of Lydia and the widow of Tmolus. During this phase of his career, Heracles was said to have been forced to wear women's clothes and to perform household duties while Omphale dressed herself in his lionskin and carried his club. Later narrators, particularly Roman poets, delighted in elaborating on this part of Heracles' life; scholars, however,

Figure 65.   Heracles battles with the river-god Acheloüs for the hand of Deianira. The horn which Heracles breaks off will become the Cornucopia, the Horn of Plenty. *Vase painting. British Museum.*

see in it either a kind of marriage rite in which partners exchanged clothing, or the reflection of an oriental cult in which a goddess is served by an effeminate consort. Be that as it may, Heracles was not prevented from performing additional feats of bravery while a slave to the Lydian queen.

Following his service to Omphale, Heracles took part in various military expeditions—the one against Troy fits into this period of his life—until he came to Calydon, where he demanded Deianira (Deianeira or Dejanira) as his wife. She was the daughter of Oeneus and the sister of Meleager who would win a name for himself in the Calydonian hunt. Deianira, however, was also being wooed by the river-god Acheloüs who claimed to be the lord of the greatest and oldest river in Greece. The two suitors engaged in a wrestling match for the hand of Deianira. Achelous attempted to wriggle out of Heracles' grip by changing his shape, first into a serpent and then into a bull. Heracles held on fast, and seizing him by one of his horns (fig. 65), threw him with such force that the horn was broken off. According to the Roman poet Ovid, the Naiads made off with the horn, filled it with fruits and flowers, and offered it to the goddess of Plenty. It was adopted by her as her symbol, the Cornucopia, the self-replenishing Horn of Plenty.

Thus Heracles won his second wife. But, as it so often happened in the hero's life, he killed someone, and even though the victim's father pardoned him, Heracles had to go into exile. While traveling with his wife Deianira, they came to a river where the centaur Nessus offered to carry them across for a small fee. Heracles needed no help to ford the river, but he gave his wife to Nessus to be carried across. Nessus, lusty centaur that he was, attempted to use her for his own pleasure. When Heracles heard her screams, he attacked the centaur and mortally wounded him (figs. 66, 67). Before he died, Nessus persuaded Deianira to take some of his blood, assuring her that it was a potent love charm. Later, when Heracles invaded Oechalia and took his revenge upon Eurytus by carrying off Iole, Deianira feared for her marriage. Believing that she possessed the means to keep her husband's love, she steeped a ceremonial robe of his in the blood of the centaur and gave it to Lichas, a messenger who had come to Trachis to get the sacrificial garment for Heracles. No sooner did the robe become warm on the body of Heracles, when the poison—Nessus' blood was no love charm but a fatal poison—began to work and caused him excruciating agony. He tried to wrench off the garment, but it stuck to his flesh and even tore off whole pieces from his body. Maddened by the pain, he

Figure 66. Heracles killing the centaur Nessus for attempting to ravish Deianira. *Vase painting. British Museum.*

Figure 67. Pablo Picasso's rendering of Heracles killing the centaur Nessus. *Lithograph, 1931, illustrating Ovid's* Metamorphoses. *Spencer Collection, The New York Public Library, Astor, Lenox and Tilden Foundation.*

threw Lichas, who had brought him the instrument of his pain, into the sea. Heracles knew that his end was near. He had himself taken to Mount Oeta in Trachis where he built a great pyre and laid himself upon it. As the funeral pyre blazed up, there was a flash of lightning, and amid peals of thunder, a cloud passed under his body and bore him to Mount Olympus. In the home of the gods, Heracles was honored with immortality—a gift given to no other man—and Zeus persuaded Hera to become reconciled with him and to give him their daughter Hebe as his Olympian wife. Prior to his immolation, Deianira, overwhelmed by the tragic consequences of her love, hanged herself.

The tortured end of Heracles by the unwitting hand of Deianira became the subject of Sophocles' tragedy *Trachiniae* (The Women of Trachis), a play of uncertain date. Four hundred years later, the same theme was treated, but with far less dramatic and emotional appeal, by Seneca, the Roman philosopher and dramatist. His *Hercules Oetaeus* (Hercules on Mount Oeta) is burdened with rhetorical bombast, portentous speeches demonstrating how Hercules endured and was superior to the pain that was killing him. The poisoned robe and the agony it caused Heracles also provided poets with an allusion for unendurable pain. Mark Antony, whose family claimed descent from Anton, a son of Heracles, could appropriately cry out in Shakespeare's *Antony and Cleopatra* when all was lost:

> The shirt of Nessus is upon me. Teach me,
> Alcides, thou mine ancestor, thy rage.
> Let me lodge Lichas on the horns o' the moon
> And with those hands that grasp'd the heaviest club
> Subdue my worthiest self.

The robe that became a shirt in Shakespeare is picked up by T. S. Eliot for *Little Gidding*, the final poem of his *Four Quartets*:

> Love is the unfamiliar Name
> Behind the hands that wove
> The intolerable shirt of flame
> Which human power cannot remove.

And when Milton wanted to describe the wild uproar of Hell in *Paradise Lost*, he compared it to the dying agony of Hercules:

> As when Alcides, from Oechalia crowned
> With conquest, felt the envenomed robe, and tore
> Through pain up by the roots Thessalian pines,
> And Lichas from the top of Oeta threw
> Into the Euboic sea.

Thus ended the eventful and stormy career of Greece's most popular hero. His end was tragic, and yet, by the agency of fire, it spelled the beginning of a new life among the immortals. Before he died, he left his bow and arrows to Poeas, or to his son Philoctetes, for having lighted the pyre which burned away his mortal nature. Heracles' arrows were later deemed a necessary token for the downfall of Troy. To Hyllus, his son by Deianira, he gave his captive concubine Iole with the command that he marry her when he reach manhood. According to legend, Heracles had at least seventy sons, fifty by the daughters of King Thespius and another twenty by various women in his life. His legendary virility extended even to Mount

Olympus where Hebe bore him two sons. But however prolific Heracles may have been, he left no ruling dynasty even though kings and peoples claimed descent from him. Stories were told of how Eurystheus threatened the children of Heracles with death and forced them to flee for their lives. It was only the work of genealogists that connected the coming of the Dorians with the descendants of Heracles.

Heracles' greatest legacy was not to politics but to art; from before the sixth century B.C. to the present, sculptors and painters, in all kind of media and in all periods, have portrayed the hero and his deeds and his agonies. Homer was also aware of the heaven and hell of Heracles: his Odysseus reports seeing his phantom in the gloomy realm of Hades, "but as for himself, he takes his pleasure at banqueting among the deathless gods, and has as his wife slim-ankled Hebe, the daughter of almighty Zeus and Hera of the golden sandals."

The tragedy of the man turned god can take yet another turn. In one of the latest adaptations of the legend, Archibald MacLeish gives us a parable of modern man who is capable of astonishing scientific accomplishments but who insanely ignores simple humanity. His poetic drama, *Herakles* (1967), borrows themes largely from Euripides' *Hercules Furens* (c. 416 B.C.) in which the hero returns to Thebes after overcoming Cerberus, only to be driven mad and kill his children by Megara. MacLeish presents not only the modern scientist in conflict with his wife over the loss of their son (Heracles versus Megara), but he also introduces a vision in which Megara waits for Heracles to reach the oracle and learn his future. Like the scientist, Heracles is both victorious and accursed, and the oracle reveals to him what he has done in his madness: he fancied his sons as his enemies and killed them. He has played god and conquered death, but it is the conquest of death without the equally important conquest of the soul.

2. The House of Minos

Europa and the Bull. One genealogical tributary has given us Danaus and his many descendants; the other takes us to the offspring of Agenor and the dynasties sprung from Cadmus and Europa (p. 289). Agenor, the king of Phoenicia and the twin brother of Belus, had a beautiful daughter Europa. This is according to popular tradition even though Homer calls her the daughter of Phoenix, son of Agenor. Zeus, who was so often attracted to feminine beauty, fell passionately in love with Europa and desired her. He sent his messenger Hermes to drive the king's cattle down to the seashore where Europa and her companions were playing. Since, as Ovid puts it "majesty and love do not mix well," Zeus put aside his lightning and his royal scepter. He then transformed himself into a magnificent white bull and mingled among cattle grazing near Europa. At first the young girl was frightened, but gradually she lost her fear, caressed him, and even put garlands of newly-plucked flowers on his horns. Innocently enough, Europa sat on the back of this wondrous creature. Slowly, with the young girl on his back, the bull made his way to the shore, plunged into the sea and made off with his prize.

Arriving in Crete, Zeus shed his disguise and confessed his divinity to Europa. Beside a spring near Gortyn, the two were joined in love; the plane trees that shaded them were granted the privilege of never losing their leaves. Europa gave the Olympian three sons: Minos, Rhadamanthys, and Sarpedon. The bull which had served as the Olympian's disguise was placed in heaven as the constellation Taurus. Zeus also presented Europa with three gifts: a bronze robot, Talos, who guarded

Figure 68. Zeus in the form of a bull carrying off Europa. *Metope from a temple in Selinus, c. 550 B.C. National Museum, Palermo. (Alinari)*

the shores of Crete against hostile invaders; a dog that would never let its prey escape; and a hunting spear that would always hit its mark. He then married Europa to Asterius, king of Crete, who adopted her children. At her death, this favorite of Zeus was accorded divine honors and was worshiped as a goddess.

The story of the abduction of Europa was rationalized by Herodotus as one of the "historical" incidents between the Greeks and the Asians that ultimately erupted into the Persian Wars. The transformation of Zeus into a bull was seen as a raiding expedition of Greeks from Crete, who came to the Phoenician shore and abducted the king's daughter, a tit for tat since the Phoenicians had abducted Io. Later, the Hellenistic poet Moschus (fl. 150 B.C.) turned the tale into an idyll with the title *Europa*, a romance filled with verbal furbelows. The romantic elements of the story also held an attraction for Ovid who used it for an episode in the *Metamorphoses*. In yet later literature Spenser describes the scene of Europa's abduction in *Muiopotmos*; Arachne (pp. 171–172) weaves the story of this illicit love and shows

> how the Olympian deceived
> Europa like a Bull, and on his backe
> Her through the sea did beare; so lively scene
> That it true Sea, and true Bull ye would weene;

Herman Melville saw in this ancient story a comparison between his white whale and the white bull into which Zeus had transformed himself for lascivious purposes. This is from his chapter on "The Whiteness of the Whale" in *Moby Dick*:

A gentle joyousness—a mighty mildness of repose in swiftness, invested the gliding whale. Not the white bull Jupiter swimming away with ravished Europa clinging to his graceful horns; his lovely, leering eyes sideways intent upon the maid; with smooth bewitching fleetness, rippling straight for the nuptial bower in Crete; not Jove, not that great majesty Supreme! did surpass the glorified White Whale as he so divinely swam.

In art, the "rape" of Europa was represented on one of the metopes of a temple in Sicily (fig. 68) and the Sicyon Treasury at Delphi, both of the sixth century B.C. A wall painting from Pompeii on the theme has survived the destruction of the city in A.D. 79. We also possess representations from the hands of such famous artists of the Renaissance as Cellini, Titian, Tintoretto, Veronese, Rubens, and Rembrandt; in more recent times, from Boucher and Bonnard.

Minos. Following the deaths of Europa and Asterius, Minos became king of Crete. Some accounts would interpose two generations and make another Minos— son of Lycastus who in turn was the son of the first Minos—the successor to his great-grandparent's realm. Homer and Hesiod, however, know only of one Minos, and on the whole the same legendary material holds for either Minos I or Minos II. From this descendant of Europa and Zeus we derive the word "Minoan," a historical term used to describe the Bronze Age civilization of the Aegean prior to the arrival of the Greeks. And as early as Thucydides in the fifth century B.C., we hear of Minos as a powerful ruler, a thalassocrat, whose navy ruled the Aegean and kept piracy in check. Behind this tradition may lie a historical reminiscence of the one-time greatness of the Minoan civilization. The reputation of Minos as an able and just administrator, one whom Zeus himself instructed in jurisprudence, earned for him a place as a distinguished judge in the Underworld. The same was true of his brother Rhadamanthys (p. 245). The third brother, Sarpedon, fought as an ally of Priam in the Trojan War, an anachronism that was overcome by claiming that he lived for three generations. In later times, Attic legend-makers blackened the character of Minos and turned him into a villain, a possible reflection of a time during the Late Bronze Age (1600–1400 B.C.) when Cretan power over Attica was contested. The close connection between Athens and Crete will soon be seen in the relationship of the legendary hero Theseus with members of Minos' family.

Minos was married to the daughter of the sun-god Helios, Pasiphaë, who bore him a number of sons and daughters, of whom Ariadne, Phaedra and Androgeus are mythologically important. When Minos competed for supremacy in Crete, he claimed that the gods had destined him to rule, and to prove this he said that anything he prayed for would be done. As he was offering up a sacrifice to Poseidon, Minos prayed that a bull might come forth from the sea, and he promised to sacrifice the animal to the god. A beautiful bull appeared in answer to his prayer and Minos became king of Crete. But Minos so admired the bull that he could not bring himself to sacrifice it. Instead, he hid the animal in his own herd and substituted another in its place. Poseidon was furious with the king for failing to fulfill his vow, and to punish him the god made Pasiphaë conceive a passion for the bull.

The Minotaur. Now it so happened that the Leonardo da Vinci of the ancient world was then in Crete. His name was Daedalus, and he was a renowned Athenian artist, architect, and master-craftsman. He had had to flee Athens with his son Icarus because in a fit of jealous rage he had killed his nephew Perdix (sometimes given as Calos or Talos) for having invented the saw and the potter's wheel. He found sanctuary in Crete and put his talents at the disposal of the royal family. So that Pasiphaë could satisfy her bestial passion, Daedalus devised a wooden cow. The resultant issue was the Minotaur, "the Minos bull," which had the body of a man but the head of a bull (fig. 78). To house this monster, Daedalus built the labyrinth, a complex maze from which no one could escape, at least not until Theseus managed to do so with the help of Ariadne and Daedalus. In his labyrinthine home, the Minotaur fed on the human flesh of young men and women who were sent to Minos as tribute, a practice that Theseus, as we shall presently see, brought to a dramatic end. (The world "labyrinth" is probably pre-Greek and connected with *labrys*, the sacred double ax of Crete; the maze itself is a widespread phenomenon associated with ritual trials and initiations of various sorts. Apart from the probable link between the Minotaur and the bull-cult on Minoan Crete, little can be said with certainty as to the original significance of this carnivorous semihuman beast.)

Daedalus and Icarus. For having helped Theseus put an end to the Minotaur, or for having helped Pasiphaë consummate her passion, Minos imprisoned Daedalus in the very labyrinth he had built to house the monster. Pasiphaë helped free the famed craftsman, but since Minos controlled all the ships on the coast of Crete, Daedalus had no means of escaping from his island prison. He faced the challenge and, as Ovid put it, "he turned his mind to arts unknown." Daedalus fashioned a pair of wings out of feathers, twine and wax, and then fastened them on his shoulders. He did the same for his son Icarus. Before setting out, he warned Icarus to follow his lead and not to fly too high or else the sun would melt the wax on his wings. Daedalus made a successful flight over the Aegean and landed safely in Sicily. But Icarus, with adolescent disregard of his father's advice, felt the thrill of bird-like-flight and flew too close to the sun. The wax on his wings melted and down he plunged into the sea off the eastern coast of Greece(fig. 69), a sea that thenceforth bore the name of the young man, the Icarian Sea. In Sicily, Daedalus came under the protection of Cocalus, king of the Sicani, and during his stay on the island he put his artistic and engineering skills to use for his benefactor. Minos, however, pursued Daedalus to Sicily only to meet his end there: the daughters of Cocalus murdered him by pouring boiling water or pitch on him; or, according to another account, Cocalus received him hospitably, murdered him in a bath, and then gave out the report that his guest had drowned. Thus the unhappy end of Minos.

As early as Homer, Daedalus was the prototype and synonym for artists and art. Socrates, himself a sculptor as his father before him, claimed descent from this Athenian progenitor of artists. In Greek, Daedalus' name was also used as a common noun or adjective (*daidalos*), meaning "artistically wrought" or "artistic"— hence Shelley's "cups of wrought and daedal gold." And in antiquity, statues made of wood and those that were believed to move, were attributed to this father of the arts. Similarly, such innovations in sculpture as the opening of the eyes, the extending of the arms free from their sides, and the opening of the distance between the

Figure 69.   Matisse. Falling Icarus.
Lithograph, 1947, from Jazz. Museum
of Modern Art, New York.

feet were said to have been due to his genius. In other fields, Daedalus was given credit for having constructed reservoirs, labyrinths, and temples. He was also the reputed inventor of carpentry—taught to him by Athena according to legend—and of the tools associated with that craft; in naval architecture, his was the invention of the mast and sailyards.

*   *   *   *

Later Greek writers, such as Lucian of Samosata (A.D. 120), saw in Daedalus a great master of astrology who taught the science to his son. The tragic fall of Icarus was rationalized as a metaphysical one: Icarus soared above ordinary truths into transcendental mysteries where he lost his reason and drowned in a sea of difficulties. (André Gide's Icarus is also a metaphysician; in Gide's *Thesée* he is a victim of soaring too close to Platonic truths.) As for Pasiphaë, she was a disciple of Daedalus in the arcane art of astrology, and the bull to which she was attracted was the constellation Taurus. Still later writers allegorized Icarus, as they had Phaethon and his unsuccessful flight through space, as presumption and rashness. In *3 Henry VI*, Shakespeare has Gloucester (later the infamous Richard III) express a similar thought when he replies to the king on the death of his son:

> Why, what a peevish fool was that of Crete
> That taught his son the office of the fowl!
> And yet, for all his wings, the fool was drown'd.

King Henry pursues the metaphor by comparing himself to Daedalus, Richard Plantagenet to Minos, his son Edward to the sun, and his other son Richard (Gloucester) to the sea:

> I, Daedalus; my poor boy, Icarus;
> Thy father, Minos, that denied our course;
> The sun that sear'd the wings of my sweet boy,
> Thy brother Edward; and thyself, the sea
> Whose envious gulf did swallow up his life.

The fate of Icarus was seen in another light by the painter Pieter Brueghel the Elder (1520–1569). In the eighth book of the *Metamorphoses*, Ovid had described the amazement of a fisherman, a shepherd, and a plowman when they saw Daedalus and Icarus flying through the sky, an event which they interpreted as an epiphany of the gods. Brueghel inverted Ovid's theme by placing the emphasis on the humble peasants who continue the labors without even a glance at the sky or at Icarus, the latter reduced to an insignificant figure that had fallen into the sea in which only his legs and his loosened wings could be seen. The *Landscape with the Fall of Icarus* (fig. 70) is seen by some as the visual representation of the proverb that no plow stops for the man who dies. W. H. Auden picks up the theme from Brueghel to illustrate man's indifference to man. In his *Musee des Beaux Arts* (1945), he writes:

> In Brueghel's *Icarus*, for example: how everything turns away
> Quite leisurely from the disaster: the ploughman may
> Have heard the splash, the forsaken cry,
> But for him it was not an important failure; the sun shone
> As it had to on the white legs disappearing into the green
> Water; and the expensive delicate ship that must have seen
> Had somewhere to get to and sailed calmly on.

Figure 70.   Pieter Brueghel. Landscape with the fall of Icarus. *Painting,*
c. 1558. Royal Museum, Brussels.

The one modern writer who has made the legend of Daedalus and Icarus his own is James Joyce. Seeing himself as the master-craftsman and innovator in letters and thought, a rebel and esthete—that and much more—he takes the name of Stephen Dedalus as the hero of his largely autobiographical novels. The epigraph to his *A Portrait of the Artist as a Young Man* (1916) is the line from Ovid's *Metamorphoses* referring to Daedalus' plan of action after Minos refused him leave to return to Athens: *dixit, et ignotas animum dimittit in artes* (he spoke and turned his mind to arts unknown). And the last line of the novel is an invocation to his patron Daedalus, as Joyce plans to flee Dublin for the Continent where he would soar into the unknown: "Old father, old artificer, stand me now and ever in good stead."

The labyrinth which this modern Daedalus set out to construct was the revolutionary *Ulysses* (1922) and *Finnegans Wake* (1939), two novels which were mazes of intricate literary and legendary, philosophical and personal allusions. In the former, the legend of Daedalus is not forgotten. Stephen's return to Dublin from Paris in response to his father's telegram that his mother was dying is turned into a touching allusion in which Stephen is cross-referenced both as Daedalus and Icarus:

> "Fabulous artificer, the hawklike man. You flew. Whereto? Newhaven-Dieppe, Steer-age passenger. Paris and back. Lapwing. Icarus. *Pater, ait.* Seabedraggled, fallen, weltering. Lapwing you are. Lapwing he."

In literature and in the arts, Pasiphaë and her half-human offspring were to become symbols of varying dimensions. In the *Inferno*, Dante and his guide found the entrance of the seventh circle of Hell occupied by the Minotaur, "the infamy of Crete, / Which was conceived in the false cow," a symbol of bloodthirsty violence and brutality of those who were punished below. Boccaccio, on the other hand, introduced a novel allegorized interpretation of Pasiphaë and the bull in his *Genealogy of the Gods*. Pasiphaë, a daughter of the Sun (Helios), is the soul, the child of God, and the true Sun. Her husband Minos, king and judge, is human reason, which

Figure 71.   Picasso. Minotauromachy. *Etching, 1935. Museum of Modern Art, New York.*

by its laws governs the soul and conducts it along the right path. Venus—Boccaccio follows a version which makes Aphrodite the cause of Pasiphaë's passion—is concupiscence and carnality, the enemy of the soul. The bull is the sensual delights of this world, and when the soul unites with mundane pleasures, the vice of bestiality, the Minotaur, comes into being.

Turning from the medieval to the modern, the prolific French writer Henry de Montherlant portrays Pasiphaë as yielding to the bull. He sees in her the rebel who is contemptuous of the moral code of the petty bourgeoisie. But his *Pasiphaé* is probably more notable for its illustrations by Henri Matisse in 1944 and Jean Cocteau in 1948. Another French artist, André Masson, whose influence spread to the United States, painted a violent and emotional *Pasiphaë* (1943); earlier, he had portrayed a surrealistic *Labyrinth* (1938), a labyrinth which exists within a monstrous Minotaur. Above all others, Pablo Picasso took the Minotaur as his own iconographic symbol, particularly during the 1930s. It was at that time that he illustrated the Skira edition of Ovid's *Metamorphoses* and provided the cover design for *Minotaure*, the magazine of the surrealists founded in 1933. In 1935 he finished his etching *Minotauromachy* (fig. 71), in which the bull-man stands out with imposing brutality amid other symbols of light and hope. In other graphic works, the symbolism of Picasso's bull-man broadens so that it covers not only savage insensate force, but also passion, pathos, ambivalence, and the bull in man.

3. The House of Cadmus

The abduction of Europa by Zeus touches off another cycle of tales that has the city of Thebes at its hub: Cadmus and the founding of Thebes; the birth and death and resurrection of Dionysus; the tragedy of the Labdacid dynasty which engulfs Oedipus and his offspring; and the downfall of Thebes in one of the great wars of Greek legend. This complex of legends and genealogies has its start in Phoenicia where Agenor, the father of Europa, was greatly disturbed at the sudden disappearance of his daughter. He commanded his sons to search for Europa and not to return home until they had found her. The only son who took this charge seriously was Cadmus; the other two, Phoenix and Cilix, never left the eastern shore of the Mediterranean. Phoenix gave his name to Phoenicia and its people; Cilix was the eponym for Cilicia and the Cilicians.

The Founding of Thebes. Cadmus and his mother Telephassa, on their mission to find Europa, arrived in Thrace and settled there. When Telephassa died, Cadmus went to Apollo's oracle at Delphi to make further inquiries as to the whereabouts of his sister. The god advised him to give up the search and instead to follow a cow with certain markings until the animal would fall down with fatigue. Cadmus found the cow in Phocis and tracked it into Boeotia (Cowland). On the spot where the animal sank down with weariness, Cadmus founded the city of Thebes with its acropolis Cadmea. When he set about to sacrifice the cow to Athena, he sent some people for water to a nearby spring of Ares, a spring that was guarded by a dragon, the son of the war-god. The dragon killed the men, and Cadmus in turn killed the dragon (fig. 72). On the advice of Athena he sowed the teeth of the dragon, and up sprang a crop of armed warriors. Cadmus threw a stone into their midst; a battle broke out in which all but five were killed. These five—Echion (Snake-man), Udaeus (Ground-man), Chthonius (Earth-man), Hyperenor (Superman or Overbearing), Pelorus (Monster)—helped Cadmus build the city. They were called *Spartoi*, the Sown Men, and legend had it that they were the ancestors of the five leading families of Thebes.

For having killed the dragon, Cadmus was compelled to serve Ares for an "eternal" year, or probably, eight common years, the usual period of banishment for a homicide. After having served his time, Athena established Cadmus as ruler over Thebes, and Zeus gave him Harmonia, the daughter of Aphrodite and Ares, as his wife. On the occasion of the wedding, said to have been the very first celebrated in Greece, all the gods came down from heaven to attend the union of Cadmus and Harmonia. The Muses and the Charites (Graces) provided the music and sang,

Figure 72.   Cadmus killing the dragon.
Vase painting. Louvre.

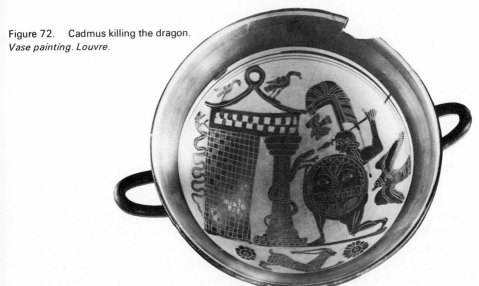

according to Theogonis (fl. 544–541 B.C.): "A beautiful thing is lovable; nothing is lovable which is not beautiful." (Two thousand years later, this thought was put into English by Keats as "A thing of beauty is a joy forever.") Cadmus gave his bride a *peplos*, akind of cloak or outer robe, and a necklace which was crafted by the god Hephaestus. These two wedding gifts were to follow the tragic house of Cadmus down to its very end. In time, Hermonia gave Cadmus four daughters (Semele, Autonoë, Ino, Agave) and a son Polydorus.

Legend made Cadmus a culture-hero in that he is given credit for having introduced into the Greek world the alphabet, the art of mining, and the worship of Dionysus. After the death of their grandson Pentheus at the hands of Agave, Cadmus and Harmonia left Thebes and settled in the western part of Greece where they reigned over the people. A son of their late age, Illyrius, gave his name to the region, Illyria, and to its people. Finally, Cadmus and Harmonia were turned into serpents, and Zeus sent them to the Greek paradise, Elysium.

In *Paradise Lost*, Milton cites the story of the serpentine transformation of this primeval couple to illustrate the beauty of the snake in Eden with which Satan had disguised himself: none lovelier, "not those that in Illyria chang'd/Hermione [= Harmonia] and Cadmus." Matthew Arnold picks up the story as a song sung by Callicles in *Empedocles on Aetna*, an idyllic picture of happiness following grief and calamity:

> There those two live, far in the Illyrian brakes.
> They had stay'd long enough to see,
> In Thebes, the billow of calamity
> Over their own dear children roll'd,
> Curse upon curse, pang upon pang,
> For years, they sitting helpless in their home,
> A grey old man and woman; yet of old
> The Gods had to their marriage come,
> And at the banquet all the Muses sang.
>
> Therefore they did not end their days
> In sight of blood; but were rapt, far away,
> To where the west-wind plays,
> And murmurs of the Adriatic come
> To those untrodden mountain-lawns; and there
> Placed safely in changed forms, the pair
> Wholly forget their first sad life, and home,
> And all that Theban woe, and stray
> For ever through the glens, placid and dumb.

The Daughters of Cadmus. The daughters of Cadmus, as we have already seen, were fated to have unenviable lives. Semele, who was wooed and won by Zeus, had to endure Hera's antagonism and the Olympian's thunderbolts, before her son Dionysus brought her up from the Underworld. Agave, married to one of the *Spartoi*, Echion, rejected the worship of Dionysus, only to be driven mad and to cause the death of her son Pentheus. Autonoë was the mother of Actaeon, the young man who was unfortunate enough to see Artemis bathing and who was punished for it by being torn apart by his hunting dogs. Ino and her husband Athamas were punished for having given refuge to the newborn Dionysus with the result that they killed their two children Melicertes and Learchus. Another story is told about Ino. When Hera drove Ino into a Dionysiac frenzy, she rushed out of the house and was away so long that Athamas thought she was dead. Not long after, Athamas took Themisto as his wife. Soon after his new wife had borne him twin sons, Ino returned with her sanity restored. Athamas placed her in his household as the nurse for his children. Themisto soon discovered the identity of the new nurse and resolved to do away with Ino's two children. She ordered her children to be dressed in white and Ino's in black, intending to have her servants kill the two with clothes of mourning. But in true folktale style, Ino, becoming suspicious of Themisto's sudden interest in how the children were to be dressed, reversed the color scheme. As a result, Themisto's children were killed, and Themisto committed suicide when she discovered to her horror that her own children had been murdered. It is then, according to this account, that Hera drove both Ino and Athamas to madness and to murder their children Melicertes and Learchus. Among the many variants to this story—it was a very popular one among Greek poets and dramatists—Ino is said to have been transformed into Leucothea, the White Goddess, and her son Melicertes into a god with the name of Palaemon.

There is yet another myth concerning Ino and Athamas that needs to be told since it provides part of the background for the cycle of tales revolving about Jason and the Argonauts. It is the story of Athamas' first marriage to Nephele (Cloud), a story that is probably connected with Orchomenus, a rival city of Thebes. According to Greek tradition, it was founded by the Minyans, one of the earliest Hellenic tribes to migrate into Thessaly and other parts of Greece. Athamas, it must be remembered, was a son of Aeolus, a brother of Salmoneus, the forefather of Jason and a probable rainmaking wizard. The story of Athamas and Nephele may also in origin have had something to do with a rainmaking rite in which the fleece of a sheep was used to attract dew; but as is so often the case, the ritual was forgotten and the myth was overlaid with aetiologies and folktale motifs—particularly that of the wicked or jealous stepmother—wthich runs throughout the stories associated with Ino and Athamas.

Phrixus and Helle. Athamas was first married to Nephele who bore him a son Phrixus and a daughter Helle. He later married Ino, daughter of Cadmus, who also bore him two children, Learchus and Melicertes. Ino hated the children of Nephele and was determined to destroy them. She contrived to have the women roast the seed-grain causing a famine in the land. When Athamas sent messengers to Delphi to inquire as to the means of averting the famine, Ino bribed them to bring back word from the god that only by the sacrifice of Phrixus, or of both Phrixus and Helle, could the land be saved from infertility and famine. When the people demanded that Athamas comply with the false oracle, Nephele appeared and rescued her children by means of a golden-fleeced ram which carried them magically to the eastern land of Colchis. On the way, Helle lost her grip and fell into the body of water which ever after bore her name, the Hellespont, modern-day Dardanelles. Phrixus successfully completed his flight to Colchis where he was welcomed by King Aeëtes, the brother of Pasiphaë and the father of Medea. Phrixus sacrificed the ram to Zeus and hung its golden fleece in a grove which was guarded by a dragon. There it remained until Jason, with Medea's help, killed the dragon and recovered the fleece. As for Athamas and Ino, they and their children had to face the wrath of Hera and the end reported in most other versions of the tale.

Figure 73. The Farnese Bull. The punishment of Dirce by Amphion and Zethus. *Marble group, second-first century B.C. National Museum, Naples. (Alinari)*

Amphion and Zethus. So much for the fate of the daughters of Cadmus. Of Cadmus' only son Polydorus there is virtually no mythology, except that he left an heir, Labdacus, the father of Laius and the grandfather of Oedipus. Labdacus also has an insignificant legendary background, leaving only a son Laius to succeed him. Since Laius was only an infant when his father died, the regency was entrusted to a certain Nycteus whose fortunes were not so notable as those of his daughter Antiope. Antiope—Homer calls her a daughter of the river-god Asopus—was a girl of extraordinary beauty and she naturally attracted the ever-roving eye of Zeus. Zeus took the form of a satyr—very appropriate to a region which was sacred to Dionysus—and made love to the girl. Fearing the anger of her father, Antiope fled and took sanctuary with the king of Sicyon. Nycteus was so shattered and despondent by what had happened to his daughter that he committed suicide; but before doing so he called upon his brother Lycus to avenge him. Lycus marched against Sicyon, killed the king, and brought Antiope back to Boeotia where she gave birth to a famous set of twins, Amphion and Zethus. The twins were then exposed on a mountain where they were discovered by a herdsman who brought them up as his own. Amphion became a gifted musician and played a lyre which was a gift of Hermes. Zethus followed the occupation of his foster-father and spent his time hunting and tending flocks. Antiope, in the meantime, had been cruelly treated by Lycus and his wife Dirce. She had been imprisoned for many years when suddenly and miraculously her chains were loosened. When Amphion and Zethus recognized their long-lost mother, they exacted their revenge by killing Lycus and by tying Dirce to a bull which dragged her about until she, too, was dead.

Other versions tell the story diffierently. Antiope was a wife of Lycus and had been seduced by the king of Sicyon. Dirce, Lycus' second wife, was jealous of Antiope and had her put in chains, but Zeus helped her to escape to Mount Cithaeron where she gave birth to her twin sons. Later Dirce doomed Antiope to be dragged to death by a bull and assigned Amphion and Zethus the task of executing the sentence. Antiope made herself known to her sons, who saw to it that Dirce died by the same punishment she had devised for their hapless mother.

The punishment of Dirce became a theme for the sculptor of the noted Farnese Bull, prime example of Hellenistic art of the second and first century B.C. (fig. 73). It was discovered in a badly preserved state in the Baths of Caracalla in 1546, and was restored considerably by a number of sculptors. The ancient work bears the names of Apollonius and Tauriscus of Tralles, but it is generally conceded to be a product of the Rhodian school of sculpture. Later artists also illustrated the story of Antiope: Correggio (c. 1525) painted a sleeping Antiope; Titian (c. 1560) and Watteau (1684–1721) portrayed Jupiter (as a satyr) and Antiope; and David (c. 1768) a Jupiter and Antiope.

With Lycus dead, Amphion and Zethus took possession of Thebes and set about fortifying the city. Zethus hefted huge boulders on his shoulders. Not so Amphion. By the magic melody of his voice and his lyre, he moved stones not only to where they were wanted, but he also had them fit themselves together so as to form a wall. Amphion afterwards married Niobe, the daughter of Tantalus, by whom he had numerous children, only to have them taken from him when Niobe boasted to Leto of the size of her brood (pp. 159–160). Some say that he killed himself when he heard of the loss of his children; others that he was killed by Apollo's arrows when he stormed the temple of the god in reprisal for what Leto's son had done to him.

The magic melody of Amphion's song was taken by Shelley as a symbol of liberty and truth in *The Revolt of Islam* and *Hellas*. Shelley's "Amphionic music" meant something quite different to Tennyson. His *Amphion* is a wistful and somewhat humorous recollection of the power of music in the mythological past:

> O, had I lived when song was great
>   In days of Old Amphion,
> And ta'en my fiddle to the gate,
>   Nor cared for seed or scion!
> And had I lived when song was great,
>   And legs of trees were limber,
> And ta'en my fiddle to the gate,
>   And fiddled in the timber!

At this milepost in the legendary history of Thebes, the pace of events quickens and a succession of misfortunes rapidly overtakes the descendants of Labdacus. With Amphion and Zethus removed from power, Laius, the son of Labdacus, returned to the city of his birth from the Peloponnese where he had been given sanctuary by King Pelops. But Laius had fallen in love with the king's son Chrysippus and had improvidently carried him off, thus providing a moral justification for the tragedy that was to befall him and his family. Pelops put a curse upon the kidnapper: that he might never have an heir; or if he did, that he should die at the hands of his son.

Oedipus.   Back in Thebes and installed as king, Laius married his cousin Jocasta (or Iocaste; Homer calls her Epicaste), daughter of Menoeceus and sister of Creon. When Jocasta failed to conceive, Laius went to the oracle of Apollo at Delphi where he received word that if a son were born to him, he would lose his life by the hand of his own child. Despite the oracle's warning, Laius lay with his wife one night when filled with drink and lust; or according to another account, both Laius and Jocasta were afflicted with madness. When Jocasta gave birth to a son,

Laius was reminded of the oracle. In order to prevent the oracle from being fulfilled, he pierced and pinned the ankles of the infant, and handed the new-born child to a shepherd to be exposed on Mount Cithaeron. It was there that a shepherd in the service of Polybus and Merope (or Periboea), king and queen of Corinth, found him—or had the child given to him by the Theban shepherd—and brought the infant to Merope who herself was childless. Polybus and Merope happily adopted the foundling as their own and gave him the name of Oedipus (Swollen Foot) because of the condition in which he was found.

The years passed and Oedipus grew to manhood. Then an incident occurred, seemingly of little significance, which affected the rest of Oedipus' life. At a banquet, a Corinthian who had had too much to drink taunted him with not being the king's son. Oedipus pressed Polybus and Merope for an answer to the question of his legitimacy, but they could only reassure him that the word of a man in his cups should not be taken seriously. Not satisfied by this reply, Oedipus went to the oracle at Delphi. He put his question to the oracle and received a reply, certainly one that he could never have expected, that he was fated to commit incest with his mother and produce children that would not be tolerated by society. The oracle also prophesied that he would kill his father. Believing Polybus and Merope to be his true parents, Oedipus resolved never to return to Corinth. On the road between Delphi and Daulis, Oedipus came upon Laius and his retinue and a dispute arose over the right of way. When the old man and his charioteer wanted to push Oedipus off the road, he became angry and killed Laius—thereby fulfilling one part of the oracle which had recently been handed to him—and all his retainers with the exception of one man who escaped.

The Riddle of the Sphinx. In the meantime another development had taken place. The celebrated Sphinx (p. 32) made its appearance in the neighborhood of Thebes. This female monster, half-woman and half-lioness, is said by some to have been sent into Boeotia by Hera who was angry with the people of Thebes for not having punished Laius for what he had done to Chrysippus. In any event, the Sphinx would put a riddle to every Theban that passed by, and whoever could not answer the riddle was snatched up and devoured. The Thebans, now beset by a new calamity, made it known that kingship and the hand of Jocasta would be given to the person who would deliver the country of the Sphinx. Oedipus came forward (fig. 74). When he approached the Sphinx, she gave him the riddle: "A being with four feet has two feet and three feet and only one voice; but its feet vary, and when it has most it is weakest." (This is but one of several versions of the same riddle.) Oedipus solved the riddle with the answer of man and his three ages: as an infant, he crawls on all fours, as an adult he goes about on two legs, and as an old man he needs the help of a staff or cane. The Sphinx was so mortified at having her riddle answered that she leaped from her high perch and killed herself on the rocks below. Thus, by killing the equivalent of a dragon, Oedipus attained the full stature of a hero and won a kingdom and the hand of the queen. But in so doing he fulfilled the oracle of Delphi: he married his mother Jocasta and became the father of two sons, Eteocles and Polynices (or Polyneices), and two daughters, Antigone and Ismene. Because of this incestuous marriage, or because the murder of Laius had gone unavenged, Thebes was visited by a plague of enormous proportions, and the entire community—its women, its fields, and its cattle—became sterile and barren.

Figure 74. Oedipus and the Sphinx.
*Vase painting, c. 470 B.C. Vatican
Museum. (Alinari)*

Sophocles' OEDIPUS TYRANNUS. It is at this point in Oedipus' life that Sophocles picks up the story for his *Oedipus Tyrannus,* "Oedipus the King," a monumental literary achievement which overshadows all treatments of the theme past and present, and one which Aristotle admiringly cites in the *Poetics* as a model of dramatic craftsmanship. Ironically enough, the date of the production of Sophocles' masterpiece is unknown; scholars place it somewhere after 430 B.C. Aeschylus had also treated the theme in a trilogy produced in 467 B.C., of which only the *Seven Against Thebes* has survived; the first two plays, *Laius* and *Oedipus,* are no longer extant, nor is the satyr-play *Sphinx* which followed the trilogy. Also lost to us are two epic cycles, conjecturally dated to the eighth century B.C.: the *Thebaid,* said by later writers to have been a work of Homer, and the *Oedipodea,* attributed to a certain Cinaethon. Homer himself briefly alludes to the story of the ill-starred couple in the *Odyssey.* He has Odysseus tell his audience of Phaeacians of the souls of illustrious women of the mythical past whom he saw in Hades' realm:

And I saw the mother of Oedipus, fair Epicaste, who unwittingly committed the dreadful act of marrying her own son, and he had killed his own father and married her. The gods soon let this be known to all. However, by the cruel plan of the gods, Oedipus remained in his beloved Thebes, ruling the people of Cadmus. But Epicaste went down to the house of Hades, the mighty keeper of the gates, and possessed by anguish she tied a noose to a roof-beam high aloft and hung herself. As for Oedipus, she left behind all the pain that the avenging curses of a mother can inflict.

Out of this critical mass of mythological material, Sophocles chose that one day in the life of Oedipus which saw him renowned beyond all others, wide-eyed and eager to help the city in distress, but a day which would see this proud and passionate man gain insight through self-blinding and end with his being a polluted outcast, his mother-wife dead by her own hand, and his innocent children fated to suffer because of the guilt of others. Through his choral odes, Sophocles read men a lesson on the human condition: its instability and its limitations, and Oedipus' fate serving as an illustration of how brief and how deluding life's good fortunes can be. All this was to be taken in the context of man's relationship to deity, for Sophocles reaffirmed for his audience the divine power of Apollo, his oracles, his prophets, and his doctrines.

Sophocles' *Oedipus Tyrannus* opens before the royal palace at Thebes. Oedipus appears as the great king whom the people of Thebes rank second only to the gods. The city is suffering from a devastating plague, and the afflicted people beg him to help as he had in the past when the city was besieged by the Sphinx. Oedipus acknowledges the pleas of his suppliants and informs them that he has sent Creon, the brother of Jocasta, to Delphi to seek the advice of the god. Creon appears with word from Apollo, clear and unambiguous, that the plague will be lifted only when the source of pollution, the murderer of Laius, will be found and driven out of the city. Oedipus then publicly invokes a solemn and deadly curse upon the murderer—without realizing that he is invoking it upon himself—and declares with tragic allusiveness that he shall root him out:

> Since I am now the holder of his office,
> and have his bed and wife that once was his,
> and had his line not been unfortunate
> we would have common children—(fortune leaped
> upon his head)—because of all these things,
> I fight in his defense as for my father.

Oedipus, in his eagerness to help the suffering city, has also sent for the blind seer Tiresias who comes before the king led by a boy. Oedipus calls upon him to use his prophetic skill, but Tiresias is very reluctant to speak. The two of them are soon at loggerheads. Oedipus, infuriated and enraged at Tiresias' refusal, accuses the prophet of being involved in the slaying of Laius. Goaded by the hot-tempered king, Tiresias blurts out that he, Oedipus, is the cause of the land's pollution. Scarcely believing his ears, the king calls upon the seer to repeat his accusation, which he does in even more explicit terms. Oedipus, now beside himself with paranoid rage, accuses Tiresias of being a false prophet and of colluding with Creon to deprive him of his throne. Before leaving, the old seer foreshadows the fate of Oedipus with these words of chilling apprehension:

> Since you have taunted me with being blind,
> here is my word for you.
> You have your eyes but see not where you are
> in sin, nor where you live, nor whom you live with.
> Do you know who your parents are? Unknowing
> you are an enemy to kith and kin
> in death, beneath the earth, and in this life.
> A deadly footed, double striking curse,
> from father and mother both, shall drive you forth
> out of this land, with darkness on your eyes,
> that now have such straight vision. Shall there be
> a place will not be harbor to your cries,
> a corner of Cithaeron will not ring
> in echo to your cries, soon, soon,—
> when you shall learn the secret of your marriage,
> which steered you to a haven in this house,—
> haven no haven, after lucky voyage?
> And of the multitude of other evils
> establishing a grim equality
> between you and your children, you know nothing.
> So muddy with contempt my words and Creon's!
> Misery shall grind no man as it will you.

Oedipus continues his passionate but misdirected pursuit of the truth by attacking Creon, but the latter, a paragon of Apollonian moderation and self-control, disavows any intent or interest in seizing power and authority; he is content with his life as it is. As tension builds up between the two, Jocasta appears and admonishes both of them for airing a family dispute in public. When asked for details of the quarrel, Oedipus tells her of the oracle that Creon brought back from Delphi. Jocasta tries to reassure him: he need not worry about such things for an oracle given to her husband Laius, that he would be killed by his son, was never fulfilled since he had been killed by brigands. Innocently enough, she lets slip that the homicide happened "at a place where three roads meet." When Oedipus hears this he is visibly shaken, and for the first time he is aware that he is personally involved in the drama that is enveloping Thebes. For the moment he is comforted when Jocasta insists that it was a band of brigands that made the attack; at least that was the report of the lone retainer who had managed to escape. Oedipus, full of trepidation, asks for this person to be brought before him. He then tells Jocasta of his own background: the slanderous charge made by a drunk at Corinth, the oracle he had received at Delphi and the homicide he had committed at the crossroads when he met an old man and his entourage.

Later, when Jocasta appears to pray to Apollo for an end to the terrors that have beset her husband for the health of the city, a messenger arrives from Corinth to report to Oedipus that his father Polybus has died. There is a sense of relief in both Jocasta and Oedipus who utter some impious remarks about oracles. Oedipus is drawn up short remembering that the oracle given him had prophesied that he would commit incest with his mother. The messenger, eager to reassure him that he need have no fear of defiling his mother's bed, tells him that he is not the legitimate child of Merope, that he was the one to whom a Theban shepherd on Mount Cithaeron had handed over an infant with pinned ankles which he, the messenger, had taken to Polybus and Merope in Corinth. While Oedipus is pressing the messenger for more and more information, Jocasta recoils with horror in the realization that the man she has married is her own son and that the oracle given to Laius had in fact been fulfilled. She begs Oedipus to cease his incessant questioning, but he misinterprets her concern as fear that she has married the son of a slave. With a shriek, Jocasta runs into the palace. Finally, when the Theban shepherd is brought before Oedipus, he is forced to admit that the story of the Corinthian messenger is true. At long last, the truth is out and Oedipus is compelled to acknowledge it. As he dashes into the palace bewailing his fate, the chorus sings:

> O generations of men, how I
> count you as equal with those who live
> not at all!
> What man, what man on earth wins more
> of happiness than a seeming
> and after that turning away?
> Oedipus, you are my pattern of this,
> Oedipus, you and your fate!
> Luckless Oedipus, whom of all men
> I envy not at all.

When the chorus concludes its homily, a second messenger appears to describe the violence that has taken place in the palace, a speech of exquisite horror and one which cannot be matched by any stage action. After describing how Jocasta threw herself on her marriage bed, calling upon her dead husband Laius and cursing the bed which produced an incestuous marriage and children through incest, the messenger continues with:

How after that she died I do not know,—
for Oedipus distracted us from seeing.
He burst upon us shouting and we looked
to him as he paced frantically around,
begging us always: Give me a sword, I say,
to find this wife no wife, this mother's womb,
this field of double sowing whence I sprang
and where I sowed my children! As he raved
some god showed him the way—none of us there.
Bellowing terribly and led by some
invisible guide he rushed on the two doors,—
wrenching the hollow bolts out of their sockets,
he charged inside. There, there, we saw his wife
hanging, the twisted rope around her neck.
When he saw her, he cried out fearfully
and cut the dangling noose. Then, as she lay,
poor woman, on the ground, what happened after,
was terrible to see. He tore the brooches—
the gold chased brooches fastening her robe—
away from her and lifting them up high
dashed them on his own eyeballs, shrieking out
such things as: they will never see the crime
I have committed or had done upon me!
Dark eyes, now in the days to come look on
forbidden faces, do not recognize
those whom you long for—with such imprecations
he struck his eyes again and yet again
with the brooches. And the bleeding eyeballs gushed
and stained his beard—no sluggish oozing drops
but a black rain and bloody hail poured down.
So it has broken—and not on one head
but troubles mixed for husband and for wife.
The fortune of the days gone by was true
good fortune—but today groans and destruction
and death and shame—of all ills can be named
not one is missing.

When Oedipus reappears, sightless and with blood streaming from his eye-sockets, he is chastened and humbled. He begs Creon to drive him out of the land or to kill him. When his two daughters Antigone and Ismene appear, he is even more overwhelmed by emotion and makes a special plea to Creon to look after them since they now are most vulnerable to insults and doomed to spinster-hood. As Oedipus and Creon leave, Sophocles has his chorus conclude the play with these words: "Call no man happy until he has ended his life free from pain."

Thus the story of the crushing tragedy in Oedipus' life. What happened to him afterwards is variously given. We have already seen that Homer has him continue to rule at Thebes even though he was tormented by his mother's curses; in the *Iliad* brief mention is made of his having fallen in battle and being honored with funeral games. According to most other traditions, however, he was compelled to surrender his rule to Creon who acted as regent for Oedipus' sons Eteocles and Polynices. Finally, Oedipus was forced to leave Thebes, the expulsion having been ordered for some unknown reason by Creon and agreed to by Eteocles and Polynices. Guided by his daughter Antigone, he wandered about, a destitute and aged pariah, until he came to the district of Colonus, a short distance from Athens. The story of Oedipus' last day on earth was told by Sophocles in *Oedipus at Colonus*, a brooding play which he wrote at the very end of his long life and which was produced posthumously in 401 B.C. Apart from the awe-inspiring effects of the play, it also had special significance to Sophocles since his birthplace was Colonus, and as a patriotic citizen of Athens he eulogizes the city for having given final honors to Oedipus.

Sophocles' OEDIPUS AT COLONUS. After Oedipus has been exiled from Thebes, his two sons, now of age, have deposed Creon and are contending for power. Eteocles has forced his brother out of Thebes; Polynices has gone to Argos where he plans to raise an army and march against the city. In the mysterious and enigmatic way in which Sophoclean gods operate, an oracle of Apollo now declares to the Thebans that the welfare of the city depends on Oedipus' presence, whether in life or death. This news is brought to Oedipus by his daughter Ismene who also tells him that Creon and her brothers know of the oracle and that they will try to exploit it for their own advantage. Oedipus, still passionate and proud, curses his sons for not recalling him to Thebes and prays to the gods that the fraternal struggle be fatal to them both. The cause of his hatred stems from their unfilial treatment: they did not raise a finger when he was cast out of the city; or according to other accounts, the sons set before Oedipus an inferior part of a sacrificial animal, the loin instead of the customary shoulder.

Oedipus offers the elders of Colonus his services and declares that he will become a protector of Athens if they will help him. When Theseus, king of Athens, appears he is kind and sympathetic and promises him sanctuary in Attica. Oedipus then rejects and rebukes both Creon and Polynices for their hypocrisy and selfishness. When they leave, peals of thunder are heard, and lightning flashes are seen in the sky. All are terrified, but Oedipus intuitively knows that it is his call to death. He asks for Theseus, for to him alone will he reveal the place designated for his grave which will protect Attica against her enemies. From the mouth of a messenger we hear how Oedipus purified himself and made a most tender farewell to his two daughters. Then the voice of a god was heard: "Oedipus, Oedipus, why do we delay? You are waiting too long." Suddenly, Oedipus, the bane become a blessing, disappears, and Theseus, who alone is permitted to be present at Oedipus' apotheosis, is forced to put his hands to his eyes as if blinded by a flashing light. The play ends with Theseus granting Antigone and Ismene permission to return to Thebes where they hope to avert the death of their brothers.

*   *   *   *

The story of Oedipus' fate has been a long-time favorite. From the ancient Greeks we possess the names of at least eight dramatists, but little else, that are attached to tragedies entitled *Oedipus*. Even Julius Caesar was attracted to the theme, and it is reported that as a young man he had composed an *Oedipus*. For Emperor Nero, the role of Oedipus was one which he loved to act, and his last public recitation was in that part. A version that has survived is Seneca's *Oedipus Rex*. In some respects it is a Latin paraphrase of Sophocles, but it can hardly be compared in power with the Greek masterpiece. In place of the intuitive Tiresias, Seneca has the seer learn of the murder by having his daughter summon up the ghastly shade of Laius through necromancy. After the discovery of the patricide and the incestuous marriage, Seneca has a self-blinded Oedipus and a motherly Jocasta in a melodramatic confrontation which ends with Jocasta plunging a sword into her womb.

Later versions take the ancient tale still further afield. In France, Corneille's *Oedipe* was produced in 1657, a play which took the simple theme of Sophocles and added a subplot of a romance between Theseus and a supposititious daughter of the deceased Laius, Dirce by name. The French Oedipus was turned into an idealized king with seventeenth-century stoic virtues. Twenty years after Corneille's play, Dryden and Lee produced their *Oedipus* which owed something to Sophocles, Seneca, and Corneille. And like the latter, Dryden and Lee introduced a romantic subplot, but this time the daughter of Laius was called Eurydice and her lover was Adrastus, king of Argos. Creon was portrayed as a hunchbacked villain who tries to force his love on Eurydice, only to be frustrated by Oedipus who reunites the two lovers. In 1718 another French version appeared; this one was from the hand of Voltaire when he was but nineteen; his *Oedipe* was somewhat Sophoclean but still encumbered with love episodes and a false accusation of Jocasta's lover as the murderer of Laius. Shelley's *Oedipus Tyrannus; or Swellfoot the Tyrant* (1820) satirizes the matrimonial affairs of King George IV; in its form and content it owes more to the comic poet Aristophanes than it does to Sophocles. In Byron's epic satire *Don Juan*, an allusion is made to the fact that only Oedipus could answer the riddle of the Sphinx. (*Davus sum* in the quotation is taken from Terence's *Andria*, Davus being a clever slave who replies to a question put to him: *Davus, sum, non Oedipus*, "I am Davus, not Oedipus.")

> But I'm not Oedipus and Life's a Sphinx;
> I tell the tale as it was told, nor dare
> To venture a solution, *Davus sum*.

In more contemporary literature, it was the Europeans, and in particular the French, who refurbished and revitalized the ancient Theban tale with new meanings. Hugo von Hofmannsthal, Austrian poet and librettist, reconstructed the events which preceded Sophocles' tragedy and produced his *Oedipus und die Sphinx* (1906). Apparently influenced by the Nietzschean concept of the superman beyond good and evil, von Hofmannsthal portrays Oedipus and Jocasta as hero and heroine for whom there is neither guilt nor innocence, who are more than gods, and who together are the world. The French novelist and dramatist André Gide saw in Oedipus a symbol of his humanistic philosophy and a parable of his own life. *Oedipe* (1930), Gide's dramatic version of the Greek myth, centers on the conflict between individualism and religious authority: Oedipus is an anticonformist and individualist, Tiresias represents religious authority and is a dogmatist, Antigone is pure faith, Creon pompous, conservative, and opportunist, Eteocles and Polynices lost souls without moral fiber. Gide's Oedipus accepts his fate with humility and joy; his blindness, unlike that of Tiresias which is accepted submissively, produces true happiness which is not based on ignorance and error. Antigone will no longer serve Tiresias; she will follow and lead her blind father. Gide would substitute for faith in the gods—that is, Christian dogma—faith in man and in man's integrity. Man, Oedipus' answer to the riddle of the Sphinx, is the true answer to life.

Jean Cocteau leads us in another direction in his adaptation of the Oedipus myth for his play *La Machine infernale* (1934). Earlier, Cocteau had provided the libretto for Igor Stravinsky's opera-oratorio *Oedipus Rex* (1928), in which he followed the general outlines of Sophocles' tragedy. *La Machine infernale* was to be something quite different and quite Freudian: the machine—in great part the Oedipus complex—is the instrument of destiny which gives man the illusion of enjoying free will, only to be destroyed by it through his weaknesses. (The poet is the one perceptive enough to see through its machinations and records, its tricks and ambiguities.) Cocteau's Oedipus is a likeable but not exceptionally gifted young man. When he comes upon the Sphinx, who is really Nemesis in disguise, he finds a beautiful young woman who dazes her victims with a barrage of words before putting the riddle to them. She is accompanied by Anubis, the Egyptian jackal-headed god of the dead, who administers the *coup de grace* to those who fail to solve her riddle. In the case of Oedipus, the Sphinx supplies him with the correct answer in hopes that he will make love to her. Now thinking he is a free agent—he has killed a man, he escaped from his parents at Corinth, he solved the riddle—he enters Thebes where he is given his reward: the hand of Jocasta and an incestuous union. Cocteau presents us with a Jocasta who is volatile and has a passion for young men. Beside her bed she keeps a cradle, a memento of the child she had to dispose of because of the fearful oracle. After seventeen years of happiness, the messenger arrives with the news of the death of Polybus. When Jocasta comes to the realization that she has married her son, she hangs herself with her red scarf, and Oedipus blinds himself. But it is only Jocasta the wife who is dead; Jocasta the mother returns—she is seen only by Oedipus, the others think he is deluded—and leads him out of the palace with motherly affection.

Tiresias.   Before picking up the story of the remaining descendants of the Labdacid dynasty, something more must be said about the most celebrated diviner in the annals of mythology, Tiresias (or Teiresias) descended from Udaeus, founder of one of Thebes' first families. His mother was the nymph Chariclo, a favorite of Athena. Blind from a very early age, Tiresias was compensated for his disability by being given the gift of prophecy. How he came by his blindness is variously told. A version already touched upon (p. 157) and one made popular by the Hellenistic poet Callimachus in his fifth hymn, *Bath of Pallas*, tells of the youthful Tiresias who came to quench his thirst at the spring of Hippocrene after roaming over Mount Helicon with his hunting dogs. Unfortunately for the young man, it was at this very spring that Athena, accompanied by Chariclo, was refreshing herself in its cool waters. When Tiresias came upon the naked goddess, she sprinkled water in his eyes and quenched his sight. Chariclo remonstrated with Athena for blinding her son, but the goddess replied that it was a divine law that whoever came upon an immortal uninvited had to pay the penalty of blindness. In lieu of his eyesight, Athena gave Tiresias prophetic powers, a long life, and post-mortem retention of mind and memory. Tennyson, who was familiar with Callimachus' hymn, tells of the blinding by Athena in his brooding poem *Tiresias* (1887):

> There in a secret olive-glade I saw
> Pallas Athene climbing from her bath
> In anger. . . .
> . . . .and I heard a voice that said,
> "Henceforth be blind, for thou hast seen too much,
> And speak the truth that no man may believe."

Another popular tradition to account for Tiresias' blindness has to do with the widespread belief that it is unlucky to see snakes coupling. It seems that when Tiresias was on Mount Cyllene or Mount Cithaeron, he observed two huge snakes mating. When he struck the female with his staff, he was turned into a woman. Some years later, the number is usually seven, he again saw two snakes mating, and this time he struck the male with the result that he was turned into a man again. Because of his experience as a member of both sexes, Zeus and Hera turned to him to settle their quarrel as to who enjoyed the pleasures of lovemaking more, man or woman. Tiresias replied that if the number ten represented the total for these pleasures, woman enjoyed nine parts, man one. Hera was so indignant at his reply that she blinded him, but Zeus made up his wife's punishment by giving Tiresias the power of prophecy and a long life which was to last seven ordinary lives. In the *Inferno*, Dante takes his cue from Ovid's *Metamorphoses*, one of the sources for this tale, and alludes to the dual sexuality of the Theban prophet when his guide turns to him and says:

> Behold Tiresias who changed his aspect, when of male he
>   was made woman, all his limbs transforming;
> and afterwards he had again to strike the two involved serpents
>   with his rod, before he could resume his manly plumes.

Dante had some influence upon Swinburne's *Tiresias* (1871), and T. S. Eliot found in these and other poets the characterization of his Tiresias in *The Waste Land* whom he cites as "the most important personage in the poem, uniting all the rest." He seems also to have been influenced by the surrealist Guillaume Apollinaire's Aristophanic comedy produced in 1917, *Les Mamelles de Tirésias* (The Breasts of Tiresias), in which an emanicipated Thérèse turns into Tiresias. Eliot uses his Tiresias to comment upon the joyless lust in the inferno of the modern world. He is "blind, throbbing between two lives," or "old man with wrinkled dugs." And after observing the spiritless love-making of the carbuncular clerk and the tired typist, he concludes the scene with this parenthetical remark:

> (And I Tiresias have foresuffered all
> Enacted on this same divan or bed;
> I who have sat by Thebes below the wall
> And walked among the lowest of the dead.)

At the end of a long life during which he witnessed the fall of Thebes, Tiresias was led away by his captors to Delphi. On the way, he drank from the spring Tilphusa and died. However, he lost none of his mental and prophetic powers in the Underworld where he will converse with Odysseus and tell him of his fate. Matthew Arnold takes the scene of Thebes' fall and the death of Tiresias to comment, in his *The Youth of Nature* (1852), upon the passing of Wordsworth, "the priest to us all."

> He grew old in an age he condemn'd
> . . . .
> And like the Theban seer,
> Died in his enemies' day.
> Cold bubbled the spring of Tilphusa,
> . . . .
> When his awe-struck captors led

The Theban seer to the spring.
Tiresias drank and died.
Nor did reviving Thebes see such a prophet again.
Well may we mourn, when the head
Of a sacred poet lies low
In an age which can rear them no more!

The Seven against Thebes.   Back to Thebes and the somber events following the unveiling of Oedipus' past. For their maltreatment of him, Oedipus laid a curse on his sons Eteocles and Polynices, and that curse was to be fulfilled: "They shall divide their inheritance with the sword." The rivalry between Eteocles and Polynices soon broke out into the open. They had agreed to rule Thebes alternately, but Eteocles refused to give up the throne on the due date. Polynices then went to Argos where King Adrastus gave him his daughter in marriage and promised to restore him to the throne of Thebes. Adrastus set about to recruit six leaders for his expedition, an expedition that under his leadership became known as the Seven against Thebes. He made his first call to his brother-in-law Amphiaraus, a seer. Knowing that the expedition would end in disaster and that Adrastus would be the sole survivor, Amphiaraus was exceedingly reluctant to enlist in the cause. But it so happened that Adrastus and Amphiaraus had had a political feud some time ago which would have had tragic consequences had not Eriphyle, wife of Amphiaraus and sister of Adrastus, stepped in and settled their differences. She also extracted a promise from her husband that in any future disagreement between himself and Adrastus, hers would be the final word in settling the dispute. Polynices found out about this agreement and also discovered that she could be bribed into forcing Amphiaraus to join the expedition with the fateful necklace of Harmonia (p. 324) which he had brought with him from Thebes. Eriphyle succumbed even though she had been told by her husband not to accept any gifts from Polynices. Amphiaraus thus was compelled to take part in a campaign which he knew would be his last. But before leaving, he instructed his sons to kill their mother.

Having mustered an army, Adrastus marched against Thebes. As the Seven approached the city, one of the leaders was sent ahead as an emissary to demand that Eteocles cede Thebes to his brother. The demand was refused. Before the walls of the city Adrastus assigned a champion to each of the seven gates of Thebes; from within Eteocles assigned an opposite number from among his chieftains to match the Seven. Tiresias was then consulted as to how the enemy might be overcome. The seer advised that the Thebans would win a victory if Menoeceus, son of Creon, would volunteer to sacrifice himself to Ares before the walls of the city; in this way Ares' anger against the descendants of Cadmus for the killing of the dragon would be appeased. Creon protested but Menoeceus slew himself before the city gates so that Thebes might live.

One by one the Seven who marched against Thebes fell before the city, all except Adrastus who escaped on the horse Arion (p. 101). As for Amphiaraus, his end was most spectacular. Zeus split the earth with one of his thunderbolts and Amphiaraus was swallowed up alive together with his horses and chariot, and so descended to the Underworld. Finally, Eteocles and Polynices met in a single combat to decide the issue of who should rule Thebes. They killed each other and fulfilled the curse of Oedipus: they divided their inheritance with the sword. Creon now became king of Thebes. He gave orders that the bodies of the invading host, including that of Polynices, be cast out of the city unburied. Antigone, Oedipus' daughter, defied Creon and gave her brother Polynices the last rites, an act of defiance which resulted in Creon's ordering her to be buried alive.

The Epigoni (Descendants). The defeat of the Seven was not to go unavenged. Ten years after the disastrous expedition, the sons of the fallen—the Epigoni (Descendants) as they are called—planned a second campaign against Thebes to avenge their fathers. An oracle foretold that this expedition would be successful, provided it was led by Alcmaeon, the son of Amphiaraus. In the meantime, a son of Polynices bribed Eriphyle, this time with the robe which Harmonia had received from the gods as a wedding gift. Alcmaeon, remembering his father's injunction, hesitated to lead the army before doing away with his mother. Eriphyle, having been bribed a second time, ordered her sons to march against Thebes. This time the expedition was successful and Thebes was brought to its knees, thus ending the legendary history of one of the great cities of early Greece. When Alcmaeon learned that his mother had been bribed, he killed her in accordance with an oracle of Apollo. Pursued by the Furies for having killed his mother, and cursed by the necklace and robe of Harmonia which he carried off with him, he led a tortured life until he was murdered. When deposited at Delphi, the robe and necklace were neutralized and caused no further anguish to their possessors.

The tale of the internecine struggle between Eteocles and Polynices was related by Aeschylus in the *Seven Against Thebes* (467 B.C.), the surviving play of a trilogy which traced the curse on the house of Laius down to the extermination of its last two male descendants. Some sixty years later Euripides produced his *Phoenissae* (The Phoenician Women), a drama quite unlike that of Aeschylus however much it was tampered with by fourth-century producers. It is in effect a series of theatrical tableaux—somewhat like a modern cinematic handling of mythological pageantry—in which Euripides trots on the stage eleven characters and four messenger speeches. Not only does Euripides tell the story of the terminal struggle of the two brothers, but he also grafts on the tragedies of Jocasta, Oedipus and Menoeceus. In his usual free-wheeling manner of handling mythological material, Euripides keeps Jocasta alive so that she can mourn over the bodies of Eteocles and Polynices and then commit suicide with a sword. This is followed by the appearance of the self-blinded Oedipus—he has been kept imprisoned at Thebes for some years— for a climactic scene in which the audience can hear from his own lips the story of his tragic life. All this and more.

In yet another genre, an epic on the Theban legend has come down to us from the hand of a Roman writer of the Silver age of Latin literature, Publius Papinius Statius (c. A.D. 45–96). The *Thebaid* traces the story from the curse of Oedipus upon his sons to the defeat of the Seven; but the story is so inflated with bombast and hyperbole, with trivial and absurd detail, with sententiousness and verbal picture-painting that he has lost his modern audience, even though Alexander Pope and Thomas Gray translated sections of it. In the Middle Ages, however, Statius was held in great esteem and his epic was much admired. He was a favorite of Chaucer and Dante; the latter regards him as a Christian and makes him an important character in the *Purgatorio*.

Sophocles' ANTIGONE. All these versions pale before another masterpiece of Sophocles, the *Antigone*. Produced for the Athenian stage about 441 B.C., *Antigone* picks up the story where Aeschylus left it in the *Seven Against Thebes*, with

Antigone's fierce determination to bury her brother Polynices even though she is forbidden to do so by the "Cadmeian state." But unlike the Aeschylean Antigone whose decision was not made in the teeth of a death penalty, Sophocles' heroine pits her defiance against the decree of one man, King Creon, whose infamous edict she brazenly flouts, knowing full well that it means her death. The dramatic conflict in the *Antigone* is simple and straightforward, a conflict between the polarized views of Antigone and Creon on several levels of related thought: between Antigone's resolution to give up her life rather than leave her brother's body unburied and the insistent demands of Creon that the laws of the state, good or bad, must be observed; between private conscience and public authority; between the sacred and the profane; or between anarchy and tyranny. But not so simple is the resolution as to which of the two principals in the play is right or wrong, hero or villain. Friedrich Hegel, the German philosopher, saw in the *Antigone* an illustration of his law of human history and states: "In the view of Eternal Justice both were wrong, because one-sided; but at the same time both were right." Shelley, attracted as always to a rebel against society, declares with Platonic inspiration: "Some of us have, in a prior existence, been in love with Antigone, and that makes us find no full content in any mortal tie." The modern literary critic Edmund Wilson describes Antigone as a psychopath who is fixated on her brother; the classical scholar Moses Hadas believes that the Athenian audience would have sided with Creon rather than Antigone. The psychoanalyst Erich Fromm views all three of Sophocles' plays on the Theban legend, which he mistakenly calls a trilogy, as being concerned with the struggle between patriarchal (Creon) and matriarchal (Antigone) systems of society. A drama that is capable of being interpreted on so many different planes is a tribute to the genius of Sophocles, not so much in the way in which he makes explicit his truths, but rather in the intensity of feeling with which he surrounds his tragic figures.

The *Antigone* opens before the palace of Creon. Antigone enters with her sister Ismene and informs her of Creon's edict: Eteocles is to be buried with full honors but the corpse of Polynices is to remain unmourned and unburied; anyone who disobeys the edict will be put to death. She asks Ismene to help her defy Creon and give the last rites to their dead brother. When Ismene indicates her unwillingness to contravene the edict, Antigone upbraids her for her cowardice, and with fierce determination sets out to do her sacred duty to the gods and to her brother. Creon enters following an ode sung by a chorus of Theban elders on how Polynices attacked Thebes with an Argive army, how Zeus repelled the attackers, and how the brothers killed each other. Creon makes known his edict to the elders and justifies the action he has taken against Polynices in terms of the welfare of the city. A guard appears and nervously informs the king that someone has performed funeral rites over the body of Polynices by sprinkling it with dust. Creon can scarcely believe what he hears. The elders suggest that it might be the work of the gods, but Creon angrily retorts that the gods do not honor the wicked. He then turns on the guard and threatens him with death if he or his comrades do not find the person responsible for the crime. As Creon re-enters the palace, the chorus of elders sing one of the best-known odes of Sophocles, the so-called Hymn to Man:

> Many the wonders but nothing walks stranger than man.
> This thing crosses the sea in the winter's storm,
> making his path through the roaring waves.

And she, the greatest of gods, the earth—
ageless she is, and unwearied—he wears her away
as the ploughs go up and down from year to year
and his mules turn up the soil.

Gay nations of birds he snares and leads,
wild beast tribes and the salty brood of the sea,
with the twisted mesh of his nets, this clever man.
He controls with craft the beasts of the open air,
walkers on hills. The horse with his shaggy mane
he holds and harnesses, yoked about the neck,
and the strong bull of the mountain.

Language, and the thought like the wind
and the feelings that make the town,
he has taught himself, and shelter against the cold,
refuge from rain. He can always help himself.
He faces no future helpless. There's only death
that he cannot find an escape from. He has contrived
refuge from illnesses once beyond all cure.

Clever beyond dreams
the inventive craft that he has
which may drive him one time or another to well or ill.
When he honors the laws of the land and the gods' sworn right
high indeed is his city; but stateless the man
who dares to dwell with dishonor. Not by my fire,
never to share my thoughts, who does these things.

The guard returns, but this time he has Antigone with him. He tells an astonished Creon of how he apprehended her in the act of repeating the burial rites after he and his men had swept the earlier dust off the rotting corpse. Antigone defiantly admits to Creon that it was she who violated his edict, that her act was premeditated. She declares that Zeus and the gods of the dead never enacted such a decree or passed such laws; their authority is eternal. Antigone not only defends what she has done, she glories in the deed and is ready to die for it. Creon is infuriated and condemns her to death. He also suspects that Ismene had some part in the criminal act and has her brought in. When she attempts to share the blame and fate of her sister, Antigone rebuffs her because she had refused to help her in burying Polynices. Ismene turns to Creon and asks whether he will kill the girl who is to marry his own son Haemon. Creon is resolved to put both Antigone and Ismene to death.

The chorus of elders sing a brooding ode on the curse on the house of Labdacus. Haemon appears before his father and at first tries to reason with him calmly, but to no avail. Losing his self-control, Haemon charges his father with tyrannical arrogance and rushes out, broadly hinting that he will share Antigone's fate. Creon now declares that he will spare Ismene, but Antigone must die. And to prevent her death from becoming a pollution to the city, he orders her to be entombed alive and left a meager supply of food. When Antigone is led before the elders of the city, she defends her act and makes a touching farewell. As she is led away for the last time, she cries out in anguish, "What law of the gods have I transgressed?"

The blind Tiresias enters with urgent news for the king. All the omens declare that he and the city are standing on the brink of fate. The gods are angry and the city is polluted because Polynices lies unburied. Creon's reply is another fit of anger. He charges Tiresias with having been bribed by the people of Thebes to frighten him, but on no condition will Polynices be buried. The aged prophet matches the passion of the king by prophesying that one sprung from Creon's own blood will be a corpse in exchange for two other corpses, because he has put in the shadows one who belongs in the sunlight, and keeps one in the sun who should belong in the world below. Tiresias leaves Creon and the elders shaken and troubled. Responding to the prompting of the elders, who remind him that the seer has always been proved right, Creon now resolves to bury Polynices and free Antigone. As he makes off, the chorus of elders sing a joyful ode in honor of Dionysus; their joy is a brief ray of light before all becomes tragic gloom.

A messenger comes on the stage to report that all is ended for Creon: his son Haemon has committed suicide. Eurydice, Creon's wife, overhears the messenger and in a state of collapse hears how Creon buried Polynices and then went to free Antigone. When he arrived at the tomb, he found that Antigone had hanged herself with a noose she had made from her veil. He also found his son Haemon embracing the dead body, and when the distracted young man saw his father, he rushed at him with his sword. Creon fled. Haemon, beside himself with grief and anguish, turned his sword on himself and died on Antigone's body. After hearing the messenger, Eurydice goes into the palace without uttering a word. Creon enters with the body of Haemon covered with a shroud. As he laments the death of his son and blames himself for his folly, a second messenger rushes in to announce that Eurydice is dead. She has taken her life by stabbing herself at the household altar, and with her last gasp she has cursed her husband. In complete and utter misery, Creon prays for death, and as he is led into the palace, the chorus sings:

> Our happiness depends
> on wisdom all the way.
> The gods must have their due.
> Great words by men of pride
> bring greater blows upon them.
> So wisdom comes to the old.

*   *   *   *

Sophocles' *Antigone* impressed itself deeply on the creative minds of twentieth-century German and French playwrights. Toward the end of World War I, the German expressionist Walter Hasenclever composed an *Antigone* in which he made a passionate plea through his heroine for pacificism and a return to ideals of humanity. Thirty years later, Bertolt Brecht utilized, though only nominally, a translation of Sophocles by the late eighteenth-century Hellenist Friedrich Hölderlin, to express his own antiwar sentiments and to present a study of the collapsing tyranny of Nazism. (The Nazis themselves had used Hölderlin's translation of the *Antigone* to express their own ideals, Antigone symbolizing feminine sensibility, Creon masculine reason.) Brecht focused his *Antigone* (1948) on the character of Creon and transformed him into a ruthless imperialist and warmonger. The prologue to the Theban tale is a scene which takes place in Berlin at the end of World War II. On leaving their air raid shelter, two sisters discover a man who has been hung, apparently as an army deserter. It is their brother. The question is raised whether one of the sisters will cut him down in face of the Storm Trooper. Brecht then picks up the story that takes place at Thebes and, to suit his dramatic needs, makes radical changes in the story. Eteocles and Polynices do not fight each other; rather both are in the ranks of Creon's army as it attacks Argos in order to acquire the city's economic resources. When Eteocles dies, Polynices is so horrified that he deserts the army. He is killed by Creon who charges him with cowardice and refuses to honor him with the ritual of burial. Antigone, who foresees the unsavory and despotic character of Creon, dies with Haemon as they witness the final defeat of the Thebans by the Argives. Brecht does not omit Sophocles' Hymn to Man, but adds to it some bitter words about man's inhumanity to man.

Among the French dramatists of the twentieth century, Antigone was to strike a different chord. In Sophocles' heroine Jean Cocteau finds his saint and a symbol of his rebellion against rules. His *Antigone* is a streamlined translation of Sophocles— "a bird's-eye view" as he calls it—which was first produced in 1922 with scenery by Pablo Picasso and music by Arthur Honegger. (The latter was to use the text of Cocteau for his opera *Antigone* which had its first hearing in 1927.) Some years later, in Paris which had been occupied by the German Nazis, Jean Anouilh produced his version of Sophocles' play. To an audience under the heel of a conquering army, the bleak theme of Anouilh's *Antigone* (1942)—death rather than compromise —seemed immediate and compelling. But as the work of Anouilh allows for a variety of interpretations, some felt that the playwright was championing the cause of the collaborationist (Creon) against the foolishly idealistic (Antigone). Since its initial performance, many have come to see his *Antigone* as tragic both for Antigone and Creon and their ideals: her aspiration for purity denies life itself and can only be found in death; Creon's equally futile hopes are lost in the harsh realities of life, and what is left for him after the loss of his son and wife is little more than a living death. As the play closes, we see Creon spiritlessly going about his duties and preparing to meet his cabinet at five o'clock.

4. The Descendants of Aeolus

The activities of the many descendents of prolific Aeolus have already been mentioned as they touched upon the lives of various gods and sundry heroes: Tyro's seduction by Poseidon; Admetus and Alcestis offering hospitality to Apollo in exile and the manner in which the god repaid them; Endymion's indifference toward Selene; Sisyphus and Salmoneus as they sojourned and suffered in the house of Hades; Bellerophon and his adventures with the winged horse Pegasus; Phrixus and Helle as they made their escape from a wicked stepmother on the back of a golden ram. There remains the story of Jason, the great-grandson of Aeolus, whose maritime expedition yielded a cycle of tales which made him one of the best-known heroes of mythological antiquity. And some nine generations removed from Aeolus, if we are to believe the genealogists of old, came Meleager who was the leader of the famed hunt for the monstrous Calydonian boar. This too remains to be told. But first the story of Jason and the Argonauts. It was a story known to Homer, related succinctly by Pindar in his Fourth Pythian Ode, and then elaborated at great length by Apollonius Rhodius in his *Argonautica* (p. 11) with all the Hellenistic love for romance and esoterica.

Figure 75.   Athena (left) overseeing
the construction of the *Argo. Roman
bas-relief, Villa Albani. (Alinari)*

Jason.   Jason was the grandson of Tyro, the young daughter of Salmoneus whom
Poseidon impregnated under a huge wave. But Jason's father Aeson did not
come into the world as a result of this spectacular union, as had his half-brothers
Pelias and Neleus, but through the more conventional means of a marriage between
Tyro and her uncle Cretheus. Cretheus was the founder of Iolcus in Thessaly and
its ruler, and when he died Pelias usurped the throne that rightly belonged to
Aeson. Then came an oracle which caused Pelias considerable anxiety: one version
of it is that he would be killed by a descendent of Aeolus; the more popular version
was that he was to beware of one coming to Iolcus from the mountains and wearing
only one sandal. Aeson, fearing for the life of his infant son Jason, feigned the
child's death and gave him to the famous foster father of heroes, the centaur Chiron,
who reared and educated the future hero on Mount Pelion. The time soon arrived
for Jason to return to the city of his birth and to claim his rightful inheritance.
Down he came from the mountain dressed in a leopard's skin and wearing only one
sandal. He is said to have lost a sandal while helping an old woman—really his
guardian deity Hera in disguise—to cross a stream. In Iolcus he found his father
alive but aged. Jason demanded of Pelias his rightful inheritance, a demand that
Pelias craftily acceded to on the condition that Jason appease the spirit of Phrixus
by bringing home the golden fleece and thereby removing the curse on the descendants of Aeolus. According to the more common tradition, Pelias recognized Jason
while he was sacrificing to Poseidon since the young man was wearing only one
sandal. After he had assured himself that Jason was the fateful one predicted
by the oracle, he asked him what he would do if he had been told by an oracle that
he would be killed by one of his subjects. Prompted by Hera, Jason replied that he
would send him to fetch the golden fleece. "Done," said Pelias, and sent the young
hero on his dangerous mission.

The Argo and the Argonauts.   The perilous mission to procure the golden fleece
at Colchis was not an easy one. Colchis could be reached only by sea, and as yet
the arts of naval architecture and seafaring were not known. Jason called upon Argus, son of Phrixus or Arestor, to help him design a craft that would enable him to
reach his destination. Argus built a fifty-oared ship, a vessel that was named *Argo*
after its builder. Athena also helped, not only with advice but also by inserting in
the bow a piece of wood with the power of speech which had been taken from the
speaking oaks in the grove of Dodona where Zeus had his oracle (fig. 75). Jason

then sent out invitations to heroes all over Greece to take part in the expedition. The number of heroes who responded is generally placed at fifty, one for each oar, and they were given the name of Argonauts. No two lists, however, agree on the names of the fifty; local patriotism, genealogists for ambitious aristocrats, and poetic invention competed with one another in making up rosters of the fifty Argonauts. Some of those listed had special abilities, such as Tiphys the pilot, Orpheus the singer, Mopsus and Idmon the seers; some were famous legendary figures such as Meleager of Calydon, Theseus, Admetus, Castor and Polydeuces (Pollux), as well as Heracles who took time off from his labors; others were the fathers of Greek heroes in the Trojan War for whom the poets provided a heroic background that would approach that of their more famous sons (for instance, Peleus, the father of Achilles; Menoetius, the father of Patroclus; Telamon, the father of Ajax the Greater; Oileus, the father of Ajax the Lesser). The rest of the expedition was made up of sons of gods and heroes of little-known reputation in the annals of Greek legend.

The Golden Fleece. Before sending off the doughty band of adventurers in the *Argo*, something further must be said about the objective of the expedition. The golden fleece, which originally may have been a ritual object (p. 325), soon attracted a number of common folk motifs and rationalizations which made of it something quite different from what it started out to be. So it is that we find a story of a sacrificial victim (Phrixus) being transported to another land by means of a remarkable creature (the golden ram), a hero (Jason) to be gotten rid of by an evil king (Pelias) sent off to a never-never land (Aea = the land) where an ogre (Aeëtes) assigns him supposedly impossible tasks (plowing a field with fire-breathing bulls), and being helped in his difficulties by the ogre's daughter, an enchantress (Medea = the cunning one, the daughter of Aeëtes, and Idyia = the knowing one). The golden fleece, therefore, becomes something of a magical treasure, the pot of gold at the end of the rainbow. In the hands of later writers, and especially in the *Argonautica* of Apollonius Rhodius, the story of the expedition becomes embroidered with geographical lore, aetiologies, Alexandrian scholarship, details borrowed from earlier epics, romance and sentimentality. As for rationalizations, the Roman historian and geographer Strabo saw the voyage as an expedition to Colchis to obtain the gold dust which the Colchians sifted from the river by means of fleeces. (The name Argonauts was given to the adventure-seekers who took part in the California gold rush of 1849). The Byzantine lexicographer "Suidas" viewed the golden fleece as a book written on parchment which told how to make gold out of base metals. Finally, if the voyage of the Argonauts was ever a historical event, its occurrence and its purpose have been irretrievably lost to us.

The Voyage of the Argo. The *Argo* was successfully launched and the heroes and demigods embarked for their adventure into the unknown. All the gods looked down from heaven that day, and crowds of people came down to the beach to bid the Argonauts *bon voyage*. The centaur Chiron also came with his wife Chariclo who was carrying the infant Achilles in her arms so that he could wave goodbye to his father Peleus. (According to ancient tradition, the expedition of the Argonauts took place at least one generation before the Trojan War.) Sailing past the mountain peaks of Pelion, Ossa, Olympus, and Athos, the Argonauts made their first landfall at the island of Lemnos. The island was ruled over by Hypsipyle, daughter of Thoas, and was inhabited solely by women who had killed their husbands and fathers—all except Hypsipyle who had saved her father Thoas—because they had brought home captive women from Thrace. Why did the men go off to Thrace looking for other women? The Lemnian women had offended Aphrodite by neglecting her cult, a neglect which the goddess of love punished by causing the women to exude a foul odor which repelled their husbands. The Lemnian women welcomed the Argonauts with open arms and invited them to share their beds. Jason chose Hypsipyle for his partner and she bore him two sons. This same Hypsipyle was later captured by pirates and sold as a slave to King Lycurgus of Nemea whose child was placed in her care. When Adrastus marched against Thebes, she showed the Seven the way to water, but while she was doing so, the son of the king was bitten by a snake and died. Amphiaraus cleared her of negligence, and the Nemean games, one of the four great national festivals of the Greeks, were instituted in honor of the unfortunate infant.

After spending a year on the island of Lemnos, the Argonauts seemed to have forgotten their mission until Heracles chided them and reminded them of what they had set out to do. They put out to sea again and made their next port of call at Samothrace where at Orpheus' suggestion they were initiated into the rites of the Samothracian mysteries. Passing through the Hellespont (the Dardanelles), the adventurers came to the land of the Doliones where they were well received by King Cyzicus; and in return for the hospitality shown by the king, Heracles and his companions overcame the armed earth-born giants who were the king's enemies. Unfortunately, however, when the Argonauts departed, they were blown back by adverse winds. The Doliones mistakenly took them for hostile invaders, and in the course of the ensuing fighting King Cyzicus was killed. His wife Clite killed herself out of remorse, and the woodland nymphs mourned for her so much that their tears turned into the spring which bears her name. After the Argonauts had paid their last respects to the king, they continued their journey only to have to put into Cios when heavy weather caused Heracles to break an oar. It was here that Heracles lost his favorite Hylas to water-nymphs when the young man went to fetch a pitcher of water, a story that has already been told. When Heracles insisted on continuing his search for Hylas, the Argonauts had to go on without him.

The next adventure took place in Bithynia in the land of the Bebryces. Amycus, a son of Poseidon and king of the Bebryces, had a penchant for challenging strangers to a boxing-match. Polydeuces, a great boxer, took up the challenge, and after a fierce give-and-take, the Argonaut knocked out the arrogant king and killed him. The Bebryces, with no feeling for sportsmanship, broke in and attacked their guests, but they were no match for the Greeks and took a sound beating. From Bithynia, the Argonauts passed through the Bosporus and landed at Salmydessus in Thrace where they met the unfortunate ruler of that land, Phineus, a seer suffering from blindness and lingering old age. He had received his gift of prophecy from Apollo, but for reasons variously given—that he had betrayed Zeus' secrets about the future, or that he had been cruel to his sons, or that he had shown Phrixus the way to Aea—he had been deprived of his sight. And that was not all: Phineus was also tormented by winged monsters, the Harpies, (p. 28) who would snatch away any food that was put before him and would render any remaining scraps inedible with a loathsome stench.

The Argonauts found Phineus in a half-starved condition and promised to help him get rid of the Harpies if he would direct them to the land of the golden fleece.

When he agreed, two of the Argonauts, Zetes and Calais, who were the winged sons of Boreas (North Wind), met the Harpies in an air battle and drove them off. Phineus then gave the Argonauts the information they needed, and in particular told them how to escape the dangers of the Symplegades, the Clashing Rocks. He advised them to take a dove along with them, and when they came to the straits, they were to release the dove just as the rocks came together like crashing symbols; then as the rocks opened again, they were to shoot through the narrows. Acting on his advice, they released the dove at the right moment. The dove got through safely except for a few tail-feathers that were nipped off when the rocks came together. When the narrows opened again, the Argonauts put their backs to the oars and rowed with might and main. But at the critical moment, the *Argo* was held back by a swift tide. Athena appeared at this moment, and holding the rocks back with one hand, she pushed the ship through with the other just as the rocks came together. And like the dove, the *Argo* suffered minor damage to her stern. After this incident, the Symplegades never clashed again, but were rooted forever in one spot close to each other.

Following this narrow escape, the Argonauts sailed into the Black Sea, and after a series of minor adventures and the loss of several men, they came to the island of Ares where they were attacked by the Stymphalian birds that Heracles had driven out of the Peloponnese with his bronze rattles and arrows. The crew of the *Argo* withstood the shower of pointed feathers by locking their shields over their heads and by making a terrible din, rattling the shields in imitation of Heracles' rattles. Before arriving at their final port of call, the Argonauts caught sight of the crags of the Caucasus and heard the tortured screams of Prometheus as the eagle plucked at his liver. At long last, they beached their ship at Colchis and saw the towers of Aea, the city over which Aeëtes ruled. Aeëtes was a son of Helios the sun-god. He was married to Idyia and had a son Apsyrtus (or Absyrtus) and two daughters, Medea (or Medeia) and Chalciope, the latter having been given to Phrixus as a wife when he came to Colchis on the golden ram. Aeetes' sisters were also well known in the mythological world: Pasiphaë, the wife of Minos of Crete, and the enchantress Circe whom Homer's hero Odysseus will encounter on his return home from the Trojan War.

Medea Meets Jason.   Now that Jason had completed the first phase of his quest for the golden fleece, he had other dangers to face, especially from a hostile Aeëtes who believed that his throne was being threatened by the Argonauts and the four sons of the deceased Phrixus—the Argonauts had found them shipwrecked on the island of Ares and had invited them, in accordance with a prophecy of Phineus, to guide them to Colchis. Help for Jason came from Athena and Hera; the goddesses prevailed upon Aphrodite to have her son Eros (Cupid) shoot a love-compelling arrow into the heart of Medea. When Jason entered the palace of Aeëtes and presented himself to the king and his family, Eros, bribed by his mother Aphrodite with a golden ball, let fly one of his arrows at Medea as she looked upon the handsome stranger. Instantly she was aflame with love, as Apollonius Rhodius describes in the *Argonautica* with Hellenistic fondness for romantic sentiment:

> . . . and the bolt burnt deep down in the maiden's heart, like a flame; and ever she kept darting bright glances straight up at Aeson's son, and within her breast her heart panted fast through anguish, all remembrance left her, and her soul melted with the sweet pain. And as a poor woman heaps dry twigs around a blazing brand . . . and the

flame waxing wondrous great from the small brand consumes all the twigs together; so, coiling around her heart, burnt secretly Love the destroyer; and the hue of her soft cheeks went and came, now pale, now red, in her soul's distraction.

Jason Wins the Golden Fleece. When Aeëtes heard that Jason had come for the golden fleece, he was restrained only by the laws of hospitality from killing all the Argonauts and the sons of Phrixus. In spite of Jason's reassurance that he had not come to harm him, Aeëtes was resolved to do away with the hero by imposing impossible tasks upon him. He agreed to surrender the golden fleece if Jason, all by himself, would yoke two fire-belching bronze bulls and plow a field with them; if successful, he was then to sow the teeth of a dragon and destroy the armed men who would spring up. (compare a similar task performed by Cadmus, p. 323). Jason accepted the challenge. Feeling sure that Jason would fail, Aeëtes planned to set fire to the *Argo* and kill the supposed invaders, including the sons of Phrixus and Chalciope. But the king had not counted on his daughters. Chalciope begged Medea to help so that her sons would have Jason's protection. Medea, now hopelessly in love with the hero, agreed. As a priestess of Hecate and skilled in the black arts, she rummaged through her pharmacopoeia to find a drug which would render Jason invulnerable to the bronze bulls and their lethal fire. From among her stock of drugs she selected one that was called Prometheus, a substance derived from a flower which grew from the Titan's ichor-like blood when the torturing eagle caused it to spill on the Caucasus. If a man would anoint himself with this drug and make sacrifice to Hecate at midnight, neither bronze nor fire could harm him for a period of twenty-four hours. When Jason and Medea met face to face, the two confessed their love for each other. Jason begged Medea to help him and promised not only marriage but also that "nothing shall come between our love till the doom of death fold us round." These words melted Medea. She instructed him in the use of the drug and told him how to meet the armed men who would spring from the dragon's teeth: he was to throw a stone in their midst and they would kill one another. Shielded by Medea's medicament and by sacrifice to Hecate, Jason successfully executed the tasks set for him by Aeëtes.

The Flight of Jason and Medea and the Return of the Argonauts. The two lovers fled before the wrath of Aeëtes, but Jason would not leave Colchis without his prize. They went into the sacred grove where the golden fleece lay guarded by a monstrous dragon. Medea closed the eyes of the coiled monster in sleep by means of incantation and by sprinkling his eyes with a sprig of juniper dipped into one of her magical potions. Jason snatched the golden fleece and the two made for the *Argo* and ordered the waiting Argonauts to cast off and head for home. Medea's brother Apsyrtus, commanding the Colchian fleet, intercepted them before they could reach the open sea. Once more Medea came to the rescue. She deceived her brother into thinking that Jason would parley with him; instead, Jason killed the young man and buried him. Another tradition holds that Apsyrtus fled with the two lovers, but when Aeëtes was about to overtake them, Medea cut her brother into pieces and cast them one by one into the sea. Aeëtes had to delay as he recovered his son's remains so that they could be given a proper burial. In any event, Zeus, speaking through the piece of Dodonian oak inserted in the bow of the ship, voiced his anger over the murder of Apsyrtus and directed the Argonauts to be purified of their crime by Circe, the sister of Aeëtes. By this time the Argonauts had reached the Adriatic—no two accounts give the same geographical details for the return trip to Iolcus—and their ship had to sail the Po and the Rhone rivers until they reached the Tyrrhenian See and Circe's island of Aeaea. Circe performed the rites which propitiated the murder of Apsyrtus and then she drove them away.

Hera, anxious for Jason to return home so that he might punish Pelias who was anathema to her, sent Iris to calm the seas. On their way the Argonauts passed the island of the Sirens and were saved from being lured to their destruction by the singing of Orpheus. Thetis and the Nereids came to their assistance when the *Argo* had to navigate the treacherous waters between Scylla and Charybdis; and when the ship was about to run afoul of the navigational hazard known as the Planctae (Wandering Rocks), the Nereids conveniently carried the craft over the rocks. Passing by Thrinacia, the island on which Helios pastured his cattle, they arrived at the island of the Phaeacians where they were hospitably received by King Alcinous and his wife Arete. Here the Colchians finally caught up with the Argonauts. They demanded of Alcinous that he surrender Medea to them. Arete, on Medea's appeal, convinced her husband that the plight of the two lovers deserved his sympathy. Alcinous therefore decreed that if Medea were still chaste, he would restore her to her father; but if she shared a husband's bed or was with child, he would not separate her from her lover. Upon Arete's prompting, a marriage was hastily arranged even though both Jason and Medea had hoped to celebrate their marriage at Iolcus. Orpheus provided marital music; nymphs sent by Hera sang and danced. The bridal bed was laid in a sacred cave and was covered over with the golden fleece. Under such circumstances Jason and Medea were joined in marriage.

Following their stay with Alcinous and Arete on the island of the Phaeacians —later writers identified this Homeric never-never land with Corcyra—the Argonauts took to their ship and renewed their homeward voyage, only to have new difficulties face them. For nine days and nights a northerly gale blew the *Argo* toward Libya and stranded her on the shoals of the Gulf of Syrtis, the graveyard of ships. With guidance from local deities, the Argonauts portaged their ship to Lake Tritonis. Their search for fresh water led them to the garden of Hesperides where they discovered that Heracles had just appeared the day before, killed the dragon Ladon and made off with the golden apples. Triton, the son of Poseidon and Amphitrite, rose from the depths of the lake bearing his name and guided the Argonauts back to the open sea. Their voyage now led them to the island of Crete. There, Talos, the bronze robot given to Europa by Zeus as a guardian for the island, prevented them from landing. Medea gave him one of her sleeping potions and then pulled the pin from his one vein, and all his life-giving fluid ran out. From Crete the Argonauts sailed without further major incident to their home port, and thus brought to an end one of the great legendary quests of a band of heroes. The rest of the story concerns itself with the life of Jason and Medea at Iolcus and Corinth.

Back in Iolcus, Pelias believed that the Argonauts would never return, and in order to secure his hold on the throne, he was determined to put Aeson and a surviving son out of the way. One tradition reports that Pelias allowed his half-brother to commit suicide by drinking the blood of a sacrificed bull. Aeson's wife took her own life and cursed Pelias with her last breath. After killing the last son of Aeson, Pelias thought himself safe, but then Jason arrived and delivered the golden fleece. (The golden fleece ultimately ended up in the temple of Zeus at Orchomenus; the *Argo* was beached on the Isthmus of Corinth and dedicated to Poseidon.) Ovid, in his *Metamorphoses*, gives another and more fanciful version of the fate of Pelias and Aeson. The Roman poet turns Medea into a nightmarish figure, an archetypal sorceress with her dragon-drawn chariot cutting a figure not far removed from a witch and her broomstick.

Medea's Magic and the Fate of Aeson and Pelias. As Ovid tells the story, when Jason arrived at Iolcus he found his father Aeson alive, but aged and infirm. He appealed to Medea to use her magic to take some of his years of youth and give them to his father. Medea replied that Hecate would forbid such a transfer, but that by the art invested in her by Hecate she would do better than that: she would rejuvenate his father. At midnight, when the moon was full, Medea invoked Hecate and all the forces of night to assist her, and off she flew in her chariot drawn by sleek dragons. For nine days she gathered herbs and drugs, and when she returned home she would not let Jason touch her or witness the rites of Hecate. Sacrificing a black ram and filling ditches with its blood as well as with wine and milk, Medea called upon the gods of the earth and the lower world to come forth. She then put Aeson into a deep sleep and purified him three times with fire, water and sulphur. What took place next is best described by Ovid.

> Meanwhile in a bronze pot her liquor simmered,
> Steamed, leaped, and boiled, the white scum foaming hot:
> There she threw roots torn from Thessalian valleys,
> Seeds, flowers, plants, and acid distillations,
> And precious stones from the far Orient,
> And sands which the spent tide of Ocean washes,
> The whited frost scooped under the full moon,
> Wings of the weird scritch owl and his torn breast,
> Bowels of the werewolf which shudder and twist
> Into a likeness of mad human faces,
> The scaled skin of a thin-hipped water snake,
> Liver of a long-lived deer, foul eggs,
> And battered head of a crow that outlived
> Eight generations. And with these a thousand things
> Without a name. When wild Medea smelled
> The unearthly brew, she dipped a wither'd wreath
> Torn from a tree that once hung rich with olives
> Into the pot—and look, even dry stems turned green,
> Then leaves crept out, and, as they flowered, the wreath
> Became an olive bough grown thick with fruit!
> And where hot foam dripped from the boiling pot,
> The earth was like a garden plot of flowers
> And green between them sprang new ferns and grasses.

And when Medea was satisfied with her witch's brew, Ovid continues,

> She flashed a knife and cut the old man's throat;
> Draining old veins she poured hot liquor down,
> Some steaming through his throat, some through his lips,
> Till his hair grew black and straight, all greyness gone.

His chest and shoulders swelled with youthful vigor
His wrinkles fell away, his loins grew stout,
His sallow skin took on a swarthy color;
And Aeson, dazed, remembered this new self
Was what he had been forty years ago.

That was not the end of it. Medea took it upon herself to punish Pelias by a diabolical scheme. Pretending that she and Jason had a lovers' quarrel, she took refuge in Pelias' house. When the king's daughters heard of how she had worked a miraculous transformation on their uncle, they were eager for her to do the same for their father. This was part of Medea's plan. And to reassure the ingenuous girls that her magic would work, she took an old ram, hacked it to pieces, and threw it into a pot boiling with her potent herbs (fig. 76). The carcass shriveled and shrank, and suddenly out leaped a lamb which went skipping off to find a ewe. Thus reassured, the daughters of Pelias were ready for the fateful operation. Medea put Pelias into a deep sleep and urged his daughters to cut his body into pieces. Although repelled by the idea, they struck at his body with their eyes closed. Medea performed the final stroke by slitting the old man's throat. She then threw the remains into a cauldron of boiling water from which, of course, she had omitted her potent rejuvenating herbs, and Pelias was lost to his world forever.

Euripides' MEDEA. Following this gruesome event, Jason and Medea left Iolcus and went to Corinth—the reasons for their leaving are variously given— where they lived happily for ten years. What we know of their lives at Corinth after those happy years is largely due to Euripides, who took the legendary material for his tragic drama *Medea*, first produced at Athens in 431 B.C. Euripides' *Medea* is a showcase for the portrayal of a passionate woman brutalized into inhumanity by a cruel and ungrateful man. It is also an *exposé* of those nonmoral forces which Euripides saw at work within the human psyche, forces which, when excessive and hence uncontrollable, lead to tragedy and tragic victims, both the innocent and the

Figure 76.   Medea giving convincing proof of her magical powers of rejuvenation to Pelias (left) and his daughters (right). *Vase painting, late sixth century B.C. British Museum.*

blameworthy. For the Greeks of his own time, Euripides had something to say about their male smugness and their arrogant treatment of foreigners. The plot of the *Medea* is a simple one, but its emotional intensity is high-pitched as it reveals the bottomless pit of human cruelty.

In Corinth, where Jason has been living with Medea and their two young sons, the opportunity arises for him to marry Glauce (some traditions report her name as Creusa), the daughter of Creon, king of Corinth. Through the mouth of the nurse for her children, we hear how unhappy and emotionally unstable Medea is over this new turn of affairs. The air is full of her threats of revenge, anguished wailings, and recriminations. When the news is brought that Creon intends to banish Medea and her children, the nurse is so fearful of what Medea may do to the children that she plans to keep them from her. King Creon enters and orders Medea to leave Corinth with her children. He admits that he is afraid of her and the evil she can do to his daughter. Although Creon has ordered her to leave at once, Medea persuades him to allow her to remain in Corinth for just one more day. It is to be a fateful day. When Creon leaves, Medea makes known that she will use the one day of grace to wreak grim vengeance on those hateful to her, regardless of the consequences. Medea, the daughter of a king and the grand-daughter of Helios the sun, will not see herself mocked and humiliated by Jason's marriage to Glauce.

Jason now comes upon the scene and tells her that her own temper and loose tongue have been the cause of her banishment. Medea charges him with cowardice and lack of manliness. She ticks off all the crimes she has committed out of love for him, and how has he repaid her? By breaking his promises, by abandoning her and her children, and by giving her no place whatever to go since she would not be welcome in either Greece or her homeland. Jason tries to refute her with sophistical replies to her argument and adds that she ought to look to the advantages of the present situation: life in the civilized country of Greece instead of barbarian Colchis, and the influence that will come to him as the husband of the king's daughter. He tries to convince Medea that his marriage to Glauce is one of convenience and is planned with Medea and her children in mind. He is also prepared to furnish her with money and give her introductions to his friends who will treat her well. Medea rejects his arguments and dismisses him.

As Medea sits in front of her house in deep despair, Aegeus, king of Athens, appears. He has just come from the oracle of Apollo where he has tried to find out whether he will ever have a son and heir. Medea sees in Aegeus the final solution to her plan of revenge. She promises him that she will work her spells and provide him with the desired son if he will give her sanctuary in his land. Aegeus agrees. Now that she has a place of refuge, Medea lays her plans for the death of Creon, his daughter, and yes, even her own children. She cannot bear to be mocked by her enemies; it must be done this way. She sends for Jason and deceitfully aks for his forgiveness; she is sorry for the way she has acted. She calls out her children to make their farewells to their father. As a final request, Medea begs her husband to intercede with Glauce to have her children remain in Corinth. She will have the children make her a present of a beautiful robe and a golden diadem—both are poisoned and part of Medea's revenge. Jason protests that such gifts are not necessary, but Medea insists and sends off the children with instructions to present the gifts to Glauce. When they return with their tutor, Medea learns that the children have been granted a reprieve by a grateful Glauce; they may remain at Corinth. Medea's next plan of action is to murder her children, but this new turn of events stirs up strong maternal feeling in her heart. She is torn between her feelings for her children and her desire for revenge, and as she decides on a course of action, she says:

> I know indeed what evil I intend to do,
> But stronger than all my afterthoughts is my fury,
> Fury that brings upon mortals the greatest of evils.

A messenger arrives and gives a grisly description of what happened to Glauce when she put on the poisoned robe and diadem, and what happened to Creon when he came to help his daughter. Blood and fire mingled, and flesh dropped or was torn from their bodies. Medea, hearing of the end of the king and the princess, now steels herself for her ultimate crime, the murder of her children. She rushes into the house, and soon the death-cries of the children are heard. Jason rushes upon the scene, eager to save his children from the people of Corinth, only to be shattered by the news that Medea has killed them. Miraculously Medea appears above the house in a chariot drawn by winged dragons—no ordinary housewife this—and with her are the bodies of her dead children. She refuses to turn over the children to Jason for burial; they will be taken where their tomb will not be defiled. In their honor an annual feast and sacrifice will be instituted at Corinth to atone for the blood-guilt. For Jason she predicts an inglorious end. And though the death of her children causes her great pain, she is comforted by the knowledge that Jason's suffering will be greater than hers. With that she flies off, leaving Jason a completely broken man. With this Euripides brings his drama to an end.

What of the end of Jason and Medea? After the death of his children, Jason wandered about Greece until he came to the Isthmus of Corinth where he had beached the *Argo*. As he sat in the shadow of its hull and reflected upon the glorious adventures he had had as commander of the Argonauts, the prow of the old ship bearing the plank of wood from the talking oaks of Dodona broke off, fell on him, and killed him outright, just as Medea had predicted. And Medea? Aegeus married her and she gave him a son Medeus. But when Theseus, whom Aegeus had sired on his way home from the oracle, came to Athens to claim his inheritance, Medea tried to poison him, but without success. She and her son then fled to Colchis, where her uncle Perses had taken over her father's kingdom. She brought about the death of the usurper and restored Aeëtes to the throne. Her son Medeus became a great soldier and eventually gave his name to a branch of the Persian people, the Medes. Some accounts even say that Medea was made immortal by Hera because she had rejected the advances of Zeus, and even more difficult to accept, that she went to the Elysian Fields where she married Achilles.

*   *   *   *

Euripides and Apollonius Rhodius left a legacy of thematic material for later generations of poets and playwrights. Ovid, the Roman poet who portrayed Medea as more witch than woman in the *Metamorphoses*, shows her as more woman than witch in the *Heriodes*. In these literary epistles, supposedly written by women of mythological fame to husbands and lovers, Medea pleads her case—perhaps too cloyingly for modern taste—as an unfortunate wife abandoned by Jason following his marriage to Creon's daughter. Ovid addresses another of these letters to Jason, but this time from the complaining hand of Hypsipyle, whom Jason had left behind with her two children on the island of Lemnos. These fictitious love letters influenced Chaucer's *Legend of Good Women*. In it he characterizes thrice-married Jason as the dragon and devourer of love, the destroyer of noble and tender women, while Ysiphile (Chaucer's Hypsipyle) and Medea are Love's martyrs. The epic tradition of Apollonius Rhodius was kept alive by Valerius Flaccus (d. A.D. 93). His *Argonautica* owes much to the Hellenistic poet—as well as to Vergil and Ovid, both of whom studied Apollonius carefully—and like many of his countrymen who used Greek mythological matter, he invests his characters with Roman pathos and Roman dignity. The modern literary descendant of Apollonius Rhodius and Valerius Flaccus is William Morris who wrote *The Death of Jason* (1867, p. 271), an epic of over 7000 lines compounded from a variety of ancient sources and classical dictionaries into a smooth poetic mixture—perhaps too bland for modern taste—of Victorian pathos and romance, melancholy and pessimism as we observe Jason dying "of love, of honour, and of joy bereft."

Among dramatists, few have attempted to match Euripides' *Medea* and his personification of vindictive passion and fury. Seneca adapted the story for a Roman audience. Like his other plays, which were designed to be read rather than performed on stage, Seneca amplifies the tragic situation with rhetoric, Stoic moralizing, and the macabre. In place of the tigress of Euripides, we have more of an Ovidian sorceress occupied with magical incantations and the supernatural, theatrical devices which were not lost upon Shakespeare and other Elizabethans. (We need only compare Medea's invocation to the infernal deities with Lady Macbeth's "Come, you spirits / That tend on mortal thoughts, unsex me here. . . .") And where Euripides has Medea murder her children offstage, Seneca has her perform the bloody deed onstage; where Euripides makes the act one of bold determination, Seneca has a half-crazed woman whipped into it by the appearance of Furies and the ghost of her brother Apsyrtus; and where Euripides eases the brutality of the infanticide by insisting on a secure burial and the institution of sacred rites in their honor, the Roman poet has Medea toss the bodies of her slain children to Jason as she flies off in her winged chariot.

Between Seneca's empurpled *Medea* and the twentieth century, there is little to recommend except a trilogy on the entire story of the Argonauts, *Das goldene Vliess* (1822) by the celebrated Austrian dramatist Franz Grillparzer. But the year 1946 saw the creation of two versions of Medea, one American and the other French. The American poet Robinson Jeffers loosely translated Euripides' *Medea*, heavily accenting the violence and fury born out of strangulated love and a passion-swept family relationship. Earlier, Jeffers had taken the story of Medea for his poem *Solstice* (1935) and transported it to a desolate locale on the coast of California. There, an untamed woman (Madrone Bothwell) murders her two children rather than give them into the custody of her estranged husband. She carries off their bodies in a battered automobile—Jeffers' version of Medea's dragon-drawn chariot —into the desert where she buries them and then disappears.

Jean Anouilh took the story of Medea from both Euripides and Seneca to explicate the aftereffects of early love and violence. *Médée*, written in 1946 but first put on stage in 1953, is the story of Jason and Medea at Corinth where the two have arrived after ten years of adventuring and brawling, loving and hating. Jason is now approaching middle age; he is tired and ready to compromise with life, "to play the game" and to become an ordinary man. He sees in Creon's daughter the purity and simplicity that will make possible for him a humble form of happiness. Medea, whom Anouilh portrays as a kind of gypsy, also has aged, but she is determined not to surrender to her present circumstances; she still dreams of recapturing the perfect communion, the ecstasy and animal excitement of her earlier life with Jason, and although she is no longer in love with Jason, she is not willing to let him go. These irreconcilable polarities produce the tragic situation. Medea strangles her children and stabs herself before plunging headlong into the flames of her burning caravan. The small talk by the guard and nurse, which immediately follows this scene and brings the one-act play to an end, is Anouilh's laconic comment on how quickly the Jasons and Medeas of this world are forgotten. Seneca's hand appears in the spectacular effects of Medea's invocation to the Spirit of Evil, in the burning scene, and in passages of rhetorical power; the overall effect of *Médée* is a closet drama much in the style of the Roman poet.

From the seventeenth century to the present, over a dozen operas have been composed on the theme of Jason and Medea—twenty, if one were to count those which include the voyage of the Argonauts—yet only one has made a place for itself in the modern operatic repertoire. Luigi Cherubini's *Médée* (1797), which has been praised for its tragic grandeur and passion, is a loose rendering of the Euripidean drama. After being spurned by Jason, Medea commits her vengeful murders and then appears before a distraught Jason surrounded by the three Furies. She holds in her hand the bloody dagger and tells him that her shade will await him at the sacred river (Styx). The temple, which she has set on fire, erupts into flames and the horrified people flee in terror.

In the field of the visual arts, only the work of the French painter Delacroix has made a stir: between the years 1838 and 1862 he gave us three renderings of Medea and her children which owe more to Roman pathos than to Euripidean horror. As for poetic allusions, Shakespeare can compare the hair of Portia in *The Merchant of Venice* with the golden fleece which makes "many Jasons come in quest of her." In the same play, an enchanted night is compared by Jessica to that night in which "Medea gathered the enchanted herbs / That did renew old Aeson." And in *2 Henry VI*, young Clifford vows revenge against the house of York with these words when he discovers the body of his father:

> Henceforth I will not have to do with pity.
> Meet I an infant of the house of York,
> Into as many gobbets will I cut it
> As wild Medea young Absyrtus did.

The Calydonian Hunt. Shortly before Jason and his band of Argonauts set out for distant lands and the golden fleece, another heroic adventure took place, the hunt for the ravaging Calydonian boar. The legendary setting for the story is within Greece proper, around the city of Calydon in the land of the Aetolians. The leading roles are played by Meleager, his mother and father Althaea and Oeneus, and his two uncles, all descendants of Aeolus. The *ingénue* of the tale is Atalanta (or Atalante), a tomboy huntress whose pedigree is either Arcadian or Boeotian. Homer tells part of the story in the *Iliad* where it is cited as an object lesson to a stubborn and petulant Achilles who has withdrawn from the battle. Achilles is approached by his old preceptor Phoenix who tells him how the Curetes besieged the Calydonians in their city when a dispute arose over the carcass of the boar. When Meleager withdrew from the defense of the city in anger over his mother, he

Figure 77.   Picasso. Meleager killing
the Calydonian boar. *Lithograph, 1931,
illustrating Ovid's* Metamorphoses.
*Spencer Collection, The New York
Public Library, Astor, Lenox and Tilden
Foundation.*

was promised all sorts of rich gifts by the Aetolians if he would rejoin the fray. He
was moved only by the tears of his wife Cleopatra, daughter of Marpessa and Idas
(p. 137), but by that time he had to forfeit the rich gifts even though he helped defeat the Curetes. Homer's version of the story may have had behind it a historical
struggle, but as the tale evolved in later times, the war between the Calydonians and
the Curetes faded into the background and the hunt became the leading episode.
It was a hunt which attracted not only heroes from all over Greece, but also a host
of dramatic incidents and folktale elements.

It so happened one year in Calydon that its king Oeneus gave thanks to the gods
for a prosperous year but neglected the altar of Artemis. The goddess, slighted by
this oversight, sent a huge boar—it was big as a bull, with tusks to match those of an
elephant, and with bristles like spears—to ravage the fields of Calydon. So monstrous was this goddess-sent creature that no one had the corrage to hunt it down, no
one except Meleager. Deciding that the dire situation required a cooperative effort,
Meleager issued an invitation to the heroes of Greece to join in the hunt. Many of
the volunteers were the same as those who later took part in the voyage of the Argonauts: Jason, Castor and Polydeuces, Peleus, Telamon, Theseus and his comrade
Pirithous. There were also Laertes, father of Odysseus, Nestor in the prime of his
life, Amphiaraus not yet betrayed by his wife, and the beautiful huntress from the
Arcadian forests, Atalanta. Meleager fell in love with Atalanta at first sight, but
for the moment he had the hunt on his mind.

The heroes tracked down the boar. The animal made its charge from the under-
brush, tossing dogs and nets left and right. Several spear-throws went wild; some of
the lesser-known heroes were killed or wounded; Nestor would not have lived to
take part in the Trojan War had he not used his spear to vault into a tree and save
himself from the slashing tusks. Atalanta was the first to wound the beast with an arrow; Amphiaraus struck it in the eye; and Meleager mortally wounded the monstrous creature with a well-aimed spear (fig. 77). The head and hide of the Calydo-

nian boar were given to Meleager as his prize, but the young man was so impressed by the beauty and skill of Atalanta that he turned over the honored prize to her. This was resented by the other heroes, and in particular by Meleager's uncles. Plexippus and Toxeus. They snatched the prize from Atalanta. Meleager was beside himself with rage and killed his offending uncles.

Back in Calydon, Meleager's mother Althaea offered sacrifices to the gods for her son's victory over the boar, but when she saw her brothers' bodies, she vowed to avenge herself on their murderer even though he was her own son. Now it happened that when Meleager was born, Althaea was visited by the three Fates and was told that the life of her newborn child would last as long as a certain log in the fire kept burning—the familiar life token or external soul. Althaea quickly had the burning log doused with water and stored in a safe place, and thus the life span of Meleager was not cut short. But the sight of her dead brothers drove the distraught mother to bring out the fateful log and to throw it into a blazing fire. Meleager, far off and unaware of what his mother had done, suddenly felt his innards burning with fever; and as the log burned more fiercely, so did Meleager until both log and hero died. Althaea completed the act of vengeance by taking her own life. Meleager's sisters were so overcome with grief at the death of their brother that Artemis transformed them into guinea hens (*meleagrides*), all except two, Gorge and Deianira. The former was to have a son, who would lead the Aetolian contingent against Troy; the latter was to be Heracles' last spouse.

Atalanta. Thus the post-Homeric account of the Calydonian hunt. But what of Atalanta? She drops from the picture of the hunt and becomes the central attraction of a competition for her hand in marriage. The story is complicated by the fact that there are two heroines by the name of Atalanta, one Boeotian and the other Arcadian. There is also an intermingling of a folk theme—many try and fail to win the hand of the princess—and an apparent by-form of the goddess Artemis (p. 153). The Boeotian tradition calls her a daughter of Schoeneus, son of Athamas; the Arcadians say she was a daughter of Iasus, son of Lycurgus and a descendant of Arcas. However that may be, the popular tale tells of how her father wanted a son and was disappointed when his wife bore him a daughter. He exposed the newborn child on Mount Parthenius (Virgin) where a she-bear came upon the infant, suckled it from time to time until hunters came upon the child. Growing up among hunters, Atalanta became expert with the bow and could outstrip any man in a footrace. Apart from her role in the Calydonian hunt, she is said to have wrestled with Peleus and won at the games honoring the death of Pelias; and some even say that she was a member of the expedition of the Argonauts. She was, however, shy of men and averse to marriage. Later, when she was restored to her parents, her father desired her to marry. She agreed on condition that any suitor who wanted to win her hand would have to compete with her in a footrace. If he won, she would marry him; if he lost, it would mean his death.

Hippomenes (or Milanion in another tradition) fell in love with Atalanta and decided to enter the competition in which so many men had met their death. One look at her new competitor melted the cold heart of Atalanta. Hippomenes prayed to Aphrodite for help, and the goddess readily responded by providing him with three golden apples from the garden near her temple on the island of Cyprus. Others say that the precious fruit came from the tree in the garden of the Hesperides. The race was on. As Atalanta was about to overtake Hippomenes, he let one of the apples drop in front of the young girl. It caught her eye; she hesitated and then slowed down to pick it up. (Or was she more than ready to take advantage of any opportunity to let the handsome young man win the race, as some accounts have it?) The stratagem worked each time as Atalanta was about to draw ahead of her competitor Hippomenes won the race and Atalanta as his bride. But the marriage had a tragic ending, and the oracle which had predicted a disastrous outcome if Atalanta married proved true. In the bliss of their newfound love, the two forgot to show their gratitude to Aphrodite, and the goddess caused them to profane the temple of Cybele (or Zeus) with their lovemaking. Cybele (or Zeus) transformed Hippomenes into a lion, Atalanta into a lioness, and the two were yoked to the chariot of the goddess Cybele. The child of this marriage—some say Meleager was the father—was Parthenopaeus (son of a maiden). Like his mother, he was exposed on Mount Parthenius, suckled by a she-bear, and rescued. His name appears in the lists of the Seven who marched against Thebes, and at Thebes he met his fate along with so many other heroes.

*   *   *   *

In the seventeenth century, the legendary lives of Meleager and Atalanta inspired painters more than poets. Rubens and his workshop produced several versions of Meleager and Atalanta as well as scenes from the Calydonian hunt. Jacob Jordaens portrayed Atalanta, once with Meleager and again with Hippomenes. Guido Reni was attracted to the race of Atalanta and Hippomenes, Nicolas Poussin to the Calydonian hunt. In the nineteenth century, it was the turn of the poets. William Morris used the story of Atalanta and her race with Hippomenes for the opening tale of his "Chaucerian" *Earthly Paradise*. In a setting that resembled medieval England more than ancient Greece, Morris has his heroine overcome more by love than by the lure of the golden apples. The story ends with the blissful marriage of the two and without a hint of the unhappy fate accorded them in the ancient tale. Several years earlier, Swinburne had completed his *Atalanta in Calydon* (1865), a poetic drama modeled along the lines of a Greek tragedy. The play, while neither Greek in spirit nor dramatic in character, made Swinburne a celebrity and caused a sensation by its anti-Christian sentiment—the words "The supreme evil, God" were so abhorrent to Christina Rossetti that she struck them from her copy. In *Atalanta in Calydon*, the ancient, including fragments of Euripides' lost tragedy *Meleager*, mingles with Marquis de Sade's doctrine of cruelty, Victorian pantheism, and lines of lyric melody.

Of Swinburne's lyrics, the best-known come from the choral hymn to Artemis which begins with:

> When the hounds of spring are on winter's traces,
>   The mother of months in meadow or plain
> Fills the shadows and windy places
>   With lisp of leaves and ripple of rain;
> . . . .
> Come with bows bent and with emptying of quivers,
>   Maiden most perfect, lady of light,
> With a noise of winds and many rivers,
>   With a clamour of waters, and with might;
> Bind on thy sandals, O thou most fleet,
> Over the splendour and speed of thy feet;
> For the faint east quickens, the wan west shivers,
>   Round the feet of the day and the feet of the night.

Shakespeare drew several allusions from the story of Meleager and Atalanta, especially that of the burning brand. He also knew of Atalanta's ability as a runner, and in *As You Like It* he has Orlando say to his brother Jaques: "You have a nimble wit; I think 'twas made of Atalanta's heels." In *2 Henry IV*, Falstaff's page apparently confuses the story of the burning log with that of Hecuba's dream of her son Paris as a firebrand of Troy. When he cries out: "Away, you rascally Althaea's dream, away!" Prince Hal asks him for an explanation of the dream. The page replies: "Marry, my lord, Althaea dreamt she was delivered of a firebrand, and therefore I call him her dream." And in *2 Henry VI*, the Duke of York complains bitterly about political machinations and compares himself to Meleager:

> So York must sit and fret and bite his tongue
> While his own lands are bargain'd for and sold.
> Methinks the realms of England, France, and Ireland
> Bear that proportion of my flesh and blood
> As did the fatal brand Althaea burnt
> Unto the prince's heart of Calydon.

5. The Descendants of Erichthonius

Apart from the two main genealogical streams already described, there comes a spate of legendary figures from one city and one region, Athens and Attica. The heroic mythology of Attica is relatively poor, and with the exception of one figure, Theseus, no Athenian could boast of a dynasty of distinguished heroes for his city, not even of an outstanding warrior in the Trojan War. As for the list of legendary kings of Athens, the names on it are often doubled or confused; it thereby comes under the suspicion of being a late compilation and artificially pieced together so as to make it impressively and respectably long. However, in the heyday of Athens, her poets clothed the city with a mythical glory which they thought appropriate for the great city of their own time; and since Athenians were eloquent and their works were better preserved than most, a good number of Attic tales have survived to the present day.

The first mythical king of Athens was Cecrops who some scholars think may have been the eponymous hero of a very early tribe, the Cecropians, that inhabited the site of the later city. Having come from Attic soil, Cecrops was represented as half-man and half-snake, and to him was attributed the institution of monogamy, the burial of the dead, and the invention of writing. The line of kings really starts with Erichthonius, whose unusual birth we have already observed in Hephaestus' unsuccessful pursuit of a celibate Athena: how his seed fell on the earth, fertilized it, and eventually produced Erichthonius. From this point we can construct an abbreviated genealogy (p. 359) that will help us through the maze of family lines and lead us to the tragic tales of Procne and Philomela, Procris and Cephalus, Nisus and Scylla, and to the Theseus cycle.

When Erichthonius reached manhood, he deposed the then reigning king and took over the throne. He is said to have introduced the worship of Athena and the festival in honor of the goddess, the Panathenaea, and to have built her a temple on the Acropolis. He also performed other services for his people as is appropriate for a kind of culture hero. And when Athena contested with Poseidon for possession of the land, he quite naturally voted in favor of the goddess. The Erechtheum, one of

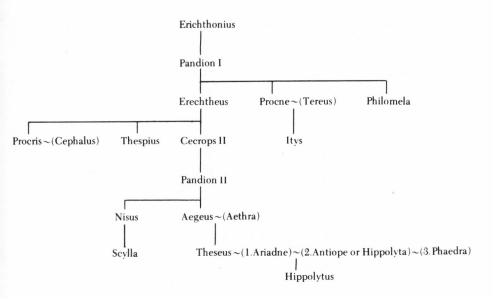

the three outstanding temples on the acropolis of Athens, has some connection with his worship or that of Erechtheus, the two often being confused. Erichthonius was succeeded by his son Pandion I, about whom there is little mythology. Tradition has it that Demeter and Dionysus came to Attica during his reign. In a war against Labdacus, king of Thebes, Pandion had the help of a certain Tereus who is commonly called a king of Thrace and a son of the war-god Ares. As a reward Pandion gave Tereus his daughter Procne in marriage, and thus begins a tragic tale. Ovid, who elaborates on the story in the *Metamorphoses*, attempts to outdo Euripides in purple patches and in showing the deadly effects of an all-consuming passion: Tereus, as is appropriate to a Thracian, is capable of any excess in order to satisfy his lust; Procne is fashioned along the lines of a vengeful Medea; and the plight of Philomela is designed to tug on our heartstrings.

Procne and Philomela. The marriage of Procne and Tereus was ill-omened from the start: the wedding was attended not by the Graces or the goddess of marriage, but rather by the Furies who lit up the wedding with torches stolen from a funeral. Under these circumstances, a child was conceived and given the name of Itys. After five years of marriage, Procne wished to see her sister Philomela and coaxed her husband to fetch her from Athens. It was there that Tereus laid eyes on the beautiful Philomela, and being a Thracian and all too quick to be overwhelmed by love, he burned with desire to possess his sister-in-law. He bided his time, however, and waited until Pandion gave his permission for Philomela to visit Procne. Tereus could hardly contain himself as his ship carried them to Thrace. But once on shore, he ravished the unwilling girl. Philomela begged her brother-in-law to kill her and raved incoherently that she would tell the world about his crime. Tereus took his sword and instead of killing her, cut out her tongue and imprisoned her. When he returned to Procne, he told her that Philomela had died on the trip to Thrace.

A year passed. Philomela in her prison had a loom to work on, and on it she wove the whole story of Tereus' infamy. She gave the tapestry (or robe) to a woman and with gestures instructed her to deliver it to Procne. Upon realizing what had happened to her sister, Procne was resolved on only one course: vengeance. She secretly contrived to free her sister from her prison. The two plotted their revenge. Noticing how much Itys resembled his father, Procne fixed on the child as a means of punishing her husband. Stifling her maternal feeling, Procne drove a knife through the child's breast, and together with her sister, hacked up his body, cooked it, and served it as a feast to Tereus. Tereus, unaware of the grisly dish, called for his son. Procne replied cryptically and cruelly: "You have within you the one you call." Again the king called for Itys. This time Philomela sprang forward and flung the gory head of Itys into the face of her ravisher. The sisters fled, pursued by a horror-maddened Tereus, and as he was about to overtake and kill them, the gods intervened. Procne was transformed into a nightingale, the tongueless Philomela into a swallow, and Tereus into a hoopoe.

According to Greek accounts, the tragic trio continued to utter the same cries which they had been emitting at the time of their metamorphosis: Procne plaintively calling the name of her son, *Itu! Itu!*; Tereus pursuing his wife with the words *Poo! Poo!*, Greek for "Where? Where?" Roman poets generally invert the transformation and make Philomela into a nightingale—perhaps attracted by a false etymology and her mellifluent name—and Procne into the inarticulate swallow.

*   *   *   *

In the Middle Ages, Ovid's version of the story was further embellished and enlarged with rhetoric and courtly love, as in the French *Philomena*. Or it became the subject of an elaborate allegory for *Ovide moralisé* (p. 129) which cautions both the body (Tereus) and the soul (Procne) against earthly delights (Philomela); when the body fixes its thoughts on these, and when the soul gives up the good life for the evil, the fruit of holy marriage (Itys) is destroyed. Chaucer found Ovid's version useful to make a more prosaic point in his *Legend of Good Women*: men are not always to be trusted.

Among the Elizabethans, the story was popular and the name "Philomel" became virtually synonymous with nightingale. In *Titus Andronicus* Shakespeare parallels the rape of Lavinia with that of Philomela, and in addition to having her tongue cut out, Lavinia's hands are also cut off so that she cannot communicate by writing. To make her situation known, she points out the story in Ovid to Titus. He then says:

> Lavinia, shall I read?
> This is the tragic tale of Philomel
> And treats of Tereus' treason and his rape;
> And rape, I fear, was the root of thine annoy.
> . . . .
> Lavinia, wert thou thus surpris'd, sweet girl,
> Ravish'd and wrong'd as Philomela was
> Forc'd in the ruthless, vast, and gloomy woods?

Elizabethan echoes did not fall uselessly on T. S. Eliot's ear. George Gascoigne's undistinguished poem, *The Complaynt of Phylomene* (1576), used the name of the Thracian king to imitate the song of the nightingale, "tereu." Another imitative sound for a bird, especially for a nightingale, was "jug." And perhaps influenced by the words of Titus Andronicus "Forc'd in the ruthless . . . woods," Eliot produced these mocking and ironic words of sexual violation apropos of Sweeney and Mrs. Porter (p. 159), Eliot's two drab specimens of the human race (from *The Fire Sermon* of *The Waste Land*):

> Twit twit twit
> Jug jug jug jug jug jug
> So rudely forc'd
> Tereu

In the preceding poem of the same collection, *A Game of Chess*, Eliot portrays another inhabitant of the human wasteland: a rich, neurotic, and loveless woman who sits before a painting which shows,

> As though a window gave upon the sylvan scene
> The change of Philomel, by the barbarous king
> So rudely forced; yet there the nightingale
> Filled all the desert with inviolable voice
> And still she cried, and still the world pursues,
> 'Jug Jug' to dirty ears.

Eliot's mentor, Ezra Pound, also recalls the ancient story in his *Canto IV*:

> And by the curved, carved foot of the couch,
>   claw-foot and lion head, an old man seated
> Speaking in the low drone . . . :
>   Ityn!
> Et ter flebiliter, Ityn, Ityn!
> And she went toward the window and cast her down,
>   "All the while, the while, swallows crying:
> Ityn!
>   "It is Cabestan's heart in the dish."
>   "It is Cabestan's heart in the dish?
>   "No other taste shall change this."

In the nineteenth century, Swinburne was drawn to the ancient story for *Itylus* (1866)—the name is taken from Homer—as was Oscar Wilde for *The Burden of Itys* (1881); but both lack the intensity of feeling that Matthew Arnold was able to achieve in setting the classical tale of "love and hate, triumph and agony," amid English lawns and moonlight. From Arnold's *Philomela* (1853):

> O wanderer from a Grecian shore,
> Still, after many years, in distant lands,
> Still nourishing in thy bewilder'd brain
> That wild unquench'd, deep-sunken, old-world pain—
> Say, will it never heal?
> And can this fragrant lawn
> With its cool trees, and night,
> And the sweet, tranquil Thames,
> And moonshine, and the dew,
> To thy rack'd heart and brain
> Afford no balm?
> Dost thou to-night behold,
> Here, through the moonlight on this English grass,
> The unfriendly palace in the Thracian wild?
> Dost thou again peruse
> With hot cheeks and sear'd eyes

> The too clear web, and thy dumb sister's shame?
>
> . . . .
>
> Listen, Eugenia—
> How thick the bursts come crowding through the leaves!
> Again—thou hearest?
> Eternal passion!
> Eternal pain!

Erechtheus.   Erechtheus, the brother of Procne and Philomela, was the king of Athens and the father of more than a dozen children. In a battle defending the city, he killed a mortal son of Poseidon, Eumolpus, who pursued his father's claim on Attica. As a result, the god demanded that Erechtheus sacrifice his daughter Chthonia, and eventually he had Zeus strike the king dead with a bolt of lightning. The fate of Erechtheus was dramatized by Euripides in a play of which fragments only survive. (These fragments were known to Swinburne who composed a poetic drama in 1876 on this obscure theme; his *Erechtheus*, like *Atalanta in Calydon*, was an attempt to reproduce a tragedy in the style of Aeschylus.) Of the many children of Erechtheus, Procris and Thespius are best known. Thespius, the reputed founder of the city of Thespiae in Boeotia, was that same king who, for eugenic purposes, introduced Heracles to his fifty daughters (p. 301). Procris, like her cousin Procne, was destined to have a tragic end to her marriage. Her story, which centers on the theme of a test of the fidelity of a spouse, was combined with several others taken from a different cycle of tales, especially that of the love of the goddess of dawn Eos (Roman Aurora) for a mortal.

Procris and Cephalus.   Procris was married to Cephalus, a son of the king of Phocis and a grandson of Aeolus. The marriage was a happy one. Once, however, when Cephalus was taking part in a hunt, he was seen by Eos who fell passionately in love with him and carried him off. (Other traditions tell of another young man by the name of Cephalus, a son of Hermes, who was abducted by Eos and became the father of Tithonus.) When he rejected the advances of the goddess, she prophesied that one day he would regret having Procris for his wife. As he returned home, Cephalus began to be filled with doubts about his wife's fidelity during his absence. He decided to test her and Eos helped by turning him into a handsome stranger. Procris at first remained unmoved by the seductive offer of rich gifts by a strange man in return for her favors. But when she started to hesitate, Cephalus could no longer restrain himself. He made himself known and burst forth with accusations of her infidelity. Procris was overwhelmed with shame and fled to the mountains where she became a devotee and favorite of the goddess Artemis. Cephalus, still hopelessly in love with his wife, recanted in time and begged her to return to him. Her hurt feelings assuaged, Procris agreed and the two lived happily as they had before. Procris presented Cephalus with two gifts which Artemis had given her: a spear which would never miss its mark and a hunting dog by the name of Laelaps (Storm) which would never lose its prey—the very same dog which Amphitryon later used when hunting the fox ravaging Boeotia (p. 299). Another tradition reports that Procris fled to Crete where Minos in gratitude gave her the spear and dog for sharing his bed and curing him of a frightening spell cast upon him by Pasiphaë whenever he had intercourse with other women.

The story now takes a turn; Procris becomes suspicious of her husband's fidelity. Cephalus was accustomed to go off on hunting trips, and when tired of the chase, he would stretch out in a shady place to enjoy the cooling breeze. At times he would call out for the breeze (*aura* both in Greek and Latin): "Come, dear Aura, comfort me and relieve the heat I'm suffering from." Someone overheard him and thought he was calling out the name of a young girl. When this was reported to Procris, she was overwhelmed with grief and anxiety. She was determined to catch him in the act; otherwise she would not be able to bring herself to believe that her husband was not true to her. On the following morning, she stole out after Cephalus and hid near the suspected trysting place. Cephalus soon arrived and stretched himself out on the grass and called for gentle Aura. Suddenly, he heard, or thought he heard, a sound coming from the nearby bushes. He sprang up, and thinking that a wild animal was concealed there, he hurled his spear, the spear which could never miss its mark, in the direction of the sound and mortally wounded Procris. As she lay dying in his arms, she begged him not to let Aura take her place in his affections. It was too late for Cephalus to explain that Aura was not a lover but "aura" the breeze.

The sad tale of Procris and Cephalus, prettified with Hellenistic romance, inspired no major work in modern literature. Shakespeare playfully alludes to the two lovers in the play-within-a-play in *A Midsummer Night's Dream* when Pyramus and Thisbe confess their love to each other with this couplet: "Not Shafalus to Procrus was so true." / "As Shafalus to Procrus, I to you." But among artists of the sixteenth and seventeenth century, various elements of the story were quite attractive, a situation that, curiously enough, did not obtain for Procne and Philomela. Piero di Cosimo painted the death of Procris, A. Caracci a fresco of the abduction of Cephalus, and Poussin a portrait of Cephalus. In the eighteenth century, Boucher pictured Aurora and Cephalus.

Scylla, Daughter of Nisus. So far, the distaff side of the descendants of Erichthonius have been the main mythological attractions, but with Pandion II, a son of Cecrops II, the male descendants—Nisus, Aegeus, and Theseus—hold the center of the stage. Pandion II, whose legendary life was as spare as that of his doublet Pandion I, was said to have been driven out of Athens and to have taken refuge at Megara, a town situated on the isthmus of Corinth. It was there that he married the daughter of the king and fathered, among other children, Nisus and Aegeus. Pandion's sons eventually reconquered Athens and placed Aegeus on the throne. Nisus remained at Megara as its king until he met his end through the treachery of his love-struck daughter. His story parallels that of Pterelaus and Meleager whose lives, Samson-like, depended on an external soul. Upon Nisus' purple lock of hair hangs a brief tale.

When Androgeus, a son of Minos and Pasiphaë, was killed at Athens, the king of Crete launched an attack at both Athens and Megara. As Minos lay siege to the town of Megara, Nisus' daughter Scylla—not to be confused with the sea-monster of the same name—caught sight of the Cretan king and fell passionately and irretrievably in love with him. As the war dragged on and the fate of the city hung in the balance, Scylla's longing drove her to a desperate act. Knowing that the safety of the city and her father's life depended on a lock of purple (or golden) hair on his head, she planned to cut it off and thereby win the gratitude and love of Minos. Although beset by misgivings and guilt, she stole in on her father as he slept and cut off the fateful lock of hair, thus cutting short his life. When Scylla presented her grim prize to Minos and confessed her love for him, the Cretan king recoiled in horror, cursed her for her impious deed, and vowed to have nothing to do with her and her professions of love. As he sailed off in his ship, Scylla dashed into the water, and strengthened by her emotions, swam to the vessel, grasped and held on to its stern. Nisus, who had been metamorphosed into an osprey, a fish-devouring hawk, saw her from the air and plummeted down to attack her. At that moment Scylla was transformed into a bird—some say a fish—called the Ciris. Other accounts which do not tell of transformations say simply that when Minos conquered Megara, he tied Scylla by the feet to the stern of a ship and drowned her.

Aegeus.   When we come to Aegeus, the brother of Nisus and father of Theseus, we are at a crossroads in Attic mythology where legend, myth, and history intersect. The name Aegeus, as we have already seen, is closely associated with the Aegean Sea and the palace of Poseidon at Aegae, the strong likelihood being that Aegeus is a by-form or humanization of the sea-god himself. And as Athens became an important maritime center in historical times, the worship of Poseidon became more and more prominent with the result that in legend the god shared in the paternity of Athen's greatest hero Theseus. At the same time, Attic legends undoubtedly preserve a reminiscence of a much earlier time, during the middle of the second millennium B.C., when Athens had close connections with Minoan Crete and may actually have been a vassal state of the Cretan empire. From the viewpoint of mythology, however, all these roads lead to one figure, Theseus.

The story of Aegeus begins with his lordship over Athens. He was twice married but neither wife bore him children. He went to the oracle at Delphi to seek a remedy to this unhappy situation. The oracle given to him was in riddling phraseology: not to open the wineskin until he reached the height of Athens. Aegeus did not know what to make of the god's response. On his way home, he stopped off at the town of Troezen in the Peloponnese where he was hospitably received by Pittheus, a son of Pelops. When Aegeus reported the strange oracle he had received, Pittheus had no difficulty in interpreting the god's meaning. He entertained Aegeus lavishly, plied him with wine, and when his guest was thoroughly inebriated, he sent his daughter Aethra to share his bed. There was a double impregnation, for on that very night Aethra had a dream which instructed her to go to a nearby island, and when she did, she was also embraced by the sea-god Poseidon. On the following day Aegeus told Aethra that if she were to bear him a son, she should bring him up in secret, and when he was of age she should send him to Athens if he could recover a sword and sandals which he had hidden under a huge rock.

From Troezen, Aegeus went to Corinth where, as we have seen, he told Medea of his difficulties in becoming a father and received her promise to help him if he were to grant her sanctuary in Athens. Back home, Aegeus was to face further problems: his brother Pallas and his fifty sons had designs on his throne, and the death of Androgeus, the son of Minos, precipitated a war with the Cretan king which resulted in Athens having to provide seven young men and seven young women annually as fodder for the Minotaur. The rest of the story belongs to Theseus, the son of Aegeus-Poseidon, Athens' hero *par excellence*. A considerable amount of that story is owed to Plutarch, the indefatigable philosopher and biographer who composed Theseus' biography, real or legendary, for the *Parrallel Lives* (A.D. 105–115).

Theseus.   At Troezen, Aethra in due course gave birth to a son whom she named Theseus. When he grew to manhood, she led him to the rock under which Aegeus had deposited the identifying sword and sandals. Demonstrating by his strength that he was worthy to be a hero, Theseus easily lifted the boulder and made it known that he was going to join his father at Athens. His mother and grandfather urged him to make the trip by sea, which was then by far the safest way to travel, but Theseus, being young and inspired by the deeds of Heracles, insisted on taking the land route which at that time was beset by sadistic brigands and terrorists. The labors of Theseus are obviously influenced by those of Heracles, but a difference should be noted: while Heracles' labors in the Peloponnese deal with impossible tasks and equally improbable monsters, those of Theseus are concerned with civilizing the land—the Athenians always prided themselves on being great civilizers—and making the roads safe for travel.

The "Labors" of Theseus. The first adventure to face Theseus on his overland route to Athens was near Epidaurus where he came upon Periphetes who was surnamed Corynetes (Club-man). He dispatched the brigand and took his club which he used ever after as a symbol of his strength in imitation of Heracles. Further along the road, near the isthmus of Corinth, he came upon Sinis who had the sobriquet of Pityocamptes (Pine-bender). This unpleasant fellow used to force travelers to help him bend down pine trees. Sinis then unexpectedly would release his hold on the tree and the unfortunate traveler would fly like a shot through the air to his death. Another version has Sinis tying his victims to two different trees, releasing them, and sending his victims to a gory death. Theseus, however, did not fall for the ruse and killed the Pine-bender by his own cruel stratagem.

The only monstrous animal Theseus had to face was a ferocious sow—some call it a boar—which lived near Crommyon and which was given the name of Phaea. Some say that this savage sow, which had been roaming the countryside and terrorizing its inhabitants, was in reality a female bandit who was given the name of The Sow because of her greed and her voracious appetite. Sow or woman, Theseus killed her and continued on his way to Athens. Near Megara he met Sciron, another murderous brigand, who forced travelers to wash his feet as he sat near the edge of a cliff. As they squatted down to carry out his orders, Sciron unceremoniously kicked them off the cliff into the sea. When it was Theseus' turn, the hero simply refused to bend down; instead, he flung the disagreeable highwayman off the cliff.

Making his way still closer to Athens, Theseus came upon Cercyon the Arcadian, a most formidable wrestler. He took him on in a wrestling match and overcame him, not as Heracles had defeated Antaeus, but by the application of the principles of scientific wrestling. Finally, just before reaching Athens, Theseus came upon yet another bizarre brigand, Damastes, better known as Procrustes (Stretcher). Whenever this sadistic fellow caught a traveler, he placed him on a bed, or on one of two beds of different sizes. If his victim was too short for it, Procrustes stretched him out to fit the bed; if he was too tall for the rack, he was cut down to size. Theseus ended his life by giving him a taste of his own medicine. The Stretcher's name, however, has survived in English as "Procrustean" to describe an action or object that has been forced into conformity by violent or arbitrary means.

With the road to Athens safer than it had ever been before, Theseus entered the city. There he found Medea and her son living with his father. The sorceress of Colchis immediately recognized him and saw in him a threat to her security. She induced Aegeus to offer the stranger a cup of poisoned wine; but just as Theseus was about to put the cup to his lips, the old man recognized the sword in his hand as the one that he had planted under the rock at Troezen and dashed the cup of wine to the ground. Medea and her son were banished; father and son were joyfully reunited. Another threat was posed by Pallas and his sons who had hoped to depose Aegeus and take over the kingdom. In short order, Theseus defeated his uncle and helped his father stabilize his rule at Athens. Then came news that the bull, which Heracles had brought back from Crete and turned loose on the plain of Marathon, had been ravaging the countryside. Theseus caught the Marathonian bull, dragged it victoriously through the streets of Athens, and sacrificed it to Apollo.

Theseus versus the Minotaur. No sooner had Theseus set things straight at Athens than the time came for the Athenians to send their periodic tribute of seven young men and seven girls to Minos. Theseus volunteered to be one of the seven young men and promised to put an end to the tribute and the deadly Minotaur. Aegeus reluctantly let his son go, but first made him promise that if he were successful in his venture, he would change the black sails of the ship to white when his ship returned. When the Athenians arrived in Crete, Minos came down to the shore and looked over the crop of young men and women. One very attractive girl caught his eye, and when he singled her out for his bed, Theseus sprang forward and declared that he, a son of Poseidon, would protect the girl. Minos laughed at him and bragged that he was a son of Zeus. To prove it, he made a sign and thunder sounded out of a clear sky. He challenged Theseus to prove his claim as a son of Poseidon by recovering a ring which he threw at some distance into the sea. (In some accounts, the contest between Theseus and Minos takes place at sea.) Without hesitation, Theseus plunged into the deep, and with the help of Poseidon's wife Amphitrite and various sea-nymphs, he not only recovered Minos' ring but he also brought back a gem-encrusted crown which he later gave to Ariadne as a wedding gift. After her death, it was placed in the heavens as a constellation.

Ariadne, Minos' daughter, had accompanied her father to the shore when the Athenian ship put in with her human cargo. As soon as she saw Theseus, she fell in love with the handsome hero. Knowing full well that Theseus would meet his death once imprisoned in the labyrinth, she offered to help her newfound love if he would carry her off to Athens and marry her. Theseus readily agreed to the proposition. She then secretly gave him a ball of magic thread designed by Daedalus (or Hephaestus) that would enable him to find his way out of the labyrinth. Theseus took the ball of thread, fastened one end over the entrance of the maze, and let it out slowly as he penetrated ever deeper into the lair of the Minotaur. When, finally, he came face to face with the miscegenated monster, he grappled with him (fig. 78), killed him, and offered him as a sacrifice to Poseidon. With the help of the unwound ball of thread, Theseus retraced his steps until he made his way out of the labyrinth.

Adriadne Abandoned. Together with his fellow-Athenians and Ariadne, the hero embarked on his ship and sailed away to the island of Naxos (Dia). What happened there to Ariadne is variously told. The most common tradition is that Theseus callously abandoned her, and that she would have put an end to her own life in despair, had she not been saved by Dionysus who made her his wife. The peculiar circumstances surrounding Ariadne—her connection with Dionysus and, as Plutarch reports, her postmortem worship on Cyprus as Ariadne Aphrodite— make scholars view her as a one-time Aegean goddess whose divinity faded with

Figure 78. Theseus killing the Minotaur. *Vase painting. British Museum.*

the passing years. However that may be, Theseus abandoned her and set sail for Athens. On his way he stopped off at various Aegean islands where he was credited with instituting various rituals and religious observances. Finally, he hove to in sight of his homeland, but he forgot to change the sails from black to white as his father had ordered as a signal of his successful return. Aegeus, who had been anxiously awaiting the return of the ship from Crete, saw the black sails from his vantage point on the acropolis, and thinking that his son was dead, leaped off the height and was dashed to death on the rocks below. This is the Greek report of his end; some Roman writers claim that he flung himself into the sea which thereafter bore his name, the Aegean. With the passing of his father, Theseus became king of Athens. The ship on which he was said to have made his historic voyage was preserved by the Athenians until the end of the fourth century B.C.

*   *   *   *

Poets, painters, and writers of musical drama have had their imaginations stirred by the romantic infatuation of Ariadne for Theseus and by her subsequent marriage to Dionysus (Bacchus). Ovid, an omnipresent influence in the arts, composed a literary epistle for Ariadne in his *Heroides* in which she charges Theseus with being a faithless lover and an ingrate, but she ends her long and pitiful complaint with a plea that he return to her. Earlier, Catullus (c. 84 – c. 54 B.C.), the greatest lyric poet of Republican Rome, described the plight of Ariadne as if one were to see it pictured on a tapestry. In a short epic, an epyllion, done in the Alexandrian style, Catullus wove the story of Ariadne and Theseus into his poem on the wedding of Thetis and Peleus. In his description of the drapery on the wedding bed, Catullus gives us a remarkable picture of the psychological state of Ariadne when she awakes and discovers that she has been abandoned (fig. 79). This is a brief portion of that description as translated by the American poet Horace Gregory:

> On this bed a tapestry weaves the legend of old heroes and
>   their deeds. See Ariadna
> gazing from the wave resounding shores of Dia, see her
>   trembling (heart torn with mad love) as Theseus
> sails upon the far horizon. Shaken from dark sleep and

dreams that betrayed her, Ariadna
gazes stricken, unbelieving at this vision of swift oars bear-
    ing him, the thoughtless lover, gone from her,
his promises now mingled with the roaring sea winds rising
    to the empty skies. She stands deserted
helpless on her lonely shore.
Now as Theseus plunges oarstruck waves, a daughter of Minos
    rises from seaweed (and like Bacchante
carved from marble, mad with tears and oceanic passion in
    her blood all grief now stripped and trembling
stand full naked) girdle fallen from her breasts and delicate
    headdress
in salt waves at her feet. But she, her mind in passion, fixed
    on you O Theseus,
cared nothing for dress, spirit, mind, body lost in darkness
that filled her brain, poor girl (the brain gone mad, hung in
    mid-air terrified)
for Venus poured maddening grief into her heart from the
    very hour that Theseus
aggressive, brave, left the embracing arms of Piraeus harbour
    and strode the palace of the Cretan King.

Figure 79.   Ariadne abandoned by
Theseus on the island of Naxos (Dia).
*An illustration in a fifteenth century
manuscript of Ovid's* Heroides.
Bibliothèque Nationale, Paris. (Giraudon)

Centuries later, Beaumont and Fletcher, in *The Maid's Tragedy* (1619), used a literary device similar to that of Catullus. Aspatia, lamenting the loss of her lover Amintor, observes her attendants weaving the sad story of Ariadne in a tapestry, and seeing that her plight parallels that of Ariadne, bids them to use her as a model. Three hundred years later, T. S. Eliot, who quotes several lines of Aspatia in his epigraph to *Sweeney Erect* (c. 1919), continues the tradition with this beautiful picture before he jars us with a lurid description of his twentiety-century vulgarian:

> Paint me a cavernous waste shore
>   Cast in the unstilled Cyclades,
> Paint me the bold anfractuous rocks
>   Faced by the snarled and yelping seas.
>
> Display me Aeolus above
>   Reviewing the insurgent gales
> Which tangle Ariadne's hair
>   And swell with haste the perjured sails.

And in a brief allusion in his *Casino*, W. H. Auden compares the labyrinth with the maze of modern life from which there is no means of escape: "The labyrinth is safe but endless, and broken/Is Ariadne's thread."

In musical drama, more than two dozen operas were composed on the events in the life of Ariadne, from Monteverdi's *Arianna* (1608) to Darius Milhaud's *L'Abandon d'Ariane* (1927). The latter was part of *Operas Minutes*, Milhaud's attempt to establish a short form of opera. The other two musical pieces of this work were also taken from Cretan and Attic mythology: *L'Enlèvement d'Europe* (The Rape of Europa) and *La Deliverance de Thésee*. The most prominent of these many operas in contemporary repertoire is Richard Strauss' *Ariadne auf Naxos* (1912) with a libretto by Hugo von Hofmannsthal (p. 334). An opera-within-an-opera, *Ariadne* celebrates with humor and melody, in an eighteenth-century setting, the melancholy of a lost love and the miracle of love regained. In a related field, ballet, the tribulations of Ariadne also provided choreographers with a theme, the latest being Balanchine's *The Triumph of Bacchus and Ariadne* (1948).

Hippolytus and Phaedra.   After Theseus had returned and killed off all those who challenged his right to succeed his father as king, he is claimed to have instituted a number of major political, social, and economic innovations at Athens: the union of various communities of Attica into one state with Athens at its head—the so-called synoecism, a historical event but like many others anachronistically attributed to the popular hero of the Athenians—a democratic form of government, the coinage of money, and the institution of various games, including the Isthmian in honor of Poseidon. There were yet other adventures in store for Theseus. His name appears on the roster of the Argonauts who joined with Jason in the legendary maritime undertaking. He also joined with Heracles or went off on his own, to invade the land of the Amazons where he won by force their queen Antiope (or her sister Hippolyta) who in due course bore him a son Hippolytus. The Amazons then invaded Attica and penetrated to the heart of Athens where Theseus defeated them after a desperate battle. After the death of the Amazon queen, Theseus married Phaedra, sister of Ariadne, who became the mother of two children. This marriage was to result in a tragedy in which the leading characters were Theseus' new bride Phaedra and his illegitimate son Hippolytus.

The story takes place in Troezen where Theseus and his entire family have gone into temporary exile following the slaying of a kinsman. Hippolytus, who has now grown into a handsome youth, has dedicated himself to the goddess Artemis and to a life of celibacy. His chastity, however, has offended Aphrodite, and for refusing to honor her and her rites, the goddess of love is determined to punish him. Using Phaedra as an instrument in her plan, she causes Theseus' wife to fall hopelessly in love with her stepson. In spite of Phaedra's determination to resist the passion that has overwhelmed her, she allows her nurse to attempt to effect a liaison between herself and Hippolytus. When the nurse approaches the young man, he is so horrified and outraged at the suggestion of a love affair with his stepmother, or with any woman for that matter, that he bursts out into a tirade against women and their deceitful ways. Phaedra, who has overheard the diastrous consequences of her nurse's plan, ties a noose about her neck and commits suicide. But so that her children would not suffer, and so that Hippolytus would also be punished, she leaves a note behind in which she accuses Hippolytus of having taken her by force. At that moment, Theseus, who had been absent from Troezen, arrives and reads the suicide note that Phaedra had tied to her wrist. Believing that his son is responsible for what has happened to his wife, Theseus prays to Poseidon to grant him one of the three wishes promised him: that Hippolytus be killed on that very day. When confronted by his father, Hippolytus insists that he is innocent and defends his character and his religious ideals. Theseus remains unconvinced and orders his son's banishment. As Hippolytus drives his chariot along the coast road, Poseidon sends huges waves and a sea-monster which frightens the horses and causes them to overturn the chariot. Entangled in the reins and dragged along by the terrified horses, Hippolytus is mortally injured. Theseus learns the truth too late: Artemis tells him that Aphrodite is responsible for the death of both Phaedra and Hippolytus.

*   *   *   *

This is the essence of the story contained in Euripides' *Hippolytus* which was exhibited at Athens in 428 B.C. When the same theme was treated some five hundred years later by Seneca in his *Phaedra*, the Greek tragedy of opposing and antagonistic powers—as seen in Aphrodite and Artemis, Phaedra and Hippolytus—was turned into a Roman melodrama in which the divine played no part at all, only the illicit lust of Phaedra. In place of the nurse acting as a go-between, Seneca preferred a confrontation between a love-tempting Phaedra and a scornful woman-hating Hippolytus. There is no letter with false accusations left behind, but there is another confrontation, this time between Theseus and Phaedra. And when the news is brought back that Hippolytus has been torn to pieces, a guilt-ridden Phaedra comes on the stage to kill herself with a sword.

In the seventeenth century, Jean Racine (1639–1699) made his reputation by adapting the ancient story for a French audience. His *Phèdre*, a terrifying portrayal of unrequited passion, called for yet other changes. Hippolytus, though chaste, is neither the religious celibate nor the woman-hater of Euripides and Seneca; he loves Aricia, a daughter of Pallas, whose family has been outlawed by Theseus. A false report of Theseus' death encourages Phaedra to make known her love for Hippolytus, only to be shattered by the news that her husband is alive and returning to Athens. Amid charges and countercharges, Hippolytus is banished and cursed by his father. On the verge of running off with Aricia, he leaves, only to be dragged to death by his maddened horses. An emotionally disturbed Phaedra appears before her distraught husband who now knows the entire truth. She reveals in her final speech that she has taken a draught of Medea's poison and calls upon death to restore her lost purity.

In the English-speaking world, the Hippolytus-Phaedra story was "discovered" by poets and playwrights in the twentieth century. T. Surge Moore's drama, *Aphrodite against Artemis*, reached the stage in 1906 and posed the two goddesses in a superhuman struggle for the possession of human souls. Moore was influenced not only by Euripides and Racine, but also by Robert Browning's *Artemis Prologizes* (1842), a fragment of a drama in which the poet intended to delve deeper into the story of Hippolytus and Aricia. The Imagist poet H. D., for whom both Phaedra and Hippolytus were the subject of four lyrics in her *Collected Poems* (1925), adapted the Euripidean tragedy for a complex lyrical drama, *Hippolytus Temporizes* (1927). The Hippolytus of H. D. loses his innocence and spiritual integrity when seduced by a passionate Phaedra who masquerades as the goddess Artemis. Even though he is told bluntly that he had slept with Phaedra, Hippolytus, unbelieving and in a state of ecstasy, goes to meet his death by being flung off his chariot. When he is revived by Helios and speaks fervidly of the intimacy which he believes he shared with the goddess, Artemis, shocked by his sensuality, orders him back to death.

Robinson Jeffers was another American poet who attempted an adaptation of Euripides' *Hippolytus* for a modern audience. *The Cretan Woman* (1954) follows Euripides in showing Hippolytus and Phaedra as tragic victims of a cruel and vindictive Aphrodite, but then Jeffers turns Senecan in his passion for confrontation and violence within an entangled family relationship. Phaedra abjectly confesses her love to Hippolytus whose "impediment of nature" suggests not religious devotion but homosexuality. When he rejects her, Medea-like she turns on him with the savage intent of hurting him. Upon Theseus' return, she convinces him that Hippolytus has defiled his bed and that she may bear his son's child. When all three come face to face, Phaedra cunningly tricks her husband into killing his innocent son with his own hand—and in full view of the audience, Immediately she turns on Theseus and pitilessly cries out that she has lied, that she loved his son and hated him, Theseus, the old manslaughterer who stinks of blood, the killer of generations of sons. Phaedra hangs herself without remorse, leaving the stage to the goddess Aphrodite who comments on the heedless power of the gods, and prophetically says that though men may control their envirnoment on earth and in space, "Let them beware. Something is lurking hidden./There is always a knife in the flowers. There is always a lion beyond the firelight."

The farthest removed from the details of the ancient tale is Eugene O'Neill's *Desire Under the Elms* which first reached the stage in 1924; since then it has had numerous revivals and was made into a film in 1962. O'Neill has set his play in bleak New England of the mid-nineteenth century, and to the theme of overwhelming passion, he has grafted on the Oedipal conflict between father and son. Eben (Hippolytus) is not the chaste and honorable figure of Euripides and Seneca; he bears a deep resentment against his father Ephraim (Theseus) for possessing both his mother and the land. He is eventually seduced by his father's new bride, the youthful Abbie (Phaedra). By her maternalism and her physical attractiveness, she lures Eben into committing incest in his mother's parlor. The liaison between son and stepmother, which at first is prompted by self-interest and sexual desire, turns into deep love. The child that is born to Abbie is advertised by Ephraim to his unbelieving and scoffing neighbors as his own. Eben rashly curses his new-born son—the curse uttered by Theseus against Hippolytus is transferred by O'Neill to Eben—and Abbie, not a supernatural force, becomes the agent of death. And like Theseus, Ephraim survives to survey the wreck of a family and a home.

Theseus and Pirithous.   There is a brief epilogue to the mythological career of Hippolytus. At the request of Artemis, he was restored to life by the legendary physician Asclepius. According to Roman accounts, he then went to the Alban Hills near Rome where he lived in a grove at Aricia—this is the source of the name of the young girl romantically linked with Hippolytus in later literature—and was identified with Virbius, an obscure male deity associated in worship with the Roman goddess Diana. As for Theseus, there were yet other adventures in store for him, adventures which he shared with the king of the Lapiths in Thessaly, Pirithous (or Peirithous) a son of Ixion or a son of Zeus by Ixion's wife. The two met when Pirithous invaded Marathon, and out of admiration for each other, the two soon became friends and allies. Pirithous accompanied Theseus on the hunt for the Calydonian boar, and according to some, went along with him on his expedition to the land of the Amazons. When Pirithous was to be married, he invited Theseus and other legendary celebrities to attend the wedding ceremonies in Thessaly. Invited also were the horse-shaped centaurs who were related to Pirithous through Ixion. Being overfond of wine, the lustful creatures lost control of themselves, and in their drunken state attempted to carry off the Lapith women; one of them even tried to asault the bride. Theseus pitched in with Pirithous and the other Lapiths and drove off the offensive centaurs.

The battle of the Lapiths and the centaurs, the so-called centauromachy, became a popular theme for ancient painters and sculptors. It is one of the mythological scenes on the famous François vase (c. 570 B.C.) now housed in the Museo Archeologico in Florence. It was also represented in a sculptural group, one of the greatest masterpieces of the fifth century B.C., on the west pediment of the Temple of Zeus at Olympia; other temples of antiquity (Bassae, "Theseum," and Parthenon) also used the centauromachy for their friezes and metopes (fig. 80). During the Renaissance, Michelangelo carved the story on a sculptural relief; Piero di Cosimo and Rubens put it on canvas.

Pirithous lost his wife soon after their marriage. Theseus and his comrade, both being widowers, sought new wives and decided on marrying daughters of Zeus. Theseus chose Helen, Zeus' daughter by Leda and later known as Helen of Troy; Pirithous chose to duplicate Hades' feat by carrying off Persephone. As Plutarch tells the story, both were attracted to Helen and cast lots for her with the understanding that the one who won her would have to help the other in getting a wife. The two went to Sparta where Helen was performing a ritual dance in honor of Artemis Orthia. They whisked her away and placed her in care of Theseus' mother Aethra at a place called Aphidna. When Theseus went off to help Pirithous find Persephone, the twin brothers of Helen, Castor and Polydeuces, recovered their sister and kidnapped Theseus' mother. As for Pirithous' enterprise, it was not so simple as the abduction of Helen, for Persephone was already married to Hades and to get to her meant a descent to the Underworld. When the descent was made, the two heroes were met by Hades who greeted them cordially enough. He invited

Figure 80. Centaur and Lapith battling one another. *Metope from the Parthenon, c. 445 B.C. British Museum. (Hirmer)*

them to sit down and immediately they found themselves stuck fast to the chairs and held fast by coils of serpents. Another version has it that the rock on which they sat grew to their flesh and held them as if clamped by a vise. There they remained until Heracles came under orders by Eurystheus to procure Hades' dog Cerberus. Heracles could do nothing for Pirithous but he managed to free Theseus. The story is also told that Theseus was stuck so fast to the rock that when Heracles tore him loose, a piece of him was left behind; and that, so the folk account goes, is the reason Athenians have such spare derrières. Plutarch rationalizes this modified motif of an attempted harrowing of hell by making Aidoneus (another name of Hades) a king of the Molossians who had a wife named Persephone, a daughter Kore, and a fierce hound by the name of Cerberus. Cerberus did away with Pirithous, and Theseus was held in confinement until liberated by Heracles.

The end of Theseus' life was not a happy one. When he returned to Athens after his adventure in the Underworld, he found that he had lost his throne and the affections of his people. He retired to the island of Scyros where he died, some say, by being pushed off a cliff by the king of the island. However, during the battle of Marathon in 490 B.C., his ghost, in full armor, was seen spurring on the Athenians against the Persians. After consulting the oracle at Delphi, his bones, or what were taken for his bones, were brought back to Athens where they were interred in the center of the city.

*   *   *   *

The checkered career of Theseus was used by Boccaccio for an ambitious literary undertaking. Dante had lamented the fact that no Italian had yet distinguished himself as a martial poet. Boccaccio saw himself as that poet. Taking as his models Vergil's *Aeneid* and Statius' *Thebaid*, he composed a "Theseid," the *Teseide* (1340–1342), which was supposedly based on the translation of a "lost" Greek romance. Although the wars of Theseus provide the background for the Italian epic, the foreground is filled with a mythological romance which is essentially Boccaccio's own creation: the story of Palamon and Arcite, a tale of love and friendship in which two Theban knights compete for the hand of Emilia, sister of the queen. The story was taken and modified by Chaucer for the *Knight's Tale* in the *Canterbury Tales*. Chaucer's version was adapted by Fletcher and Shakespeare for *The Two Noble Kinsmen* (1613) and then paraphrased by Dryden in heroic couplets for his *Palamon and Arcite* (1699). Shakespeare has the marriage of Theseus and Hippolyta as the central event for *A Midsummer's Night Dream*; for this play he undoubtedly used the background material available to him in Sir Thomas North's translation (1579) of Plutarch's life of Theseus.

Six hundred years after Boccaccio's *Teseide*, a French writer was to gain distinction, possibly greater than the Italian poet's, by another approach to the life of the Athenian hero. André Gide found in the character of Theseus, and in the many legendary figures surrounding him, the medium through which he could evaluate the long experience of his life as well as the means of attaining self-understanding. *Thésée* (1946), the last and most celebrated of Gide's myth-based works, is a complex of symbols, philosophical and self-confessional, which embrace a wide range of his moral, religious, social, and political views. The story is told in the first person and begins with this revealing statement:

> I wanted to tell the story of my life as a lesson for my son Hippolytus: but he is no more, and I am telling it all the same. For his sake I should not have dared to include, as I shall now do, certain passages of love; he was extraordinarily prudish, and in his company I never dared to speak of my attachments. Besides, these only mattered to me during the first part of my life; but at least they taught me to know myself, as did also the various monsters whom I subdued. For the first thing is to know exactly who one is . . . later comes the time to assess and adopt one's inheritance.

The Trojan War

Is this the face that launched a thousand ships.
And burnt the topless towers of Ilium?
Christopher Marlowe—*Dr. Faustus*

Four miles to the east of the Aegean entrance to the Dardanelles, on a plain near the Scamander River in Asia Minor, lay the ancient city of Troy. It was also known by the name of Ilium. Sometime toward the end of the second millennium, about 1200 B.C., the Troy of Priam and Hector was burned by an invading host and her physical remains were covered over by succeeding cities until the spade of the archaeologist unearthed the charred ruins of the once great city. Whoever it was that made the attack could hardly have dreamed of its consequences, for in the history of the world no war of any magnitude worked more on the imagination of poet and artist. The literature of the Western world opens with Homer's monumental epics which prominently display the effects of that war. From Homer and other Greek writers, the legends of the Trojan War passed to Rome and into the Latin language, and thus became a living force and a living tradition for both Greeks and Romans. And even when the tale of the Trojan War began to fade in late antiquity, two short prose narratives, originally written in Greek (now lost) and translated into Latin in the fourth and sixth centuries A.D., communicated the story in easy-to-read Latin for yet later generations. The writers of both these narratives—one a Cretan, the other a Phrygian—claim to have antedated Homer and to have been actual eyewitnesses to the events. Both claims have long since been shown to have no foundation in fact, but to the audiences of late antiquity and the Middle Ages, the attractiveness of having eyewitnesses to such a famous conflict was not complicated by scholarly investigation. One must keep in mind that Western Europe believed in the tradition developed by the Romans that they originated in Troy; in England, for example, "New Troy" (London) was settled by Brutus the Trojan.

375

Dictys Cretensis, who said he was a member of the contingent from Crete, wrote *A Diary of the Trojan War* (*Ephemeris belli Troiani* in the Latin translation); and Dares Phrygius, who claimed to have fought with the Trojans, wrote *A History of the Destruction of Troy* (*De excidio Troiae historia*). These two narratives endeared themselves to the public of late antiquity and the Middle Ages by avoiding Homer's divine machinery, debates in heaven, and battles between gods and humans. At the same time, they appealed to the prevailing sentiment by providing romantic episodes which were not prominent in Homer's epics. Above all, they were seminal for the writers of the Middle Ages and helped preserve the Trojan saga until scholars of the Renaissance retrieved earlier Greek and Roman literature.

Dares and Dictys were the main sources for Benoît de Sainte-Maure's *Roman de Troie* (c. A.D. 1160), a pioneer work of medieval romance. To this French poet, we owe the story of Troilus and Cressida, the romance of Achilles and Polyxena, and other love-episodes. Guido da Colonna's *Historia Troiana* (1272–1287) is a prose version of Benoît's *Roman* and received wide circulation since it was written in the international language of the time, medieval Latin. For English readers there was John Lydgate's *Troy Book* (1412–1420) which was based on Guido da Colonna, and William Caxton's *Recuyell of the Historyes of Troyen*, (1468–1471), the most widely known form of the Trojan saga in English, which was a translation from the French of Raoul Lefèvre's expanded version of Guido's *Historia*.

When Homer sang of the wrath of Achilles in the *Iliad*, he picked up the story in the tenth and final year of the Trojan War, and then further confined the action to some forty odd days of that convulsive year. But what of the beginnings? and what of the background of the principal families embroiled in that epic struggle? Homer's audience did not have to be told; presumably they were so familiar with the story of the war and its participants that the poet was free to develop his theme on the explosive situation which arose late in the war. It was left for later poets and mythographers to fill in the gaps for us. So that the names which Homer so casually drops will have the full range of meaning they must have had for his contemporaries, it is necessary to look at the family lines that produced the Younger Heroes who took active roles in the climactic struggle at Troy. The leading figures come from four main families: the families of Peleus, Atreus, and Tyndareus on the Greek side; the family of Priam on the Trojan.

The Leading Families

Peleus

Peleus, the father of Achilles, could trace his descent, like most Greek heroes, from the great Olympian. His family goes back to the time when Zeus came upon Aegina, the daughter of the river-god Asopus, and finding her attractive, carried her off to an island which later bore her name. When Asopus went to search for her, it was Sisyphus, the trickster from Corinth, who told Asopus what had happened; and for indiscreet tattling, Sisyphus was assigned a painful task in the Underworld. In time Aegina gave birth to a son Aeacus. Hera, in her usual fit of jealousy against her husband's paramours, ravaged the island by a plague or a monstrous dragon with the result that the population was decimated. In answer to Aeacus' prayers, Zeus repopulated the island by turning ants into men, and thus by popular etymology (myrmex = ant), Aeacus became king of the Myrmidons, the host that

Figure 81. The baptism of Achilles in the river Styx. *A caricature by Honoré Daumier from his* Histoire ancienne, *a series of lithographs published in* Charivari, *Paris, 1841–1842. Museum of Fine Arts, Boston*

Achilles would later lead against the Trojans. Aeacus, renowned for his piety and sense of justice, was rewarded after death by being made a judge in the Underworld.

Aeacus had two sons, Peleus and Telamon. The latter also sired two sons who took active roles in the Trojan War: Teucer, considered the best archer among the Greeks at Troy, and his stepbrother Ajax (or Aias) who, next to Achilles, was the bravest of the Greeks. Telamon himself was said to have been a great friend of Heracles and to have accompanied him against Laomedon of Troy. Both Peleus and Telamon were members of the Argonauts and also took part in hunting down the Calydonian boar. When they had the misfortune to kill a stepbrother of theirs, Telamon went off to Salamis where he became king of the island—his son Ajax eventually led the Salaminian contingent against Troy—while Peleus, at the head of the Myrmidons, went off to Phthia in Thessaly where he too became king.

As is fitting for a hero and the father of an even greater hero, Peleus had his share of adventures and unfortunate love affairs, but no incident in his life was so significant as his marriage. When Zeus and Poseidon learned that if they had a son by the Nereid Thetis, he would be stronger than the father (pp. 43; 74), the sea-goddess was given to Peleus for his virtue and for being the most deserving of mankind. The marriage of Peleus and Thetis not only produced the greatest hero of all time, but also put into motion the events that ultimately resulted in the Trojan War. When Achilles was born, Thetis attempted to make him immortal by burning or boiling away the mortal parts which he inherited from his father. Peleus, not understanding what Thetis was up to, was terror-struck and cried out so loud that she was prevented from completing her work. Thetis left her husband's house in anger and returned to her sister-Nereids. The popular tale of how Thetis attempted to make Achilles immortal by dipping him into the river Styx is first reported by the Roman poet Statius. The attempt was only partially successful, for Thetis had to hold the infant by his heels or ankles which therefore were not touched by the river's immortalizing waters; hence the phrase for vulnerability, one's Achilles' heel (fig. 81). With no mother to take care of the child, Peleus turned Achilles over to the wise old centaur Chiron who nourished him on the flesh of wild animals and instructed the future hero in riding, hunting and lyre-playing (fig. 82). Achilles had one son, Neoptolemus (also called Pyrrhus) who, after the death of his father, was

Figure 82.   The centaur Chiron instructing young Achilles in the art of playing the lyre. *Roman wall painting, first century A.D. Pompeii. National Museum, Naples. (Alinari)*

summoned to Troy where he showed himself to be a mighty warrior like his father. The family line of Peleus can be summed up by this genealogical tree:

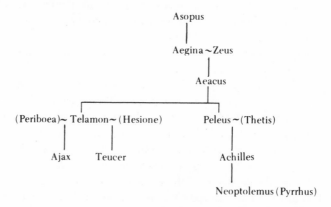

One illustration of the very early years of Achilles' life under the tutelage of Chiron is given by Matthew Arnold in *Empedocles on Etna*. In the opening lyric of Callicles, who sings of a time when the world was idyllically beautiful and untroubled, Arnold romanticizes Achilles' education; it is hardly the kind that an early Greek poet would prescribe for an epic hero.

> In such a glen, on such a day,
> On Pelion, on the grassy ground,
> Chiron, the aged Centaur, lay,
> The young Achilles standing by.
> The Centaur taught him to explore
> The mountains . . .
>
> . . . .
> He show'd him Phthia far away,
> And said: O boy, I taught this lore

To Peleus, in long distant years!
He told him of the Gods, the stars,
The tides;—and then of mortal wars,
And of the life which heroes lead
Before they reach the Elysian place
And rest in the immortal mead;
And all the wisdom of his race.

Atreus

Agamemnon, commander of the Greek forces at Troy, and his brother Menelaus, spouse of Helen and the world's most famous cuckold, were sons of Atreus, and as such they were often called by their patronymic "Atreides." The family of Atreus, both forebears and descendants, was calamity-ridden, its history one of crime and punishment. The story of this family was exploited by tragic poets who added choice bits of Gothic horror and violence to a tale so well known by Homer's time that all the poet had to do—as he does in the opening scene of the *Odyssey*—was mention the name of Aegisthus, and it immediately conjured up a picture of incest, adultery, and murder. Atreus' antecedents begin with Tantalus, a son of Zeus and a king in Asia Minor. His various attempts to trick the gods, as we have already witnessed, led to his eternal punishment in the Underworld. His daughter Niobe, who had the presumption to denigrate the maternity of Leto, the mother of Artemis and Apollo, had an equally unhappy fate on earth. But first, here is a somewhat trimmed family tree to help us through the ramifications of this legendary house.

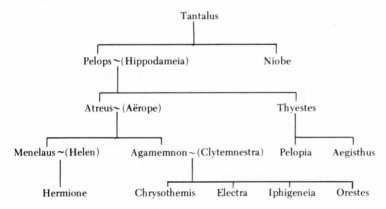

Pelops. Pelops, son of Tantalus, was slaughtered by his father, cooked and served up as a feast to the unsuspecting gods. When the gods, with the exception of the grieving Demeter, divined Tantalus' plan to deceive them, they punished him and reconstituted his son. Pelops then made his way to Greece where, by virtue of his great wealth and by marrying Hippodameia (or Hippodamia), he became king of Pisa in Elis and eventually gave his name to the great southern peninsula of Greece, the Peloponnese, "Pelops' isle." How he won the hand of Hippodameia is a tale of treachery and murder.

Hippodameia's father Oenomaus was king of Pisa and a son of Ares. He was told by an oracle that he would be killed by his son-in-law, and hence he refused to give his beautiful daughter to anyone in marriage. Some say that he was in love with his own daughter and that was why he was loath to surrender her. When suitors appeared, Oenomaus declared that he would give his daughter to the man who would defeat him in a chariot race, but if the suitor lost, he would have to forfeit his life. Another version has it that Hippodameia would be permitted to go off with a suitor in his chariot, but if Oenomaus caught up with him—as he always did since his horses had been given to him by the god Ares—the suitor would be killed and his head nailed to the king's house. When Pelops came a-wooing and saw the grim relics of the unsuccessful challengers, he had misgivings about his chances to defeat Oenomaus. In order to insure his success, he promised Myrtilus, the king's charioteer, half the kingdom if he would help him win Hippodameia. Myrtilus agreed and saw to it that the wheels of the chariot were not properly fastened. The plan succeeded, for in the race Oenomaus was killed when his chariot overturned; but before he died he laid a heavy curse on his venal charioteer. When Pelops returned to Pisa with his bride, he rewarded Myrtilus by throwing him off a cliff into the sea, and as Myrtilus sank he cursed Pelops and his whole race. The curse was not to fall on Pelops' head but was inherited by his descendants.

Atreus versus Thyestes. Pelops had many sons and daughters by Hippodameia, of whom Atreus and Thyestes had leading roles in playing out the tragedy of the family. One son, Pittheus of Troezen, was to achieve renown through his daughter Aethra who became the mother of Theseus. Pelops had a favorite son Chrysippus born to him by a nymph, the same Chrysippus whom Oedipus' father carried off to his regret. Hippodameia hated this child that was so favored by her husband, and she induced her two sons Atreus and Thyestes to murder their stepbrother. In fear of their father's wrath, the two fled to Mycenae where they were given sanctuary. Atreus eventually became king of Mycenae, but how this came about is a tale of unmitigated horror.

Those accounts which omit the story of the murder of Chrysippus tell us that the Mycenaeans were instructed by an oracle to invite a son of Pelops to become their king. Accordingly, they invited both Atreus and Thyestes to come to Mycenae. Now it so happened that Atreus had once promised to sacrifice the finest of his flocks to the goddess Artemis, but when a golden lamb appeared among his sheep, he throttled it and put it into a box. Aërope, the wife of Atreus, turned the box with the golden lamb over to Thyestes, her lover and seducer. When the two brothers turned up at Mycenae, Thyestes claimed that the kingship should go to the one owning the golden lamb. Atreus agreed, but much to his surprise, his brother produced the prized lamb. The gods, however, saw to it that Atreus became king by a remarkable change in the course of nature: they made the sun rise in the west and set in the east.

Atreus banished Thyestes from his kingdom, but when he later discovered that Thyestes had committed adultery with his wife, there was no limit to his vengeance. Pretending that all was forgiven, Atreus invited his brother to return to his court, and at a sumptuous banquet he had the flesh of Thyestes' children served up to him as a dish. After Thyestes had feasted, Atreus showed him the arms and bones of his children. Thyestes recoiled in horror at the enormity of his brother's crime. He cursed Atreus and his whole line, and then fled the city. Helios the sun was also horrified by Atreus' infamous banquet: some say that he turned his face away from the frightful scene; others that he changed his course from east to west on that day.

Seeking vengeance, Thyestes went to the oracle for advice. He was told that he could accomplish his purpose if he were to have intercourse with his daughter and beget a son. Thyestes accordingly lay with his daughter Pelopia who bore him his avenger-son, Aegisthus. Other versions elaborate the events which followed the cannibalistic feast. Atreus took Pelopia for his wife in belief that she was the daughter of a certain Thesprotus. At the time of the marriage, however, she was bearing Thyestes' child, and after having given birth to Aegisthus, she exposed him. The infant was found by shepherds who gave him to be suckled by a goat. Atreus later sent for him and brought him up as his own child. At all events, when Aegisthus grew to manhood and learned that he was a son of Thyestes, he killed Atreus and placed his father on the throne. (During the Trojan War, Aegisthus became the paramour of Agamemnon's wife Clytemnestra and later colluded with her in the murder of her husband.) As for the two sons of Atreus, Agamemnon and Menelaus, Aegisthus expelled them when he and his father occupied the kingdom of Mycenae. The two brothers made their way to Sparta where they were received by Tyndareus. Menelaus married Helen and eventually succeeded Tyndareus as king of Sparta. Agamemnon married Helen's half-sister Clytemnestra and returned to Mycenae where he peaceably succeeded Thyestes. According to other accounts, he expelled his uncle and usurped the throne. At the outbreak of the Trojan War, Agamemnon was the most powerful prince in all Greece, "king of many islands and of all Argos."

The story of the curse-afflicted family of Atreus is central to Aeschylus' *Agamemnon*, the leading play of the *Oresteia* (p. 9). It was also dramatized in plays, now lost, by Sophocles (*Atreus*), Euripides (*Thyestes*), and by the Augustan poet Varius Rufus (*Thyestes*). Seneca's *Thyestes* has survived the vagaries of literary tradition. It is another of the closet dramas of the Roman poet, replete with ghost scenes, gore, and fustian rhetoric. Seneca's play, however, made an impression upon playwrights of the Renaissance who cannibalized the play for lines—the best translations of Seneca in English are by Elizabethan poets—and for themes, particularly that of revenge. In *Titus Andronicus*, a play of revenge and counterrevenge, Shakespeare fuses two classical tales, the rape of Philomela and Seneca's Thyestean banquet. Titus kills the two sons of Tamora, queen of the Goths, for having raped and mutilated his daughter Lavinia, and then serves them up in a pie to their mother. In *Paradise Lost*, Milton recalls the Sun's horror at Atreus' deed at the time that Adam ate the forbidden fruit: ". . . At that tasted Fruit/The Sun, as from Thyestean Banquet, turn'd/His course intended." In more modern times, Louis MacNeice ponders the question of self-complicity in his *Thyestes*:

> When the King sat down to the feast and the golden lid revealed
> The human cutlets and the Graces sang
> Their lays of love returned and lovers meeting.
> Did his blood tell him what his mind concealed?
> Didn't he know—or did he—what he was eating?

Tyndareus

Leda and the Swan. Helen, the young beauty who is better known as Helen of Troy, came from a family that could trace its descent back to Aeolus. When Tyndareus, king of Sparta, had to seek political asylum among the Aetolians, he met Leda, the daughter of King Thestius. She was given to him in marriage and he took her back to Sparta when his kingdom was restored. The two had a number of children. Up to this point the married life of Tyndareus and his spouse had nothing unusual about it. But one night Zeus appeared to Leda in the form of a swan and made love to her; and later that very night Tyndareus also made love to her. The result of this double union was most unusual and hardly two accounts give the same versions. Common tradition has it that Leda bore Helen and Polydeuces (latinized to Pollux) to Zeus, Clytemnestra (or Clytaemnestra) and Castor to Tyndareus.

Another version reports that Helen was a daughter of Nemesis and Zeus and that her birth came about in this fashion: Nemesis, attempting to escape from the passionate embraces of Zeus, changed herself into a goose. Undaunted by this transformation, Zeus turned himself into a swan and so had his way with her. As a consequence of this love affair, Nemesis laid an egg which a shepherd found and brought to Tyndareus's wife. Leda put the egg in a chest and kept it there until it hatched. Out came Helen whom Leda brought up as her own daughter. In some versions, Leda herself is represented as having brought forth two eggs: Castor and Polydeuces are born from one, Helen from the other. In yet another account, Zeus is called the father of Helen and Polydeuces, and Tyndareus the father of Clytemnestra and Castor. Our earliest source, Homer, considers only Helen to be the daughter of Zeus by Leda; Castor, Polydeuces and Clytemnestra are said to be children of Tyndareus and Leda. The egg which Leda brought forth after her encounter with Zeus became a sacred relic; Pausanias, that indefatigable traveler of the second century A.D., reported that he saw it hanging by ribbons from the ceiling of a temple at Sparta.

*   *   *   *

The story of how Leda conceived her children was represented by one of the finest artists of the Renaissance, Leonardo da Vinci. *Leda and the Swan*, now in the Spiridon Collection at Rome, depicts the version of the two eggs out of which were hatched Helen and Polydeuces, Clytemnestra and Castor (fig. 83). Other artists of the period who put Leda on canvas were Correggio, Veronese, and Tintoretto. A modern approach to the ancient story was painted by the surrealist Salvador Dali, his *Leda atomica* (1945). In literature Spenser used the tale in the *Faerie Queene* when describing the mythological tapestries which hung in the house of Busyrane, the "vile Enchaunter," Spenser's symbol of unlawful love. But Spenser's description of Leda's encounter with Zeus hardly makes profane love seem evil and gross.

> Then he was turnd into a snowy Swan,
> To win faire Leda to his lovely trade:
> O wondrous skill, and sweet wit of the man,
> That her in daffadillies sleeping made,
> From scorching heat her daintie limbes to shade:
> Whiles the proud Bird ruffing his fethers wyde,
> And brushing his faire brest, did her invade;
> She slept, yet twixt her eyelids closely spyde,
> How towards her he rusht, and smiled at his pryde.

No painter and no poet was to find in Leda—and in her fateful children as well—a symbol more complex and more involuted than W. B. Yeats, a symbol that embraced the philosophical and esthetic, the mystical and occult views of the poet. To Yeats the union of Leda and the swan symbolized, as he tells us in *A Vison* (1925), the opening of a two-thousand-year cycle which came to an end with the birth of Christ and which in turn marked the beginning of another cycle; it was "the annunciation that founded Greece as made to Leda, remembering that they showed in a

Figure 83. Leonardo da Vinci (or his school). Leda and the Swan. *Painting. Spiradon Collection, Rome. (Mansell)*

Spartan temple, strung up to the roof as a holy relic, an unhatched egg of hers; and from one of her eggs came Love (Helen and Clytemnestra) and from the other War (Castor and Polydeuces)." Yeats' finest lyrical statement on the ancient story of the primal embrace of god and mortal appears in *Leda and the Swan* (1924), a fusion of mythology, sexuality and prophecy.

> A sudden blow: the great wings beating still
> Above the staggering girl, her thighs caressed
> By the dark webs, her nape caught in his bill,
> He holds her helpless breast upon his breast.
> How can those terrified vague fingers push
> The feathered glory from her loosening thighs?
> And how can body, laid in that white rush,
> But feel the strange heart beating where it lies?
>
> A shudder in the loins engenders there
> The broken wall, the burning roof and tower
> And Agamemnon dead.
>
>   Being so caught up,
> So mastered by the brute blood of the air,
> Did she put on his knowledge with his power
> Before the indifferent beak could let her drop?

Yeats returned to the theme, but with far less violence, in the final stanza of *Lullaby* (1931). "Sleep, beloved," he says

> Such a sleep and sound as fell
> Upon Eurotas' grassy bank
> When the holy bird, that there
> Accomplished his predestined will,
> From the limbs of Leda sank
> But not from her protecting care.

Castor and Polydeuces (Pollux).   The twin sons of Leda, Castor and Polydeuces, known collectively as the Dioscuri, "the sons of Zeus," made a reputation for themselves in taming horses, fencing, boxing, and cavalry tactics.   To them were attributed the invention of the war dance and warlike music. They had their share of adventure in two heroic undertakings: the expedition of the Argonauts and the hunt for the Calydonian boar. And when their sister Helen was abducted by Theseus, they invaded Attica and brought her back home along with Theseus' mother. Castor, the twin generally regarded to be mortal, had a violent end. In a dispute over some cattle which they helped run off—or over the abduction of the two daughters of Leucippus—Castor was killed by a certain Idas. Polydeuces was inconsolable over the loss of his brother. He begged Zeus to be allowed to die with Castor, a request which was impossible to grant because of his immortality. Polydeuces was finally permitted to spend alternately one day among the gods on Olympus, the other with his brother in Hades. According to another account, the god marked his approval of their love by placing them in the sky as twin stars, the Gemini. In their astral aspect, the inseparable brothers came also to be regarded as the twin lights of St. Elmo's fire. The Romans took the twins into their pantheon as Castor and Pollux when the two were said to have appeared on the side of the Romans at the battle of Lake Regillus (c. 496 B.C.), an adaptation of a Spartan story that was picked up by later historians and given a Roman setting.

Clytemnestra and Helen.   On the distaff side of the family, Clytemnestra was married off to Agamemnon with a minimum of legendary fanfare. The situation was quite different with Helen. Agamemnon and Clytemnestra had four children, three girls and one boy: Iphigeneia (Iphianassa according to Homer), Electra (or Laodice in Homer), Chrysothemis, and Orestes. All will be deeply involved in the fate of the house of Atreus when their father returns home from the Trojan War. As for Helen, when Tyndareus believed it was time for her to settle down with a husband, he was beseiged by a horde of eligible suitors. Lists of the men seeking Tyndareus' permission to marry his daughter give the names of two or three dozen men from the finest legendary families of Greece. Among some of the better known were Odysseus, Diomedes, the greater and the lesser Ajaxes, Patroclus, and Menelaus. (Shakespeare with but modest poetic hyperbole in *The Taming of the Shrew* could rightly say "Fair Leda's daughter had a thousand wooers.")

Seeing the abundance of suitors on hand, Tyndareus was afraid that if he preferred one over the other, he would precipitate a deadly quarrel among them. Odysseus came forth, as he usually did, with a solution to the problem. But first he received Tyndareus' promise of help in securing Penelope, daughter of Icarius, for his bride. When this was agreed to, Odysseus suggested that before making his choice, Tyndareus should exact an oath from all the suitors that they would defend the man he chose against any wrong that might be done him with regard to the marriage. After Tyndareus had the suitors swear a mighty oath over the severed pieces of a sacrificed horse, he then chose Menelaus as Helen's husband. And following the passing of Castor and Polydeuces from the mundane world, Tyndareus made Menelaus heir to the kingdom of Sparta.

The beauty of Helen aroused the emotions not only of her many suitors, but of countless poets. To the German poet Goethe, the Helen of his *Faustus* (Part II) was more than a symbol of transcendent physical beauty; she was Greece and the perfection of Greek art, a prize difficult to attain by ordinary means and impossible to hold even when attained. Her union with Faustus is the marriage of Classical and Romantic art. To Edgar Allan Poe (1809–1849) the beauty of Helen evoked not only "the glory that was Greece / And the grandeur that was Rome" but a serenity and a tranquillity to the poet who long roamed "desperate seas." These are the opening lines of Poe's *To Helen*:

> Helen, thy beauty is to me
> Like those Nicaean barks of yore,
> That gently, o'er a perfumed sea,
> The weary, wayworn wanderer bore
> To his own native shore.

Priam

Turning now to the Trojans, Priam, the ruling king at the time of the Trojan War, was one of the prolific kings of legend. Homer tells us that he had fifty sons—to say nothing of daughters—nineteen of whom were given to him by his wife Hecuba (or Hecabe), the rest came from various concubines in his palace. According to genealogists, Priam traced his line back to Dardanus, a son of Zeus and the Pleiad Electra (p. 163). Before the great Deluge, so goes one story, Dardanus lived on the island of Samothrace and survived the flood by floating to the region of Troy on a raft or an inflated hide. He married the daughter of the local king and eventually, as so often happened to legendary figures, inherited the kingdom. Some of the more prominent descendants of Dardanus are given in this family tree:

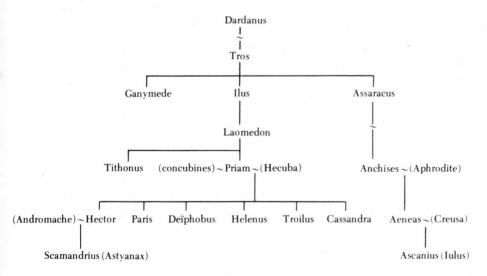

Tros, the grandson of Dardanus, is little more than eponym for Troy, the Troad, and the Trojan people. His three sons were somewhat more distinguished. Assaracus was the progenitor of the line that would produce the great hero Aeneas. Ilus gave his name to Ilium (or Ilion), another name for Troy, and he is also believed to have founded the city itself. The story is told that one of the prizes he won at a wrestling match among the Phrygians was a dappled cow. In obedience to an oracle, Ilus followed the cow—just as Cadmus had done in founding Thebes—until it came to rest at the foot of a hill. It was there that he built a city and gave it his name, Ilium. He then prayed to Zeus for a divine sign. The god let fall from heaven the Palladium (pp. 164; 170), a statue of Pallas (Athena). Ilus built a temple to honor this heaven-sent talisman, and on this statue depended the safety of the city. The Palladium was in effect a life token for Troy, and later it had to be removed by the Greeks before the sack of the city could be effected.

Ganymede. Quite different from the story of Assaracus and Ilus was that of Ganymede (or Ganymedes). Homer is the first to tell us that he was the most beautiful of mortal men and that the gods carried him off to serve as the cupbearer of Zeus. Later writers report that Zeus took the form of an eagle, or sent his eagle, to carry off the youth to Olympus where he replaced Hebe as the cupbearer for the great Olympian (fig. 84). In compensation for his loss, Ganymede's father was given a pair of divine horses or a golden vine. The romanticizers of mythology pictured Zeus as having fallen in love with the youthful Ganymede, much to the annoyance of Hera, and as having fashioned an eagle which brought the boy to Olympus. The eagle ultimately found its way into the heavens as the constellation Aquila, Ganymede being Aquarius, the waterbearer. When the Romans pronounced the name Ganymede, it came out as Catamitus. From the Latin came the English word "catamite"; its pejorative connotation taken from the view that Ganymede was the youthful lover of Zeus.

*   *   *   *

As early as the fourth century B.C. the story of Ganymede's rape was rationalized and allegorized. Plato thought that the myth was coined by Cretans to justify the love between men and young boys. A contemporary of Plato, Xenophon (c. 430–c. 354 B.C.), treated the myth as an allegory, taking the name of Ganymede to mean "the enjoyment of the intellect." Xenophon interpreted the story of the rape as proving that intellectual qualities win the love of the gods and that intellect was superior to the body. The same approach was taken by the allegorizers and moralizers of the Middle Ages and the Renaissance. Ganymede was the unsullied soul, the incarnation of the innocent soul finding its joy in God. He prefigured St. John the Evangelist who was transported to heaven; he was human intellect beloved by Jupiter, to wit, the Supreme Being. A favorite also among artists of the Renaissance, Ganymede was drawn or painted by Michelangelo—two drawings of the rape were sent to his friend Tommaso Cavalieri—by Correggio, Rubens and Rembrandt.

The two opposing conceptions of Ganymede are reflected in literature. In Marlowe's *Hero and Leander*, the temple of Venus at Sestos had a picture of "Jove slylie stealing from his sisters bed, / To dallie with Idalian Ganimed." And in Tennyson's "lordly pleasure-house" in *The Palace of Art* (1842) this bit of sensuous picture painting: "Or else flush'd Ganymede, his rosy thigh / Half-buried in the eagle's down." The English representative of the allegorizing school is George Chapman (1559?–1634?), the famed English translator of Homer. Ganymede's translation to heaven in the *Hymnus in Cynthiam* is described in the highest moral tones:

> His beauty was it, not the body's pride,
> That made him great Aquarius stellified.
> And that mind most is beautiful and high,
> And nearest comes to a Divinity,
> That furthest is from spot of Earth's delight,

Figure 84. Zeus abducting Ganymede. *Terracotta, c. 470 B.C. Olympia Museum. (Hirmer)*

> Pleasures that lose their substance with their sight,
> Such one, Saturnius ravisheth to love,
> And fills the cup of all content to Jove.

Laomedon. The history of the royal family of Troy continues with Laomedon, the double-dealing king whose relationships with Poseidon and Heracles have already been told. It was Poseidon who helped Laomedon build the famed walls of Troy while Apollo cared for the king's flocks. But when Laomedon refused to honor his contract with the gods, they—or Poseidon himself—sent a monster from the sea to ravage the country. An oracle called upon the Trojans to appease the beast through the sacrifice of a young girl. When the lot fell to Hesione, the daughter of Laomedon, Heracles, who happened to be in Troy at the time, stepped forward and agreed to save Hesione for a price: the pair of divine horses which were given to Ilus in compensation for the loss of Ganymede. Heracles lived up to his part of the bargain and saved Hesione, but Laomedon again reneged on his promise. In revenge, Heracles sailed with a squadron of Greek ships against Troy, killed Laomedon and most of his sons, and carried off Priam and Hesione. The latter was given to Telamon as a wife and ultimately bore him a son Teucer. Hesione was able to ransom her brother Priam who returned to Troy and succeeded his father as king.

Tithonus and Eos. Priam had a brother Tithonus whose misfortune it was to catch the fancy of a deity. The goddess of dawn Eos loved this young son of Laomedon and carried him off to her home in mythical Ethiopia. She had carried off Cephalus in a similar fashion, but he did not return her love as did Tithonus. Homer paints a domestic picture of Eos rising from her bed where she sleeps with Tithonus, to bring light to immortals and to mortal men. Through the goddess' prayers, or through his own, Tithonus was given the gift of immortality, a boon that turned into a bane, since the request did not include eternal youth to accompany a deathless life. All too soon Tithonus began to turn gray and Eos was no longer interested in sharing her bed with him although she continued to take care of him. When he became senile and immobile, the goddess shut him up in a room where he continued to babble on endlessly. Some say that Tithonus was transformed into a grasshopper or a cicada whose musical chirping would forever sound in the ears of the goddess. Out of this relationship between goddess and mortal came a son, Memnon, who became king of Ethiopia and later enlisted on the side of the Trojans in their conflict with the Greeks.

The finest rendering of this tale in ancient literature appears in the *Homeric Hymn to Aphrodite*. After recounting the stories of both Ganymede and Tithonus, the goddess of love reassures her mortal lover Anchises that immortality will not be his fate. At the same time she excuses her falling in love with a mortal by claiming that the royal line of Troy is almost divine. Tennyson picks up this brief episode in the Homeric hymn for his dramatic monologue *Tithonus* (1860), in which he dwells on the *weltschmerz* of Tithonus—and of his own?—and in the sad realization that "after many a summer dies the swan." Tennyson's Tithonus calls upon the goddess of dawn to release him from the gift of immortality which the gods granted him:

> Yet hold me not forever in thine East;
> How can my nature longer mix with thine?
> Coldly thy rosy shadows bathe me, cold
> Are all thy lights, and cold my wrinkled feet
> Upon thy glimmering thresholds, when the steam
> Floats up from those dim fields about the homes
> Of happy men that have the power to die,
> And grassy barrows of the happier dead.
> Release me, and restore me to the ground.
> Thou seest all things, thou wilt see my grave;
> Thou wilt renew thy beauty morn by morn,
> I earth in earth forget these empty courts,
> And thee returning on thy silver wheels.

Hector. The early life of Priam as king of Troy was uneventful, with the exception of the large brood of children he fathered on Hecuba and other women within his palace. The eldest son of Priam and Hecuba was Hector. He was to become the bravest of the Trojan warriors, and when the Greeks attacked, the defense of the city was entrusted to him. In time Hector married Andromache, the orphaned daughter of Eetion, the king of Cilician Thebe. Hector married her after her father and brothers fell under the sword of Achilles during the early stages of the war. Andromache bore her husband a son Scamandrius whom the people of Troy called Astyanax (Lord of the city.) At the end of the Trojan War, Scamandrius, who was yet but an infant, was to suffer a premature end at the hands of the Greeks.

Paris. Paris, also known as Alexander, was a son of quite a different stamp. He was the second eldest child of Priam and Hecuba. Before he was born, Hecuba had a dream that she had given birth to a firebrand which enveloped the city and destroyed it. This dream was interpreted to mean that Hecuba would bring forth a son who would be responsible for the downfall of Troy. Accordingly, she was advised to expose the child when it was born; some say was told to kill the child, but she could not bring herself to do this, and Priam had to order the exposure of the newborn infant. However that may be, Hecuba's child was given to a shepherd with instructions to take it to Mount Ida and abandon it there. When the shepherd returned to the spot five days later, he found the infant still alive and being suckled by a she-bear. He took the child home, gave him the name of Paris, and reared him as his own.

Paris grew up in the environs of Mount Ida where he soon earned a reputation as a valiant defender of men and flocks. Eventually he discovered his true origin through Cassandra, his prophetic sister. He was restored to the bosom of his family, and Hecuba's fateful dream was for the moment forgotten or disregarded. Before his involvement with Helen, Paris loved the nymph Oenone, a daughter of a river-god of the Troad, whom he had met while tending the flocks on Mount Ida. Being prophetic, Oenone warned Paris not to sail off in pursuit of Helen. When she failed to persuade him, she told him to come to her in the event that he was wounded since through her skill alone could he be healed. Thus tragic consequences followed for both Paris and the nymph who loved him so. The sad tale of the nymph's love for "her playmate on the hills" is told by Tennyson in two poems, *Oenone* (1842) and *The Death of Oenone* (1892).

These then are the four main families involved in the Trojan War and some of their more important members. Now for the war itself: how it came about, the gathering of the host and the early years of the conflict, the action contained in Homer's *Iliad*, its conclusion. It must be kept in mind that a synthesis of the epic conflict is derived from a variety of Greek and Roman sources spanning two millennia, from poets, mythographers, and commentators. The conventional approach is to describe what took place prior to the *Iliad* (the so-called ante-Homerica), the events made known to us by Homer (in the *Iliad*), and those which followed (post-Homerica).

The Ante-Homerica

The Wedding of Peleus and Thetis. It all began at the wedding feast of Peleus, king of Thessaly and father-to-be of Achilles, and Thetis, the sea nymph whom Zeus and Poseidon found desirable yet unattainable. For those who sought an explanation for the cause of the conflict in the will of the gods, Zeus and Themis were said to have used the occasion of the wedding to trigger the Trojan War. Another version has it that Zeus had a specific objective in mind, namely, that he felt that the earth was heavily overpopulated, and to deal with the problem he was resolved to bring about the Trojan War so that "the load of death might empty the world." In any event, a quarrel broke out at the wedding banquet of Peleus and Thetis. All the gods had been invited to this great occasion, all except Eris, the goddess of strife. (Whoever sent out the invitations would naturally consider it inappropriate to invite Strife or Discord to a wedding.) Eris, in a fit of anger and pique, took her revenge by tossing among the guests a golden apple inscribed with the words "For the Fairest." Three goddesses immediately laid claim to the apple and its inscription: Hera, Athena, and Aphrodite. Unable to decide among themselves who rightfully should be given the prize, they were on the verge of a battle when Zeus intervened. They appealed to him for a decision as to which of them was the fairest, but Zeus wisely and shrewdly said that he would not decide the matter himself. Instead, he directed them to go to Mount Ida where they would find a shepherd by the name of Paris, who was known for his discriminating taste and ability to judge pulchritude. This is how the celebrated Judgment of Paris came about.

The Judgment of Paris. The three goddesses guided by Hermes approached the youthful Paris on Mount Ida where the was living happily with the nymph Oenone (fig. 85). Each of the goddesses made the handsome young man an offer if he would award her the golden apple. Hera promised him rule over all Asia and great riches. Athena assured him of victory in all his battles. Aphrodite promised him Helen, the most beautiful woman in the world, for his wife. Without hesitation, Paris declared Aphrodite to be the fairest and deserving of the golden apple (p. 187). By so doing Paris earned Aphrodite's friendship and gratitude; he also won the everlasting hatred of Hera and Athena for both himself and all Troy.

Later, when Paris discovered his true origins and returned to Troy, he asked for a fleet of ships to sail to Sparta. In spite of prophetic announcements by Cassandra and Helenus that the voyage would result in a calamity for Troy, Priam allowed Paris to sail. When he arrived at Sparta, Menelaus and Helen received him with all the courtesy and hospitality required for a royal guest. Then it happened that Menelaus had to go to Crete for the funeral of his maternal grandfather, leaving the obligations of a host in the hands of his wife Helen. No sooner had Menelaus departed than Paris persuaded Helen to go off with him. Traditions differ as to whether Helen was forced to leave Sparta or went off willingly. According to some, Helen, influenced by Aphrodite, followed her seducer without resistance, abandoning her child Hermione and carrying off a considerable amount of treasure. Later accounts claim that there was no elopement but rather a rape, that Paris forcibly carried her off during a hunt or a festival.

Figure 85. The Judgment of Paris. Hermes leading Athena, Hera and Aphrodite to Paris on Mount Ida. *Vase painting, 490–480 B.C. State museum, Berlin.*

Different stories are also told of the voyage back to Troy. The common tradition is that Paris and Helen sailed to Troy without further incident. Others have it that the gods allowed only a phantom, fashioned out of clouds and resembling Helen, to accompany Paris to Troy while the real Helen was put under the protection of King Proteus of Egypt, and that she remained there until Menelaus reclaimed her after the war (pp. 7; 104).

*   *   *   *

Literature and art put the Judgment of Paris and the "rape" of Helen to good use. Like many other popular themes, they found their way into countless poetic allusions; they were also satirized, allegorized, and modernized. Lucian of Samosata (born c. A.D. 125), a philosophical satirist and a hater of sham, cynically presents the Judgment in a burlesque of conventional mythology. Hermes has just approached Paris on Mount Ida, leading the three goddesses. Paris at first is frightened by the divine presences and by having been selected to judge a beauty contest. He quickly gains his composure and insists that the goddesses exhibit themselves in the nude. From Lucian's *Dialogues of the Gods:*

Paris. God of wonders! What a sight! They're so beautiful, so lovely! Oh, that virgin! And this queen—she's dazzling, superb. She deserves to be the wife of the king of the gods. And how sweet this lady's look is, what a charming and seductive smile! But enough of this bliss. Ladies, if there are no objections, I'd like to look each one of you over individually. Right now I'm confused. I don't know where to look—my eyes are drawn every which way.

Aphrodite. Let's let him.

Paris. Hera, will you please stay! And you two step aside?

Hera. With pleasure. And after you've looked me over carefully, there's something else I want you to give thought to—whether you'd like the gifts I can offer in return for your vote. You see, Paris, if you decide in my favor, I'll make you lord of all Asia.

Paris. Sorry, I'm not selling my verdict for gifts. You may go now. I'll vote as I think best. Athena, will you please step forward?

Athena. Here I am. Now Paris, if you vote in my favor, you'll never lose a battle. You'll always be victorious. I'll make you a conquering hero.

Paris. War and battles don't interest me, Athena. As you can see, Troy and Lydia are at peace; no one's challenging my father's rule. But don't worry—your chances won't be hurt even if I'm not letting gifts influence my decision. You may get dressed and put on your helmet. I've seen enough. Aphrodite's turn now.

Aphrodite. Standing right by you. Look me all over, every detail. Don't skip a thing. Spend all the time you want on every part of my body. Now, my handsome young man, if you don't mind, I'd like to tell you something. I noticed a long time ago how young and handsome you are; I don't think there's another to match you in all of Troy. I congratulate you on your good looks—but I don't at all approve of your living here among these cliffs and rocks instead of in the city and ruining your good looks in this desert. What good do these mountains do you? What good do your looks do these cows of yours? You should have been married by now—not to one of the country girls you have around here, but to a Greek girl, someone from Argos or Corinth or Sparta. Like Helen, for example. She's young, every bit as beautiful as I am, and—what's more important—the amorous type. One look at you and I know she'd give up everything, surrender herself to you completely, follow you home, and live with you. I'm sure you've heard all about her.

Paris. Not a word, Aphrodite. And I'd be very happy to hear all you can tell me.

Aphrodite, of course, easily bribes Paris who had just been so moralistic in dealing with the offers made by the other two goddesses. She offers to serve as his
matchmaker and promises to deliver Helen even though she is married. At that,
Paris hands Aphrodite the golden apple and declares her the winner of the beauty
contest. In quite a different vein, Fulgentius, a mythographer of the fifth century
A.D. whose influence was strongly felt in later ages, allegorizes the Judgment. The
three goddesses become symbols of the active (Hera), contemplative (Athena), and
amorous (Aphrodite) life; Paris' choice thereby becomes a philosophical one. And as
an example of modernization of the ancient tale, John Latouche wrote a libretto for
the musical comedy *The Golden Apple* (1954) in which the judgment and abduction take place in the opening years of the twentieth century, the scene being set in
a small American town near Mount Olympus on the Pacific coast.

Painters and sculptors were drawn particularly to the scene of Paris interviewing
the trinity of goddesses, but less so to the abduction of Helen. Among Greek vase
painters, the goddesses were represented as appearing before the Trojan youth fully
clothed (fig. 85). Roman artists took to representing the goddess of love in the nude,
an iconographic motif that, under the influence of representations of the three
Graces, soon spread to the other two goddesses. Lucas Cranach the Elder painted
several versions of the Judgment of Paris with medieval overtones; one of the best
known (c. 1528) is now in the Metropolitan Museum of Art. The sensuous exuber-
ance of the seventeenth century has given us several versions of the beauty contest
from the brush of Peter Paul Rubens. The painting (c. 1635) hanging in the National
Gallery in London shows us the goddesses appearing before Paris in varying degrees
of undress but with their identifying attributes placed close by: Hera's peacock,
Aphrodite's winged Eros, and Athena's Gorgon-headed shield. And in a cloud
above the scene is Eris herself, brandishing the torch that will mark the destruction
of Troy. The twentieth century is best represented by Pierre Auguste Renoir (1841–
1919), the French impressionist, who like Cranach and Rubens, painted several
versions of the Judgment (fig. 86) and in addition turned out several bronze reliefs
on the same theme.

Jacques-Louis David's *Paris and Helen* (1788) is an eighteenth-century rendering of the two lovers in a boudoir setting. Helen is portrayed as leaning languor-
ously on Paris who holds a lyre in his left hand as he looks longingly into her down-
cast eyes. The painting is thought to have been inspired by Gluck's opera *Paride
ed Elena*. Calzabigi's text for the opera has no basis in Greek literature—Helen, for
example, is betrothed, but not married to Menelaus—and juxtaposes an ingenuous
Spartan girl against an urbane and passionate Paris. David's painting resembles the
third act of the opera in which Paris sings ardently of his love and pleads his cause.
Helen is torn by her doubts and by her pledge to Menelaus. Love wins out in the
end, and as the curtain falls the lovers board a ship for Troy.

The Call to Arms. When Menelaus returned to Sparta and found that Paris
had made off with his wife and property, he went to his brother Agamemnon
and asked him to raise an army to be sent against Troy. Agamemnon invoked the
oath of Tyndareus (p. 384) and summoned the princes of Greece to Argos where
by virtue of his superior power he was chosen as the commander-in-chief of the
Greek forces. Two heroes, however, did not show up for the roll call, Odysseus and
Achilles. Odysseus (Roman Ulysses) had married Penelope, a cousin of Helen, and
had just been presented with a son, Telemachus. For that reason he was extremely

Figure 86.   Renoir. The Judgment of Paris. *Painting, c. 1915. Collection of Henry P. McIlhenny. Philadelphia Museum of Art.*

reluctant to leave his wife and child to go off on a punitive expedition. Homer tells us that Agamemnon made a special trip to Odysseus' home on the island of Ithaca and with great difficulty persuaded him to join forces with the other Greek princes.

A more colorful story is told in later accounts. A Greek by the name of Palamedes was sent to convince Odysseus that he was bound by the oath of Tyndareus. When Palamedes arrived in Ithaca, Odysseus pretended to be insane; he yoked an ass and an ox to a plow and sowed his fields with salt. Palamedes tested his sanity by taking the infant Telemachus and placing him in front of the oncoming plow. According to another account, he snatched the child from Penelope and drew his sword as if to kill the child. Fearing for the safety of his son, Odysseus gave up the charade and joined the expedition against Troy. But Odysseus never forgave Palamedes for forcing him to go to war, and later on he took out his revenge on Palamedes with a Machiavellian strategem. He planted a forged letter in Palamedes' tent which implicated him in an act of treason. The result was that Palamedes was stoned to death. Another version has it that Odysseus and Diomedes induced Palamedes to go down into a deep well and then buried him with a shower of rocks.

Figure 87.   Poussin. Achilles on the island of Scyros. Achilles (right) reveals his identity to Odysseus who is disguised as a merchant. *Painting, 1653–1654.* *Museum of Fine Arts, Boston.*

With Odysseus as a member of the expedition, his cleverness was put to use in bringing in the other "draft dodger." When Achilles was but nine years old, Calchas the seer declared that Troy could not be taken without him. Achilles' mother Thetis, knowing that the war would be fatal to her son, disguised him as a girl and hid him among the daughters of Lycomedes, king of the island of Scyros, where he was known under the name of Pyrrha (Ginger or Carrot-top) because of the color of his hair. However his masculinity did not remain hidden for long, since one of the daughters of Lycomedes, Deidamia, became the mother of his son Neoptolemus (also called Pyrrhus). When the report reached Odysseus that Achilles was on the island of Scyros, he disguised himself as a merchant and went to Lycomedes' palace. There he spread out his wares of women's finery and weapons before the women. Unlike the others who made a grab for the feminine attire, Achilles was attracted only to the weapons (fig. 87). Crafty Odysseus had no difficulty in identifying his man. Another account tells of a different ruse. When Odysseus had his wares spread out, he had a trumpet sound an alarm. Achilles, thinking that the island was under attack, tore off his women's clothing and grabbed a spear and a shield, and thus revealed himself. Achilles owned up to the call to arms and went with a complement of Myrmidons to join the other Greeks. He came accompanied by his old tutor Phoenix and by his comrade in arms Patroclus, a son of Menoetius.

The Greek Forces at Aulis.   Agamemnon and his Greek princes assembled their forces at Aulis in Boeotia, and in preparation for the amphibious operation against Troy, they had a fleet of over one thousand ships riding at anchor in the harbor. While preparations were being made, a remarkable omen took place. Following a sacrifice to Apollo, a speckled serpent darted from the altar, slithered up a plane tree, devoured eight sparrows in a nest together with the mother sparrow, and then turned to stone. Calchas the seer interpreted this as a sign from Zeus indicating that the war would consume nine years before Troy would fall in the tenth year. With this and other prophecies confirming a decade of conflict, the Greeks sailed from Aulis in the general direction of Troy. But the course to their objective was not well known. Some say that the first landing was made at Mysia in Asia Minor, and that the Greeks ravaged the city, mistaking it for Troy. In the conflict, Telephus, king of the Mysians and a son of Heracles, was seriously wounded by Achilles. The Greeks returned to Aulis in a state of confusion; there was no one who could show them the way to Troy. Telephus, whose wound would not heal, applied to Apollo for help. The god advised him through his oracle that he could be cured only by the one who wounded him. Telephus went to Aulis and begged Achilles to help him, promising to lay a true course to the city of Troy in return. Achilles agreed and healed him by scraping off the rust of his Pelian spear on to the wound. Telephus thereupon provided the information which he had promised, and its accuracy was confirmed by Calchas through the art of divination.

There was yet another difficulty that lay ahead before the Greeks could set sail from Aulis and make their landing at Troy. Agamemnon had offended the goddess Artemis who then created weather conditions making it impossible for the ships to sail out of the harbor at Aulis. Calchas was again consulted. He reported that the goddess was angry at Agamemnon and demanded the sacrifice of his daughter Iphigeneia. The nature of Agamemnon's offense, how Iphigeneia was summoned to Aulis under the pretext of being married to Achilles, and the results of the sacrifice have already been detailed in the biography of Artemis (pp. 154–155).

Philoctetes. With directions in hand, and with the gods offering no further obstacle to their departure, the Greeks hoisted sail and made their way out of the harbor. En route to Troy they had to stop on the island of Lemnos where they put ashore one of the leading Greeks. Philoctetes had been bitten by a snake at Aulis and the stench of his festering wound became so unbearable to his comrades that they forced him to leave the expedition and gave the command of his seven ships to another man. This was the same Philoctetes who had prepared the funeral pyre for Heracles and who was rewarded by the great hero for his friendship and service with his bow and never-erring poisoned arrows. According to the common tradition, Philoctetes remained on Lemnos for most of the war until Odysseus and Diomedes (or Neoptolemus) came to him in the tenth year with word that an oracle had declared that Troy could not be taken without the arrows of Heracles. In spite of his antagonism toward his fellow-Greeks for having abandoned him to a wretched and painful existence on Lemnos, Philoctetes was persuaded to rejoin the army at Troy. There he was cured of his wound by one of the army physicians, and soon thereafter mortally wounded Paris with a Heraclean arrow and witnessed the fall of the city.

The Landing at Troy and the First Casualty, Protesilaus. Shortly after Philoctetes had been abandoned on the island of Lemnos, the Greeks sent an embassy composed of Menelaus and Odysseus to Troy to demand the return of Helen and the misappropriated property. The Trojans indignantly refused and threatened to kill the envoys. Antenor, Priam's wise counselor, interceded on their behalf and gave them safe conduct out of Troy. The Greeks at long last made their landfall on the Troad within sight of their objective. On this landfall hangs another tale, a story of a warbound husband and a lovelorn wife. An oracle had predicted that the first Greek to touch land would meet his death. This fate befell Protesilaus, the leader of a contingent of troops from Thessaly. When the other Greeks hesitated to disembark, Protesilaus patriotically and bravely leaped from his ship on to the shore. He was soon killed by Hector who came down with his Trojan host to oppose the landing.

Protesilaus' wife Laodamia loved her husband dearly—they had been married for only a very short time before Protesilaus had to leave—and when the news was brought to her that her husband had been killed, she prayed to the gods for permission to converse with him for three hours. Her weeping and grief were so intense that the gods could not refuse her. Hermes brought Protesilaus up from the Underworld and Laodamia had her three hours with her husband. When the allotted time had passed, Protesilaus died a second time. Laodamia was again beside herself with grief. She is said to have fashioned a bronze image of her husband which she hid in her room. When her father learned that she was kissing and embracing the statue, he insisted that it be burned along with other sacrificial offerings. Laodamia, whose anguish knew no limits, threw herself on the pyre and joined her husband in death. Nymphs are believed to have planted elm trees around Protesilaus' tomb and the foliage which faced Troy grew green and faded earlier than the rest.

Initial Forays and the Death of Troilus.   Under the driving leadership of Achilles, the Greeks soon established a beachhead and drove off the Trojans. During the early stages of the conflict on the Troad, Troilus, the youngest son of Priam, was killed by Achilles; according to some accounts he fell in the Thymbraean temple of Apollo where, ironically enough, Achilles was to meet his own end. The Greeks were unable to penetrate the defenses of Troy, but the surrounding region fell prey to Achilles and the raiding Greeks. Twelve towns were taken by sea, eleven by land. During these forays, two women—Chryseis and Briseis—who were to become the source of contention during the climactic tenth year of the war, fell into Greek hands as part of the spoils of war. In the division of the booty, Chryseis was awarded to Agamemnon, Briseis to Achilles. It is at about this point that Homer picks up the story in the *Iliad*.

*   *   *   *

The name of Troilus cannot be passed over without some mention of his romantic connection in later literature with Briseida or Cressida—both names derive from Briseis and Chryseis. Classical antiquity has nothing to say about Troilus ever meeting with either of these two women, but from Dares Phrygius' account of the war, in which Troilus is portrayed as a brave Trojan warrior throughout the war, medieval poets extended and enlarged upon the character of this little-known hero. Benoît de Sainte-Maure and Guido da Colonna tell the story of a faithless Briseida who forsakes her lover Troilus for the Greek Diomedes. When Boccaccio, sad and lonely in Naples because of the absence of his love, looked about for material to express his unhappiness, he took the story of Benoît and Guido and turned it into a full-blown story of parted and unhappy lovers. Briseida was changed into Griseida (Cressida), and the character of Pandarus was added as a dissolute gallant and friend of Troilus. His name is taken from the Trojan saga but this is about all. Boccaccio called his story of love and friendship *Il Filostrato* (The Man Overwhelmed by Love).

It was to Boccaccio's romance that Chaucer went for the main source of his

Troylus and Cryseyde (1372–1386), a poem that emphasized character and the frailty of human love, not the passion and sensualism of Boccaccio. Chaucer's tale was continued by the Scotch poet Robert Henryson (1430?–1506) who, in the *Testament of Cresseid,* tells of the pathetic latter days of Cressida and the retribution that came upon her in the form of leprosy. By the time the story reached Shakespeare and his contemporaries, the characters had become so stereotyped that an Elizabethan audience expected to see a Cressida who was a wanton, a Troilus who was an eager young man brought to grief by his love for a disreputable woman, and a Pandarus who was a procurer and a "pander"—an English word derived from his characterization in literature. Thus the clown in Shakespeare's *Twelfth Night*, asking for a second gratuity, says that he "would play Lord Pandarus of Phrygia to bring a Cressida to this Troilus"; and in *Henry V*, Pistol calls Doll a "lazar kite of Cressid's kind." Shakespeare follows these characterizations in his *Troilus and Cressida* with amplification of details about the Trojan War available to him in the works of Lydgate and Caxton as well as from Chapman's translation of Homer's *Iliad.*

The story of Protesilaus and his devoted wife also deserves a word regarding its treatment in modern literature, specifically by William Wordsworth. In antiquity, the story of Laodamia's love for her husband and her suicide was supposed to tug on the heartstrings and elicit a sympathetic response for the lovelorn woman. In *Laodamia* (1814), Wordsworth rejects the passion of the ancient heroine; instead he calls for "reason," "self-government," and "fortitude" as if he were a Vergilian Stoic. This is part of the conversation Protesilaus has with his wife when he is brought up from the Underworld:

> And Thou, though strong in love, art all too weak
> In reason, in self-government too slow;
> I counsel thee by fortitude to seek
> Our blest reunion in the shades below.
> The invisible world with thee hath sympathised;
> Be thy affections raised and solemnised.
>
> Learn, by a mortal yearning, to ascend—
> Seeking a higher object. Love was given,
> Encouraged, sanctioned, chiefly for that end;
> For this the passion to excess was driven—
> That self might be annulled: her bondage prove
> The fetters of a dream opposed to love.

The Iliad

In the tenth year of the war, a seemingly minor incident takes place which touches off a chain reaction of events and emotions which, within a short period of time, yields tragic consequences for many Greek and Trojan heroes. We owe to Homer and the *Iliad* the finest rendering of the dramatic episodes that take place in forty odd days of the war; and although the war itself is not the theme of this epic, but rather the wrath of Achilles and its effect on others, Homer employs the saga of Troy to give us a sense of human life, its vitality and its joy, its sorrow and its tragedy. The *Iliad*, after stating its theme, begins with the incident which triggered a quarrel between Achilles and Agamemnon; it ends with the burial of the Trojan hero Hector.

The Wrath of Achilles. What brought Agamemnon and Achilles into open conflict? Chryses, a priest of Apollo and the father of Chryseis, came to Agamemnon to ransom his daughter. Agamemnon curtly refused the offer for the attractive girl who was his prize of war, and sent her aged father away with threats on his life. The old man then prayed to Apollo and asked the god to avenge him. The god answered his prayers by sending a devastating plague upon the Greek forces. After nine days of unremitting death, Achilles summoned an assembly of the army to deliberate on how to placate the gods and avert the plague. As was usual in crises of this sort, Calchas the seer was consulted; but he hesitated to speak out because he feared Agamemnon's displeasure. When Achilles promised to protect him, Calchas put the onus upon Agamemnon and declared that the plague would not end until Chryseis had been returned to her father and the god Apollo appeased by a sacrifice. Agamemnon was infuriated when he heard Calchas and burst out with the demand that he be given another woman equal in merit to Chryseis. He pointed his finger at Ajax, Odysseus, and Achilles and threatened to take a captive woman of theirs for himself. Ajax and Odysseus said nothing, but Achilles could not restrain himself since he and many others had no quarrel with the Trojans but were fighting for the sake of Agamemnon and Menelaus. Thereupon, Agamemnon insisted that he would take Achilles' woman Briseis to teach him a lesson that he, Agamemnon, was more powerful and that his word was law. With this challenge, Achilles' anger mounted and reached the point where he said that he would have nothing more to do with the war and that he was going to take his troops home. Words flew thick and fast, and Achilles was at the point of reaching for his sword and killing Agamemnon when Athena came down from heaven—no else could see her—and checked him. She urged him not to use violence and to be patient, for he would be compensated more than threefold for the loss of Briseis. Achilles agreed and turned on Agamemnon and stung him with such words as "Drunk!" and "Coward!" He then threw down his gold-studded staff and swore a mighty oath that he would no longer fight in the war. The argument had reached such a pitch that Nestor, the wise old counselor from Pylos, attempted to reconcile the two men but without success.

Achilles and Agamemnon finished their battle of words, and the assembly broke up. Odysseus was chosen to escort Chryseis back to her father and to perform the necessary propitiatory rites. At the same time, Agamemnon sent two men to Achilles' tent to fetch Briseis. Although Achilles bitterly resented having to surrender his prize of war, he did not interfere. Instead he went down to the seashore and prayed to his mother, the sea-goddess Thetis, and when she appeared he asked that she intervene with Zeus on his behalf. He asked her to go to the Olympian and to get him to promise that he would see to it that the Trojans would carry the field and drive back the Greeks. In this way Agamemnon's leadership would be brought into question and recognition would be given to Achilles for his part in the war. Thetis, knowing full well that her son would have an early death, bewailed her lot and that of her ill-fated son; but she promised that she would approach Zeus as soon as he had returned from the land of the Ethiopians where he and the other gods were enjoying Ethiopian hospitality.

Thetis Intercedes for Achilles. Twelve days later, Thetis went up to Mount Olympus and petitioned Zeus on behalf of her son (fig. 88). At first Zeus hesitated, fearing the reciminations of his wife, but Thetis prodded him until he granted her request. Hera, who sided with the Greeks, saw Thetis make her appeal to Zeus and suspected that her husband would allow the Trojans to be victorious so that Achilles could save face. God and goddess began to quarrel. Zeus, losing his temper, threatened Hera with more than mere words (p. 95). Hephaestus stepped in and reminded his mother of Zeus' strength and asked her not to spoil the day-long feast of the gods. Hera finally accepted a cup of nectar from her son and laughed.

Figure 88.   Ingres. Thetis appealing to Zeus on behalf of her son Achilles. *Painting, 1811. Aix-en-Provence Museum. (Giraudon)*

The other Olympians had witnessed the quarrel between husband and wife and were somewhat tense, but they burst out laughing when they saw gimpy Hephaestus as he bustled about ladling out nectar to the gods. With the tension eased, the gods feasted while Apollo played the lyre and the Muses sang. At evening they returned to their homes; Zeus went to bed and "beside him was Hera of the golden throne." Thus ends Book I of the *Iliad*, a book of contrasting moods and colors, of anger and revenge, of tears and laughter, of human sadness and carefree gods.

Agamemnon's Plan of Action. The pace of events now begins to quicken. Zeus sends Agamemnon a dream which deceives him into thinking that if he takes the field immediately it will result in the fall of Troy. On the following morning, it is agreed at a council of chieftains to test the morale of the troops by indicating that the war cannot be won and by urging a withdrawal. Agamemnon carries out the plan before a general assembly. Contrary to expectations, the troops receive the news with unrestrained joy and make a rush for the ships. Odysseus, incited by Athena, restores a semblance of order by both his eloquence and strength. Thersites, who is described as the ugliest and most abusive of the Greeks who came to Ilium—bowlegged, lame in one foot, stooped shoulders, a pointed head with only a tuft of hair on it, a scandalmonger—harangues the troops and calls on them to leave Agamemnon and his unending greed. Odysseus brings his scepter down on Thersites' back and soon shames him before the other men. The army is brought back into line by reminding the men of Calchas' words that Troy would be taken in the tenth year of the war. When Agamemnon calls his men to battle, Homer takes the opportunity to catalog the Greek forces; and when Hector receives word of the enemy's preparations, he too summons his men and their allies, and there is a muster of the Trojan forces.

Paris Challenges the Greeks. As the two opposing forces march toward each other, Paris steps from the ranks of the Trojans and dares any one of the Greeks to fight him. When Menelaus comes forward to accept the challenge, Paris flees back to his lines. Hector sneers at his brother, "Pretty-boy Paris, you woman-crazy seducer," and gives him a tongue-lashing for causing the Trojans to lose face in front of the enemy. Paris admits to his faults, but proposes a duel between himself and Menelaus on the condition that Helen and her wealth go to the winner. Hector makes the proposal to the Greeks; they accept the challenge and the terms. When Helen hears of the approaching fight between Menelaus and Paris, she mounts the tower at the Scaean gate. When the Trojan elders see her, there is a murmur of appreciation for her beauty, but they also wish that she would go home and let their people live in peace. King Priam, however, does not hold her to blame; it is the gods who caused the war. He then asks Helen to point out for him and the other elders some of the Greek heroes on the battlefield. She spots her brother-in-law Agamemnon, Odysseus, the greater Ajax, and the King of Crete, Idomeneus.

Paris and Menelaus Duel. Before the duel takes place, both sides make appropriate sacrifices and take awesome oaths respecting the terms of the agreement. Menelaus and Paris arm themselves, and the duel is on. Paris hurls his spear without effect. Menelaus throws his spear and pierces his opponent's shield, but little more. Then drawing his sword and striking Paris' helmet, Menelaus is dismayed to find his weapon shattered in four pieces. With nothing left but his hands to fight with, Menelaus grabs Paris by his helmet and starts to drag him toward the Greek lines.

Paris would have been choked to death by his chin strap if Aphrodite had not intervened on behalf of her favorite. She releases the chin strap, wraps him in mist, and whisks him off to his room in Troy. The goddess, in the disguise of an old woman, goes to Helen to inform her that Paris awaits her in his bedroom. Helen at first is furious both with Paris and the goddess—the disguise does not fool her—but she is easily won over by Paris and his passionate desire for her.

Men and Gods Join the Battle. At a conference of the gods, Zeus taunts Athena and Hera. They have not taken as good care of their favorite as Aphrodite has of hers, and it looks as if Troy will survive now that Menelaus has defeated Paris. Athena quietly disguises herself as a Trojan and approaches Pandarus, an expert archer and the leader of the contingent from Lycia. She eggs him on to shoot an arrow at Menelaus and thereby win fame for himself. Pandarus is persuaded, but his arrow is deflected by Hera, and Menelaus is only slightly wounded. With this, the sacred oaths are violated and the truce is broken. The two sides rally their forces and the battle rages once more. Diomedes, inspired by Athena, performs prodigious feats of valor, even taking on the gods in battle. He kills Pandarus although the famed archer has wounded him with one of his arrows. He would also have snuffed out the life of Aeneas with a huge boulder if Aphrodite had not come to protect her son. As she removes him from the battlefield, Diomedes wounds the goddess in her hand with his spear. Aphrodite manages to escape in Ares' chariot and makes her way back to her mother Dione (p. 182) who comforts her and heals her wound. Diomedes is not put off from his attempt to kill Aeneas, but Apollo steps in to save the Trojan hero. As the battle rages back and forth, Diomedes comes face to face with Ares—mortal versus the god of war. Inspired once more by Athena and protected by the goddess, Diomedes takes on Ares and deals him a spearwound in the lower part of his belly. Ares lets out a howl equal to the yell of ten thousand men, and he runs off to complain to Zeus about the encouragement Athena is giving Diomedes. Zeus has no sympathy for this son of his (p. 180), but he sees to it that the physician of the gods heals his wound.

The battle continues with many Trojans falling before the onslaught of Menelaus, Ajax, and the indomitable Diomedes. Helenus, the brother of Hector and a seer, advises both Aeneas and Hector to rally their forces to make a stand. He also advises his brother to return to the city and to have the women offer sacrifices and prayers to Athena for the sake of the city's safety. In the meantime Diomedes is about to square off with Glaucus, another leader of the Lycian allies of Troy. Diomedes discovers that Glaucus is a descendant of Bellerophon, the famous hero who killed the Chimaera and performed many other feats of valor. He realizes that both of them are guest-friends, since his grandfather had entertained Bellerophon. Instead of fighting each other, Diomedes and Glaucus exchange armor as a token of their newfound friendship, Diomedes getting the better of the bargain since his bronze armor is worth only nine oxen, while Glaucus' is made of gold and is worth a hundred.

Hector and Andromache. The scene now shifts to Troy. After Hector has returned to the city and instructed his mother in how to appease Athena, he takes the opportunity to visit with his wife Andromache and their child. The encounter, one of the most touching in literature, is a startling contrast to the relationship of Paris and Helen, and even to that of Zeus and Hera. Andromache tearfully reminds Hector of the tragic fate that befell her family at the hands of Achilles. She asks Hector to have pity on her and not make her a widow and their child an orphan; he is all she has, he is father, brother, and mother to her as well as her beloved husband. She pleads with him to take a defensive position in the city and not expose himself to danger on the battlefield. Hector replies with these words:

All that, my dear, is surely my concern. But if I hid myself like a coward and refused to fight, I could never face the Trojans and the Trojan ladies in their trailing gowns. Besides, it would go against the grain, for I have trained myself always, like a good soldier, to take my place in the front line and win glory for my father and myself. Deep in my heart I know the day is coming when holy Ilium will be destroyed, with Priam and the people of Priam of the good ashen spear. Yet I am not so much distressed by the thought of what the Trojans will suffer, or Hecabe herself, or King Priam, or all my gallant brothers whom the enemy will fling down in the dust, as by the thought of you, dragged off in tears by some Achaean man-at-arms to slavery. I see you there in Argos, toiling for some other woman at the loom, or carrying water from an alien well, a helpless drudge with no will of your own. "There goes the wife of Hector," they will say when they see your tears. "He was the champion of the horse-taming Trojans when Ilium was besieged." And every time they say it, you will feel another pang at the loss of the one man who might have kept you free. Ah, may the earth lie deep on my dead body before I hear the screams you utter as they drag you off!

With that, Hector holds out his hands to take his child Scamandrius, but the boy is frightened by his father's helmet and its horsehair plume. He takes off the helmet, picks up his child, kisses him, and then prays to Zeus: "O Zeus and all you other gods, grant that this son of mine may be like me pre-eminent among the Trojans; may he be as brave and strong as I am, and may he be a great king of Ilium. And may men say of him when he returns from battle, 'He is far mightier than his father.' And may he bring home with him the blood-stained spoils of his enemy and make his mother happy." (An ironic prayer since the child will die with the fall of Troy.)

Hector returns the child to Andromache and reassures her that no man is going to kill him who has not been destined to do so. Hector leaves his sorrowful wife and returns to the battlefield. He is immediately joined by Paris whose character and vitality is summed up by Homer in an extended simile. Positioned as it is following the tender and loving scene between Hector and Andromache, Homer emphasizes the contrast between the two brothers.

Paris had also been quick and had not lingered in his lofty house. Directly he had put on his splendid armor with its trappings of bronze, he hurried off through the town at full speed, like a stallion who breaks his halter at the manger where they keep and fatten him, and gallops off across the fields in triumph to his usual bathing place in the delightful river. He tosses up his head; his mane flies back along his shoulders; he knows how beautiful he is; and away he goes, skimming the ground with his feet, to the haunts and pastures of the mares. So Paris, Priam's son, came down hotfoot from the citadel of Pergamus, resplendent in his armor like the dazzling sun, and laughing as he came.

Hector and Ajax Duel to a Draw. In spite of Hector's premonition of impending doom, the end was not yet to be. When Hector returned to the field, he challenged the bravest of the Greeks to fight. Nine accepted the challenge, but Ajax was chosen by lot to face Troy's defender. The duel lasted all day without either of the contestants being able to overpower the other. Hector and Ajax agreed to a draw and parted with great respect for each other. After a short truce to allow each side to give the last rites to soldiers who had fallen in battle, the conflict was renewed. But this time it was the Greeks who were given a taste of defeat; they were driven back in panic before the might of Hector and his troops.

Overtures to Achilles. Agamemnon was now thoroughly disheartened by the course of the war, and he wept openly and without shame. He called another council of his bravest and wisest leaders and proposed—this time in earnest—that they give up the fight and sail home to Greece. A debate ensued. Nestor advised Agamemnon that Achilles' help was imperative and that he should placate him with an apology and with gifts. Agamemnon agreed and drew up a list of peace offerings: the return of Briseis with assurances that he had never slept with her, seven new tripods, twelve polished cauldrons, ten talents of gold, twelve horses noted for their swiftness, seven beautiful and talented women from the island of Lesbos; and after the capture of Troy, a shipload of bronze and gold and the pick of twenty Trojan women. On top of all this, Agamemnon offered one of his daughters in marriage and a dowry of seven well-populated cities. Three men were then carefully selected to carry Agamemnon's handsome offer to Achilles: Odysseus, Ajax, and Phoenix.

When the three envoys approached the disaffected Achilles in the camp of his Myrmidons, they found him playing the lyre and singing of the deeds of famous men. Opposite him sat Patroclus. Before the business at hand was taken up, the customary guest-privileges were observed; they ate and drank. Odysseus then laid before Achilles the desperate military situation and Agamemnon's offer of gifts for his return to the battlefield. Achilles was unmoved by the offer; he could not forgive Agamemnon the insults and the lack of recognition which should have been his. With contempt, Achilles also turned aside the offer of gifts saying that he would reject them even if they were more than twenty times the present offer. And as for the hand of Agamemnon's daughter, he would not have her even if she matched Aphrodite in beauty and Athena in handiwork. Furthermore his mother Thetis had told him that the Fates had laid two courses open for him: if he should stay and fight at Troy, he would have a short life but undying fame; if he should return home, he would have a long life, but lose his good name. Achilles opted for the latter and decided to sail for home on the following day.

The envoys were stunned by Achilles' response. Phoenix, Achilles' old tutor, tried to move him with an emotional appeal, reminding him that even the gods are swayed by prayers and sacrifices. He recalled to Achilles his own tragic past and that of Meleager who was overcome by anger. Achilles, however, was not moved by Phoenix's appeal and offered to take the old man back with him when he sailed. Ajax, who was never known for subtlety, burst out with the charge that Achilles had no regard for the affections of his comrades; that for the sake of one woman he had worked himself up to such an emotional pitch; and here they were offering him seven of the very best and much more besides. Achilles reiterated that he could not abide the arrogant treatment given him by Agamemnon. Ajax and Odysseus returned to Agamemnon and reported the failure of their mission.

Odysseus and Diomedes Raid the Trojan Camp. The battle was renewed. Both sides reconnoitered each other's positions. As Odysseus and Diomedes made their way toward the Trojan lines, they captured Dolon who had volunteered to scout the Greek camp. After Dolon revealed the purpose of his mission and provided information on the disposition of the Trojan forces, Diomedes killed him with a stroke of his sword. Odysseus and Diomedes next raided the Trojan camp and made off with the horses of Rhesus, the Thracian ally of Priam; they also killed Rhesus and twelve of his men. Feeling that the balance of battle had changed in their favor, the Greeks took to the field and killed many Trojans before Zeus tipped the scales in favor of Hector. In quick succession Agamemnon, Odysseus, and Diomedes were wounded and the Greek forces withdrew to the defensive installations around their ships. For the first time since he withdrew from the fight, Achilles became interested in what was happening on the battlefield. He sent Patroclus to get information from Nestor. The wise old man from Pylos saw an opportunity to exploit Patroclus' close relationship with Achilles. In a long speech Nestor appealed to the young man's desire for glory, admonished him to be a man of action, and urged him to put on Achilles' armor and lead the Myrmidons onto the battlefield.

The Battle at the Ships. In the meantime, the situation became much more desperate for the Greeks. Hector and his Trojan forces breached the defensive wall protecting the ships and forced a retreat to the ships. The situation would have been far worse had Poseidon not made his appearance in the guise of Calchas the seer and roused the Greeks to make a stand and hold the Trojans at bay. Agamemnon was again dispirited and advised a withdrawal from Troy. Odysseus and Diomedes took Agamemnon to task for recommending such a course of action. Poseidon, this time in the guise of an old man, prophesied the defeat of the Trojans and the fall of Troy. Another divinity lent her hand on the side of the Greeks. Hera was intent on drawing the attention of Zeus from the field of battle. The goddess, dressed up in her finest and armed with a love charm which she managed to secure from Aphrodite by trickery, approached her husband on Mount Ida. When Zeus saw Hera it awakened memories of his early passion for her (pp. 5;94). He embraced his wife and soon fell asleep. With Zeus thus distracted, the tide of battle now shifted in favor of the Greeks. Hector was felled by a huge boulder which Ajax had hefted and thrown at the Trojan commander. As Hector was dragged off the field by his comrades, the Greeks, assisted by Poseidon, took heart and drove back the Trojans.

Patroclus Fights and Dies. When Zeus awoke from his love-induced sleep and took stock of the military situation, he was appalled to find Hector wounded and the Trojans in retreat before the advancing Greeks. He turned on Hera and threatened her bodily punishment for her part in changing the course of battle. A messenger was sent to Poseidon ordering him to stop aiding the Greeks, and Apollo was dispatched to revive Hector and to inspire him with courage. In short order the Trojans were back in the field and the Greeks were forced to retreat. When Patroclus saw his comrades fighting with their backs to the sea, he rushed to Achilles and pleaded for the use of his armor and the Myrmidons. As the two were talking, flames burst from one of the ships. Achilles had no second thoughts. He armed Patroclus and gave him command of the Myrmidons with strict orders to drive the enemy from the ships but not to pursue them to the walls of Troy.

The sight of Achilles' armor and the Myrmidon host had a startling effect on both the Greeks and the Trojans. Thinking that Achilles had come back to fight, the Greeks were inspired and regained the will to resist; the Trojans, fearing that their indomitable foe had taken to the field, were dismayed and hastily drew back from their advanced positions on the beach. Patroclus drove all before him, killing among many others Sarpedon, the best of the Lycian allies. After a fierce struggle for the armor of Sarpedon as a prize of war, Patroclus swept the field and appeared before the walls of Troy. Casting aside Achilles' orders, he attempted to scale the walls. Three times he made the attempt, and three times Apollo himself forced him back. At the fourth try, Apollo's voice boomed out that the city was neither fated to fall to his spear nor to Achilles, who was a far better man than he. At that, Patroclus retreated only to be stunned by a karate-like chop from Apollo's hand. His helmet rolled off, and while he was dazed by the blow, he received a wound. Hector then closed in on Patroclus for the kill and mortally wounded him with a spearthrust at close quarters. Stripping Patroclus of Achilles' armor, he cast aside his own and put on the famed armor which Achilles' father had received from the gods as a wedding gift. A fierce struggle ensued for the body of Patroclus. The Greeks managed to recover it and carry it back to their camp.

Achilles Ends His Feud with Agamemnon.   When Achilles hears of Patroclus' death, he is so overwhelmed with grief, so distraught, that a comrade has to hold his hands for fear that he will commit suicide. Even in the depths of the sea, Thetis and her sister Nereids beat their breasts and weep for the loss of Patroclus. Thetis rises from the sea to comfort her son, only to hear him say that she will have much more sorrow to bear since he has no wish to live unless he makes Hector pay with his life for the one he took from Patroclus. Thetis replies tearfully that he indeed will have a short life, for death awaits him soon after Hector's end. Achilles responds to this prediction with passion and with some observations on the effects of anger:

> Then *let* me die forthwith since I have failed to save my friend from death. He has fallen, far from his motherland, wanting my help in his extremity.... Ah, how I wish that discord could be banished from the world of gods and men, and with it anger, insidious as trickling honey, anger that makes the wisest man flare up and spreads like smoke through his whole being, anger such as King Agamemnon roused in me that day! .. As for my death, when Zeus and the other deathless gods appoint it, let it come. Even the mighty Heracles did not escape his doom, dear as he was to Zeus the Royal Son of Cronos, but was laid low by Fate and Hera's bitter enmity. And I too shall lie low when I am dead, if the same lot awaits me.

Thetis bids Achilles not to rush out on the field unarmed; she will have the master-craftsman of the gods Hephaestus fabricate a new suit of armor within a day's time (fig. 37). While Thetis is on her way to Mount Olympus, the Trojans launch an attack in an attempt to make off with Patroclus' body, but Achilles frightens them off with his terrifying war cries. On the following morning Thetis appears with the armor she has promised her son; it is magnificently crafted out of precious metals and elaborately decorated, a product that could have come only from the workshop of a god (pp. 177–179). Achilles, suitably armed, makes his appearance before the assembled host. He announces that he is ready to end his feud with Agamemnon, to let bygones be bygones, and to pit his might against the enemy. Agamemnon on his part confesses his error in insisting on taking Briseis and lays the blame for his rashness on Ate, the goddess of infatuation. Although Achilles sees no need to accept the gift-offerings, he does so at the urging of Odysseus who sees it as a formal act to end the feud. Achilles cannot wait to take the field, and reluctantly bides his time while the men eat and drink; he himself will not touch a bit of food until he avenges the death of Patroclus. When Briseis is returned and sees the body of Patroclus, she throws herself on the corpse and tearfully eulogizes his nobility and kindness.

Achilles Takes to the Field.   Armed and ready to take the field in his chariot, Achilles suddenly hears one of his horses speak—for the moment Hera has given the animal the power of speech—prophesying his death at the hands of a mortal and a god. Undaunted by this phenomenon, Achilles raises a battle cry and rides off to avenge the death of Patroclus and win glory for himself. At an assembly of the gods, Zeus announces that the gods may also take part in the coming conflict, although he himself will remain neutral. Hera, Athena, Poseidon, Hermes, and Hephaestus line up on the side of the Greeks; on the Trojan side there are Ares, Apollo, Artemis, Leto, the river-god Xanthus, and Aphrodite. Once in the field, Achilles is filled with a rage and a thirst for vengeance so great that he is irresistible. Apollo cautions Hector to keep his distance, but he urges Aeneas to take on the indomitable Greek warrior. Just as Aeneas is about to be defeated by Achilles, Poseidon intervenes and saves him since fate has decreed that he is to be Priam's successor as the ruler of the Trojans.

The Trojans retreat before the onslaught of Achilles to the river Xanthus (Scamander). The carnage so chokes the stream that the river-god Xanthus voices his objections to Achilles who disdainfully turns them aside. Xanthus then causes the river to overflow its banks and threatens to overwhelm Achilles. He is saved when Hera commands Hephaestus to set the river afire and dry up its waters. The gods take to fighting and squabbling among themselves. Athena quickly routs Ares and Aphrodite. Hera boxes Artemis' ears and sends her arrows flying. Apollo parries a challenge by Poseidon and refuses to fight.

The Death of Hector. The climactic confrontation between Hector and Achilles is now at hand. Apollo has made it possible for the remnants of the Trojan forces to find safety within the walls of Troy by appearing to Achilles in the form of a Trojan and leading him on a wild goose chase. When the gates of the city are closed, one Trojan is left outside the walls, Hector. Priam and his wife Hecuba beg and plead with him not to stand up to Achilles but to take refuge with them within the city. Hector ignores the pleas and tears of his parents. As he awaits the coming of Achilles, he indulges in an internal debate. He knows that if he seeks protection within the gates of Troy, he will have to face the recriminations of his brother Polydamas who advised him to withdraw his troops when Achilles took the field. He cannot bear that, nor can he bear to hear the Trojans say that he sacrificed an army because of his own perversity and misjudgment. He has another thought. Perhaps he can lay aside his arms and make a deal with Achilles to return Helen with all her property, and in addition offer half of all the chattels that Troy possesses. No, he knows that would not work, for if he tried to approach Achilles unarmed, he would be killed outright. The only course left open to him is to fight.

While Hector debates his position with himself, Achilles draws near. And when Hector sees him brandishing his mighty spear, sees his armor flashing like a blazing fire or the rising sun, he begins to shake all over; he cannot stand his ground and runs away in terror and fear. Like a dove fleeing a hawk, or a fawn trying to escape from a hound, Hector runs before Achilles. He runs around the city of Troy three times before Zeus decides to see whose fate hangs in the balance. He takes out his golden scales and in the pan on either side he puts a sentence of death. When he raises the scale, the pan bearing Hector's lot sinks down. Hector is fated to die and the gods cannot forestall the event.

The divine machinery goes to work to effect the decree of fate. Apollo deserts his favorite, while Athena informs Achilles that now is the moment of truth, that together they will kill Hector. Disguising herself as Hector's brother Deïphobus, Athena appears at Hector's side and leads him to believe that he has his brother's support. Achilles and Hector come together in the duel of death. Hector attempts to come to an agreement with his opponent on the disposition of the body of the loser. It is bluntly rejected. The fight is on. Achilles hurls his spear; it misses its mark. Then Hector hurls his weapon only to have it strike Achilles' shield and rebound. Turning around to get another spear from his brother, Hector finds to his astonishment that he is alone. He knows now that his end is near, but he is determined to go down fighting. He draws his sword and charges his opponent. Achilles sees his chance and drives his spear through the gullet of the oncharging Hector. It is a mortal blow, and as Hector lies dying in the dust, he begs Achilles to allow his parents to ransom his body so that it can be given the last rites on the funeral pyre. Achilles scowls at him and says:

> You dog, don't talk to me of knees or name my parents in your prayers. I only wish that I could summon up the appetite to carve and eat you raw myself, for what you have done to me. But this at least is certain, that nobody is going to keep the dogs from you, not even if the Trojans bring here and weigh out a ransom ten or twenty times your worth, and promise more besides; not if Dardanian Priam tells them to pay your weight in gold—not even so shall your lady mother lay you on a bier to mourn the son she bore, but the dogs and birds of prey shall eat you up.

As Hector gasps out his last breath, he foreshadows the death of Achilles at the hands of Paris and Apollo at the Scaean gate; and then, Homer says, "the shadow of death came down upon him, and his soul flew forth from his limbs and went down to the house of Hades, bewailing its fate and the vigor and youth that it left behind." Stripping the armor from Hector's body, Achilles pierces the tendons near the ankles and lashes the feet to his chariot. Then mounting the chariot, he brutally drags the body of Hector back and forth in full view of the Trojans. At the sight of their son being dragged in the dust, Priam and Hecuba are grief-stricken. The sounds of Trojan mourning and wailing reach the ears of Andromache as she works at her loom. With beating heart she goes out to the battlements, and when she sees Achilles dragging the body of her husband, she falls into a dead faint. Once revived, Andromache laments the fate of her orphaned child and the loss of her husband.

The Last Rites for Patroclus. Back in the camp of the Greeks, preparations are underway for the funeral of Patroclus. Achilles falls into a deep sleep; he is thoroughly exhausted after a day of fighting which culminated in his chase of Hector. He is visited by the soul of Patroclus who begs him to give his body the ritual of fire so that he can pass through the gates of Hades. And since Achilles is fated to die under the walls of Troy, Patroclus also asks that their bones be buried together. Achilles agrees and tries to embrace the ghost-like soul of his comrade, only to have it disappear like a puff of smoke. On the following morning a magnificent funeral pyre is built for Patroclus. Achilles surrounds the body of his friend with slain cattle, horses, dogs, jars of oil and honey; and finally, twelve Trojan prisoners are put to the sword and placed on the pyre. When Patroclus' body is consumed by the flames, the bones are placed in a golden urn to await those of Achilles when he dies. The rites are concluded with games of all kinds: chariot-racing, boxing, wrestling, archery, shot put, and javelinthrowing. To the winners of these athletic contests, Achilles awards rich prizes.

Priam Ransoms the Body of Hector. Even though Patroclus was given the last rites befitting a hero, Achilles cannot dispel the grief he feels for his comrade. Day after day, Achilles assuages his pain by hitching up his chariot and dragging the body of Hector around the grave of Patroclus (fig. 89). Apollo sees to it, however, that Hector's body is neither lacerated nor disfigured; and after some days of witnessing Achilles' inhumanity, Apollo forcibly brings the matter to the attention of the gods on Mount Olympus. Zeus sends for Thetis and asks her to take a message back to Achilles telling him that the gods are angry with him for his senseless rage over the body of Hector and his refusal to part with it. When Thetis informs Achilles of Zeus' displeasure, he agrees to accept a ransom for Hector's body. At the same time, Zeus sends a messenger to Priam with word that he is to go into the camp of the Greeks alone with rich gifts as a ransom for his son's corpse; he need not have any fear for Hermes will escort him. Priam, reassured by an omen from Zeus, heaps a wagon full of treasures. Protected by Hermes, he makes his way unseen through the Greek camp to the hut of Achilles (fig. 90). Startling everyone by his sudden appearance, Priam goes to Achilles and kisses his hands, the terrible man killing hands that had slaughtered so many of his sons. And before anyone can speak, the old man makes this plea to the man who has just killed his favorite son:

> Most worshipful Achilles, think of your own father, who is the same age as I, and so has nothing but miserable old age ahead of him. No doubt his neighbors are oppressing him and there is nobody to save him from their depredations. Yet he at least has one consolation. While he knows that you are still alive, he can look forward day by day to seeing his beloved son come back from Troy; whereas my fortunes are completely broken. I had the best sons in the whole of this broad realm, and now not one, not one I say, is left. There were fifty when the Achaean expedition came. Nineteen of them were borne by one mother and the rest by other ladies in my palace. Most of them have fallen in action, and Hector, the only one I could count on, the bulwark of Troy and the Trojans, has now been killed by you, fighting for his native land. It is to get him back from you that I have come to the Achaean ships, bringing this princely ransom with me. Achilles, fear the gods, and be merciful to me, remembering your own father, though I am even more entitled to compassion, since I have brought myself to do a thing that no one else on earth has done—I have raised to my lips the hand of the man who killed my son.

Priam's plea touches Achilles. It sets him thinking of his father and evokes compassion for the old man before him. The two begin to weep, Achilles for his father and for Patroclus, Priam for Hector. Achilles then assents to deliver the body of Hector for the ransom. He also agrees to a twelve-day truce so that Hector can be honored with a proper funeral. Although Achilles invites the old man to spend the night with him, Hermes alerts Priam to the need to leave the Greek camp as soon as possible. When Priam approaches the city with the body of his son, the air is filled with cries of grief. Andromache throws herself on the body of her husband and tearfully laments his untimely death. She is followed by Hecuba whose words cause a fresh wave of weeping. And even Helen sheds tears of sorrow for Hector whom she loved best of all her Trojan relatives. At Priam's orders, a funeral pyre is prepared for Hector, and at the end of the ritual of fire, his bones are placed in a golden urn and buried in a gravemound. And then the *Iliad*, which has been surging with varied emotions and movements, comes to a simple and quiet end with these words: "Such were the funeral rites for Hector, tamer of horses." Or in Pope's translation: "Such honors Ilium to her hero paid,/And peaceful slept the mighty Hector's shade."

*   *   *   *

Figure 89.   Achilles dragging the body of Hector past the tomb of Patroclus.
Vase painting, early fifth century B.C. Metropolitan Museum of Art.

Figure 90.   Priam approaching Achilles
to ransom the body of Hector (below).
*Vase painting, c. 480 B.C. Kunsthistor-
isches Museum, Vienna.*

The *Iliad* had an inhibiting effect on major poets of all ages; they did not dare to challenge the genius of Homer by reinterpreting his version of the forty-seven critical days in the tenth year of the Trojan War. Artists, however, felt no such restraint; the epic stirred their imagination and impelled them to creativity. In antiquity, episodes from the *Iliad* were illustrated on media of all kinds: vases, metal cups and jugs, mosaics and manuscripts, and even on sarcophagi. When the volcanic dust was swept from the ruins of Pompeii, it revealed Roman homes decorated with frescoes and mosaics depicting such scenes as Athena restraining Achilles, the surrender of Briseis, Priam begging for the body of Hector. Of course, the interior decorators of old did not neglect themes taken from the ante-Homerica; for example, Achilles on Scyros and the sacrifice of Iphigeneia (fig. 31). Following the Revival of Learning, illustrations of themes taken directly or indirectly from the *Iliad* become legion. Sometime before 1643, Rubens painted eight oil sketches for a set of tapestries on the history of Achilles—such tapestries were popular in the seventeenth and eighteenth centuries—and of the eight, half were on subjects taken from the *Iliad*. A hundred years later, the Italian artist Giovanni Battista Tiepolo (1696–1770), decorated one of five rooms in the Villa Valmarana near Vincenza with scenes from the *Iliad*. Like many other artists, he, too, was attracted to the story of Achilles on the island of Scyros—Nicholas Poussin also painted two

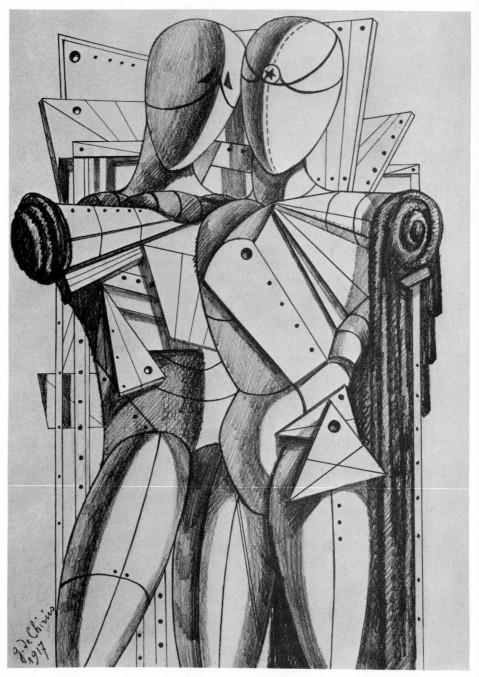

Figure 91. Giorgio de Chirico. Hector and Andromache. *Pencil drawing, 1917.*
Museum of Modern Art.

versions of the episode (fig. 87)—and to the sacrifice of Iphigeneia. Representing
the French school, Jacques-Louis David painted a portrait of Hector and one of
Andromache bewailing Hector. His compatriot, Jean-Auguste-Dominique Ingres,

depicted Thetis making her plea to Zeus on behalf of Achilles (fig. 88), and the envoys of Agamemnon at the tent of Achilles. And to conclude this sampling, there is the work of Giorgio de Chirico, an Italian artist who had spent his youth in Greece and for whom Hector and Andromache had a special attraction. Between 1916 and 1926, de Chirico painted four versions of the devoted couple, and although he painted them as mannequins and faceless, the effect is one of poignant and eloquent concern for one another (fig. 91).

The Fall of Troy

Homer's poem of the wrath of Achilles is concluded with the rites for the fallen Hector. There still remain other battles for Achilles to fight before his young life is brought to its prophesied end, and there also remains the saga of the fall of the sacred city of Troy. The story is told in part by Homer in the *Odyssey*, by the dramatists Aeschylus, Sophocles, and Euripides, by Vergil in the *Aeneid*, and by numerous poets and mythographers of later antiquity. It is the story of the defeat of two allies of Troy at the hands of Achilles, the death of the great Greek hero, the fulfillment of conditions necessary for Troy's fall, the stratagem of the Wooden Horse, and lastly, the fall of the city and the fate of the royal family.

Penthesileia. After the death of Hector, Penthesileia, an Amazon of extraordinary beauty, came to help in the defense of Troy. It is said that this queen of the Amazons appeared with her followers during the twelve days of truce set aside for the funeral rites of the Trojan hero. When Achilles came face to face with her on the field of battle, he had no way of knowing that his antagonist was a woman. Penthesileia fought valiantly, only to fall when Achilles' spear pierced her breast. When her helmet rolled off, Achilles was stunned to find a woman of remarkable beauty instead of a man. Thersites, the ugliest of the Greeks, is said to have gouged out the eyes of the dead Amazon and to have ridiculed Achilles' grief at having taken the life of the female warrior. He was killed out of hand by an outraged Achilles.

Memnon. On the heels of Penthesileia came Memnon, the son of Tithonus and the dawn-goddess Eos. Leading his Ethiopian troops and wearing armor fashioned by Hephaestus, Memnon soon was to face the challenge of Achilles in battle. But since the two were sons of goddesses, a special decision was needed from upon high as to which one should die. Zeus took out his golden scales to settle the issue, the same scales of fate that had decreed Hector's end. The pan holding the lot of Memnon went down, and thus Memnon fell before the spear of the great Achilles. Eos mourned for her dead son, and it is said that her tears are remembered by men as drops of morning dew.

The Death of Achilles. Now came Achilles' turn. Elated by his victory over Memnon, Achilles was irresistible. He drove the Trojans back into the city through the Scaean gate; but as he charged after the enemy, he was struck in the heel by an arrow, in that one vulnerable spot which had not been bathed in the river Styx. Hector's prophetic words were realized; Achilles died at the Scaean gate by the hand of Paris and Apollo. Some say that Paris shot the arrow that was aimed by Apollo; others say that it was Apollo in the guise of Paris who sent the arrow into Achilles' vulnerable heel; still others say that Achilles met his death by the shafts of Apollo alone. But dead he was at the Scaean gate. Immediately there was a fight over his body, and it was only through the bravery of Ajax and Odysseus that the corpse of the Greek hero was recovered and brought back to their camp.

The late romanticizers of Greek legend offer another version of Achilles' death. At one occasion or another, Achilles had seen Polyxena, a daughter of Priam, and had fallen in love with her. When Priam saw that his daughter had captivated Achilles, he offered him her hand in marriage on condition that he lift the siege of Troy. Achilles agreed to influence the Greeks to make peace. When he went alone and unarmed to the temple of the Thymbraean Apollo to negotiate the terms of the peace and of the marriage, he was greeted by Deïphobus, a son of Priam, who embraced him, seemingly in a gesture of friendship. Paris then treacherously assassinated him with a sword. Other accounts say that Paris hid behind a statue of the god and shot a death-dealing arrow at Achilles. Later the ghost of Achilles demanded that this same Polyxena be sacrificed on his grave.

Back in the Greek camp, the body of Achilles was stripped of its armor and laid out in state. Thetis, accompanied by her sister Nereids and the Muses, mourned over the fallen hero and sang dirges. The period of mourning stretched over seventeen days, and on the eighteenth the body of Achilles was laid on a funeral pyre and burned. His bones were united with those of Patroclus and were put into a golden urn crafted by Hephaestus which Dionysus had given to Peleus and Thetis as a wedding gift. This urn was buried by the army in a huge gravemound at the entrance of the Hellespont, a mound so high that ships could see it from a great distance. When Alexander the Great crossed the Hellespont with his army in 334 B.C., he honored his favorite hero by making appropriate offerings and by running naked around the mound as was the custom. Such was the death and burial of the greatest hero of Greek legend. But while his mortal remains were buried in the Troad, his shade paced the Plain of Asphodel in the kingdom of the dead. Later reports have him residing on Leuce, the White Island, in the Black Sea near the mouth of the Danube. It is there that he is said to dwell with his wife—variously given as Helen, Iphigeneia, or Medea—and with his friend Patroclus.

The Contest for the Arms of Achilles. In the games which were a part of the funeral rites for Achilles, Thetis offered her son's armor as a prize to the one who was judged the bravest of the Greeks. The contest narrowed down to two names, Ajax and Odysseus. Odysseus was declared the winner and was given the prize. How the judgment was made is variously given. Some say that the contest was settled by Agamemnon with the advice of Athena; others that it was on the testimony of Trojan prisoners; still others that it was decided by the report of a conversation between two Trojan girls which had been overheard by Greek scouts. When Ajax saw the prize go to Odysseus, he turned stark raving mad. In the middle of the night, he rushed out and attacked the flocks and herds of the Greek army and dragged dead and living animals into his tent in the insane belief that they were his enemies. Some say that he originally intended to attack his comrades, but Athena turned his hand against the animals and caused him to think that they were the ones who had wronged him. When Ajax came to his senses and saw what he had done, he was so ashamed that he committed suicide with the sword Hector had given him as a present (fig. 92). It is said that his body was refused the ritual of fire and was buried in a coffin; other accounts have it that Odysseus persuaded the Greek leaders to give Ajax the customary funeral rites of a warrior. Later traditions with a penchant for metamorphoses state that when his blood flowed into the ground, there sprang up a deep-red flower which bore the letters *AI* on its leaves—compare Hyacinth (p. 138). The letters were taken from the beginning of his name (Aias in Greek); they also signify a cry of anguish and woe. Ajax even kept his grudge against Odysseus in the kingdom of the dead: he refused to acknowledge his opponent when the hero attempted to converse with him in the house of Hades; he simply turned on his heel and walked off without uttering a word.

The Death of Paris. Achilles was dead and Troy still stood. Diviners and oracles were consulted as to what had to be done to inspirit the Greek army and to debilitate the enemy. The Greeks were informed that it would be necessary to bring the bones of Pelops, the ancestor of Agamemnon and Menelaus, to Troy. They were also told that Achilles' son Neoptolemus as well as Philoctetes and the bow which Heracles had bequeathed him would have to be there. A further condition for the fall of Troy was the removal of the Palladium from its precinct within the city. The bones of Pelops were accordingly brought from their resting-place in Greece. Neoptolemus was summoned from the island of Scyros and, wearing the armor of his famous father which Odysseus graciously surrendered, soon distinguished himself in battle. As for Philoctetes, an embassy was dispatched to the island of Lemnos, where he had been abandoned. After much difficulty and soul-searching, Philoctetes was persuaded to rejoin his comrades before Troy and to bring with him Heracles' bow and arrows. After he had been cured of his festering wound, Philoctetes took to the field and within a short time wounded Paris mortally with one of his Heraclean arrows. Paris retreated to Mount Ida and sought the help of Oenone, the nymph who loved him. Although Oenone had it within her power to heal him, she refused to do so because he had abandoned her for Helen. But she soon changed her mind and rushed after Paris with her remedies. It was too late; Paris had died. In her grief Oenone committed suicide either by hanging or by throwing herself on the funeral pyre of the man who had once loved her. After the death of Paris, two of his brothers—Helenus the prophet and Deïphobus—quarreled over who was to have Helen for his wife. When Deïphobus was given the nod over Helenus, the latter left Troy and was soon captured by the Greeks. It is said that Helenus was the one who was forced to reveal to the Greeks the conditions under which Troy could be taken, all except the one involving Philoctetes and his bow.

Figure 92. The suicide of Ajax. *Enlarged impression of a carnelian scarab. Etruscan, late fifth century B.C. Museum of Fine Arts, Boston.*

Figure 93. The theft of the Palladium. Diomedes has removed the image of Athena from her altar. *Vase painting, early fourth century B.C. Ashmolean Museum, Oxford.*

The Palladium. There still remained the problem of removing the Palladium from its hidden shrine deep within the palace of Priam. Odysseus volunteered as a spy to gather information on the location of the fateful statue. Disguised as a ragged beggar he made his way into the city where he chanced to come upon Helen, now the wife of Deïphobus. She longed for the child and the home she had left behind in Sparta; she was ready to be reconciled with her Menelaus. Helen had no difficulty in penetrating Odysseus' disguise and in recognizing her former suitor. She swore not to betray him and provided the information he had come for. Before returning to the Greek camp, Odysseus killed many Trojans. Disguising himself once more as a beggar, and accompanied by Diomedes this time, he made his way back into the city and carried off the life-token of Troy (fig. 93). Accounts differ as to which one of the heroes, Odysseus or Diomedes, had the major role in carrying off the Palladium.

The Stratagem of the Wooden Horse. Still the city did not fall. The wily Odysseus, inspired by Athena, came up with a plan, the stratagem of the Wooden Horse, popularly known as the Trojan Horse. According to one account, this plan had been conceived before the Palladium had been removed from the city: it called for the construction of a wooden horse, a horse so large that the Trojans would have to breach their walls in order to bring it within the city. The horse would be hollow so that a number of warriors could hide within it. The plan also called for the pretense of preparations to abandon the siege; the Greeks would break camp and sail away as if to return home, but in reality they would sail to the island of Tenedos to await a signal that the Wooden Horse was within the city. The signal was to be given by Sinon, a cousin of Odysseus who had volunteered to be left behind ostensibly as a deserter. His job was to convince the Trojans that the siege had been abandoned and that if Troy wished to gain supremacy over Greece, the Wooden Horse would have to be drawn with their own hands into the city. Once the walls were breached and the Horse was within the city, the ships would return and there would be a coordinated attack by the forces hidden in the belly of the steed and those coming from the sea. Although the plan was called cowardly by some Greek leaders, it was approved and put into effect. Epeius the architect, was given the task of constructing the Wooden Horse. He built it with the help of Athena. The finished work was marked with the votive inscription "A thank-offering to Athena from the Greeks for their return home." Odysseus and a band of chosen men entered the belly of the Horse—the number of men is variously given as 23, 30, 50, even 3000—the campfires were doused, and the ships sailed away to their rendezvous behind the island of Tenedos.

Laocoön. All went as planned. The Trojans rushed out of the city to explore the campsite of the Greeks and to marvel at the wooden prodigy they had left behind. While they stood there gaping at the Wooden Horse and debating whether it should be taken within the city as a trophy, the priest Laocoön came rushing down from Troy to berate his countrymen for even thinking of the idea. "What insanity is this!" he cried out, "Do you think that the enemy has sailed off, or that a Greek could offer a gift without treachery in it? Whatever it may be, I fear the Greeks even when they bear gifts." (*Timeo Danaos et dona ferentes.*) As he finished his tongue-lashing, he threw his spear with all his strength into the side of the Wooden Horse. It struck and gave off a hollow sound like a groan.

The Trojans began to have second thoughts, but just at that moment a group of Trojans appeared dragging forward someone who seemed to be a Greek prisoner. It was Sinon. Sinon spun out his tale with great histrionic skill. Yes, he was a Greek and he had been left behind by a vindictive comrade. As for the Wooden Horse, it was a propitiatory offering to the goddess for the theft of the Palladium. It had been made so huge so that it could not be carried within the city, for Calchas the seer had told them that if the Trojans did so, they would triumph over the Greeks. So convincing was Sinon and his trumped-up story that the Trojans were ready once more to change their minds. All doubts were swept away by what came next. Now it so happened that Laocoön was a priest of Apollo—or a priest of Poseidon in some accounts—and had offended one of the gods: the hostility of Athena was directed against him for having thrown his spear against the Wooden Horse; or Apollo was angry at him for having married contrary to his wishes and for having begotten children in his temple; or Poseidon, who was hostile to the Trojans, wanted to illustrate the fate that they all deserved through Laocoön. Whatever the reason, just as Laocoön was sacrificing a bull, two monstrous serpents arose from the sea and in full view of all strangled the priest and his two sons (figs. 94, 95). This is how Vergil's hero describes the scene in the *Aeneid:*

> . . . From Tenedos over the still deep, two serpents coiled in vast circles are seen breasting the sea, and moving side by side toward the shore. Their breasts rise erect among the waves; their manes, of blood-red hue, tower over the water, the rest of them floats behind on the main, trailing a huge undulating length; the brine foams and dashes about them; they are already on shore, in the plain—with their glowing eyes bloodshot and fiery, and their forked tongues playing in their hissing mouths. We fly all ways in terror: they, in an unswerving column, make for Laocoön, and first each serpent folds round one of his two sons, clasping the youthful body, and greedily devouring the poor limbs. Afterwards, as the father comes to the rescue, weapon in hand, they fasten on him and lash their enormous spires tight around him—and now twice folded round his middle, twice embracing his neck with their scaly length, they tower over him with uplifted head and crest. He is straining with agonizing clutch to pull the knots asunder, his priestly fillets all bedewed with gore and black poison, and raising all the while dreadful cries to heaven—like the bellowing, when a wounded bull darts away from the altar, dashing off from his neck the ill-aimed ax. But the two serpents escape glidingly to the temple top, making for the height where ruthless Minerva is enthroned, and they shelter themselves under the goddess' feet and round her shield.

Troy's Final Hours. When the Trojans saw what happened to Laocoön and his sons, they rushed to tear down their defensive wall and to drag the Wooden Horse into the city; unfavorable omens and the prophetic shrieks of Cassandra were of no avail. All day long the Trojans celebrated their "triumph" with singing and gay

Figure 94. Laocoön and his sons being strangled by serpents sent by Apollo. *Marble group (right arm incorrectly restored), second-first century B.C. Vatican Museum. (Alinari)*

Figure 95. El Greco. Laocoön (with a view of Toledo in the background). *Painting, c. 1601–1606. Samuel H. Kress Collection, National Gallery of Art, Washington D.C.*

Figure 96.   Greek warriors pouring out of the Wooden Horse. *Vase painting.*
Bibliothèque Nationale, Paris. (Giraudon)

Figure 97.   Neoptolemus (Pyrrhus)
killing the child Astyanax and the aged
king Priam. At the left Ajax the Lesser
seizes Cassandra. *Vase painting, c.*
465 B.C. Museum of Fine Arts, Boston.

festivities, and when night came they fell into a deep, exhausted sleep. Sinon now
began to carry out the final phase of the operation plan. He signaled the ships lying
off Tenedos and released the soldiers within the Wooden Horse (fig. 96). The
Greeks rushed about the city, killing and burning. Achilles' son Neoptolemus
(Pyrrhus) broke into the palace in pursuit of Polites, the youngest son of Priam and
Hecuba. Priam had taken refuge with his wife and daughters at an altar, and when
Polites died at the feet of his father, the old man weakly tried to attack the on-
rushing Greek. He was mercilessly cut down by Neoptolemus (fig. 97). Deïphobus,
the latest husband of Helen, was brutally mangled and killed. The only members
of the royal family to escape were Aeneas, his son Ascanius, and his father Anchises.
More will be said later of their adventures in exile.

Figure 98.   Menelaus, overcome by the beauty of Helen, drops his sword.
Vase painting, fourth century B.C. British Museum.

What was the fate of Helen and of some of the other women? While the city was being put to the torch, Helen hid in a temple or in the palace, racked by doubts and fears. However, when she came face to face with Menelaus, there seems to have been little difficulty in effecting a reconciliation. One account tells how Menelaus drew his sword and was ready to kill her, but when he caught a glimpse of her bare bosom, he let his sword fall to the ground (fig. 98). Helen back at home in Sparta rationalized her seduction by Paris: she had been blinded by Aphrodite's infatuation. The fate of the other women was not as fortunate as that of Helen. When the spoils were divided, Andromache was given to Neoptolemus, Hecuba to Odysseus, and Cassandra to Agamemnon after she had been assaulted by the lesser Ajax in the temple of Athena. As for Polyxena, she was slaughtered on the grave of Achilles; and Astyanax, the infant son of Hector and Andromache, was thrown to his death from the battlements. Thus died the legendary city of Troy.

*   *   *   *

Sophocles' PHILOCTETES.   The post-*Iliad* events leading to the burning of Troy had a most lasting effect through the efforts of the dramatists of antiquity even though only four of their dramas have survived to the present day: the *Ajax* and *Philoctetes* of Sophocles; the *Trojan Women* and *Hecuba* of Euripides. The *Philoctetes,* the penultimate play of Sophocles—he was well over eighty when he wrote it— was produced in 409 B.C. It has as its subject the mission of Odysseus and Neoptolemus to the island of Lemnos for the invincible bow of Heracles. Sophocles' invalid hermit is one of the poet's mysterious god-chosen mortals who is both bane and boon, a man who is strong but mutilated, humiliated yet honored. Odysseus is presented as an unscrupulous, self-serving patriot who would stoop to any means to accomplish his objective. Neoptolemus appears as an ingenuous young man who first is persuaded by his cynical comrade but has a change of heart and responds to the higher claims of simple humanity. At the play's end, Heracles appears and convinces a hate-ridden Philoctetes to go to Troy, instead of returning home; Zeus has promised the suffering Greek a cure and an opportunity to win glory.

Almost two and a half millennia after Sophocles had produced his play, the theme of the agonized Philoctetes was revived by André Gide. His *Philoctète* (1899) is a philosophical drama which pits the artist and moralist—Gide himself—against the outworn conventions and concepts of society. Total disinterestedness and total serenity are achieved by Philoctetes once he surrenders his bow and arrows; only in isolation and as an outcast can genius thrive and develop. Another approach inspired by Sophocles is Edmund Wilson's *The Wound and the Bow* (1929), seven critical essays on literature which end with a study of Sophocles' *Philoctetes*.

Sophocles' AJAX.   The *Ajax*, the earliest surviving play of Sophocles (produced sometime before 441 B.C.), takes as its subject the madness and death of Ajax, following his dispute with Odysseus over the arms of Achilles. Sophocles has turned this episode into a struggle between the forces of hate and those of humanity, one in which humanity, reason, and respect for the dead triumph over immoderation and intransigence. The play contains some elements which are novel and unexpected for a classical drama: the horrifying scene of a deranged Ajax sitting in his tent among the sheep he slaughtered, torturing others in the Athena-inspired belief that they were his enemies, and the unexpected sight of Ajax committing suicide in full view of the audience. The death scene occurs after Ajax recovers his sanity and is overwhelmed by remorse at the realization of his shameful behavior. As preparations are made for Ajax' burial, Menelaus appears and delivers the verdict of the army: the body of the suicide is to be left unburied as if he were a traitor. A tense situation develops between Teucer, the half-brother of Ajax, and Agamemnon: the former insists on last rites for Ajax, the latter furiously forbids them. The conflict is resolved by Odysseus—not the cold-blooded, scheming villain of the *Philoctetes*, but the Sophoclean model of the just, moderate, and wise man—who sees to it that Ajax has an honorable burial.

Euripides' TROJAN WOMEN.   Turning to the two plays of Euripides, the *Trojan Women* (often cited as the *Troades*) was produced in 415 B.C. during the Peloponnesian War and shortly after the infamous Melian episode in which the island of Melos, though neutral, was ruthlessly sacked by the Athenians under the guise of political necessity. Euripides may have been addressing himself to the *Machtpolitik* of the Athenians, but the play is an eloquent polemic against war and its attendant miseries. In a series of tableaux, in which Hecuba stands as a central figure, we hear how the captive women have been distributed to the victors; and through Cassandra, who had been attacked by the lesser Ajax in the temple of Athena, we hear a prophetic pronouncement of the agonies that await both Greeks and Trojans. When Andromache comes on the scene, she informs Hecuba that her daughter Polyxena has been sacrificed on the tomb of Achilles. At the same time Andromache learns that her son Astyanax must die for political expediency; Odysseus has advised the Greeks that a hero's son must not be allowed to live. When Menelaus and Helen come before Hecuba, a bitter debate ensues in which the queen tears apart Helen's defense of her actions and urges Menelaus to kill her. She is so eloquent that Menelaus is shaken and promises to execute her when they reach home. The play ends with the body of Astyanax being brought to Hecuba who tearfully laments his fate and proposes an epitaph that will read: "Here lies a babe whom the Greeks killed because they were afraid of him." As Hecuba and the chorus of captive women leave the stage, Troy is put to the torch and bursts into flames.

Euripides' HECUBA. The *Hecuba* of Euripides was exhibited ten years before the *Trojan Women* in 425 B.C. Again Hecuba is the central figure about whom two episodes are joined, the sacrifice of Polyxena and the murder of her son Polydorus. For this drama Euripides gives us a portrayal of a shattered and pathetic old woman turned into a vengeful demon. Hecuba learns that before the Greeks can sail for home, her daughter Polyxena must be sacrificed to the ghost of Achilles. Even though Agamemnon has opposed the sacrifice, Odysseus has persuaded the Greeks that it must be done. When Polyxena hears of what has been planned for her, she accepts her fate quietly and courageously: to her it is better than the life of a slave. Hecuba pleads with Odysseus to spare her daughter and to allow her to take the girl's place. To no avail, and Odysseus takes Polyxena away. The aged queen is then struck another blow. She learns that her son Polydorus, whom she has entrusted to Polymestor, king of Thrace, for safekeeping along with a considerable amount of gold, has been treacherously murdered and that his body has been thrown into the sea. When Agamemnon comes upon the stricken queen to ask her to remove Polyxena's body, he finds her with the corpse of Polydorus in her arms. She begs him to allow her to take her revenge on Polymestor for his treachery. He agrees and sends the Thracian king with his two sons to Hecuba's tent where she blinds Polymestor and kills his two sons. Agamemnon condemns Polymestor for having violated the guest-laws. Polymestor then prophesies a strange end for Hecuba—transformation into a dog with fiery eyes—and tells Agamemnon of the bloodbath that awaits him at home. Agamemnon orders that the blinded king be marooned on a desert island. And since a favorable breeze has sprung up following the sacrifice of Polyxena, Agamemnon bids Hecuba to bury her dead and the other captives to board the Greek ships.

This picture of a brutalized and dehumanized Hecuba is picked up by Ovid in the *Metamorphoses* and then transmitted to the Middle Ages. Hence Dante introduces her in the *Inferno* with the words *trista, misera e cattiva:*

> Hecuba, sad, miserable, and captive, after she had seen
> Polyxena slain, and, forlorn, discerned her Polydorus,
> on the sea-strand, she, out of her sense, barked like a dog:
> to such a degree had the sorrow wrung her soul.

And she is the "mobled queen" of Shakespeare's *Hamlet*, as one of the traveling players gives the young prince a sample of his histrionic talent with a tearful speech on Hecuba's witnessing the death of Priam at the hands of Pyrrhus. This leads to Hamlet's soliliquy and the lines: "What's Hecuba to him, or he to Hecuba,/That he should weep for her?"

In our own time, Jean Giraudoux has selected details from the full range of incidents and characters of war. Although Giraudoux had in mind the struggle between France and Germany just prior to World War II, his theme transcends both the legendary and modern war. Entitled *La Guerre de Troie n'aura pas lieu* (The Trojan War Shall Not Take Place)—an ironical title to begin with—the play which was produced in 1935 has often been restaged in English as *Tiger at the Gates*. The drama is an imaginative reconstruction of the events just before the Trojan War. In addition to the well-known legendary figures, Giraudoux has added other characters such as Demokos, an aging chauvinistic poet eager to celebrate the deaths of war heroes, and Busiris, an international lawyer for whom a legal victory is worth more than a world holocaust. Hector is put in the role of a serious diplomat and soldier whose efforts to prevent the war by returning Helen to Menelaus fail because the world is not ruled by sense and logic. When Demokos protests the return of Helen, Hector strikes him in order to prevent him from sending up a war chant. It is an act of violence, but ironically enough it is done in the name of peace. Not to be denied his war, Demokos with his dying breath accuses Ajax of murdering him. In reprisal the Trojans kill Ajax and thus provoke the war which should not have taken place.

In the field of art, one post-*Iliad* theme was to surpass all others: the strangling of Laocoön and his sons by serpents. One representation of this scene comes from antiquity and is in marble; the other is from the seventeenth century and is in oil. In January of the year 1506, a work of monumental proportions was discovered in a vineyard on one of the hills of Rome. Pope Julius II had it restored and placed in the Vatican Museum as one of his prized possessions (fig. 94). From notices in Pliny the Elder, the Roman encyclopedist of the first century A.D., the marble group was identified as the *Laocoön* which Pliny says stood in the palace of Emperor Titus. He reports that it was the work of three Rhodian sculptors and that it was carved out of a single block of stone. In his judgment it was the finest work of art ever to come from the hand of man. The *Laocoön* as it now stands is said by some to date from the last half of the first century B.C.; others would place it earlier, from the middle to the first half of the second century B.C. Whatever its date, it proved to be a popular and influential work of art. Michelangelo admired it as did Goethe. Winckelman (p. 269) and Gotthold Ephraim Lessing saw in the *Laocoön* the dignity and restraint—there is agony but it is restrined and limited to a groan instead of Vergil's shriek—which characterized the Greek classical spirit. This view is not shared by modern critics. In 1766 Lessing published an essay entitled *Laocoön* in which he attempted to delineate the limits of figurative art and poetry. Using the Hellenistic statue to prove his thesis, he directed attention away from the moral and philosophical values Winckelman and others had seen in the work; rather he focused on the esthetic principles of the artist and the limitations imposed on him by his medium. These learned discussions helped stimulate the formulation of the neoclassical principles of the nineteenth century.

The *Laocoön* (c. 1601–1606) of the Spanish painter El Greco, now hanging in the National Gallery of Art in Washington, shows the Trojan priest staring at the fangs of the serpent and on the point of death (fig. 95). The two nude figures to his left have been variously interpreted as either Apollo and Artemis or Poseidon and Cassandra. Recent scholarship, however, has demonstrated otherwise. It is now apparent that the two mysterious nudes are representations of Adam (looking at an apple in his left hand) and Eve. In other words, El Greco has painted a moralized version of the ancient myth which is linked to the Biblical story of the original sin: Laocoön is being punished for having violated his vow of chastity and for begetting children in the temple of Apollo.

Laocoön's tale inspired artists, and sometimes the artist's work inspired the poet. Thus Lord Byron in *Childe Harold* bids us to go to the Vatican and see

> Laocoön's torture dignifying pain—
> A father's love and mortal's agony
> With an immortal's patience blending:—Vain
> The struggle; vain, against the coiling strain
> And gripe, and deepening of the dragon's grasp,
> The old man's clench; the long envenom'd chain
> Rivets the living links—the enormous asp
> Enforces pang on pang, and stifles gasp on gasp.

For concluding words on the fall of Troy, Matthew Arnold's *Palladium* (1867) is an interpretation of the life-token of the city as that of the individual, a symbol of the soul that sends "upon our life a ruling effluence."

> We shall renew the battle in the plain
> To-morrow;—red with blood will Xanthus be;
> Hector and Ajax will be there again,
> Helen will come upon the wall to see.
>
> Then we shall rust in shade, or shine in strife,
> And fluctuate 'twixt blind hopes and blind despairs,
> And fancy that we put forth all our life,
> And never know how with the soul it fares.
>
> Still doth the soul, from its lone fastness high,
> Upon our life a ruling effluence send,
> And when it fails, fight as we will, we die;
> And while it lasts, we cannot wholly end.

The Homecomings

Tell me, Muse, of that resourceful man who
wandered far and wide after he had destroyed
the sacred citadel of Troy . . . .

Homer—*Odyssey*

The nightingales are singing near
The Convent of the Sacred Heart,
And sang within the bloody wood
When Agamemnon cried aloud,
And let their liquid siftings fall
To stain the stiff dishonoured shroud.

T. S. Eliot—*Sweeney Among the Nightingales*

The end of the Trojan War did not bring an end to the legends of the heroes who survived the clash of arms on the battlefield; nor did these heroes, as Hesiod reported, continue to live untouched by sorrows on the Islands of the Blessed. Once they set sail from Troy, there were sorrows aplenty and there were "slings and arrows of outrageous fortune" for both the victors and their victims. In the epic cycles, these events were recorded in the *Homecomings* (*Nostoi*) and in Homer's *Odyssey*. Of the former we possess merely a few fragments, but it must have been known to the tragic poets and later mythographers who give us a connected account of the final days of the Heroic Age. In the main we are presented with a tragedy—the fate of Agamemnon, his family and intimates—and a comedy, that is, the happy ending for Odysseus and his family after a long period of trial and tribulation.

The Return of Menelaus. But first, what happened after the sack of Troy to Menelaus and Helen, to Diomedes, to the lesser Ajax, and to Idomeneus, the leader of the Cretan contingent? All had god-inspired difficulties at sea after they set sail for home. Menelaus' fleet was beset by a storm which forced part of his ships onto the coast of Crete, while five others, his own included, were shipwrecked on the shores of Egypt. After this Menelaus was buffeted about for eight years in various parts of the Mediterranean until his wanderings brought him to the island of Pharos off the coast of Egypt. It was there that Menelaus was told that if he was successful in a wrestling match with Proteus, the Old Man of the Sea, he would find out how he might reach home safely (p. 104). Once pinned down by Menelaus, Proteus revealed that a fair sailing wind would spring up if he would go to Egypt to propitiate the gods with sacrifices. This Menelaus did, and at the same time he erected a cenotaph in memory of his brother Agamemnon whose death at the hands of Aegisthus and Clytemnestra had been reported to him by Proteus. Next to Odysseus, Menelaus was the last of the heroes to return home, and he arrived at Sparta on the very day on which Orestes, having avenged the death of his father, was burying his mother Clytemnestra and her lover Aegisthus. When Menelaus was visited by Odysseus' son Telemachus, he was preparing to send off his daughter Hermione as a bride for Neoptolemus. Menelaus lived in peace and comfort with Helen at Sparta until, as Proteus prophesied, the gods transported him to Elysium in recognition of his being a son-in-law of Zeus. This is the story that Homer tells in the third and fourth books of the *Odyssey*.

Euripides picks up the tale of Helen in Egypt, the story of how only her phantom went to Troy while the real and chaste Helen remained in Egypt under the protection of King Proteus. For his *Helen*, first exhibited in 412 B.C., Euripides composed a tragicomedy on the surprise meeting of Helen and her husband in Egypt after the Trojan War—a war ironically fought over a mere apparition—and after Menelaus' years of wandering. The two, happily reunited, plan to escape from the clutches of the new king of Egypt Theoclymenus who has designs on Helen. By an elaborate ruse, which includes a mock funeral, Helen easily outwits Theoclymenus and escapes with Menelaus to Sparta. This same story, compounded with fairy-tale elements, was taken over by Hugo von Hofmannsthal for the libretto of Richard Strauss' opera *Die aegyptische Helena* (The Egyptian Helen) which had its first performance in 1928. As for the later years of this couple, the poet Rupert Brooke makes this wry and cynical comment in his *Menelaus and Helen* (1915):

> So far the poet. How should he behold
> That journey home, the long connubial years?
> He does not tell you how while Helen bears
> Child on legitimate child, becomes a scold,
> Haggard with virtue. Menelaus bold
> Waxed garrulous, and sacked a hundred Troys
> 'Twixt noon and supper. And her golden voice
> Got shrill as he grew deafer. And both were old.
> Often he wonders why on earth he went
> Troyward, or why poor Paris ever came.
> Oft she weeps, gummy-eyed and impotent;
> Her dry shanks twitch at Paris' mumbled name.
> So Menelaus nagged; and Helen cried;
> And Paris slept on by Scamander side.

The Fate of the Lesser Ajax. As for the lesser Ajax who assaulted Cassandra in the temple of Athena, his life was snuffed out shortly after the departure of the fleet from Troy. A storm drove his vessel onto the rocks, and only with Poseidon's help did he manage to make his way to shore. But then he arrogantly boasted that he had saved himself in defiance of the gods. For this blasphemy Poseidon took up his trident and split the rock over Ajax' head. Part of the rock struck him and thrust him into the sea where he drowned. Some say that it was Athena who killed Ajax with a flash of lightning for his maltreatment of Cassandra in the goddess' temple.

Diomedes' Return. Diomedes was more fortunate than Ajax, at least for a while. He is said to have reached home without any difficulty, but other reports say that

Aphrodite caused his ship to be wrecked on the shores of Lycia where he would have been killed by the king, had the king's daughter not taken pity on him and helped him to escape. When he arrived home in Argos, he discovered that his wife had taken a lover. Diomedes was driven out of his kingdom by his unfaithful wife, and after traveling about in Greece for some time, he took a ship for Italy and settled in Daunia (Apulia). There he took the daughter of King Daunus for a wife and became the legendary founder of a number of Greek cities in southern Italy, among them Beneventum and Brundisium. Of his last years, there are differing accounts: some say that he died of natural causes at an advanced age; others say that King Daunus murdered him out of jealousy of his wealth and power; still others tell us that he returned to Argos or simply disappeared.

Idomeneus and his Son.   The buffeting of the Greek fleet by stormy seas led to a pathetic tale which has a parallel in the Biblical story of Jephthah's daughter in *Judges 11.* It contains a folktale motif known in many parts of the world: the rash vow of a father. When Idomeneus, king of Crete, was on his way home from Troy and was caught in a storm, he prayed to Poseidon to save him. He vowed that he would sacrifice to the god the first thing or person he encountered on landing. As folktales would have it, the first to meet him was his own son. According to some accounts, he carried out his vow to Poseidon and sacrificed his son; according to others, he tried to do so, but did not succeed. As a consequence, Crete was afflicted by a plague which the people attributed to their king's cruelty. Idomeneus was exiled and first migrated to Calabria in Italy where he founded a temple of Athena. He then went to Asia Minor where he died and was buried. The story of Idomeneus' vow attracted the musical genius of Mozart; in 1781, he composed the *Idomeneo,* a heroic opera in three acts. To the traditional story, Mozart's librettist added these romantic details: the love of Idomeneus' son for Ilia, a daughter of Priam; a monster that comes out of the sea; the willingness of Idomeneus and Ilia to sacrifice themselves in place of the victim; and finally the god's renouncement of the vow in the face of such love and readiness for sacrifice.

The Homecoming of Agamemnon.   No homecoming of a hero was as tragic as that of Agamemnon, for it touched not only his life but all those around him. The story in its outline is a simple one. After being driven off-course by storms at sea, Agamemnon arrives home only to be killed by his wife's lover Aegisthus or by Clytemnestra herself. His death is subsequently avenged by his son Orestes and his daughter Electra. Homer is our earliest source for many of these events; the poet has the story of Agamemnon's fate run like a contrapuntal theme throughout the *Odyssey* to contrast the sagacity of Odysseus and the fidelity of Penelope with a guileless Agamemnon and an unfaithful Clytemnestra. When the tragic poets pick up the story, the details of the deception, murder and countermurder are accented and amplified for dramatic effect and to explicate a point of view. Sophocles' *Electra* (418?–410? B.C.) is perhaps the most Homeric in spirit; the vengeance exacted by Electra and Orestes is accepted as a justifiable and necessary homicide. There is no suggestion of Furies pursuing Orestes for having killed his mother; there is no hint of divine punishment for brother and sister. Sophocles' portrait of Electra is a heroic one; with inflexible will and obsessive hatred for her mother, she finds redemption in the slaying of her father's killers. Euripides had other insights into the character of this daughter of Agamemnon. His *Electra* (413 B.C.) is a study of a brutalized and sexually deprived woman, a hate-filled victim of her mother and her mother's lover. It is Euripides at his best, mocking the traditional view of the gods and denying heroic stature to the legendary figures of old. His answer to the actions of Electra and Orestes is that violence is no solution to violence.

The Oresteia

Both Sophocles and Euripides had treated the consequences of Agamemnon's murder, not the full range of the legend from Thyestes' curse (pp. 380–381) to the vindication of Orestes of the crime of matricide. The most complete dramatization of these legends had already taken place in 458 B.C. when Aeschylus exhibited his *Oresteia*, now the only surviving trilogy of antiquity and probably the finest in the repertoire of ancient theater. Aeschylus took the grim tales of the Atreid family and employed them in an almost undefinable complexity. Through the use of choral lyric and verbal imagery, through stunning stage effects and thrilling scenes, he evolves a moral vision which proceeds from anarchy and ambiguity—social, political, and cosmic—to harmony and balance both in heaven and in Athens. The *Oresteia* is in effect a *summa*, a Divine Comedy in dramatic form. The trilogy is made up of three connected dramas—the *Agamemnon*, the *Libation Bearers* (also known as the *Choephoroe*), the *Eumenides*—each having a character and an ambience of its own but at the same time linked together by the development of the dramatic vision.

THE AGAMEMNON.   In the gloom before dawn, a watchman on the roof of Agamemnon's palace in Argos awaits a beacon signal that will announce the end of the Trojan War. He has been waiting for a whole year by order of Clytemnestra, a woman with a "man-strong heart." And when he tries to pass the time in song, he falls to weeping because all is not well within the house that was once so great. Suddenly, a flash of fire from a distant beacon. For a moment the watchman is overjoyed at this sign that Troy has been taken and at the prospect of Agamemnon's return. As he rushes off to give Clytemnestra the news, his momentary happiness is brought up short by the thought of the tangled domestic situation within the palace. He closes his prologue with a guarded and gloomy statement:

> The house itself, could it take voice, might speak
> aloud and plain. I speak to those who understand,
> but if they fail, I have forgotten everything.

The chorus of Argive elders comes on stage, as yet unaware that Troy has fallen. In chant and song they review the background of the war in moral terms: the gathering of the armada to punish Troy for the guilt of Helen and Paris, the heaven-sent omens, the call to sacrifice Agamemnon's daughter Iphigeneia so that the ships could sail, and Agamemnon's ambivalence giving way to heedless ambition and sin in sacrificing his daughter for a war brought about by a woman. A confused mass of rights and wrongs. These brooding observations by the chorus are interspersed with prayers to Zeus who punishes men for their sins and teaches them wisdom through suffering. When Clytemnestra informs the elders that Troy has fallen, they are bewildered and wonder whether she has not been misled by womanly fancies and hope. Clytemnestra describes for them the complicated relay of beacons that transmitted the news across the Aegean Sea to Argos, and ends with a cutting remark that it is a woman who has brought them this news. The elders acknowledge that she speaks like a man, and then they go on to comment that Zeus has judged Troy, that the sinner suffers in his longing until at last temptations overcome him, as longing for Helen overcame Paris. The suffering of those close to Helen is small in comparison to the grief of those who mourn their loved ones lost in the war. The one who commits bloodshed does not go unobserved by the gods; punishment is in store for him.

After an interval of several days, a herald arrives before the elders and rejoices at his return home after ten long years of hardship at Troy. He brings news that Paris and Troy have been punished and that Agamemnon will soon arrive in Argos. The elders take the edge off the herald's joy by intimating that all is not well at home. While the herald is told of the sufferings of the army at Troy and how the ships were stormed at sea, Clytemnestra makes her appearance. She greets the herald with a speech that is filled with intentioned deceit. She bids him to return to Agamemnon with this message:

> Come, and with speed, back to the city that longs for him,
> and may he find a wife within his house as true
> as on the day he left her, watchdog of the house
> gentle to him alone, fierce to his enemies,
> and such a woman in all her ways as this, who has
> not broken the seal upon her in the length of days.
> With no man else have I known delight, nor any shame
> of evil speech more than I know how to temper bronze.

These words are received with a cryptic remark by the chorus of elders, and after receiving further information from the herald about Menelaus' difficulties at sea, they sing again of Helen and of her marriage-song turned into a dirge. Her reception at Troy is compared to a playful lion cub that is reared as a pet, but in time turns into a ravening, uncontrollable beast, a blessing made into a curse. It is not true, as men say, that gods envy man's prosperity; if wealth is innocently derived, there is no vengeance. It is sin that breeds other evil acts; pride and ruthlessness brings retribution and justice. Justice loves the humble and the innocent.

Agamemnon arrives on the scene in a chariot; behind him in another chariot is, among other spoils of war, Cassandra. The elders greet their conquering hero, though admitting they were not pleased when he marshaled an army to recover Helen. After Agamemnon gives thanks to the gods for his victory and return, he is met by Clytemnestra. In another speech filled with deceit, she tells of her agony and anxieties while Agamemnon was fighting at Troy. She gives excuses as to why she meets him with dry eyes and why Orestes, their son, is not there to meet him. As a token of his superhuman glory in trampling Troy and to prompt him into a prideful act, Clytemnestra urges Agamemnon to enter the palace by means of a purple (crimson or blood-red) carpet which she orders her servants to spread before him. Agamemnon responds with coolness. At first he rejects the carpet as an oriental display befitting a god, not a mortal (p. 122,) but Clytemnestra insists and easily tempts her husband to tread the carpet. He does so but with great feelings of guilt and fear of offending the gods. As he enters the palace, he asks that Cassandra be treated gently even though she is a slave. Clytemnestra follows her husband into the palace with a plea to Zeus that he answer her prayers.

Left alone, the chorus is tense and overwhelmed by fears of impending doom. Clytemnestra appears at the door of the palace and invites Cassandra to enter and take part in the sacrifice. Cassandra is silent. Impatiently, Clytemnestra dismisses her with words that are filled with double meanings—"the victims are at the altar ready for the knife"—and goes back into the palace. The chorus is filled with pity for the captive girl, but soon they are terrified as Cassandra, in a state of prophetic frenzy, calls upon the god Apollo who now possesses her. To the horror of the elders, she alludes to the murder of the children of Thyestes, the Thyestean banquet, and Clytemnestra's adultery with Aegisthus. In her god-possessed frenzy, Cassandra also sees the imminent murder of Agamemnon:

> See there, see there! Keep from his mate the bull.
> Caught in the folded web's
> entanglement she pinions him and with the black horn
> strikes. And he crumples in the watered bath.
> Guile, I tell you, and death there in the caldron wrought.

The chorus of elders cannot penetrate her meaning, even though time after time she alludes to the murder both of Agamemnon and herself. Cassandra tears off the symbols that mark her as a priestess of Apollo (p. 126), and as she is about to enter the palace where she knows death awaits her (fig. 99), she recoils for a moment, repelled by the anticipated stench of the bloodbath. No sooner has Cassandra disappeared within the palace, than Agamemnon's agonized cry is heard: "Uh-h! I am struck—a blow—deadly and deep!" The elders are in a state of confusion upon hearing their king's death-cry. They are about to enter the palace when the doors open, revealing Clytemnestra, spattered with blood, standing over the bodies of Agamemnon and Cassandra. Triumphantly she admits that her act was not unpremeditated; she exults in her accomplishment. In vivid language, she describes how she struck down her husband and her ectasy at having done so:

> I stand now where I struck him down. The thing is done
> Thus have I wrought, and I will not deny it now.
> That he might not escape nor beat aside his death,
> as fishermen cast their huge circling nets, I spread
> deadly abundance of rich robes, and caught him fast.
> I struck him twice. In two great cries of agony
> he buckled at the knees and fell. When he was down
> I struck him the third blow, in thanks and reverence
> to Zeus the lord of dead men underneath the ground.
> Thus he went down, and the life struggled out of him;
> and as he died he spattered me with the dark red
> and violent driven rain of bitters savored blood
> to make me glad, as gardens stand among the showers
> of God in glory at the birthtime of the buds.

In a debate with the elders, Clytemnestra tries to rationalize her crime by placing the onus upon Agamemnon: his sacrificing Iphigeneia and his adulterous relationship with Cassandra. She views herself not only as the avenger of her daughter's death, but also of the crime done to Thyestes by Atreus, a sin inherited by Agamemnon from his father. Her paramour Aegisthus enters and admits his complicity in the murder. He threatens the elders with violence, but a now-subdued Clytemnestra restrains him. The elders pray for Orestes to come as an avenger. Clytemnestra asserts that she and Aegisthus will now rule, and with a strong hand.

Figure 99. Clytemnestra killing Cassandra. *Vase painting, c. 430 B.C. National Museum, Ferrara. (Hirmer)*

THE LIBATION BEARERS (CHOEPHOROE). Several years have passed. Orestes, who had been taken to Phocis as a child and reared by King Strophius, arrives in Argos with his friend Pylades, a son of Strophius. The two approach the tomb of Agamemnon on which Orestes lays a lock of his hair as a token of his grief. He prays to the gods for power to avenge the murder of his father. The two young men stand aside as they see Electra entering with a number of foreign women dressed in black. These women, the chorus, are slaves and at Clytemnestra's bidding are carrying libations to be poured on the burial mound of Agamemnon. (The second part of the trilogy takes its name from these women, the libation bearers.) Clytemnestra, it seems, has been having terrifying dreams and hopes to propitiate Earth by making offerings on the grave of Agamemnon. The chorus has no sympathy for a "godless woman" with blood on her hands. Electra, at a loss as to how to offer a prayer to her father on behalf of her mother, asks the chorus for guidance. The women advise her to pray for an avenger, one to kill those who took a life. In a chilling prayer to Hades and Hermes, Electra pours out a libation and calls upon the spirit of her father for the return of Orestes and

> for our enemies,
> father, I pray that your avenger come, that they
> who killed you shall be killed in turn, as they deserve.
> Between my prayer for good and prayer for good I set
> this prayer for evil; and I speak it against Them.
> For us, bring blessings up into the world. Let Earth
> and conquering Justice, and all gods beside, give aid.

As the chorus also offers prayers for an avenger, Electra notices the lock of hair on the tomb. By this and other signs she knows that her brother must be near. When Orestes comes forward and identifies himself by yet another token—a piece of weaving done by Electra's own hand—the two embrace each other lovingly. Orestes offers a prayer to Zeus filled with powerful imagery:

> Zeus, Zeus, direct all that we try to do. Behold
> the orphaned children of the eagle-father, now
> that he has died entangled in the binding coils
> of the deadly viper, and the young he left behind
> are worn with hunger of starvation, not full grown
> to bring their shelter slain food, as their father did.

Orestes then tells his sister that the oracle of Apollo has ordered him to kill his father's murderers under pain of disease and death. And even if oracles are not to be trusted, he is under obligation to his father and to those brave men who brought down Troy to act; the state should not be subject to two women, Clytemnestra and Aegisthus. At Agamemnon's burial mound Orestes, Electra, and the chorus chant and sing in operatic fasion: the women cry for blood to avenge spilled blood, an eye for an eye; Orestes laments the manner in which a great warrior has died and prays for vengeance upon his mother; Electra calls upon Zeus for justice for the wrong done not only to her father but to herself as well. The prayers strengthen the wills of Orestes and Electra; the chorus calls for action. When Orestes asks the reason for the offerings at the grave of Agamemnon, he is told of Clytemnestra's nightmare: she dreamed that she gave birth to a snake thinking that it was a child, and that when she put it to her breast, the snake sucked blood and milk. Orestes sees himself as part of the dream and gives this interpretation:

> If this snake came out of the same place whence I came,
> if she wrapped it in robes, as she wrapped me, and if
> its jaws gaped wide around the breast that suckled me,
> and if it stained the intimate milk with an outburst
> of blood, so that for fright and pain she cried aloud,
> it follows then, that as she nursed this hideous thing
> of prophecy, she must be cruelly murdered. I
> turn snake to kill her. This is what the dream portends.

Orestes contrives a plan to lull Clytemnestra and Aegisthus into a false sense of security. The chorus sings of women's passion and the destructive consequences that arise from this force. Examples are cited from the canons of legend: Althaea, who brought about the death of her own son; Scylla, bribed by Minos, caused the death of her father Nisus; and the women from Lemnos who slew their husbands out of jealousy. Yet, justice will prevail and there will be vengeance even though the crime may have been commited some time ago.

The scene shifts to the front of the palace. Orestes and Pylades call out to be admitted. When Clytemnestra comes out, Orestes pretends that he bears a message from King Strophius in Phocis that Orestes is dead. Not having seen her son for many years, Clytemnestra does not recognize him. She receives the news with assumed grief. Orestes and Pylades are invited into the palace while a messenger—she hap-

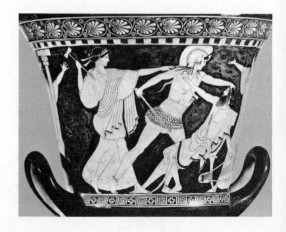

Figure 100.   Orestes about to kill Aegisthus; Clytemnestra, ax in hand, tries to prevent her son from killing her lover. *Vase painting, c. 460 B.C. Museum of Fine Arts, Boston.*

pens to be Orestes' old nurse—is sent to Aegisthus to tell him of this new development. On the way, the nurse is intercepted by the chorus. The women hear her
grief and how Clytemnestra "put a sad face on / before the servants, to hide / the
smile inside her eyes." The chorus, now a part of the plot, tells the nurse to alter the
message to Aegisthus: he is to come to the palace without his armed guard. When
Aegisthus arrives before the chorus of women, he questions them about the report;
he has little faith in female credulity. The chorus refers him to the messengers
within the palace. No sooner does Aegisthus enter the palace when a death cry is
heard (fig. 100). A servant rushes out shouting that Aegisthus is dead and calls for
Clytemnestra:

> where
> is she, does what? Her neck is on the razor's edge
> and ripe for lopping, as she did to others before.

Clytemnestra rushes in. She is quick to realize that Orestes is alive; she is also
ready to kill him. With swords drawn, Orestes and Pylades confront Clytemnestra.
She appeals to her son to pity his mother. Orestes is shaken by the thought of killing
his mother and turns to Pylades for advice. Pylades reminds him of Apollo's oracle
and the oath he has sworn to avenge his father. Line by line, Orestes forces his
mother back into the palace, rejecting all her appeals and prepared to accept a
mother's curse.

The chorus sings exultingly of the triumph of justice and that in time the wicked
will be found out and punished. The doors of the palace then swing open and reveal
Orestes standing over the bodies of Clytemnestra and her lover—a scene that parallels one in the *Agamemnon* but with a difference in mood. There covering the
bodies is the same bloodied robe which Clytemnestra used to entangle Agamemnon
and kill him. But instead of reveling in the act of homicide, as had Clytemnestra,
Orestes is subdued and sorrowful: though he has won a victory by killing the two
tyrants of the state and avenging a crime done to his father, he can take no pride in
the act. Since Apollo's oracle had commanded him and had declared that he could
take these lives with impunity, he will return to Delphi to seek refuge. The chorus
sees no evil in his action; he has freed the city by killing the two snakes, Clytemnestra and Aegisthus. At that moment, Orestes is set upon by the Furies (Erinyes) Gor-
gonlike and robed in black, repulsive spirits sent to hound him for killing his
mother. Though unseen by anyone else, Orestes is tormented and agonized by these
avenging spirits and rushes off as if driven mad. The chorus wishes him well and ends
the second part of the trilogy with a question: when shall this procession of murder
and countermurder come to an end?

THE EUMENIDES.   The scene is Delphi. The Pythian priestess appears before the
temple of Apollo and in an invocation gives a short history of the powers that once
held the seat of prophecy (pp. 120–121). She enters the sanctuary and soon reappears, horrified at what she has found within. There at the *omphalos*, the holy navel
stone, sits Orestes with blood still dripping from his hands and sword, and around
him sleep the loathsome Furies. In a vivid speech she describes their repelling
stench and their hideous appearance. The doors of the temple open revealing Orestes, the Furies—who now take the part of the chorus—Apollo, and Hermes. Apollo
reassures Orestes that he will not desert him, and that he will bring an end to the
pursuit by these hags who are hated both by men and gods (fig. 101). He instructs
Orestes to go to Athens where the goddess Athena will find the means to judge his

Figure 101. Orestes embracing the sacred *omphalos* (naval stone) at Delphi while Apollo fends off one of the Furies. *Vase painting, National Museum, Naples. (Hirmer)*

case and free him from the afflictions caused by a god's injunction. As Hermes leads Orestes away, the ghost of Clytemnestra appears on the scene and furiously rebukes the sleeping Furies for having allowed her murderer to escape. The ghost disappears and the Furies awaken. They charge Apollo, one of the "younger gods," with having violated the rights and privileges of the older gods in permitting the matricide to escape. Referring to the Titanomachy, they claim that the Olympians have ruthlessly abrogated the traditional powers of the older generation of gods. Apollo turns on the black-robed goddesses threateningly and berates them as being blood-thirsty and barbarous; his temple is no fit place for their likes:

> The whole cast of your shape is guide
> to what you are, the like of whom should hole in the cave
> of the blood-reeking lion, not in oracular
> interiors, like mine nearby, wipe off your filth.
> Out then, you flock of goats without a herdsman, since
> no god has such affection as to tend this brood.

After Apollo and the Furies briefly debate their differences over the nature of the two homicides, the scene shifts to Athens where Orestes has come as a suppliant. As he prays at the statue of the goddess Athena, the Furies enter and insist that spilled blood must be repaid with blood, that Orestes must pay for the death of his mother. Orestes claims that he has been absolved of the crime at Delphi and calls upon Athena to come to his rescue. In a long choral ode, the Furies relate how from the time of their birth they were given the power of exacting vengeance on those who commit murder; they hound them not only in life but also in death. They resent interference by the Olympians in their ancient privileges. Athena enters and questions first the Furies and then Orestes. After explaining the circumstances of his matricide, Orestes pleads guilty and implicates Apollo since he had been acting under the command of the god. Athena decides that the issue is a complex one since there is some justice on both sides; she will impanel a jury of Athenian citizens to hear the case. The Furies are enraged at this challenge to their authority; without the ancient restraints, men will commit the most heinous crimes.

Twelve Athenian citizens led by Athena come onstage, the first courtroom scene in Western literature. The Furies and Orestes give their testimony. When Orestes asks why the Furies did not punish Clytemnestra for the murder of Agamemnon, they reply that the man she killed was not bound to her by ties of blood. Orestes has no answer to their charge and turns his case over to Apollo. The trial now takes on a new dimension and a new confrontation. Apollo declares that he speaks on the authority of Zeus, that the death of Agamemnon, a warrior-king who holds a scepter granted by Zeus, is not to be compared with that of a treacherous wife. As for the primacy of maternal bloodties, the mother is only the nourisher of the seed planted by the father; the male predominates over the female. In proof of this biological principle, Apollo points to Athena who had not been born from the womb of a woman. Concluding his testimony, Apollo promises greatness for Athens and its people.

The hearing is concluded. Athena formally establishes the court which will henceforth try cases of homicide in Athens. (Thus the vendetta, which started several generations ago with Atreus and Thyestes, ends in a court of law.) The goddess lays down the criteria for practical justice in a democratic state: that justice will be the mean between tyranny and anarchy, that fear will play a role in making men act righteously—these principles are derived from the Furies, and Athena wisely absorbs the old into the new—that the court be uncorrupted, serious, and the country's protector. Athena further declares that if the ballots cast by the jury are even and end in a tie, she will vote for Orestes since she sides with the male and Olympian point of view. And this is what happens when the votes are cast.

The Furies are enraged at the Olympians for having deprived them of the right to avenge the crime of bloodguilt. They threaten Athens with blight and a rain of death. Gradually and forcefully, Athena persuades the Furies to accept a new role within the state: they will become goddesses of fertility and prosperity, protectors of Athens. (Once more Athena absorbs the old into the new.) The trilogy ends in a magnificent pageant in which the Furies exchange their black robes for robes of purple; and instead of being known as the Furies, they shall now be called the Eumenides, "the Kindly Ones." In a triumphant procession the venerable goddesses are led to their new home in a sanctuary near the Areopagus, the hill which gave its name to the new court established by Athena.

*   *   *   *

The dramatic possibilities inherent in the postbellum events enveloping Agamemnon and his unhappy brood were best realized by the dramatists of the twentieth century. Taking their inspiration from Aeschylus, Sophocles, and Euripides, the legends of the becursed house were used by Hugo von Hofmannsthal to portray a woman's psychosis, by Robinson Jeffers to dramatize the psychosexual violence of two women and the mystical union of a man with nature, by Eugene O'Neill to unfold a Freudian case history, by Jean Giraudoux to pose a confrontation between a politican and an idealistic rebel, by T. S. Eliot for the expression of religious and philosophical ideas, and by Jean-Paul Sartre for the exposition of existentialist philosophy in a political setting.

At the opening of the century, Hugo von Hofmannsthal, the Austrian poet and dramatist, turned out a drama, *Elektra* (1904), in which he attempted to outdo Euripides in his portrayal of a woman stripped of every vestige of humanity and morality. The dramatist presents us with an Electra whose life is one long blazing pathological obsession: to avenge her father's murder. And when she finally hears Clytemnestra's agonized death-cry, she is filled with a Maenad-like ecstasy; with her head thrown back, she dances wildly and passionately until she collapses. Having fulfilled her only reason to live, she dies. Richard Strauss translated this drama of von Hofmannsthal into an opera, *Elektra* (1909). Through the angularity of his musical phrases and the use of harmonies unprecedented in his day, Strauss was able to convey the savagery and shattering emotional conflict von Hofmannsthal attempted in his drama.

In 1925 Robinson Jeffers published the *Tower Beyond Tragedy*, a verse drama in which the poet exploited the scenes of violence in the first two plays of Aeschylus' *Oresteia* and seasoned them highly with sexual symbolism. In a departure from Aeschylus, Cassandra does not die with Agamemnon but is kept alive to act as medium for the dead Agamemnon who possesses her body (p. 126). She urges his soldiers to kill his treacherous wife. While awaiting help from Aegisthus, Clytemnestra holds off the threatening soldiers, tantalizing them with a display of her body and performing a kind of striptease. When her lover arrives, he is more interested in hunting than in the affairs of state. He goes off in his chariot, only to be met and killed by Orestes who is on his way to the palace. Encouraged by both Cassandra and Electra, Orestes kills his mother, and in his bewilderment also plunges his sword into Cassandra. Brother and sister are reunited, but Orestes wanders away into the wilderness "to find his mother." He returns later, much changed and strangely abstracted. In an effort to persuade Orestes to take his rightful position as king, Electra offers herself to her brother as a lover. But Orestes is no longer interested in human affairs; he has transcended the world of introverted concerns and has entered into a mystical union with nonhuman surroundings. Orestes is Jeffers' hero who finds salvation from the madness of self-centered humanity by "falling in love outward" with nature devoid of humans. Orestes has, as the final line of the play puts it, "climbed the tower beyond time, consciously, and cast humanity, entered the earlier fountain."

Eugene O'Neill took the tragic story of the house of Atreus and transferred the scene of action from a palace in ancient Argos to a New England mansion with a Greek-temple facade shortly after the Civil War. For the moral and religious issues of Aeschylus' *Oresteia*, O'Neill substituted Freudian determinism brought about by sexual repression and Oedipal strivings (p. 282); and for the royal family of Atreus, we have a New England Brahmin family, the Mannons. *Mourning Becomes Electra* (1931) is a play in three parts: *Homecoming* is O'Neill's *Agamemnon*, *The Hunted* parallels *The Libation Bearers*, and *The Haunted* would be the equivalent of the *Eumenides*. When General Ezra Mannon (Agamemnon) returns home from the Civil War, he finds that his wife Christine (Clytemnestra) has been having a love affair with Adam Brant (Aegisthus), a member of a rival branch of the family and the captain of a clipper ship. The hatred of Christine for her husband is so deep that she poisons him after he attempts to effect a reconciliation. In the second part of the trilogy, Orin (Orestes) and Lavinia (Electra)—Lavinia happens to be a rival of her mother for all the men in Christine's life: Ezra, Adam, and Orin—kill Adam whereupon Christine commits suicide. In the third part of the trilogy, Orin is tormented by a guilty conscience (the Furies) even though his mother had committed suicide willingly and gladly. He becomes so neurotically dependent on his sister that he will not permit her to marry anyone; she becomes in effect a mother-surrogate for her abnormal brother. The curse on the house of Mannon comes to a dramatic climax when Lavinia drives Orin to suicide and shuts herself up for the rest of her life in the family mansion to punish herself and renounce all chances of happiness.

T. S. Eliot's *Family Reunion* (1939) is another treatment of the Orestean theme in a modern setting. Far more knotty than O'Neill's "trilogy of the damned," Eliot's play is a complex of secularized Greco-Christian doctrines intertwined with psychoanalytic procedures His house of Atreus is the house of Monchesney, a depressing titled English family. The curse which falls on Harry Monchesney (Orestes) is his father's infatuation with a certain Agatha, and his father's plot, never carried out, to murder his wife Amy when she was bearing Harry. (Earlier drafts of the play had taken the original sin back to a mad Thyestean great-uncle.) Sin begetting sin according to the ancient Greek formula, Harry wills his wife's death. The Furies that pursue a neurotic Harry are represented by an overwhelming sense of guilt over the death of his wife who either fell or committed suicide from the deck of a ship. Harry does not believe that his conscience is the only cause of his suffering; it is the world in which he lives that is diseased. In psychoanalytic fashion, this modern Orestes exorcises his family's past, and in so doing he is liberated from his purgatory. The Furies, now turned into the Eumenides, impel him toward a good and saint-like life; beatifically he will "follow the bright angels."

Two French playwrights found no need to provide modern settings for their treatment of the legends of the house of Atreus—since the Renaissance, the French have periodically rewritten classical dramas, most recently during the 1930's and 1940's. Jean Giraudoux freely adapted the Euripidean version of the legendary heroine for his *Electre* (1939), a play that alternates urbanity and wit with political allegory and mordant tragedy. With the political antagonism between France and Germany prior to World War II before him, Giraudoux sets an Electra, obsessed with revenge and the abstract laws of justice, against an Aegisthus who has been transformed from a craven adulterer into a practical politician. In working out her obsession, Electra not only brings down her mother and Aegisthus, but her country and its inhabitants as well. As chaos and destruction roll over the city, Electra resolutely clings to her belief that in having justice she has everything. Giraudoux employs the Aeschylean Furies as nasty, impudent little girls who grow in size until at the end of the play they are of the same height and figure as Electra. They leave her to pursue Orestes until they drive him mad and he commits suicide cursing his sister.

Some few years after Giraudoux' *Electre*, at a time when France was occupied by the Germans, Jean-Paul Sartre (1905–   ) wrote the existentialist version of the Orestes legend, *Les Mouches* (The Flies, 1943). Dramatizing his protest against the occupation and the government which supported it, Sartre also dramatized his philosophy of personal involvement (*l'engagement*). To the cast of legendary figures, he added a tutor in philosophy for Orestes, and a Jupiter who appears in the guise of an Athenian merchant—for stage use Sartre preferred to use the Roman name for Zeus. His Jupiter is a satanic figure who regrets having made man free because once man realizes that he is free, the gods have no control over him. However, he delights in torturing his creations with feelings of guilt, fear, and remorse. It is Jupiter who has sent the avenging Furies to blood-guilty Argos in the form of huge, evil-smelling flies. And in place of the stately elders of Aeschylus, Sartre has substituted the dregs of the community, a community that is ridden with guilt and superstition and hardly worth saving. Into this political and social maelstrom comes the exiled

Orestes who has a yearning to return home to be with his own people. Jupiter and others attempt to dissuade Orestes from liberating the city from its illegitimate ruler (Aegisthus) and his collaborator (Clytemnestra). But once he comes to recognize his freedom, Orestes becomes the authentic man who acts in perfect good faith and who readily accepts the consequences of his action. He kills his mother and her lover for the sake of justice and for the people of Argos. The result is that Electra is overcome by remorse and turns on her brother; the people of Argos cry out for his blood. The flies now swoop down on him; they can torment him but they cannot kill. Orestes is alone, alienated, but he exists and is free. He refuses to repent and boldly goes off into the light and into a new life.

Each age has its own Orestes and its own Electra. Jack Richardson took Orestes as a symbol of the alienated youth of his own time. The alienation the American playwright portrays in *The Prodigal* (1960) is not of the Sartrean kind; it is the cool, dispassionate variety of the "beat" generation. He places in the crucible an Orestes who cannot communicate with his parents, who rejects his father's ambition and pursuit of power, who will not conform either to the standards of society or to the demands of his station. He is the antihero of the twentieth century, a rebel against the idealism of his elders' generation. Agamemnon goes to his death, knowing that society will force his son to assume a conventional role. And this is what happens. Richardson's Orestes comments bitterly:

> The world demands that we inherit the pretensions of our fathers, that we go on killing in the name of ancient illusions about ourselves, that we assume the right to punish, order, and invent philosophies to make our worst moments seem inspired. Who am I to contradict all this any longer?

The Odyssey

The last of the Greek heroes to return home after the Trojan War was Odysseus whom the Romans called Ulixes and who is now known popularly as Ulysses. His ten years of wandering after the conclusion of the war have been immortalized by Homer in the *Odyssey*. Homer not only told a rattling good tale about Odysseus' adventures, but he also sang the praise of those virtues which made a man and the world he lived in civilized: cunning and sagacity, loyalty, close family ties, and the recognition of established rights and customs. But what is perhaps most remarkable of all—certainly for the eighth century B.C. and for many centuries afterwards—is Homer's view that man, not deity, is responsible for most of his suffering in life. He strikes this note at the very outset of the epic when, at a council of the gods, Zeus remarks that men blame the gods for their suffering and regard them as the source of their troubles; but the truth is that it is their own wickedness that causes them suffering beyond what is ordained them by their lot in life. Many episodes in the *Odyssey* are cross-referenced with this point of view; and at the very end of the epic the same thought is reiterated by a wise old man who berates the fathers of the slain suitors: "It is your own wickedness, my friends, that is to blame for what happened."

What had set Zeus thinking on the matter of personal responsibility for suffering was the death of Aegisthus at the hands of Orestes. The Olympian had sent Hermes to advise Aegisthus not to kill Agamemnon nor to make love to his wife, for Orestes was bound to avenge the deed as soon as he became of age and returned home. But

Aegisthus did not take the advice and suffered for his lack of good sense. Through-out the *Odyssey*, the events surrounding Agamemnon's ill-fated homecoming are cited as instances of poor judgment or disloyalty. In particular, the ingenuousness of Agamemnon and the treachery of Clytemnestra are contrasted with the acumen of Odysseus and the loyalty of his wife Penelope.

The Situation at Ithaca. The arrangement of the *Odyssey* is not chronological. The opening scene takes place in the tenth year after the end of the war, and for the first four books we hear a good deal about Odysseus but never do we catch a glimpse of him. We first find Athena planning to obtain Odysseus' release from the island where the nymph Calypso holds him as a prisoner of love. Then we are brought to Odysseus' palace on Ithaca where Penelope is being besieged by suitors who are making merry at the expense of her husband's estate. Telemachus, Odysseus' son, is furious at the suitors for wasting his property and he demands that they leave forth-with. They refuse and insist that Penelope choose one of them as her husband. At the prompting of Athena, in disguise of course, Telemachus goes off in search of news about his father. These first four books may be considered a small epic on Tele-machus' coming of age and a demonstration that he has inherited all the noble char-acteristics of his father. At the palace of Nestor at Pylos, he hears from the lips of the old monarch an account of the homecomings of some of the heroes and of the shame-less murder of Agamemnon. Several days later, Telemachus is hospitably received by Menelaus and Helen at Sparta. From this famous couple he hears several of Odysseus' exploits at Troy and receives a tantalizing bit of information that his father has been seen as an unwilling captive of Calypso. No one, however, can give Telemachus any assurance that his father is still alive. Back at Ithaca, meanwhile, the suitors are disturbed by Telemachus' sudden aggressiveness and plan to ambush him when he returns home.

Calypso's Isle. The scene now shifts to a mythical island in the Mediterranean, Ogygia, where Calypso, a daughter of Atlas, has had Odysseus all for herself for seven years. At Athena's urging, Zeus sends Hermes to Ogygia with orders to Calypso to release Odysseus and to send him on his way. When Hermes arrives at Ogygia, he is struck by the remarkable beauty of the island; it is a veritable paradise. Calypso receives the Olympian's command with anger and complains of the jealousy of the gods when a goddess takes a mortal for her consort. She will obey Zeus nevertheless. When she goes to tell Odysseus that he may leave the island, we get our first glimpse of the great hero. This is how Homer tells it:

> Calypso found Odysseus sitting on the shore. His eyes were never dry of tears, and life's sweetness was ebbing away as he mourned for his return home. He no longer found the nymph attractive, but at night he would sleep with her as needs he must, unwilling lover with a willing woman. In the daytime, however, he would sit on the rocks and on the beach, straining his soul with tears, and groans, and griefs, and through his tears he would look wistfully over the watery wilderness.

Characteristically of Odysseus, he receives the news from Calypso with suspicion and caution; he will not act upon it until she swears an inviolable oath that she will not plot to harm him in any way. Calypso does so, and the two go into her cavern-home where the nymph first serves him his meal before having her servants wait upon her. She cannot understand why Odysseus wants to leave her; after all Penel-ope cannot be as attractive as she is, since it would be unseemly for a mortal to compete with a goddess in beauty. And then, too, if he stayed with her he would never taste death, enjoying immortality and eternal youth. Odysseus respectfully declines her offer; in spite of the sufferings he will have to endure, he longs for home.

In a few days' time Odysseus, with Calypso's help, fashions a seaworthy craft. Setting out from Ogygia and about to make a landfall after seventeen days at sea, he is spotted by Poseidon as the god is returning from the land of the Ethiopians. Ever since Odysseus had blinded his son Polyphemus, the god has made life difficult for the hero and has kept him from reaching home. In fact, it was while Poseidon was among the Ethiopians that Athena made her plea to Zeus for the release of her favorite. Seeing Odysseus sailing on a calm sea is too much for Poseidon and he rouses the winds to cause a mighty storm. Mountainous waves shatter Odysseus' craft and the hero fears that he will drown. At that moment, the sea-goddess Ino Leucothea comes to his rescue and offers him a magic veil that will keep him from drowning and enable him to reach the island of Scheria, the mythical land of the Phaeacians. Odysseus, ever cautious, accepts the magic veil but does not rely on it entirely; he holds on to the planks of his boat until a huge wave breaks his grip and plunges him into the sea. After two days of swimming, he barely manages to make the shore of Scheria. Naked and exhausted and crusted with brine, Odysseus first returns to the sea the magic veil which helped save his life, and then he falls into a deep sleep in a bed of leaves under a clump of bushes.

Nausicaa. Athena comes to the land of Phaeacians to help her favorite. She appears in a dream to Nausicaa, the nubile daughter of Alcinous and Arete, king and queen of the Phaeacians (p. 348). So that Nausicaa may come to Odysseus' aid, the goddess puts the thought into her head that it is time she think of marriage. And what better way is there to attract a young man than by advertising her domesticity, that is, by taking her family's wash through the town down to the river? When she awakes, Nausicaa asks her father for a wagon to take the laundry down to the river. She says nothing about marriage, but Alcinous is not deceived and readily grants her wish. Together with her attendants, Nausicaa goes to the river, not far from the place where Odysseus lies fast asleep. There they wash the clothes and set them out in the sun to dry. The girls then have a picnic and amuse themselves with a game of ball. When Athena causes Nausicaa to throw the ball into the river, the screams of the girls awaken Odysseus. Naked and looking more like a wild animal than a human being, Odysseus frightens off the young girls when he steps out of his hiding place with just a leafy branch to cover his nakedness. Only Nausicaa holds her ground. In an exceedingly clever speech, Odysseus flatters her by comparing her beauty to that of Artemis. He quickly informs her of how he had been shipwrecked and asks her to help him. And quick to notice that Nausicaa is of marriageable age, he ends his plea with these words, a definition of an ideal marriage (the kind that he shares with Penelope): "And may the gods give you all that your heart desires: a husband and a home, and a mind that is one with his. There is nothing nobler or more to be admired than when a man and his wife see eye to eye; to their enemies it causes grief, to their friends great joy, as they themselves know best."

Nausicaa is very much taken by this stranger. There is something about him that shows he is no ordinary man. She orders her attendants to provide him with clothing, and after modestly going off at a distance to bathe himself in the river, Odysseus returns looking exceedingly handsome and attractive. Nausicaa remarks to the girls that he is just the kind of man she would like to have as a husband. Fearing unpleasant gossip if she is seen coming through the city with a stranger, she advises Odysseus to wait in her father's garden outside the city; and when she has had time to reach home, he is to make his way to the palace and approach her mother Arete and beg her to help him. In the meantime, Athena covers Odysseus with a cloud of mist that will make him invisible. In disguise once more, the goddess directs him to the palace, and as he follows her he marvels at the sight of the harbors, the ships, and the battlements of the wealthy seafaring Phaeacians. The palace is also a marvel to behold, and Odysseus is astonished at the wealth of silver and gold that decorate the building. Everything is perfection, even the king's garden outside the court-yard: it is unique in that it produces fruit the year round, winter and summer. (Like Calypso's island, the land of the Phaeacians is another paradise which Odysseus will be offered and which he will reject in favor of his own home and family.)

The Palace of Alcinous.   Odysseus makes his way unseen to the court where Al-cinous and Arete and the Phaeacian noblemen are gathered. As he grasps the queen's knees, the mist of invisibility is lifted. All are startled at the sudden appearance of the stranger who begs Arete to help him complete his homeward journey. Aware of his duty as a host, Alcinous offers him a place at the table and gives him food and drink. The king suggests to his council that a meeting be held on the following day to de-cide on how best to help the stranger. With extreme delicacy Alcinous and Arete query him as to his true identity, but Odysseus cleverly parries their questions and avoids giving them his name. The king is so impressed with this stranger—he finds him like himself—that he openly admits that he would like to have him as a son-in-law. Yet, if his guest wishes to leave, he will provide him with the means of reach-ing his destination.

On the following day, Alcinous commands that his visitor be royally entertained. Demodocus, the blind minstrel, is brought in and sings of an episode that took place between Odysseus and Achilles. Odysseus is touched to tears but he manages to keep his emotions from being noticed by his host. At various competitive games in his honor, Odysseus is invited to take part. He courteously declines until one of the Phaeacians insults his aristocratic status by contemptuously referring to him as a merchant. Returning the insult, Odysseus leaps up and with ease hurls the heaviest discus far beyond the mark of all the other discus-throwers. More musical entertain-ment follows. This time Demodocus sings of infidelity in heaven, the racy tale of how Ares seduced Hephaestus' wife Aphrodite and how Hephaestus forged the in-visible net that caught the adulterers in the very act of their adultery (p. 177). Al-cinous then proposes that the princes make their guest handsome gifts to speed him on his way home. When Demodocus appears to entertain them once more, Odysseus requests him to sing of the stratagem of the Wooden Horse at Troy. As the bard sings, Odysseus is so moved that he breaks down and weeps bitterly, this time openly and in full view of all. Alcinous calls a halt to the music and again asks his guest to give them the courtesy of knowing who he really is. Odysseus agrees, gives them his name and tells them where he hails from. He then relates his adventures from the time that he left Troy at the end of the war to the time of his imprisonment on Ogygia, Calypso's island. These adventures take up four books of the *Odyssey*, ad-ventures which take place in other never-never lands—with perhaps one excep-tion—where the hero encounters strange and improbable beings.

The Cicones.   After leaving Troy, Odysseus tells his Phaeacian hosts, he led his twelve ships of Ithacans to Thrace and to Ismarus, the city of the Cicones, where he and his men sacked the city, killed off the men, and divided up the booty. (A pirati-cal raid of this kind was a legitimate occupation of the early seafaring Greeks.) But instead of making off with their spoils, as Odysseus advised them to do, the crew in-sisted on feasting on the livestock and wine of the Cicones. This gave the Cicones an opportunity to rally their forces and launch a counterattack. In the pitched battle which followed the Greeks were driven off with a loss of six men from each ship.

The Lotus-Eaters. When they put to sea once more, Zeus sent a raging storm, which ripped the sails and exhausted the men as they attempted to row to the safety of land. The ships almost made the southern coast of the Peloponnese but adverse winds caused them to drift past the island of Cythera. Nine days later they made a landing in the country of the Lotus-eaters (Lotophagi). After replenishing the sup-ply of drinking water, Odysseus sent three of his men to investigate the people who inhabited this unknown land. They discovered that the Lotus-eaters were a peaceful folk who doted on the lotus plant. When Odysseus' men ate the lotus offered them, they found themselves so tranquilized that they lost all desire of returning home; all they wanted to do was to stay with the Lotus-eaters and forage for more lotus plants. Odysseus had to force his men to return. Fearing that the rest of his men might become addicted to the plant and lose their will to return home, he gave orders for his ships to cast off and to be on their way again.

Polyphemus the Cyclops. The next landfall was on the island of the Cyclopes (p. 22). These uncivilized one-eyed people did not cultivate the land, nor did they have lawmaking assemblies and established customs. There were cave-dwelling shepherds who lived off their flocks and what grew wild on the island. After a day of rest and relaxation, Odysseus was consumed with curiosity as to the character of the inhabitants of the island. Taking with him twelve of his men, a supply of food, and a jar of potent wine, he went off to explore the island. They came upon a large cave whose owner was absent at the time. Upon investigation they found it stored with quantities of cheese, pails and bowls filled with milk, and pens of lambs and kids. Odysseus' men suggested that they make off with the cheeses and drive the lambs and kids down to their ship. But Odysseus would not fall in with the plan; he wanted to stay and meet the troglodyte who made his home here.

It was not long before they heard the approach of a Cyclops—Polyphemus was his name, a son of Poseidon and Thoosa. He laid down the huge bundle of firewood he was carrying and drove into the cave the sheep and goats that had to be milked. After he entered, he rolled an enormous stone against the cave's mouth, a stone so heavy that twenty oxen-drawn wagons could not budge it. After milking his ewes, his one eye spied Odysseus and his men, and in a booming voice asked who they were and how they came. Odysseus gave him a thumbnail description of the glory they had won at Troy and then asked Polyphemus to reverence the gods by observ-ing the laws of hospitality and the rights of a guest. The Cyclops merely scoffed at his fear of the gods, claiming that the Cyclopes were stronger than Zeus and the other gods. Reaching out, he seized two of Odysseus' men, dashed their heads on the ground and made a meal of them. After washing it all down with a bowl of milk, he fell into a deep sleep. Odysseus turned his mind to how he might extricate himself and his men from this terrifying predicament. At first he considered driving his sword into the sleeping Polyphemus, but he thought better of it since their escape would be barred by the immense stone blocking the egress from the cave.

Next morning, Polyphemus made a breakfast out of two more of Odysseus' men

Figure 102. Odysseus and his men blinding the drunken Polyphemus (note the cup in the right hand of the Cyclops). *Vase painting, mid seventh century B.C. Eleusis Museum. (Hirmer)*

and then went out with his flocks, He kept his "guests" penned up within the cave by again blocking the entrance with the huge boulder. Odysseus kept racking his brain for a scheme that would get them free and at the same time repay Polyphemus for having murdered his companions. The best plan he could come up with was this. He had his men take a great pole of green olive wood Polyphemus had cut for a staff. They trimmed it down, sharpened the end to a point, and then hardened it in the blazing fire. The weapon, for now such it was, was hidden under the heaps of dung which littered the floor of the cave. Odysseus selected by lot four men who would help him manipulate the weapon when the opportunity afforded it.

Polyphemus came home that evening with his flocks, and this time he drove all of them into the cave and blocked the entrance. After the monster had made a meal of two more men, Odysseus approached him with a bowl of unmixed wine which he poured from the jar he had brought along with him, and invited him to use it to wash down his meal of human flesh. Polyphemus found the bouquet and taste much to his liking and asked for another bowlful. After three helpings of the potent drink, the Cyclops began to feel its effects. Odysseus then offered to tell his enemy his name in exchange for a gift: "My name is Noman (or Nobody, *outis* in Greek). Noman is what I am called by my father and my mother and all my friends." Polyphemus offered a cruel joke as his gift: Noman will be eaten last of all the men. With that the Cyclops fell into a drunken sleep.

Odysseus and his men sprang into action. They took the olive pole from its hiding place and heated the point in the fire until it was on the point of bursting into flame; then placing it close to the monster's only eye, they plunged it deep into the socket while Odysseus used his strength to twist it about like a ship's carpenter boring a hole in a beam (figs. 102, 103). Polyphemus awoke with an agonized shriek, and Odysseus and his men ran for cover in the cave. Hearing his bellowing and his cries for help,

Figure 103. Matisse's rendering of the blinding of Polyphemus. *Lithograph, 1935, illustrating an edition of Joyce's* Ulysses. *Rare Book Division, The New York Public Library, Astor, Lenox and Tilden Foundation.*

the other Cyclopes gathered outside his cave and asked what was ailing him. From within the cave Polyphemus replied: "My friend, Noman is killing me with craft, not by violence." They answered, "Well, if no man is attacking you when you are alone, you must be sick. Best pray to your father Poseidon to help you." With that they returned to their caves on the heights.

Polyphemus rolled away the stone blocking the entrance of the cave and planted himself there in hopes of catching his tormentors as they tried to leave. Odysseus was not taken in by this ploy, and after turning over in his mind one stratagem after another, he came up with a plan of escape. For each of his men he lashed three rams abreast and placed him under the breast of the middle animal. For himself he chose a ram that was the pick of the flock, and he too clung to the fleece of its belly (fig. 104). Next morning, when the flocks bleated to be let out to pasture, Polyphemus let them out of the cave, running his hands over their backs as they passed by. Once in the clear, the Greeks drove a good part of the flock to their ship and cast off. At a distance from shore, Odysseus could not restrain himself from taunting Polyphemus, even though his men advised him to curb the impulse. He ended up, not very wisely, giving the blinded Cyclops his full name and address:

> Cyclops, if anyone should ask you how you happened to come by your unsightly blindness, tell him that it was I who did it, Odysseus, the sacker of cities, the son of Laertes, whose home is in Ithaca.

Knowing the true name of his tormentor, Polyphemus now prayed to his father Poseidon to avenge him: to see to it that Odysseus would never reach home; or if he was destined to do so, that he would come home late and under the worst circumstances. Poseidon heard his son's prayer. And so through his imprudence—Homer's paragon is also human in that he occasionally errs—Odysseus earned the continuing enmity of Poseidon.

Aeolus, Keeper of the Winds. The next adventure took Odysseus to the floating island of Aeolia which was ruled over by Aeolus, a favorite of the gods and the keeper of the winds. After being entertained hospitably for a month, the Greeks took their leave. Aeolus gave Odysseus a bag in which all the unfavorable winds were tightly secured, and he sent a favorable breeze to blow his ships on a direct course for Ithaca. For nine days all went well, and on the tenth they were in sight of Ithaca. But Odysseus, exhausted from continuous duty at the helm of his ship, fell asleep. While he slept, his crew grew curious about the mysterious bag which Aeolus had given their captain. Thinking that it contained a treasure which would not be shared with the crew, they opened the bag. As soon as they undid the silver thong, out rushed all the boisterous winds which blew the ships back to Aeolia. Aeolus refused to have anything further to do with Odysseus, asuming that what had happened was a sign from the gods that he and his men had fallen into their disfavor.

The Laestrygonians. In the absence of any kind of wind, the Greeks were forced into the back-breaking labor of rowing their ships. Seven days later they came to the island of the Laestrygonians. There they found an excellent landlocked harbor and crowded their ships into it, all except Odysseus who moored his vessel just outside the cove—wisely as it turned out. Seeing smoke rise in the distance, Odysseus sent three of his men to investigate. Unfortunately, the Laestrygonians turned out to be a race of giant cannibals. They pelted the ships crammed together in the narrow harbor, sinking or overturning them. Then they speared the men in the water as if they were fish and carried them off to make a meal of them. Only Odysseus' ship which lay outside the cove managed to escape.

Circe. Completely dejected by what had happened to their comrades at the hands of the Laestrygonians, the remaining Greeks pressed on in their remaining ship, and in due course they came to the island of Aeaea, the home of the goddess Circe. After two days of rest, Odysseus set out to see if he could discover any sign of habitation. He caught sight of smoke rising from Circe's house and returned to his shipmates with his information. At his suggestion that they investigate, they broke down and wept for they remembered what had happened when they reconnoitered the land of the Laestrygonians. But Odysseus insisted and divided his men into two bands; he took charge of one party, and a certain Eurylochus was

Figure 104.   Odysseus makes his escape from the cave of Polyphemus under a ram. *Vase painting, c. 475 B.C. Museum of Fine Arts, Boston.*

placed in charge of the other. It was Eurylochus and his men who came upon Circe's house. The goddess cordially invited them to enter, which they did in their innocence, all except Eurylochus who was suspicious. The enchantress, for that she was, served the men a dish of drugged delicacies, and with a touch of her magic wand, turned them into swine. Circe penned them in sties and left them to wallow in the mud and to grub for pigs' fodder.

Eurylochus ran back to Odysseus and reported the dreadful transformation of his men. Odysseus set out as a rescue party of one. On the way he was met by Hermes. The god advised him of the dangers he was facing at the hands of Circe and instructed him how to counteract her magic. He gave him a plant called *moly* which would act as an antidote to Circe's drug. And when the goddess would touch him with her wand, Hermes told Odysseus, he was to spring at her with his sword. At that, Circe would invite Odysseus to share her bed, which he should do, but first he must get her to swear an oath not to harm him, otherwise she could unman him and strip him of his courage.

All went as Hermes said it would. Circe took Odysseus as her lover and treated him magnificently. He saw to it that his men were turned back into human form and he persuaded his other shipmates to join them in Circe's house. Day after day they were royally entertained until a year had passed and Odysseus had to be reminded that it was time to think of Ithaca and of returning home. Circe had no objection to her guest's leaving, but she said that he would first have to make a journey to the house of Hades and Persephone. There he was to consult the soul of the Theban seer Tiresias who alone of the shades had kept his intellectual powers and who would tell him how to reach Ithaca. Odysseus was shattered when he heard this, for no one had ever sailed a ship to the dreaded house of Hades. Circe gave him sailing instructions and advised him on the rituals of sacrificing to the infernal deities and the souls of the dead. Odysseus prepared his men for the trip—he did not tell them the exact course he was laying until the very last minute. In the hustle and bustle of getting ready to leave, there was a casualty. Elpenor, the youngest member of the crew, had had too much to drink the night before and had gone on the roof for fresh air and sleep. Roused in the morning to make his departure, he forgot about the ladder and fell from the roof breaking his neck.

The House of Hades.   The wind sent by Circe blew Odysseus' ship to the earth's end and the world-encircling Ocean. Disembarking, Odysseus dug a trench to receive the offerings and the blood of the sacrificial animals; and as he performed the rituals prescribed by Circe, up came the spirits of the dead. The first to approach the trench was Elpenor who had not been given the last rites when his shipmates set out for Hades' realm (fig. 105). He begged for the ritual of the funeral pyre and received his captain's promise that it would be tended to. Then came Tiresias. He told the hero of the hardships Poseidon would foist upon him for having blinded Polyphemus. The seer cautioned Odysseus against doing any injury to the cattle of Hyperion the sun-god when they came to the island of Thrinacia; if they did, there would be a disaster both for the men and their ship. Tiresias concluded with instructions on how to appease the wrath of Poseidon, and with a prophecy on how Odysseus would end his life: a most gentle death coming from the sea when he was very old and surrounded by a happy people.

While in Hades' kingdom, Odysseus took the opportunity to speak with the shade of his mother Anticleia. She told him how things were at home, and that his wife

and son were still loyal to him and yearning for his homecoming. As for her own death, she had wasted away longing for him. Odysseus' heart was touched by his mother's words and he stretched out his arms to embrace her, but three times she slipped through his arms like a shadow or a dream. As he spoke to his mother, Persephone drove before her the souls of other women, and Odysseus was privileged to see those women of legendary fame such as Tyro, Antiope, Alcmene, Epicaste (Jocasta), Phaedra, Procris, and Ariadne.

Dramatically, Odysseus stops the account of his adventures at this point and suggests to his audience that it is late and time to go to sleep. The Phaeacians, spellbound by his story, protest; they want to hear more. Arete suggests that they promise to give their honored guest rich gifts before he leaves, and Alcinous begs him to finish the story of his adventures. Odysseus agrees and picks up the thread of his tale with his encounter in Hades with some of the souls of his former comrades-in-arms, Agamemnon, Achilles, and Ajax.

After Persephone drove off the souls of the women, Odysseus was approached by the shade of Agamemnon, and when the hero asked him in what glorious way he met his death, Agamemnon bitterly reported to him the shameless way in which he and Cassandra had died, ending with a warning that what had happened to him should serve as a lesson to Odysseus: not to trust anyone and not to sail openly into his home port. He inquired if Odysseus had any news of his son Orestes, but Odysseus could give him no information.

Next to appear was the shade of the great Achilles. When Odysseus addressed him as a mighty prince among the dead, Achilles replied that he would much rather be a lowly serf than king of the dead and departed. Like Agamemnon, Achilles was anxious to have news of his son. This time Odysseus could report that Neoptolemus had conducted himself gloriously on the field of battle and most effectively in the councils of men. At that, Achilles turned on his heel and went off happy. Then came the soul of Ajax. When Odysseus tried to speak to him, there was nothing but silence, for Ajax still bore his grudge with Odysseus over the unhappy contest the two had had over the arms of Achilles.

After describing the agonies of the three arch sinners—Tityus, Tantalus, and Sisyphus—and sighting the souls of several other notable men, Odysseus made his way out of the house of Hades, boarded his ship and returned to Circe's island. There he fulfilled the promise he had made to Elpenor and gave him a hero's funeral. He reported back to Circe who exclaimed with wonderment on the remarkable feat of descending alive to the house of Hades; now he and his men would have two deaths instead of one. After a day's rest, Circe sent them on their way with suggestions on how to avoid the dangers of the Sirens and of Scylla and Charybdis. She also repeated the warning given by Tiresias that if they expected to reach home, they must not kill any of the cattle of Hyperion the sun-god.

The Sirens. Once more Circe sent a spanking breeze to send the Greeks on their way, but as their ship approached the island of the Sirens, they were becalmed and had to put their backs to the oars. Heeding the instructions he had received from the goddess, Odysseus plugged the ears of his crew with beeswax so that they would not hear the siren call of these deadly sea nymphs whose enchanting music could lure a man to his death. Odysseus, however, was not to be deprived of a recital. He had his men lash him to the mast and ordered them to tighten the ropes which bound him whenever he pleaded to be released (fig. 106).

As they rowed past the island of the Sirens and out of earshot of their music, Odysseus was released. But just then they saw the threat of the Wandering Rocks, and once more following Circe's advice, Odysseus steered his ship past the marine hazard and headed for the equally hazardous course that would take them through the straits which separated Scylla and Charybdis (p. 101). On the one side was Scylla, a fearful monster of the rocks, barking like a dog, with twelve feet, six long necks, and mouths with three rows of teeth each; on the other was Charyb-

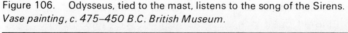

Figure 106.   Odysseus, tied to the mast, listens to the song of the Sirens.
Vase painting, c. 475–450 B.C. British Museum.

dis, a whirlpool that sucked water three times a day right down to the sandy bottom of the sea and three times a day spewed it forth. Odysseus chose the course set for him by Circe—he did not tell his crew what was in store for them in order to avoid panic among them—even though it meant losing some of his men. He steered his craft close to the rock which housed Scylla, and while his men kept a close eye on Charybdis, the monster grabbed off and devoured six of his men.

The Cattle of Hyperion. After the terrifying experience of Scylla and Charybdis, Odysseus' ship reached the island of Thrinacia where Hyperion kept his cattle. To avoid any risk of offending the sun-god, Odysseus suggested that they bypass the island. But no, Eurylochus insisted that the men were exhausted and in need of rest. As for the cattle of Hyperion, he assured Odysseus that they would not be harmed. Once on shore, however, a gale blew up, and for a whole month adverse winds forced them to remain on the island. When their food gave out, Odysseus went inland to pray to the gods in hope that one of them might provide him with the means of escaping death from starvation. Eurylochus took advantage of his captain's absence and persuaded his shipmates to slaughter some of Hyperion's cattle in order to survive and to repay the sun-god later by building him a temple in Ithaca. When Odysseus returned and saw his men roasting the meat of the sacrosanct animals, he was horrified and outraged. Equally outraged was Hyperion who went to Zeus and declared that if the culprits were not punished, he would go down to Hades and shine among the dead. Zeus mollified the offended god by guaranteeing disaster for the sinners. The gods also let their displeasure be known to the men by having the beef "moo" on the roasting spits and the hides crawl on the ground.

For six days the crew feasted on Hyperion's cattle, and when the storm abated on the seventh, they put out to sea again. Zeus was as good as his word; he sent a furious storm and shattered the vessel with one of his lightning bolts. All the men drowned, all except Odysseus who had wisely refrained from eating the forbidden meat. He managed to stay afloat on some of the wreckage of his ship. The storm blew him back to the straits between Scylla and Charybdis, and just as his improvised raft was sucked down by the whirlpool, he managed to grab a fig tree on the rock above and held on to it until Charybdis spewed up the timbers of his craft. Paddling with his hands, he got as far away as he could from Scylla and Charybdis. He drifted for nine days, and on the tenth he landed on the island of Ogygia, the home of Calypso, where he spent seven years of his life.

At this point Odysseus concludes the narration of his adventures. There is silence in the hall; the Phaeacian nobles are spellbound. Alcinous suggests additional gifts for their honored guest, the burden of which will be met by a tax on the people. On the following day, a Phaeacian ship is readied to take Odysseus home to Ithaca. He gives thanks to his hosts and embarks with his cargo of fine gifts. When the ship reaches Ithaca, Odysseus is in a deep sleep. The Phaeacian sailors deposit their sleeping passenger and his treasure under an olive tree and depart. The kindly Phaeacians have yet to reckon with the anger of Poseidon for rescuing the man who blinded his son. When the ship is in sight of their native island, the god turns it into a rock; at the same time he rings the city of the Phaeacians with high mountains, thereby cutting off the livelihood of the city. All this comes about, as it often does in such tales, in accordance with a prophecy Alcinous recalls after Poseidon has petrified both the ship and the approach to the city.

Odysseus in Ithaca. The scene now shifts to Ithaca. Odysseus awakes and for the moment thinks he is in a strange land. After checking to see that his gifts are all there, he asks a passing shepherd, who is really Athena in disguise, where he is and who inhabits the land. The goddess teases him a bit and ends her speech by telling her favorite that he is in Ithaca. Odysseus is overjoyed at the news, but he does not let his joy carry him away. With his usual caution, he does not reveal his true identity; instead he tells the "shepherd" a long cock-and-bull story about how he came to land on the island. Athena smiles at Odysseus' crafty ways which she finds so admirable since she too is skilled in trickery. She changes her appearance and reveals her divinity. The goddess then gives him a report on conditions within the palace and proposes a course of action. After helping Odysseus carefully store away his shipload of gifts in a cave, she disguises the hero by turning him into a ragged old beggar and tells him to seek shelter at the hut of his loyal swineherd Eumaeus while she goes off to Sparta to summon Telemachus home.

In Eumaeus' Hut. Odysseus, though in all appearances an out-and-out beggar, is received by Eumaeus with kindness. The swineherd soon lets it be known how much he misses his king and master, and how intolerable he finds the behavior of the suitors. Eumaeus, however, is suspicious of the beggar since others of his ilk have come to the island with all kinds of stories about Odysseus, pouring them out to a gullible Penelope in hopes of being given a gift. The old swineherd is convinced that his master is dead. Odysseus tells the unbelieving Eumaeus that his master will come home and then spins out a long tale of how he heard that Odysseus was on his way to the oracle of Dodona to find out how he should return home, openly or in disguise.

Telemachus Returns and Meets his Father. In the meantime, Athena appears to Telemachus in a dream. She urges him to return home and warns him of an ambush laid by the suitors; until it is safe for him to return to the palace, she suggests that he stay at Eumaeus' hut. Telemachus follows the advice of the goddess and arrives safely in Ithaca. He makes for the hut of Eumaeus where he is warmly received by the old swineherd. To the stranger in the hut, the young son of Odysseus is courteous and shows his respect for his elders. Telemachus queries Eumaeus about his mother and hears that she has not chosen a husband from among the suitors. He then sends the swineherd to inform Penelope that he has arrived home safely.

While Eumaeus is on his way to the palace, Athena appears to Odysseus and tells him that he should make himself known to his son. She changes him from a beggar into his former vigorous self. Telemachus can hardly believe his eyes until Odysseus convinces him that he really is his father who at long last has come home. Father and son tearfully embrace each other. Odysseus learns from Telemachus that there are over one hundred suitors in the palace, and although the youth is dismayed at the thought of the two of them taking on the suitors by themselves, Odysseus does not let the odds overwhelm him. He begins to lay his plans. In his disguise as a beggar he will go to the palace, and Telemachus will see to it that all the weapons in the great hall are removed, all except those which they will need for themselves. And Telemachus is to tell no one that he has returned, not even Eumaeus or Penelope. There is also the need to discover who among the servants is loyal and who is not. Back at the palace, the suitors have learned that Telemachus has escaped their ambush, and after much discussion, they decide to

Figure 107.   Odysseus in the guise of a beggar approaches a sorrowing
Penelope. Telemachus and Laertes stand behind Penelope; the swineherd
Eumaeus is seated on the ground. *Greek terracotta relief, c. 460 B.C. The
Metropolitan Museum of Art, Fletcher Fund, 1930.*

abandon further plans of putting Telemachus out of the way. Penelope, who has
learned of the plot to kill her son, turns on the suitors and gives them a tongue-
lashing, especially Antinous, the most arrogant of the horde of unwanted guests.

Odysseus in the Palace.   On the following day, Telemachus sets out for the
palace after asking Eumaeus to take Odysseus, now again disguised as a beggar,
to the palace where he can beg for some scraps of food (fig. 107). When Penelope
sees her son, she bursts into sobs and throws her arms around his neck and kisses
him. Manfully, Telemachus rejects her emotional display and orders her to her
room. Penelope is taken aback, but she does as her son bids her. Toward evening,
Eumaeus escorts Odysseus to town, and on the way they are met by Melanthius, a
self-seeking goatherd who sides with the suitors. When he insults and kicks Odysseus, it is only with considerable restraint that the hero keeps from shedding
his disguise and killing the offensive Melanthius. As Eumaeus and his beggar-
companion approach the courtyard of the palace, Odysseus' old hunting dog, Argus, recognizes his master. When Odysseus sees his favorite hound wag his tail and
drop his ears in a sign of recognition, he is moved to tears but he manages to conceal his emotions from Eumaeus. Seeing his master again after an absence of
nineteen years, old Argus dies.

Within the palace Odysseus is constantly abused and maltreated by the suitors;
yet there is always something in the way he reacts to situations which causes the
suitors no little amazement. As for Penelope, her contempt for the suitors is hardly

restrained even though she teases them into giving her gifts. She reiterates her longing and love for Odysseus, but she is in an ambivalent position. If Odysseus is really dead, she should take another husband as her parents urge her to do; if she remains in Odysseus' house, the suitors will squander the estate that rightfully belongs to Telemachus. Telemachus, verging on manhood, wishes to be recognized as an adult. He is not the child his mother sees in him, and he bitterly resents the suitors who are eating him out of house and home.

Finally, the occasion arises for Penelope and Odysseus to meet in private. Still in the guise of a beggar, he tells her of the imminent arrival of her husband. To conceal his identity, Odysseus tells her a number of tall tales, but he proves that he has seen Odysseus by describing his clothes and the details of a brooch. Penelope is moved to tears although she cannot bring herself to believe the beggar's statement that her husband will come home soon. She has confided to this strangely attractive beggar a dream which clearly foreshadows the death of the suitors; and she has also told him of how she put off the suitors for more than three years by a clever stratagem. Announcing that she could not make a decision until she had finished weaving a shroud for Odysseus' father Laertes, she would work at the loom all day, and at night she would unravel all that she had woven during the day. She was able to deceive the suitors in this way until one night her maids discovered what she was doing. Now she is being forced from all sides to make a decision.

Eurycleia Recognizes Odysseus. Just before Penelope tells Odysseus her dream, a recognition scene takes place. Wishing to repay the beggar for his information, Penelope offers him a bath and a clean bed. Assenting to Odysseus' request to have one of the older servants bathe his feet, she orders Eurycleia, a servant in the household for many years, to do so. Eurycleia notices the resemblance between this dirty beggar and her long-absent master. And as she washes his feet, she recognizes on his leg an old scar which resulted from a boar-wound he had received many years ago while hunting with his grandfather Autolycus. She is about to blurt out to Penelope that her husband is here—Penelope for the moment being distracted by Athena—when Odysseus grabs her by the throat and chokes off her words. He makes her swear, which she does most willingly, that she will tell no one that Odysseus is in the house.

The time has come for Penelope to choose a husband from among the encamped suitors, and to select a mate she has decided on a test of skill in archery. It is a plan which she outlined to Odysseus when they met in private and which he encouraged her to put into operation. Odysseus himself sees his own plan of action more clearly. On a pretext, Telemachus has removed all the weapons from the great hall in which the suitors are assembled. Disloyal servants are marked for later punishment and a faithful retainer, Philoetius the herdsman, is cited as a future ally. All is in readiness for the long-awaited denouement.

The Great Bow. Penelope descends to the storeroom where the material wealth of the household is stored and from among the treasures she picks out Odysseus' great bow. The very touch of it moves her to tears. She announces to the suitors that whoever strings the bow and shoots an arrow through the hafts of twelve axes set in a row will be her choice as a husband. Telemachus sets out the axes in a

Figure 108.   Odysseus slaying the suitors. *Vase painting, c.450 B.C. State Museum, Berlin.*

straight line and announces that he will have the first try at stringing the bow and
shooting an arrow through the axes; if he is successful, his mother can leave his
house with whomever she pleases. Three times he strains to string the great bow,
and on the fourth try he might have been successful, but he gets a disapproving
nod from his father. The young man acknowledges that he has failed and turns
over the unstrung bow to one of the suitors. While the contest is going on, Odysseus takes Eumaeus and Philoetius aside and reveals his identity to them by
showing them the scar on his leg. He instructs them to clear the hall of servants
and to bar the door to the courtyard so that no one can escape. Suitor after suitor
tries to string the bow without success. Odysseus then asks for a chance. The
suitors are shocked at the presumption of the beggar, even though Penelope
registers no objection. After some discussion Telemachus asks his mother to leave
the hall, and Eumaeus hands Odysseus the bow. He first tests the bow and then
strings it without difficulty. He plucks the string and its music sounds throughout
the hall. Picking up an arrow, he takes casual aim and shoots it through the hafts
of the twelve axes. Telemachus arms himself and moves to the side of his father
for the slaughter which is about to begin.

The Fate of the Suitors.   Odysseus sheds his beggar's rags and leaps to the
threshold with his bow and quiver full of arrows (fig. 108). His first arrow is for
Antinous, the most arrogant of the suitors, who is struck in the neck just as he
reaches for a cup of wine. When the other suitors realize that the supposed beggar
is Odysseus himself, they blanch in fear. One of them attempts to persuade
Odysseus that Antinous was to blame and begs him to spare his fellow-Ithacans
who will repay him and more for all they have consumed in his house. Odysseus is
unrelenting; he will forgive no one. Seeing that they have no way to escape, the
suitors choose to fight with their swords. One by one they are slaughtered by
Odysseus' arrows. Together with his son, Eumaeus, and Philoetius, Odysseus continues cutting down his enemies. Telemachus replenishes their weapons with armor
and spears from the storeroom. One of the besieged suitors sends Melanthius, the
sycophant goatherd, for reinforcements. He is intercepted in the storeroom by Eu-

maeus and Philoetius who tie him up and suspend him from the ceiling. He will hang there until the end of the fighting when he will be mutilated and killed for his unconscionable treachery.

Athena now comes to the side of Odysseus in the guise of Mentor, the old Ithacan to whom the hero had entrusted his household and the education of his son Telemachus—a name that has come into English as "mentor," a wise and trusted counselor. The goddess spurs on her favorite and then leaves without taking an active part in the fighting. Finally, all the suitors are killed off in the bloody battle. Only two are spared on the plea of Telemachus: Phemius the bard and Medon the herald. Odysseus calls in Eurycleia and has her summon the women-servants who were disloyal to him. They are to clean the hall of the blood and gore and to carry out the bodies of the slain suitors. When they have finished fumigating the great hall, Telemachus takes them outside and strings them up by their necks to die a painful death.

Odysseus and Penelope Reunited. The carnage is over, the disloyal servants have been meted out their punishment, Odysseus is once more the master of his house. What is the reaction of Penelope when Eurycleia rushes in to tell her that the stranger in the palace is the husband she has been longing for for so many years? She is unbelieving. And when she comes face to face with Odysseus, she is silent and reserved. Telemachus cannot understand his mother's attitude, but Penelope assures him that if the man seated opposite her is really her husband, they will recognize each other by the secrets which only the two of them share. Odysseus is patient and orders a bath and new clothes. He emerges looking handsome and irresistible. Still no reaction from Penelope. Odysseus exclaims in exasperation that he cannot understand her; no other woman could have kept from rushing into her husband's arms after an absence of so many years. He asks Eurycleia to make a bed for him apart from his wife's. Penelope replies that he is still strange to her and orders Eurycleia to remove the great bed that Odysseus himself had built and to place it outside the bedroom. This was Penelope's test of Odysseus—cautious and resourceful, she is the female counterpart of her husband—for the secret that they shared was the unmovable bed which Odysseus had fashioned out of a living olive tree. When her husband bursts out demanding to know whether the tree has been cut through and his bed moved elsewhere, Penelope is given proof positive that the man standing before her is truly Odysseus. She melts and tearfully embraces her husband, pleading with him not to be angry with her for putting him to the test. After Odysseus gives Penelope an account of his adventures, the two go to bed, and Athena holds back the dawn so that they can have their fill of love.

The curtain does not fall on the *Odyssey* with the hero and heroine in each other's arms; the parents of the slain suitors have to be dealt with. We are also treated to another scene in the Underworld to reinforce the contrast in the domestic lives of Agamemnon and Odysseus. There in the Underworld where Hermes has delivered them, the souls of the suitors meet Agamemnon and Achilles who happen to be reviewing the last moments of each other's life. One of the suitors, in reply to Agamemnon's query, tells him the sad story of how Penelope deceived them for years by weaving and unweaving Laertes' shroud, and how Odysseus descended on them disguised as a beggar and then dispatched them in a bloody battle. After hearing the story, Agamemnon has these words of high praise for the ideal couple:

Oh happy son of Laertes, resourceful Odysseus, you indeed have a most excellent wife, good and wise Penelope, who has shown herself so loyal to her husband. Her glory shall never perish from the earth; rather the deathless gods will make a song for mortal men glorifying the constant Penelope. How unlike Clytemnestra and her infamous deed when she killed her wedded lord! Her song shall be hateful among men, and she has ruined the reputation of her entire sex, even of honest women in it.

Odysseus and Laertes. At dawn of the following day, Odysseus goes off to visit his aged father Laertes who has retired from active affairs to take care of his orchard and vineyard. As is his usual custom, Odysseus makes an indirect approach, at first pretending that he has come for information about Odysseus and telling a tall tale about himself. When Laertes breaks down and weeps upon hearing his son's name, Odysseus reveals his true identity and reports that he has killed all the suitors who besieged his household. Laertes, in the family tradition, is suspicious and unbelieving. Not until his son shows him the scar on his leg and tells him the exact number of fruit trees he planted a number of years ago, does Laertes believe him. After a tearful reunion, Laertes warns his son that the friends and relatives of the slain suitors will seek to avenge their murder. Odysseus is confident that they can meet the situation when it develops and suggests that they go into the farmhouse to have their meal.

The End of the Feud. The news of the suitors' death finally has leaked out— Odysseus has managed to keep it quiet for a time by a ruse—and the kinsmen and friends have gathered to seek redress. Rejecting the advice of a notable gray-beard, they arm themselves and march upon Laertes' house to punish Odysseus. Together with his son and father and a handful of retainers, Odysseus arms himself to meet the angered crowd. Laertes, old as he is, gathers his strength, hurls his spear, and lays low the leader of the mob. The battle is joined. Telemachus and Odysseus charge into the front ranks, and they would have killed them all had Athena not intervened, shouting for them to stop their fighting and to separate. The sound of the goddess' voice panics the Ithacans; they drop their weapons and flee for their lives. Not so Odysseus. With a war whoop he pounces on the fleeing men, but Zeus sends a flaming bolt of lightning to fall at Athena's feet, and the goddess calls Odysseus by his royal titles and orders him to stop, since otherwise Zeus will be offended. Odysseus agrees and the goddess brings about peace between both sides. On this harmonious note, Homer concludes his saga of Odysseus the soldier, adventurer, lover, and lately, the family man.

There is little more to report on the subsequent career of Homer's cunning and eloquent hero. Late tradition, quite un-Homeric, has it that Telegonus, a son of Odysseus by Circe, was sent by his mother to seek out his father. A storm cast him up on Ithaca, and driven by hunger he began to plunder the land. He was attacked by Odysseus and Telemachus, and in the ensuing battle Telegonus killed his father. Athena ordered Penelope and Telemachus to carry his body to Aeaea, Circe's island, where they buried him. We then hear that Telemachus married Circe and sired a son Italus who gave his name to Italy. As for Penelope, she married Telegonus and bore him a son Latinus. (Hesiod calls Latinus a son of Odysseus and Circe; other traditions provide various parents for this lengendary Latin figure.) In addition to giving his name to a people and a language, Latinus was also the father of Lavinia who became Aeneas' wife when he migrated to Italy.

*   *   *   *

Over the centuries, the character of Homer's versatile and adaptable hero rarely remained Homeric. As early as Sophocles and Euripides—and even earlier with Pindar—the selfish cunning and deceit of Odysseus were deprecated by poets and philosophers. In a world in which ethical values were constantly scrutinized and debated, these Homeric virtues could hardly be recommended as models of desirable conduct. Plato, of course, objected to both Homer and Odysseus on moral grounds. In the *Philoctetes*, Sophocles portrays Odysseus as a tempter and corrupter of the youthful Neoptolemus; he is a liar and a coward, one who would do anything to achieve his ends. Similarly in Euripides' *Hecuba*, Odysseus is brutally callous in rejecting Hecuba's plea for mercy though he is under obligation to the aged queen. And in the *Trojan Women*, although Odysseus does not appear on the stage, we are told that he urged the death of Hector's son Astyanax; and when Hecuba learns that she has been assigned to him as his slave, she describes him in an emotional outburst as being abominable, treacherous, an enemy of justice, double-tongued, a lawbreaking monster, a brute, and a breaker of promises. Roman poets, particularly those with anti-Greek sentiments, continue this unflattering portrait of Homer's hero. There were exceptions of course. During the Hellenistic and Roman periods, Stoic philosophers found in Odysseus an exemplar of patience, prudence, and fortitude, and their views found expression in the works of Cicero, Horace, Plutarch, and some ecclesiastical writers. Two of the Church Fathers, Origen and Hippolytus, went so far as to compare Christ on the Cross with Odysseus bound to the mast as he sailed past the island of the Sirens. In general, however, the Middle Ages clung to the anti-Homeric literary tradition; the Renaissance, with its more liberal attitudes and greater familiarity with Greek and Latin texts, was able to appreciate the finer qualities of Homer's Odysseus.

Apart from an appreciation of Odysseus-Ulysses as a symbol of a saint or a Satan, it was also possible for a poet to find something of himself in the legendary hero. In more modern times, Tennyson found an outlet for his despondency over the death of his friend Arthur Hallam by proposing an un-Greek Odyssean adventure of "going forward and braving the struggle of life." *Ulysses* (1842) is a lyrical monologue, influenced by Dante's picture of Ulysses in the *Inferno* where we hear that the hero never reached home, but that upon leaving Circe he pursued his inordinate desire for knowledge and experience of the unknown world. Tennyson's Ulysses is this kind of restless adventurer; he is not satisfied with being a family man and mouldering in Ithaca with his aged wife. "I cannot rest from travel; I will drink / Life to the lees," he says and desires "to follow knowledge like a sinking star, / Beyond the utmost bound of human thought." He then bids

> Come, my friends,
> 'Tis not too late to seek a newer world.
> Push off, and sitting well in order smite
> The sounding furrows; for my purpose holds
> To sail beyond the sunset, and the baths
> Of all the western stars, until I die.
> It may be that the gulfs will wash us down;
> It may be we shall touch the Happy Isles
> And see the great Achilles, whom we knew.
> Tho' much is taken, much abides; and tho'

We are not now that strength which in old days
Moved earth and heaven; that which we are, we are,—
One equal temper of heroic hearts,
Made weak by time and fate, but strong in will
To strive, to seek, to find, and not to yield.

Tennyson took another theme from Homer to play upon his Victorian melancholia and ennui. The *Lotus Eaters* (1833, rev. 1842), more Lucretian than Homeric, is a plea for tranquillity, for release from the obligations of life, from striving and "eyes grown dim with gazing on the pilot-stars." In a similar vein, Matthew Arnold took snatches of Odyssean themes to say something about himself and his art. The *Strayed Reveller* (1849) concerns itself with poetic inspiration, its ecstasies and its penalties. In place of Homer's enchantress, Arnold gives us a more motherly Muse-like Circe whose draught is not a beast-transforming drug, but a cup of intoxicating wine. In the same year Arnold published the *New Sirens* in which the poet hears the seductive voices of the bodily senses calling to him, a call which he halfheartedly rejects in favor of disciplined and critical thought.

Ezra Pound, the twentieth-century Dante and poet-voyager into the realm of the creative imagination, opens the *Cantos* with Odysseus' adventure in the house of Hades, a syncopated version of the eleventh book of the *Odyssey*. In *Canto XX*, he returns to the Odyssean theme with a cynical query by the Lotus-eaters of the hero's fearless search for beauty:

> "What gain with Odysseus,
> "They that died in the whirlpool
> "And after many vain labours,
> "Living by stolen meat, chained to the rowingbench,
> "That he should have a great fame
>   "And lie by night with the goddess?
> "Their names are not written in bronze
>   "Nor their rowing sticks set with Elpenor's;
>
> . . . .
>
> "Nor lay there with the queen's waiting maids,
> "Nor had they Circe to couch-mate, Circe Titania,
> "Nor had they meats of Kalüpso
> "Or her silk skirts brushing their thighs.
> "Give! What were they given?
>   Ear-wax.
> "Poison and ear-wax,
>   and a salt grave by the bull-field. . ."

T. S. Eliot, unlike his mentor Pound, made little use of Odyssean themes. In *Sweeney Erect* he makes a parenthetical allusion to "Nausicaa and Polypheme," an incongruous collocation of characters in which the gross and lustful Sweeney is compared with Polyphemus, the epileptic woman with Nausicaa. This "Polypheme" may be a cross between Homer's unnoble savage and the Sicilian Polyphemus of the Hellenistic pastoral tradition (p. 12). The story, as we find it mainly in the *Idylls* of Theocritus and in Ovid's *Metamorphoses*, is of the uncouth one-eyed shepherd Polyphemus who is hopelessly in love with the sea-nymph Galatea, but she loves Acis, a son of Faunus and a river-nymph. To win the love of Galatea, Polyphemus tries to make himself attractive by grooming his unkempt hair and beard and by serenading her with lugubrious songs of his passion. When he comes upon the two lovers after having poured out his heart in a song, he is so enraged that he picks up a huge boulder and crushes poor Acis with it, while Galatea escapes by diving into the sea. The nymph is joined by her beloved, when his blood turns into the Sicilian stream that bears his name and flows into the sea. This tale is celebrated in John Gay's libretto for Handel's opera *Acis and Galatea* (1720)—in the eighteenth century there were at least seven other operas on this story, including one by Haydn—and in art by Raphael, Carracci, Tiepolo, and others. In Thomas Lodge's *Rosalynde* (1590), a pastoral romance, we hear a love-struck shepherd pouring out his heart in euphuistic song to a coy shepherdess Phoebe, comparing his suffering to that of "Polypheme":

> The lovesick Polypheme that could not see
> Who on the barren shore
> His fortunes doth deplore,
> And melteth all in moan
> For Galatea gone,
>
> . . . .
>
> Alas, his pain is nought;
> For were my woe but thought,
> Oh how would Phoebe sigh if she did look on me!

Until the twentieth century no one had attempted to compete with Homer in giving epic treatment to the character of *homo ulixeanus*, the Odyssean man. François Fénelon, the French prelate, had attempted it for Telemachus in his *Les Aventures de Télémaque* (1699), a romantic narrative in elegant prose, and like the *Iliad* and the *Odyssey*, in twenty-four "books." Fénelon had written it for his pupil, the Duke of Burgundy and the second heir to the throne of Louis XIV, and designed it to instruct him in the art of good government. Telemachus (Burgundy), accompanied by the goddess of wisdom (Fénelon) travels all over the Mediterranean and has adventures far in excess of those which his Homeric father enjoyed or suffered. He also had his Mentor, the goddess Minerva (Fénelon) in disguise, to provide him with moral discourses on happy kingdoms and wicked kings. But the real challenge to Homer in heroic epic came from an Irishman, James Joyce (1882–1941), and a Greek, Nikos Kazantzakis (1885–1957), both of whom—if we were to consider sheer bulk only—easily surpassed the blind bard of Scio's isle.

Joyce's *Ulysses* takes us through a day—specifically, eighteen hours and forty-five minutes of Thursday, the 16th of June, 1904—in the inner and outer and imaginative lives of two Edwardian Dubliners. (Compare Homer's forty-one days in the tenth year of Odysseus' wanderings.) Joyce took from the *Odyssey* a series of correspondences, and using it as a structural frame, he constructed a complex study in compassionate humanism, of man in megalopolis (Dublin vs. Homer's Mediterranean), of self-identification (Dedalus-Bloom-Joyce), of multilayered meanings and symbols in the tradition of Dante. All this and much more. Stephen Dedalus is Joyce's Telemachus, and for the first three books (chapters), we follow him as he seeks not his blood-father, but a father-surrogate and "the consubstantiality of the Father and the Son." We then pass to the adventures of Joyce's Ulysses, Leopold Bloom, the wandering Jew, cosmopolite, polymath, agnostic, aesthete, cuckold, and yet the prudent, the versatile and adaptable man. He is married to Molly, the inverted Penelope, an overripe beauty who is continually unfaithful to him. She also doubles as Calypso and as various aspects of a fertility goddess. As Bloom wanders through Dublin, the microcosm of the universe, he goes to a public bath (Lotus-land) where he luxuriates in a narcotic-like torpor. At the funeral of Paddy Dignam (Elpenor), he is taken to the cemetery whose caretaker is John O'Connell (Hades). There he notices the statue of Parnell (the shade of Agamemnon) who, like his atavar, came to an unhappy end because of a woman. Aeolus' cave of the winds becomes a Dublin newspaper office; the Laestrygonian cannibals are found in a restaurant where Bloom is repelled by the people gorging themselves. Scylla and Charybdis are found in the National Library where Bloom escapes from the metaphysical and literary Scylla of dogma (Aristotle and Shakespeare's Stratford) and the Charybdis of mysticism (Plato and Elizabethan London). Joyce's Polyphemus is a drunken Irishman, violently anti-Semitic, who routs Bloom from Barney Kiernan's public house (the Cyclop's cave) by throwing things at him and by sicking his dog after him. This leads Bloom down to the beach where he sees an adolescent daydreamer of love, Gertie MacDowell (Nausicaa), about whom he has sordid and lewd thoughts. When Stephen Dedalus invites his friends out for a drink and a night on the town, they are led to Bella Cohen's brothel (Circe's house) where men are turned into beasts and where Dedalus and Bloom experience the phantasmagorical horror of seeing their submerged thoughts, fears, memories, dreams, and visions materialize and live before their eyes. This episode is called the *Walpurgis* Night or Pandemonium of *Ulysses*.

These are but a few obvious, and not-so-obvious parallels of Joyce's work with Homer's *Odyssey* without the multidimensional overlay of liteary and legendary allusions, of cross correspondences, of rhetorical devices. Joyce, to whom force and violence were repugnant, handles the slaying-of-the-suitors scene with considerable ingenuity. Bloom's victory over the suitors (that is, his suspicions, jealousies, fears) is a psychological one. He achieves a peace of mind (Ithaca) by ignoring his faithless Penelope and by falling asleep. Joyce is satisfied, says one critic, "to complete his modern *Odyssey* by showing how a modern Everyman without religious faith, without high philosophic principles or a highly cultivated humanism, without true friends or even a loyal family, can, by self-knowledge, prudence, humility, and resignation, regain his kingdom in Ithaca."

The epic hero of Kazantzakis, in contrast with the Leopold Bloom of James Joyce, was not one to be restricted to a square mile or so of Dublin, or by the unity of time, but he was to travel from Ithaca to Crete, Egypt, Africa, and south to the Antarctic region where he was to die. For his *Odyssey, A Modern Sequel* (1938, translated into English in 1958), Kazantzakis chose to give us a spacious and symbolic portrait of the post-Homeric life of Odysseus. It is a portrait of a restless, incurable wanderer in the tradition of Dante and Tennyson, a man questing for meaning in life, a rebel with a passion "to drink life to the lees, to follow knowledge like a sinking star." This modern Odysseus has a philosophical bent of mind that embraces Plato, Moses, Marx, and Yoga. Like Homer's hero, he is a man of action; and unlike his ancient prototype, he is a man of change and self-discovery who frees himself from the bonds of society to seek spiritual freedom and God through asceticism.

Disenchanted with Ithaca and Penelope, Kazantzakis' Odysseus sets out with a small band of men for further adventures. When he comes to Sparta he finds a fat, self-satisfied Menelaus, and a Helen who yearns for the excitement of another Paris. Together they run off to Crete where Helen will mate with a Dorian barbarian—there is no carnal bond between Odysseus and Helen—and will bear a child who will be the ancestor of a new Greek world, uniting the decaying Achaean civilization with the new blood of the Dorians. While on Crete, Odysseus helps the Dorians overthrow the old order and establish a new one with the local proletariat. His wanderings take him to Egypt where he again fights on the side of the revolutionaries to overthrow a tyrannical and decaying civilization. It is in Egypt that he begins his search for God. After escaping from an Egyptian prison with a handful of Egyptian riffraff, the scum of the earth, he treks with them to the wilderness where he will build a new city, a city which is a composite of Plato's Republic, Augustine's City of God, and a Marxian Utopia. Descending from a mountain from which he has received divine dispensation for a new Decalogue, he builds his city only to see it destroyed by a volcanic eruption during the ritual of its inauguration. Alone and in shock over the destruction of his creation, Odysseus abandons his desire to change the social and political order of the world. He now begins a new quest, a search for his true inner self. This leads him to the life of an ascetic, a holy man who is completely divorced from the social order. Ultimately, as Tiresias had predicted for him, he goes off to meet his death in the half-frozen seas in a skiff shaped like a coffin. There on a huge iceberg a peaceful death descends upon him. His quest is over; he has gained the freedom which he sought, death, and in death he has gained life in that he has merged into the divine essence of the world.

Aeneas and the Quest for a New Troy

I was a poet and I sang of that upright
son of Anchises who came from Troy after
proud Ilium was burned.

Dante—*Inferno*

The third greatest epic of classical antiquity, the *Aeneid*, although ostensibly the story of a Trojan who struggled valiantly to establish a new Troy on Italian shores, is more than a tale of the adventures of Aeneas; it is a testament to the "glory and destiny of his descendants." In short, the hero of the *Aeneid* is Rome. The work comes from the hand of Vergil, the poet who sang of shepherds and farmers (pp. 14f.), and who was to become the most outstanding poet in the Latin language. Maecenas, a patron of literature and the unofficial secretary for the advancement of Roman culture under Octavian (Emperor Augustus), brought this promising poet to the attention of Rome's new ruler who urged him to undertake writing the Latin epic he had been contemplating. Between 29 B.C. and his death in 19 B.C., Vergil labored over his creation, line by line, giving shape to the pageantry of Roman history, to the mission and destiny of Rome, and imparting a sense of optimism in the new era of leadership under Augustus. At the time of his death he was not satisfied with his work and ordered it destroyed. Augustus, however, countermanded the order and turned the manuscript over to two literary executors who published the work as it now stands.

Vergil modeled the *Aeneid* broadly on the *Iliad* and the *Odyssey*. "Arms and the man I sing," are his first words. The first six books on "the man" are his *Odyssey*, the story of Aeneas' struggles to make his way from Troy to the promised land; the second six books on "arms," are his *Iliad*, the battles of the Trojans to establish themselves on Italian soil. But why did Vergil use the Trojan cycle instead of a native Latin theme as the basis for his epic? Simply stated, whatever had been native had long been Hellenized or was unsuitable for epic treatment. Why did he not fabricate a new Achilles or Odysseus out of a legendary Greek hero? It would not have been politically appropriate since Rome had conquered Greece and a Greek would not have been acceptable as the prototype for the founder of the Roman nation. There was, in addition, a strong xenophobic sentiment among the Romans: they viewed the Greeks as clever scoundrels, thieves, wizards, actors, blackmailers, and double-talkers. The Greeks known to the Romans were very different from Homer's heroic figures or from the great men of the Classical Age, and even those had suffered denigration—Odysseus, for example—at the hands of later writers. A century after Vergil we hear the voice of a Roman blue-blood saying, "It's that the city has become Greek that I cannot bear." As for the Trojans, they had long since faded into the legendary past, ideal material for coining new legends. And of all the Trojans, Aeneas was the one Trojan for whom Homer had prophesied survival for himself and his descendants. In the *Iliad* we hear Poseidon say: "For Zeus has cursed the line of Priam and now Aeneas' might shall rule the Trojans, and his children's children who will be born of his seed." Further, a tradition was already in existence in early Latin literature connecting Aeneas and the Trojans and the founding of cities in Sicily and Italy; it was a tradition fostered by Hellenistic poets and genealogists who wished to curry favor with Roman political power which was then in ascendancy in the Mediterranean. But in spite of all the Greek legendary apparatus, the *Aeneid* and its crusading knight are transformed completely into symbols of Rome and Roman ideas: seriousness, loyalty, duty, piety, and patriotism. Above all, Vergil gives us an apocalyptic vision of Rome, not as a state to be known for its arts—that was reserved for the Greeks—but as a great civilizing power. This is best expressed by the shade of Anchises in the Underworld who gives his son a sense of the mission of Rome:

> Others, for so I can well believe, shall hammer forth more delicately a breathing likeness out of bronze, coax living faces from the marble, plead causes with more skill, plot with their gauge the movements in the sky, and tell the rising of the constellations. But you, Roman, must remember that you have to guide the nations by your authority, for this is to be your skill, to graft tradition onto peace, to show mercy to the conquered, and to wage war until the haughty are brought low.

Juno's Hostility.   The *Aeneid*, like its Homeric congeners, plunges *in medias res*, right into the middle of the story. Aeneas and his band of men who survived the holocaust of Troy have been wandering through the Mediterranean for seven years in search of the site on which to build a new Troy. Under Aeneas' leadership, twenty-one ships have just set sail from Sicily to Italy when Juno—Vergil, of course, uses Roman names of the gods—sets in motion a new disaster for the remnant of the Trojan people. Why is this goddess hostile to Aeneas and the Trojans? Juno favors the Phoenician city of Carthage, which is just then being built. She hopes that its destiny is to rule the world; but she has heard that the Trojans are destined to build a city which one day will overthrow Carthage. There are also historical reasons for Juno's anger: the judgment of Paris, which was an insult to her beauty; the descent of the Trojan line from an illegitimate son of Jupiter; and Trojan Ganymede displacing her daughter Hebe as cupbearer of the gods. Hence Juno has kept the Trojans from reaching their promised land during the past seven years. Now as the fleet comes into sight of Italy, Juno calls upon Aeolus, king of the winds, to stir up a fierce storm to scatter the Trojan ships. All would have been lost for Aeneas and his men had Neptune not been provoked by the sudden commotion of his waters. He orders the winds to depart, calms the seas, and helps free the ships which have been grounded on the sandbanks. Aeneas and seven of his ships make their way to the coast of Africa where they anchor. Aeneas sees to it that his men are provided with food and their morale bolstered; he himself is depressed and discouraged but he takes pains not to show it.

In the meantime, Aeneas' mother Venus lodges a complaint with Jupiter. Why are her son and the other Trojans suffering so? And what of the promise he had made that Aeneas' descendants would rule the seas and a mighty empire? Jupiter mollifies his daughter by assuring her that she shall see her son found the city of Lavinium. He goes on to prophesy the future history of Aeneas and Rome: victory in war over the confederacy of Italian armies, the building of Alba Longa by Aeneas' son Ascanius, the birth of the twin sons of Mars, Romulus and Remus, the founding of Rome by Romulus, victory by the Romans over Greece, and the coming of Augustus who will close the gates of war and bring peace upon the earth.

The Trojans at Carthage. On the following day, Aeneas and a companion set out to reconnoiter the land. He is met by Venus disguised as a huntress, and when he respectfully asks for information, she tells him that she is a Carthaginian and that the country is ruled by Phoenicians from the city of Tyre. She then recounts the story of how Dido, queen of Carthage, came to Africa. She had been the wife of Sychaeus, a wealthy landowner whom she loved deeply. Her brother Pygmalion, king of Tyre, killed Sychaeus for his money. Dido knew nothing of the murder until the ghost of her husband appeared and told her what had happened. He urged her to leave Tyre with a secret cache of gold and silver. Gathering others who hated the king, Dido fled to Africa where she was now busily engaged in building the city of Carthage. Venus also gives her son news of his missing ships and bids him to go on to Carthage. After revealing her divinity to Aeneas, she covers him and his comrade in a thick mist so that they can enter the city unobserved.

At Carthage, Aeneas is overwhelmed at the sight of bustling activity; everyone is industriously at work building a new city. In a temple under construction, he sees painted scenes of the Trojan War, a sight that moves him to tears. While he is absorbed in looking at the pictures, Dido enters surrounded by her entourage and accompanied by the Trojan captains who had been separated from Aeneas at sea. When Aeneas sees his lost shipmates, he is bursting with anxiety to embrace them, but he restrains himself prudently until he can be assured that the Carthaginians are friendly. Dido receives the Trojan captains graciously. After apologizing for the rough treatment given them when they were captured, she offers them her assistance and a place of refuge at Carthage. At that moment, Aeneas, seeing that the Carthaginians are friendly, bursts out of the cloud of invisibility and addresses the queen. Dido is struck with awe at the sudden sight of the handsome stranger—Venus has helped by improving his appearance—but when she recovers, she offers Aeneas provisions for his men and invites them to attend a banquet at the palace.

Aeneas sends his comrade back to the ships to fetch the men and his son Ascanius. (Vergil often calls Ascanius by his other name, Iulus.) Venus, however, is still an anxious mother; she fears that Juno may plot some new disaster for the Trojans. In order to make sure that her favorites will not be harmed, she plans to make Dido fall desperately and irrevocably in love with Aeneas. She turns to her son Cupid and tells him to assume the appearance of Ascanius so that when the Carthaginian queen embraces him at the banquet, he will inflame her with love for Aeneas. And so it comes about. At the banquet, Dido, with the disguised Cupid on her lap, fondles and kisses the boy she thinks is Aeneas' son, all the while falling deeper and deeper in love with the handsome stranger. She finds Aeneas so attractive that she cannot take her eyes off him. To keep him from leaving, she questions him about the Trojan War. Finally, she persuades him to tell the story of the fall of Troy and his seven years of wandering. Although it is painful for Aeneas to recall the sad events of his life, and although the hour is late, he complies with the queen's request.

Aeneas Tells of Troy's Downfall. Troy's man of destiny begins his story with the strategem which led to his city's downfall, the Wooden Horse: how the Greeks pretended to have given up the fight and how they sailed away leaving behind the engine of war with its cache of soldiers hidden within it; how Sinon, "with all the cunning of a Greek," deceived the Trojans into believing that the Wooden Horse was left behind to appease Minerva, and that once it was within the walls of the city, Troy would be invincible; how Laocoön warned his countrymen to beware of Greeks bearing gifts, and how Laocoön and his two sons were crushed to death by sea-serpents; and how, when Troy was asleep, Sinon signaled the Greek forces to return and let loose the soldiers hidden within the Horse. Aeneas then tells of what happened to him on that fateful night when the Greeks poured into the city. He had been asleep when the ghost of mangled Hector appeared to him in a dream and told him that the city was doomed and that its defense was no longer possible. The specter then advised Aeneas to flee and to find a new home for the Trojans and their gods. Aeneas awoke and rushed out to find the city in flames. He gathered about him a group of Trojans and attempted to stay the burning flood of Greek arms. To no avail. No matter how many of the enemy fell before them, more and more kept coming. Aeneas broke off the fight and rushed to Priam's palace, only to witness the blood-crazed son of Achilles, Pyrrhus (Neoptolemus), killing the aged king. This made Aeneas think of the safety of his own father, his wife Creusa, and his son Ascanius. As he was about to leave, he caught sight of Helen cowering at an altar in fear for her life. He was about to kill the cause of Troy's anguish when Venus appeared and dissuaded him by revealing the awesome sight of the gods fighting against the Trojans and helping in the destruction of the city. Troy was destined by the gods to fall!

Protected by Venus, Aeneas made his way through the flames and the fighting to his own home. His father Anchises refused to leave the city; he had lived long enough and did not wish to burden his son. Creusa begged Aeneas to let her and their son die with him. Just then several heaven-sent omens appeared and convinced them to flee the city. Aeneas placed his aged father on his shoulders—Anchises held in his hands the revered household gods, the Lares and Penates—and taking Ascanius by the hand he made his way out of the city. (fig. 109). Creusa was to follow right behind them, but in the confusion she became separated from her husband. A distracted Aeneas rushed back into the burning city to find his wife. Suddenly, her ghost appeared before him; she was no longer among the living. Creusa told her husband that her death was part of the divine plan; she was fated to die at Troy, but he was to go on as an exile to a western land where a new kingdom and a new wife awaited him. Her last words for him were to care for their child. A grief-stricken Aeneas made his way back to the spot where he had left his father and son. He found gathered there a group of Trojan men, women, and children, all ready and eager to follow him to whatever land he chose as their new home.

Figure 109.   Bernini. Aeneas fleeing Troy with Anchises and Ascanius.
Anchises holds the household gods in his hands. *Marble group, 1619. Borghese
Gallery, Rome. (Alinari)*

The Departure from Troy. By the following summer Aeneas and his followers had built a fleet of ships and set out to find their promised land. Their first landfall was Thrace where a site was chosen on which a new Troy was to rise. But as he was preparing to offer a sacrifice to Venus and the other gods, Aeneas pulled up some myrtle bushes from the ground to garland the altar. To his horror, the broken twigs began to drip blood and a moan was heard coming from the earth. It was the voice of his kinsman Polydorus, who had been murdered by the king of Thrace (p. 420), asking why his grave was being disturbed. In fear of founding a city in an accursed land, the Trojans gave Polydorus a new burial and quickly departed.

The next port of call was the island of Delos where the oracle of Apollo was consulted. A voice came from the shrine which gave an ambiguous response: "Seek your ancient mother; there the race of Aeneas shall live and bring all the other nations under their sway." Anchises interpreted the oracle to mean the island of Crete since one of Troy's ancestors and the goddess Cybele were said to have come from that ancient land. But Crete also proved to be a false lead. The Trojans set to work building their city only to be afflicted by a devastating plague and famine. Anchises suggested to his son that he get further advice from Apollo, but on that night the household-gods appeared to Aeneas in a dream. They had been sent by Apollo to tell him that the god had not meant Crete but Hesperia (Italy) since Dardanus, the founder of the Trojan line, had come from this western land. Anchises confirmed the dream and recalled that Cassandra had prophesied that Italy would be the future realm of the Trojans.

The Harpies. Once more the Trojans set sail. A storm drove them to the Strophades, the island home of the Harpies in the Ionian Sea. Exhausted from days on the turbulent waters, the Trojans slaughtered some cattle they found on the island and prepared for a feast. Just then the Harpies swooped down screeching, and what they did not seize in their claws they befouled with their filth and stench. Aeneas called upon his men to fight off these horrible winged creatures, but the monstrous intruders were too quick and their feathers protected them as if they had been clad in armor. One of the Harpies, Celaeno by name, cursed them for having slaughtered their cattle and prophesied that they would reach Italy, but that they would not build the walls of their city until hunger forced them to eat their tables. The Trojans wasted no time in raising sail and putting to sea again. They made their way up the western coast of Greece sailing past several islands, among them Ithaca, "the land that had nourished savage Ulysses." After pausing at Actium to perform sacrifices and to hold games, Aeneas and his countrymen continued their northward course past Phaeacia, Alcinous' island home, until they sighted Epirus and the city of Buthrotum.

Helenus and Andromache. At Buthrotum, the Trojans heard a remarkable tale; they could scarcely believe what they heard. Helenus, the prophetic son of Priam (p. 125), was the king of this Greek kingdom. He had been captured by Achilles' son Pyrrhus and brought to Epirus where he had been accepted by the Greeks as their ruler when Pyrrhus died. That was not all. Andromache, Hector's wife, had been taken by Pyrrhus as part of the division of the spoils and had been forced to marry her conqueror. She was later given in marriage to her brother-in-law Helenus, and thus she was reunited with the Trojan line. When Aeneas came upon her, she was tearfully offering sacrifices to the shade of her first love, Hector. After recovering from the shock of seeing Aeneas, she told him the story of her life after the fall of Troy. Because of Pyrrhus' passion for Hermione, the daughter of Helen and Menelaus, he soon abandoned her to Helenus. Orestes, who had been married to Hermione, was insane with jealousy and stabbed Pyrrhus to death at his household altar. In this way Helenus became king of Epirus and she his wife and queen. After Andromache had finished her story, Aeneas was joined by Helenus who received his kinsman with joy. After some days of rest and hospitality, Aeneas was anxious to set out again. He asked Helenus to use his prophetic powers to interpret the will of Apollo and to tell him how to avoid more calamities. Helenus reassured him that he was destined by the powers above to reach Italy, but that his voyage there would be a long one. He also advised him to avoid certain perils: Scylla and Charybdis for one, and the anger of Juno for another. And when Aeneas was to reach the shores of Italy, he was to go to the Sibyl at Cumae (p. 128) who would give him further information about what the future would bring.

The Cyclopes Again. Armed with detailed instructions from Helenus and loaded with gifts, Aeneas and his fellow-Trojans took to their ships. They proceeded on a course which soon took them within sight of the southeastern coast of Italy. To have landed on the Italian coast at this point would have meant traversing the Straits of Messina and the dangers of Scylla and Charybdis. With Helenus' advice in mind, Aeneas plotted a western course which would take his ships around the coast of Sicily. A landing on the island placed them near Mount Etna and the home of the Cyclopes. The Trojans were terrified by the sight of Etna belching fire, smoke, and hot lava. On the following morning a gaunt stranger was seen rushing out of the woods towards them. It was Achaemenides, a Greek who had been trapped along with Ulysses in Polyphemus' cave. He had been left behind by his comrades when, after gouging out the eye of the Cyclops, they had rushed pell-mell down to their ship. Achaemenides begged the Trojans to take him off the island; he had been living on berries and roots for three months, and death at their hands would be better than being eaten alive by the Cyclopes. As he spoke, they saw Polyphemus coming down the mountainside to wash his bleeding eye socket in the sea. The Trojans hastened to their ships, taking Achaemenides along with them. Polyphemus heard the sound of their oars, headed towards them, and raised a fearful shout. The other Cyclopes rushed down to the shore, a sight that so frightened the Trojans that they frantically threw on as much sail as they could. Once clear of the threat of danger, they made for Drepanum in western Sicily. It was here that Anchises died, another blow for which Aeneas was not prepared. And it was from Drepanum that Aeneas sailed with his twenty-one ships when he ran into the storm inspired by Juno which drove him onto the coast of North Africa near Carthage.

Dido and Aeneas. This concludes Aeneas' account of his adventures. Vergil now gives over the stage—book four of the *Aeneid*—to the queen of Carthage who gives a stunning performance of the pathological effects of love and passion. Dido is utterly consumed with love for the handsome and noble stranger. She confides to her sister Anna that she is being racked by her emotions, but that she is resolved to remain true to the vow she made after her husband's murder: she would remain celibate, she would never give her love to another man. Anna reminds her sister that Carthage is surrounded by enemies and that Aeneas' coming was more than fortuitous; a marriage with the Trojan hero would help the city survive and win glory for it. Anna's words give Dido hope and weaken her already wavering resolve to quench "the old fire" which Aeneas has revived. Deeper and deeper the flames of love eat into Dido. In the presence of her beloved she is tongue-tied; she hangs breathless on his every word. And when he is out of her sight she still hears his voice and feels his presence. The queen neglects the needs of the city; all building activity ceases as does the military training of the young men.

Juno, alarmed at seeing Dido subverted by her love for the Trojan hero, approaches Venus with a proposal: let Dido and Aeneas marry—Carthage and its inhabitants will serve as a dowry—and the two goddesses shall jointly share in ruling the city. Venus sees in the proposal Juno's intention to keep Aeneas from reaching the land destined for him. She suggests that Jupiter be consulted. Juno parries the suggestion and lays a plan whereby the two lovers will be isolated and then joined in a "marriage." On the following morning, Aeneas and Dido leave the city with an entourage gaily decked out for a day of hunting. It is not long before the sky becomes threatening and a rainstorm sends everyone scurrying for shelter. Dido and Aeneas are separated from the others and make their way to a cave where, witnessed only by the forces of nature, they consummate their love:

> Primeval Earth and Juno, Mistress of the Marriage, gave their sign. The sky connived at the union; the lightning flared; on their mountain-peaks nymphs cried their joy. On that day were sown the seeds of suffering and death. Henceforward Dido cared no more for appearances or her good name, and ceased to take any thought for secrecy in her love. She called it a marriage; she used this word to screen her sin.

The goddess Rumor, ever-swift and fearful, spreads both fact and fiction about Dido and Aeneas: the two are lovers, and so lost are they in their shameful passion that royal duties are being neglected. When Rumor pours this gossip into the ear of Iarbas, king of a neighboring realm and a rejected suitor of Dido, he prays to his father Jupiter and complains of mistreatment and injustice. Jupiter hears his son and acts. He sends Mercury to Aeneas with a message: it was not for this that Venus saved him twice from his Greek enemies; he has a destiny to fulfill in Italy and is to be the founder of a line of rulers who will subject the earth to the rule of law; he must set sail for Italy. Mercury wings his way to Carthage where he finds Aeneas dressed like a Carthaginian and supervising the construction of the city. Mercury delivers Jupiter's message and reminds him forcefully that he has forgotten his destiny. The effect on Aeneas is startling. He gives word to his men to fit out the fleet for an immediate departure. But how to tell Dido? He chooses to say nothing.

"But who can ever deceive a lover?" Intuitively Dido divines what is happening and when Rumor brings her the news that the Trojan fleet is being readied to leave, she loses all control of herself. Raging like a Maenad celebrating the rites of Bacchus, she flies wildly about Carthage until at last she confronts Aeneas. She runs through a gamut of emotions and pleas: tears, regard for their love, pleas for pity, reproaches for his ingratitude, threats of suicide. She turns to blaming him for having incurred the enmity of the neighboring Africans and her own people, for having lost her honor and good name, for leaving her to face death at the hands of her enemies. The concluding appeal is for him to stay long enough to give her a son whose likeness will remind her of him.

Aeneas is torn between his feelings for Dido and his call to duty. His reply is brief. He is grateful for all that Dido has done for him and he will always remember her. As for their relationship, he insists that he never had a formal marriage in mind. Further, he has been divinely commanded to go to Italy, and Italy must dominate his feelings. This cool and rationalized response hardly comforts Dido. Now completely out of control, she pours out a bitter stream of insults, threats, and ill wishes. She is so emotionally distraught that she cannot continue. She runs off to fall in a dead faint.

"Ah, shameless love, to what lengths do you not force the human heart to go?" Dido, now having lost all sense of pride and self-respect, sends her sister Anna to Aeneas time and again to beg him to delay his departure. All appeals are in vain. Though his heart is touched and tears roll down his cheeks, Aeneas stands firm in his determination to leave. Dido soon sees that all is lost; she is now totally deranged. She is overcome by delusions and hallucinations and nightmares—all point the way to death. In this highly disturbed state of mind she plans her suicide. Assuming an appearance of calm determination, Dido tells her sister that she is working on the means to expunge her love for Aeneas through magic. Anna, innocent of Dido's true intention, is prevailed upon to build a huge pyre on which she places Aeneas' clothes, his armor, and the bridal bed which the two lovers shared. Meanwhile, Mercury makes another call on Aeneas to urge his departure and to caution him on the dangers that lurk in Carthage as long as he remains there. "Woman is ever a thing of changing moods," he says and flies off. Aeneas is galvanized into action; he gives orders to his men to cast off.

At dawn of the following morning, Dido, after a sleepless night, sights the Trojan fleet at sea and under full sail. She raves insanely and calls upon the gods in heaven and underneath the earth to bring Aeneas to an untimely death. She prays further for an avenger to arise from her bones, one who would pursue with fire and sword all the descendants of Aeneas for all time to come. (This prayer is a prophetic pronouncement of Hannibal and the Punic Wars between Rome and Carthage.) In Vergil's words Dido,

> bewildered and maddened by her great determination, rolling her bloodshot eyes, her quivering cheeks stained with fiery streams, and pale with the shadow of death, bursts the door of the inner palace, and frantically climbs the high funeral pyre, and unsheaths the Trojan sword, a gift given for far different purposes.

After kissing the bridal bed, she plunges the sword into her breast. The wailing and screams of the women in the palace bring Anna to the room where Dido lies dying. Desperately she tries to stem the streams of blood flowing from the deep wound. To no effect. Finally, Juno, out of pity for Dido's agony, sends her messenger Iris to release the soul of the tortured woman. Iris cuts a lock of Dido's hair as an offering to the god of the Underworld, and at once all warmth leaves her body and she dies.

En Route to Italy. On the high seas and en route to Italy, Aeneas looks back to Carthage and sees the sky aglow from the flames of Dido's funeral pyre. The Trojans of course can only surmise what has happened. All too soon the skies become overcast and a squall threatens the fleet. Palinurus, the helmsman, sees that the ships cannot hold their course for Italy and suggests putting in at Sicily. Once more the Trojans are hospitably received by the king of the island. It has been a year since Anchises had died and was buried there. Aeneas proclaims a celebration on the anniversary of his father's death. Sacrifices are performed with attending favorable omens. Nine days later, under a cloudless sky, athletic games in honor of Anchises are held by Trojans and Sicilians.

Juno, meanwhile, was planning more mischief for the man of destiny. Recognizing that the Trojan women are weary to the bone from traveling and enduring constant hardships, she sends Iris into their midst disguised as a Trojan woman of an illustrious family. Iris goads the other women into refusing to go on; Sicily is a good enough site for their new city. She picks up a torch and flings it at one of the ships. When she is recognized as a divinity, she soars into the heavens, leaving a giant rainbow in her wake. The women are stirred by this sight to imitate the goddess; they rush to throw torches at the ships. When Aeneas rushes to the scene, he is dismayed at what he sees. All efforts to extinguish the flames are useless until, in answer to Aeneas' prayer, Jupiter produces a sudden downpour of rain and saves all but four of the ships from being destroyed.

Palinurus. Italy at Last. Aeneas now begins to have doubts whether to proceed to Italy or whether to remain in Sicily. An old and faithful seer, Nautes, suggests to Aeneas that he leave behind in Sicily those who are feeble and unwilling to go on and to sail for Italy with the most hardy. That night, while Aeneas is anxiously pondering the best course to follow, Anchises appears to him in a vision and bids him to follow Nautes' advice. He also urges his son to visit him in Elysium when he reaches the shores of Italy; the Sibyl will guide him to the Underworld. The next day, Aeneas selects the site for the colony of Trojans who will settle in Sicily; the city will be called Acesta in honor of King Acestes who has been so kind to them. After nine days of sacrifices and feasting, Aeneas sets out for Italy with the remainder of his company. Venus, however, is still concerned over the safety of her son, ever fearing the hostility of Juno. She approaches Neptune and seeks a guarantee from him that all will go well for Aeneas and his ships. The god of the sea agrees but on condition that one Trojan life be given to him. Neptune calms the seas and Aeneas orders full sail for the ships. Palinurus sets a course for Italy, but it is to be Palinurus whom Neptune selects as his victim. The loyal helmsman is overcome by Somnus, the god of sleep, and is flung overboard. In spite of the loss of Palinurus, the ships continue on course until the sound of the surf beating on the Siren's rocks is heard. Aeneas then discovers his ship drifting aimlessly. He takes the helm and leads the ships to a landing at Cumae. At long last, the Trojans have arrived at the shores of Italy.

Aeneas in the Underworld. The trip from Carthage to Sicily and Cumae is an interlude which introduces another main scene: Aeneas' visit to the Underworld—book six of the *Aeneid*. Unlike Homer, Vergil does not use the visit to exalt an individual engaged in a unique adventure, but rather to give us a pageant of the past and future, a gallery of national history, a procession of the legendary and historic figures of Rome, all leading to a vision of a new golden age and a universal empire. When Aeneas emerges from this experience, he has lost his ambivalence and uncertainty; he is a self-assured leader, a conscious instrument of destiny.

On shore at Cumae, while the Trojans joyfully set about exploring the environs of this new land, Aeneas makes his way to the home of the Sibyl. No sooner does he make himself known than the priestess of Apollo is possessed by the god, and in her frenzy she prophesies more afflictions for the Trojans—war and Juno's continued antagonism—because of another foreign bride (that is, Aeneas' future wife; Helen was the other foreign bride). When the Sibyl comes to herself, Aeneas implores her to lead him to the Underworld where his father will reveal to him his future and that of his descendants. She agrees but tells him that he first has to find a golden bough in the forest which will serve as an offering to Proserpine. With Venus' help he finds the magic bough, his passport to the Underworld, and all is ready for the great descent.

Proper sacrifices having been made to the infernal goddesses, Proserpine, Hecate and the Furies, Aeneas and the Sibyl plunge into the depths of a hellmouth near the Stygian lake of Avernus. There at the entrance of the dismal land of the dead, lie the horrible spirits that afflict mankind: Grief, Avenging Care, Diseases, Old Age, Fear, Hunger, Toil and Poverty, Death and Sleep, War, and False Dreams. There too are the iron beds of the Furies and of insane Strife; and there too are the monstrous hybrid creatures: Centaurs, half-human Scyllas, hundred-handed Briareus, the hissing Hydra and the fire-breathing Chimaera, Gorgons, Harpies, and triple-bodied Geryon. Aeneas and the Sibyl make their way to the banks of the Acheron where Charon the ferryman is loading his skiff with the souls of the dead. He accepts only those souls for passage across the river Styx whose bodies have received a ritual burial; those who have not, will have to wander on the banks of the infernal river for a hundred years before he will accept them. At that moment, Aeneas sees the shade of his faithful helmsman Palinurus who met his death by drowning. Palinurus begs to be allowed to accompany them across the river Styx. The plea is rejected. The Sibyl assures Aeneas that his comrade's body will be found on the shore and will not only be given a ritual burial and a tomb, but that the spot where he was found will be known as Cape Palinurus.

When Charon sights Aeneas, living and armed, he angrily demands to know what right he has to be in the land of the dead. The Sibyl explains the hero's mission and produces the golden bough. Without another word the squalid old man ferries them across the infernal river. In Hades proper they hear Cerberus barking and howling from his three throats. The Sibyl tosses the menacing hellhound a drugged cake that soon puts him to sleep. The first to meet the two voyagers are the souls of infants who died before their time. Near them are those who died because of false accusations. Minos reviews the account of their lives and the charges made against them. Then come the souls of those who hated life and took their own lives; and not far from them in the Fields of Mourning wander these who died because of unrequited love, among them Phaedra, Procris and Laodamia. Out of the gloom, Aeneas sees the soul of Dido with her self-afflicted wound still fresh upon her. Tearfully, Aeneas begs for her forgiveness and tries to explain that the decrees of the gods forced him to abandon her. Dido says not a word; she turns on her heel and walks off to join the shade of her husband Sychaeus.

Proceeding through the gloom, Aeneas and his guide come to the souls of the heroes who died in battle. The Trojans excitedly crowd around him, the Greeks, on the other hand, tremble when they see their former enemy. Aeneas converses with Deïphobus who tells him how he was betrayed by Helen and murdered by Menelaus. Aeneas is eager to hear more from his old comrades, but the Sibyl hurries him away; time is getting short and he must not forget the purpose of his visit. They come to a fork in the road (p. 237); the path to the right leads to Elysium where he will find the soul of his father; the one to the left leads to Tartarus, the city of the damned. Aeneas looks back and sees the triple walls of Tartarus surrounded by the fiery river of Phlegethon, and sitting at a gate of adamant he spies Tisiphone, one of the avenging Furies. From within come groans, the crack of whips, the creaking of iron, and the clanking of chains. Terror-stricken, Aeneas asks his guide what kind of crimes could produce these horrible sounds. The Sibyl replies that Tartarus is ruled by Rhadamanthys with an iron hand. He forces the souls to confess their crimes done in life which the perpetrators foolishly thought could be concealed. Tisiphone scourges them mercilessly with her whip of knotted serpents and then turns them over to her sister Furies. The Sibyl continues her description of the pit of hell and tells of some of the legendary figures who are eternally punished there, among them Salmoneus, Tityus, Ixion, Sisyphus, and Tantalus. She then outlines the kind of crimes that send souls to Tartarus for punishment: hatred for a brother, striking a parent, fraud, greed, adultery, treason, perversion of laws. The Sibyl concludes her description with these words: "No, not even if I had a hundred tongues and a hundred mouths and a voice of iron, could I detail all the types of crimes, nor could I run through all the names of the punishments for them."

Aeneas is urged to be on his way to Elysium. The Trojan hero sprinkles water on his body in a rite of purification and deposits the golden bough in fulfillment of his obligations to the goddess Proserpine. They now enter Elysium, the land of joy, the happy groves and the homes of the blessed. Aeneas observes some happy souls engaged in the sport of wrestling, others are dancing or singing. Orpheus is there playing his lyre. There too are the souls of the founders of Troy, patriots who fought for their fatherland, uncorrupted priests, noble poets, inventors who benefited mankind. Aeneas is directed by Musaeus, the first bard, to his father. He comes upon Anchises who happens to be reviewing the future character and deeds of his descendants who one day will ascend to the world above. Anchises greets his son with deep affection. Aeneas questions him about a group of souls who are gathered at the river Lethe. His father tells him that they are the souls who will take on a body for a second time, but first they have to drink of the river of forgetfulness. Aeneas cannot understand why souls living in Elysium would want to return to the world of dreary matter. Anchises proceeds to give his son a philosophic explanation of the nature of the soul and the doctrine of transmigration of souls. It includes a description of how souls are purged of their sins over a period of one thousand years, and how they are brought to the river Lethe prior to their reincarnation so that the memory of their former existence will be effaced.

Anchises next reveals to Aeneas the souls of his descendants and the great future in store for them. Outstanding among these are Silvius, his son by his future Italian wife Lavinia; he will be a king and a father of kings-to-be. He points out the soul of Romulus, the founder of Rome, and then says:

> Now . . . look at that family, your own true Romans. For there is Caesar, and all the line of Iulus, who are destined to reach the brilliant height of Heaven. And there in very truth is he whom you have often heard prophesied, Augustus Caesar, son of the Deified [Julius Caesar], and founder of golden centuries once more in Latium, in those same lands where once Saturn reigned; he shall extend our dominion beyond the Garamantians [interior of Africa] and the Indians in a region which lies outside the path of the constellations, outside the track of the year and of the sun, where Atlas the Heaven-bearer holds on his shoulder the turning sphere, inset with blazing stars . . . Can we now hesitate to assert our valor by our deeds? Can any fear now prevent us from taking our stand on Italy's soil?

Anchises follows this glowing revelation with a panoramic survey of five centuries of key historic figures, both the famous and the infamous, of kings and consuls, of generals and politicians. Last of all is seen the soul of Marcellus, Augustus' nephew, whom the emperor had designated as his successor but who had died prematurely at the age of twenty. Anchises delivers a tender and tearful eulogy on the youthful soul. (Augustus' sister Octavia is said to have fainted when Vergil gave a reading of this portion of the epic). With this, Anchises concludes his review and Aeneas ascends with the Sibyl to the upper world through the Gates of Sleep. He rejoins his men and gives orders to up anchor and to sail for Latium.

The Promised Land. "A greater sequence of events comes before me; I now attempt a greater enterprise," says Vergil as he opens the second half of the *Aeneid*. This will be Vergil's *Iliad*, and for the poet, it is a greater enterprise than the first half since Aeneas' wars in Italy are intimately involved in the founding of Rome. After Aeneas leaves Cumae and heads north towards Latium, a favoring wind sent by Neptune sends the fleet past Circe's land where the Trojans hear the howls of the men whom the enchantress has transformed into animals. At dawn, the Tiber is sighted and the order is given for the fleet to head into the mouth of the river and to make a landing. The promised land at last, but it is already rules over by King Latinus, son of Faunus (p. 216), and his wife Amata. It so happens that Latinus is old and has no male heir; his daughter Lavinia, however, is eagerly sought after by the neighboring princes. Although Amata favors Turnus, the powerful king of the Rutilians, as a husband for her daughter, Latinus opposes the match because of various portents and an oracle he has received from his father. The latter has come to him in a dream, indicating that Lavinia is destined to marry a stranger and that their descendants will bring eternal glory to his name. By the time Aeneas lands, Rumor has spread the story of the oracle throughout the land.

The Fulfillment of the Prophecy. The Trojans beach their ships and satisfy their hunger by preparing flat mealcakes and placing on them whatever fruits they can forage from the countryside. Seeing the men eat the cakes, Ascanius jokingly says, "We are even eating our tables." This innocent remark is the fulfillment of the prophecy made by the Harpy Celaeno. Now convinced that this is truly the land of destiny, Aeneas sends Ascanius and a number of men as envoys to King Latinus to ask for friendship and alliance. There is mutual admiration on both sides; Latinus has in mind that the leader of the Trojans may be the very stranger prophesied by the oracle. He is most cordial to the Trojans; he tells them of the fateful oracle and immediately offers the hand of his daughter Lavinia in marriage to Aeneas. The envoys are sent away loaded with rich gifts and an invitation to Aeneas that he come in person so that the king can welcome him appropriately.

Allecto Stirs up Conflict. Juno is unhappy about the prosperous state of affairs for the man of destiny. Even though she cannot change the will of heaven, she is determined to delay the success of Aeneas' undertaking. The goddess summons one of the Furies from the Underworld, Allecto (or Alecto), who delights in stirring up war and violence, and orders her to do her hellish work. Taking a snake from her viperine coiffure, Allecto thrusts it under Amata's clothing. When the old woman feels the effects of snake's venom, she rages and runs wild through the city stirring up a frenzy among the other women. Allecto turns her attention to Turnus, the suitor Latinus has rejected, and visits him in a nightmare. He is so frightened that he bolts from his bed, shouts for his arms, and calls the Rutilians to defend Italy. The Fury still has more work to do. When she sees Ascanius hunting, she puts his dogs on the scent of a tame stag, the favorite of Silvia, daughter of Latinus' herdsman. Ascanius' arrow wounds the stag which has only enough strength left to limp home and die at Silvia's feet. The girl cries for help; the neighboring herdsmen rush for their weapons and attack the hunting party, only to be repelled by the Trojans who spring to Ascanius' help. Blood flows on both sides. Allecto has done her work well and Juno sends her back to the Underworld.

War Between the Trojans and the Latins. Hysteria for a war against the Trojans mounts. Latinus as chief magistrate is urged to perform the sacred rite of opening the gates of the temple of Janus as a signal for the formal declaration of war. He resists and ultimately is forced to abdicate as the leader of his people. Juno, however, comes down from the sky and with her own hands bursts open the gates of war; immediately the whole country is aflame with warfever. A roster of Italian forces is given. Among the many Latin allies is Mezentius, the Etruscan tyrant in exile, and his son Lausus, a young man of nobler character than his father. At the head of the confedereacy is Turnus, noble, proud and very volatile. This chief of the Rutilians wears a helmet crowned with a fire-breathing Chimaera which belches flames and smoke in proportion to the heat of the battle. Also present is Camilla, Amazon-like, a huntress and warrior in the service of the goddess Diana. She came by her unusual profession in the following way. When her royal father was expelled and pursued by his subjects, he tied his infant daughter to a spear and hurled her across a river swollen by rains. He himself then swam after her, and upon reaching the opposite bank, he found the child miraculously safe and uninjured. Camilla was suckled by mares and other wild animals, and from an early age was taught how to use the weapons of the hunt and of war. Devoted to Diana, she would have nothing to do with men or marriage.

Alliance with Evander. With this array of forces against Aeneas and his Trojans, help comes in the form of advice from the river-god Tibernius. He appears to Aeneas in a dream and advises him to seek an alliance with Evander, the aged king of the Arcadians, who has long been at war with Turnus and the Rutilians. When he awakes he sees the portent predicted by Tibernius—a sow with a litter of thirty young—a sign that Ascanius will found the city of Alba Longa thirty years hence. Aeneas sails up the Tiber to Pallanteum, Evander's town of some scattered huts but destined to be the future site of Rome. Evander and his son Pallas accord the Trojan leader a friendly reception. After identifying himself, Aeneas reminds Evander that they are distantly related. The old king peers closely at Aeneas and then sees his resemblance to Anchises whom he had met some time ago. An alliance is readily agreed on and Aeneas is invited to participate in a local festival in honor of Hercules. Afterwards, Evander gives his guest a guided tour of the site on which the city of Rome will later rise. He points to the sacred monuments of the past and to places that will become famous landmarks when Rome itself becomes famous. That night, while Aeneas sleeps in the rude hut which is Evander's palace, Venus moves to arm her son for the coming battles. She approaches her husband Vulcan and wins over the smithy-god with kisses, caresses, and love-making. Vulcan rushes off to Sicily and Mount Etna where the Cyclopes have their forges. He finds his Cyclopean smiths busily engaged in fashioning a thunderbolt for Jupiter, a chariot for Mars, and a piece of armor for Minerva. Vulcan orders them to lay aside their present projects and to produce a new suit of armor for Venus' son.

The next day, Evander and Aeneas discuss their alliance. Evander knows that his armed forces are too slim to give material support to the Trojans. He suggests that Aeneas look to the powerful Etruscans who have revolted against Mezentius and sent him fleeing to a sanctuary with Turnus. The Trojan hero stands a good chance because there is an oracle which anticipates a foreign leader for the Etruscan armies. Accompanied by Pallas, Aeneas sets off for Etruria, and as they are about to reach the Etruscan encampment, Venus appears with the new suit of armor which Vulcan had produced in a night's work. There is also a marvelous shield decorated with scenes of the future history of Rome: the she-wolf mothering the twins Romulus and Remus, the rape of the Sabine women, the alliance of the Sabines and the Romans, the siege of Rome by the Etruscans under Lars Porsena, treasonous Catiline in Tartarus, Cato in Elysium, the Battle of Actium and the defeat of Antony and Cleopatra, the triumph of Augustus. Aeneas proudly lifts the shield, the glory and the destiny of his descendants, onto his shoulder.

Turnus Attacks the Trojan Camp. While Aeneas is away enlisting the support of the Etruscans, Juno incites Turnus to launch a surprise attack on the Trojan camp. He assembles his Rutilians and attacks, only to find his adversaries deeply entrenched behind a protective stockade. Frustrated by the unwillingness of the Trojans to meet him on an open field, Turnus turns to their ships and sets them afire. But divine help is at hand. The ships have been constructed of wood sacred to Cybele, and by an appeal to Jupiter the Great Mother goddess sees to it that the ships are turned into nymphs and that the flames are extinguished. The sight of this miracle terrifies and disheartens the Latin forces. Turnus bolsters the morale of his men and orders a siege of the Trojan encampment.

Nisus and Euryalus. Anxiety overcomes the Trojans. How can they meet the new threat? How can they warn Aeneas of the present danger? Nisus and Euryalus, adventurous comrades-in arms, volunteer to make their way through the enemy lines and to get word to Aeneas. They get the approval and admiration of their commanders and are promised rewards for the success of their mission. Youthful Euryalus has only one favor to ask: not to distress his aged mother by letting her know that he is engaged in a dangerous mission. Concealed by the darkness of a moonless night, Nisus and Euryalus cautiously creep into the enemy's camp, and finding no one on watch, they decide to take a toll of the sleeping men before continuing on their way. They go through the ranks killing as many as they can without alerting the others. As they make their way out of the camp, Euryalus cannot resist taking a beautiful white-plumed helmet as part of his booty. The helmet proves their undoing. The two Trojans are surprised by an approaching cavalry unit; the white plumes betray their presence. Nisus and Euryalus dash into the forest for safety. Euryalus loses his way and falls into the hands of the enemy. Nisus, heedless of his own safety, retraces his steps, attacks his friend's captors and kills some of them, including the leader of the unit. In revenge, Euryalus is slaughtered before Nisus' eyes. Insane and ignoring the impossible odds against him, Nisus charges into the body of men and invites his own death. When the dead are brought into camp, Turnus impales their heads on pikes and displays them to the horrified Trojans. Euryalus' mother is so stricken with grief that she has to be restrained from leaping from the defensive wall into the thick of the enemy. Turnus now redoubles his attack on the Trojan defenses. When some Trojans recklessly open the gates of their fortification to meet the Rutilians head on the slaughter is horrendous. With difficulty the gates are closed, entrapping Turnus within the camp. The Rutilian chief narrowly escapes death by diving, armor and all, from the battlements into the Tiber.

The Death of Pallas.   Jupiter, who is unhappy to see the Trojans and the Italians fighting each other, convenes the gods on Mount Olympus and asks them to put an end to the dissension. Venus and Juno debate their causes, each blaming the other and causing the gods to take sides. Jupiter decides to remain neutral and leaves the settlement of the dispute to the Fates. The bloody battle is renewed. Meanwhile, Aeneas, having formed an alliance with the Etruscans, is on his way to relieve his garrison with a force of thirty ships. On the way he is met by the Trojan ships that had been transformed into nymphs of the sea. One of the nymphs informs him of the desperate situation of his Trojans and helps Aeneas' ship speed on its way by a tremendous thrust of her hand. By daybreak the relief force is in sight of the beleaguered camp. In a strategic move, Turnus diverts his men from the field of battle in an attempt to prevent Aeneas and his men from landing on the beach. Desperate fighting takes place. Pallas, Evander's young son, bravely rallies his retreating forces. On the opposing side, Mezentius' son Lausus is equally heroic in spurring on his men. And when the two young men are about to confront each other, Turnus comes thundering in his war chariot and compels Lausus to retire while he takes on Pallas. It is an unequal match. Although Pallas fights bravely, Turnus kills the youth with a spear thrust through his heart. In a noble gesture, the Rutilian prince allows Pallas' friends to carry his body off the field; the only spoil he takes is Pallas' massive sword belt. It turns out to be a fateful trophy.

Aeneas Kills Lausus and Mezentius.   The news of Pallas' death turns Aeneas in a raging warrior; he is pitiless, and pitiless is the force of his arm in battle. Juno fears for the safety of her favorite, and with Jupiter's begrudging help, she has Turnus pursue a phantom which he believes to be Aeneas. When he realizes that he has been tricked, he is so chagrined and humiliated that he would have committed suicide, had not Juno prevented him from doing so. While Turnus is absent from the battlefield, another fierce warrior takes his place, Mezentius, the deposed king of Etruria. Mezentius boasts to his son Lausus that he will soon be wearing Aeneas' armor. The two meet in combat, and in the exchange Mezentius is wounded in the groin and is forced to give ground. Lausus bravely covers his father's retreat, but he is no match for Aeneas. The youth persists in his insane attack until Aeneas buries his sword deep in Lausus' belly. The Trojan prince is filled with pity for the young man who was so loyal to his father. Aeneas, however, has no such compassion for Mezentius. The cruel Etruscan hears the cries of grief that accompany the death of his son and is touched to the quick. Wounded though he is, he mounts his horse and gallops back to renew his fight with Aeneas. He hurls spear after spear at his adversary, but because of his weakened condition they have little effect. Aeneas then takes careful aim and hurls a spear that strikes Mezentius' horse in the head. The horse rears and throws Mezentius to the ground where he is pinned down by the animal as it rolls over him. Knowing his end is near, the deposed tyrant begs to have his body spared the fury of his own people and to be buried with his son Lausus. Aeneas delivers the *coup de grâce* by plunging his sword into Mezentius' throat.

A Truce.   After the furious pace of this battle, there is a pause. Aeneas erects a war trophy made of Mezentius' arms and proposes an attack on the Latin stronghold of Laurentum, Latinus' city. With a military escort of one thousand men, Pallas' body is sent back to Evander who in his grief calls for his own death and vengeance upon Turnus. Emissaries appear before Aeneas and ask for twelve days of truce so that the dead can be buried. The Trojan prince readily grants the request. He goes further and says that he would be willing to end the war which was not of his making. There is a clear feeling on the part of some of the nobles of Laurentum that the time has come to conclude an alliance with the Trojans. Smoke rises from the funeral pyres as both sides perform the ceremonial rites for those fallen in battle.

The Death of Camilla.   When word comes from Diomedes—the old enemy of the Trojans who has now settled in Italy—that he will not join forces with Turnus, King Latinus is even more ready to make peace and grant the Trojans territorial concessions. One noble in support of Latinus recommends that Lavinia be given in marriage to Aeneas as a guarantee of a peaceful settlement. Turnus will have none of it; he is prepared to die fighting. Just then word comes that the Trojans and their Etruscan allies are approaching the city. Turnus leaps up to lead his men against the enemy. Camilla, the huntress-warrior, persuades Turnus to let her and her cavalry unit take the brunt of the attack. After a fierce battle, she is killed by Aruns, an Etruscan; in revenge Diana sends one of her nymphs to take Aruns' life.

The situation of the Latins is now desperate. Turnus takes it upon himself to settle the entire issue by a duel between himself and Aeneas; Lavinia and peace will be awarded to the winner. Aeneas agrees. But once more Juno is fearful for her favorite's life. She plots with Juturna, Turnus' sister and a nymph, to prevent the duel from coming about. When the terms of the combat are solemnized with oaths and sacrifices, Juturna stirs up the Rutilians to attack the Trojans and thus cause the battle between the opposing sides to rage once more. Aeneas receives an arrow-wound in the knee. The wound does not respond to treatment until Venus comes to her son's aid with a miracle herb that helps remove the arrow and heal the open wound. The Trojan prince returns to the battle and sweeps all before him. Turnus, however, is not to be seen; his sister manages to keep the two antagonists from meeting. When Aeneas turns his Trojans to attack Latinus' city, the inhabitants are thrown into panic. Amata, believing that the city has fallen into the hands of the enemy and that Turnus is dead, commits suicide by hanging. All is grief and gloom within the palace.

Aeneas and Turnus Duel.   When Turnus hears of the calamity that has befallen Laurentum, he rushes back to save the city and his good name. He orders his men to stop fighting. Aeneas and Turnus at last come face to face for a duel to the finish. They clash in close combat. Turnus breaks his sword—not his own, which was made by Vulcan, but his charioteer's—as he brings it down on Aeneas' shield. He flees in his chariot calling upon his men to get him his own weapon. Aeneas pursues him and throws a spear which misses its mark and embeds itself deep in the stump of an olive tree. Juturna, Juno's agent, brings Turnus his sword; Venus frees Aeneas' spear. At this moment, Jupiter intervenes and calls upon Juno to cease persecuting the Trojans and intervening in the course of destiny. The goddess consents to peace and the marriage on the condition that the Trojans give up their name, and that the two people become united under the names of Latins. Jupiter agrees to have all Latins speak one language; the union of the two races will produce one race of mixed Italian blood that will be superior to all others in performing its religious obligations and in honoring Juno's rites above those of all other deities.

Aeneas and Turnus come face to face again. The two men taunt each other. Turnus picks up a huge stone and hurls it at Aeneas. It misses by a wide margin. Turnus is alone: no refuge, no sister, no place to flee. Aeneas lifts his spear, aims, and throws. It whistles through the air and wounds Turnus in the thigh. The Rutilian prince falls to the ground, a ready prey to the death blow. He asks for no mercy except that his body be given to his kinsmen for burial. Aeneas, his sword in hand, hesitates and is on the verge of sparing his enemy's life, but then he sees the sword belt which Turnus had pillaged from Pallas' body. Pity leaves him and rage returns; his arm comes down and he buries his sword deep in Turnus' chest.

*Post-*AENEID *Events.* With the death of Turnus, Vergil brings the Aeneid to a close. But the story of Rome's origins does not stop here. Genealogists and mythological historians recognized the gap in time between the events following the Trojan War and the traditional date of the founding of Rome, a gap of some four hundred years. Vergil, of course, was well aware of this and in his Underworld scene closed the gap by having Aeneas review the souls of his descendants. In the hands of prosaic chronographers, the time between Aeneas and the twin founders of Rome is made up by a list of legendary kings of Alba Longa who are descendants of Aeneas' son Ascanius. By the time we come to Numitor, the chronology is more or less harmonized with the traditional date of Rome's founding in the eighth century B.C.

Romulus and Remus. Numitor, king of Alba Longa, had a younger brother Amulius who deposed him but permitted him to live. However, fearing political repercussions if he allowed Numitor's children to survive, he had his brother's male heirs murdered and forced perpetual chastity on his daughter Silvia (Rhea Silvia or Ilia) by making her a Vestal Virgin. One day, as Silvia went into a sacred grove to draw water, she came upon a wolf and had to flee to a cave for safety. It was there, on a day of a total eclipse of the sun, that Mars ravished her. The god consoled the poor girl by promising her that she would become the mother of outstanding children. When Silvia gave birth to twin-sons, Amulius imprisoned her and ordered the infants to be drowned. The twins, however, were placed at the edge of the Tiber which happened to be in flood. They were carried downstream in their cradle-like craft until it drifted ashore at the foot of the Palatine hill. A she-wolf came upon the infants and carried them to her den nearby where she suckled them (fig. 110). A woodpecker, an animal which like the wolf is sacred to Mars, helped sustain the twins by bringing in other food. Soon afterwards they were found by Faustulus, the king's herdsman, who brought them to his home where he and his wife reared them and gave them the names of Romulus and Remus. The twins grew up along with the twelve sons of their foster parents. But as is often the case with children sired by a god, they soon distinguished themselves from those around them by their good looks and their outstanding bravery. In time, circumstances brought Romulus and Remus before their grandfather Numitor who recognized them as his daughter's sons. The twins were now determined to avenge the wrong done their family, and with the help of their comrades, they killed Amulius and restored Numitor to his rightful position on the throne.

The Founding of Rome. Romulus and Remus undertook a new project. They decided to build a city of their own on the site where they had been found and reared. But a problem arose. Which of the twins was to have the authority to deter-

Figure 110. The she-wolf of Rome, nurse of Romulus and Remus.
*Etruscan (?) bronze, late sixth or early fifth century B.C. Conservatori Museum,
Rome. (Alinari)*

mine the exact site of the new city, to be its founder and namegiver? It was agreed
to leave the question for the gods of the countryside to decide; they would send a
sign indicating their preference. Romulus took a position on the Palatine hill;
Remus a short distance away on the Aventine. Remus received the first sign when
he spotted six vultures flying above him. No sooner had this news been brought to
Romulus than twelve vultures were seen flying past. Each brother claimed the
augury in his own favor, one claiming priority of the sign, the other basing his
claim on the greater number of birds. Open conflict broke out between the two
brothers, and some say that it was then that Remus was killed. The more popular
account holds that Romulus proceeded to mark out the site of the new town and to
build its walls. Remus, still brooding over the wrong he believed had been done
him, scornfully jumped over the half-built walls. Infuriated at being mocked in
this way, Romulus killed his brother, saying, "So die whoever else shall leap over
my battlements." He was now in undisputed control and gave the newly-built
city his name, Rome.

*   *   *   *

Through Vergil and the *Aeneid*, Rome found a valid legendary past and a divinely ordained future. The poet not only gave permanence to a legend, but he also became a legendary figure himself. On publication the *Aeneid* was an immediate success; it was widely quoted and imitated by other poets; it was used as a school textbook. At the same time a mystical aura gathered around Vergil as a man who possessed profound learning and secrets of the future. Only a little more than a hundred years after his death, we hear of his works being used to foretell coming events: the *Sortes Vergilianae*. The works of the poet would be opened at random and the first line on which the eye or the finger fell would be taken as an omen to foretell the future. In this respect the *Aeneid* takes its place along with the Bible and Homer's two epics. In Rabelais' *Pantagruel* (1532), Panurge resorts to the *Sortes* when he decides whether or not to marry. Charles I, King of England, is reported to have looked to the *Sortes* only to have his eye fall on the passage of Dido cursing Aeneas as he left her.

Vergil held a special place in the affection of the people of the Middle Ages. The *Aeneid* was the backbone of Latin studies and the most widely read secular work; it was better known to some churchmen than the Bible. Among pre-Christian writers, Vergil alone was regarded as a prophet of Christ, as an *anima naturaliter Christiana*, a spirit by nature Christian, an authority on the world beyond the grave. He gained this reputation through his so-called Messianic Eclogue (p. 15), through his "still sad music of humanity," and through his deep religious sentiment. It is not surprising, therefore, to find him among the Hebrew prophets in the cathedral of Zamora in Spain, or to find him in the *Divine Comedy* guiding Dante through the Inferno and Purgatory to the gates of Paradise.

Rome's descent from Trojan heroes, the legend which Vergil legitimized, was carried into other countries. In England, for example, Geoffrey of Monmouth (1100?–1154) gives an account of the kings who ruled Britain before the time of Christ. The founder of the British race, according to Geoffrey's *Historia Regum Britanniae*, was Brutus (or Brute), a grandson of Ascanius. This Brutus had the misfortune to kill his father and had to flee to Italy. Gathering a number of Trojans, he migrated to England, uninhabited at that time except for a few giants, where he founded Troynovant or New Troy (nowadays London). From this descendant of Aeneas, sprang a line of British kings, including "Old King Cole, the merry old soul," and King Arthur.

In time, poetic interest in Rome's destiny fell by the wayside, but Vergil's influence in matters concerning epic form, cadence, and diction was to continue through the centuries. During the Renaissance, Ariosto's *Orlando Furioso* (1532), Tasso's *Gerusalemme Liberata* (1581), and Camoen's *Lusiads* (1572), just to mention a few seminal European works, were all fashioned on the Vergilian epic. And from Chaucer's time to the twentieth century, it would be difficult to name a major English poet—Spenser, Shakespeare, Milton, and Tennyson to name a few—who was not in some degree influenced by Vergil. Such influences aside, the later life of the *Aeneid* was to take an unexpected turn. Vergil's sensitive rendering of Dido's tragic passion entranced a public more interested in romance and sentiment than in duty and destiny. We hear St. Augustine's rather shamefaced confession that he was moved "to weep for Dido's death because she killed herself out of love for Aeneas." Only short years after Vergil's death, Ovid took up the plight of Dido in the *Heroides*, where he portrayed the hapless queen of Carthage addressing a letter to the man who abandoned her. To tug all the more on the heartstrings of his readers, Ovid has his heroine accuse her faithless lover of leaving her pregnant with his child. "A part of you lies hidden in my body," she says and warns him that he will cause not only her death but also that of his unborn child.

In later ages, Vergil's story of Dido and Aeneas, as well as that of the entire *Aeneid*, was infected with Ovidian romance, a case of an epic turning into a love story. In the *Legend of Good Women*, for example, Chaucer opens his treatment of the legend of Dido with words of high praise for Vergil: "I shal, as I can./Folow thy lantern, as thou goest biforn." But the tale he tells is more Ovidian than Vergilian. Aeneas is little better than a cad and a bounder, a "traitour" who wins Dido's love and swears to be true to her forevermore. But when he wearies of her, he invents a vision of his father who appears in a dream and tells him that he must be off to Italy. Dido passionately begs him to stay and ends her futile plea, "I am with childe and yive my child his lyf. / Mercy, lord! have pite in your thought!"

There was a return to Vergil in Christopher Marlowe's *Tragedy of Dido, Queen of Carthage* (1593). In this earliest play of the Elizabethan poet which incorporates large sections directly translated from the *Aeneid*, Aeneas is once more the man of destiny, and Dido is once more at the mercy of the gods and part of the divine plan that will send her lover off to Italy to found Rome. But in the poetic language of the age, Aeneas was usually the false and faithless lover, Dido the heroic woman who is destroyed by love. Shakespeare, who alludes to Dido and Aeneas in ten of his plays, employs the theme with great versatility. In *Cymbeline*, Imogen brings together Aeneas and the infamous Sinon in this comparison:

> True honest men being heard like false Aeneas,
> Were in his time thought false; and Sinon's weeping
> Did scandal many a holy tear, took pity
> From most true wretchedness.

In *A Midsummer Night's Dream*, Hermia agrees to tryst with her lover and seals her promise with a vow, swearing

> . . . by that fire which burn'd the Carthage queen
> When the false Troyan under sail was seen,
> By all the vows that ever men have broke
> (In number more than ever women spoke),

And in the moonlight duet between Jessica and Lorenzo in *The Merchant of Venice*, there is a lyrical allusion to the lovelorn queen:

> In such a night
> Stood Dido with a willow in her hand
> Upon the wild sea-banks and waft her love
> To come again to Carthage.

In *Titus Andronicus*, however, Shakespeare turns back to Vergil for an undramatic reminiscence from the *Aeneid*. In a lovely part of the forest, Tamora calls upon her ruthless lover Aaron for lovemaking as

> The wand'ring prince and Dido once enjoy'd,
> When with a happy storm they were surpris'd,
> And curtain'd with a counsel-keeping cave.

More dramatically, when Antony receives a false report of Cleopatra's death, he is ready to forfeit his own life and calls upon his friend Eros to kill him. From *Antony and Cleopatra*:

> Eros!—I come, my queen.—Eros!—Stay for me.
>   Where souls do couch on flowers, we'll hand in hand
> And with our sprightly port make the ghosts gaze.
> Dido and her Aeneas shall want troops,
> And all the haunt be ours.

Themes from the *Aeneid*, particularly those involving Aeneas' stay at Carthage and Dido's tragic end, were put on canvas by the master painters of England and the Continent. Rubens and Sir Joshua Reynolds (1723–1792), among many others, portrayed the death of Dido. J. M. W. Turner (1775–1851), the prolific English painter, turned out a number of canvases depicting Dido building Carthage, directing equipment, and accompanying Aeneas on the morning of the hunt. Other paintings of his show Aeneas telling Dido the story of his adventures, Mercury being sent to Aeneas to tell him that he must leave Carthage, the departure of Aeneas' fleet, and Aeneas and the Sibyl.

Pre-eminent among the operatic compositions based on Vergil's *Aeneid* is the spectacular and monumental work of Hector Berlioz (1803–1869), *Les Troyens* (The Trojans). First performed in its entirety twenty-one years after the composer's death, it was written in two parts: *La Prise de Troie* (*The Capture of Troy*) and *Les Troyens à Carthage* (*The Trojans at Carthage*), the first serving as a kind of prologue. Vergil had been a favorite of Berlioz' since childhood, and when the opportunity arose to challenge Richard Wagner's projected *Ring of the Nibelung*, he chose the *Aeneid* for his musical epic. The idea of putting a Greco-Latin legend opposite a Germanic one attracted Berlioz. Although rarely performed—its cut version has been staged more often since the 1950's—the symphonic interlude, *The Royal Hunt and Storm*, is well known through concert performances.

In the eighteenth century one name connected with Dido and Aeneas stands out above all others, Pietro Metastasio (1698–1782). His drama, *Didone abbandonata* (Dido Abandoned), written in 1724, was set to music by at least fifty composers and enjoyed a tremendous success throughout the century. But perhaps the most famous of all operas based on Vergil's epic is the *Dido and Aeneas* of Henry Purcell (1658?–1695). Dido's aria "When I am laid in earth" is one of the most celebrated vocal pieces in operatic literature. *Dido and Aeneas*, Purcell's only true opera, was composed some time during 1689 for a performance at the Chelsea girls' school. The libretto was written by Nahum Tate, who was famous not so much because he was the poet laureate of England but because he revised Shakespeare's *King Lear* so as to give it a happy ending. Tate took similar liberties with Vergil's story. Not only did he introduce witches and a sorceress, and a chorus of sailors who urge their mates to "take a boozy short leave of your nymphs on the shore," but he also changed the character of the two leading figures. His Aeneas is no longer a man of destiny or a "false Troyan," but a love-sick creature willing to "offend the gods and love obey." Tate's Dido is a warhearted woman who is torn by her queenly dignity and her love for the Trojan hero; she is far removed from Vergil's love-possessed widow who is driven to insanity and suicide by uncontrollable emotions. This is how the Dido and Aeneas of the Restoration confronted each other:

Aeneas: What shall lost Aeneas do?
How, Royal fair, shall I impart
The Gods' decree, and tell you we must part?

Dido: Thus on the fatal banks of Nile,
Weeps the deceitful crocodile!
Thus hypocrites that murder act,
Make Heaven and gods the authors of the fact!

Aeneas: By all that's good!

Dido: By all that's good, no more!
All that's good you have forswore.
To your promised empire fly,
And let forsaken Dido die.

Aeneas: In spite of Jove's command I'll stay,
Offend the Gods, and love obey!

Dido: No, faithless man! Thy course pursue,
I'm now resolved as well as you.
No repentance shall reclaim
The injured Dido's slighted flame.
For 'tis enough whate'er you now decree,
That you had once a thought of leaving me!

Aeneas: Let Jove say what he will, I'll stay!

Dido: No, no! away, away!

Aeneas: I'll stay, and love obey!

Dido: No, no! to death I'll fly if longer you delay!

Away, away!

Nahum Tate should not be faulted for taking such liberties with Vergil; he no doubt had in mind the Chelsea school and the young ladies for whom the work was commissioned. In this respect, however, he differs little from Vergil and from those who came before and after him, who for a great variety of reasons—historical, political, artistic, ethical, or religious—adapted the myths and legends of the past to serve a new purpose and a new end. To show the multifaceted aspects of mythology has, in large part, been the aim of this text.

Bibliography

A working list of books on classical mythology and its uses is difficult to compile since the literature is so vast and the subject has been approached from so many widely differing points of view. Listed here are a number of books, all in the English language and many available in paperback editions, which may be found serviceable to those who wish to dig deeper into the varied strata of Greek and Roman mythology. Many of the books have detailed bibliographies which can be useful on technical points of scholarship or to supplement those listed below. Any omission, particularly among translations of ancient source material, does not imply depreciation; it is due only to the demands of brevity.

Ancient Sources

AESCHYLUS. See *Greek Dramatists*.

APOLLODORUS. *The Library* (Bibliotheca). 2 vols. Trans. Sir James George Frazer. Cambridge, Mass.: Loeb Classical Library, 1921.

APOLLONIUS RHODIUS. *The Argonautica*. Trans. R. C. Seaton. Cambridge, Mass.: Loeb Classical Library, 1912.

_____. *The Voyage of the Argo*. Trans. E. V. Rieu. Baltimore: Penguin Classics, 1959.

APULEIUS. *The Golden Ass* (The Metamorphoses). Trans. Jack Lindsay. Bloomington, Ill., 1962.

BION. See *Greek Bucolic Poets*.

CALLIMACHUS. *Callimachus and Lycophron*. Trans. A. W. Mair. Rev. ed. Cambridge, Mass., 1955.

CATULLUS. *The Poems of Catullus*. Trans. Horace Gregory. New York, 1956.

DARES OF PHRYGIA. *The Trojan War: The Chronicles of Dictys of Crete and Dares the Phrygian*. Trans. R. M. Frazer, Jr. Bloomington, Ill. and London, 1966.

DICTYS OF CRETE. See *Dares of Phrygia*.

EURIPIDES. See *Greek Dramatists*.

GREEK BUCOLIC POETS. *The Greek Bucolic Poets*. Trans. J. M. Edmonds. Rev. ed. Cambridge, Mass.: Loeb Classical Library, 1938.

_____. *The Greek Bucolic Poets*. Trans. A. S. F. Gow. Cambridge, 1953.

GREEK DRAMATISTS. *The Complete Greek Tragedies*. Eds. Richmond Lattimore and David Grene. Chicago, 1957. (The University of Chicago Press edition is available in the Modern Library series and in the Washington Square Press editions.)

_____. *The Complete Greek Drama*. Eds. Whitney J. Oates and Eugene O'Neill, Jr. New York, 1938. All the extant tragedies of Aeschylus, Sophocles, and Euripides and the comedies of Aristophanes and Menander.

_____. Individual plays and groups of plays are available in numerous editions. See, among many others, translations by Dudley Fitts, Robert Fitzgerald, Edith Hamilton, Louis MacNeice, George Thomson, Philip Vellacott, Rex Warner, and E. F. Watling.

HERODOTUS. *The Histories*. Trans. Aubrey de Selincourt. Baltimore: Penguin Classics, 1954.

HESIOD. *Hesoid, The Homeric Hymns and Homerica*. Trans. Hugh G. Evelyn-White. Cambridge, Mass.: Loeb Classical Library, 1914.

———. *Hesiod*. Trans. Richmond Lattimore. Ann Arbor, 1959.

———. *Theogony*. Edited with prolegomena and commentary by M. L. West. Oxford, 1966. (Greek text, but highly useful for detailed introduction and analysis.)

HOMER. *The Iliad*. Trans. E. V. Rieu. Baltimore: Penguin Classics, 1950.

———. *The Iliad*. Trans. Richmond Lattimore. Chicago, 1951.

———. *The Odyssey*. Trans. E. V. Rieu. Baltimore: Penguin Classics, 1946.

———. *The Odyssey*. Trans. Richmond Lattimore. New York, 1968.

HOMERIC HYMNS. See *Hesiod*.

HYGINUS. *The Myths of Hyginus*. Trans. Mary Grant. Lawrence, Kan., 1960.

LUCIAN. *Selected Satires of Lucian*. Trans. Lionel Casson. New York, 1962.

LUCRETIUS. *The Nature of the Universe*. Trans. R. E. Latham. Baltimore: Penguin Classics, 1951.

LYCROPHON. See *Callimachus*.

MOSCHUS. See *Greek Bucolic Poets*.

NONNUS. *Dionysiaca*. 3 vols. Trans. W. H. D. Rouse. Cambridge, Mass.: Loeb Classical Library, 1940.

OVID. *The Metamorphoses*. Trans. Rolfe Humphries. Bloomington, Ill., 1955.

———. *The Metamorphoses*. Trans. Horace Gregory. New York, 1958.

———. *The Metamorphoses*. Trans. Mary M. Innes. Baltimore: Penguin Classics, 1955.

———. *Heroides and Amores*. Trans. Grant Showerman. Cambridge: Loeb Classical Library, 1921.

———. *Heroides, Amours*. Trans. Henry T. Rile. London: Bohn's Libraries, 1919.

PAUSANIAS. *Description of Greece*. 5 vols. Trans. W. H. S. Jones et al. Cambridge, Mass.: Loeb Classical Library, 1918–1955.

PINDAR. *The Odes of Pindar*. Trans. Richmond Lattimore. Chicago, 1947.

PLATO. *The Dialogues of Plato*. Trans. Benjamin Jowett. 4th ed. Oxford, 1953.

———. *Great Dialogues of Plato*. Trans. W. H. D. Rouse. New York, 1956.

———. *The Republic of Plato*. Trans. F. M. Cornford. Oxford, 1941.

PLUTARCH. *The Lives of the Noble Grecians and Romans*. Trans. John Dryden and revised by Arthur H. Clough. New York: Modern Library, 1932.

———. *Plutarch's Lives*. 11 vols. Trans. Bernadotte Perrin. Cambridge, Mass.: Loeb Classical Library, 1914–1926.

SENECA. *Tragedies*. vols. 8–9. Trans. Frank J. Miller. Cambridge, Mass.: Loeb Classical Library, 1917, 1929.

SOPHOCLES. See *Greek Dramatists*.

THEOCRITUS. See *Greek Bucolic Poets*.

VERGIL. *The Aeneid*. Trans. W. F. Jackson Knight. Baltimore: Penguin Classics, 1956.

———. *The Aeneid*. Trans. Rolfe Humphries. New York, 1951.

———. *The Aeneid*. Trans. C. Day Lewis. New York, 1952.

———. *Pastoral Poems* (Eclogues). Trans. E. V. Rieu. Baltimore: Penguin Classics. 1949.

——— *The Georgics*. Trans. by C. Day Lewis. New York, 1947.

Bibliographies, Dictionaries, and Encyclopedias

BALDENSPERGER, F. and FRIEDRICH, W. P. *Bibliography of Comparative Literature. University of North Carolina Studies in Comparative Literature*, Chapel Hill, 1950 (Book 2, Parts 2–4; Book 3, Part 2, for Greek and Roman influence on modern literature.)

BLOOM, E., ed. *Grove's Dictionary of Music*. 5th ed. London, 1954.

BROWN, H. *A Bibliography of Classical Influence on English Literature. Harvard Studies in Philology, 18*. Cambridge, Mass., 1935.

CARY, M. et al., eds. *The Oxford Classical Dictionary*. Oxford, 1949. Second edition (ed. N. G. L. Hammond and H. H. Scullard), 1970.

HUBBARD, W. L., ed. *American History and Encyclopedia of Music*. Toledo, 1908.

LAW, HELEN H. *Bibliography of Greek Myth in English Literature. American Classical League Bulletin XXVII*, 1932; *Supplement*, 1941.

LEACH, MARIA, ed. Funk and Wagnalls *Standard Dictionary of Folklore, Mythology and Legend.* 2 vols. New York, 1949–1950.

LEMPRIÈRE, J. *A Classical Dictionary.* (The editions of 1804, 1806 and 1847 were used by English poets of the nineteenth century.)

NORTON, D. S. and RUSHTON, P. *Classical Myths in English Literature.* New York, 1952.

SMITH, W., ed. *A Dictionary of Greek and Roman Biography and Mythology.* 3 vols. London, 1876.

SONNECK, O. G. T., ed. Library of Congress. *Catalogue of Opera Librettos Printed before 1800.* 2 vols. Washington, 1914.

Handbooks

GAYLEY, C. M. *The Classic Myths in English Literature and Art.* Boston, 1911.

GRANT, MICHAEL. *Myths of the Greeks and Romans.* London, 1962.

GRAVES, ROBERT. *The Greek Myths.* 2 vols. Baltimore: Penguin Classics, 1955.

HAMILTON, EDITH. *Mythology.* Boston, 1940.

KERÉNYI, C. *The Gods of the Greeks.* Trans. N. Cameron. London and New York, 1951.

_____. *The Heroes of the Greeks.* Trans. H. J. Rose. New York, 1960.

ROSE, H. J. *A Handbook of Greek Mythology.* 6th ed. New York, 1958.

Approaches (Anthropological, Psychological, etc.) To Mythology

ABRAHAM, KARL. *Dreams and Myths.* Trans. W. A. White. New York, 1913.

CAMPBELL, JOSEPH. *The Masks of God: Occidental Mythology.* New York, 1964.

_____. *The Hero with a Thousand Faces.* 2nd ed. Princeton, 1968.

CARPENTER, RHYS. *Folk Tale, Fiction, and Saga in the Homeric Epics.* Berkeley, 1946.

CASSIRER, ERNEST. *Essay on Man.* New Haven and London, 1944.

ELIADE, MIRCEA. *Myth and Reality.* Trans. W. R. Trask. New York, 1963.

FONTENROSE, JOSEPH. *The Ritual Theory of Man.* Berkeley, 1966.

FRAZER, SIR JAMES GEORGE. *The New Golden Bough.* Ed. T. H. Gaster. New York, 1961.

FREUD, SIGMUND. *The Interpretation of Dreams.* Trans. J. Strachey et al. 2 vols. (Standard Edition of the Complete Psychological Works, 4–5). London, 1953.

GASTER, THEODORE H. *Thespis: Ritual, Myth, and Drama in the Ancient Near East.* New York, 1950.

HOOKE, S. H., ed. *Myth, Ritual and Kingship.* Oxford, 1958.

JUNG, C. and KERÉNYI, C. *Essays on a Science of Mythology.* Trans. R. F. S. Hull. New York, 1949.

JUNG, C. G. *The Archetypes of the Collective Unconscious (Collected Works of C. G. Jung,* 9,1). New York and London, 1959.

_____, ed. *Man and His Symbols.* New York, 1964.

KIRK, G. S. *Myth. Its Meaning and Function in Ancient and Other Cultures.* Berkeley, 1970.

MALINOWSKI, BRONISLAW. *Myth in Primitive Psychology.* New York, 1926.

MULLAHY, PATRICK. *Oedipus Myth and Complex.* New York, 1948.

RAGLAN, LORD. *The Hero.* London, 1936.

RANK, OTTO. *The Myth of the Birth of the Hero.* Trans. F. Robbins and S. E. Jelliffe. New York, 1952.

SEBEOK, T. A., ed. *Myth: A Symposium.* Bloomington, Ill., 1965.

THOMPSON, STITH. *The Folktale.* New York, 1946.

Greek and Roman Civilization

BAILEY, C. *Phases in the Religion of Ancient Rome.* Berkeley, 1932.

BALDRY, H. C. *Greek Literature for the Modern Reader.* London, 1951.

BARROW, R. H. *The Romans.* Baltimore, 1949.

BIEBER, M. *A History of the Greek and Roman Theater.* Princeton, 1961.

BURN, A. R. *The Lyric Age of Greece.* London, 1960.

DODDS, E. R. *The Greeks and the Irrational.* Berkeley, 1951.

FINLEY, M. I. *The World of Odysseus.* Rev. ed. London, 1956.

GRANT, MICHAEL. *The World of Rome.* New York, 1960.

GUTHRIE, W. K. C. *The Greeks and Their Gods.* Boston, 1954.
———. *Orpheus and Greek Religion.* London, 1952.
HALLIDAY, W. R. *Greek and Roman Folklore.* London, 1927.
HARRISON, JANE E. *Themis. A Study of the Social Origins of Greek Religion.* Cambridge, 1927.
JAEGER, WERNER. *Paidea: the Ideals of Greek Culture.* 3 vols. Trans. G. Highet. Oxford and New York, 1939–1944.
KERÉNYI, C. *The Religion of the Greeks and Romans.* Trans. C. Holme. New York, 1962.
KITTO, H. D. F. *Greek Tragedy: A Literary Study.* Rev. ed. New York, 1954.
———. *The Greeks.* Baltimore, 1951.
MURRAY, GILBERT. *Five Stages of Greek Religion.* London, 1935.
NILSSON, M. P. *The Mycenaean Origin of Greek Mythology.* Berkeley, 1932.
———. *A History of Greek Religion.* Trans F. J. Fielden. New York, 1925.
ROSE, H. J. *A Handbook of Greek Literature.* New York, 1965.
———. *A Handbook of Latin Literature.* London, 1954.
———. *Ancient Roman Religion.* London, 1948.
SNELL, BRUNO. *The Discovery of the Mind: The Greek Origins of European Thought.* Trans. T. G. Rosenmeyer. Cambridge, Mass., 1953.
SOLMSEN, F. *Hesiod and Aeschylus.* Ithaca, 1949.
STARR, CHESTER G. *The Origins of Greek Civilization.* London, 1961.
STEWART, J. A. *The Myths of Plato.* Ed. G. R. Levy. Carbondale, Ill., 1960.
WALCOT, PETER. *Hesiod and the Near East.* Cardiff, Wales, 1966.
WEBSTER, T. B. L. *From Mycenae to Homer.* 2nd ed. New York, 1964.

The Literary Heritage

ANDERSON, M. J., ed. *Classical Drama and Its Influence.* London, 1965.
BALDWIN, THOMAS W. *William Shakspere's Small Latine and Lesse Greeke.* 2 vols. Urbana, Ill., 1944.
BELLI, ANGELA. *Ancient Greek Myths and Modern Drama: A Study in Continuity.* New York and London, 1969.
BOLGAR, R. R. *The Classical Heritage and its Beneficiaries.* Cambridge, Mass., 1954.
BREWER, WILMON. *Ovid's Metamorphoses in European Culture.* 3 vols. Boston and Francestown, N.H., 1933–1957.
BUSH, DOUGLAS. *Mythology and the Renaissance Tradition in English Poetry.* Minneapolis and London, 1932.
———. *Mythology and the Romantic Tradition in English Poetry.* Cambridge, Mass., 1937.
BUTLER, E. M. *The Tyranny of Greece over Germany.* Cambridge, 1935.
CHISLETT, WILLIAM. *The Classical Influence in English Literature in the Nineteenth Century.* Boston, 1918.
COMPARETTI, D. *Vergil in the Middle Ages.* Trans. E. F. M. Benecke. New York, 1895.
CURTIUS, E. R. *European Literature and the Latin Middle Ages.* Trans. Willard R. Trask. New York, 1953.
FORCE, WILLIAM F., ed. *Orestes and Electra: Myth and Dramatic Form.* New York, 1968.
FRIEDMAN, JOHN B. *Orpheus in the Middle Ages.* Cambridge, Mass., 1970.
GILBERT, STUART. *James Joyce's Ulysses: A Study.* New York, 1931.
GORDON, G. S., ed. *English Literature and the Classics.* Oxford, 1912.
GORDON, R. K., trans. and ed. *The Story of Troilus.* London, 1934.
HATHORN, RICHMOND Y. *Tragedy, Myth, and Mystery.* Bloomington, Ill. and London, 1962.
HIGHET, GILBERT. *The Classical Tradition: Greek and Roman Influences on Western Literature.* New York and London, 1949.
JONES, EARNEST. *Hamlet and Oedipus.* New York, 1949.
KALLICH, M. et al., eds. *Oedipus: Myth and Drama.* New York, 1968.
KERLIN, ROBERT T. *Theocritus in English Literature.* Lynchburg, Va., 1910.
KITTO, H. D. F. *Form and Meaning in Drama.* London, 1956.
———. *Poiesis: Structure and Thought.* Berkeley, 1966.

LEVIN, HARRY. *The Broken Column. A Study in Romantic Hellenism.* Cambridge, Mass., 1931.

MACKAIL, J. W. *Virgil and His Meaning to the World of Today.* New York, 1963.

MERIVALE, PATRICIA. *Pan the Goat-God: His Myth in Modern Times.* Cambridge, Mass., 1969.

MURRAY, GILBERT. *The Classical Tradition in Poetry.* Cambridge, Mass., 1927.

NITCHIE, ELIZABETH. *Vergil and the English Poets.* New York, 1919.

ROBERTSON, JOHN G. *The Gods in German Poetry.* Oxford, 1924.

SHEPPARD, J. T. *Aeschylus and Sophocles: Their Work and Influence.* New York, 1927.

STANFORD, W. B. *The Ulysses Theme. A Study in the Adaptability of a Traditional Hero.* Rev. ed. Oxford, 1963.

STARNES, D. T. and TALBERT, E. W. *Classical Myth and Legend in Renaissance Dictionaries.* Chapel Hill, 1955.

THOMSON, J. A. K. *The Classical Background of English Literature.* London, 1948.

―――. *The Classical Influences on English Poetry.* London, 1951.

TREVELYAN, HUMPHRY. *Goethe and the Greeks.* Cambridge, 1942.

WIND, EDGAR. *Pagan Mysteries in the Renaissance.* New Haven, 1958.

YOUNG, ARTHUR. *Troy and Her Legend.* Pittsburgh, 1948.

Art and Music

ARIAS, P., HIRMER, M., and SHEFTON, B. B. *A History of Greek Vase Painting.* London, 1961.

BEAZLEY, J. D. *Attic Black Figure Vase Painters.* Oxford, 1956.

―――. *The Development of Attic Black Figure.* Berkeley, 1951.

―――. *Potter and Painter in Ancient Athens.* London, 1944.

―――. and ASHMOLE, B. *Greek Sculpture and Painting.* Cambridge, 1932.

BIEBER, M. *The Sculpture of the Hellenistic Age.* New York, 1954.

BOARDMAN, JOHN. *Greek Art.* New York, 1964.

―――. *Island Gems.* London, 1963.

CLARK, K. *The Nude.* London, 1957.

COOK, B. M. *Greek Painted Pottery.* London, 1960.

GOMBRICH, E. H. *The Story of Art.* London, 1962.

HARRISON, JANE. *Myths of the Odyssey in Art and Literature.* London, 1882.

LULLIES, R. and HIRMER, M. *Greek Sculpture.* London, 1960.

MARTENS, FREDERICK H. *A Thousand and One Nights of Opera.* Chaps. 2 and 3. New York and London, 1926.

PANOFSKY, DORA and ERWIN. *Pandora's Box: The Changing Aspects of a Mythical Symbol.* Rev. ed. New York, 1962.

PANOFSKY, ERWIN. *Renaissance and Renascences in Western Art.* Stockholm, 1956.

―――. *Studies in Iconology: Humanistic Themes in the Art of the Renaissance.* Oxford, 1939.

RICHTER, G. M. A. *Ancient Italy.* Ann Arbor, 1955.

―――. *Archaic Greek Art.* Oxford, 1949.

―――. *Attic Red Figure Vases: A Survey.* New Haven, 1958.

―――. *A Handbook of Greek Art.* London, 1959.

RIIS, P. J. *An Introduction to Etruscan Art.* Copenhagen, 1953.

ROBERTSON, C. M. *Greek Painting.* Geneva, 1959.

SCHEFOLD, KARL. *Myth and Legend in Early Greek Art.* London, 1966.

SCHERER, MARGARET R. *The Legends of Troy in Art and Literature.* New York and London, 1963.

SEZNEC, JEAN. *The Survival of the Pagan Gods. The Mythological Tradition and Its Place in Renaissance Humanism and Art.* New York, 1953.

SMITH, PATRICK J. *The Tenth Muse.* A Historical Study of the Opera Libretto. New York, 1970.

Index

For the reader who wishes to have some guide lines without elaborate phonetic transcriptions, we offer these few general rules for the pronunciation of mythological names. Where necessary we have marked accents and long vowels. In a matter so disputed as "correct" pronunciation, especially for Greek names that have been both latinized and anglicized, it is difficult for anyone to claim special authority. We have attempted to give those pronunciations which are generally accepted and widely used.

1. A word of two syllables receives its accent on the first syllable (e.g. A' jax).
2. Final *e* or *o* are treated as long vowels and are pronounced long (e.g. Antigone and Juno).
3. Final *es* is pronounced like the word "ease" (e.g. Hermes).
4. *ch* is given the sound of "k" (e.g. Achilles).
5. *c* and *g* before *e, i, ae, oe* and *y* are pronounced soft, as in "Caesar" and "Giant."
6. The diphthongs *ae* and *oe* are given a long "e" sound, again as in "Caesar." (Oedipus and Aeschylus, of course, are exceptions.)
7. The diphthong *ei* is most often given the sound of a long "i." It is often simplified to "i" (Teiresias > Tiresias), less often to "e" (Medeia > Medea).
8. *eu* – a difficult combination – is most often pronounced like the eu in "euphony." It is sometimes given the value of two syllables.

A B C D E F G H I J   9 8 7 6 5 4 3 2 1